THE THABO MBEKI I KNOW

THE
THABO MBEKI
I KNOW

❧

EDITED BY
SIFISO MXOLISI NDLOVU AND MIRANDA STRYDOM

PICADOR AFRICA

Thabo Mbeki
FOUNDATION

Dedicated to Africa's Renaissance

First published in 2016 by Picador Africa
an imprint of Pan Macmillan South Africa
Private Bag X19, Northlands
Johannesburg, 2116

www.panmacmillan.co.za

ISBN 978-1-77010-341-2
eBook ISBN 978-1-77010-342-9

Project management by Reneé Naudé
Editing by Pam Thornley
Proofreading by Sally Hines and Sean Fraser
Design and typesetting by Triple M Design, Johannesburg
Cover photograph: Mail & Guardian / Oupa Nkosi / Africa Media Online
Cover design by K4

Printed and bound by Shumani Mills Communications, Parow, Cape Town
SW61507

CONTENTS

❧

ACRONYMS

❦

AAM	Anti-Apartheid Movement
ACDEG	African Charter on Democracy, Elections and Governance
Africom	United States Africa Command
AGOA	Africa Growth and Opportunity Act
AIDS	Acquired Immune Deficiency Syndrome
AIT	African Institute of Technology
ANC	African National Congress
ANCYL	African National Congress Youth League
APF	African Partnership Forum
APRM	African Peer Review Mechanism
ASA	African Students' Association
ASEAN	Association of Southeast Asian Nations
AU	African Union
BBC	British Broadcasting Corporation
BCM	Black Consciousness Movement
BEE	Black Economic Empowerment
BPC	Black People's Convention
CDITP	Centre for Development of Information and Telecommunications Policy
COD	Congress of Democrats
CODESA	Convention for a Democratic South Africa
COMINT	Communications Intelligence
COMSEC	Communications Security (formerly Electronic Communications Security Pty Ltd)
COPE	Congress of the People
COSAS	Congress of South African Students
COSATU	Congress of South African Trade Unions
CPSU	Communist Party of the Soviet Union

DBSA	Development Bank of Southern Africa
DG	Director General
DIA	Department of International Affairs (ANC)
DIP	Department of Information and Publicity (ANC)
DOTforce	Digital Opportunity Task Force
DRC	Democratic Republic of the Congo
EC	European Commission
ECOWAS	Economic Community of West African States
ELINT	Electronics Intelligence
EU	European Union
EW	Electronic Warfare
FAPLA	Força Armadas Populares de Libertação de Angola (People's Armed Forces for the Liberation of Angola)
FDI	Foreign Direct Investment
FESTAC	Festival of Arts and Culture
FNLA	Frente Nacional para Libertação de Angola (National Liberation Front of Angola)
FOSAD	Forum of South African Directors
FOSATU	Federation of South African Trade Unions
FRELIMO	Frente de Libertação de Moçambique (Mozambique Liberation Front)
G8	Group of Eight (highly industrialised nations)
G77	Group of 77 developing countries established in 1964
GAC	Government Advisory Committee
GCIS	Government Communication and Information System
GDR	German Democratic Republic
GEAR	Growth, Employment and Redistribution (Plan)
GNU	Government of National Unity
HAART	Highly Active Antiretroviral Treatment
HIV	Human Immunodeficiency Virus
IBA	Independent Broadcasting Authority
ICANN	Internet Corporation for Assigned Names and Numbers
ICASA	Independent Communications Authority of South Africa
ICBMs	Intercontinental Ballistics Missiles
ICT	Information and Communications Technology
IDASA	Institute for Democracy in South Africa
IEC	Independent Electoral Commission
IFP	Inkatha Freedom Party
IMF	International Monetary Fund
IPC	Internal Political Committee (ANC)

ISAD	Information Society and Development
ISSA	Institute of Satellite and Space Applications
IT	Information Technology
ITU	International Telecommunications Union
IUEF	International University Exchange Fund
KZN	KwaZulu-Natal
LEO	Low Earth Orbit
MAP	Millennium Africa Plan
MARNET	Military Area Radio Network
MDM	Mass Democratic Movement
MERG	Macro-Economic Research Group
MK	Umkhonto we Sizwe
MPLA	Movimento Popular de Libertação de Angola (People's Movement for the Liberation of Angola)
MRC	Medical Research Council
NAASP	New Asian-Africa Strategic Partnership
NAFCOC	National African Federation of Commerce
NAI	New Africa Initiative
NAM	Non-Aligned Movement
NATO	North Atlantic Treaty Organisation
NCC	National Communications Centre
NDR	National Democratic Revolution
NEC	National Executive Committee (of the ANC)
NEMISA	National Electronic Media Institute of South Africa
NEPAD	New Partnership for Africa's Development
NGC	National General Council (ANC)
NLM	National Liberation Movement
NUMSA	National Union of Metalworkers of South Africa
NUSAS	National Union of South African Students
OAU	Organisation of African Unity
OTB	Overberg Test Range
PABX	Private Automatic Branch Exchange
PAC	Pan Africanist Congress
PF	Patriotic Front
PMC	Politico Military Council (ANC)
PSCBC	Public Sector Collective Bargaining Chamber
RENAMO	Resistência Nacional Moçambicana (Mozambican National Resistance)
RPMC	Regional Political Military Committee (AAM)
SABC	South African Broadcasting Corporation

SACP   South African Communist Party
SACTU   South African Congress of Trade Unions
SADC   Southern African Development Community
SADCC   Southern African Development Coordination Conference (forerunner of
              SADC)
SADF   South African Defence Force
SALT   Southern African Large Telescope
SALT2   Strategic Arms Limitation Talks 2
SANDF   South African National Defence Force
SANSCO   South African National Students Congress
SASO   South African Student Organisation
SATRA   South African Telecommunications Regulatory Authority
SIDA   Swedish International Development Cooperation Agency
SIGINT   Signals Intelligence
SITA   State Information Technology Agency
SRC   Students' Representative Council
SWAPO   South West Africa People's Organisation
TAC   Treatment Action Campaign
UDF   United Democratic Front
UN   United Nations
UNCTAD   United Nations Conference on Trade and Development
UNDP   United Nations Development Programme
UNECA   United Nations Economic Commission for Africa
UNISA   University of South Africa
UNITA   União Nacional para a Independência Total de Angola (National Union
              for the Total Independence of Angola)
USSR   Union of Soviet Socialist Republics
WCC   World Council of Churches
WFDY   World Federation of Democratic Youth
WIPHOLD   Women's Investment Portfolio Holdings Limited
WHO   World Health Organization
WSIS   World Summit on Information Society
WTO   World Trade Organisation
YWCA   Young Women's Christian Association
ZANLA   Zimbabwe African National Liberation Army
ZANU   Zimbabwe African National Union
ZANU-PF   Zimbabwe African National Union Patriotic Front
ZAPU   Zimbabwe African People's Union
ZIPRA   Zimbabwe People's Revolutionary Army

FOREWORD

※

BARNEY AFAKO

A book that sets out to honour Thabo Mbeki in fact unveils some quite remarkable women and men who make this collection absorbing reading. Presidents, bodyguards, busy mothers, passionate economists, judges, lawyers, insurgent diplomats, tenacious politicians and many others who have come into his orbit share stories of the Thabo Mbeki they know. This is no anthology of praise songs. Here you will find affection but also candid portraits of the man who detests personality cults.

In these pages, you will find fellow combatants with Mbeki in the African cause, such as former Nigerian president, Olusegun Obasanjo who, with Mbeki, has recorded remarkable successes, including the New Partnership for Africa's Development (NEPAD). Meles Zenawi, Ethiopia's late prime minister, another formidable African intellect in the trenches, admires Mbeki's insistence that Africans must be allowed to think for themselves and to chart their own course.

Inevitably, Mbeki's immense contribution to the peaceful transition in South Africa traverses the book: it is clear this was the culmination of years of dogged hard work and dedication. The well-honed communication skills and deep reservoirs of political empathy served their purpose in those intensive and complex negotiations. Willie Esterhuyse, who first looked across the room at 'the enemy' Mbeki, succumbed to the trust, and is now a close friend. Courage courses through this book in large measure.

'No day or night' – the Mbeki work ethic

Mbeki is about hard work. For Frank Chikane, who oversaw his office at the presidency, and the others in the president's office, there was 'no day or night'. Joel Netshitenzhe and Alec Erwin's accounts of their work bear out this work ethic. Together with Welile Nhlapo's chapter, they paint a picture of a competent, hard-working and committed team, while also shedding light on key stages of the history of the struggle and sharing their insights into the difficult business of managing the economy. Many will not know that South Africa was almost bankrupt when the ANC took power, and it was the tireless Mbeki and his team that set out to rescue the economy. Others, like George Nene, remember receiving the Mbeki drafts under the door having said goodnight to him in the small hours. Many today will know well the 3am email from 'TM' that requires the attention of their partner.

The pan-Africanist – 'Africa's uber diplomat'

And Mbeki has always been about Africa. Chris Landsberg describes him as the foremost international stalwart and statesman of his generation in Africa. He has always worn two hats: a South African leader, and a leader of the continent. Dr Salim Ahmed Salim of Tanzania rightly refers to him as 'one of the most outstanding emissaries of Africa in dealing with African problems'. His clear vision of an African Renaissance drives him on. Sir Ketumile Masire and others describe the hours the South African president later devoted to peace in the Democratic Republic of Congo, Zimbabwe, Côte d'Ivoire and countless other African countries, where he invariably brought years of accumulated knowledge and experience to bear in addressing those challenges.

You will meet courageous diplomats, uncowed by the global stage: Thandi Lujabe-Rankoe, Aziz Pahad, Dumisani Kumalo, Nozipo January-Bardill and George Nene all provide fascinating insights into the workings of geopolitics and the challenges of defending Africa's interests on the world stage. Miranda Strydom's engrossing tales from covering Mbeki's trips bring a journalist's eye to that stage on which the restless and incisive intellectual energy of Mbeki ensured that South Africa 'punched above its weight', always in the defence of the continent and the dignity of all

Africans, including those in the diaspora.

When in March 2011 Father Jean-Bertrand Aristide chose to return to Haiti from exile in South Africa, Mbeki was worried. I still recall that night in Khartoum when I received an advanced tutorial in Haitian political history, as he explained to me the difficult context into which Aristide was returning. Randall Robinson's synopsis in these pages of Haiti's history and his excerpts from Mbeki's St Domingue speech in the 2004 bicentennial celebration of the Haitian Revolution are a must-read for an illustration of pan-Africanist solidarity.

Emotional intelligence

The observant and considerate young man whom Tiksie Mabizela and her husband Stan hosted in their Manzini house in Swaziland still retains that emotional intelligence and the twinkle in his eye. In probably the most intimate portrayal of Mbeki in a domestic setting, Tiksie describes how Thabo became a member of her family, a fun-loving uncle and lasting friend to her children. Thabo always defused any tensions and looked out for others' needs. In 1991, Thandi Lujabe-Rankoe, the ANC representative in Oslo, also 'discovered his soft heart' when Mbeki was first to notice that visiting ANC leaders needed warmer clothes. Tau Thekiso, his bodyguard as president, remembers how President Mbeki sought tips from him for a campaign rally, incorporated Thekiso's ideas, and credited him and his colleagues publicly.

Another close-up view of Mbeki is provided by Mpho Ngozi, his secretary at the presidency. Her chapter serves up several gems, including the time when Mbeki threw Essop Pahad out of his office because he had not sought Ngozi's permission to enter. She also reveals Mbeki's love of photography and butterflies in particular, of archaeology and palaeontology, confirmed by Tanzania's Ambassador Ami Mpungwe who arranged for the Mbekis to visit Olduvai Gorge, Tanzania, while on a holiday Madiba had ordered Mbeki to take.

The life partner

Although no specific chapter is dedicated to Zanele, Mbeki's wife of over 40 years, her personal warmth and influence as a political actor in her own right cannot be hidden. A close friend to Brigalia Bam over the years, we see Zanele encouraging and nurturing young South Africans, such as Gloria Serobe, who then went on to bigger roles in transforming South Africa. It has often fallen to her to bring some balance into TM's punishing schedule – 'your friend is going to die in his library', she teases George Nene. It is Zanele who arranges for their friend, the late Danny Schechter, to speak frankly to Mbeki in Switzerland in that 'explosive' confrontation about the management of his image. Mangosuthu Buthelezi, whose relationship with the ANC survived difficult patches, has continued to value Zanele's warmth and friendship even after leaving government.

The formidable women in this book speak volumes about Mbeki's feminist credentials. We find him encouraging Brigalia Bam and opening his inner circle to Advocate Mojanku Gumbi, among others. As president, Mbeki gave quality time to the Presidential Working Group for Women, led by Gloria Serobe – a group that has since been left to wither. And it was Mbeki who in 2005 appointed Phumzile Mlambo-Ngcuka to be his deputy president.

The bruising business of governing

The Mbeki presidency attracted its share of controversy, and the authors do not skirt around the issues. Indeed the question of the HIV/AIDS controversy is tackled head-on. Anthony Mbewu, in particular, provides a detailed riposte to the critics, tackling the distortions of Mbeki's position. Although others consider that the questions that Mbeki posed were important and had to be asked, some think that Mbeki's intellectual curiosity and commitment to rational policy-making drew him too deep into the minutiae. Danny Schechter, who confronted Mbeki, thought the president had tried his best to ride the many contradictions of his party and country.

Anders Möllander, Swedish friend for many years, and others point out that it was in fact Mbeki who was at the forefront of securing cheaper antiretroviral drugs for South Africans and the continent; arguably, the single intervention with the furthest reaching consequences in the fight against AIDS on the continent. Even those who, like Albie Sachs and Anne Page, have disagreed with some of the positions Mbeki took, start with memories of his remarkable gifts, and have retained their friendship and respect.

Inevitably the ghosts of Polokwane and of Mbeki's 'recall' by the ANC linger. Alongside the obvious pain, there is also reflection. Bheki Khumalo and others consider that the issue of the succession to the ANC presidency could have been handled differently. Anne Page thinks that Mbeki became caught up in leading, and was less able to listen. Mavuso Msimang, a friend going back to younger days, thinks Mbeki was unable to imagine that ANC people could be corruptible, and therefore failed to see, in time, when others acted in their personal interests. For Möllander, seeking re-election as ANC president was 'a very rare but obvious miscalculation' on Mbeki's part. These candid observations of the people close to Mbeki make for a rounded book.

Although his resignation was undoubtedly a traumatic experience, Mbeki's composure and dignity when the world around him appeared to collapse shines through. Rallying his shocked and demoralised supporters, Mbeki declined to fight the ANC in court, despite the advice of some. This was the Mbeki leadership: putting country and party first; providing pastoral care to others.

'A gift to all Africans'

But South Africa's loss became Africa's gain. Few can argue with Patricia McFadden that Mbeki is a gift to the continent. To its credit, the African Union moved quickly to make the most use of him. In 2009, Mbeki was invited to chair first a panel on Darfur and then another on Sudan and South Sudan. His formidable skills and energy shepherded through the process of the secession of South Sudan, including the important Cooperation Agreement between the two states in September 2012. The patience and humanism that President Pedro Pires sees in him underpin Mbeki's work across the continent. Another key recent contribution is Mbeki's stewardship of the High Level Panel on Illicit Financial Flows from Africa. The 2015 final report, which carries Mbeki's indelible ink, should be required reading for every African government, organisation and citizen concerned about the continuing plunder of the continent.

That social ease, observed by Bheki Khumalo and others throughout the book, of being able to sit with world leaders and royalty one day and then with humble villagers the next, remains. That facility with words; expressing ideas with precision and clarity, formulating powerful oral argument when it matters most (see Albie Sachs and Smuts Ngonyama on his courageous 1993 sanctions speech) have been put at the disposal of the continent. Mbeki the mentor continues to push others to fulfil their potential. Through his Leadership Institute he is helping to nurture the next generation of leaders, in the same way O.R. Tambo invested in him. Mbeki the teacher, listening intently, priest-like (accordingly to Dumisani Kumalo), will share his knowledge, usually recommending a good book from his vast reading as additional material.

'Hell, he can sing!'

Some say that being out of power has allowed Mbeki to let his hair down more, but Essop Pahad insists that Mbeki could always relax and, indeed, hold a tune. His love of music and jazz in particular runs like a riff throughout this book. Veteran jazz maestro Jonas Gwangwa is grateful for Mbeki's support in the formation of *Amandla*, the protest musical of the South African struggle for freedom. We learn too that Mbeki has found more time to play his piano.

Countless others could share their own personal experiences of Mbeki. This is a rich collection of lessons in history, visionary and practical politics and of courage in adversity. The authors, often unwittingly, reflect the image of the Chief whose genius is to inspire and mobilise others, from presidents to bodyguards, to serve and fight for causes bigger than themselves.

One summer, having concluded my presentation on Africa and international justice at the Summer School of the University of Leiden in The Hague, one of the graduate participants wanted to know more about my background. When I explained that I also worked with Mbeki on the panel he leads on Sudan and South Sudan, she nodded and broke into a wide smile: 'I am not surprised!' she said in triumph. We both laughed. She meant it as a compliment – to Thabo Mbeki.

Abingdon, Oxfordshire
April 2016

FOREWORD

MAHMOOD MAMDANI

Call them reminiscences or testimonials, the collection of writings in this book presents a combination of personal and political accounts of Thabo Mbeki, his passage from youth to manhood, from political apprenticeship under Oliver Tambo to the presidency of South Africa, and his fall from that dizzy height. The writers range from close friends and colleagues to sympathetic critics and political adversaries. Some defend him out of personal loyalty, others out of intelligent conviction, and yet others remain respectfully neutral.

By any measure, Thabo's political journey is remarkable. He emerges as both the strategist of the growing consensus around a negotiated end to apartheid and the one who articulates its purpose alongside Nelson Mandela.

From armed struggle to negotiations
We associate the South African transition with the heroic figure of Nelson Mandela. The contributors to this book twin Mbeki with Mandela, often citing Mandela's statement that he had been more of a ceremonial president with Mbeki as the de facto president of the country. The challenge this generation of political leaders faced was huge: to dismantle the legacy of a regime that had been the bulwark of minority racial privilege for centuries, and in its place to build the political, social and institutional foundations for a new South Africa. How do you respond to the long-suppressed aspirations of the majority, but at the same time do so without stoking the fears of

the minority? If the country needed political reconciliation, it also needed social justice. The challenge was to avoid not one but two possible pitfalls: on the one hand, to reconcile without embracing the bitter legacy of apartheid; on the other, to pursue justice without turning it into a vendetta, a project of revenge.

Mbeki would later sum up two sides of the dilemma in two separate speeches: 'I am an African' and 'Two Nations'. Though two sides of the same coin, these dilemmas tended to appear at very different moments, the first at the dawn of the post-apartheid era, the second in the aftermath of the first perceived failure to respond to the legitimate aspirations of the majority oppressed under apartheid. Eventually, his critics on the left and right came together in a single chorus, claiming that in addressing the two questions at separate times, he was moving from one extreme to another: those on the left claimed he had embraced reconciliation in the absence of justice, and those on the right accused him of turning to the question of justice for demagogic reasons, Mugabe-style, so as to turn the demand for justice into a racial vendetta.

The discussion that ensued led to the Harare Declaration of 1989, calling for a negotiated end to apartheid. At the same time, the situation had changed decisively at all levels – within the townships, the region, and the globe (Salim Salim). A triple development had brought the regime to consider the possibility of a negotiated solution: internally, a raging popular struggle in the townships; regionally, military defeat at the hands of a joint Cuban-Angolan force at Cuito Cuanavale in Angola; and, globally, the end of the Cold War and thus the fear that the ANC could turn out to be a Soviet Trojan Horse.

The shift of emphasis from armed struggle (or insurrection, in Thabo's words) to a negotiated settlement was first evident in 'The Path to Power', drafted for the 7th Congress of the South African Communist Party (SACP) held in Cuba in 1989. It had the support of the Frontline States, and Nyerere in particular, daunted as he was by the human cost of an attempted insurrection (Essop Pahad).

Thabo's role was pivotal in the multiple negotiations that unfolded over the next several years. His negotiating partners ranged from the internal wing of the township uprising (mainly United Democratic Front

[UDF] leaders and the trade unions), the official leadership of the South African government, big business and government-allied intellectuals, and the United States. In spite of President P.W. Botha scuttling a meeting planned for earlier in 1985 – 'We do not talk to murderers' – the first talks took place in Lusaka in 1985. They were with captains of industry and led to public talks in London. Then followed secret talks in Switzerland. Aziz Pahad tells us that the ANC's objective in the talks with big business was to remove 'the curtain of ignorance and fear' that had stoked white anxieties as a prelude to a series of talks with the more organised Afrikaner establishments. Dissident Afrikaners – Frederik van Zyl Slabbert and Breyten Breytenbach – flew to London, and the Cape Town-based Institute for a Democratic South Africa (IDASA) organised 45 prominent Afrikaners to meet the ANC in Dakar. The year 1987 was marked by several meetings. One of these was a get-together with Afrikaner intellectuals from Stellenbosch. It was led by Willie Esterhuyse, who writes: 'Mbeki, more than anyone else from the ANC, helped me to "deconstruct" my concept of "the enemy". He liberated me in this respect'. Another was a meeting with the US Secretary of State. The high point was a meeting with Niel Barnard, head of the National Intelligence Service. Four more secret meetings followed with the Intelligence Service, all in Switzerland, in 1989 and 1990.

Mbeki participated in several of these meetings, including those with the South African Intelligence Service. He had chaired the SACP congress that adopted 'The Path to Power'. This document presented negotiations as the conclusion of a successful armed struggle, thus complementary to armed struggle rather than an alternative to it: 'Armed struggle cannot be counterposed with dialogue, negotiation and justifiable compromise, as if they were mutually exclusive categories. Liberation struggles have rarely ended with the unconditional surrender of the enemy's military forces …' (Geraldine J. Fraser-Moleketi). Thabo was part of the group that agreed on key concessions to the National Party, known as the Sunset Clauses, including a power-sharing agreement (Aziz Pahad, Alexander Erwin).

It was not the exile-based armed struggle but the internal uprising that had brought the apartheid regime to the negotiating table. The contributions to this book suggest that Thabo Mbeki played a critical role in convincing the internal movements – come together as the UDF – to line up behind the negotiation strategy. The coming together of the exile and the internal wings of the anti-apartheid struggle was not a foregone conclusion. If forging that coalition was Mbeki's great achievement, to make that unity durable would be his biggest political challenge. It is growing cracks within that united front that gave his opponents the opportunity to remove Mbeki from office.

Zimbabwe

Zimbabwe was arguably one of Thabo Mbeki's great successes; the other, in spite of the furore and the controversy it generated, in hindsight, as I shall argue later, was the HIV/AIDS campaign.

Zimbabwe was the great NO, no to regime change, no to external dictation. It was at the same time a great YES, yes to reform as the alternative to punishment, yes to regionalism as a way to stem the tide of growing external interference. It was through the South African initiative that Africa was able to force the European Union to invite Zimbabwe for the consultative meeting with Europe.

It is Western powers, in particular Britain, and big capital in South Africa, that wanted a regime change in Zimbabwe (Essop Pahad). Contributors to this book give two arguments against regime change. One, regime change has brought disaster wherever it has been attempted, in Afghanistan, Iraq, Libya, Syria (Alexander Erwin). To be sure, regime change would have deepened the internal crisis in Zimbabwe in the name of resolving it; the cost would have been staggering, much more than the one to three million Zimbabwean refugees currently in South Africa (Anders Möllander). Second, South Africa would have been the next target of regime change had it succeeded (Aziz Pahad). But then, we may ask, was it not anyway?

It was possibly in Zimbabwe that Western powers fine-tuned an alternative strategy for regime change – linking up with domestic forces in a pincer movement that would take full advantage of an internal crisis. That strategy called for building a grand coalition, of three different oppositions, one within the regime, the second outside the regime, and the third within civil society. Welile Nhlapo points out that the Movement for Democratic Change (MDC) was being sponsored through the so-called Freedom/

Democracy programmes and that Britain was one of Morgan Tsvangirai's main sponsors through Freedom House.

Mbeki's response to regime change was to promote internal reform, in particular that of the electoral and governmental system, and to build a regional consensus behind it. One instance of growing support for the strategy, not just in the southern African region but also elsewhere in the continent, is provided in Dumisani Kumalo's account of the Burkinabe representative at the United Nations (UN) defying his president to vote against a regime change resolution. The irony of his resolute stance was that though Mbeki succeeded in making Zimbabwe safe from regime change, he was unable to inoculate South Africa from that same fate. We shall turn to this question later.

The thinking that informed South Africa's Zimbabwe policy was born of its own internal experience: a negotiated outcome called for more than just a reconciliation that turned one's back on the past; it also required internal reform to build a more durable future. South Africa succeeded in transporting this lesson to other countries in the region, especially Burundi and the Democratic Republic of Congo (DRC) (Ketumile Masire). The DRC set a precedent: for the first time in any UN mission, the lead state was not a major Western power, but an African country (John Stremlau). Equatorial Guinea presents a different kind of example: there, South Africa intervened to prevent an armed coup that would have resulted in a regime change. The Congo agreement was signed on 16 December 2002. With Thabo's departure, much changed, not only internally but also in foreign policy. The dramatic change at the UN is illustrated by the contrast between how South Africa responded to two regime change initiatives. During Mbeki's time, South Africa rallied African opposition to a unilateral US intervention in Iraq; under Zuma's leadership, South Africa buckled under US pressure and in spite of an AU resolution to the contrary, supported intervention in Libya. One gets the sense of a fresh breeze that was blowing across the continent during the opening years of the 21st century from reading accounts in this book. Its effects, small and often no more than symbolic, were evident in many a place. It took a symbolic face-off between French and South African troops in Abidjan in 2004 to get the French to believe that an agreement had been reached between political adversaries in a Francophone country

(Ivory Coast) without France's direct involvement in favour of their proxy, in this case Alassane Ouattara (Dumisani Kumalo, Miranda Strydom). In Haiti, Mbeki turned up as the only foreign head of state at the 200th anniversary of the revolution of 1804 led by Toussaint L'Ouverture. And when Aristide was ousted in an America-sanctioned operation, Mbeki hosted him back home in South Africa (Mavuso Msimang, Randall Robinson). Another initiative, important in both symbolism and reality, was the project to preserve the Timbuktu manuscripts (Mavuso Msimang). This, then, was quintessential Mbeki, unafraid to go into battle, to lead the frontlines, some (in this collection) say no matter the odds.

Economic policy

The signature documents of the ANC's economic policy are known as NEPAD and GEAR. The former put together a global agenda for Africa, and the latter put forward an agenda for the new South Africa. Immediately, the debate focused on whether these marked a step forward or a retreat.

To read Meles Zenawi's contribution to this book is to get some idea of the frame of mind of Africa's leaders in the closing years of the 20th century. There is a sense of being boxed in, with little choice but to bide time until there is some fresh air. Read Meles' account of 'those very dark and menacing days': 'We needed foreign aid and loans to keep body and soul together … Whether we liked it or not, we knew we had to do what everyone else on the continent was doing: reform our economy … The informal and heartfelt advice that the leaders of our delegations got from every African country they visited was very simple. You have to say "yes" to whatever they, meaning the IMF and the World Bank, tell you: Say yes, and if you can't, whenever you can, you must try to play around with the implementation of things you do not like.' Meles' sober but not very edifying conclusion: 'The most we could do to counter it was never to accept it, but also never to challenge it in public and all the time seeking a better way out … A Swedish diplomat in Tanzania had … publicly stated that ownership means that Africans do what you tell them to do, but they do it willingly.' This is how Obasanjo recalls the humiliation of those times: the three African leaders – Mbeki of South Africa, Bouteflika of Algeria and Obasanjo of Nigeria – 'were sent' to meet the G7+Russia, who were themselves meeting in

Okinawa. But they met the big boys and girls in Tokyo and were 'dismissed as African leaders in 30 minutes or so'. It was this moment of shame that forced a reckoning – 'that we had to do something tangible' – that led to the birth of NEPAD.

The policy differences with the World Bank and the Washington Consensus were minimal: NEPAD broadened priorities beyond primary education and good governance to include higher education and infrastructure. Was not NEPAD really a face-saving device, voluntarily taking on board 'reforms' that would otherwise be forced by external creditors? Or was it a gesture of independence at a time when the word was rapidly losing meaning?

NEPAD was born in a bleak ideological landscape that allowed no space for independent thinking by Africans. For its advocates, what distinguished NEPAD from the generic Structural Adjustment Programme was not its economics but its politics, that it was home-made, African! Meles thought NEPAD was more than an economic programme; he credited NEPAD and the Peer Review Mechanism with 'resisting shotgun democratisation, externally driven regime change and colour revolutions ... rather successfully'.

If NEPAD was a time-saving device for the leaders who championed it, it was more of a face-saving anathema for the political left, which saw it as a home-baked version of neoliberalism. Even as tacticians embraced NEPAD, those with an acumen for strategy turned away from it. As the logic behind NEPAD came to inform domestic economic policy, the political cost was high, especially to Mbeki: it opened a crack in the coalition that had stood behind the ANC's turn to a negotiating strategy in the late 1980s.

The confrontation came to a head over domestic policy in South Africa with the unveiling of a new 'reform' economic programme, GEAR. By 1996, the lines were drawn. The ideological left was divided. On one side were those in the Congress of South African Trade Unions (COSATU) and the SACP; on the other side those in government. Yesterday's comrades stood on different sides with lines redrawn and redefined: insults were hurled across the barricades, at the 'class of 96' and 'neoliberals' on one side, and 'ultra-leftists' on the other. The reader can get a taste of the theoretical shift in the position of the ANC leadership in government from the contribution of Wiseman Nkuhlu, who became Chairman of the Development

Bank of Southern Africa in 1992/93. Nkuhlu argues as a born-again pragmatist: 'All of us in the 1970s were strongly socialist, but as years went by we
got a better understanding of the economic policies followed by successful countries, especially the Nordic countries, and also later on the Asian
countries.' He sums up the lesson as follows: to have a sustainable welfare
programme you needed a strong enough tax base, and to have a strong
enough tax base you needed incentives for the private sector to invest in
the economy and to have faith in the future. GEAR was that confidence-
building exercise.

In this volume, the reader will find essays that give the point of view of
the practitioners, their sense of reality as a set of constraints that they had
little choice but to take into account, informing their conviction that their
response was not only correct but also effective. After all, the balance of
payments was in a surplus when Thabo left office. Alexander Erwin, one of
Thabo's economic ministers, justifies the belt-tightening that was GEAR
on technical grounds (effectively dealing with 'gaps in terms of economic
policy ... monetary policy, deficit policy, interest rate policy, exchange rate
policy, tariff policy') and on grounds of realism ('we had inherited an economically bankrupt country from the apartheid regime'). Others (Smuts
Ngonyama, Miranda Strydom, Frank Chikane) nod in agreement. But the
debate was not about constraints but about choices: how should the ANC
respond to these constraints? The ANC's historic position as a liberation
movement had been that the apartheid debt should not be paid because it
was an 'odious debt'. But now, the ANC in government argued that since
'only 6% or so was foreign debt' the government had an obligation to pay
it. The critics on the left and in civil society disagreed: they pointed out
that not only was the debt mainly to 'white' pension funds, it was anyway
owed to the wealthier section of society, whereas the burden of paying it
would fall disproportionately on the shoulders of the black poor. Thabo
would later sum up the divide between these two sides as that between 'two
nations'. But by then it would be too late, for both Thabo Mbeki and the
left coalition in the country.

Danny Schechter points out that big business was not interested in incentives. It wanted certainty. And that surety could only be political, the result
of a regime change. The irony is that Schechter, a journalist from outside

South Africa, is the only one among the contributors who exposes the shaky political ground upon which the Mbeki administration now stood: the assumption that the strategic interest of big capital was compatible with those of the people over the short run was no longer tenable.

By 2006, all the pieces needed for regime change were in place: big business, the left in COSATU and the SACP, and the ANC right wing. Nkuhlu, however, believes the exercise paid off since 'when Mbeki left government we had a surplus and we were in a strong economic position'. What he does not tell us is that by then 'we' were no longer in a political position to follow a social democratic programme for the simple reason that the political coalition that would have enforced such a programme was no longer in power! The political price this coalition paid for a positive balance of payments was regime change: what had begun as a shouting match in 1996 would end with the sacrifice of Thabo Mbeki a decade later.

The single most puzzling thing about the essays in this collection is their inability to come to grips with the political defeat that was Thabo's ouster from office. Most, like Essop Pahad, think it was the result of a failure of communication. None entertains the possibility that it may have been the result of a policy failure that made for a broad and politically unsustainable coalition of forces – left, centre and right – that would topple Thabo and dissolve the morning after.

The confrontation continued from GEAR to the controversy over HIV/AIDS. The sacrificial rites would come to a close only with the consummation of Thabo Mbeki.

The HIV/AIDS debate

Though researchers identify 1990 as the onset of HIV/AIDS in South Africa, the controversy around the disease began only in mid-1995/96. That same year, Anthony Mbewu, a medical professional, came from England to work at the Medical Research Council (MRC). Mbewu became the lead person in the research team on HIV/AIDS at the MRC. Nineteen ninety-six was also the year Mbeki inaugurated the Partnership Against Aids. Mbewu argues that 'Mbeki was one of the first who understood that this was not just a disease, but was something that affected every sector of society and whose spread and impact was closely interwoven with all sorts of aspects of South African life'.

HIV/AIDS was a new and little understood disease and was perceived as a global threat. The controversy around it focused on several issues. Two early cases, one in the West and the other in Africa, shaped the discussion around HIV/AIDS. During its early spread in the US and UK, HIV/AIDS came to be known as a lifestyle disease, of gay men and drug-users. Lessons pointed not just to the virus but also to a context that suggested that multiple factors were fuelling the epidemic: 'multiple sexual partners, drug use and so on'. By the time AZT came on the scene, which was 1985, the epidemic was 'beginning to come under control within the gay and artistic communities in London'. In those days, when there was neither a drug nor a vaccine, 'change in sexual behaviour was the first method of control: I used to say to people, technically we have a cure for AIDS called the condom. If you and your partner are both negative and use a condom, the chances of your getting HIV are almost zero' (Anthony Mbewu).

The second important case was that of Uganda, hit by an epidemic known as 'slim disease' in the late 1980s. Without the local availability of equipment to test for HIV antibodies, scientists in the US said it was 'just a severe immune deficiency caused by malnutrition, particularly by vitamin B12 deficiency'. But within a few years this same epidemic was labelled HIV/AIDS. Debate was no longer seen as healthy. An officially sanctioned version of the truth took over. Anthony Mbewu says a 'gospel truth' was rolled out, and it became 'blasphemous to question the causation of HIV/AIDS'.

Not everyone agreed. Among these was Luc Montagnier who had discovered the HI virus. His point of view was that, true, 'AIDS was caused by HIV, but there were other aspects to consider'. Montagnier asked, 'Why did it hit Africa so hard but not the United States and Europe? What else was there that makes HIV prevalence escalate dramatically in African countries but not in European countries?' Other scientists argued that it was malnutrition, alongside HIV, that destroyed the immune system. Mbewu highlights the example of tuberculosis (TB), which 'used to kill about 70 000 people a year in South Africa but that has come down to less than 50 000'. That 'the key to managing TB is drugs' should not obscure the fact that 'the course of TB in a population is not primarily determined by the availability of drug treatment' but 'by overcrowding, lack of sanitation, by malnutrition, by many social variables and challenges'. Luc Montagnier went on to elaborate the point: 'We should push for more, you know, a combination of measures; antioxidants, nutrition advice, nutritions, fighting other infections – malaria, tuberculosis, parasitosis, worms – education of course, genital hygiene for women and men also, very simple measures which [are] not very expensive, but which could do a lot. And this is my, actually my worry about the many spectacular actions for the global funds to buy drugs and so on, and Bill Gates and so on, for the vaccine.'

This is where the role of pharmaceuticals in setting limits on the public debate became evident. In Mbewu's words, 'medical research is driven primarily by commercial interests -- not primarily by the major health problems that afflict a population'. The driver behind research is 'largely a commercial one and not primarily a humanitarian one. It was an issue of antiretroviral drugs having to find a market.' Contradicting expectations, the disease had not spread in Europe and the US, but was raging like a wild fire in large parts of Africa. HIV prevalence in the UK was 1%, but in South Africa it was 14%. No wonder commercial interests focused on South Africa, one of the richest countries in Africa.

At this time, scientists had begun withdrawing from asking uncomfortable questions because 'if they did, they would not get grants, journals would ban their papers, their careers would be destroyed'. It is at this juncture that President Mbeki entered the fray. The Presidential International Aids Panel he set up in 1999 laid out a welcome mat to those asking uncomfortable but relevant questions. There was a furore: 'How could President Mbeki, who was not even a scientist, ask these questions and cast doubt in people's minds about the causation of HIV and AIDS?'

With pharmaceutical interests in the driving seat, the AIDS lobby labelled critics denialists, as questioning that HIV causes AIDS. And yet the most telling argument made by critics did not concern the cause of AIDS but why it was spreading so much faster in Africa than in Europe and the US. The AIDS lobby succeeded in shaping the public perception and thus public narrative around the debate. Instead of testimony to the integral necessity of debate in the pursuit of science, the debate was perceived as socially irresponsible, and those involved in the debate were vilified as 'denialists' who should be ostracised both in the scientific community and in the public at large. The accusation of being a 'denial-ist' became potent and powerful because it evoked other contexts: the denial of the Holocaust in particular, and genocide in general. The *Mail & Guardian*, asked in April 2001, as it had in 1996, if Mbeki was fit to rule (Bheki Khumalo). Some even suggested that Mbeki be taken to The Hague and tried as a denialist.

That the thrust of the debate was not to question whether HIV caused AIDS, but to shine a light on contributing factors is clear from the report of the International Presidential Aids Panel: '… antiretrovirals are useful in the management of HIV and AIDS but they are not the primary solution'. The 'media hype around antiretrovirals' was claiming that 'if we could only get our hands on antiretrovirals, the HIV epidemic would be contained and of course that is not true'. Why ignore the experience of the gay commu-nity in the US, where HIV declined from 1980 mainly because of changes in sexual behaviour? To take that and other experiences into account one needed to focus on not only the cure for AIDS but its prevention so as to check its spread. The Report presented the views of both sides to the debate and raised a lot of questions – like the need for further research, both on more than 2 000 plants that are used in traditional medicines, and 'on issues around poverty and socio-economic deprivation, important in terms of the pathogenesis of HIV as in the cause of TB'. But the report was ignored by the scientific community and the pharmaceutical industry, which refused to fund the recommended research. Mbewu labels it a spectacular case of self-censorship.

The HIV/AIDS case in South Africa is a powerful illustration of three facts: (1) the power and muscle of the corporate sector, in this case the pharmaceutical companies; (2) the counter-force that the state can muster to corporate interests in middle-income countries like South Africa; and (3) the decisive role of society (often called 'civil society') in shaping the outcome of the contest between the corporate power and the state.

The power of the state in mustering a counter-force capable of with-standing the greed and ambition of commercial interests became clear in the aftermath of Clinton's 2003 visit to South Africa. Following it, the Clinton Foundation assembled around 50 of 'the world's leading HIV/AIDS scientists'. With their help, the MRC wrote the Operational Plan for Prevention, Treatment and Care for HIV/AIDS, emphasising a 'comprehensive approach to HIV and AIDS treatment' on the premise that 'it was not just a matter of rolling out antiretrovirals' but focusing on 'the whole of the health system, all of South African society' with a comprehensive programme that combined prevention and treatment. The outcome can only be described as a stunning victory against the pharmaceutical industry. Although the cost of treatment per patient in the global market had gone down from US$10 000 in 1997, it was still US$3 000 in 2000, clearly unaffordable for a middle-income country like South Africa. South Africa turned to Indian pharmaceutical companies for an affordable generic substitute. The pharmaceuticals agreed to discuss the basics, starting with their cost of production, provided each of the Indian companies that participated could be guaranteed one million patients on treatment. The final agreement reduced the cost per patient per year to US$250 by early 2004. Antiretroviral therapy began in 2004. That same year, Anthony Mbewu informed the Science and Technology Portfolio Committee in parliament 'that South Africa had the largest antiretroviral programme in the history of the planet'. By 2009, there were 900 000 people on treatment, a figure that has grown to 2.2 million people today. None of this would have been possible without the search for an affordable, generic replacement for brand names that guarantee superprofits for pharmaceutical companies.

Apart from the scientific research underlying the HIV/AIDS controversy, we need to understand that the very specific politics of AIDS made it a potent political force in the ongoing anti-Mbeki campaign. In this, the role of the gay community was pivotal. This stemmed from the fact that AIDS had first affected the gay community in the early 1980s. From the start, AIDS was stigmatised as *the* gay and drug-user disease. The stigma rationalised official neglect of a growing epidemic in the US, compelling the gay community to mobilise to combat the spread of HIV/AIDS. When it came to South Africa, it became possible to portray Thabo Mbeki as uncaring, this time not just with regard to the concerns of the gay community or those who suffered from AIDS, but in a larger sense, unsympathetic to minorities.

Did Mbeki try to use his position as president of South Africa to impose an official truth, just as the pharmaceuticals were using their financial muscle to do? Or did he seek to use the power of the presidency to keep open a discussion of great importance for the South African people? Several writers in this volume disagree with Mbeki's views (Mangosuthu Buthelezi, Mavuso Msimang, Albie Sachs). But none holds him responsible for the kind of crime he was charged with by AIDS activists. Danny Schechter sums up the middle ground: 'To raise questions in that period was akin to some of us denying the Holocaust ... The issue had by then become highly emotional and many were convinced that there was only one way to fight AIDS: hand over the national budget to buy overpriced AIDS medicines. He rejected that ... ever since mainstream media narratives of the world have looked at him negatively. Once they brand you, they keep you branded in a simplistic world of good guys and bad guys.'

There can be no doubt that Mbeki used his position as president to further certain objectives which he was convinced were in the larger public interest. The first was to ensure that the debate remains open on an issue of great public interest. Though not a single contribution to this book raises the question, there is little doubt that Mbeki believed that the argument that disassociated the spread of the disease from its context – the abject poverty of large sections of the black population – was an incitement to a racist anti-black discourse. The second was to pursue the search for an affordable drug, one affordable in a middle-income country with a poor majority.

The Mbeki government took on the pharmaceuticals in two ways. The first was to get access to generic drugs. In 1997, during the Mandela presidency, the South African government passed a law setting up, among other things, a marketplace for medicines based on affordable prices. Clause 15c relied on two practices agreed under the World Trade Organisation's guidelines. The first, called compulsory licensing, 'allows businesses in a country in a state of emergency to manufacture generic products paying only a royalty to the patent owner'. The second, called parallel importing, 'lets a nation import drugs made more cheaply in one country than in another'. As we know now, the difference between using brand names and generics was that between US$10 000 and US$250 per AIDS patient per year. The legislation was labelled 'piracy' by PhRMA (the Pharmaceutical Research and Manufacturers of America) – 'a formidable alliance' of the 100 biggest drug companies in the US.[1] The big pharmaceutical companies threatened South Africa should the country break patent laws. This is the battle that Mbeki took on and won in 2001.

The roll-out of AZT began after 2001. Critics held Mbeki responsible for the delay and the deaths of hundreds of thousands in the interim. Could South Africa have rolled out AZT at US$10 000 – even US$3 000 – a year per user? If so, how much of the health budget, and more, would it have consumed, and at what collateral damage? The second victory against the pharmaceuticals was to generate a debate on co-factors, to expand the discussion beyond treatment to prevention. The second victory was not just to roll out affordable AZTs but to make possible a countrywide discussion leading to making AZT part of a comprehensive programme.

Was it morally irresponsible to keep asking questions in a situation of national emergency? It is imperative in an emergency that one must act, but also that one must keep thinking even as one acts. If we must act even on the basis of incomplete information, we must continue thinking and thus know that every action remains provisional and thus subject to revision. Mbewu writes: 'A scientific hypothesis or a scientific theory is only true until an alternative explanation comes along and debunks it. Scientists all ask questions, scientists do not believe anything.'

Fall from power
Thabo Mbeki made two notable speeches during his time as president: 'I am an African' and 'Two Nations'. Together, they give a comprehensive account of his understanding of the new South Africa, its promise and its challenge. His critics took each speech on its own, wrenched from a larger context, and painted him either a born-again neoliberal who had capitulated to powerful vested interests, or a racial demagogue setting up a minority against the majority.

The promise was articulated in 'I am an African', one of the most remarkable political documents of the 20th century. This speech was made on the occasion of the adoption of the Constitution Bill by the Constitutional Assembly of the Republic of South Africa on 8 May 1996. Its focus was on

---

1 'How Drug Giants Let Millions Die of Aids', published in *The Guardian*, UK http://www.theguardian.com/uk/1999/dec/19/theobserver.uknews6.

the future: Would yesterday's settlers be today's migrants, citizens of the new de-racialised South Africa, or will they be flushed out of the colony, like the *Pieds Noirs* in Algeria, to make way for a racially cleansed independent country? Mbeki's answer was unequivocal: 'I am formed of the migrants who left Europe to find a new home on our native land. Whatever their own actions, they remain still part of me … I am the grandchild who lays fresh flowers on the Boer graves at St Helena and the Bahamas, who sees in the mind's eye and suffers the suffering of a simple peasant folk: death, concentration camps, destroyed homesteads, a dream in ruins … I am an African!' South Africa, Thabo was saying, will take a road different from Algeria, another famed settler colony at the northern end of the continent. The consequences would be enormous for both the native and the settler. It was a grand vision, Lincolnesque, fitting for a statesman at the helm of the new South Africa.

If building a shared future was the promise of the new South Africa, its challenge was the realisation of social justice for the vast majority who had been forcibly excluded from this common journey until only yesterday. This stark history had given rise to *two nations*, the subject of Mbeki's second speech, given at the opening of the debate in the National Assembly on 'Reconciliation and Nation-Building' on 29 May 1998. Patricia McFadden, citing Vusi Gumede, evokes the critique from the left: whereas in 'I am an African' Mbeki had 'described being South African fundamentally in historical terms', 'Two Nations' was finally coming to grips with 'the difficult but inevitable challenges posed by white class privilege'. Though some on the left welcomed the speech as addressing so much unfinished business, for many it was a rhetorical gesture that had come too late. Those on the right said it was not 'reconciliatory at all to talk like that' for he had been widely perceived as 'playing the race card' (Mangosuthu Buthelezi).

While none of the writers in this volume celebrates the departure of Thabo Mbeki from the presidency, none is able to make political sense of this moment when a broad coalition came together with a single agenda, to oust him from office, falling apart as soon as the agenda had been accomplished.

To understand the power of the coalition, one needs to understand its contradictory components. It included big capital and organised labour, pharmaceuticals and AIDS activists, ambitious politicians and marginalised groups. If big capital saw in Mbeki and those around him the potential capacity to organise a social coalition against powerful vested interests (such as the pharmaceutical lobby or the Zimbabwe lobby), organised labour and social activists saw Mbeki as already having capitulated to big business (GEAR) or uncaring of vulnerable groups when it came to social catastrophe demanding urgent attention (HIV/AIDS).

Some (Essop Pahad) think that Mbeki's failure was a failure of communication. Others think of it as a personal tragedy of Shakespearean proportions (Bheki Khumalo), and yet others argue that his fall was not only preventable, but was a greater tragedy for South Africa than for Thabo Mbeki (Danny Schechter).

The Americans among these writers compare him to Bill Clinton (Danny Schechter) or to Al Gore (John Stremlau). But Mbeki is neither a Clinton nor a Gore. The AIDS/HIV controversy was more of an epic saga than a sex scandal. Al Gore was awarded with a consolation Nobel Prize for having subordinated personal ambition to national interest; Thabo Mbeki is unlikely to accept a consolation prize, more likely to continue to pursue the same objectives that led him into that fateful encounter with international pharmaceuticals and domestic big capital.

Mbeki's fall from the presidency evokes other parallels: with Morsi in Egypt, and the possible fall of Rousseff in Brazil. In both cases, having failed to do the job on their own, powerful interests turned to aggrieved social movements to tip the balance. In South Africa, that mobilisation was done by a combination of AIDS activists and trade unionists.

Thabo Mbeki was removed from office barely seven months before his term as president expired. Even his political adversaries – such as Buthelezi – recognise that his removal was not necessary: 'it was done just to humiliate him'. And, one may add, as a lesson for others who may follow in his footsteps.

The strength of the essays in this book is that they give the reader insider views of developments, each from a different vantage point. But they do so in piecemeal fashion. What is missing is an account of the full picture from those who combine involvement with detachment and proximity with distance, two conditions necessary for a comprehensive reflection. And because that overall view is missing, the book does not take on the question of why a palpably unfair and unconstitutional ouster from power was possible less than two decades into the era of political democracy. My hunch is that the answer to that question will say more about what has happened to the ANC than it will about Thabo Mbeki. My hope is that this book will prepare its readers to ask that question and draw lessons from it.[2]

April 2016

2 I would like to thank Lyn Ossome and Suren Pillay for critical comments on an earlier draft of this Foreword.

I

FAMILY FRIENDS

BRIGALIA BAM

❖

I was introduced to Thabo Mbeki by Zanele Dlamini, who later became his wife, at Mazisi Kunene's house in London in 1967. Mazisi Kunene's home was a meeting place for many South Africans in exile. Mazisi was a poet and at the time of our meeting he was a representative of the African National Congress (ANC) in the United Kingdom. I had known Zanele Mbeki and her family since 1954 in Alexandra township where her father was a minister of religion. Later I worked for the Young Women's Christian Association (YWCA) in Durban; Edith Dlamini Grenville-Grey, Zanele's older sister, had recruited me and she was my boss. That year I was spending my Christmas holiday in London with Khushu Dlamini, another of Zanele's sisters, who was doing a postgraduate course in nursing.

To provide a context of the reason why I first met Thabo Mbeki in London: I left South Africa in September 1967 because the World Council of Churches (WCC) in Geneva, Switzerland, had offered me a job. I had waited for my passport for four years. And that December I went to London for my vacation and to meet the South Africans who were in exile there. There were hardly any Africans from South Africa in exile in Geneva.

The amenable working relationship between the WCC and the ANC provided another platform for Thabo and I to meet occasionally. This was because the general secretary of the WCC, Dr Eugene Carson Blake, had decided to invite the members of the ANC to the WCC Assembly. In 1968, the 4th assembly of the WCC took place in Uppsala, Sweden, and Joe Matthews was the official representative of the ANC at that meeting.

3

The assembly of the WCC takes place once every seven years and brings together member churches from all over the world.

I had heard of Thabo Mbeki before meeting him and I knew of his parents who were well known and respected in South Africa. My own father and grandfather had in the early days of the Transkei Council (Bhunga) worked with Thabo's father Govan Mbeki. I also knew his uncle Manasseh Moerane who was the editor of one of the leading black newspapers of the time. Later in life I met Thabo's siblings who were also in exile. They were Moeletsi, his younger brother, and Jama, his older brother. Moeletsi would engage in interesting debates with Scrap Ntshona over dinners prepared by Scrap himself and their deliberations were often about ideological issues and geopolitics. Ntshona was a member of the Unity Movement and also a Trotskyite. I met Jama in Botswana when he represented my aunt, Mazonke Mei, in a court case that she eventually won.

When I first met Thabo in London he was a very quiet, rather shy young man, and very good looking. We engaged in a conversation about our old school, Lovedale. I left Lovedale in 1952. Thabo enrolled at Lovedale for his secondary school education in 1955 but according to the records he was then only 12 years old and had been in the group at Lovedale that had participated in the 1959 strike and as a result was expelled the same year. I was very pleased to meet him because although Lovedale was a famous missionary college, on reflection it was very racist. The living quarters of the black and white teaching staff were separate. The missionaries had better housing and even at the evening services at Lovedale, the teachers sat separately. At the time when we met Thabo was only 24 years old, and I was 34. I was so pleased to meet one of those youngsters who had been courageous and challenged racism and those of us who had been at Lovedale were very proud of this courageous younger generation. We also had a conversation about Robben Island prison because I had visited my brother, Fikile Bam, who was incarcerated on the island together with Thabo's father, Oom Gov Thabo had not been as fortunate as I was to visit the island. The conversation saddened me because Thabo had not seen his parents for years.

My first impression of Thabo Mbeki was that he was very reserved, and I did not find him to be a light-hearted person. Most of the South Africans would walk into Mazisi Kunene's home in London and start joking in their usual jovial way, but he was reserved. He was not the type of person to talk much but Kunene would always be able to start conversations with Thabo; he was not a pushy person who just took over any conversation. What I remember as I got to know Thabo better is that he was not very good at small talk. Whenever we South Africans met in exile we enjoyed gossiping about things that we had heard from home and it was a wonderful way for us to relieve the stress. Talking about apartheid and the struggle would hurt us, so to be able to enter into lamentations about home helped to distract us.

At that time Thabo already had a relationship with Zanele and I knew that they were special friends. But together with Mazisi we unilaterally assumed the role of matchmakers without being asked by the people concerned. On one occasion at Mazisi Kunene's house the latter said, 'I think that those two should get married', and I totally agreed. Mazisi emphasised that I had to find a way to convince Thabo to marry Zanele. We were of the view that Thabo and Zanele were intellectuals and both had very solid family backgrounds but different political backgrounds. Zanele was originally a member of the Unity Movement and Thabo had always been a member of the ANC.

I remember this as if it were yesterday. I am not sure when they decided to get married, but years later I got a call from Zanele and she had kept this secret away from me and wanted to surprise me. She said to me on the phone, 'I'm getting married.' I was overjoyed. The wedding took place in Edith's home, Farnham Castle in England. On his wedding day Thabo just looked the same – very serious, although he smiled frequently. When we congratulated him, he did not say much, but he smiled even more!

I met Thabo a few times in Europe before our meeting in Lusaka. I was travelling in the region on a WCC mission and I had also gone to visit Botswana. The ANC had decided that they wanted to meet my colleagues and me. I actually spent half a day with the executive of the ANC. They wanted to know what was happening with the anti-apartheid groups because at that time the WCC had organised a lot of debates focusing on issues such as sanctions against apartheid South Africa, which was one of our strongest campaigns.

One of my tasks was to organise women in exile. This was done on a personal level but with the support of the WCC. I will never forget the empowering support I got from Zanele and Thabo after the ANC had rejected my idea of forming an inclusive women's movement that included members of all liberation movements and those women who were not official members of these exiled liberation movements such as the ANC, Pan Africanist Congress (PAC) and Unity Movement. Gertrude Shope organised a problem-solving meeting between me and some of the NEC members of the ANC. The meeting was held at Thabo and Zanele's home in Lusaka. Thabo was decisive in this meeting for he was the one who resolved the matter by supporting my initiative.

On one occasion I had to deliver a speech at a big international conference of the World Methodist Church, which was held in Nairobi, Kenya. Thabo was visiting Zanele who was now working for the United Nations High Commissioner for Refugees and was based in Nairobi. As a representative of the WCC, I was asked by the conference organisers to deliver a speech. I had written this speech in Geneva and my colleagues had read and approved it. Whilst at Zanele's house Thabo asked to read my conference speech. I asked myself the question, why did he want to read it? That day while I was at the conference and Zanele had gone to work, Thabo spent time in the house rewriting my speech.

When I read Thabo's speech – not my speech – I was given a standing ovation by the audience attending the international conference. I could not believe that a politician like him could write a speech for the church. He emphasised the idea of a just war and linked it to apartheid South Africa and, believe me, Thabo quoted the Bible in a responsible manner. On one of the evenings, the leadership of the Methodist Church visited the flat to spend time with Zanele and Thabo.

It was impressive that Thabo was able to engage the leadership of the Methodist Church on religious matters – as a politician he was able to engage and understand the institution of the church. Of course one did not ask what his religious background was and what he knew about the church or even what he knew about the biblical references, ethics, or morality that he was able to articulate during the discussions. It was clear to me that he was an avid reader.

Another incident that I remember is related to the fact that on one occasion in London again, I solicited Mazisi and Thabo's views on an idea that

Johnny Makhathini whom I had known and worked with for some years in Durban doing ANC work, had put to me. He had suggested to me that I should be trained to do underground work for the ANC. He promised to arrange for my training in France. Mazisi and I had been giving support to the ANC office in Algeria. The ANC at that time was not able to raise enough money to support their representatives abroad. Both Thabo and Mazisi discouraged me and as a result I rejected Makhathini's proposal. Thabo felt that there were already a number of South African ANC representatives engaged in all forms of training. He then went on to talk about the importance of international global institutions and felt that my presence in the WCC and the work we were doing against apartheid was very important. He articulated, to my greatest amazement, the role of religion in the world and its role in the liberation struggle. I was very pleased with the discussion and felt that I was working with an organisation (at that time) that was important in supporting our struggle. It did not surprise me that when Thabo was deputy president and president of our country, he retained the respect of religious leaders and churches. Nor did it surprise me that he and Mandela invited the Reverend Frank Chikane to be their adviser and later director general in the presidency.

It was then that O.R. Tambo gave me very strict instructions after being informed about Makhathini's proposal. He said that I should remember that when I was at the WCC, I was not representing the ANC; I was there as the ambassador for South Africa. He said that I should forget about my ANC membership and rather see myself as speaking for the oppressed majority in the country. It was a wonderful release because in my work at the WCC, I could not be speaking for a liberation movement anyway. This would not be the last time Thabo Mbeki discouraged me from doing things that were not clear-cut.

In 1987, Desmond Tutu recruited me and tried to convince me to return to South Africa to be the general secretary of the South African Council of Churches (SACC). Desmond had been the previous general secretary and Beyers Naudé had been asked to be the interim general secretary while they looked for a person to fill the post. Again in 1987, Thabo phoned me when he was still in Lusaka and said, 'I hear that Desmond [Tutu] and others want you to return to South Africa as the SACC general secretary.' He said that he was not sure about it because the SACC was then the only organisation that held hope for us and because of that the apartheid government was really watching the SACC.

Thabo said this to protect me and prevent me from returning home. He told me that the government was intensifying the repression in terms of securocrats and the military forces being the dominant groups in charge of the country. But then he went on to say that Zanele did not agree with his view. She felt that I should return home and that I could manage it and she believed that I had the courage and the competencies to become the general secretary of the SACC. Zanele also felt that the time had arrived when a woman should occupy that position. But Thabo Mbeki responded, 'Sisi Hlophe, I am not doubting your competencies; I am just talking about the harsh political climate.'

Beyers Naudé and Desmond Tutu were relentless in their drive to recruit me because they kept phoning me but I thought that perhaps it would be a dangerous move. I would be returning to South Africa as a Swiss and as a Transkeian. I was no longer a South African as my South African passport was taken away from me by the apartheid regime. So I would be returning to work in my country for the SACC as a foreigner and I was scared. I phoned my brother Fikile Bam to tell him about these developments and what Thabo had told me. My brother wanted to consult a few people but said that his own immediate reaction was that Thabo was correct; the apartheid security system would crush me. I was not even sure that the churches in South Africa themselves were ready to support a woman in this position because when you become a general secretary you are in charge of all the churches. It is a very high position in the SACC as an institution and by tradition the leadership is dominated by males.

Indeed, when my brother got back to me after consulting his colleagues, he said that it was not advisable for me to return. So I called Desmond and Beyers and explained that I could not come back to South Africa. But then they both proposed that I come back to assist Frank Chikane who was then employed by the SACC. I would be there to give backing because they needed access to the international community, which I was in touch with. I knew most of the anti-apartheid groups. This time, I had no choice. Something just happened one day and I asked myself, 'What am I doing in Switzerland?' I had lived there for 21 years. There were people in South Africa who had made big sacrifices. I decided that I was going back home. I was more than ready.

During the same year, 1987, Thabo called me just before Oom Gov Mbeki was released from prison. He said, 'Sis Hlophe, you must have been hearing in the press that my father might be released soon. We do not know when but it is clear from the discussions that he will be released.' He said somebody had told him that my brother Fikile Bam was very friendly with his mother. My brother at the time was working in Idutywa where Thabo's mom lived. So I confirmed that this was true and that the person who introduced my brother to his mother was Oom Gov himself, because they were on Robben Island together. Oom Gov had given my brother many messages and had instructed him that, when he left the Robben Island prison, he must take care of his wife.

My brother Fikile was very pleased to be introduced to Epainette (Thabo's mother) and he found her amazing company. He could not believe that at that time they could engage with Thabo's mother on such deep political issues. He could not believe that someone living in a rural area was so articulate and so informed about politics. She became my role model because I wished that I could be like her. Thabo asked me to ask my brother if he would be kind enough to give support to his mother.

Then came the moment when Zanele was due to come back to South Africa. I often say that these were times when I discovered the caring human side of Thabo. He phoned me from Zambia and asked me if I could please help Zanele resettle. He said that he was really nervous about her coming back home and he wanted to make sure that she was safe and that the security forces did not harass her. I assured him that I would do my best.

We decided with Zanele that she should not spend the first night with me. So she spent her first two nights boarding at the Roman Catholic church in Yeoville. It was the safest place for her. We had to call Lusaka to assure Thabo that Zanele was safe. Even though it was normal for someone to worry and care that much, it underscored for me what a great man Thabo is.

The SACC arranged to go to Lusaka to conduct official discussions with the ANC about how the returnees would be repatriated. The Swedes had given the SACC funds so we hired two planes to Lusaka to meet the ANC. Thabo Mbeki was among the team that briefed us about the returnees. That, for me, was really the time of discovering Thabo more deeply because I was never with him for extended periods – usually our meetings were short encounters. Thabo and his colleagues informed us about the complexities of exile life, including the fact that there were several categories of returnees.

The first category was the youth, that group of young people who left South Africa with their parents as infants and within this group there were those who were born in exile. They had never been to South Africa. The second group were young adults who had grown up in exile. The third group were South African adults, some of them were already in their fifties and sixties. They had been residing in camps for the greater part of their life in exile. The fourth group was a limited number of those who had been living in Zambia and Tanzania in family units. Very few of them had been in employment. Their support was mostly provided by the ANC or the political party to which they were affiliated.

The returnees had lived in different countries during their time in exile. Even those who had been in employment had no insurance or pensions. Their original homes in South Africa were not recorded by the ANC for security reasons. We had no statistics of those who had particular skills or professions that would allow them to be absorbed in formal employment. We did not know some of the people who were coming back home; we did not know their correct names; we did not know where in South Africa they originated. Some of their parents had passed on while they were in exile and they did not know. My own observation was that those who came directly from the camps would have special problems adjusting.[1]

One of the things that we tried to do was to get a correct profile of the different groups among the returnees. Thabo Mbeki tried very hard to explain to us what it meant for people who had been staying in military camps and the kind of different reception they needed; this was contrary to somebody who had been at school/university or had a normal job in exile – missing home like everybody else but able to be in contact with

---

1 On these matters see S.M. Ndlovu, 'The Return of the ANC "Exiles" and other Challenges in the Early 1990s' in South African Democracy Education Trust, *Road to Democracy in South Africa*, Volume 6 (Pretoria: UNISA Press, 2013), Chapter 16.

people at home. But according to him it was different for somebody who had undergone military training as a member of Umkhonto we Sizwe and lived in military camps in Tanzania, Angola and Uganda; it meant moving from a military camp straight back home as a civilian.

I was at that time coordinating the project and I realised that as the representative of the SACC this was one of the most challenging projects to handle. When I reflect on this particular phase in our history maybe we should have created a long-term structure that would assist the returnees not only materially but also in the healing process. Maybe as the SACC we should have persuaded the transitional government to make this pro-gramme compulsory. Some of the returnees had no homes; their original families had been affected by the forced removals carried out by the apart-heid regime. Others were searching for the graves of their parents, siblings and extended family members. Some of the returnees had been traumatised by the loss of their loved ones while they were in exile through torture and killings by the South African apartheid agents. We had instances where families did not want to receive their relatives because they were still fearful of the apartheid regime's destructive security policies. On reflection, the SACC and the interim government could have handled this process differ-ently, but we knew no better. The pre-election period between 1990 and 1993 was the most challenging one because we were not actually in gov-ernment at the time. Thabo Mbeki was conscious of most of the challenges that faced returnees. He was one of the people who tried to help us defuse the situation. We used to agonise about these issues with Zanele and Thabo – about the lack of proper preparation for different categories of returnees.

But then we all came home and it was great and we all started preparing for the first democratic elections in 1994. The ANC decided to compile lists of people to go to parliament after winning the elections. At that stage, we were all excited about the idea of being parliamentarians. We used to conduct workshops through a non-governmental organisation (NGO) I had established – the Women's Development Foundation – every weekend to prepare ourselves for parliament. One day, lo and behold, I received a midnight call from one of the National Executive Committee members who had been asked to inform me that they had removed my name from the list of those people who they were recommending for parliament. I was so upset. I thought that parliament was the most important institution in South Africa. All I could think was 'How could Thabo do this to me?'

In my mind, he should have been taking care of my position in the ANC. I didn't sleep that night because I was really angry. I was waiting for six o'clock to phone Thabo. I thought, let me be decent and let him sleep, I will phone early in the morning and give him a tongue-lashing. I called him at six o'clock the following morning. The phone rang once and he picked up the call on the second ring. I never gave him a chance to speak. I told him how angry I was at being told at midnight that I had been removed from the list. How could I be removed from the list because I wanted to go to parliament like everybody else? Thabo is such a good listener; he did not say a word while I went on and on, demanding that my name be put back on the list.

When he did respond, he was cool and calm and he explained that in fact he had just walked into their Johannesburg flat after working throughout the night and that was why he picked up the phone. He confirmed that my name had been removed from the list. They had been discussing the names throughout the night and that was why he had only got home at that hour in the morning: he had not slept. By this time, I was feeling very ashamed to have reprimanded poor Thabo and he had not slept all night. He went on to confirm that the ANC had decided to remove quite a number of people from the list. He explained that they realised that they were thinning out the people who should remain within the broader society and other institutions that were important and that they needed people to head these institutions and continue playing a leadership role, especially in the NGOs and other institutions of government. He emphasised that they would need people with experience, like me, to work outside parliamentary structures.

I informed Thabo that I was disappointed that I was not chosen to be a parliamentary representative. And then he said to me, 'Sis Hlophe, you can't be serious about going to parliament. Do you know what is going to happen to you in parliament?' He then started educating me about processes and procedures governing parliament. He elaborated on the fact that I had been working all my life in a situation where I personally had to make decisions. He clarified that in parliament I would have to work within the constraints of my political party. Secondly, I was used to public speaking and expressing personal opinions about challenging matters affecting us as South Africans. Thabo asked me if I could imagine sitting in parliament for hours and hours listening to other parliamentarians and that if I got to address parliament once for a few minutes, I would be very lucky. It was not possible to be able to stand up in most instances and express my independent views, being confined by parliamentary rules and procedures. He asked, 'Is that what you want to do?'

Truly, when I think about it now I do not know what was going through my mind – but we all thought that parliament was the most important thing as we would all be engaged in dismantling the hideous apartheid system. By the time he had finished telling me all those things about parliament, thanks to Thabo, I was through with my fancy notions of being a parliamentarian. Now every time I watch the parliamentarians on television I am glad that I did not go there. In the end what was good for me was that Thabo Mbeki had said that they would need my experience where it mattered; that was an affirmation for me.

Then in 1994 we conducted elections that catapulted us into a non-racial, democratic, free South Africa and it was all great and exciting. The Independent Electoral Commission (IEC), led by Judge Kriegler, had been in discussions with the government about its independence and Thabo Mbeki and I were also involved in those talks because I was appointed as a commissioner in 1997 and then became deputy chair to Judge Kriegler. This was the first important discussion that had taken place and the IEC was granted its independence but Judge Kriegler later resigned. To provide the context of Kriegler's resignation, South Africa had never had an electoral commission and so our understanding of its independence was not clear. It had been assumed that the IEC would fall under Home Affairs and this quickly became a problem when we started to discuss budgets. We felt that the IEC budget was supposed to be part of the budget of Home Affairs.[1]

Deputy President Thabo Mbeki and his team led the discussions and I had never heard him talk tough in the manner in which he did then. In this instance he was emotional but constructive. We relied entirely on the deputy president to help us through the transition of our independence as a Chapter 9 institution and this process involved a lot of challenges.

---

1 On these issues see B. Bam, *Democracy: More Than Just Elections* (Johannesburg: KMM Review Publishing, 2015).

The idea of Chapter 9 institutions was a new one. I admire the wisdom of the drafters of the constitution who felt that it was important to appoint independent commissioners who would be responsible for elections. The greatest challenge was the independence of these institutions that are accountable to parliament. The major difficulty for the electoral commission in its early days was precisely over the budget. Home Affairs had assumed that the budget of the IEC would be approved and submitted to parliament. These serious tensions affected the relationship between Home Affairs and the commission. Finally Judge Kriegler resigned and I was asked, as the deputy, to take over as the chairperson of the IEC in 1999.

I made an appointment to see Deputy President Thabo Mbeki who had been given the responsibility by President Mandela to oversee all matters related to elections. I was desperate; the elections were due to be held a few months after the departure of Judge Kriegler and I told Mbeki that we would not be ready to have elections that same year. I had written a long list of things that had to be done. This list included the voters' roll, the problem of identity documents (IDs), demarcation, lack of infrastructure in the villages, no facilities at the voting stations, especially in the rural villages where there was no water, toilets or electricity. I also mentioned that all the different race groups had different identity documents, and that the Home Affairs Department did not have an updated population register. We were a little behind on the training of the IEC staff and finalising their employment contracts. We were also battling with dismantling the apartheid legacy on separate amenities. I had hoped that he would agree that we postpone the elections.

I came out empty-handed but full of confidence because Mbeki was against the postponement of the elections. He assured me that I would manage if I abided by the discipline of our values defined by honesty, integrity, transparency and hard work. Mbeki responded in his usual calm way. 'You know, Sis Hlophe, we are all in this government and none of us have ever been to a university on how to run a government, but we have had to learn. As long as one has the passion, discipline, integrity and commitment and is prepared to read and learn, one can do it.' I never forgot those words; they stayed with me for years. This kind of affirmation is so important and empowering. After our protestation Thabo resolved our budgetary challenges and we were able to complete the first common voters' role in South Africa. This was achieved in 1999.

And so when Thabo eventually became the president of the Republic of South Africa, some of us caucused around him and how we could try to change his serious public image so that people would be aware of the softer side of the president when he addressed the public; we thought he should try to hold and kiss babies and rehearse all those other things that go with being a president appearing in the public sphere in order for him to connect with the people. I was asked by this self-appointed advisory group to be the one to advise him.

I went to consult Moeletsi Mbeki, the president's younger brother, to inform him that I was one of the people who was going to work on Thabo's public image because he needed to look 'presidential' when he was with ordinary people and make them laugh and all those things. Moeletsi was amused and his response was, 'You are going to do that with whom? Don't waste your time.' I immediately shelved my plans: I just could not and would not have dared to try. I think that some people are just born like that. Mandela had an aura that overwhelmed people and so did Thabo Mbeki, but their public images were very different.

I am one of the people in this country who can give testimony to President Mbeki's unwavering belief in and commitment to empowering women: the team of women cabinet ministers and the portfolios they held; women were also included as ambassadors and high commissioners to a number of countries. President Mandela and Deputy President Mbeki established a tradition of honouring women. The greatest breakthrough was appointing women as ministers and deputy ministers in ministries such as Home Affairs, Foreign Affairs, Education, Justice, Science and Technology and Intelligence. The appointment of his deputy, Phumzile Mlambo-Ngcuka, was also commendable.

Then there was the establishment of a women's forum representing every sector – institutions, NGOs, civil society, organisations from rural communities. This forum gave women an opportunity to interact with the president of the country and share with him their stories of success, challenges and frustrations. This was one of the best innovations in communication. There are thousands of citizens of this country who have never had the opportunity to enter the Union Buildings. One of the projects that was initiated through this forum was the creation of a pension fund for women who work in informal sectors, including domestic workers where employers do not provide pension funds.

I also benefited from Thabo's generosity. One night we were all waiting to brief him at his office and it was late and by the time it was my turn, it was around 00:45. He really was a hard worker. He asked, 'You are still here?' And at that time I had no driver. At the end of our session, he decided that I had to be driven home and that one of the security personnel would drive my car home. He questioned why the IEC could not make arrangements for me to have a driver. This was not in the books about the benefits for the IEC chairperson – I had to drive myself both night and day. This sounds like small talk but it made a big difference in my work when it was agreed that I should have such benefits.

What I also recall and appreciate about Thabo as both deputy president and president of the Republic of South Africa was his selfless commitment to the people of the African continent. I am therefore grateful to him for cultivating love of the continent of Africa. I had been fortunate to attend the inauguration of Mwalimu Julius Nyerere during the early 1960s. What an honour in my life to shake hands and hold a conversation with him when he visited South Africa prior to our democratic elections. This encounter ended in a conversation with a message that one day South Africa would be free. One of the greatest tributes paid to Nyerere by President Thabo Mbeki reads as follows:

> Today the wretched of our continent have begun to walk with a firm tread in their step, confident of a better future for themselves and for the African motherland. They walk tall, with straight backs, no longer afraid to look into the eyes of those who had sought to set themselves up as rapacious demi-gods. On the shoulders of these generations rests the duty to answer the drawn-outs cries of those who were enslaved and colonised by strangers and abused by their own kith and kin. They rest on firm ground because they stand on the foundation of stone that Mwalimu Julius Nyerere built.

One of Thabo Mbeki's outstanding contributions during his term as president was his support and encouragement to the South African Electoral Commission to partner with the African Union (AU) in organising a conference on governance and elections in 2003. This was the first time such a path-breaking conference had been held and most African countries were represented. The seeds of the African Charter were sown at this conference. For once, as Africans, we produced our own charter drawn from the experiences of managing our own elections and on challenges our younger democracies faced on governance. This led to the AU officially adopting the charter and several African governments ratified it.

Another important contribution he made was in Dar es Salaam, Tanzania, at an annual general meeting of the Southern African Development Community Electoral Commissions Forum in 1999. He was our guest speaker on the theme 'Achieving African Renaissance'. He made reference to what had characterised many African countries, that the only way to ensure good governance and stability was to establish one-party states while allowing elections to take place within this system. But he went on to say that 'this system has now collapsed' and continued to elaborate, 'I do not know of any serious contemporary African politician or intellectual who today argues in favour of such a system. We had no choice but to construct genuine democratic systems of governance within the specific context of our national realities.' Thabo played a prominent role in promoting good governance in the African continent. The final conclusion and a parting note was: 'You who are gathered here, as the Electoral Commissions of our region, have a great and historic contribution to make to this outcome without which there can be no African Renaissance.'

I was devastated about his recall and there was also an element of disbelief when it was actually announced; it did not sink in. I knew that President Mbeki was supposed to go to the United Nations (UN). I had heard that his appearance at the UN was meant to be his farewell as it would be his last as president of the Republic of South Africa.

What hurt me most was the humiliation at the UN. He had only six months left in office. He was not only our pride; he was the pride of the African continent. I wondered what the world would say and what the people of the African continent would express about this matter. I thought of all the constructive work that he had persuaded us to do. He would say, 'Sisi Hlophe, could you go to Mozambique and support our counterparts with the elections?' – not to mention the first democratic elections in the Democratic Republic of the Congo (DRC). During those elections one would have thought that we were part of the official DRC election team as we had to play a proactive role in helping the country achieve its goals. It was obvious to us that Thabo Mbeki's heart and soul had been in those first ever democratic elections in the DRC. This went much deeper because it was part of the anti-colonial struggle in Africa that had cost so many lives.

So when he was recalled, I thought of all his hard work in these African countries and all his peacekeeping efforts on the continent. In fact, I was not even thinking about how hard all of us fought for the freedom of the oppressed majority in apartheid South Africa, and now we were fighting amongst ourselves. When President Mbeki was recalled, as a democrat I took it as my duty to read the constitution and I sent extracts of it to some legal people to find out about the constitutionality of his removal. Thabo had no other life outside the ANC and the driving force in his entire life was the liberation struggle and the fight for a non-racial democratic South Africa. He imbibed his politics from his parents, aunts and uncles.

To me, because the president was removed by a ruling party and not by parliamentary rules, it is still not clear why Mbeki never challenged it constitutionally. What hurt me afterwards was that the president could not even address parliament when he resigned; he was not allowed to do so by the ruling party. What does the constitution say about that? Because he was elected into power by ordinary South Africans who were not necessarily members of the ruling party, he would have been addressing South Africans in parliament because through the ANC as the victorious political party, Mbeki was voted into power by a majority of ordinary citizens. The removal of a president in this manner convinced me that an electoral system that gives power to few representatives from a ruling party to remove a president of a state cannot be a system that is democratic.

It is my hope that the South African constitution and the electoral system in the future will give an opportunity to citizens to be involved or consulted when such an action has to be taken. It was the worst thing we could ever have done as a nation to a president whom we had put in power and who had performed excellently. This was a man who had never been corrupt and who was our pride. I am not saying that he did not make mistakes – he is human after all. We all make mistakes. Like all presidents, he did things that people did not like, but if you take the totality of his leadership, and especially his recognition of women, he was an excellent leader. I was among the first women in the world to hold my position as chair of the IEC and there were many more women who were respected and affirmed by his presidency. Our history will be incomplete if the ANC leadership does not explain to South Africans the reasons behind Thabo Mbeki's removal. Many South Africans were not active members of the ANC, but we were citizens of South Africa and we need to be given a proper explanation. It was not only Thabo Mbeki's humiliation; it was a humiliation for many South Africans and also for South Africa as a democratic country. That is why it still hurts to this day.

The greatest legacy that Thabo Mbeki left is the affirmation of us as human beings – the affirmation of who we are, pride in our African identity, respect for our humanity and human solidarity. This is something that is not commodified. Mbeki is somebody who recognised you as a fellow human being. He cared for other people, he stood up for them and he fought for his continent. As the continent, and as black people in particular, we had been underdogs who were made to believe that we lacked culture and that we added no value to the world. But Thabo Mbeki's statement, 'I am an African', gave us back our dignity and allowed us to stand tall and affirmed us as black people. In Thabo Mbeki we had a person who was able to lift us as a people, giving us recognition: to me these are things that are intangible and not measurable.

Whenever he made a profound statement it was in such a cool, calm way. It was never made in an arrogant way and it was accompanied by overtones of wisdom.

Also constituting part of his enduring legacy, Thabo Mbeki respected the IEC's independence as a Chapter 9 institution and never ever interfered with our work. He always appreciated the visits we initiated and undertook as members of the IEC to brief and update him on our activities. There are two gifts that he valued and appreciated from the IEC. One was the copy of the South African voters' roll, the first of its kind, that had been compiled prior to the elections of 1999. The second gift was the National Election Atlas of Results. A unique compilation of the results, he even made some suggestions regarding the content so that it could be a useful tool for national development planning. Also, President Mbeki extended a special invitation to me as the chair of the electoral commission to brief a few members of cabinet about the planning of the voting processes for prisoners. This was after the Constitutional Court had made a ruling on prisoners to be enfranchised. The cabinet had been concerned because prisoners had not been registered and they were conscious of the challenges and the mammoth task that faced the IEC. A large number of prisoners did not have IDs. Thabo offered to provide additional help that the IEC needed in implementing their plans for prisoners to be able to exercise their democratic right to vote for a political party of their choice. Both President Mbeki and the cabinet greatly appreciated the commitment of the IEC.

Interviewed June 2015, Pretoria

TIKSIE MABIZELA

I was born in the former Transkei in a village called Tsomo, which is a neighbouring village of Idutywa where Thabo Mbeki comes from. Apart from two in my family, we all went to Lovedale. The younger ones did not make Lovedale because it had changed. I cannot recall whether it changed to a boys-only school or a girls-only school, but the apartheid government did something that caused my younger brother, together with Thabo Mbeki, to leave Lovedale.

After school, I chose nursing. I had dreams about nursing but those dreams only went as far as nursing education at Natal University so that I could teach nurses how to look after the sick. I taught at Edendale Hospital in Pietermaritzburg. That also did not last very long because after I had taught there for about six months I had to follow my husband into exile in Swaziland. Stan Mabizela, my husband, was arrested when I was in the process of applying to do my nursing education and I was admitted in 1966. That was the year that Stan came out of prison. He was in prison from 1964 to January 1966.

So he came to Pietermaritzburg for us to buy an engagement and a wedding ring. In January 1966 in the Transkei Stan skipped the country after we got married and I was starting my nursing education diploma at Natal University. I joined him in about April 1967 because by then a baby was on the way. Indeed the baby was born in Swaziland like the other two that followed. Swaziland had not quite gained independence then; it only got independence in 1968. I tried to get a job and applied to Barclays Bank. I was given a column of figures to add and a job that paid the bills. By this time Stan was teaching at Salesian High School.

It is important to note that building the African National Congress (ANC) underground in Swaziland took some doing. When we got to Swaziland, there were the likes of M.B. Yengwa, Mandla Sithole, Dr Zami Chonco – these are the names that I remember. My husband reported his presence to the ANC membership that he could identify. Not much was happening in Swaziland until Salazar gave up on the Portuguese colonies in 1974 and Mozambique opened up. As soon as that happened the floodgates opened for the ANC. Members of the ANC were then going to both Mozambique and to Swaziland. The structures then started being consolidated, not in the form into which they developed much later, but it was clear that underground work could now be done on a serious note in Swaziland, which was what brought Thabo Mbeki there. Thabo had actually come to Swaziland to do the groundwork for Oliver Tambo's visit to find out who on the side of the government of Swaziland would be suitable to meet with the president of the ANC in his efforts to establish formal relations for accepted representation of the ANC in Swaziland.

One day, two young men knocked at my door. Stan had told me to expect some people from Lusaka because he was not going to be home. He asked me to keep them at the house until he returned from work. These two young men came to the door at the schoolhouse we were living in; a shortish one and a slightly taller one, who was lightish in complexion. Stan had told me their names. He said they would be Max Sisulu and Thabo Mbeki. As soon as I opened the door, I asked 'Which one of you is Nontsikelelo's (Sisulu's) son?' I was in such a hurry to meet him. I knew of Sisi Ntsiki through my mother who thought that she was the most beautiful lady in the region. I had also heard of Govan Mbeki because he was already incarcerated on Robben Island. Any politically minded person would have known that and this made his son Thabo Mbeki a known person as well. The name Govan Mbeki had also dropped a few times from my father's lips when the Cape African Teachers' Association was formed to oppose 'Bantu' Education.

So there were Thabo and Max but they were both rather reserved. This was in 1975 and it was my first encounter with Thabo, who had a twinkle in his eye but was really reserved when I first met him. At the time, I think that I did most of the talking because I wanted to know how they had travelled, which way they had come, and we also discussed family stuff. They did not stay long in Swaziland on that visit. I think that they had been dispatched by the National Executive Committee to talk to Stan about how he saw the situation and what he saw as possibilities after having lived in Swaziland for almost seven years. They did not stay with us; I think that they were accommodated in a hotel.

These two young men then went back to report to the ANC leadership and Oliver Tambo eventually undertook his visit. I think this was in 1975. We never had a fully open representative mission in Swaziland because the Swazis were divided in their attitude to the presence of the ANC. There were circles, including the king, that were very sympathetic and I think that is what helped to keep the mission's head above water; the fact that the king was on the side of the ANC. The Swazi security forces tended to work more with the apartheid regime because the South Africans were not going to allow the ANC to operate that close to their borders and so they intimidated the Swazi security forces. But even then, some of the security forces were sympathetic to the ANC.

This was when Stan got involved in the underground because Mozambique was open and the groundwork had been done to recognise some kind of presence of the ANC in Swaziland. Hence it became possible for Umkhonto we Sizwe (MK) cadres and those who worked in the ANC underground to move between Swaziland and Mozambique. Tambo's visit to Swaziland lasted less than a week and when he left Thabo Mbeki remained behind and later Albert Dlomo arrived from London to reinforce Thabo because Stan was a full-time teacher until he had to go away for about six months for training. And so Thabo and Albert were on their own. Stan went to the Soviet Union and Thabo and Albert lived in my house. Actually my home became the unofficial office of the ANC.

I vividly remember that on Oliver Tambo's visit, I actually bought him a tie as a present and I had knitted a jersey for Thabo. That jersey helped Thabo a great deal when he was in jail in Swaziland. I enjoy knitting. I used to knit for my family, and Thabo's jersey was the first I had knitted for a comrade in the liberation struggle.

Thabo Mbeki has this amazing ease with people. He soon developed a social network composed mostly of university students: Tokyo Sexwale, Lindiwe Sisulu, Mpule Mogodi, Samkele and even Sbu Ndebele were at the University of Swaziland. They were regulars; every evening there was something to be discussed. He networked beyond the students, also reaching the lecturers like Patricia McFadden. Every South African at that time had something to offer and Thabo's networking and socialising evolved around this. It was this capacity he had for networking that made him get on so well with a section of the Swaziland security forces, in spite of the situation.

Thabo Mbeki came to our home as a guest and soon became a member of the family. The children were still very young and he became like a real uncle to them. Stan's mother was a Dlamini and Thabo's clan name is Dlamini, so they had a kind of *mzala* thing going on. He liked the children and they liked him a lot. I remember him sitting on a sofa one day and Phola, who was five then, was also sitting on the sofa but she stood up and, holding Thabo by the ears, she asked, 'Uncle Thabo, why are your ears so small?' and Thabo's response was, 'Phola, the reason my ears are so small is so that I should not hear everything that people are saying.' Phola did not forget that and she would sometimes say that she wished that she had Uncle Thabo's ears so that as a grown-up she could not hear everything that people were saying. Then there was the day I came home from work and Thabo, Andile, Vuyo and Phola were all jumping on the bed and humming something. And I said to him, 'You, too, have you been shrunk?' He just responded, 'Hayi Tiksi siyadlala apha.' It was unbelievable, this Sussex graduate jumping on the bed with the children, but that just showed you the versatility of the man and his ability to fit in at any level.

But for him, my house was home. Thabo could even tell when I was not myself. He had a way of defusing situations around the house. If there was tension with the house help, he would make a joke and say, 'Hey Eunice, u Sisi udiniwe namhlanje ungakumenzeli I cup yetiye'. (Eunice, Sisi is tired today please make her a cup of tea). He read the family as if they were his own. For all that, he did not spoil my children. When they needed discipline, he would very quietly administer it.

We went to Arusha for the Socialist International conference and I had gone along to Tanzania to visit Stan. The children were with me. We went on a safari drive and Phola was sitting on the same side of the vehicle as Thabo. We saw lions, which had just made a kill, and Phola was so excited. She was on the point of jumping out and immediately Thabo grabbed and shouted, 'Phola, what do you think you are doing?' It was a reflex action as if he was protecting his own child from danger. Stan and I had barely noticed anything.

In this socialising of Thabo Mbeki's, he and some others went out one evening with one of the guys who had come from home in South Africa. They came back singing at the tops of their voices, and when they came into the house Thabo presented me with this jazz record that I still value so much. He said, 'Sisi, this is for you.' This was on 13 May 1975 as indicated by his note on the sleeve of the jazz record. Thabo loved his music, especially classical music and jazz. I do not know at what point they bought this record because they came back in the dark, singing, and very late. I asked them what was up with them; they were all very happy and it was not normal because we were living on the edge all the time knowing that we were being watched by the security forces.

There was a relationship between a certain section of my family and the Transkei homeland. When the Bantustans were established, my brother and my brother-in-law served under Kaiser Matanzima – that was Koyana and T.T. Letlaka who was once a member of the Pan Africanist Congress. At one time, my brother was foreign minister for the Transkei in London. In terms of political camps, so to speak, my family was divided. Uncle Wycliffe Tsotsi was a member of the political organisation that I had previously supported, namely the Unity Movement, in which both Zanele and I had cut our political teeth as students!

My family used to visit close to the end of every year and they really made life in exile very light during their visits. The Letlakas came too. My family visited while Thabo Mbeki was with us in Swaziland. Thabo never judged them in terms of their different politics: not to themselves and not to me. Mbeki's regard for my own standing in the ANC as an organisation was not affected at all by my family who had different political persuasions and were even serving under the Bantustans. Instead the atmosphere was one of family; originally, we had all come from the Transkei, we knew the same people and the conversations were easy and tension-free.

I had been quite tentative about my family and their political positions but Thabo put me completely at ease without saying anything at all. As far as he was concerned, they were who they had chosen to be for now, and let them be. In my view, this is a very commendable trait; what human beings do so often is to start by judging people. While he knew about these strange affiliations in my family, Thabo did not talk much about his family. But we did become close enough for me to quiz him a few times. That was how I got to know, for instance, that his mother was running a shop in the countryside in Idutywa. That was how I got to know that he had a sister called Linda and two brothers, Moeletsi and Jama.

At one time while he was still with us, I obtained a Transkei passport so that I could travel home to take my children to visit my parents and their family. I told Thabo that I was going to go to his home to see his mother in Idutywa and tell her that he was staying with us in our home in Swaziland and that he was fine. This had been easy to do because I had been staying with my brother in Umtata and my father was teaching at Ngcobo secondary school at the time and I wanted to visit him. Idutywa was in between those two places. So I went to visit Epainette Mbeki at her shop in Idutywa and we sat and talked over tea. It was amazing for me. This was the wife of Govan Mbeki and the mother of Thabo Mbeki. It was very special, particularly since at that time her own son was living in my house in Swaziland. I bought a memento in her shop; it was a very nice piece of beadwork, which I still have today.

I do not think that Thabo Mbeki did not speak much about his family because he was reserved; I think it was more of a security mechanism for Thabo to keep his family to himself. Sometimes, even though so much is happening, you reserve a corner in your head to go to and be by yourself. I think that his family was that kind of corner in his head for him. For instance, he said very little about the death of his brother Jama. I heard from other people about the disappearance of his son. He never spoke about it.

But Thabo's networking in Swaziland helped a great deal in that the Swazi security forces would now and again turn a blind eye to some things, which, under different circumstances, they would have taken up because of the pressure from their South African counterparts. They were not unaware that there was an influx from South Africa. For instance, while our home (house No.1 in Salesian High School in the teachers quarters) was the place where ANC cadres arrived and were then sent to forward areas, there was another residence in another township and they (the security forces) knew that it was an ANC residence. The other place was in Fairview. Thabo Mbeki's networking even went as far as his friendship with Bishop Zwane, a very good bishop and a friend of ours. He was a good shepherd, he came to our houses and sat with us and talked with us. Bishop Zwane and Thabo clicked very well. I think that he did a lot of ANC underground work with Thabo, but I would not know specifically what they did. It was even strongly rumoured that Bishop Zwane's death was carried out by the enemy because of his connection with us as part of the ANC underground.

Bishop Zwane was a very sociable person. He would go with us to a nightclub and we all looked very happy and above board, but Thabo was doing his social networking right there in the nightclub. Sometimes, there were people from home with whom he was meeting right there and nobody would have detected that he was doing ANC underground work. This was usually at the Why Not nightclub in Ezulwini, which was our favourite haunt. I was trying to remember how Thabo dances, and it actually struck me that I had never seen him dancing. Even though we went to the nightclubs, he was mingling and socialising and doing his ANC underground work. We would all be there with Bishop Zwane and others and it would be a happy evening, but underground work had been done.

The ease that Thabo Mbeki had with people was classless. He networked with students and lecturers, but he was also very much at home among the ordinary people. When he was with them, you would not say that this was a University of Sussex graduate; he was just one of the guys. It was an amazing thing he had with people. When ANC cadres came to report and take directives, he would say, 'Sisi, do you have anything for them to eat or a cup of tea?' This person in my house would probably be someone that I would never see again. Thabo had a way of just walking into people's hearts. In part, I think it has taken him a long way in his own political career.

The George Hotel in Manzini was another place where Thabo and Albert went in the evenings. Sometimes they would carry out their ANC underground work there and would make their phone calls from there. I think that the George Hotel had given them a special facility to be able to make their contacts because if that had not been the case, a lot of people whom they contacted telephonically might have been in trouble. I think that there was one phone at the entrance that they would use and I think that some of the sympathetic staff also helped them. But it also exposed them to detection; for instance Craig Williamson, the apartheid regime's spy, eventually tried to poison Stan at the George Hotel because he had become aware that they frequented the hotel.

When Thabo and Albert were staying with us, there was this incident that took place while Stan was away. They were getting merry at the George Hotel and Albert was apparently carrying a weapon for self-protection. He accidentally fired it at the wrong place at the wrong time. The next thing I knew, one of the security guys came to the house and asked whether these men lived at my house because they had given my address. So I said yes, and I asked where they were because they had not come back the previous night. The security men told me that they were in the Matsapha jail. It was not my business to ask why. So I asked if I could visit them and they gave me the visiting times. I was able to go and see them. What I cannot remember is why Albert, who had actually let the gun go off, was released before Thabo. I used to take him food and a change of clothes in prison. One day he was wearing that jersey that I had knitted for him. He had stretched the jersey because it was so cold in the cells. He was detained for close to a month.

My own thinking is that it was good for certain forces in Swaziland to have Thabo Mbeki detained because they would have been targeting him anyway. Many representations and negotiations had to be carried out in order to secure his release. There was a guy who used to show up at my place at about 10.30 at night to give me a briefing on what was going on and he also provided suggestions as to who could help resolve this matter. According to Hugh Macmillan, who I met long after the incident, I sent him to deliver a secret message to the ANC in Botswana to inform them that Thabo Mbeki had been arrested. Hugh Macmillan was at the University of Swaziland in Manzini. He was a historian and a friend and also an adopted son of my father. I had asked him to stop by my house before he left for Botswana. He said the message I gave him was that he must tell this person (I had written Tsitsi Matthews' name down) that she must pass it on; she would understand its import. Hugh reminded me that that was how I managed to get the message through to Lusaka within a few days of Thabo Mbeki being detained. That message then activated the senior machinery of the ANC to negotiate for his release with the Swazis.

I do not know whether perhaps Thabo Mbeki's capacity for networking and his ease with people was evidence of the kind of diplomat that was already ingrained in him. He was very unemotional on the surface but you could tell the depth in Thabo. One would utter one sentence and if it struck something in him, he would ask you to repeat what you had said, but he would not tell you what he thought or what the importance was of what you had just said. You could be sure that Thabo was working on his own thoughts and intellect.

For instance, I remember one day asking how Comrade Nelson Mandela could say that the ANC must work on the M-Plan. I asked how long that was going to take in terms of time and logistics and I wondered how sure Mandela was about the security of house-to-house networking. Thabo asked what I had said and I repeated my thinking and then he clammed up. But much, much later, he said that in our campaign as the ANC for the release of Nelson Mandela we had to be conscious of things that would work and those that would not work. So when the armed struggle was implemented, it replaced something else that would never have worked and that would have been the M-Plan as proposed by Mandela.

I do not think that I have ever seen Thabo Mbeki angry or expressing anger in words. But I once saw him really riled when one of the guys from the Gang of Eight came to visit us in Swaziland, Mzimkhulu Makiwane, the younger brother of Tennyson Makiwane, who had been in the same class as my older brother at Lovedale. His visit was quite a surprise. I did not know that Stan knew Makiwane. But we just took it they were South Africans in exile and our house was open to all and this was how we also admitted spies who had actually come to Swaziland to destroy the ANC underground. In one instance, I had a whole family of South African exiles visiting and later it turned out that it was a false family who were dining with us and sleeping in our house.

So Makiwane came to visit. Thabo was around. Then when he left after a couple of days, we took him to the Nomahasha border. What does Thabo see when Makiwane is showing his passport? It was a Zairean passport. Now the question is, during the Mobutu days, who was going to move around on a Zairean passport? The ANC did not have a relationship with Mobutu's Zaire. Thabo did not say anything at the time but when we got home, he was livid. He said, 'How can he do this to us, he is carrying a Zairean passport and he comes and lives with us here.' That was the one time I saw him really upset.

My little brother Thabo Mbeki could not drive when he arrived in Swaziland. I had a Volkswagen and my brother and I shared it and whoever was with Thabo could drive him around. They used the car when I was at work at the bank. Eventually the ANC head office gave them money to buy a car, a rusty coloured Peugeot, so that they had a car that they could use at any time of the day. They went all over the place in that rusty Peugeot. He learned to drive in that car.

Thabo would sit up late at night with his pipe, and he would likely have a glass of his drink, and he would write until the early hours of the morning. I did not know that you could write reports or letters on toilet paper. He would unroll it and roll it again and give a cadre a roll of toilet paper to take across the border. I did not know that biscuits could carry money. These were tins of biscuits with the biscuits' insides being used to transport cash. I got to learn some of the tricks myself. When Thabo was in jail, I had to report to him that some or other cadre had arrived and there was a need for money at home. I was also their treasurer because I knew that there was money reserved for the ANC underground work. And Thabo told me that I would have to send a tin of biscuits home. That was all he said and I knew what he meant. There was an art to packing the money with the biscuits in the tin and sealing it so that it looked completely untouched.

In 1976, things started getting really hot in Swaziland and by the end of the 1970s our people were being ambushed and killed and there were a couple of bomb blasts in our own area. We were now being watched quite intensely and intrusively. After the 1976 student uprising, hordes of kids crossed over the border and many of them ended up on my doorstep. While it was a lot of hard work cooking and taking care of all these young people, it was also enjoyable. Thabo had left Swaziland by then.

One day the children came back from school and showed us a photograph, which they said a white man had given them. And it was a picture of the kids. We took this to be a message that the South African security police would get the kids. That really set us on alert to strategise about our continued stay in Swaziland. The other thing that prompted our new strategy occurred when Stan's car was stolen from our yard. It was a car that had been allocated to him by the organisation after Thabo left. The organisation had bought him the later version of the Peugeot.

We both agreed that the family was now at risk. At this stage, the house could have been dynamited with all of us inside it. This was the period when letter bombs were going off and then there were the Trelawney Park bombings and it was just becoming too risky. The family relocated to Mozambique for security reasons.

Just to go back to Thabo Mbeki's networking skills. The networks that he had already established in the diplomatic corps were remarkable. We were close to the Swedish community in Mozambique and there were a lot of people in the diplomatic corps who already knew Thabo Mbeki. Some would have met him in Angola and others in Zambia or overseas. His network was really very widespread. This meant that we also found ready-made friends in Mozambique because people like Thabo Mbeki already knew them. Those connections continued to support us for a long time while we were in exile.

We kept the connection when Thabo Mbeki left Swaziland. Stan was the political person and I did not want anything to interfere with his ANC underground work. I was looking after the family, bringing up the children. When we were in Mozambique we sometimes went for two years without seeing Stan because he would think he was coming in December and then ANC work demanded that he did not come to visit his family. The kids would see Uncle Thabo on a visit; for instance, when we went to Arusha, and it was always great for the kids. They loved their reunion with their uncle. When I meet Thabo Mbeki even now I say 'come and greet your big sister'. He has not changed much. The essential Thabo is still there.

Interviewed May 2014, Port Elizabeth

II

AFRICAN LEADERS

OLUSEGUN OBASANJO

Thabo Mbeki was an active member of the African National Congress (ANC) when I first met him in the United Kingdom. I cannot quite remember, but I think that it was in a university setting. Then he became the ANC representative in Nigeria when I was a military head of state (1977). I know that when he was in Nigeria, he did great work because his own direct involvement and his relations with Nigeria brought greater awareness of the struggle against apartheid. One of the officers in my office was assigned to work with him. My first impression of the young Thabo at the time was that he was a clear-minded, bright and smart young man. He knew what he was talking about and he was committed. That first impression has lasted throughout our relationship up until today. He has not changed much – except that he is getting older.

I met Thabo Mbeki again when I was a member of the Commonwealth Eminent Persons Group (1986). When we were in Zambia, we met Oliver Tambo and Thabo Mbeki was present at that meeting, and of course we met Nelson Mandela in Pollsmoor prison. I was the first to meet Mandela there and this deepened our relationship with the ANC. We wanted to know what the important areas of negotiation were, what the no-go areas were or, if you like, the minimally acceptable areas. As a member of the Eminent Persons Group, and also as the spokesperson for the group, I was particularly clear in my mind when we met Mrs Thatcher who was talking about reforming apartheid that this was not going to be the case. I said to her, 'Look, apartheid is like Satan. If God felt there was a way of reforming Satan, he would not have driven him out of his abode in heaven.' So I told Thatcher that apartheid was not reformable; it just had to be exorcised.

We did not say that the ANC should abandon the military route into power. We believed that anything that would bring an end to apartheid should be embarked upon. Of course, we could not put that in our report but it was understood. If you read that report today, you will also see that the word 'sanctions' does not appear because if we had used the word 'sanctions' in that report Mrs Thatcher would have rejected it and all that was needed for the Eminent Persons Group to fail was one important member of the Commonwealth rejecting the report. So instead of the word 'sanctions', we used the phrase 'other means'. Mrs Thatcher said 'other means' could be anything, so she was able to live with it. Then we went to the United States. We did not meet President Reagan, we met the then Vice-President (George H.W.) Bush, who later became president, and we also met members of the Congress. The first time that the American Congress passed a resolution against the apartheid regime in South Africa was as a result of our work with the US Senate. As a group, we worked very hard to ensure that our report was acceptable – and it was. Oliver Tambo described the report as a 'watershed'. It contained all the required ingredients to bring an end to apartheid but in a language acceptable to all. Thabo Mbeki was privy to all this information because he was Oliver Tambo's right-hand man and he also had to deal with these matters as the person in charge of the ANC's Department of International Affairs. I never thought then that Mbeki would one day become president of South Africa. Of course he had the qualities and the makings of a president. He was smart, committed, serious-minded and intellectual. He had the potential.

The idea about conceptualising the New Partnership for Africa's Development (NEPAD) arose when President Thabo Mbeki was the chairman of the Non-Aligned Movement. I was the chairman of the G77+China, which held a meeting in Havana, Cuba. President Abdelaziz Bouteflika was the chairman of the Organisation of African Unity (OAU) in 1999; the OAU held its meeting that year in Algiers. And separately, without consultation among those three organisations, each of us was sent to the G7+Russia. I think that the conveners went to one of the Japanese islands that year after meeting briefly in Tokyo. It must have been Okinawa. So they met us briefly in Tokyo, but they dismissed us as African leaders within 30 minutes or so. The three of us went back to our hotel and said, 'Look, if they had asked us what is Africa's programme we would have had nothing to put on the table.' So there and then we decided that we had to do something tangible and that was the beginning of NEPAD.

President Thabo Mbeki, President Bouteflika and I all contributed experts to work on developing the concept; we agreed that President Thabo Mbeki should host these experts and that was the genesis and things developed from there. In the process, President Abdoulaye Wade of Senegal came up with what he called the Omega Plan. I think what we called our economic plan at the time was the New Africa Initiative, not NEPAD. When President Wade came up with Omega, we decided that we had to accommodate him but felt that if we continued to call it the New Africa Initiative, he might think that his own plan had not been incorporated, so we came up with the New Partnership for Africa's Development. And everybody accepted it. And, of course, from NEPAD, the African Peer Review Mechanism (APRM) was developed.

I think there was confidence and a belief in African leaders during the first decade of the twenty-first century. President Thabo Mbeki had been deputy president of South Africa (1994-1999) and he had worked with President Mandela so he was an insider of the ruling party in South Africa. He came with loads of confidence, which was consolidated by the fact that he had garnered international experience when he worked closely with Oliver Tambo. I had been a military head of state and had what you may call interregnum for 20 years before becoming head of state; I had fought in the Nigerian civil war and brought that war to an end. During that period of interregnum, I met the who's who of the international community. I was a member of a group called the InterAction Group, made up of German Chancellor Helmut Schmidt, Pierre Trudeau, Jim Callaghan, among others. So together with Mbeki and others we had considerable experience of working with the international community; that is the first point. The second point is that as African leaders we worked together and we were very clear about where we believed Africa should be going. We had differences, but we were clear about what had to be done and we moved together on issues relating to the African continent. It was a kind of teamwork with trust among us. I think it was the orientation, the vision, mission and the focus of all of us that stood out and we were not competing for anything. For instance, the unwritten rule among us was that if South Africa wanted something, Nigeria would not compete for the same thing. It was akin to a consensual leadership style.

Let us look at the United Nations (UN) Security Council. I believe that there was and that there still is a need for a UN Security Council that has Africa as a permanent member, otherwise it is not democratic enough. We must also bear in mind that at the time that the UN came into being not many African countries were really independent; I think that it was only Ethiopia, Liberia, Libya, Egypt and Morocco. To me, what matters most is African representation and not a particular country. It does not matter whether it is Nigeria or South Africa. I really did not see competition between me and President Mbeki. For me, if South Africa is a member of the Security Council, it is well and good. If Nigeria is a member of the Security Council, she cannot work against the interests of South Africa and vice versa. What use does it serve that we compete and thereby lose the opportunity for Africa to become a permanent member of the UN Security Council?

I think that at present there is a need for re-energising. There is also a need for refocusing. People would ask what it was at that time that drove myself, Mbeki and others. We could argue that it was because we believed in Africa and we had confidence in ourselves as leaders of the continent. African leaders today must understand and appreciate the world in which they live and operate in a proactive manner; that is very important. African leaders today must also properly define Africa's interests; protect the continent and promote it like we did with Mbeki and others. It is very important to do that as was the case during the first decade of the twenty-first century. Any nation's interest promoted and protected at the expense of African interest must be both myopic and futile.

We have a plethora of resolutions and policies that were developed when, together with Thabo Mbeki, we were still part of the affairs of the African continent. I believe that NEPAD and the APRM, as African Union (AU) programmes, are adequate if you are talking of strategic partnerships with the international world. In the acronym NEPAD, the important word is *Partnership*, which will be partnerships within and between communities, states and within Africa. This includes the issue of Africa's regional integration and moving the continent forward. We must also focus on the partnership between Africa and the international community – different regions of the world, different continents – so it is all there and we do not need to reinvent the wheel. We just need to do what needs to be done and we must have the political will to move forward. All that Africa needs to make progress can be found in Africa. These matters are also dear to Thabo Mbeki.

In terms of conflict prevention, I deferred to President Mbeki on Zimbabwe because he was closer to the issue and, although we were always in communication, I think that rightly, as African leaders, we gave him the space to try to resolve that matter. I was also the one who said, for instance, as a West African I am probably too involved in Côte d'Ivoire and because Mbeki was a little bit distant, I asked him to come and help. That is the way that I saw it. Of course, there was also the Liberian national conference in West Africa, which was convened in Ghana. When the time came to implement the report, as they had worked on their own programme, again I made it a continental issue; we did not limit it to West Africa and hence the involvement of President Mbeki. Even if it started as a sub-regional issue, where necessary, we quickly made it a continental issue and that was how we carried it. In that way, if the continent starts on something and stands firmly, it is difficult for anybody or any region or any group to make us break rank. Unity and teamwork based on African interest should be all that African leaders need to move the continent forward holistically.

Having worked with Mbeki for a long time, to me his recall from office remains regrettable. Naturally he felt that he did not get what he deserved when he left public office. I share a bit of that. But he got over that, as we all get over anything untoward happening to us. At present he is continuing his assignments in the African continent and there is always work for all of us to do for Africa until we breathe our last. Mbeki is working very hard for the continent to become a better place for all and it is admirable of him to do so. He should continue to do it until he either becomes too old and feeble to be able to do it or until God calls him unto His bosom. But until then, we shall all continue to serve our local communities, Africa and humanity. I know Thabo shares my views in this respect. God bless him.

Interviewed July 2014, Dar es Salaam

MELES ZENAWI

⊰⊱

Keynote address at a Gala Dinner hosted by the Women's Investment Portfolio Holdings Limited (WIPHOLD) in honour of President Thabo Mbeki, 19 June 2008

Your Excellencies, comrades and friends, I wish to start my speech today by sincerely thanking the organisers of the gala dinner to celebrate President Thabo Mbeki's work to empower women and to promote the African Renaissance. I am grateful for the honour bestowed on me as the keynote speaker on this joyous occasion. I really am overjoyed and humbled by your gesture. I would like to focus my speech on President Mbeki's work on the African Renaissance. I'll not attempt to present the learned treaties on the matter, because that will be tantamount to doing a monstrous injustice to a task better done by better-equipped people. I will limit myself to personal testimony on the matter. I will not attempt to make a comprehensive review of President Mbeki's work on the African Renaissance based on my recollection, as you would all be fast asleep by the time I finish. I will therefore limit myself to a few personal recollections merely to highlight some of his work on the issue.

It is difficult to fully understand the significance of President Mbeki's work on the African Renaissance if one cannot grasp the circumstances in which it was articulated and I have very vivid recollections of those very dark and menacing days. We (the Ethiopian People's Revolutionary Democratic Front) took over in Addis Ababa at the beginning of the summer of 1991 and inherited a completely shattered nation. A nation that was poor to begin with, had become even poorer with the dysfunctional command economy superimposed on its very fragile body. We needed foreign aid and loans to keep body and soul together, to say nothing about development and growth. It was very clear to us that we could get none of these unless we could engage in economic reforms and get a clean bill of health from the International Monetary Fund (IMF) and the World Bank. Whether we liked it or not, we knew we had to do what everyone else on the continent was doing: reform our economy.

We wanted to learn from the experience of other African countries before we embarked on it and we sent a couple of delegations all over the continent. A couple of weeks later, the leadership of our movement met to discuss the report of the leaders of the delegations. Our comrades told us how every African country was eager to share their experience with us, how they explained the mechanics of the reform programmes during formal meetings and how, at the end of it, all the leaders of our delegations were pulled aside and given informal and heartfelt advice. The informal and heartfelt advice that the leaders of our delegations got from every African country they visited was very simple. You have to say 'yes' to whatever they, meaning the IMF and the World Bank, tell you: Say yes, and if you can't, whenever you can, you must try to play around with the implementation of things you do not like. The message was as clear as it was depressing. You have to agree to whatever you are told to do. The report of our leaders of delegations reminded me of the joke in our midst that was popular during our armed struggle of how Chinese communists always counted in threes. It seems to me that Africans could only count in ones, because everywhere we went we were faced with the one whatever, whatever the IMF says, you had to agree to it.

We had a series of discussions about the matter and we came up with the compromised formula that we should never stop the search for the paradigm of development that would help us chart a course of fast and independent development. That we should never accept the neo-liberal paradigm in total, only elements of it that are compatible with our own agenda. And that we should never challenge the fundamentals of the new liberal paradigm in public and should try to highlight the compatibility of our parts of independent development with elements of the new liberal paradigm.

Having defeated a one-party dictatorship in our country, we began to learn to live in a one-party world where the poor were expected to worship at the altar of new liberalism if they were to get the aid they needed to live another day. As one writer pointed out, the IMF had told the African leaders to fear God, meaning the fear of challenging new liberal orthodoxy. The most we could do to counter it was never to accept it, but also never to challenge it in public and all the time seek a better way out. We could try countering the challenge by replacing the one whatever that was almost universal in the continent by the three nevers. The one-party neo-liberal dictatorship that had reigned throughout the African continent funded by the IMF and World Bank is so pervasive and so Orwellian in its choice of words that anyone who was uncomfortable with the orthodoxy was overpowered with a feeling of perpetual suffocation.

One of the best examples of this Orwellian world and choice of words was the word 'ownership', which became popular on the African continent in the early to mid-1990s. Initially we were puzzled when we were told to 'own' our own reforms. We asked ourselves whether we will get the minimum assistance we needed if we 'owned' our reform programmes and rejected the new liberal paradigm, before we made costly mistakes. We were persuaded away from any attempt to give the word 'ownership' its own dictionary meaning.

A Swedish diplomat in Tanzania had given the definitive meaning of the word. He had publicly stated that ownership means that Africans do what you tell them to do, but they do it willingly, and so, Africa on the basis of the one whatever, said yes to the ownerships professed by the Swedish diplomat in Tanzania. Partnerships and many other words were given a similar Orwellian twist. The concept of the African Renaissance as pursued by President Mbeki emerged at a time when African governments had lost the right to think and act for themselves.

The new liberal orthodoxy had been imposed on the continent with very little space for policy experimentation, and African economies were mired in their debt, low growth and low investment trap. The concept of the African Renaissance emerged at the time when we had lost confidence in ourselves and in building a better future in our countries. It emerged at a time when Africa had been totally marginalised economically, politically and diplomatically. The African Renaissance was articulated by Mbeki when Africa was seen as a basket case and pundits in the West were publishing articles in respectable magazines such as *The Economist* as to whether the direct recolonisation of the continent would be the only option to push African societies towards modernisation.

The only bright light across the dark African skies of the 1990s was the liberation of South Africa. The end of apartheid in South Africa was the crowning achievement of the struggle against all forms of colonialism. And, as such, every African was and had every right to be proud. Even with the desolate political landscape in Africa at the time, many Africans felt that South Africa would be a great success and prove to the rest of the world that Africans are not destined to fail and be the playthings of world powers.

Progressive forces in Africa were especially pleased that their strongest contingent on the continent, the African National Congress (ANC), had taken power in the most economically advanced country on the continent. They were convinced that this would be an enormous boost for all progressive forces on the continent. How this would be achieved was not initially clear. Some felt that the ANC would have to focus on transforming the desolate political landscape on the continent, because if it failed to do so it would be isolated and vulnerable. Others felt that the ANC should focus on transforming South Africa first, and should not prematurely tackle the new liberal hegemony on the continent. Only after consolidating itself in South Africa, could it take on such a task.

The consensus in our own movement was that the latter would be the prudent option. Given the fact that our own tactic was never to challenge the new liberal paradigm publicly until circumstances changed to give us a fighting chance in that struggle, we assumed that the ANC would pursue a similar policy. You can therefore understand our initial response to President Thabo Mbeki's ideas of the African Renaissance. Naturally, we assumed that this was one of the Orwellian words floating around at the time and admired him for the speed with which we thought he was catching up with the rest of us in mastering the vocabulary of the day and making a new contribution to it. That is where we left the matter until the precursor of the New Partnership for Africa's Development (NEPAD) programme, the Millennium Africa Plan (MAP), was unveiled. I had the opportunity to participate in a meeting held in Tanzania to discuss MAP and I was elated and confused at the same time. I was elated because I read the document that boldly charted a new course for the continent, one around which progressive forces in the continent could rally. I was confused because at the meetings in Tanzania the participants included, among others, the president of the World Bank, whose institution epitomised the new liberal paradigm. Later on, MAP was modified to accommodate views of some African leaders and endorsed by the Organisation of African Unity/African Union (AU) as the plan for the regeneration of the African continent.

In so doing, MAP became a framework for the broad church rather than a document of a rather narrow group of progressives on the continent. The NEPAD framework is to me the essence of the programme for the renaissance of Africa, and both MAP and NEPAD are rightly associated with President Thabo Mbeki. The NEPAD framework creates enough holes in the new liberal paradigm for a whole contingent of a progressive army to pass through, while at the same time opening doors for others to do better without necessarily adopting a progressive alternative to the new liberal paradigm. It charts a new course for continental diplomacy, which would allow Africa to productively engage not only the Western powers but also the emerging powers in pursuit of its own strategic interests. It outlines a programme for democracy and good governance for Africa. This is fundamentally different in its approach from the reigning neo-liberal orthodoxy because it recognises that such political transformation is possible only when it is a free choice of every nation, and that it is a process, not an event, that each nation may wish to embark upon in its own way and at its own pace. It recognised that such political transformation cannot and should not be imposed from our side, either through military invasions of regime change or the so-called coloured revolutions.

Your Excellencies, comrades and friends, we now know what the African Renaissance and its strategy, NEPAD, have achieved. Some people asked me, what had NEPAD really achieved? How many roads, railways, power stations has NEPAD built? What is the specific result of NEPAD in terms of actual economic development? What has it really done to promote democracy and good governance? Unfortunately I think the line of reasoning behind these questions has raised, perhaps subconsciously, the effects of neo-liberal hegemony. What NEPAD inherited is a bleak ideological landscape that allowed no space for independent thinking by Africans. It inherited a landscape where progressive thinking had to go deep underground and hibernate to survive. That has now been completely transformed, largely because of NEPAD and the way it was very skilfully marketed. With the necessary price paid in terms of delusion of the progressive elements of NEPAD, it was possible to get it endorsed by the AU and the United Nations (UN). The G8 were first on board, which meant that while they did not necessarily fully endorse it, they could not reject it outright either. It provided an internationally accepted and legitimate platform on the basis of which African governments, both progressive and other governments, could then articulate their own strategies of independent development. That for me is the biggest success of NEPAD. And one that is vastly more important than bridges and roads.

There is no hope of Renaissance in Africa, no matter how many bricks and windmills we build, if there is no liberation of the African mind from the straitjacket of fatherlism/paternalism and pessimisms associated with the neo-liberal orthodoxy. NEPAD has gone a long way in bringing about that liberation, and it is only a matter of time before we see its impact on the economic transformation of our continent. Indeed, it could be argued that we are already seeing its impact. For example, in Ethiopia our concept of independent development based on the establishment of a democratic developmental state is no longer buried deep underground and in hibernation, hiding from the IMF and the World Bank. We are now fully free to articulate it openly and publicly, and hence effectively mobilise our people around that platform. We are now free to openly and publicly criticise the new liberal paradigm. We are thus now free to fully implement our alternative vision. As a result of this, for the past five years we have seen our economic growth as slightly above 11 per cent per year and our exports grow at around 25 per cent per year.

The liberation of the mind is indeed the precursor of (political) liberation and economic liberation. This in turn is the basis for the consolidation of the liberation of the mind. NEPAD inherited a political landscape where Africa was marginalised as a basket case in the perspective with which African issues were dealt with by major powers. NEPAD proposed two broad strategies to correct that. It articulated the strategic interest that major powers had in Africa and what Africa can bring to the table in that regard. It established the basis on which we could interact with them on a more equitable basis. It also articulated a framework for inter-African solidarity and solidarity with newly emerging powers. By combining the two, we now have a situation where Africa is no longer marginalised. The G8 has consistently been inviting African leaders to its summits to discuss Africa's concerns. We have had a series of summits with emerging powers. Africa is now being courted with a passion that has not been seen before. That is a fundamental transformation brought about to a large extent by the NEPAD strategy for inter-African and international engagement.

This is of fundamental significance because there can be no hope of an African Renaissance in a globalised world without a productive and mutually beneficial engagement with the rest of the world. In spite of what we hear from the international media, we have made enormous progress on the issues of democracy and governance too, and that is because of NEPAD and its Peer Review Mechanism. This unique process is based on two principles that fundamentally differ from the neo-liberal agenda. First, it is based on the clear recognition of every country's right to chart its own course of political development. This principle is reflected in the fact that African governments accede to the peer review process only if they wish to do so. And quite a few African countries have chosen not to join that process. It is also reflected in the fact that the parameters on which every country is being reviewed are set by African governments and can't be modified as and when we agree to do so. The second basic principle on which it is based is one of peer learning rather than attacks and threats. We peer review each other so that if we so wish, we learn from each other's experience. No one is threatened, forced or cajoled to do anything.

Everyone is given the opportunity to learn from the experience and that of others in the hope and expectation that they would use the opportunity to improve governance and consolidate democratic reforms. Some people will tell you that Zimbabwe has proved conclusively that the Peer Review Mechanism is toothless and hopeless. I would argue the exact opposite is the case because I believe democratic political transformation has more to do with the brain, rather than the trees and clouds. No matter what the motive might be, democracy and good governance in Zimbabwe or elsewhere in the African continent cannot be imposed from outside through threats, demonisation or invasion. It can only come from inside, supported by peer learning and solidarity. NEPAD has promoted the only sustainable means of political transformation in Africa through its Peer Review Mechanism and by resisting shotgun democratisation, externally driven regime change and colour revolutions and has done so rather successfully. Africa has taken a firm stand on Zimbabwe and rejected a summit with Europe that does not include Zimbabwe.

After several years of such resistance, Europe, in a manner that would have been unheard of in the 1990s, accepted Africa's position and invited Zimbabwe. This is a dramatic illustration of the transformation of Africa's global position, and how quickly Africans have learned the fear of God of the 1990s. Africa took such a position, not because it sided with any party in Zimbabwe or because it condones violence and repression, but because it rejects externally driven regime change. The results of the NEPAD approach might not be spectacular in the short term, but it is NEPAD's contention that democratisation is a process and not an event that is susceptible to short cuts. The history of democratisation globally shows that NEPAD is on the right path and the new liberal project of democratisation is a dead end. Short-term spectacular change, in favour of apparent democracy on a path that is really on a dead end is not what the African Renaissance means.

An appropriate path that eventually leads to the successful transformation, however protracted the journey might be, is the only path to the African Renaissance. Charting such a course and resisting the dead end of new liberal democratisation has, in my view, been one of the proudest achievements of NEPAD. And so the African Renaissance has proved to be something very different from the Orwellian vocabulary that we had learned in the 1990s. It has, through NEPAD, very significantly contributed to the liberation of the African mind, to the dramatic improvement of Africa's global economic position, and to the charting of a correct path of democratisation and good governance on the continent.

The African Renaissance is being successfully implemented in front of our eyes. I think only those whose eyes are impaired because of the neo-liberal blinkers that they have put on them can fail to see the enormous progress. This is why we have every right to celebrate tonight the work of President Thabo Mbeki on the African Renaissance. Your Excellencies, comrades and friends, I know enough of the ANC and the government that it leads, to know that the progressive agenda pursued by President Mbeki is not a personal crusade but a reflection of the ANC's principled positions. I know that, in a way, President Thabo Mbeki was merely representing the fundamental views of the ANC and the government it leads when he embarked on the struggle for the African Renaissance.

But I am confident that you will also agree with me that he has represented those institutions with distinction and that in doing so he has brought to the table some unique personal qualities that had a very significant impact on the success of the project. Let me start with the obvious one. President Thabo Mbeki has brought to the table an extraordinary intellect. I know this is a double-edged sword; he has sometimes been accused of being too scholarly and not charming enough. Indeed, this has been some sort of irritation for people such as me, who are neither charming nor scholarly. A source of irritation because just listening to him is enough to understand the full meaning of his arguments. You have to, at the same time, think in order to fully understand him. People such as myself find it difficult to listen and think at the same time and therefore missed some of his points. More often he forces us to exercise our mental faculties when we would rather not do so. In other words, it is as much our problem as it is his.

In any case, his intellect has been of vital significance in winning the arguments for NEPAD and designing the appropriate tactics and approaches to neutralise opposition and mobilise support for it. I know of too many great ideas that flounder because of wrong approaches and tactics to undermine the significance of what President Thabo Mbeki has brought to the table in the struggle for African Renaissance. President Mbeki has also been very patient and flexible in the pursuit of the ideals of the African Renaissance. I have seen him suffer many fools patiently and focusing on doing just enough to carry the day or making it possible for progressive forces to fight another day. The meeting in Tanzania that I mentioned earlier on, and the watering down of MAP to build a broad consensus around NEPAD, is a case in point.

I personally thought that the progressive content of MAP should be protected by all means, most importantly, by keeping others away from it and I was confused, at times frustrated, that that was not President Mbeki's preferred approach. Fortunately because he chose such an approach, NEPAD was saved from becoming an idol of worship for a narrow sect of self-declared progressiveness and became the African framework accepted as such by its friends and adversaries alike. As a result, it became an infinitely more effective weapon for progressive forces across the African continent. I have, at times, been very angry with him because I fail to notice anger in his arguments when I am burning inside and amply exhibiting it. I have been very angry because he did not exhibit anger when I felt he should have done so. Fortunately, as a result of his patience and flexibility, every time we have been engaged in heated arguments, his arguments with our colleagues on the continent or elsewhere, we have either won without wounding the pride of our colleagues or successfully avoided defeat so that we would continue with the struggle on another day. As a result, all my anger against his lack of anger has never survived the end of the debates that we have been involved in. I know too many great ideas that have been defeated for lack of tact and patience for me to undermine the significance of what President Thabo Mbeki personally brings to the table.

Lastly, the president has shown that he has nerves of steel and that he is willing to stand firm. He is willing to stand firm like the Drakensberg mountains against powerful waves and storms, if and when the fundamental interests of the continent and the African Renaissance are at stake. I have a feeling that his mother may have something to do with it.

The firm stand that he has taken in the sometimes silly debates on the so-called United States of Africa is a case in point. His firm stand on Zimbabwe is also a case in point. I have always been amazed and proud of his nerves of steel. I know of too many promising revolutionary endeavours that have collapsed because of the lack of the necessary nerve on the part of the leadership to undermine the significance of what President Thabo Mbeki brings to the table. In other words, while the credit for the progressive stand of the South African government that he heads goes to the ANC, the credit for very ably representing these progressive views and providing the critical leadership that I mentioned belongs to him personally. If you are inclined to count in threes like the Chinese do and like I have done this evening, you might call these the three leadership qualities of President Thabo Mbeki.

Let me conclude on a very personal note and, Mr President, I was planning to tell you this the day after you leave office as president of South Africa, but I want to say it now because we are close enough to that day. Over the past decade, there have been few events that have given me unqualified happiness. This is so because most of the victories that have given me some happiness, I have had challenges within them. Getting to know you, having you as comrade and friend, has been one of these very few sources of unqualified happiness for me.

I therefore want to use this occasion to say: thank you so very much. The British have a famous saying: 'The King is dead, long live the King.' I wish to paraphrase, and say: 'Goodbye, Comrade President, and long live the architect of the African Renaissance.'

I thank you!

PEDRO PIRES

❧

In being entrusted with the honourable and delightful task of presenting a personal view of my friend and comrade in the struggle for African liberation, President Thabo Mbeki, I was immediately taken with the need and concern to transcend my sentiments of friendship and affection and seek to discover more information about the man, freedom fighter and statesman, without the pretension, however, of embarking upon a biographical narrative. I did not have the opportunity to associate with Thabo Mbeki during the times of resistance and of the fight for the liberation of our respective countries and peoples. I did, however, have the pleasure and honour of meeting and fraternising with various other African National Congress (ANC) leaders, including Oliver Tambo, Alfred Nzo and Johnny Makhathini, among others. I only met Thabo Mbeki when he was already carrying out government functions.

This led to me asking myself how to elaborate upon the vision of this statesman without being familiar with his life history or with the day and age that nourished his personality? And it was in search of an answer to this question that I wrote the narrative that I am now presenting to you, founded on contexts and circumstances that I believe contributed in a marked manner towards the formation of the character and personality of the person, the African man, the politician and the leader that is Thabo Mbeki.

To begin with, the family and social environment that surrounded Thabo Mbeki's adolescence and youth were deeply marked by disquiet and by the permanent fight for justice and dignity. This conquest demanded systematic and firm opposition to the humiliating and rampant designs of ambition of absolute power over all of the country's resources controlled by a minority, representing less than 10 per cent of the South African population. In summary, the white minority apartheid regime claimed perpetual and total political and economic domination over the country, depriving the African, Indian and coloured populations of the most basic political and social rights. In order to achieve this end, the white minority instituted a programme aimed at the physical, intellectual and spiritual denigration of the black majority. This programme was mainly characterised by administering inferior quality education to the majority; instituting their confinement into 'Bantustans'; excluding them from property rights over the vast majority of arable and productive land; subjecting them to hunger and poverty; and, finally, encouraging their transformation into an urbanised proletariat geared to serve the interests of large white-owned companies and to provide cheap manual labour to extractive industries.

Out of this complex context of human drama arose the unease that would pursue Mbeki throughout his life. With the pride I feel as an African who was also once a victim of oppression, I cannot but highlight the importance of the role played by the cultural component in South Africa's struggle for freedom, which was particularly visible in the iron-clad and lucid desire on the part of black elites to invest in scholarship and knowledge as an integral part of the liberation strategy, thus overcoming the obstacles erected by the racist regime through the most diverse means. I believe that this was not the struggle of a single generation. On the contrary, I suspect that previous generations, which include Pixley ka Isaka Seme, a founder of the ANC, likely had the same stance and dedication with regard to access to education. This is the lucid and wise posture that is able to explain the emergence of the generation of freedom fighters and intellectuals of the stature of Nelson Mandela, Walter Sisulu, Govan Mbeki, Oliver Tambo, Desmond Tutu and so many others.

Indeed, it was from this generation, through his parents and their friends and comrades, that Thabo Mbeki got his determination to acquire an academic education characterised by thirst for knowledge and human solidarity. The reversals of fortune and obstacles both clumsy and trite – at times even farcical – that the young Thabo Mbeki had to go through in

order to attain meaningful access to a fundamental right, the right to a dignified and useful education, could not but lead to revolt and to personal and
collective dedication to the fight against and destruction of the political and
social regime that embodied them. It was in this context and circumstances
of rejection of the apartheid system and struggle for dignity and the right to
a future of equality, justice, respect, progress and well-being for all in South
Africa that the rich personality of the future politician and statesman Thabo
Mbeki was forged.

The most marked elements defining the context into which Thabo
Mbeki's parents, extended family and relatives had to insert their choices
and experiences in the education and formation of the young Mbeki's
values led me to the conviction that it was along this journey that he
developed the profile of a perceptive, sensitive person averse to injustice,
endowed with mental and spiritual strength and sagacity able to feed his
irreducible persistence in his firm aim of fighting for the edification of
an inclusive Africa for all, an Africa characterised by respect for humanity.
These qualities, allied with the later development of the diplomat, within
the complexity of globalisation, contributed, I believe, towards forging the
lucid and brilliant statesman and embodiment of the African Renaissance
that I would come to know.

In contrast, it is difficult to understand the inner workings of the minds
of the founders and leaders of apartheid, for their socio-political practice
was founded on irrational feelings and postures devoid of reason and rea-
sonability. What is more, the blind cult of racial superiority and the right
and power to humanly and psychologically dominate, humiliate, alienate
and destroy the Other based on absurd and inhuman principles and practices could only but foreshadow a disastrous ending, generating general
repudiation both inside and outside of the country, and bringing about the
mobilisation of efforts of the oppressed for their eradication. How was it
possible to think in that manner? A plausible answer cannot easily be found.

The condition was an extremely dramatic one, as the political system
left one with two alternatives: either acceptance of racial inferiority, which
was impracticable, as it would amount to denying oneself as a human being
and delving into the inferno of depersonalisation and collective dementia;
or courageously assuming the responsibility of the ceaseless battle for its

elimination, taking on the resulting risks, costs and human losses. Certainly the challenge of and urgent need for the eradication of apartheid influenced and quickened the political awareness of the young Thabo Mbeki's generation.

I believe that the oppressive circumstances that curtailed any personal or collective project of natural, social and intellectual advancement deeply assaulted the intelligence and hope of African youth, forcing them to grow up all too quickly and anticipate their social and political intervention. Such an oppressive and repressive atmosphere was an invitation and a call to combat for its extirpation.

In actuality, some of Thabo Mbeki's initiatives while still a young man corroborate my presumptions. Early on, he decided to move to the centre of the political fight against the racist and fascist powers that be, the township of Soweto, where his political participation and intervention would be taken note of by security services as he was detained overnight at the border between South Africa and what was then Bechuanaland on his way into exile. In the meantime, with the intensification of the persecutory actions of the apartheid state, he opted for political exile, but with the predefined and express objective of continuing his education and personal capacity, as well as pursuing from abroad the fight against apartheid. Indeed, these intents were fulfilled, the fruit of high levels of dedication, sacrifice and merit.

I am led to believe that, despite the distress and anguish that characterise all situations of political exile, his time in the United Kingdom was useful and fertile. It allowed him to free himself temporarily of the pressures and uncertainties of the daily experience of political resistance in his country, to act in an environment of greater freedom and personal safety, and to deepen his serene assessment of the racist regime and of the long and arduous path necessary for its deconstruction and eradication.

His activities as a militant within a multinational and pluralist student community allowed him to enrich his personal vision of the world in general, and of Africa and South Africa in particular. And it may have contributed to the beginnings of a humanistic vision of the South Africa of the future, indivisible and inclusive, freely encompassing all of its human components – in other words, anticipating the democratic political alternative

to the apartheid system. In addition, as a student leader in exile, he contributed to the expansion and consolidation of the presence and influence of
the ANC within this important international community.

His commitment to the fight for liberation embodied and led by the
ANC was also a constant during his time in the UK, associated with his
efforts to expand knowledge of the strategies of African liberation struggles
and to make it possible for South African freedom fighters to take advantage of them.

Once his academic training had been concluded, Thabo Mbeki joined
the sensitive and complex 'battle front' of international relations, in which
he stood out as an exquisite and convincing diplomat, providing an important contribution to the international isolation of the apartheid regime.

He was later a part of the ANC's upper leadership and was prominent
in the coordination, orientation and intensification of political and armed
action inside the country, with which he was able to further aggravate
the political weakening, social isolation and progressive breakdown of the
political and social foundations that sustained apartheid. He participated in
political mobilisation and orientation work and in diplomatic actions in the
various countries bordering South Africa, where he was able to witness the
strong sense of solidarity of their respective peoples with the ANC. He also
bore witness to the systematic destabilising actions of the apartheid regime
against neighbouring countries, the weaknesses of the latter's security and
defence systems and, at times, complicit conduct vis-à-vis the repudiated
and historically condemned regime. This experience was doubtless advan-
tageous for the improvement of political leadership methods and for the
tightening and consolidation of political alliances.

During the 1980s, the apartheid regime began to show signs of collapse
for different reasons and motives. It had, while sustaining extremely high
material, moral and political costs, failed or obtained results far below those
expected with its costly and criminal military incursions against the recently
independent neighbouring states of Angola and Mozambique, with the
obvious intention of creating a security belt along its borders and installing
'buffer states' led by African collaborationists. On the external plane, the
political isolation and international discrediting of apartheid was also on
the rise, with the regime finding itself under pressure from its own foreign

investors and former allies, who no longer believed in the regime's future or capacity to protect its interests without wide-reaching political changes.

It was the apartheid system itself that planted the seed of its future undoing, although it fought to ensure the opposite through all means available. Its obtuse policies, utterly devoid of a sense of future, were the origin of the gestation, growth and development of the forces that came to fight it. It was the urbanised labourers and the black petit bourgeoisie concentrated in the townships that ensured this change. In the midst of these processes of struggle, there is a strategic dimension that those who dominate and oppress peoples have largely ignored: the limits of the employment of brute force they have at their disposal. In the specific case of South Africa, the blind use of force and repression regardless of the possible consequences would have led to the country's economic and social collapse, something that would have constituted a catastrophe. Under such circumstances, there was only one plausible way left to resolve the impasse: a change in path and negotiation with the adversary.

Personally, I have been fascinated by the evolution of post-apartheid South Africa, a fascination that has led me to wonder how it was possible to contain and neutralise the many ingredients that could easily have led to violence, chaos and revenge and threatened the success of the political solution that had been found.

On the domestic level, while political and armed resistance and their destructive consequences increased, the apartheid regime's leadership gradually lost confidence in the effectiveness of the armed and discriminatory and repressive methods employed against the black African majority, which had until then been used in an attempt to halt the fight for freedom that was under way. Distrust and uncertainties with regard to its future grew. The more enlightened factions of the leadership concluded that apartheid had become exhausted as a political model, that the use of armed aggression against South Africa's neighbours and of brute force and internal repression had outlived their utility as tools for staunching the advance of the struggle for freedom, and, finally, that the time had come to reform the racist regime. There arose, then, the imminent need to prepare for negotiations that would lead to the organisation of the complex process of transition from a racist white minority regime to a democratic, inclusive and non-racial regime.

At that moment in which the direction of events began to turn, the great challenge of political innovation and re-elaboration of the strategy to be employed presented itself. In addition, in a situation of political radicalisation, any change in political orientation demanded, above all else, a great deal of lucidity, immense moral courage and a clear vision of the future, as well as realism and a sense of possibility. It was vital to maintain the clairvoyance and wisdom required for the conception and leadership of the complex process of political and societal transition and reform of the minority regime.

I wish to highlight the clarity, generosity, humanism, humility and political intelligence of the ANC leadership, which gained my personal admiration and respect. Indeed, these were the human and political qualities that, associated with a lofty sense of patriotism, would usher in the birth of the new South Africa in 1994 – a democratic, inclusive, indivisible and progressive South Africa.

Nevertheless, ingredients liable to generate chaos were present in South African society, leading to a real risk of the situation sliding out of control. The urgent need to neutralise the political and social factors on which these ingredients relied thus proved crucial in order to avoid the deterioration of the situation. As a consequence, it was urgent to moderate excessive euphoria and arrogance on the part of the victors, attenuate the justified impatience of the black majority and prevent it from being used for political advantage, ensure the trust of the minority of European descent and dispel its fears about the future, and, finally, to neutralise the temptations of tyranny of the majority with the establishment of institutional checks and balances.

The country found itself faced with the need for a true art of political leadership, one in which there should prevail general trust in the respect for commitments, in the defence of the interests of all South Africans, regardless of their origin, race or ethnic identity, in the integration of the various components of the national population and in the protection of the interests and unity of the new emerging nation. It was necessary to ensure the transmission of the trust and hope in a different and better future for all, inspiring and ensuring its appropriation and defence on the part of all components of South African society. This, incredibly, is what happened, but its conservation and consolidation continue to this day to demand continuous renovation through encouraging moral attitudes, corresponding public policies and good governing practices.

How was such a miracle possible? I believe that the success must be attributed to leadership in the different sectors of South African society, including political, religious, union and business leaders and civil society organisations. However, it was an exceptional historical personality, President Nelson Mandela, who, with an extraordinary vision of the future, with great generosity and wisdom and with unsurpassed intelligence, had the great merit of leading the complex process of political change and laying down the political, ethical and institutional foundations of the newly emerging democratic, humanistic, inclusive and progressive South Africa.

Thabo Mbeki's three mandates, one as deputy president and two as president, were in fact of decisive political importance to the progressive installation, initiation, functioning and consolidation of the political, social and institutional foundations of the new South Africa. Indeed, his was the period of implementation, experimentation, adaptation and perfecting of the institutions of the democratic rule of law and of the dawning of individual and collective life in a different society, one of equality among people, of democracy, of plurality and of inclusiveness. It also constituted a time of political, social and cultural rupture with the practices and values of the apartheid regime and the composition of new social and institutional equilibriums.

Even so, in order to guarantee the success of the transformation and reform process, a great sense of realism was indispensable, as was gaining the confidence and respect of the various components of society for the new political order and for its institutions; containing the possibility of impatience; guaranteeing the country's stability and security; stimulating national concord and harmony and encouraging the adoption of the common destiny that gives body to and inspires the entire nation. Under those circumstances, trust and hope constituted subjective factors vital to a successful transition.

It was also essential to guarantee the growth and sustainability of the economy, the key to reducing unemployment and ensuring more income for families. As such, the confidence of investors and business communities operating in the country, as well as of the labour unions, had to be maintained. Indeed, the sensibility, courage and precaution with which the new leadership decided to maintain many of the existing economic structures was widely recognised, even though these could easily be perceived and criticised as being tied to the old regime.

For the subsequent substitution of the political and legal institutions installed by the white minority regime, it was necessary to edify new institutions under the democratic rule of law, obeying the norms and guarantees established by the recently approved constitution, with the introduction of the principle of majority representation. In addition to the elaboration and approval of norms, it was fundamental to ensure the full and effective functioning of institutions, which called for careful and permanent monitoring.

The next pressing requirement was reform in state administration, associated with the democratisation of public institutions and accompanied by the institution of a new ethics and a new organic structure able to ensure the promotion of equal opportunities for all citizens regardless of their ethnic or social origins. In the same manner, there was an urgent need to redefine territorial administration, adapting it to the country's new political reality, so as to respect local cultures and values and guarantee the democratic and fair representation of its populations. In summary, a balanced management was required in accordance with the ethnic and cultural plurality of the nation that was about to be born.

The institutionalised discrimination, oppression and distancing of the black majority in the management of public affairs cut across all areas of the country's social, economic, financial and academic life. This practice had generated a perverted and sick society that required comprehension, humanism, courage and vision to promote its progressive change and recovery. In order to achieve such an objective, it was necessary to conceive and implement a wide-reaching reform programme encompassing the areas of the economy, education, health and housing.

The social and cultural heritage of apartheid was extremely burdensome and demanded the application of innovative and daring public policies to confront it and achieve its progressive reduction and elimination. In addition, inequalities in terms of status and income needed to be decisively overcome in order to conquer and maintain confidence in the future on the part of the popular classes, something that constituted a fundamental element in domestic political and social stability.

Public acknowledgement of the internal and external credibility of the organs of state power was another political priority that had to be ensured. As a consequence, the appropriate, realistic and prudent management of very sensitive areas of power, such as justice, security, public order and national defence, remained fundamental, while at the same time promoting their reform and ensuring their efficiency.

On the external or international level, Thabo Mbeki's mandates coincided with the new South African regime's period of international affirmation and the elimination of the isolation into which the previous regime had driven the country. He was thus the eloquent spokesman for the promotion and affirmation of South Africa's new image in the most important international forums and in regional and pan-African institutions. He was additionally a coherent defender of the interests of both his country and Africa in general in negotiations on strategic issues of global reach, garnering him affection, respect and prestige in pan-African and international institutions.

On the national level, I believe that it is worth highlighting and acknowledging Thabo Mbeki's strategy of preserving the political alliances that had been the mainstays of the victorious struggle against apartheid and which would later constitute the political and moral reserve for the preservation of the new regime's political and social stability, a precondition for the continuation and success of the wide-reaching reforms being implemented. Another decisive factor in the success of the transition under way was the judicious and pragmatic decision to transform the ANC into an institutional, moderate party that respected its commitments to its political partners.

In summary, the leadership of President Thabo Mbeki was fundamental in guaranteeing a peaceful and successful regime transition and in the establishment and consolidation of the foundations of the South African democratic rule of law, the guarantor of stability, security and healthy coexistence among South Africans and of the promotion of the country's socio-economic progress.

During my time in office as president of the Republic of Cabo Verde, I followed with particular interest the evolution of South Africa's reforms and policies and, consequently, the actions carried out under the leadership and drive of Thabo Mbeki, first as deputy president and subsequently as president of South Africa. In this context, we had the opportunity to exchange ideas and opinions about the future of Africa, as well as about the great challenges faced by the continent.

Indeed, the edification of a future of peace, unity, prosperity, solidarity and autonomy for independent Africa was and remains a constant concern of Thabo Mbeki. His proposal for the ideal of the African Renaissance represents a vision of Africa in transformation, an Africa of peace, prosperity and solidarity that is politically and economically integrated, and serves as a path towards the expansion and consolidation of the African liberation process begun some 50 years ago. It also represents a visionary programme for the fulfilment of pan-Africanist ideals.

The New Partnership for Africa's Development came to be one of the fundamental proposals for the reconstruction and economic modernisation of Africa currently under way. Among these proposals, I would like to highlight the prominence and priority that have been given to providing the continent with infrastructures and electrification, associated with the innovative design of mobilising intra-African resources for their financing and realisation of a better future for the continent. Indeed, it would not be realistic to consider promoting African integration without having reliable and modern communication structures available and depending exclusively on foreign direct investment for their materialisation. In the same manner, development, socio-economic transformation and modernisation cannot be truly achieved without easy, reliable and permanent access to electrical energy.

Lastly, I believe it pertinent to highlight Thabo Mbeki's continuing concern for and unyielding efforts in contributing to the reduction of external interference in Africa, in favour of greater African political and military autonomy.

In my esteemed friend Thabo Mbeki I see a humanistic, patient leader who possesses a strategic vision for his country and for the African continent. He has, furthermore, proven to be a statesman gifted with a solid, lucid, realistic, pragmatic and reform-minded outlook. Instead of fractious solutions and sudden substitutions, the development of which would always have been unpredictable, he preferred patience, gradualism and the progressive transformation of South African society and the South African economy. And, precisely at a time in which populist and vengeful sentiments could very well have prevailed, he resisted radical decisions. In reality, the edification of the new South Africa calls for a transformational transition, monitored in an intelligent and properly understood manner in a long-term perspective.

No less important, once no longer in power, he adopted a posture of great dignity and respect, and revealed a profound sense of purpose, offering his talents to serve his country and Africa as a continent, successfully undertaking a number of delicate and highly complex missions. The creation of the Thabo Mbeki Foundation, motivated by noble and forward-looking intentions, represents a major contribution to the training and education of new generations of South African leaders, and confirms his political stature as a leader committed to the future.

Finally, I would like to express my appreciation for the opportunity I have been given to outline, in this brief presentation, the profile of my distinguished and esteemed friend, Thabo Mbeki, and I take advantage of the occasion to pay him genuine and brotherly homage.

Praia, May 2015

KETUMILE MASIRE

❦

Word reached us one day in 1962 that a 'football team' from South Africa had crossed into Bechuanaland Protectorate (as Botswana was then known) and that it was to pass on to Southern Rhodesia (present-day Zimbabwe). The border control between Botswana and South Africa back in 1962 was not really strict so the team experienced no problems coming through to Botswana. But there were problems when the team got to Southern Rhodesia because the authorities wanted all sorts of documents and they decided that these young fellows had entered the country illegally. And they decided to send them back to South Africa.

I heard of this travelling party because at the time I was a member of the Legislative Council that had been formed the previous year. This was the first ever structure to run the country and make the laws under British rule.

We were told that there was a bright young fellow leading this team that had been thrown back at the Rhodesian border and the Bechuanaland government had arranged for them to fly out to Tanganyika (Tanzania), which was where they were actually headed. The young man was Thabo Mbeki. There was a gap of about 10 years before I heard of him again because he had proceeded to study in Britain.

In the meantime we had gained our independence from Britain in 1966, while the (South African) liberation movement had become more active. Oliver Tambo, the president of the African National Congress (ANC), having found that Botswana could be a bridge, used to come to the country frequently and that was when I once again met Thabo Mbeki, who was now Oliver Tambo's secretary, so to speak. He was young but wise and mature beyond his age. He impressed me. He was a ball of fire, and ultimately became a sort of foreign minister for the ANC.

The ANC once presented a very delicate request to President Seretse Khama. They asked to establish an ANC presence in Botswana, and the request was put to President Khama verbally at an Organisation of African Unity (OAU) summit in Ethiopia. Oliver Tambo was told to put the request in writing. The entreaty was indeed put in writing, but the response was not.

We told them that we had considered their request, but that we found it difficult to accede to it because we did not want the apartheid regime to use such presence to justify its lingering suspicion that we were militarily aiding the liberation movement. However, ANC members would be allowed into Botswana if they could come in quietly. Thabo was one of the ANC members allowed to settle in Botswana during the early 1970s and one of his major tasks was to try to establish a diplomatic working relationship between the ANC and the Botswana government.

Then came the next request from the ANC, which was whether we could facilitate a military training venue. Much as the ANC struggle was ours as well, we had to weigh other options. An ANC military training facility in Botswana would give the apartheid regime the much-needed justification to accuse us of being actively at war with them. Our major contribution in the struggle had been our moral voice in international forums against apartheid.

We told Tambo and Thabo that apartheid South Africa already had a lingering fear that liberation movements were going to use Botswana as a base. Therefore, if the apartheid government learned that we had allowed the ANC a military training facility, they could come into our country claiming to be in pursuit of these groups, and that would create more complications.

So we presented an alternative, somewhat audacious plan: 'If you can come through in a way that we cannot see you, then we will not have seen you.' So we agreed on those terms. Our official policy was that we did not allow the liberation movements to use Botswana as a springboard to launch military attacks on neighbouring countries. If the ANC managed to infiltrate arms and guerrillas through Botswana, we would claim not to have seen them pass through our country.

So we lived for quite some time in that mode. Whenever we felt the need to discuss matters with the ANC we called Oliver Tambo and he always brought Thabo with him.

A conduit, albeit a secret and unofficial one, was extended – and the apartheid regime felt the heat. Pik Botha, the regime's minister of foreign affairs, once asked if we needed their assistance in trying to plug the hole, wherever it was, to which we responded that we did not need assistance from anybody to patrol our borders.

We had a tricky balancing act to follow. To show that we were not an official conduit for the liberation armies, our police would occasionally arrest some of them. They would be tried for illegal possession of arms, be sentenced, serve a short term, and get a presidential pardon.

And then the raids and bombings started. Refugees were killed but there was a lot of collateral damage and many of our people died. As a government, we had to defend the country, but we did not have the wherewithal to do it.

When you have no power, you use your ingenuity. So our biggest strength was our moral stand. The Geneva Conventions stipulated that refugees had the right to sanctuary. As a signatory to the Geneva Conventions, we said that the South African regime's actions were not only an affront to Botswana's sovereignty, but to the United Nations (UN) itself. The UN would send delegations to come and see the damage inflicted on our country by the regime. Throughout, Oliver Tambo and Thabo Mbeki would come to express sympathy, attend funerals, or just to comfort both the Batswana and South Africans whose families had been killed by the regime's security forces.

The winds of change were certainly blowing on the subcontinent. In 1979, the minority regime in Rhodesia was on its knees, and a democratic Zimbabwe was going to rise from the ashes of a bitter war of liberation. When the parties to the conflict met at the Lancaster House talks to map Zimbabwe's future, the Botswana government had two observers, Archibald Mogwe and Joseph Legwaila. Thabo represented the ANC.

After Zimbabwe's independence in 1980, it would be a decade before Namibia also became an independent state. By now the demise of the apartheid regime was imminent. Indeed, this happened when Nelson Mandela was sworn in as president of a democratic Republic of South Africa in 1994, with Thabo Mbeki as one of his deputies.

In the region, we had been seized with the question of what would happen post the liberation struggle. Thabo Mbeki, as the deputy president of South Africa, seemed also to have thought long and hard about how to bring southern Africa together and what should be done to get the whole of Africa to work together. When he delivered his epoch-defining 'I am an African' speech in the South African parliament in 1996, he forced all of us to think again about our continent and where we really wanted to steer it.

That was the genesis of initiatives like the New Partnership for Africa's Development and the African Renaissance. At the time when he was championing these important initiatives, I had left office, and he had succeeded Mandela as president. He asked me as an elder statesman to drive the African Renaissance as its executive secretary. Unfortunately, my hands were already full because I had just been in Rwanda and I was moving to the Democratic Republic of Congo (DRC) as an envoy of peace, promoting the conflict prevention efforts of the Southern African Development Community (SADC) and the African Union (AU). I could not handle all these commitments without being unfair to one or all of them.

Then there was the question of the difficult work that I was doing in the DRC, a country that really drove Thabo Mbeki's and my resolve in terms of building a democratic state. It is important to provide historical context related to our collective role in promoting peace and preventing conflict in the DRC because that will explain why, in the name of the African continent, President Mbeki had to commit resources belonging to the South African people to build a democratic state in the DRC. Our effort to promote democracy and a stable political landscape in the DRC was part of the broader African Renaissance.

The Inter-Congolese Dialogue was a protracted and taxing process. The country's problems were as unique as was its history. The Congo was a colonial possession that had never had a colonial administration, so it had no knowledge of how a central government worked. Unlike other colonies, the Congo had not been run by a colonial power that had put in administrative structures to service the metropolis. King Leopold of Belgium had owned it as a foreign estate or personal fiefdom, which he looted as he liked. The coming of independence only continued the country's tragic story. Mobutu proceeded the plunder for personal enrichment. Of course, Laurent Kabila's rebel movement unseated Mobutu. After Kabila's assassination, his son Joseph Kabila was immediately made president and he had to pick up the pieces.

And that was when President Mbeki became involved. The Inter-Congolese Dialogue process really tested his resolve and he proved his mettle as an important leader on the continent. What also came to the fore was his deep conviction that the time had come for Africans to take the lead in rebuilding Africa. He was conscious of the fact that the economic and socio-political development of the DRC was very crucial for the African continent and its renaissance. He really worked very hard for the DRC to conduct its first democratic elections and in the process promote peace building.

Another important initiative in which President Mbeki was instrumental was the transformation of the OAU to the AU. The OAU had become an annual gathering for politicians to exchange pleasantries, without achieving much in terms of transforming the continent. President Mbeki felt that the AU could be a vehicle to drive Africa's developmental agenda.

Regarding Mbeki as a person, he has always been very articulate. He puts his points clearly and forcefully without appearing to be coercive. As a public speaker, he is an orator of great note. I believe one of his best speeches was when he stepped down from office. Here was a man who accepted his fate with grace. It was a telling moment; a great example to the rest of our continent that a leader, even a president, must always subject himself to the will of those he leads.

Interviewed April 2014, Gaborone, Botswana

SALIM AHMED SALIM

❖

I followed the political developments in South Africa as a young student in Zanzibar, but I was not that conversant with the issues. My real education of the South African situation was when I went to Havana, Cuba. I had gone with two other Zanzibaris to open an office there in 1961. Within months, the African National Congress (ANC) representative by the name of Mzimkhulu Makiwane arrived in Cuba. He had also come to Havana to open the ANC office. As we were accommodated in the same villa we had a lot of time to discuss issues, especially those pertaining to developments in Africa with special emphasis on the liberation struggle. He gave us the political background to what was going on in South Africa and so that gave me a real insight into the situation.

When I was in the student and youth movements, we always followed events in Africa; we always sympathised and supported the struggle in South Africa. But we did so more out of emotion and out of the conviction that apartheid was wrong. We were really not aware of the ghastly details of what was going on in South Africa. Eventually, of course, things became much clearer.

Subsequent to my visit to Cuba in 1961, when I went to the United Nations (UN) as the ambassador of Tanzania, I became much more involved in the liberation struggle. The UN had three committees dealing with colonial problems, all of which were presided over by Africans. We had the Special Committee Against Apartheid (presided over by the Nigerian ambassador), the Special Committee on Decolonisation (which I presided over) and the UN Council for Namibia (presided over by the Zambian ambassador). So we had a very strong team that collaborated and worked together. We were very active in the efforts towards mobilising support for the policies of the apartheid regime to be considered a crime against humanity. In a sense you could not completely divorce the responsibilities of the Committee Against Apartheid from those of the Committee on Decolonisation, nor could they be divorced from the Council for Namibia because they all related to apartheid South Africa as the main bulwark of oppression and repression and the central supporter of the colonial regimes in the area. So we worked together as Africans and exchanged views. The UN played a very important role in the struggle against apartheid in terms of mobilisation of international opinion and also in terms of the isolation of the regime.

We were privileged at that time to have a South African nationalist and a top ANC freedom fighter: Johnny Makhathini. We used to debate with him and although we did not agree with everything that he had to say, he was so articulate and effective that he boosted our morale and also helped us to understand things much better at the UN. I spent two years in the Security Council from 1975-76 and one of the most important issues at the time was the African agenda, which meant dealing with issues of liberation. In the Council, I dealt with South African issues on a number of occasions. The Soweto uprisings were really an important turning point in the South African liberation struggle. For us, it demonstrated the extent of the criminality of the apartheid regime and its total disregard for human beings.

I recall that during the debate in the Security Council there was an attempt by some to justify the regime's actions by claiming that the situation was being exaggerated because nobody had been there. Yet the fact remains that the international media was extensively reporting on the sad evolution of the situation there. We were distressed and infuriated by the images of armoured cars being used in fighting against little school kids. We were not talking about grown-ups; we were talking about little school kids being shot at point blank by security police. We also had occasion in the Security Council to deal with the South African aggression against Angola.

In terms of international solidarity we dealt with the South African situation in many other forums. For instance, I presided over a special international conference in Paris. We worked consistently to impress upon the international community the need to get more involved in understanding what was going on in apartheid South Africa and the crucial importance of lending support to the struggle. We organised lectures in parts of the United States to talk about the South African struggle. We worked with concerned African Americans and also with a number of white Americans who were very concerned about the struggle. My own president, Mwalimu Julius Nyerere, was a central figure in the promotion of the liberation struggle in Africa.

Through my human solidarity work and engagements, I might have come across Thabo Mbeki during the late 1960s when he was still part of the ANC Youth and Student Section, but more so in the early 1970s because that was when the Africa Group at the UN became more involved in the South African situation. I served in the UN from 1970 to 1980 and that was the period when so many of these events were taking place.

Of course, Thabo Mbeki had always been a fighter, and he was also extremely articulate in explaining the situation about the struggle. Indeed, he used every occasion to highlight the South African struggle. I remember that we once travelled together to Cairo in the 1980s when I was Tanzania's foreign affairs minister and he was the head of the department of international affairs of the ANC, having taken over that portfolio from the late Johnny Makhathini. He spoke at that African meeting and he was very articulate. This was something for which he was always respected because it is one thing to argue emotionally, but quite another to argue rationally so that the people whose support you are seeking understand the crux of the problem and are able to sympathise.

Those were the years when the Western world as a whole, except for a few countries, notably the Scandinavian countries, was doing very little or nothing to create problems for the apartheid system. Every time we came with ideas in terms of putting more pressure on South Africa, the Western countries became defensive. We had to work with the liberation movements to fight against pro-apartheid Western countries. Mbeki, as Oliver Tambo's right-hand man, was much involved in this struggle.

In 1971 when we rejected the credentials of South Africa to the UN, the Africa Group took the position that we could no longer continue with the interpretation of the ruling, which held that the rejection of the credentials of the South African regime meant that we were giving the regime a solemn warning.

I interacted with Oliver Tambo at the UN, but more so when I returned to Tanzania where we interacted not only on issues of strategy, but also on the issue of the ANC freedom fighters. Comrade Oliver Tambo came to Dar es Salaam quite often. With Mandela incarcerated in jail, Oliver Tambo was a towering figure and he was the one everybody associated with the liberation struggle in South Africa. He was a very calm person who hardly displayed any anger. He was eloquent and effective in explaining the case for a liberated South Africa and I respected him a lot. I think this may be where Thabo Mbeki acquired his mannerisms because I have never seen him angry.

Thabo Mbeki would be justified in showing anger but he does not manifest that unless it is absolutely necessary. He is very polished, articulate and effective both in general conferences and in bilaterals. I would say he was part of the cream of the ANC leadership. You had Madiba, Oliver Tambo and you had the next layer, which included Thabo Mbeki. He became an important factor for us in terms of understanding the situation because despite our best intentions and efforts, the final analysis rested with the ANC people who were in a better position to tell us what was going on. I should also say that at the same time we were dealing with the Pan Africanist Congress.

Later, when I had returned to Tanzania from the UN, I was deputy prime minister and minister of defence when Oliver Tambo came to Dar es Salaam to consult us about possible substantive political negotiations in South Africa and I was privy to discussions because I was actively dealing with the liberation movements. The truth is, the ANC position as it was then articulated, did not differ fundamentally from the position taken by the Organisation of African Unity (OAU) in the 1969 Lusaka Manifesto.[1] As I recall, the Lusaka Manifesto was very clear that the OAU would prefer a negotiated solution, a peaceful transition rather than a continuation of violence. But when everything else was blocked, when obstacles contin-

1 The reference is S.M. Ndlovu, 'The ANC's Diplomacy and International Relations' in South Africa Democracy Education Trust, *Road to Democracy in South Africa, Volume 2 (1970–1980)* (Pretoria: UNISA Press, 2006) 616-20.

ued to be placed in the way of a non-violent solution, there was support for an armed struggle. That was the crux of the matter and in a sense the (1989) Harare Declaration was more or less a continuation of the Lusaka Manifesto which had been proposed and adopted by the OAU 20 years earlier. Perhaps there was a question of tactics, which led to a stalemate, but in principle it was not a departure from the position, which was adopted earlier by the OAU. Actually, that was a very important point because there was an attempt to make the international community believe that the ANC and others were communist rabble-rousers who wanted to overthrow the white minority regime in South Africa. But in reality nobody wanted to fight for the sake of fighting. Wherever there were opportunities to achieve objectives through negotiated solutions, you went for that. The ANC therefore presented the Harare Declaration to both the Frontline States and the OAU. I think this was one area where people like Oliver Tambo, Thabo Mbeki and others were very effective, as a collective, in articulating and explaining the situation to us as outsiders.

The Nordic countries were very strong supporters of the struggle against apartheid, but of course they were finding it difficult to entertain the idea of armed struggle. At least they saw that there might be no alternative. They did not have to support this position but simply to have their understanding was critical. So the Lusaka Manifesto and then later the Harare Declaration were very helpful to Nordic countries.

When Oliver Tambo and Thabo Mbeki came to see Mwalimu Nyerere about the Harare Declaration, we cautioned them on the possible implications of negotiating with the Pretoria regime. Mwalimu was following the struggles in southern Africa very closely, especially in South Africa, in its minutest details. I had to know what I was going to present to him. Whenever I went to see Mwalimu at his house at Msasani, I had to be well prepared. He was not only following these international events; they affected him personally. Our friends from the Western world understood Mwalimu's commitment to the liberation struggle – and remember South Africa was the last country that had not been liberated. So I had to understand what Oliver Tambo and Thabo Mbeki were bringing to Mwalimu Nyerere as the president of Tanzania.

Throughout the struggle for national liberation in South Africa, we were talking about dialogue with apartheid South Africa during the 1960s. There were very distinguished groups of African leaders, such as Houphouët Boigny of Côte d'Ivoire, who championed this position together with other respected Africans – and you must understand that the Ivorian leader and those who thought like him were not stooges or sympathisers of the apartheid regime; they were not trying to sell out, but during the 1960s they genuinely believed that dialogue with South Africa was the only way. So to take African leaders away from that position and to achieve a consensus position required people like Mwalimu and Kenneth Kaunda, among others to say to Houphouët Boigny and his supporters that it was not that they did not want a dialogue with the apartheid regime, but that it was impossible to have a dialogue with the deaf.

We knew what an armed struggle meant – there would have been death and destruction. That was Mwalimu's position, and also that of the Frontline States and Africa in general. It is true that as the South African government became more intransigent, our position then became more focused on the armed struggle rather than on a diplomatic solution. But then the Harare Declaration of 1989 changed all this because it championed the diplomatic solution. Collective credit must be given to Oliver Tambo and his team, which included Thabo Mbeki, because Nyerere had seen and heard it before when Houphouët Boigny and others tried to convince the OAU to rubberstamp talks with the apartheid regime during the 1960s.

Tambo, Mbeki and others had to convince us why the Harare Declaration was fundamentally different from the Lusaka Manifesto. I had the task of selling the Harare Declaration to the OAU. I supported the ANC position, and presented to the OAU a declaration on fundamental changes in the world and how this had an impact on Africa. Because of that, we then deliberated on issues around democratisation, respect for human rights, majority rule, release of political prisoners, formation of an inclusive interim government and so on, issues that were not addressed effectively by the Lusaka Manifesto.

Frankly, it was good timing. The gate was opening not only because Madiba and other political prisoners were released but it was also the end of the Cold War. The Cold War affected Africa because you were either seen as the allies of the Soviet Union and China or the allies of the Western countries. So the end of the Cold War meant that Africa could assert itself. The mandate of the OAU insofar as liberation was concerned was coming to an end because South Africa was about to become free. In reality, the whole of Africa became free when South Africa attained its liberation and that was one of the primary objectives of the OAU. Mbeki followed these issues very closely because these political dynamics and changes would later influence him to spearhead the formation of the African Union (AU) which replaced the OAU.

Now that we were free and our countries no longer had to deal with the question of liberation as such, what next? The priorities became somewhat different and strengthening of the OAU became necessary. We went to Tripoli at the invitation of 'Brother Leader' Muammar Gaddafi. When we arrived there, 'Brother Leader' had already prepared his own ideas and produced some documents for us to peruse and discuss. I did not know about this, but he had asked experts from different African countries to work out a new charter for the AU, which would have had one government, one defence ministry, etc. It was very ambitious. I think that he was well-meaning but it was not realistic.

So the challenge in Sirte, Libya, in 1999 was how to make good of an admirable idea, but one that was too ambitious and not realistic politically speaking. This was where people like Thabo Mbeki played a very important role. President Thabo Mbeki, President Abdelaziz Bouteflika of Algeria and President Olusegun Obasanjo of Nigeria were among those people who played a critical role in arriving at the Sirte Declaration, which was a very mild version of what Brother Leader had intended to achieve. It was a very important development because the Sirte Declaration talked about the transformation of the OAU into the AU. It took the best elements of the OAU and dropped those that could create confusion.

For example, after the freedom of our countries, one of the main issues we needed to focus on was the question of conflicts on our continent: internal conflicts and inter-state conflicts. When the OAU was established, the thinking was that we would have to deal with inter-state conflicts but there were hardly any. There was the conflict between Morocco and Algeria at one time, but the problems were mainly internal conflicts and coups. The OAU had a provision for non-interference in the internal affairs of member states. Personally, I think it was a good provision and well-intentioned. But then people started misusing it. Some leaders committed atrocious things on the African continent, but nothing could be done because of the 'non-interference' factor. If, for example, a crisis was looming, even if we needed to offer advice, as the OAU, we could not intervene because it would be seen as interference in the internal affairs of a member state. So one of the significant and radical changes that took place in Libya was a shift towards the 'collective concern of Africa'. This meant that the AU had a right to intervene in situations of massive violation of human rights, especially in cases such as genocide or war crimes. The right to intervene was part of the transformation from the OAU to the AU, which was launched in Durban (in July 2002) and chaired by President Mbeki. This was really a commendable political milestone. The creation of the AU Peace and Security Council was clearly a significant development.

I think that the demonstration by African leaders that they were prepared to be involved in conflict prevention and peace diplomacy was extremely important. The conflict situations in the Democratic Republic of the Congo, Burundi, Sudan and Somalia meant that African countries were prepared to act and Mbeki's role in conflict prevention proves the point. We still have a long way to go and there are still some limitations. For example, I was the chief AU representative in Sudan on the issue of Darfur and one of our most frustrating experiences was the lack of necessary resources. Even at the time when we had the UN/AU Hybrid force, and we appealed for helicopters, we were told that there weren't any. So for a long time the mission in Darfur was very difficult. Personally, I do not believe that Africans are so poor that they cannot afford to provide the necessary support when there is a need to assist in a peace process. These are some of the difficult challenges that Mbeki has to deal with as a peace envoy for both the AU and the UN.

Every epoch has its own leaders but it is a fact that the leadership, which was demonstrated by the founding fathers of the OAU, was committed to liberating the African continent from colonialism and minority white rule. Those leaders had just come out of the freedom struggles and they felt that they wanted to assert Africa's identity: her personality and her independence, and they did that. We are talking about people like Mwalimu

Nyerere, Kwame Nkrumah, Modibo Keïta, among others. My own experience while I was in New York was that the African ambassadors that formed the African Group were so strong and powerful because we had our unity and integrity and we spoke with one voice. There was no such a thing as Anglophone, Lusophone, Francophone, Arabphone, Swahiliphone: we were all Africans. That was the difference and Johnny Makhathini and Mbeki had access to us. At present, the position of the Africa Group in the UN has been somehow weakened but efforts have been made to address the situation.

Thabo Mbeki achieved a lot, first of all by being what he is. I am talking about at the African level. He is respected because he respects other people. He is articulate and he articulated issues that were the concerns of all Africans and in particular ordinary Africans. President Mbeki's patriotism and his commitment to the transformation of the African continent are beyond doubt. His pan-Africanism is beyond doubt. He is, of course, one of the architects of the philosophy of the African Renaissance. He is also one of the founding architects of the New Partnership for Africa's Development. And in the context of how things are on our continent, Mbeki was the leading figure calling for democratic change. He has made use of the experiences that he accumulated during the liberation struggle and he continues to support good causes and to solidify cooperation with other African countries; he has undoubtedly made a major contribution in the continent. Despite the difficulties he had in South Africa with his recall from office Mbeki did not give up. He is now one of the most outstanding emissaries of Africa in dealing with African problems.

Since President Mbeki left office, he has spent time in Sudan. Mediators are not always the most popular people in any given situation and yet I think that he has been able to establish himself and to give the AU the respect that it deserves. He has managed to convince even the most intransigent African leaders that he is genuine and that he is not in it for himself; he gains nothing personally. Mbeki will go down as one of the most outstanding leaders of our continent. Of course, you must remember that he is in Mandela's country and Madiba was larger than life. But even in that situation, Mbeki has been able to have his own impact in Africa.

When you analyse the way Mbeki addressed conflict prevention in

Zimbabwe you need to ask yourself the question: from whom did the criticism come? He was supposed to go there and try to help find a solution. The Southern African Development Community countries did not give him a mandate to go and tell Robert Mugabe to retire from politics. Our powerful friends in the West would have liked that to have been the mandate given to Thabo Mbeki – to be the cheerleader of regime change. But that was not possible because Mugabe is respected in this continent and in the region. No doubt he made his grave mistakes, but there is a history to contend with and that history is an important part of our liberation struggle. I remember that at the World Summit on Sustainable Development in Johannesburg (in 2002) when Mugabe took to the podium and addressed Tony Blair, he told him to keep his Britain and he would keep his Zimbabwe. Mugabe got a standing ovation from the audience that day. This must tell you something. Rightly or wrongly, Mugabe is an important factor on this continent. I do not think that it was Thabo Mbeki's role or that of any envoy of the AU to tell Mugabe to leave office or even to create conditions for him to leave. I do not think that it was fair to criticise Mbeki because he was not ruthless in dealing with President Mugabe and enforcing a regime change. It is up to the people of Zimbabwe to vote him out of office.

I was sad when Mbeki was recalled from office by the ANC. Without wishing to interfere in the internal affairs of South Africa, I thought that since he had only seven months to go before his term ended, he should have been left to complete it because South Africa was just beginning to lead as an example to all of us in Africa. I was really sad and you will find that a lot of Africans were sad, even today. We do not want to get involved in the internal politics of the ANC because we support them, but if I had to give my opinion, I would have advised the ANC leadership that the matter should not have been sorted out in that way.

As a true leader of the liberation struggle, Thabo Mbeki handled himself in a very dignified manner. Even the act of accepting resignation from office: that was a magnanimous act. He was not elected into office by the ANC alone, there are many other South Africans who elected him. Once you are elected president, you become president of South Africa; you are not president of the ANC only. I can understand the politics of the ruling party, but I think that in the circumstances, he made a dignified exit. That is why he is so respected in the African continent. At the Thabo Mbeki Africa Day lecture that I delivered in 2014 at the University of South Africa, I noted that when he entered the hall he received a standing ovation from the audience. This bears testimony to what I am saying about how well respected he is in his own country. He is well respected here in Tanzania, and in many other parts of the African continent. This does not mean that everything that Thabo Mbeki did was right; he made mistakes, but I think that everybody knows that he is a person of impeccable integrity; his credentials really talk in terms of his passion and unwavering commitment to seeing a better Africa for all who live on the continent.

Interviewed August 2014, Dar es Salaam

DUMISO DABENGWA

✦

I joined the liberation struggle just after it started in Southern Rhodesia after I had matriculated in 1956. I taught for a while at a mission near Bulawayo. It was a temporary job merely to assist the mission because they did not have a teacher for their Standard 4 class and I was asked to take on that class. I then left for Bulawayo and got a job with the Bulawayo city council as a clerk in the social welfare department. It was while I was there in 1959 that the Southern Rhodesia African National Congress (ANC) chapter was banned.

I was given the task of facilitating the visits by the relatives of the African nationalists who were detained at Khami maximum prison, which is in Bulawayo. There were prisoners from Bulawayo, Zambia and Malawi – I am talking here of members of the ANC of Nyasaland (Malawi) and the ANC of Northern Rhodesia (Zambia). Among other things, I helped arrange transport for the relatives whose visits I facilitated.

I think it was in 1962 when we started getting young men from the ANC in South Africa who were trying to find their way north to Zambia on their way to Dar es Salaam to join the liberation struggle. Thabo Mbeki was among the students and youth who came to Rhodesia on their way to Tanganyika (Tanzania). I was the secretary of the youth wing of the Zimbabwe African People's Union (ZAPU) in the western region and my attention was drawn to the presence of these young men from South Africa. We had heard and read about Govan Mbeki and we knew that Thabo, who was among those arrested by the police, was the old man Govan Mbeki's son. The police had intercepted the young men and wanted to deport them back to South Africa.

We got one of our best lawyers to advise on how best the young students and youth from South Africa could be handled. It was the late Leo Baron who helped us. He later became chief justice of Zimbabwe. Leo Baron, who was our party (ZAPU) lawyer, interceded and made sure that deportations back to South Africa were not carried out. He argued that if they had to be deported, they should be sent to the north to Zambia or back to the country of entry, which was Botswana.

I do remember very well that Thabo Mbeki was young, on the quiet side, but when he explained things he was very articulate about what he wanted. He made it clear to us that whatever happened, he would not allow himself to be deported back to South Africa. At that time he said we should rather put him in prison in Zimbabwe, but he certainly was not going back to South Africa. I think the legalities were that the Rhodesians were hoping that when the police finally agreed to have them released, they could only send them to Botswana. Zambia was not yet fully independent in 1962; it got its independence in 1964 and it had been semi-autonomous but it was not yet independent.

I think Leo Baron argued that if the young men and women went to Zambia, the white governor of Northern Rhodesia (Zambia) might collaborate with South Africa and might decide to send Thabo Mbeki and his comrades back to South Africa. So it was arranged that they be sent to Botswana.

That was the last time I saw Thabo Mbeki and his young comrades and we did not meet again for a long time. In 1963, the following year, I left Rhodesia to go to Zambia en route for military training in the Soviet Union. We were in Zambia for some time. Because the ANC already had an office in Lusaka, we enquired about what had happened to Thabo Mbeki and his group. We were told that he had gone to study abroad. So we did not have any contact then but went for training in the Soviet Union and after training there and in other countries such as China, Cuba and Egypt we converged in Lusaka. Our military wing, the Zimbabwe People's Revolutionary Army (ZIPRA), had not been formed into an army then. There we formed the first semblance of what one would call a military command structure and ZIPRA became the military wing of ZAPU. We formed an alliance with the ANC, which led to the 1967/68 Wankie and Sipolilo military campaigns.

We met up with Thabo Mbeki again in Zambia around 1972/73. Thabo came to Lusaka and we remembered each other and started working together. He worked very closely with Oliver Tambo. We used to exchange quite a lot of experiences, briefing each other on an almost weekly basis about what was happening on the ANC front and what was happening on the ZAPU front. We would strategise and discuss how best to proceed with the struggle for national liberation in our countries. Our interactions continued right up to the time when Zimbabwe got its independence.

Thabo Mbeki was not on the military side. At that time, I was in charge of intelligence, both in ZAPU, the party, and in ZIPRA, the military wing. When our president Joshua Nkomo was released from prison, ZAPU formed the War Council of which I was secretary. A lot was also happening on the ANC front. We shared notes on the political discussions that Mbeki had been involved in but those were very discreet discussions and we kept them to ourselves.

After Robert Mugabe and Joshua Nkomo had both been released from prison we decided to form the Patriotic Front made up of the ZAPU and ZANU (Zimbabwe African National Union) liberation movements. We first started by trying to bring in Bishop Muzorewa but that did not work. Finally, we concentrated on trying to find common ground and a united front for both ZAPU and ZANU. Most of the discussions were held in Mozambique and from time to time we flew to Mozambique to meet with the Zimbabwe African National Liberation Army (ZANLA), the military wing of ZANU, and to have discussions on the Patriotic Front. By the time we went to Lancaster House (1979), we had already formed the Patriotic Front.

While still based in Lusaka, Thabo Mbeki and I discussed issues linked to the liberation struggle and the future of our countries. I would brief him on where the Zimbabwean situation was going. We would try to analyse the two scenarios; apartheid South Africa and Rhodesia. We had boers this side that might contemplate political negotiations after Mozambique and Angola had gained their independence. Later on Ian Smith, the prime minister of Rhodesia, initiated negotiations with John Vorster, the prime minister of South Africa, and we could anticipate the changing political trend, including what might happen in South Africa if substantive negotiations were to take place.

Later Smith came to Nkomo and said, 'I am ready to hand over political power.' This was sometime around 1977/78 before the Lancaster House negotiations. He had a meeting with Nkomo in Nigeria, which was facilitated by Olusegun Obasanjo. But Nkomo said, 'Smith, if you are serious about what you are saying, let us have a meeting with Mugabe.' He emphasised the point that Robert Mugabe, the leader of ZANU, had to be there because he did not want to have a political arrangement with Smith and then have Mugabe say that Nkomo had been a sell-out – that Nkomo had agreed to a political settlement with Smith outside the liberation movement's formal structures represented by the Patriotic Front. Nkomo told Smith that if he was serious about a political settlement, Mugabe must be brought into the picture. Smith did not go ahead with his proposed plan of handing over power because this was a divide and rule strategy and its ultimate goal was to weaken the Patriotic Front.

Thabo Mbeki and I compared all these situations and our analysis was correct that whatever Vorster and the leaders of apartheid South Africa were doing behind the scenes as advisers to Ian Smith, they were possibly pushing for a split between ZANU and ZAPU. That same line of thinking might be used in future to split the ANC if substantive negotiations were to commence in that part of the world. We had to be careful how we advised our leadership on how to tackle these sensitive issues.

When the Lancaster House negotiations about the future of Zimbabwe commenced, we maintained contact with Thabo Mbeki and again we weighed the issues equally. We got to understand exactly how substantive negotiations might proceed on the South African scene as well; we had to take that future into account. Thabo was my ANC point man in London during those Lancaster House negotiations, which he attended in order to take notes for a future dispensation in South Africa.

During the negotiations at Lancaster House, we presented ourselves as the Patriotic Front. I was then leading the ZIPRA delegation and my counterpart was Josiah Tongogara on the ZANLA side. We discussed a ceasefire

arrangement and other issues with the British generals. We agreed towards
the end of that conference, when it was clear that we were now going to go
back home, that we were going to fight the elections as one – the Patriotic
Front, and not as ZANU and ZAPU.

Due to cultural, historical and political ties, we as ZAPU continued assisting the Umkhonto we Sizwe (MK) comrades when I was in Zimbabwe
during the ceasefire period; we actually had MK comrades who came
in together under the ZIPRA name. The white minority government
in South Africa got wind of this. I do not know to this day how it was
leaked, but they got information and it was accurate because they then
went to President Mugabe – who was prime minister then – and told
him that there were 25 ANC cadres in the ZIPRA camp, which was situated towards Beitbridge. The South African Defence Force (SADF) wanted
them removed at once and if they were not removed, the SADF would
bomb the camp. The ultimatum was that if they were not removed by sunset that day, South Africa would attack and if they suspected that there were
even more of them, they would attack more of our camps.

President Mugabe called me. I was in the Joint High Command with
General Wallis who was in the defunct Rhodesian military forces. Mugabe
said that he called me because he did not want to discuss the matter with
my other colleagues in the command because it was only ZIPRA that was
affected. He told me what South Africa was threatening and he said he
wanted those MK guys removed from the camp and sent back to Zambia
immediately. I made arrangements and got my commanders to select – I
think that the proportion was 13 – those whose features were obviously
South African. The other 12 could have passed as either South Africans or
Zimbabweans and we said they could remain. So they remained up to the
end and those MK cadres demobilised together with the ZIPRA cadres.
After that we knew where to deploy them among the villages and they
remained there to carry out the tasks that were given to them by MK.

I am narrating this story to prove that we would not betray the ANC,
considering the deep friendship I had with Thabo Mbeki and others in
the organisation. This might help others to understand why later Mbeki,
as the president of the Republic of South Africa, stoically stood up against
the British and Americans when they wanted to intervene in Zimbabwe's

internal affairs. He understood what happened during the negotiations at Lancaster House because we were constantly in touch. That relationship with MK continued right up to the period of South Africa's new dispensation.

I worked with Thabo Mbeki right through to the time when President Mandela took over political power in 1994. We went with Thabo to Mandela's house because the latter had complained that each time I came to South Africa I never bothered to stop by to say hello to him. At that time I was Zimbabwe's minister of home affairs after I had come out of detention. Thabo Mbeki arranged the meeting and we had a very interesting two-hour discussion.

After Thabo Mbeki became president in 1999, we were embroiled in many political problems in Zimbabwe and it is still the same to date. My view is that Thabo meant well. We had been in constant contact over this matter. At one time I had attended an international conference at which he delivered the opening address. It was one of the Scandinavian conferences that were held on Robben Island and I led the Zimbabwean delegation. When we finished business for the day he asked that I should see him. We spent about three hours in discussion at his house in Cape Town, sharing notes as we used to do in Lusaka.

The funny thing about that meeting was that Mbeki was supposed to be meeting the queen or the king from one of those small countries – it could have been Belgium. We were deep in conversation until it was almost time for him to go and meet his foreign guests and his wife Zanele kept reminding him: Thabo do not forget to go and collect your guests. His response to Zanele was that she could also go and pick them up because, he told her, 'We are busy on important issues which involve Zimbabwe.' But then I said to him, Thabo it is not right, you are the head of state, so please go and attend to your guests, we will always find time to meet and discuss the political scenario in Zimbabwe.

This scenario reminded me of the discussions we used to have while we were both based in Lusaka during the 1970s. I would usually be accompanied by my wife and we would use Zanele's flat as a meeting place. It had a balcony and we would sit on the balcony with a bottle of whisky and carry out our elaborate political discussions. My wife would keep Zanele busy

on the other side and they were not privy to the main content of our discussions. Even our wives were treated on a need-to-know basis and never
ever did I give even a hint of what we were discussing. As far as my wife
was concerned we were discussing general issues related to the alliance and
solidarity between the ANC and ZAPU.

When that incident occurred in Cape Town and Mbeki was now the
president of the Republic of South Africa, we had been analysing the
complex political situation in Zimbabwe. I was still in government and I
informed him about how the old man Robert Mugabe was beginning to
lose touch with the actual political situation in Zimbabwe and that there
was a need for our president to be advised on how to handle the political
challenges. He was really putting the whole legacy of the liberation struggle to shame, judging by the manner in which he was handling issues that
affected the future of the country.

Each time I came to South Africa on official or unofficial business, I
would meet Thabo Mbeki and we would share ideas and discuss the
Zimbabwe situation. After the 2005 elections in Zimbabwe, when Mbeki
came to facilitate the Zimbabwean situation, he tried his best to assist the
simmering situation in Zimbabwe. The political roadmap proposed by
Mbeki, and the idea of drafting a new constitution that would really be
democratic, was a constructive proposal intended to address a dicey political
situation. But unfortunately, I personally think that to some extent Mbeki
was too trusting and did not realise that he was dealing with a cunning old
fox, meaning that President Mugabe would listen with one ear and let some
of Mbeki's constructive suggestions go through the other ear and continue
with his manipulations. To this day I have never discussed this personally
with Thabo. I really hope that as close comrades who have come a long way
together we can talk about this at some stage. The last time I saw Thabo
was at a conference in Algeria in December 2010 and we promised that we
would sit down and review some of these things but unfortunately we did
not have the time.

My personal reflection on him is that, first and foremost, Thabo Mbeki is
a real pan-Africanist: he believes in pan-Africanism. I think that he would
genuinely like to see democracy embedded throughout the continent of
Africa, not just in South Africa or in Zimbabwe or the Southern African

Development Community, but in the whole of Africa. I think that his effort is for real democracy to be achieved in Africa. I think that this is something that he is very genuine about and this is why I said that his intervention in Zimbabwe was genuine, from the heart, and it was for the good of Zimbabwe and, in actual fact, it was an effort to try to promote a democratic Zimbabwe. Unfortunately he did not succeed. But what drives Thabo Mbeki the person is his belief in a democratic Africa and this is something that he is genuinely committed to and something that he has been prepared to fight for throughout his life.

Interviewed October 2014, Johannesburg

III

CABINET AND GOVERNMENT

ESSOP PAHAD

My first recollection of meeting Thabo Mbeki was when he initially came from the Eastern Cape to Johannesburg. Obviously when he came he was under the tutelage of Tata Walter Sisulu and Duma Nokwe, who both resided in Orlando West, Soweto. I met him at Macosa House in Johannesburg on the corner of Bezuidenhout and Commissioner streets, which was where we also had the offices of our football club called Dynamos. My father had an office there and the movement took the top floor and turned it into a club office and used it as a place where a lot of the African National Congress (ANC) young people would come and meet because the ANC had been banned. That was when Thabo came. Tata Sisulu and others sent him and Sindiso Mfenyana to me to discuss the formation of the African Students' Association (ASA), which was formally launched on 16 December 1961.

My first impression of Thabo was of a very young, handsome-looking fellow with a warm personality and already at that time you could tell that he had a very sharp political brain. He is three years younger than I am, so I was involved in the struggle before him. By the time I met him I was already on the executive committee of the Transvaal Indian Youth Congress. From the beginning one was very impressed by him: his personality and his warmth. We went to a number of parties together in the white suburbs in those days. I am not sure that he wants to remember this, but one of the songs that he used to like was 'We will take the country the Castro way'. So that was where we established a friendship and a political relationship. My younger brother Aziz and I were already students at Wits University and Thabo was about to do his A levels.

Thabo Mbeki and I clicked immediately, at least from my side. I was impressed by this young man's depth of political thinking and his sense of fun and enjoyment. I think this is very important to note because people think that, from a young age, he was always a very serious person, which is just not true, not even in his old age. He loved to party and he loved to sing freedom songs. He denies it but, hell, he can sing! When we were in exile, he used to sing bass in our youth choir. Thabo was the recognised leader of the ASA, at least as far as I am concerned. Even when he went abroad he was recognised as the person who was the leader of the ASA, and this was before we formed the ANC Youth and Student Section in England.

My own view is that everybody who came into contact with the young Thabo Mbeki was impressed by him. Therefore this also applied to the ANC leadership: whether it was Tata Walter Sisulu or Duma Nokwe. Of course he did not come without credibility; he came as the son of Govan and Mama Mbeki who were already well known in political circles. But what was good about him was that he never used his father's name. He seldom talked about his father, partly because he did not want to be seen as Govan Mbeki's son. At that time, Govan was the more famous one; Mama Mbeki was not that well known. Oom Gov was already on the Central Committee of the Communist Party and so the relationship with him was of a different kind.

But already then, you could tell that in terms of the leadership of the ANC Youth and Student Section, not only ASA, Thabo was recognised as capable, even at that early age. I attribute this to his depth of knowledge, his commitment and his passion for the liberation struggle. All of these quali-ties meant that he had the potential to emerge as one of the leaders of the movement. Thabo had the advantage of spending time with people like Duma Nokwe because he lived with Duma and his wife Tiny in Orlando West. Duma would already have been a member of the Party underground at that time. I think that it was from Duma that he picked up a lot about a Marxist/Leninist approach, which then led him in the direction of the Communist Party itself and he became one of its leaders.

To come back to his other skills that emerged later on: when he reads documents or articles or books, Thabo Mbeki has a greater capacity to really get to grips with the content and central points more quickly than most people I know. I will give you an example. After he came back from the Lenin Party School in Moscow (which he attended in 1969 with Ahmed Timol and Ann Nicholson) he was in London and we were having a general discussion about the post-independence South African economy. He asked me if I had read Lenin. I responded that of course I had read Lenin. He then asked if I had read Lenin's book entitled *The Impending Catastrophe and How to Combat It*. I had not, but I listed all the works that I *had* read. He asked me to go and read it. He was the first person ever to point me in that direction and it was remarkable because it was one of Lenin's significant works, which most people have ignored although it is in his collected works. It is where Lenin argues about a new economic policy. When I read it, I thought this chap was quite right. Another example: I was asked by the Party to attend a conference on Engels in Berlin in the German Democratic Republic (GDR) sometime in the 1970s. Thabo happened to be in London and I asked him, 'Chief, what do you think, what should one say at the conference?' He said, 'Have you read Engels on *The Second Peasant War in Germany*?' I said no. He suggested that I read it and that I would then know what to talk about regarding Engels.

Fortunately, I had all the books at home. I went and found the book, which is a remarkable piece of work about how you needed another agrarian revolution to change a society and Engels explains the importance of an agrarian revolution in this respect. Of course, I went to the conference in Berlin and I was the only one who presented Engels' perceptive views about the Second Peasant War in Germany. My point is that whilst most of us who were in the South African Communist Party (SACP) at the same time more or less concentrated a great deal on some of the best-known works – whether it was the *Communist Manifesto* or Marx's other well-known works – Thabo Mbeki had the capacity to find things that were not that well known and also not that popular but that had a profound impact if you read them carefully. That is Thabo's strength and it distinguished him from us even though we were of the same generation. It was something that enabled him to grow, develop and mature politically and theoretically much faster than most of us.

I did ask him one day: 'What happened to you, Chief, what drugs are you taking? You must be taking something. We are more or less the same, we

have had more or less the same experiences, the same years of involvement
in the struggle and yet you are ahead of most of us.'

He developed into a very, very good writer of articles and documents
and not for nothing did he become Comrade Oliver Tambo's main speechwriter. I think this partly had to do with the fact that he studied a lot
of speechwriters. Oliver Tambo could tell that he was ahead of his own
generation.

Thabo went into exile in 1962 and then went to the University of Sussex.
Aziz and I left for London in December 1964. My father was already there
and we stayed in a one-bedroomed place. Aziz and I had to share a double
bed and we slept in pullovers and socks because it was so cold and my poor
father had only one small electric heater. Whilst in London, I made contact
with Thabo through Dr Yusuf Dadoo and then we met at the ANC offices. At
that time the ANC's small office was in Earl's Court Square in London and
the ANC chief representative was Mazisi Kunene. We started having discussions about what to do. We talked about what was happening in South Africa
because we had just arrived from home. We talked about the solidarity movement, the international youth and student movement. Suddenly he told me
that I must go to Sweden. The Social Democrats used to organise summer
schools for the youth. I had no passport, just a piece of paper, but he told me
how to get my passport and directed me to the British Home Office where I
was issued with a travel document. This was a way for him to consolidate the
point that international solidarity among the youth and students of the world
was very important for us as ANC youth and students.

An important thing that we often discussed with Thabo was trying to
mobilise South African students who were studying in England; there were
not that many, but the aim was to bring them under a South African students' body. The then leaders of the British National Union of Students
belonged to the right wing of the Labour Party, approved of the National
Union of South African Students and they did not really want to work
with us but preferred to work with white South African students. ASA was
like a no-no to them. That was what we had to discuss and consider how
we should go about mobilising South African students. You must remember that at that time the ANC was not open to non-Africans.

One day Thabo said we should go to visit Comrade O.R. Tambo. At that

time, Mama Adelaide had a flat in Highgate. He told me that we were going
to discuss with Comrade O.R. Tambo the opening of an ANC Youth and
Student Section in England, but basically in London. When we got there,
Thabo raised the matter with Oliver Tambo and you know how he explains
things; he goes round and round and then he comes straight to the point
that he believes the Youth and Student Section in England should be open
to members of other races. Oliver Tambo said, 'But Thabo, Essop, why did
you come here?' I tried to say, 'Well, as Thabo has explained …' but he kept
asking, 'But why did you come to me?' Then Oliver Tambo said, 'Just go
and do it.' That was how we started the non-racial ANC Youth and Student
Section in England.

We discussed how we could strengthen the ANC Youth and Student
Section in London and whether there were people that we could bring in
from outside South Africa. Thabo and I were very instrumental in getting
Mandela scholarships for South African students. The main tasks we then
set for ourselves were first to mobilise the South African students and second, to make a real impact on the British youth and students section.

Thabo already had good connections with the British Young Communist
League whom he knew quite well and had met even before I arrived in
London. We built on his contacts and in the end the Young Communist
League became one of our main support bases. If you want to understand
Thabo, you have to look at what impact all those experiences had, including working with people from the Young Communist League and with
some of the Communist Party leaders, both in Britain. He had his own
connections with people in the British establishment. People were charmed
by this young man who was so clever, spoke very good English and was
polite and gentle.

Because we were in Europe and because Thabo Mbeki was a recognised
leader of the ANC Youth and Student Section, he developed links with the
International Union of Students, an organisation of the Social Democratic
Youth, which was in opposition to the World Federation of Democratic
Youth. As leader of the ANC Youth and Student Section, Thabo had con-
tacts with all of these organisations.

We went to the World Youth Festival in Sofia in 1966. The London
branch of the ANC Youth and Student Section formed a choir because

we wanted to do something to project the image of the ANC at the World Youth Festival. Fortunately we had Theresa Maimane who had a very beautiful soprano voice and Sobizana Mngqikana who was a brilliant musician; he played the saxophone and he was our choirmaster. So we formed the ANC Youth and Student choir, which impressed Comrade Oliver Tambo no end when he first heard us practise in the ANC offices. Thabo sang bass in that choir and he was also part of the gumboot dancing group.

Thabo was without doubt our recognised leader. We travelled to Sofia through the GDR where along the way we picked up some of our people who had come from Lusaka, Morogoro and Dar es Salaam. When we got to Sofia, a big shock awaited us. I do not know if Thabo knew about it, but when we got to our first meeting we found that Johnny Makhathini was the leader of our delegation. The ANC students from the Soviet Union were in revolt; they wanted to know who Johnny Makhathini was and who had appointed him as the leader of the ANC delegation. We had just arrived in Sofia and our meeting was taking place in one room and it was quite tense because Johnny was being openly confronted. We were a big group from London and we were well prepared with documents and our choir was ready to show off its talent. In those heated discussions, we followed Thabo Mbeki's leadership. We had our own meeting while the young people from the Soviet Union met in another room and the people from the African continent also met on their own.

Following Thabo's leadership, we said we were going back into the joint meeting of the ANC Youth and Student Section to support Comrade Johnny Makhathini. In the end the decision was made that Comrade Johnny was the leader of the ANC Youth and Student delegation in Sofia and those from the Soviet Union were told in no uncertain terms that they had to accept his leadership, which they reluctantly did. Again, this was where Thabo Mbeki's leadership was evident because without him it would have been very difficult for Johnny Makhathini to lead that delegation.

If you want to understand how Thabo Mbeki has such a broad understanding of the world, this is informed by the amount of work he was doing in England and in the rest of Europe and meeting with other student and youth leaders. And then of course the mass student uprising took place in Europe in 1968, which meant that we had to engage with a great number of these radical international students who were not necessarily sympathetic to the communist parties of those countries. The Communist Party of France was a very powerful party at that time, but those young French people had a view that was different from the Communist Party. With Mbeki, we engaged in theoretical discussions with them. One of the main things we discussed was that it was not possible for the French students to carry out the revolution on their own, no matter how militant they were. Our own theoretical training said that they would need the strength of the organised working class. They were already hostile to the communist parties and they were even hostile to some of the trade unions in France. Here again, Mbeki excelled. It was very difficult for them to counter him because he could argue radical politics from a very powerful Marxist/Leninist base.

With him and a few others we also had discussions with the Black Power Movement of the United States. Of course we already had good relations with the Communist Party in the USA and those who were active and in the leadership of the World Federation of Democratic Youth and the International Union of Students.

By that time Thabo Mbeki had already been recruited into the SACP. Aziz and I were recruited later. I was not in the same Party unit as Thabo but our involvement enabled us to have more extensive and robust discussions about what was going on inside South Africa, in Europe, on the African continent and how the SACP should approach issues. This helped us to advance our own political thinking. In my view, it made us better revolutionaries with a greater understanding of the requirements of the struggle.

Mbeki had a very good friend involved with the Iraqis in England. The Communist Party in Iraq had some valuable people in London. One day Mbeki said, why don't we form an international grouping of youth and students in England? So we started it with a woman colleague connected to the Iraqis (I have forgotten her name) acting as the coordinator. Thabo and I were there from the ANC Youth and Student Section. We had as members Iraqis, Iranians and Greeks, among others. This move was essentially to mobilise international students who were living and working in England. They were all obviously in the same situation as we were as exiles. So we had some commonalities. For example, after the Greek colonels' coup d'état we organised demonstrations in support of the progressive Greek forces.

One of the biggest youth and student demonstrations ever held in London was the Vietnam War demonstration in the late 1960s and this was when Mbeki lost half of one of his front teeth. He and I represented the ANC Youth and Student Section on the committee organising the Vietnam War demonstration. We went to Grosvenor Square where the US Embassy is and at the end of the demonstration we walked home peacefully. But there was a lot of confrontation with the police, especially with the anarchists who were trying to storm the fences of the US Embassy, which were being guarded by police on horseback. Some of the anarchists were trying to enter the US Embassy from one side and others from the other side, trying to divert and outflank the police.

As our ANC delegation was walking home, Thabo Mbeki was carrying an ANC flag. The next thing he disappeared from sight. We thought he might have met an acquaintance and decided to go off on his own and so we thought that we would meet up with him later. Later, however, we discovered that, although we were walking together, the police had swiftly pulled both the flag and Mbeki out of the crowd. He was holding on for dear life to his beloved ANC flag. One of his shoes was left behind, so he was arrested wearing only one shoe and clutching the ANC flag, and he lost half his tooth during the commotion. He has never had that tooth fixed because it is a commemoration of the Vietnam War demonstration.

We found out only afterwards that when he was sitting in the police van he was asked what he had been doing, so he gave the policeman a long lecture about the Vietnam War and the meaning of the demonstrations and he won the policeman over. The policeman said he wished he could release him but he couldn't because he was under arrest. So they had to take him to court. The reason that I am raising this is so that you understand the way that we worked as a collective; it went well beyond our own personal struggles and our own friendships. It encompassed the world, it encompassed other international struggles and that is why people were, and still are, surprised about the depth of our understanding and knowledge about what happens in other parts of the world today.

Thabo Mbeki became head of the ANC's Department of International Affairs after Johnny Makhathini passed away, which gave him a new insight into geopolitics and a better understanding of the African continent and the world and how to work with other people, even if you disagree with them. Internationally, a lot of the time we had to work with people who we did not necessarily agree with. That was the experience we accumulated from living in England.

For example, even though he knew very little about cricket when the West Indies came to play the Sussex county team in Brighton, Thabo suggested that we organise a party for them. Kenny Parker and I shared a flat and Thabo proposed that we invite the West Indies cricket team so that we could talk to them and politicise them to make sure that they would never play in South Africa. So we organised the party and they came, the whole West Indies cricket team, and it was a very nice party too!

We used the occasion to talk to the West Indies team and we instilled in them a better understanding of the situation in apartheid South Africa, explaining about the sports boycott and why they should support it. All this was Thabo Mbeki's idea, but of course it was not his flat so Kenny and I had to do all the work, organising the party and all the food and as far as I can remember I do not think he contributed anything – except of course the idea of the party, but it does not really matter because it turned out to be a great party.

This was Thabo's foresight. It was Thabo at his best. It never occurred to me or Kenny, both of us politically involved, to think of inviting the West Indies cricket team, not only to a party but to use the occasion for the politicisation of the international cricket team. Thabo has never forgotten it and I think that was when he began to take an interest in cricket as a sport because before then I do not think that he had ever been to a cricket match.

I think that our lives in Europe and later when Thabo Mbeki was in Lusaka constituted a great learning experience and a good opportunity to interact with people from different parts of the world. It was a wonderful chance to connect with left-wing, progressive people. It enhanced our own knowledge of politics and the world and it helped us to expand our understanding. To this day, it has helped us to really understand something like the political crisis in Ukraine; we are able to come to the correct conclusions. It is what helped to mould us. It is what helped Thabo Mbeki to emerge as the kind of leader he ultimately became so that when he became head of the ANC's Department of International Affairs he did not start from scratch; he started with a profound experience base that he had developed in Europe.

In my view, Thabo Mbeki must take credit for creating the ANC Youth and Student Section and using it to broaden the South African struggle and popularise the ANC abroad. With a number of others, he also played a very important role in getting the ANC projected internationally as the dominant liberation movement, and not the Pan Africanist Congress or the Unity Movement.

When we moved into the ANC office in Rathbone Place in London it was filthy and he said that what we needed to do was go down on our hands and knees and scrub ... and we scrubbed for nearly two weeks to make it at least relatively presentable. Of course we could have hired people to do the scrubbing, but we thought that it was part of our own political work and training. It was at that time that Thabo saw Zanele Dlamini. He asked me if I knew her. So he introduced me to my wife Meg, because they were studying together at the University of Sussex, and I introduced him to Zanele who I knew from our days at Wits University.

We were really trying to get the ANC office going. We not only cleaned the office, but we helped to run it, and we helped to do the ANC's work because we were students and we had more time and since we were on scholarships we had a little bit of money. We had to travel sometimes at our own expense using our scholarship money. The ANC had a little bit of money so it would give us a few pounds and we were able to go to conferences and meetings.

Those of us who had the privilege and honour of meeting and working under Comrade Oliver Tambo regarded him as one of the greatest South Africans who ever lived. I think that what Thabo Mbeki learned from Oliver Tambo was how he conducted meetings of the National Executive Committee (NEC), which were very difficult at that time. They both had this ability to sit and listen in a meeting. I remember in NEC meetings – especially when Terror Lekota was the chairperson – there would be a lot of hard discussion. Even as the president, Thabo did not speak in the NEC meetings except when he gave a political overview. Then at the end of the meeting, the chairperson had to sum up and when Terror summed up, hands flew up; we could not agree with him. Then Thabo would intervene and say, no, what Comrade Chair is saying ... he would never say that Terror was wrong but he would sum up and as soon as he had finished everybody in the NEC – without fail – agreed with his summary of the discussions. I think that this is what he learned from Oliver Tambo. It is a very difficult skill, bringing together a number of conflicting views in a way in which everybody is satisfied that it is an accurate reflection. At the same time it also brings us together as a liberation movement, so that the decisions of the NEC become acceptable to everybody. That is why those who say today that Thabo Mbeki was a dictator are talking nonsense; it is just not true.

Of course, Comrade Oliver Tambo was a stickler and even more difficult than Thabo to write speeches for. We could go to conferences and sit up all night writing, and he would say, but why is the comma there and why the full stop there – and what about that word? A lot of the time Oliver Tambo would say the speech was okay and then write his own. I think that this was where Thabo began to be more careful with words; what you say and what you write must be something that you are able to defend, and so you would write with caution and not with anger. In the end, Thabo was the only one who could write speeches for Oliver Tambo that O.R. did not change. Most of Oliver Tambo's speeches were written by Thabo, which was quite a remarkable achievement. Oliver Tambo had full confidence that what Thabo Mbeki wrote was what Oliver Tambo thought. The same thing applied to Mandela; he also had such confidence in Thabo who wrote some of his main speeches before he became president.

We went to the US with Mandela in about 1990 – Thabo came to London and asked me to join them. Mandela had to make a major speech to the US Congress. Thabo told Ngoako Ramatlhodi and me to leave him alone and he sat in his hotel room writing the speech. We went to Congress and as were sitting there, Madiba asked where Thabo was and I replied that he was coming. One thing about the Americans is that they have great respect for speechwriters. It is an American political tradition. Anyway, I stepped out and approached one of secret service men and told him that Madiba's speechwriter was staying in the hotel across the road and because they had blocked off all the roads, he was not going to be able to bring the speech in time because they did not know who he was.

So we waited and Madiba was getting worried that Thabo had not arrived, but as we prepared to go into Congress, Thabo arrived with the speech. I must say Mandela read it beautifully. What I am saying is that Madiba had not seen the speech before he read it, but he and Thabo had discussed the line that should be taken. Mandela did not fully comprehend the history of the US but Thabo did and that was how he was able to go back into US history as part of the speech. It was a beautiful, beautiful speech. Mandela got several standing ovations. As is well known, Thabo Mbeki has a very good command of the English language and the capacity to use the English language in a way that is not over-elaborate but is very rich in ideas.

Let me give you an example. We had this huge anti-apartheid conference in Arusha, Tanzania, essentially paid for by the Soviet Union, where we brought together anti-apartheid forces from around the world. Salim Ahmed Salim was chairing the meeting with Comrade Oliver Tambo who gave Thabo an instruction that the documents needed to be written up by the next morning. Now that was a hell of a job. So Thabo roped in me and English lawyer Mike Siefert, who had come to say hello to us and we made him sit down and work. We worked the whole night. Salim Salim kept asking Oliver Tambo where the documents were. I think that the conference was going to finish around one o'clock. By 12 noon we had finished. Salim Salim was astonished because he did not believe that we would be able to produce the documents. That was the kind of confidence that Oliver Tambo had in Thabo: he knew he would deliver.

One of Thabo's greatest strengths is his unbelievable ability to put himself in another person's shoes. He is a very good listener and by putting himself in the other person's shoes he was able to understand, even if he did not agree, why the person had a particular viewpoint. He would respond on the basis of an understanding of what they were saying. But he was also able to bring them round to a position that was different from where they had started the conversation. This is a very challenging skill: to lend a sympathetic ear even if you do not agree with the other side. I think that this helped him a great deal in all his interactions when he became president of South Africa: whether it was with President Chirac of France, Prime Minister Blair of the UK or President Bush of the US, he could really use this skill. They would come with preconceived positions on Zimbabwe and a whole range of issues, but Thabo was able to bring them round without using anger in his arguments. I have never heard him say to a person, I do not agree with you.

Thabo was one of the first people to consider a shift to a negotiated settlement in South Africa rather than insurrection, and I think that he then convinced Oliver Tambo, but they had to be very careful about how they raised it with the NEC. The negotiations had to be secret because the apartheid regime did not want it to be known that they were talking to us and nor did we want people to know that we were having negotiations with representatives of the regime.

Thabo chaired the meeting that drafted the document 'The Path to Power' at the Communist Party congress in Cuba during the late 1980s. He did it in such a masterful manner that everyone at that congress could not but admire Thabo for the way he dealt with the meeting and the drafting and the way that he intervened because there were a lot of arguments about the inclusion or exclusion of words. In the end, the document was a bit lopsided because it still projected an insurrectionary approach but we did manage to include the element on negotiations.

People underestimate the great difficulties we had when we took over in 1994. Remember, there was a lot of violence in the country at the time. Mangosuthu Buthelezi had been brought in as minister of home affairs, Ben Ngubane had been brought in as minister of arts and culture as well as one or two others from the Inkatha Freedom Party. They came from very different and even contradictory and conflicting political cultures; even the manner of working was totally different.

One day Deputy President Mbeki phoned me and told me that he was sending his car to collect me and we were going to Pretoria to the Union Buildings. He did not have an office there yet and was working from their flat in Johannesburg.

We arrived at the Union Buildings, which we had only seen from the outside. They had allocated Mbeki one white guy and one white woman for his office. De Klerk had his staff of 60 people, which he came with as the former president of South Africa. The two white compatriots were very welcoming. They said, 'Mr Deputy President, we will show you the offices and then you can choose.' And the first nice office I saw I took. It was a lovely office on the first floor with wooden panels. I said, okay, Deputy

President Mbeki will take this office – and that was how he got his first office. There was no paper, no pens, not even paper clips; there was nothing and we had to start from scratch. We had no experience of running a state so we relied on the white lady and the white gentleman who had been allocated to us by foreign affairs and I must say that they were very good to us. Without them we would not have known what to do.

Jakes Gerwel wanted the deputy president's office to be separate from President Mandela's office and that's what more or less happened. We started recruiting for Mbeki's office, but we felt that not everybody should be ANC members. That was how we found our legal adviser, Advocate Mojanku Gumbi – an African woman, a lawyer, whom I had met through the Independent Electoral Commission for which she was working. Then we needed an economic adviser. I knew Moss Ngoasheng from when he came to do a course at the University of Sussex and I took him and Ketso Gordhan for political study classes. Then we brought in the Reverend Frank Chikane as an adviser on policy issues. So we now had three advisers, Mojanku, Moss and Frank. Tebogo Mafole was recruited to head his office assisted by the very able Nomsa Ngakane.

When I was his parliamentary councillor I sat in on almost all of Deputy President Mbeki's meetings, including those with heads of state. This was also a tremendous eye-opener for me because I saw things in Mbeki that I was never aware existed, although I had known him for so long. For me, this was a beautiful, steep learning curve, just sitting and listening to him on domestic issues as well as issues about the African continent and the world. And it was obvious how others appreciated his brilliant mind and his thinking.

But he himself was learning to govern. It is true – and Madiba himself admitted it – that Thabo Mbeki had taken on a large part of Madiba's responsibilities in terms of cabinet governance. We inherited an economy that was bankrupt, and you can imagine what it meant to develop prudent financial and economic policies. Unlike more established democracies, post-1994 we had to devise new policies. We couldn't take the old apartheid policies and just tinker with them as you might do in the UK or the US.

On the issue of Zimbabwe, I think that what needs to be understood was the opposition that we were facing, the hostility of the major Western powers. They had decided that they wanted regime change in Zimbabwe, especially the British. One of Thabo's strengths – or what others might regard as a weakness – is that once he is convinced that a position is correct, it does not matter who brings the pressure or how powerful they or it may be, he will not be browbeaten or blackmailed into taking standpoints just because relationships with certain powerful people need to be maintained. I think he understood that the powerful people that he was talking to and hugging and smiling with were trying to undermine him and also using their intelligence agencies to undermine him to safeguard their own. When these people take a position, the temptation is just to go along with it simply because it was said by the rich and powerful countries, even if it does not serve our interests in South Africa.

But they could not move President Thabo Mbeki, and he was not alone. The positions he took on Zimbabwe were consistent with the positions that many of us had taken. Of course he just articulated it better and of course he was the president of the country, but this was a position that we took as the ANC, as government and as a cabinet. If he had taken those positions by himself, he would have been long gone. We all understood why a regime change in Zimbabwe would have devastating consequences for us in South Africa; they could do the same thing to us if they did not like our policies; they could initiate a regime change.

One thing is clear and that is that the superpowers understood that they could not impose their views on Mbeki and his government and the ANC. But in discussions with him they also understood that his positions were correct, which is why President George Bush of the US called Thabo 'our point man on Zimbabwe'. But there were other pressures on them from their own people who wanted a different approach to Zimbabwe, who were hell-bent that President Mugabe should go. But Mbeki stood firm against the most powerful forces in the world. He stood firm when he reported to the NEC as president, taking them through the whole history of Zimbabwe, and there was not a single dissenting voice in that meeting. He did the same thing with big business, explaining everything from the time of Ian Smith to the land question and its importance. The big business delegation agreed with him and we issued a joint statement afterwards with Saki Macozoma who was part of the business delegation. This demonstrated once again Mbeki's powers of persuasion and the logic of his arguments and the correctness of his position.

But the other forces were very powerful and so he got into a situation in which he was not trusted because he was a clever black man and he was not so nice to the powerful and mighty. He had some very robust things to say about the economy and the role of big capital and people who read carefully what he wrote every Friday (his *ANC Today* column) could see that he was still influenced by a Marxist methodology and they did not like that. The French did not like him pissing in their own backyard, whether it was Côte d'Ivoire or other places that they regarded as their territory. The US administration would hug, laugh and smile but it was unhappy that we were taking positions on major issues that were not consistent with their self-serving stances. I did lots of imbizos with President Mbeki and his support amongst the masses of our people was incredible. So the hostility around the Zimbabwe issue came from certain sections of big capital here and from the major Western powers, not from the majority of South Africans.

Could we have done better to communicate our position? Possibly yes, but then I must take a lot of the blame because I was head of government communications.

On the HIV/AIDS issue, first of all I must say that I do not think he was wrong. In my view, what happened was that, as usual, when Mbeki is confronted with a problem, he wants to understand it in all its complexities. He is never satisfied with scanty information. He will get down to some serious reading and research and try to understand what he is confronting. He started reading to familiarise himself with the disease. You must remember that when Madiba was the president, Thabo, as deputy president headed the HIV and AIDS campaign. All the government's HIV and AIDS campaigns after 1994 were done when Mbeki was in charge, including the responsibility of setting up the South African National Aids Council. So the idea of forming a broad-based strategy to deal with HIV and AIDS started with Thabo.

My understanding – and I might be wrong – was that when he began to delve deeper into the issue, he began to see that something was wrong with the science, not necessarily that HIV does not cause AIDS – it does – but that there was this great push for antiretrovirals to be rolled out, and yet people were not taking into account the broader social issues like nutrition, safe sex, single partners and other important factors.

But then we were dealing with the huge multinational drug companies, how were we going to compete with them? We were faced with this huge lobby of the major pharmaceutical companies in the world, including South Africa. If they did not sell antiretrovirals, they would lose billions of dollars; they were not interested in the other issues we were raising about poverty and nutrition and so on.

If people go back to the questions that Mbeki posed to the experts on the Presidential International Advisory Panel, they will find that he was very correct in the issues that he raised. He never intervened in those debates. That panel was designed to be totally independent from the government and that was why Manto Tshabalala-Msimang who was then the minister of health was not on it either. Part of the problem was that those who were referred to as 'dissidents' were then abusing Mbeki's name. Of course, anything they said, the media would turn into headline news.

After enormous pressure, Mbeki backed off. Remember that he made that statement to the effect that he was no longer going to speak on the matter. We did say to him as cabinet that he was president and that the time had come for his ministers to take the rap and do the talking, although we knew that none of us were as articulate as he was. My own view to him was that he needed to be careful. I said to him that he was just the president of this little country at the bottom of the African continent, the powers that be had killed many people before, like Patrice Lumumba, and they would have no problem with killing him too if he was seen as a major stumbling block. His response was, 'And then what, you want me to keep quiet and watch my people being ripped off by the major pharmaceutical companies?'

But the pressures were quite strong, even from Madiba. Looking at it with hindsight, if Mbeki had taken a less public offensive on the issue and allowed his ministers to handle it, he would not have been associated with everything. Sometimes the way that he expressed himself was not always the best way. For example, it was a correct argument to say that if HIV is a syndrome by the very definition of the word it means that there are a number of causes. But he said that and people labelled him a denialist! You can go back to all the Government Communication and Information System documents, and I mean ALL the documents, and there is not a single line anywhere where he ever said HIV did not cause AIDS. Mbeki had said that antiretrovirals on their own were not the only solution but he did not say no to antiretrovirals.

Thabo Mbeki's argument, which still holds water, was that malaria and diabetes were bigger killers in the African continent, but the world is only coming with this argument now; he said it back then. The debate was how to move effectively and efficiently utilise a limited health budget because the budget also had to cater for other things and education was taking the bulk of the money.

The budget rose exponentially because the minister of health was convinced that we needed to put in more money. By the time Mbeki was re-elected in 2004, our budget for HIV – and that can be checked with the budget plans – was already between R3 to R4 billion. We were the only country in the continent that was spending its own money on HIV and AIDS; all the others were receiving money from the US. The misunderstanding on this matter was not accidental if you recognise who we were up against but perhaps we could have argued it better and perhaps he should have played a less frontal role.

In terms of Mbeki's weaknesses, sometimes I think that he tends to be too trusting. When he trusts somebody and he likes somebody, then he will work with that person even if that person's work begins to deteriorate. It is a weakness because he cannot bring himself to say that someone is not pulling their weight. There were very few cabinet reshuffles when he was president. He relied on the people he appointed to do the jobs that they were doing, and perhaps he did not pay sufficient attention to following through whether or not they were doing their jobs effectively. It was very difficult to reshuffle the cabinet as often as problems were detected. As president he had such immense responsibilities, but sometimes he ended up doing the job of the ineffective cabinet minister. We started monitoring and evaluation but it had not really got going. I do think that some of his appointments were not necessarily the best ones he could have made in terms of some of the premiers, ministers and deputy ministers. But that was his prerogative and he did consult with ANC officials beforehand. I will not mention names but at times I felt that he was not appointing the right people to do the job for the people of South Africa.

I think that he could have spent more time, not just doing the imbizos, with the ANC provincial leadership structures, and he could have spent more time interacting with the Congress of South African Trade Unions (COSATU) although by that time a lot of the COSATU leadership were already moving away. I think that he should have tried harder to keep the alliance together but the hostility from the Communist Party leadership and COSATU made it difficult. We did have our alliance meetings but they did not always come out in the open about their issues.

It is impossible when you become president to find the time to attend social events and he did not do what Madiba did with famous Hollywood or Bollywood stars – meet them and have a photo opportunity. He was of the view that he was not a showman but that meant that in the eyes of the public he did not emerge as a friendly and warm person. He gave the impression that he was aloof, which he was not, because of the way he responded to the masses and they to him. But I do believe that the responsibility and the burden of governance weighed on him in a way in which he could not always behave and act in the kind of social way that we knew from our time in London. He never had the time for that.

Thabo Mbeki took governance very seriously. He read all the documents, he knew what was happening in terms of policy positions. That left very little time for doing those social things that endear you to the masses. He went to football matches but he could have gone to more sporting events. There were many things that we as ministers and deputy ministers could have done better, which could have cast him in a much more favourable light. We all made mistakes by not supporting him when it mattered; we are human after all. Mbeki is also a human being: he has likes and dislikes. He made mistakes like everyone else.

Big capital was opposed to Thabo Mbeki from the beginning because they knew that in him they had a serious opponent; an economist who understood the economy but who was determined that we needed to change the patterns of ownership of our economy, that we needed to empower the majority of our people, we needed to implement Black Economic Empowerment policies and positions and we needed to take positions on international issues. Big capital did not like this and nor did the major Western powers. So obviously, in the course of what he was doing, Mbeki had a lot of opponents and ruffled many feathers.

Speaking as head of government communications, I can tell you that he was not the easiest person to get to communicate because he had his own very rich ideas about how to communicate. You could not get him to do things premised on soundbites. It was one of my biggest gripes. It meant that in terms of communication, you missed the boat because he hated soundbites. He wanted to know that when he spoke you must get an in-depth understanding of the issue rather than just the superficial one-liner that does not say anything and runs into the danger of being misquoted by the media. We had set up a system where we were going to have what were called the off the record briefings and unfortunately it was the media that messed it up. We catered for journalists to be part of the imbizos and we even tried to start the presidential (press) corps with his agreement. It was unfortunate that the media really could not get it together.

There was the media thing about Mbeki having to fill Madiba's shoes. He did not have to fill Madiba's shoes; he did not have to fill anyone's shoes because he was his own person. You cannot be a president and act and behave as if you are filling someone else's shoes. You will never succeed. You have got to come in and show that you have the capacity to govern. You have got to earn the respect of your ministers and deputy ministers, officials and the country. You have to do things differently and I do not think that President Mbeki ever thought of filling anyone's shoes. The policies were ANC policies, and they had to be implemented and could only be changed at ANC conferences or at NEC meetings. So it was not like he was taking up the position with a clean slate. That is how his response about filling Madiba's shoes can be contextualised.

You will recall that the ANC had asked Comrade Kgalema Motlanthe to join the government so that he should get some experience in government. Prior to that his experience had been in the unions and in the ANC as secretary general and so I do think that this was a very good learning curve for him. It was a good decision, even if it was taken for the wrong reasons. But it was the beginning of the indications that some of the NEC members wanted to remove Thabo Mbeki from office. And some of those on the NEC let the media know that this was one of their intentions. Many of us felt that this was a likely scenario and I think that he obviously was also aware of it. I think that some warning signs were there but nothing was said. So whether or not they had removed Thabo Mbeki, the chances were that Kgalema was going to become deputy president after the next elections.

I went to see President Mbeki that same morning after the NEC decision to recall him and there were already other people at the house who had come to commiserate – but he was not commiserating. I told him that he must expect my letter of resignation the next morning. I also told him that the ANC would also receive a letter from me resigning as a member of parliament. He said, but who asked you to resign? I have not asked you and the ANC has not asked you to resign. So I told him that I had not come to ask for his advice. I had come to inform him that I had taken this decision. I said, look, Chief, the way that we have grown up all our lives is that we are what we are because of the ANC and the Communist Party. If I cannot serve the ANC as honestly and as diligently as I should then I do not see how I can take up a position in a government run by the same ANC. Secondly, I said, I have a very strong view that the decision to recall you is unjust and undemocratic, the timing is wrong and the reasons given asking you to step down are also very wrong. And so because I cannot serve the ANC leadership, the NEC, then I feel that I have to resign as a matter of principle because, as I insist, the ANC and the Communist Party, to some extent, moulded us and we only got into positions in government because of the positions that we occupied in the ANC.

So then he said that he understood. Of course there were others who came and who also indicated that they were going to resign, but it was an individual decision that each one of us had taken. He was very calm that day.

I think that after Polokwane anything could have happened. There was an NEC meeting to which he was invited and they also invited those of us who were ministers. I think that at that NEC meeting, a number of us felt that there was a growing hostility towards him. There was a feeling that there were some in the NEC who were determined to find

some way to act against President Thabo Mbeki. Some in the leadership
of COSATU and certainly in the leadership of the SACP had, for some
reason, become very hostile because they thought that he was negative
towards both COSATU and the SACP. Prior to that, when he addressed
the SACP congress, he did admonish them about some of the positions
that they had taken, but it was something that Madiba had done before
him. But I think that there was this growing hostility, certainly within
some powerful elements in COSATU and very powerful elements in the
SACP, who then used the opportunity to work together with those who
felt that now was the time to strike.

I must say that again Thabo Mbeki demonstrated calmness under pressure. I know that I felt quite a bit pain for him but he did not show it. Then
he said that he would call a cabinet meeting at which he said goodbye.
There were some cabinet ministers who were practically in tears. People
spoke and said what they thought about him. But here again, he demonstrated his depth of political understanding and his great respect for the
decisions of the ANC, that even though you do not agree with it, once a
collective decision is made, you support it.

The manner in which he resigned and stepped down showed his commitment to the ANC because if he had not agreed to the wrong decision,
if he had decided to contest the decision, it could have caused a great deal
of political tension and conflict because the ANC would then have had to
make a decision to follow the procedure of impeaching him in parliament.
To impeach him meant that you would have had to call a special session of
the National Assembly and if it was going to be by secret ballot, you could
not be sure that the majority of the ANC members, or enough of them,
would agree to carry the vote and support those who wanted to impeach
him. Obviously, the opposition parties, just in order to defeat the ANC,
would have not voted for it. It would have created great tension in all of the
ANC structures throughout the country.

Notwithstanding what happened in Polokwane, Thabo Mbeki still commanded a great deal of respect and support within the ANC leadership and
obviously in the country among the majority of our people. Upholding his
own principles of always respecting the decisions arrived at by the leadership of the ANC, he complied with a decision however badly it might affect

him. Again at that moment in time, he demonstrated his capacity to take rational decisions even though they impacted negatively on his own life. He did not know what he was going to do after that; in fact none of us knew what we were going to do after we had resigned.

In the end we needed to respect the way President Mbeki handled the matter and the way that he went onto national television and the calm manner in which he announced that he was stepping down. I think that the long-term impact has been negative for the ANC. One hopes that, as time goes on, the ANC leadership will work in such a way that there is no repeat of what happened. There really was no reason to ask Thabo Mbeki to step down. The elections were coming in seven months.

It was very painful and tragic – in my view not only for us and Thabo Mbeki. It was painful because the top leadership of this organisation that we had given our lives to and that we will still continue to love and respect, could behave in the manner that they did. The organisation had taken a step that had never before been made in its history and it was really tragic that the NEC could arrive at that decision not fully comprehending its enormity. It put the ANC in a very difficult position and it also led to the formation of the Congress of the People.

I think that when historians look at this event later with an objective approach – and if they can find the people who can really talk about what actually happened in that fateful NEC meeting – then I think that we will find that the decision was arrived at mainly because there were some people who felt determined to see the humiliation of Thabo Mbeki. For me, the humiliation was not Thabo Mbeki's, the humiliation was the ANC's and that is what makes it so much sadder. As I said, the ANC will always remain our organisation and we will always remain faithful to it. But its act in recalling Thabo Mbeki was one that I think led it into some disrepute. The long-term impact has been that it has introduced wrong ways of working inside the organisation. Some of the bad elements were there already and what has happened is that the bad elements in the ANC have been strengthened in a way that is not in the interests of the organisation. This remains true to this day.

Interviewed April 2014, Johannesburg

MANGOSUTHU BUTHELEZI

⚎

Whenever I talk to Mr Thabo Mbeki, I always refer to him as 'Zizi' because that is one of his clan names. He once told me that, according to his father, the Mbeki clan originated from Okhahlamba in KwaZulu-Natal. I remember one day when the Inkosi of the Zizis was present, I jokingly referred to Mbeki as Inkosi Zizi's 'subject'. We all had a good laugh about that.

To appreciate my relationship with Mr Mbeki, one must understand my roots in the African National Congress (ANC).

My early education was in Nongoma where I stayed at the palace of my uncle, King Solomon kaDinuzulu, the grandfather of the present king. Later, I went to Adams College for my secondary school education. I believe Mr Mbeki's parents taught at Adams College.

I grew up in the ANC because its founder, Dr Pixley ka Isaka Seme, was my uncle. He was married to King Dinuzulu's eldest daughter, Princess Phikisile Harriet, who was my aunt. I often visited my aunt and cousins at home, and on occasion Seme would send for me to assist him with his correspondence. At that time, he had had an operation that left him with only one eye. So he would dictate his letters to me. I would write them and he would sign them. During this time, he often spoke to me about Mr Govan Mbeki.

I joined the ANC Youth League at Fort Hare University and immediately became politically active. In 1950 we demonstrated during the visit of Governor General Gideon Brand van Zyl, who was then the head of state

114

in South Africa. I was expelled for my participation, though I prefer to say that I was rusticated from Fort Hare.

After that I became close to Inkosi Luthuli, before he became the ANC president. Through him I first made contact with Mr Oliver Tambo, in 1963, after he was sent overseas to set up the external mission of the ANC.

It was on Mr Tambo's and Inkosi Luthuli's instruction that I took up the leadership of the KwaZulu homeland, so that we could undermine the apartheid system from within. I did this as a loyal ANC cadre.

In October 1979, Mr Tambo sent a message requesting that I go to London with a delegation so that we could talk about sanctions and the armed struggle. Thus we met at the Excelsior Hotel for two-and-a-half days. Amongst other things, we were shown films of Umkhonto we Sizwe cadres in training.

That was when I first met Mr Thabo Mbeki in person. He was present at that meeting in London as part of Mr Tambo's delegation. I was very impressed with him, especially with his intellect. I could see that he was deeply involved in the ANC's international affairs, working with Johnny Makhathini.

Our discussions ended with Mr Tambo promising that they would come back to me in December that year: there was going to be a meeting of the National Executive Committee of the ANC and they would contact me thereafter. Sadly, that never happened.

Instead, on 26 June 1980 the secretary general of the ANC, Mr Alfred Nzo, launched a blistering public attack on me. It was the first of many international attacks questioning my participation in the KwaZulu government, despite my participation being an instruction of the ANC's leadership.

On 29 January 1991, during the height of the violence between the ANC and Inkatha, our two parties held a joint meeting. Madiba and I were both there. The scribe for the ANC was none other than our future president, Mr Thabo Mbeki. The scribe on our side was Walter Felgate. They did all the writing and prepared a joint communiqué. One decision contained in that communiqué was that, from then onwards, we would organise joint rallies. Unfortunately the ANC reneged on that agreement almost immediately.

Nevertheless, that meeting was very constructive and, from around that time, I really got to know Mr Mbeki. He was one of those leaders of the

ANC who I felt was genuinely friendly towards me. From the moment
we met, I could say that on a personal basis we got on like a house on fire.
There was a certain synergy between us.

When the substantive negotiations concluded, our interim constitution
created the Government of National Unity (GNU), and Madiba appointed
me as minister of home affairs. Mr Mbeki was deputy president with Mr
de Klerk. But Mr de Klerk then left the GNU. Although he told me about
his quitting and tried to influence me, I was not prepared to quit because
too many innocent people had died and I thought that reconciliation was
important.

What many people do not realise is that Mr Mbeki managed South
Africa from 1994. Madiba attended hardly any of the meetings of cabinet.
Mr Mbeki actually chaired those meetings. Madiba himself used to say, 'I
am the *de jure* president of South Africa, but the *de facto* president is Thabo
Mbeki.' It was not a joke. It was the truth. Madiba, of course, did much for
the important issues of reconciliation, social cohesion and so on, includ-
ing visiting Orania. But whether people like it or not, the truth is that Mr
Mbeki ran the country.

I do not think that Mr Mbeki was intolerant of dissent during cabinet
meetings. But we have to admit that he has a very powerful brain and I
think that people tended to be overawed – they were scared of disagreeing
with him. But it was not because he did not allow for debate; there was
debate. I think people just tended to be intimidated by his intellect.

At times in cabinet, we disagreed without being disagreeable. Even on
the issue for which everyone crucified him (his denial of the connection
between HIV and AIDS), I remember that we used to argue intensely, but
without acrimony. He has always been a very decent person, and intellectually he is someone that I will respect for the rest of my life.

Whenever I sat next to President Mbeki in cabinet meetings we would
talk about this issue of HIV and AIDS. I would tell him about the many
funerals I attended when I went home to Mahlabathini, and how these
were funerals of people who had died of AIDS. He asked how I knew that,
and we would argue about it because he did not believe that it was AIDS.
He argued as though I did not know what I was talking about, and he spoke
about HIV being a syndrome and so on in a very scientific manner, while I

was talking about practicalities and realities.

But I was shocked when he returned from a trip abroad where he had said that he had not met anyone who had suffered from AIDS. My own son had died of AIDS, and then my daughter. Each time I announced the causes of their deaths it was to try to remove the stigma, because people did not want to talk about AIDS. Soon after that Madiba's son iNkosi MaKgatho died of AIDS and Madiba also spoke up, in an effort to remove the stigma of this illness.

I must say, though, while I was having these scientific arguments with my friend Mr Mbeki, his wife showed enormous compassion. For as long as we live, my wife Princess Irene and I will never forget the kindness of Mrs Zanele Mbeki. Each time we lost one of our children, she would come to Mahlabathini to grieve with us at their funeral.

With the 1999 elections, the GNU expired. Just before the election, Mr Mbeki invited me to Oliver Tambo House and said that although the interim constitution had expired and there was no longer a requirement for us to work together, he thought that for the sake of the reconciliation of the country we should continue to work together. He went further and said that he wanted me to be his deputy president.

After the election, he invited me again to Oliver Tambo House to offer me the position. But then he pointed at seats and said, 'You know, I offer you this position, but you know all these seats here have been for members of the ANC in KwaZulu-Natal.' Then he said, 'They [the ANC members] came here to say that if I appoint you as my deputy, then you must give the premiership of KwaZulu-Natal to the ANC.' It did not come from him.

Of course, I would not agree to that. I declined, saying that I could not be deputy president under those conditions because the voters in the province were democratically entitled to the leadership they voted for.

Once we reached that impasse, he still thought that we should continue to work together. He insisted that he wanted me in his cabinet. So I thought about it and I said, 'Well, Zizi, it is up to you what position you offer me.' He replied, 'I want you back in the same position as minister of home affairs.' So I was minister of home affairs for five more years by the grace of Mr Mbeki. I will always respect him as a person who genuinely wanted reconciliation.

I think it was unfortunate that his speech about two nations in South Africa was misunderstood, because it was actually perceived that he was playing the race card. He talked about the South African nation and then he went on to talk about the two nations within the country. For a head of state, I think that it was not reconciliatory at all to talk like that. It was as if he was talking from both sides of his mouth on this particular issue. I did not agree with that position at all.

During the last days of my time as a minister, I had a very difficult time in cabinet. In truth, it was not only during Mbeki's time. There were several laws passed in this country with which I did not agree. So very often I would, for the record, issue a memorandum and go to cabinet with the memorandum to distance myself from what cabinet had decided.

Even on the important issue of the Truth and Reconciliation Commission (TRC), for example. Madiba came to cabinet and sat next to Mr Mbeki and me, and announced that he was proposing the name of my archbishop, His Grace Archbishop Tutu, as chairperson of the TRC. I objected, explaining that I did not regard the archbishop as impartial. He had made no secret of his alliance with the ANC.

But I had many problems operating as President Mbeki's minister. For instance, there were arguments over the Immigration Bill. Throughout my time in cabinet, that is the only bill that I remember being debated for three hours. President Mbeki then sent it to his ministers to tear apart. In spite of the fact that we got on so well, like a house on fire as I have said, it seemed to me that he did not trust me.

Of course I know that as far as they were concerned, the problem was my ministerial adviser, Dr Mario Oriani-Ambrosini, because some of them wanted me to get rid of him. They did not trust him and I was chided for allowing him to be resident in South Africa. I consider it a sign of weakness on the part of the president for having done that to me. As a cabinet, we took joint responsibility for our decisions and actions, but the manner in which my bill was treated simply because they did not trust my adviser was truly shocking and it put me under pressure.

Even the way I exited cabinet was shocking. I was in my house in the Bryntirion Estate when a letter was delivered at midnight. It was from Mr Mbeki, who was due to be installed the next day for his second term. His letter informed me that, after his installation, he no longer required my services. I just thought that the way he did it was unnecessary.

But I still remained in contact with him. Even on his 70th birthday, which was long after he left office, I went to his house to pay tribute to him. Because of our relations with Mrs Mbeki, I bear no resentment or enmity towards him. But it was really regrettable that I was fired in that manner.

I openly condemned his recall from office because I was quite shocked. Whatever the differences within the ANC, he was my president; he was our head of state.

Before all of this, I had tried to introduce a Private Member's Bill to separate the two positions of head of state and head of the executive. I believe that the president should represent us all, even though he belongs to a specific political party. But of course the ANC torpedoed my idea.

I can never forget the time when I was in Durban when the Indian prime minister, Mr Singh, was visiting on an official occasion. ANC members were singing derogatory songs and flinging all sorts of expletives at Mr Mbeki. Even in parliament I tried to caution them, saying that he was still our head of state and that if they did this to him, it could happen to any other president of the country, even to Mr Zuma whom they were supporting.

In fact it did happen, as I predicted. Consider what Mr Malema has done to Mr Zuma, whereas at the time the ANC approved of this behaviour. And Mr Malema himself has said that he was prompted by Zuma and others to do this to President Mbeki.

President Mbeki's recall was unnecessary and I do not think that he deserved it. It was just a few months before the end of his term. It was done just to humiliate him. I lost some respect for those leaders of the ANC who orchestrated that. It cannot be defended; it was wrong whichever way you want to look at it.

Interviewed July 2014, Cape Town

AZIZ PAHAD

※

I met Thabo Mbeki in the early 1960s when we were going through an exciting time as well as a very difficult time in apartheid South Africa. Mbeki had been sent from the Eastern Cape to the then Transvaal, to use it as a base to mobilise the African Students' Association (ASA) but he was also very active in broader Congress work and, of course, he was a link to all the senior leaders including Nelson Mandela, Walter Sisulu, Oliver Tambo, and he was living with the (Duma) Nokwes in the Soweto township of Orlando West. He spent a lot of time in Johannesburg. From that time you could see that Mbeki was going to be driving the campaign for the mobilisation of the youth and students. His task and focus was on the African students and I was not directly involved, but we used to meet as youth and students in the broader Congress activities where we would discuss what they were doing, but it was separate from what we were working on. Other comrades from the Transvaal Indian Youth Committee and the Congress of Democrats (COD) also worked with him at that time. Thabo visited many major cities to help establish the ASA.

Thabo Mbeki was actively involved in the Macosa House Social Club, which was established when the liberation movement was banned. It was directly opposite where we lived in Ferreirastown, Johannesburg. It was a front for the ANC under the pretext of being a social club where ballroom dancing was taught, but it was also a place where we would meet the leadership and have discussions.

In those days you could only go to the houses of white comrades in the

COD for non-racial parties; they had homes in the historically white areas that could accommodate such parties. So we went a lot to those social gatherings. Needless to say many political discussions took place. These were the few occasions when you could meet seniors and youth from other racial groups. They were always monitored by the security police because of their multiracial character and also because alcohol was served.

One day Mbeki disappeared and I did not know where he had gone. I concluded that he had gone into exile and had been redeployed.

Later we heard that Thabo was in London and enrolled as a student at the University of Sussex; we had totally lost touch with him. We learned that it had been decided that he should go to the United Kingdom to complete his studies and then start full-time work for the ANC. The next time I met him was when I went into exile in 1964 and Thabo was already a university student. He came to London regularly. The ANC Youth and Student Section in London was very active and Thabo was the link to Mazisi Kunene, the African National Congress (ANC) chief representative in England. At that time the only ANC structure that was open to all races was the London branch of the Youth and Student Section. Before the decision to open the structure to youth of all races, Thabo, Essop Pahad and others had discussions with Comrade Oliver Tambo, president of the ANC.

The Youth and Student Section, under Mbeki's leadership, became a very dynamic structure that had the task of mobilising South African youth in exile within the ANC and then using that collective strength to help develop and grow the anti-apartheid movement. But we were under strict instructions not to seek to turn the anti-apartheid movement into an ANC support group. It had to continue to be a broad-based solidarity movement in support of the democratic struggle in South Africa.

The 1960s was really the raving era in Europe and the United States. It was a time of hostility and opposition by young people to government structures and authority. It took form in both a political and a social way. It was a period of 'free love', the 'flower children', the burning of bras, the intensification of the fight for gender equality, and the smoking of marijuana. It was also a period of massive mobilisation against the American aggression in Vietnam, the campaign for nuclear disarmament and anti-racism. In terms of political development, we were concretely experiencing and therefore developing a better understanding of internationalism and anti-imperialism. The Vietnam and Cuban struggles were crucial in this respect. The ANC Youth and Student Section leadership, represented by Thabo and Essop, sat on the Vietnam Solidarity Committee. They played a very important role in the ideological struggle because this was a broad movement encompassing all sections and classes of society.

A few years after I arrived in London, Thabo Mbeki completed his studies at Sussex but was not immediately recalled to Africa. He was still commuting between London and Sussex while doing his postgraduate degree. I did not study at Sussex while he was there but Essop did. They had their own group and they had renewed their friendship. When Essop and Kenny Parker were students at Sussex, they had a house, which became another political/social meeting place. I was aware that Thabo Mbeki was giving leadership to build a strong anti-apartheid movement on the University of Sussex campus.

At that time various Trotskyite organisations had a prominent presence at the university. Under Thabo Mbeki's leadership they were manageable. At least we did not have to 'reach for guns each time we met a Trotskyite'. The discussions were sharp but not antagonistic. They were very dogmatic and I always wondered why they criticised us as the 'black bourgeoisie' not working for 'socialism now' in South Africa. But in reality they were weak politically in their own country and I saw no signs of a socialist revolution in the UK. While they were against the US war in Vietnam they were also hostile to the Vietnamese National Liberation Front. Indeed they opposed all liberation movements that they erroneously saw as Soviet 'puppets' and which did not support some form of Trotskyism.

While we were very active in the anti-apartheid movement in England, we were also very active in the Vietnam, Cuban and Palestine campaigns. London, Sussex and Europe generally had many students from other Third World countries like Chile and Argentina where the military juntas had seized power. There were also Iraqi and Iranian students who were in exile because of persecution by the Shah in Iran and by the Saddam Hussein regime in Iraq. We were in close contact with them in the UK. The ANC Youth and Student Section built very good relations with other oppressed and persecuted students in the Middle East, Latin America and Asia.

Thabo Mbeki, as the leader of the Youth and Student Section, provided active guidance and leadership to us on all these issues.

The ANC was very active in the Organisation of African Unity (OAU), the Pan African Youth Movement, the Afro Asian Peoples' Solidarity Committee, the Non-Aligned Movement, the World Peace Council, the World Youth Federation, the International Students' Union and various women's organisations, including the World Federation of Democratic Women. We were probably one of the strongest youth groupings of the ANC in exile who were deeply involved in other struggles and we were able to build a network between these and struggles in southern Africa. There were other ANC youth and student sections in the Soviet Union, Romania and the German Democratic Republic (GDR).

We were fortunate to be guided by a leadership that had a far deeper understanding of the international situation and the hostile forces we were facing. It was to the credit of the ANC leadership and our concrete experience that we developed our ideological and political understanding.

Under the London ANC Youth and Student Section, led by Thabo, we participated almost every week in anti-apartheid, anti-Vietnam war, anti-racist and anti-nuclear weapons demonstrations. We were also in touch with other African students, so we were involved in demonstrations against some African countries, especially Zaire. The ANC leadership based in Lusaka had advised us to be very tactical and sensitive in demonstrating against African countries because we had to carry the torch against Afro-pessimism and avoid creating reasons/excuses for further restriction of our activities on the African continent and creating more fertile conditions for some countries' co-option by apartheid South Africa. It was also important to try to move them out of the imperialist and neo-colonial camps. This did not stop us taking part in demonstrations outside the Zairean, Rhodesian and Portuguese embassies.

There were other liberation movements with which the ANC had good working relations; these included the People's Movement for the Liberation of Angola (MPLA), the Mozambique Liberation Front (FRELIMO), and the South West Africa People's Organisation (SWAPO).

There was a consistent struggle for international support with the Pan Africanist Congress (PAC), the National Union for the Total Independence of Angola (UNITA) and the Zimbabwe African National Union (ZANU). These organisations had some government support but they failed to get much backing from the international solidarity movement.

We were also actively involved in the struggle against Western governments that supported the apartheid regime and other repressive governments in southern Africa and the rest of the world. I do not know of any major university campus in Europe and North America that did not participate in solidarity activities in support of the Vietnam struggle against the US war of aggression, the anti-apartheid, anti-Smith and anti-Portuguese campaigns.

As I explained earlier, many of the European students of the 'left', especially Trotskyites, saw Thabo Mbeki and other ANC comrades as 'representatives of the black bourgeoisie' and Soviet 'imperialism'. They had accepted the propaganda that the ANC was an instrument of the South African Communist Party (SACP), which was an instrument of Moscow, so anti-Sovietism in many ways became anti-ANC simply because the ANC was seen as being part of the 'non-socialist bourgeoisie'.

Whenever Comrade President O.R. came to London, Thabo Mbeki spent a lot of time at his house to get guidance and direction on the work of the Youth and Student Section and ANC work generally. Thabo was one of the organisers and led our delegation to the first youth festival in Bulgaria. When we got to Bulgaria, our students who were studying in Moscow and other socialist countries, such as the GDR, led an offensive against the leadership of Johnny Makhathini, which became a battle amongst ourselves. The first meeting of our delegation in Sofia was very tense because I did not know most of our students. Thabo might have known some of them as members of the ANC, the SACP or the ASA when he was still at home, or when he went for military training in the then Soviet Union. I am not sure whether our students from Russia and other regions had caucused, but to our surprise at the first meeting they went into an offensive against Makhathini. They wanted to know who had imposed him on us as the leader of the delegation. They argued that as the youth and students from South Africa, it was their task to choose a leader of the delegation. Again, it was Thabo Mbeki's leadership that helped to contain the volatile situation. The meeting agreed that Makhathini would be the leader. Tensions disappeared and we went on to have an excellent political and social experience, the first such experience for most of us.

Suddenly in the early 1970s Thabo disappeared. It was only later that we learned that he had gone to the Lenin School in the Soviet Union. After the visit to the Soviet Union, Thabo was recalled to Lusaka and later deployed to Nigeria as the ANC chief representative. He developed extensive contacts with all levels of society, establishing strong support for the South African struggle, and played an important role in minimising initiatives to start a 'third force' South African organisation supported by some forces in Nigeria. Before settling in Nigeria he was deployed to Botswana to make contact with all sectors of South African society.

When he was deployed to be head of the ANC Department of Information and Publicity he had excellent contacts internationally and it was therefore necessary for him to travel regularly to Europe and the US. When he went to other parts of Europe or to the US, London became a stopover. So the interaction between us went on for many years. By that time I was in the Revolutionary Council and together we were meeting a lot of internal leadership members in the UK and Europe. Thabo was also very involved with the public and in secret meetings with the Afrikaner delegations in the UK and Switzerland. He travelled to the UK regularly to prepare for the meetings and lead the delegations when the meetings took place. Because of the need-to-know rule, many comrades in Africa and London were not aware of these meetings. Only the committee chaired by Comrade O.R. Tambo was aware of them. Thabo had to attend meetings with representatives of South African society on the African continent, in London, Europe and the US. In London he was very involved in our discussions with internal leadership represented by the likes of Jakes Gerwel, Frank Chikane, Allan Boesak and others before the launching of the United Democratic Front. During the 1980s he was also actively involved in the planning of the meeting of South African progressive trade unionists, which was held in London and where the launching of the Congress of South African Trade Unions (COSATU) was discussed. Thabo Mbeki was also meeting people from the British, European and American establishments in Lusaka during the early 1980s. He and Comrade O.R. attended many such meetings. Both had a style of arguing and outlining ANC positions, including the armed struggle, the alliance with the SACP and sanctions, that did not antagonise the European and US establishments.

In 1986 Oliver Tambo led an ANC delegation, which included Thabo, Mac Maharaj and me. It was the first time the ANC addressed such a meeting with big business in the House of Commons. The meeting was convened when the crisis of apartheid became severe because the ANC had called for the country to become ungovernable. The situation in southern Africa was also changing. The British establishment did not alter their position of supporting apartheid, but they wanted apartheid to reform in a way that would prevent what they feared would be a revolution, which would have affected their economic interests not only in South Africa but on the whole of the African continent. I think that Oliver Tambo and Thabo Mbeki managed to explain ANC policies and weaken their resolve to continue uncritically to support the apartheid regime and to minimise their hostility to the ANC.

Thabo Mbeki was also involved in Oliver Tambo's meeting with Chester Crocker. There were sharp debates in Lusaka about whether Tambo should meet Crocker. There were some elements that felt that he (Crocker) was not senior enough in terms of political leadership in US and they did not see the importance of the meeting. Eventually it was agreed that the meeting should take place in the Zambian Embassy in London and it led to the first ever official meeting between the ANC and the US secretary of state in 1987.

With regard to the importance of ANC–South African white big business talks, the ANC came to the conclusion that our tactic must be to break 'the curtain of ignorance and fear' about the ANC that had been built around whites and that we should start a series of talks with the more organised Afrikaner establishments. That first meeting with the white captains of industry held in Lusaka in 1985 later led to the first public talks with the Afrikaners in the UK and the secret talks in Switzerland during the late 1980s. The 1985 Lusaka meeting opened up the floodgates and destroyed the fear syndrome among white South Africans. Whites from all sectors – Afrikaner politicians, religious leaders, students, poets, writers and many members of the Broederbond – came to meet the ANC after this path-breaking meeting. In fact it opened up possibilities for many subsequent meetings. Thabo was one of the coordinators of the Lusaka meeting as well as the public and secret meetings with the Afrikaners.

When Frederik van Zyl Slabbert and Alex Boraine resigned from the South African parliament as leaders of the opposition party, Thabo Mbeki was very much in touch with them. Van Zyl Slabbert came to London accompanied by Breyten Breytenbach from Paris. The first meeting took place in Van Zyl's friends' flat in Knightsbridge where we planned the Dakar meeting. The Institute for a Democratic Alternative for South Africa organised about 45 people from the Afrikaner establishment to meet the ANC for the first time in Dakar. Some comrades in the ANC leadership rejected in principle any such meetings. Eventually the leadership agreed and comrades like Pallo Jordan and Mac Maharaj did come to the meetings in Dakar and Burkina Faso. After that there were two other such meetings. The Dakar meeting was with the Afrikaner establishment; in Paris we met with Afrikaners as well as some English-speaking South Africans, politicians, big business and representatives of the Mass Democratic Movement (MDM). In Leverkusen, Afrikaner and Soviet intellectuals met the ANC. These were very crucial meetings that discussed white fears, black aspirations, the armed struggle, sanctions and the future political dispensation for South Africa.

As might have been expected, the reaction of the apartheid regime was negative and hostile. South Africans from across the spectrum, especially after Zimbabwe and Mozambique became independent, were holding meetings with the ANC. So there were hundreds of meetings taking place in many countries of the world. Mbeki made invaluable contributions to these discussions. There was great interest in these meetings both in South Africa and internationally. Later, when we met Niel Barnard, the head of the apartheid regime's National Intelligence Services, he said some people were treating them like 'stupid boers' but they knew what was going on in the public and secret meetings of the ANC. He also hinted that National Intelligence, Military Intelligence and the apartheid security police had infiltrated all levels of the Tripartite Alliance and the MDM.

In many ways, my own political development cannot be separated from the influence of Thabo Mbeki. He provided guidance and leadership right through the days when we were in London to the days when I visited Lusaka and especially after the Kabwe conference when I was elected to the National Executive Committee of the ANC, and when I was in the Revolutionary Council and later in the Political Military Committee. We had very dynamic contacts because Thabo was participating in many meetings with South Africans from home. I was head of the Political Military Committee in London; however, because of the need-to-know rule, I was not informed about everything. To Mbeki's credit, what you did not need to know, you were not told. Regardless of your position or whether you socialised with him, you were told only what you were supposed to know. So I cannot claim that I was aware of all information relating to internal reconstruction that he was aware of. We knew the broad guidelines and we worked accordingly.

There were four secret meetings of the ANC with the apartheid regime's National Intelligence Service in Switzerland in 1989 and the early 1990s, all of which were led by Thabo Mbeki. He and Jacob Zuma represented the ANC at the first meeting. I joined Mbeki for the second meeting and Joe Nhlanhla and I joined him for the third meeting. Again, I also joined Mbeki in the fourth meeting. The issues discussed included the release of Nelson Mandela and other political prisoners, the unbanning of the ANC, SACP, PAC and all other banned organisations and the consequences thereof, indemnity to enable the return of exiles to South Africa, the first meeting of the ANC and the apartheid government in South Africa, and the setting up of committees to deal concretely with these issues. Mbeki was involved in the preparations for the first ANC group to return to South Africa led by Zuma in March 1990. Nhlanhla and I joined the team a few weeks later. We constituted the steering committee to deal with the issues identified in the secret talks in Switzerland.

During the 7th SACP congress held in Cuba in 1989, the 'Path to Power' document was finally adopted. I always argued that it was an insurrectionary document that did not take into consideration developments inside South Africa, the growing political and economic crisis of the apartheid regime and the consequences of the collapse of socialism; also, many people were not aware of the secret talks with representatives of the regime or did not believe that the 'enemy' were genuinely holding talks. Comrade O.R. Tambo and the committee that the National Executive Committee had mandated to deal with negotiations understood that the apartheid regime wanted to negotiate reform and not genuine democracy based on one person, one vote, but circumstances demanded that we start the process for negotiations.

The decision to adopt 'Path to Power' was a majority decision. In line with democratic centralism, once the majority took a decision, it was binding and the decision was accepted. Mbeki and I went to the party congress in Cuba after one of our secret meetings with representatives of the apartheid regime in Switzerland. Thabo Mbeki's leadership qualities were apparent in that we had come from a secret meeting with representatives of the South African National Intelligence Service where we had discussed concrete measures to start negotiations, and then he successfully chaired the SACP conference in Cuba, which adopted the 'Path to Power', knowing that within months we would be returning to South Africa.

Thabo knew that the struggle was not over because negotiations had yet to take place, but he understood that the struggle now had to continue in the political terrain of substantive negotiations.

After 1990 I was deputy head of the ANC Department of International Affairs (DIA). Of course, we saw each other more or less every day because Thabo was the head of the DIA.

In all our public and secret meetings with the apartheid regime and representatives of the MDM, he clearly understood that, given the balance of forces and their control of the South African Defence Force and security, some of the fears of the whites would have to be taken into consideration, although always in the context of black aspirations. He understood that because we were going for the bigger goal, we had to make some compromises; but compromises such as the Sunset Clause and a Government of National Unity could not be permanent. If the political arrangement establishing the Government of National Unity was to continue, this had to be based on the objective realities and not because it was written in the democratic constitution of South Africa. Deputy President F.W. de Klerk did not understand this and that was why the National Party walked out of the Government of National Unity. He wanted power-sharing with the white minority group to be written into the democratic South African constitution. The ANC was not opposed to bringing into government representatives of other organisations as long as they were willing to work within the perspectives of genuine democracy and democratic centralism.

This was the approach used by the progressive forces during the Convention for a Democratic South Africa (CODESA) negotiations. Mbeki and Zuma played important roles during the CODESA talks, especially in dealing with whites who were threatening civil war and in influencing Chief Buthelezi.

Unfortunately there has been much misguided criticism of the compromises that had to be made. The critics have given no credible alternatives. I believe that there was no alternative to preventing a disastrous violent racial confrontation. However, 21 years later one can openly debate whether in implementation of economic policies we could have been bolder.

On the question of leadership, although the ANC perspective has been, quite correctly, that liberation movements make individuals, history is full of examples of individuals within a liberation or political movement who have a certain capacity for analysis, understanding and commitment to detail in challenging issues and therefore give important leadership at crucial times. Mbeki was such an individual. I also saw this attribute when he was in government. He understood economic diplomacy and international relations. For him economics and international relations were two sides of the same coin and a priority to consolidate South Africa's democracy and create a better life for all.

On the question of Mbeki's 'aloofness', arrogance and authoritarian style of leadership when he was the deputy president and president of South Africa, such criticisms were never substantiated and were based on distortions and half-truths.

The reality is that it was under his presidency that the cluster system of ministers and deputy ministers was established. The clusters met regularly and discussed fully any issue that was going to be submitted to cabinet. Mbeki did not attend the cluster meetings so how could he dictatorially impose his positions?

He listened to every view, whether it was in the cabinet or in the lekgotla meetings, and then he summed up. That was why I always sympathised with the first clusters, which had to do their presentations in the lekgotla because that was when he was at his sharpest and he had read all the documents and submissions. Many cluster reports in the first one-and-a-half days of lekgotla meetings had to be redone and resubmitted by relevant cabinet ministers. But that was not because of Mbeki's authoritarian leadership. Some were long reports and did not distinguish what I called the 'trees from the forest'. After long discussions he was able to get to the core issues and debate how we intended to deal with matters of delivery and he would want to know our recommendations for the way forward.

Another issue that was used to demonise Mbeki was HIV/AIDS, about which there were very sharp debates. Mbeki had read every bit of information that he could lay his hands on. He read what the medical scientists were saying, including the 'dissidents'. He argued that there seemed to be two opinions and asked why we could not bring the two groups together and let them debate so that we could see what could be the way forward for us as a country and for the African continent. He was wrongly accused of being a 'denialist'. In the end, he was advised by the cabinet to back off from the debate because the issue was being abused to achieve other objectives, and he accepted that. I recall that Mbeki always asked why it was that the ministers and their deputies did not speak up on issues impacting on their portfolios. He argued that this was not how a collective works. It was the task of ministers to speak out after discussions in their clusters and decisions in cabinet. Indirectly, he was challenging us to defend cabinet decisions taken collectively.

To understand Mbeki's approach to issues both in Africa and internationally you need to be familiar with the history of the ANC, SACP and the South African Congress of Trade Unions alliance which was based on anti-imperialist, anti-colonialist and pan-Africanist perspectives. Many documents published by the ANC since 1912 raised such matters. Of course, President Mbeki was able to intellectualise this position and implement it even before we were in government. When he became deputy president he started laying the foundations of a progressive pan-African position. It was not mere lip service. Everything that we did was related to our vision of an African Renaissance stemming from the early history of the ANC. Mbeki was inspired by our founding fathers and the leadership that followed, which included Comrades O.R. Tambo, Dr Yusuf Dadoo, J.B. Marks, Michael Harmel, Bram Fischer and Moses Kotane.

We were very fortunate that in a historical moment there was an African leadership that was not only anti-colonialist but, in broad terms, progressive. For example, you had Olusegun Obasanjo from Nigeria, Abdelaziz Bouteflika from Algeria, Meles Zenawi from Ethiopia and Mandela and Mbeki from South Africa. Because there was a leadership that had a progressive vision, it was possible for progressive ideas to gain ground. Inadvertently, there was a 'cabal' of four countries that could influence issues within the African Union (AU), although they never imposed their positions. Then we also had, at that time, a united Southern African Development Community (SADC) – united because of our common experiences as liberation movements and countries that suffered destabilisation by the apartheid regime. The SADC collectively discussed progressive ideas and developed common positions and then argued for these positions in the OAU/AU. But this is not the case at present – there is a different leadership on the African continent. Now you look around and you ask where is the leadership in Africa that can take us back on the road to a progressive African Renaissance like that which was led by the collective consisting of Obasanjo, Bouteflika, Meles and Mbeki during the early years of the twenty-first century. The World Bank report that positively approached the question 'Can Africa Claim the 21st Century?' is increasingly becoming unrealistic.

On domestic issues, particularly the Polokwane debacle, I think that the ANC alliance was too confident after 1994. We thought that the ANC could never be weakened and divided because we were approaching our 100th birthday; we could only be divided from within the movement, which we believed was not possible. No outside force could divide us because of the liberation movement's history and experience. But in reality we did not understand that once we went into government, we allowed the structures of the liberation movement to be weakened because the best cadres joined the government at national, regional and provincial levels, including the civil service and state-owned enterprises. So by the time we woke up to a campaign of destabilisation against the progressive National Democratic Revolution (NDR), organisationally we had little capacity to counter it. We should look at the Zimbabwe, HIV/AIDS and the arms issues in this context. I am confident that history will show that this was not accidental and that the demonisation of Mbeki was an old tactic used against many independent and progressive leaders in many Third World countries.

We understood that if Zimbabwe had gone through a regime change, which some foreign powers and other forces were working on, then South Africa would have been the next target. I think that although we appreciated it intellectually, we did not think that foreign powers and other interests could succeed in exploiting our organisational and leadership weaknesses to dilute and divide the ANC. From 1994 Deputy President Mbeki had an advisory committee, which Jacob Zuma took over when he became deputy president. It was intended to support the effective functioning of the office of the deputy president. President Mbeki did not have an organised/formal committee, which the newspapers ignorantly or naively referred to as a 'kitchen cabinet', a sort of cabal that influenced all major decisions. The suggestion was that it was a cabal of stooges used to impose Mbeki's dictates. This was a distortion of the reality and another tactic in the divide and rule campaign against Mbeki and ultimately against the ANC.

Our organisational experience post-1990 led to weaknesses in the structures of all the alliance members; it led to factionalism and divisions, culminating in the Polokwane events. I still thought that at Polokwane we were dealing with challenges that afflict any liberation or political movement post-liberation and that we could handle the challenges politically. I think that some ANC leaders are now beginning to understand that we opened up a Pandora's box that is threatening the unity and progressive content of the ANC.

On the issue of the unprecedented recall of President Mbeki, I believe that if he did not see himself as a politically disciplined cadre of the ANC and had no regard for the interests of the country, he could have mobilised the military, the police, the intelligence services and the 40 per cent who voted for him at the Polokwane conference to defy his recall. I think his recall was unconstitutional. It was based on an absolutely flawed judgment of Judge Chris Nicholson. I really do not know how he came to that judgment, but he gave the ANC leadership a reason to take the decision to recall President Mbeki. The president only had seven months to the end of his term. It was the wrong decision for the country and for the ANC, the SACP and COSATU and I think that we are going to pay a heavy price for that. Nicholson's judgment was later challenged and we all know that it could not stand the test of a higher court. Julius Malema is already publicly reflecting on his role at Polokwane. He has alleged that he was part of a 'dirty tricks' campaign. The former secretary general of COSATU, Comrade Zwelinzima Vavi, has publicly apologised for being part of a plot to undermine President Mbeki. History has many examples of individuals who were part of factionalism and who later expose details in public. The question that you are asking is, was it expected? I was surprised.

With regard to my resignation as deputy minister – I did not resign from government because I was an 'Mbekite'. I and other ministers and deputy ministers resigned because we understood that President Mbeki's recall would have long-term repercussions for the liberation movement. I was re-appointed by President Kgalema Motlanthe after I resigned but I did not accept the appointment and explained why I had resigned. Comrades resigned because they understood that the recall was politically wrong and organisationally dangerous for the ANC.

Another consequence was the formation of the Congress of the People (COPE). Some of the finest comrades left the ANC and joined COPE or withdrew from politics. If these comrades had stayed in the movement they would have strengthened many other comrades in the ANC who are convinced that organisationally the ANC faces many challenges. Hence in the interests of the ANC and the country, it is vital to ensure that the ANC regains its progressive vision, policies and values. Polokwane and the recall set in motion a lot of dangerous tendencies.

As regards the rift between Thabo Mbeki and the SACP, I believe that the SACP made a tactically wrong decision at our last Central Committee meeting held in Lusaka after the unbannings to decide to become a mass party. This weakened the ideological base of the SACP and gave rise to unscientific analysis. Some comrades post the unbannings did not believe in the SACP's historical perspectives of 'colonialism of a special type' and did not want to accept that the NDR had not been completed. In the new circumstances post-1990 the role of each member of the alliance had to be based on this understanding. This issue came up consistently in National Executive Committee meetings. So-called 'informed sources' systematically briefed the media and 'analysts' about 'Mbeki's group' and its anti-commu-nist and neo-liberal positions.

When the Growth, Employment and Redistribution plan was

implemented they began to campaign against the 'Class of 96' and 'neo-liberalism'; thus the slogan 'prepare for socialism now' became the SACP mantra. There was no credible attempt at scientific analysis of the South African economy and a progressive developmental state. They conveniently ignored the experiences in Lenin's writings of the early years of the Russian Revolution. Some of the SACP leaders are aware that at crucial stages some comrades argued that the Party was displaying unMarxist tendencies and that the Party's decision to go it alone should be encouraged. It was Mbeki who argued that the Party was important to deepen the ideological content of the NDR and to counter 'populist Marxism-Leninism'. Mbeki argued that the Party was important to explain the relationship between national and class struggles. It seemed that some of the SACP leadership began to believe that the role the Party was to take over leadership of the NDR and we witnessed some of the worst manifestations of 'entryism'. This ignored the historical role of the SACP of understanding the relationship between national and class struggles, deepening the ideological foundations of the ANC and ensuring that progressives ideas influenced the 'broad ANC family'.

But we had many lighter moments with Thabo Mbeki. We socialised a lot. Many of our meetings in exile ended with drinks and a lot of singing of freedom songs. Freedom songs were very important to maintain morale and discipline. We had a slogan, 'Freedom in our Lifetime'. There were times when some us did not believe that it would happen. That was why we sang the freedom songs. I do not know what the British people thought of us. It is possible that they were asking what was going on with these 'noisy foreigners'. We used to party like hell, even though we did not allow this to interfere with our work. Mbeki was a good singer and dancer and partici-pated in many social activities in London.

There are many fond memories after we came back from exile. When I returned I stayed at the homes of various family members. Later Comrade Yusuf Saloojee (Jojo) and I bought a house near Mayfair, which became a social base for many comrades, including Joe Modise, Mbeki, Penuell Maduna, Jackie Selebi, Mathews Phosa and Anthony Mongalo. I was a bad singer. When the ANC Youth and Student Section in London was prepar-ing to go to the World Youth Festival in Bulgaria in 1966, after many choir rehearsals, a decision was taken that if you could not sing, you could not be part of the delegation and they chucked me out. In the end Mbeki intervened on my behalf and convinced others to keep me in the delegation if I contributed to the political preparations.

On a serious note, much of what I have learned about international relations and diplomacy, I learned from Mbeki. In terms of weaknesses, as I said earlier, we did not fully appreciate the offensive launched against the ANC or were too confident that efforts to weaken and divide the ANC and its alliance partners would not succeed.

I think that the government communications strategy to deal with many challenges post-1994 made the mistake of believing that our people would not fall for the media distortions and the demonisation of Mbeki. Add that to the organisational weaknesses of the ANC and the SACP and you have a combination of factors that creates conditions for things to go wrong. The communications strategy has to improve to counter the misinformation by the press and analysts. Many people will remember that Thabo Mbeki used to write for the *ANC Today,* which was a way to keep the public engaged on relevant and topical issues. How he managed to do this every week is a mystery to me. It reminded me of Lenin's polemics at crucial stages of the Russian Revolution. The media and experts must take time to read past issues of *ANC Today* and Mbeki's speeches when in government. Knowing the past better will help all of us to deal better with the present challenges.

To this day, there are continuing distortions that Mbeki was 'out of touch with the people', he was aloof, opinionated and authoritarian. Some critics fail or refuse to acknowledge the pressures of the domestic and international programme of a deputy president or president. As I said earlier, they make allegations without any substantiation, ignoring the reality. On occasions I reflect on whether some find it difficult to accept a black person who can intellectualise and enter into debates on many issues. They yearn for the stereotype of a subservient singing and dancing black person.

To return to the present. In terms of conflict prevention and other challenges facing the African continent, Mbeki is chair of the AU committee dealing with the outstanding issues between North and South Sudan. He is also involved with the internal democratic processes in North Sudan. Thabo Mbeki knows his subject matter well. His negotiating skill is his ability to listen to the other side, to understand what is driving the other side to adopt certain positions. In the broader context, in a conflict situation he would want to know and get to the bottom of what the root causes are. He has used the same approach in Zimbabwe, Sudan, Ivory Coast, the Democratic Republic of the Congo or whenever he discusses conflict situations. In essence, these are basic negotiating tactics, but they are seldom applied by other facilitators or negotiators in dealing with African conflicts.

There is also a growing tendency in negotiations to impose decisions. That is why the big powers cannot get anything right in terms of finding solutions. Besides their militaristic approach, they impose political solutions. Thabo Mbeki's negotiating skill, from what I saw in all the public and secret meetings with representatives of the apartheid regime and later in CODESA, was not to say 'this is our position, you take it or leave it'. He would try to convince the other side why their interests coincided with our interests as a liberation movement, which was in the best interests of all South Africans.

In 2014 the Economic Commission for Africa chose Mbeki as chairman of a commission to investigate the illegal transfer of money from Africa. The final report is excellent and it should serve as a guideline to African governments and non-governmental organisations on the extent of the problem and what should be done to deal with the problem.

Interviewed May 2014, Johannesburg

ALEXANDER ERWIN

❖

The path to my political activism started at a point in my youth that
eludes me – no doubt, though, the product of humane and interested
parents. Clearer political memories start in the late sixties and early seven-
ties of the last century – talking in centuries is in itself cause for thought.
When I think back to the South Africa of that time and the country I now
live in, then I am humbled. I have lived through an amazing and, in essence,
humanising period of history. It was fraught with difficulty, danger, brutality
and sadness. Yet it was inspiring; it made one glimpse the soaring aspiration
of the human spirit, it lent profound meaning to existence. I was fortunate
to work with workers and leaders whose nobility of cause lent an energy
and integrity to my being.

This is not an account about me. It is about an exceptional leader –
Thabo Mbeki – known first as a clandestine figure of the underground tract
or Radio Freedom and then as a human being I grew to respect deeply and
towards whom I feel a profound friendship – a comradeship. He is of the
category that led our movement, the African National Congress (ANC), to
fight for and achieve democracy; they are heroes and heroines no matter
what a modern media might capriciously decide in the pursuit of commercial whim. As a nation we are fortunate that in the long and often pitiless
tide of history we were endowed with that category of thinkers, humanists
and doggedly determined freedom fighters.

For me personally there were precursors of this category before I met
Mbeki: Harold Nxasana, William Khanyile and Judson Khuzwayo, among

others. I invoke these four men as they had the properties of the ilk of that ANC leadership. They never jumped to conclusions; they analysed and they studied in order to analyse. Dogma was a product of the lazy mind and the uncertain soul (used in a figurative sense). Despite all – personal lives were unstable, to say the least, under the rule of the apartheid regime – they were at peace with their chosen path and the conviction that there was a better world ahead. I wish that one could reminisce with them now.

I am pretty certain that the first time that I met President Mbeki was around 1987/88. There came a time when we inside could leave the country on a passport. The sequence of events is hazy for me now, but the memory is vivid. There is a strange hotel off Piccadilly Circus where we met representatives of the South African Congress of Trade Unions (SACTU) in the afternoon. That evening we got into cars and were blindfolded for our own protection so we did not know where we were going. The home was suburban – we saw only the inside. It was the people who were important. Thabo Mbeki, Steve Tshwete, Aziz Pahad and, if I recall correctly, John Nkadimeng. Jay Naidoo, Maxwell Xulu (hamba kahle, Max, a memory of great pain) and I were a Congress of South African Trade Unions (COSATU) delegation from the inside.

At that meeting in London, we analysed, exchanged information and strategised. For me, a relationship of trust developed. I respected the process – thought, information, accuracy or, in other words, praxis in the Marxian sense. We had to deal with harsh realities and brutalities, but we could also explore politics in its more profound sense. By this I mean it is more than the manoeuvre of the moment – the electoral gain of a political party or factional advance – it is about how humans choose to govern themselves, about how they choose to build civilisations that embody the best of humanity and fulfil its aspirations for nobility.

This group, along with Chris Hani, helped trade unions towards unity. They persuaded us of the merit of a strong union federation. There were still some tensions between the general workers' unions and the industrial unions. Then we had another big meeting with Mbeki, Hani and others at the Pamodzi Hotel in Lusaka. There was quite a big COSATU delegation at that meeting.

They also worked closely with us in dealing with devastating violence in

KwaZulu-Natal (KZN) – in effect a major internal civil war. They and current President Zuma guided us through and participated in a long series of clandestine meetings with Inkatha to try to mitigate a potentially disastrous situation. One cannot do anything other than form a spirit of comradeship in such a situation. A sad irony was that individuals grew in understanding, wisdom and compassion out of this national pain.

In 1989, a big delegation went to Harare, where Oliver Tambo addressed us on the Harare, Declaration. Jay Naidoo, Johnny Copelyn and I, and someone else (can't remember who), then spent the whole night, as I recall it, with Thabo Mbeki and Aziz Pahad, where they persuaded us that the Harare Declaration approach would make the most sense. Then we had to come back to try to sell the idea to the trade unions and workers. I would say without any hesitation that Thabo Mbeki was the key person who persuaded the COSATU leadership that the ANC was serious. I think that what impressed us was that here was someone who was a better Marxist than all of us and who understood profoundly what unions were doing and what they could do. I always found it strange that a later generation of COSATU leaders saw Mbeki as hostile to unions – despite the fact that we told them time and again that the ANC leader who best understands unions is Thabo Mbeki. It is proving a costly mistake for many!

I would not hesitate to say that Thabo Mbeki was definitely the person who got some of the left-orientated and critical trade union leaders on board. He did it because of his intellect. He did not try to dictate and tell us what to do; he persuaded us. We argued for hours – and we were quite a team of trade unionists to argue – on the merits of the Harare Declaration, which clearly favoured substantive negotiations.

We were divided ourselves, but we tended to favour pushing harder in terms of insurrection so that we could get better terms from the apartheid regime; others said we were not going to get better terms and that we should move now and negotiate. We had started with a limited degree of self-defence but in the end what turned it for all of us in COSATU and made it possible for Thabo Mbeki to persuade us was that we had all started to see this uncontrolled violence and its brutality. Things like necklacing were horrific. Some of the self-defence units in various townships were completely undisciplined and you could see that criminality was moving into them.

It was on that trip to Harare where, because we had all these problems, we said to Hani and Mbeki – I think it was just Jay Naidoo and me – that we needed money. People were dying because of the violence; we needed guns to defend ourselves. We had started to tap supportive business people here in South Africa for funds and we were buying pistols through white guys who had licences. We did not want to link with Harry Gwala because we thought he was too radical. Then we found a route to bring in AKs for northern KZN, but we needed money to purchase the weapons. I cannot remember if it was on this particular trip or later; all I remember is that Thabo Mbeki said go home and Zanele gave me a brown paper packet with money in it. Murphy Morobe and I then took the chance of bringing this back in. Mbeki said when you get back to South Africa, you should immediately fly to Cape Town to meet Trevor Manuel and Cheryl Carolus to give them a message that Margaret Thatcher was prepared to come and meet South Africa's leaders – now whether this message was true or not, I do not know. Manuel and Carolus probably knew what it meant. We brought in quite a lot of money to help finance that anti-violence period. I guess that we must have met with Thabo Mbeki five or six times.

Fortunately, all the South African leadership started to see that violence begets violence in terrible ways; it brutalises societies and people no longer know what a human being is. I am sure that most of my colleagues at the time would go with my assessment that Thabo was the key person in terms of addressing this matter. Chris Hani played an important role, especially when he came to KZN, because he was widely respected; even the Inkatha guys respected him. When Walter Sisulu and Andrew Mlangeni and others came out, they also played a very important role in helping us to negotiate peace and to try to reduce the violence in KZN. Jacob Zuma was also very important in calming us down.

For me personally in meeting and spending a lot of time with Thabo Mbeki, I really appreciated the depth of his historical, intellectual, humane and Marxist thinking. You walked away from him thinking that this was a hell of a serious intellectual leadership: this was a leadership that was thinking; it had strategies, which was often different for the ANC operatives on the ground. And it was after we met and engaged with Thabo Mbeki that the whole COSATU leadership swung solidly behind the ANC.

We had that big, important meeting in Paris in 1989 where Thabo Mbeki was present. We gave a paper on the economy. Then we met with the South African Communist Party (SACP) and when Joe Slovo wrote that paper distancing himself from Soviet orthodoxy, a number of us joined the Party – John Gomomo, myself, Moses Mayekiso and many others. We were members but we were never very active in the structures. We agreed with the alliance structure but we were more left than the ANC. So the party was a home for many of the trade union leaders.

By the time Thabo Mbeki and others came home from exile, I would say that the working relationship was very good because, as have I said, he had already persuaded us in the trade unions of the merits of the alliance structure. For most of that period, what took up most of my time was the violence in KZN. So many contacts at that point were with Thabo Mbeki, Chris Hani until he was killed, and Mandela directly. Mandela played an important role on the frontline in that violence because Buthelezi's approach was that he only talked to Mandela. Buthelezi also respected Thabo Mbeki a lot; it had to be either Mbeki or Mandela. But for the political symbolism, Buthelezi wanted it to be more Mandela and also because Mandela, like himself, was of royal lineage.

From then on we worked very closely and I was often up from KZN to work out tactics. Mandela was very strong and very clear on what he was going to do and his approach was slightly different from Thabo Mbeki's. Mandela's approach was 'I will go and meet the leaders of the IFP', while Thabo wanted to set up processes, which was more our approach.

We won the first democratic elections in 1994 and I do not think that I had really contemplated that I would go into government. I have always enjoyed working with Thabo Mbeki because he is a hell of a good economist. It was a whole dimension of my involvement with Mbeki that for me was very personally fulfilling and exciting because he took a keen interest in the economic research we were doing. He understood what we were doing and he could make inputs. I would say that Thabo Mbeki was the intellectual mentor in that whole evolution of the economic policy and when we started doing Ready to Govern and then later the Reconstruction and Development Programme (RDP). So I had two levels of work with him: one was on the violence side and the other was on the economic side.

I guess that by the time that we put together that task team in late 1993, Jay Naidoo, myself and few other trade union leaders effectively moved full time to work with the ANC to prepare policy. We had the Economic Transformation Committee first chaired by Max Sisulu and then by Tito Mboweni and Trevor Manuel. Then there was also the Macro-Economic Research Group (MERG) – that whole arena of economic research preparation was very exciting and we worked very closely with Thabo Mbeki, who led the economic policy programme of the ANC. I enjoyed that a lot. Tito Mboweni and I were the two trained economists. Trevor Manuel and others learned as they went along and they learned very quickly and very well.

When I was brought into the post-1994 government, I came in as deputy minister of finance and it was a surprise. I got a phone call from Naidoo, who said, 'Alec, you are going to be a deputy minister.' I said, 'Oh, okay, that's lekker,' not believing him. But then I said, 'What?' when I realised that he was being serious. He emphasised, 'You are going to be deputy minister of finance.' Finance was not my number one because I preferred trade and industry, but I was very fortunate because Derek Keys was the finance minister and we had done a lot of work with him before. He had been minister of finance and trade and industry in the last years of the National Party government. So I had personally met him many, many times and we set up the motor industry task group. I was delighted to be able to work with Derek; he was a fantastic teacher and Jay and I worked with him a lot.

Then I worked very closely with Mbeki as the deputy president of South Africa. By the time we got to the RDP, all the key economic thinkers or players were largely at one. The people who still objected were characters like Patrick Bond and some of the more ultra-left academics. We debated some of the key issues, things like macro balance; should you risk inflation by increasing the deficit and spending more or should there be a more cautious approach, usually referred to as macro balance? One of the questions we asked ourselves was the importance of inflation. We had pretty much reached agreement on that. The independence of the Central Bank had been debated extensively and we reached agreement on that too. It was the trade unions that pushed more for the RDP. The ANC's department of economic policy was less keen to do this broad programme because they felt that we were making commitments that we may not meet in terms of available resources. Whereas on the trade union side we argued that we wanted to make those commitments so that we could hold the democratic government accountable to them. But by that time we had actually crafted the RDP, a large measure of agreement had been reached. There was a big team of economists working on that, people like Alan Hirsch, David Lewis, Steven Gelb, Moss Ngoasheng, Max Sisulu. By the time we went into government, the key economic ministers had a short book, what we called the 'Yellow Book', which outlined the first year or so of policy action that we needed to work on.

I worked more on the trade and industry side of that, but then came in on finance. Just before the elections we had frequent preparatory meetings with Keys and his senior officials. I recall one meeting at night at the Development Bank of Southern Africa. I think that this is what Sampie Terreblanche calls the 'secret meeting'. I think it was Tito Mboweni who asked, 'Derek, what is South Africa's debt?' He responded, 'How do I know?' So we were perplexed and one of us commented, 'But you are the finance minister.' He replied, 'I can tell you what the debt of this South African central government is; but I cannot tell you the debt of Transkei, Ciskei and all of these other bantustans and endless development corporations. We tried to find out, but we really do not know.'

So, funnily enough, my first job as deputy minister of finance was to sort out all that debt: to go find out what the debt was, what the international banks and financers were owed. I worked with Iraj Abedien, checking what all those development corporations owed, the pension funds, excess employment – it was bad. So that was the first warning we got that there were huge problems in terms of the economy of South Africa. That was where the team, which included Deputy President Mbeki, started to think that we had to be more cautious. When we came in we had had a strategy to try to raise finance on the international capital markets: both to show that we were respectable and not terrorist lunatics, but also to try to put a discipline on the economy so that we would not be forced to do crazy things. We were reasonably successful.

I travelled with Keys and then with Chris Liebenberg to raise those bond issues but when we came back we said to Thabo, Trevor, Tito and others,

'Our economic policy is not technically credible. It has a lot of socio-economic aspirations but it is not technically credible.' We were being asked how we were going to manage our exchange rate and what the exchange rate policy was. When you read the RDP, it does not mention the exchange rate policy. When people are being asked to invest in South Africa, what is going to happen to the exchange rate? What is the attitude to inflation? What are we going to do with tariffs? The tariffs we had worked out in the negotiations with the World Trade Organisation (WTO). So Growth, Employment and Redistribution (GEAR) was that: it was the more technical dimension, trying to address the gaps in terms of economic policy. It spelled out monetary policy more carefully – deficit policy, interest rate policy, exchange rate policy – and it linked technically from an economics point of view to the tariff level. The depreciation of the currency meant that the effective level of protection for South African industry was rising. This defeated the policy objective of lowering this level of protection over a number of years to increase the competitiveness of our industry. Technically, therefore, we should have lowered tariffs faster. However, in the end we did not do this, preferring a 'softer landing' for the economy.

Now because we were so preoccupied with influencing our exchange rate and the capital markets, we could not have a public debate around GEAR, because if you do that the capital markets respond to everything that you say. In hindsight we were too cautious. We should have probably warned the trade unions a bit earlier that we had inherited an economically bankrupt country from the apartheid regime. I then moved to trade and industry and Trevor Manuel took over as finance minister before GEAR. But I was given the job of going to explain it to the trade unions. So, according to them, I was the 'Class of 1996' criminal. It gave a lot of ammunition to ultra-left groups that we had left out like Patrick Bond and many others in the trade union movements. They said, 'You see, we told you that these guys are bringing us a World Bank/Washington Consensus rubbish.'

I am often asked whether we regret it and I think that most of us – me, Tito, Trevor and certainly Thabo – would say that we do not regret it because if we had not done, it we would have had serious economic problems. It formed the bedrock that allowed us to move to the kind of position of surplus that we had and hence, by the end of Thabo Mbeki's term as president, we were in a healthy economic position. This is certainly being eroded in recent years by inconsistent policy. What was wonderful about working with Mandela was that you just had to give a short summary of where we were going, these are the arguments for and against, and we recommend you go this way and he would listen and say get on with it. But with Thabo Mbeki you would be able to thrash things out and say this is a judgement call, that is, a mix between politics and economics and on an informed basis Mbeki could say, 'Okay, let us go this route.' So in the preparation for GEAR, Mbeki and the economic ministers had long discussions and we said we have to go for it. But it was a tough period and the difficulty was that if you had precipitated high inflation as a result of an undervalued currency it would have been a difficult time for South Africa's economy.

It has never been my experience that Mbeki came across as a dictator. There were three areas where I worked with him. The other area, which I have not mentioned before, was his understanding of the global economy and the importance of multilateralism and what multilateralism meant and why Africa was important. He was a good economist and I think that he has a profound respect for constitutionalism and the protection of rights. For me, Thabo Mbeki has an extremely profound understanding of what that means and how sometimes your own personal interests had to be subordinated if you wanted those principles to apply. I am making this point because all too often cabinet ministers who did not understand their own portfolios well enough did not understand that he already had a vision of where he thought that you should be going. I think that ministers who were often not clear might have been intimidated by the fact that he knew where he wanted to go. I never saw him dictating. My own view is that I thought that sometimes he might have been too weak with some of those ministers. I think that he should have kicked some of their arses.

In the economic cluster, we were lucky because we had come to similar conclusions and we were often able to debate issues with him, but we understood the vision that he was seeing. One of the nicest areas of interaction, which he still hammers us on, that we have not written on, was the long discussions we held about the effects of globalisation and how capitalism was working. Thabo Mbeki is a good Marxist in that he understands the capitalist economy better than the capitalists themselves, and that is the strength of Marx. If you are a Marxist, you understand capitalism better than the capitalist can.

I think that Madiba was often a bit tougher than Mbeki. If you messed up, Mandela would bomb you from a hundred miles. My own view is that allegations of dictatorship were often an excuse for cabinet ministers and people who were not prepared to take on his arguments. Instead of taking on the critical arguments, they just sat. If they could not take it on because they did not know as much as he did, then he would naturally come across as running the show. If they did know enough but were not brave enough to do it, it was not Mbeki's fault and many did not want to take responsibilities. But I never ever felt at any time that I could not argue a point with Thabo. Often I disagreed with him; sometimes he persuaded me, or I might have persuaded him to adopt my arguments.

I think that one of the problems in running a complex modern state is that you need a leadership that is capable of understanding that complexity – not in the abstract, but in minute detail. For me the great merit of Mandela was that he had more of a strategic, instinctive understanding of what was right and wrong, but he had not been much exposed to the nitty-gritty of these things, whereas Thabo Mbeki had really been exposed. Thabo shared those instincts with Mandela, but had far more technical and intellectual training, which enhanced his understanding. I am absolutely convinced that if modern states do not have that core of capable intellectual leadership, they start to stand still; they vacillate, they do not know where to go and then political factionalism becomes paramount. In the absence of a core that is driving the state, it becomes difficult to govern effectively.

An area in which I absolutely and thoroughly enjoyed working with Thabo Mbeki was the global one. He supported me fully when I was chairman of the United Nations Conference on Trade and Development (UNCTAD); he could understand what I was driving. We had a vision; it was not that it was just a nice position in UNCTAD. He said, 'Let us try and do something with this.' Even with the EU-SA (European Union-South Africa) agreement, we knew what we wanted to do. When we got to those WTO negotiations, we knew what we wanted out of them. And South Africa punched well above its weight. Mbeki supported me so strongly in the WTO.

Much could be said about Comrade Thabo Mbeki, but for me there are three areas that make him stand that one small step above the rest of us. He offers great intellectual capabilities and used them fully to be a key architect of the fledgling democracy and nation we proudly call South Africa. Mbeki is, for me, the classic organic intellectual – an intellectual who springs from and then grows within the struggle for national liberation. He is a historian and economist or – the more accurate description – a political economist (a love of poetry lends a heavy dose of humanism to this mix). This makes him an astute reader of the balance of forces – but not just the local balance of forces, as in the tactics of factions, but rather the global balance of forces. Mbeki wisely counselled us young socialist hotheads against a futile attempt to take on the full force of capitalism as it entered its heyday moments of globalisation. He counselled a more cautious approach, which was to build a solid beachhead from which we could engage capital. For the pure ultra-left and the populists, this did not go down well and what Mbeki stood for seemed just to be some sell-out by a '96 Class project' – matters that we now need to assess soberly, particularly as reflection will undoubtedly uncover unintentional error on all sides that is now in need of correction.

The hallmark of revolutionary success is the correct reading of the balance of forces by the revolutionary leadership and not the purity of its theories. Precipitate advance can destroy a movement and failure to seize an opportunity will also weaken a movement. The ilk of ANC leadership that I unabashedly lionise were masters in this area and Mbeki stands at the very forefront of that. I think that Joel Netshitenzhe played a key role that is often left out of the account. Understanding the conjuncture and seizing the moment require the ability to determine the balance of forces and this requires the effort to fully understand and respect the historically determined positions of all the participants in shaping that balance of forces. To stigmatise an opposing force, which is what the ultra-left and their sympathisers did by labelling us as the 'Class of 96' rather than understand us, is to eschew the opportunity to analyse the balance of forces.

About the New Partnership for Africa's Development (NEPAD) programmes and how they began: a few of us accompanied Mbeki to a beautiful centre near Oporto in Portugal and first French President Chirac and then Italian Prime Minister Romano Prodi, with commendable frankness, said effectively: Africa you are on your own since Europe has to watch its eastern fronts. They were right and the popular adage that 'black man (read Africa), you are on your own' took on an immediate sense. Thabo Mbeki, Frank Chikane, Titus Mafole and I were flying back from that meeting. Thabo said, 'So those guys said there is no plan for Africa; we are going to write it.' We started then and spent six hours discussing it. We talked about what it should be and what it should look like. When we got home, we convened some meetings and we got in Wiseman Nkuhlu and others to write papers and we had debates. But that was where NEPAD started: in that aeroplane.

Clearly, in our minds, we had been thinking about Africa for a long time, but when Prodi made that point that there was no economic plan for the African continent, it was Thabo Mbeki who said, 'Fine, we are going to write this plan.' To get the plan through, we had to push our way through into the G7 and get to that summit. It was fortunate in that we could talk to President Bouteflika of Algeria and President Obasanjo of Nigeria, who were both strong leaders. So there were some powerful African leaders at the time whom Thabo Mbeki could persuade to move.

After an internal debate in South Africa and inputs from great Africans from around the continent, a new vision – NEPAD – emerged. It ignited the African Renaissance, and we heard far less about the hopeless continent after that intervention. Being the historian, humanist and scholar he is, Mbeki knew that one had to define what it meant to be African. Can this be defined more lyrically than in 'I am an African'?

On the HIV and AIDS issue, I am prepared to be labelled along with him as a dissident. I supported what he was doing. I did not do as much homework as he did. I tried to do as much as I could, but I was also of the view that there was something logically and epistemologically incorrect with what was being said. So we needed to be critical and ask relevant questions. If you are saying that this is a syndrome, it means that there is a multiplicity of causes. But then you are saying that it is a virus that is causing a syndrome. So one of the explanations must be scientifically at fault. It is either that you thought that it was a syndrome or you are finding that it is a virus. In my own economics studies, I am always fascinated by the history of economic thought and particularly fascinated by a very famous book by

Thomas Kuhn on paradigmatic change. It is also linked to Gramsci and others with the concept of hegemony and structures. For it was a fertile thing when Thabo Mbeki started raising critical questions because it immediately looked to me like a paradigmatic problem. When I studied the history of medicine and how it unfolded, you could immediately see that it is very easy in the history of medicine for paradigms to get things wrong and to change prior assumptions.

The questions he was asking were profoundly correct because he was arguing that if you are saying that it is a syndrome, then we should have many responses to it as a government. So he was asking them to tell him which responses the government needed to take or prioritise. If it was just a virus, then why was it a syndrome, according to others? So it was an attempt to work that out because at the time there were many scientists in Australia, among other places, saying that it was not a virus; it was the effect of various free radicals or other things that are happening, and that it is a modern condition. It is a genuine syndrome in that so many things are impinging on the human organism that they are causing a collapse. So there were many plausible theories. This has implications in terms of what policies to adopt as a government.

The questions raised by Mbeki were absolutely correct policy-wise. Deaths were taking place, but they were not being accurately measured. When we looked at the South African statistics, it was very difficult to find an accurate measure of what the cause of death was because people were not registering it properly. So if that was happening, what was the treatment package that would make sense? Hence Mbeki said that once you say that there is a form of treatment available, such as antiretrovirals, then there ought to be clinical support for that treatment. So where was that clinical support in our health system in South Africa? It was not there; we had not trained anyone to implement it. The question was whether the South African government was going to give away, free of charge, these drugs, which are said to have serious and dangerous side effects. I think that Mbeki asked the perfectly correct questions.

I also sided with Joel Netshitenzhe, who articulated the view that in a sense Thabo Mbeki was unable to suppress his intellectualism. We told him that we knew that those who blindly supported pharmaceutical companies and their interests were talking rubbish, but it did not help us politically or publicly for him to take them on at that point; just put the issue in your back pocket and we will deal with it later as government. I think that the international medical profession and others were being dishonest, and that much of the evidence that is coming out now creates a very complex picture as a result of complex questions that were raised by the likes of Mbeki and others.

In the end, what we agreed upon as a government – and what we never got out enough – was that we put out a perfectly sensible policy, which led to a massive programme. That is to say that it had to be safe but not lethal to those who were affected. So we started slowly rolling out the clinical capacity that was lacking before, bringing in the drugs – and what was also important was that we had that fantastic victory over the pharmaceutical companies and their lobby groups when we lowered the cost of drugs. The cabinet was divided. I think that for those who were taking pain under the media and had not bothered to do much homework, it was seen as a mistake. I think that a lot of the people – my guess is many of them ministers – then started to say that Thabo Mbeki was dictatorial. But when he made his presentation to the cabinet, they did not take him on. The question is, why did they not do that?

My view is that if you are in cabinet and you disagree with policy, then you had better say why. If the majority persuades you that they are right or if you still hold your disagreement, but do not think that it is fundamental to governance, then you go along with the cabinet decision. But if in your view what is being done is fundamentally wrong, then you should not stay in cabinet, which is why some of us resigned when Thabo Mbeki was recalled by the ANC. This is just the way things work in high positions. It is going to be very interesting to see what retrospect looks like in five or ten years from now. But our actions were not irrational; they were not some mindless dissidence; they were not based on a view that AIDS did not exist. None of those things is what Thabo Mbeki said. I agreed with what he was saying intellectually. I think that his greatest achievement, like all great statespersons, was that he was prepared to take on big causes.

Regarding Zimbabwe, I totally agreed with what he was saying and so should every rational thinking person. If you look at the mess that exists in most of those other countries where this purported intervention and regime change was meant to be a solution and move towards democracy, it has been absolutely disastrous in terms governance and human lives. Look at what happened in Afghanistan, Iraq, Libya and now in Syria. I respect Thabo Mbeki for his profound sense of how nations are built and how difficult it is to overcome racial distinctions. One does not mess lightly with those processes.

I admire him greatly for that courage and when Africa looks back one day, it is going to say thank you. Zimbabwe is not Libya, it is not Sudan, it is not Somalia, it is not the Middle East. It has its problems but it is alive, whereas if you look at all those other interventions, they are just massive failures. I do not think that regime change has done very well in Côte d'Ivoire; all that it has done is to create a divided nation. We might have made tactical errors, but at the end of the day, I think that for most of us it was Thabo Mbeki's intellectual honesty that earned him respect. His honesty did not allow him to come out with half-baked stories. He is honest to a fault.

Polokwane was a political disaster. One thing for me personally, having being a trade unionist for 20 years, is that you learn that human beings are fairly volatile and the way you learn that in a union movement is to have a strike; you are a hero and then the next day everyone goes back to work and you are isolated again. I am a bit less surprised by these political movements and I kind of knew that was lurking in the ANC somewhere and that there was a fight and we lost. I think that Thabo Mbeki sees it like this too. These were forces that were coming to a head. We had a crack at fighting it. We started too late because we misjudged the mood in the ANC and we also misjudged the extent of the resources that Zuma had managed to build around him. As soon as you start attacking an individual, you must know that the attackers have no vision; because they have no other ammunition, they start looking for the individual. That was what happened and we were too late to counter it. It was painful, as is any defeat. One prospect that was explored before Polokwane, when it became fairly clear we were not going to win this thing, was whether Thabo Mbeki should stand down, which I think he contemplated, but I for one and a few of us against argued that.

I am cognisant of the annoying danger of overstatement. Thabo Mbeki, like all, is human and not boring enough to be a paragon. But in my view he is a great leader and thinker. It is also my view that in politics one should never follow an individual qua individual but rather the vision and programme that the individual articulates convincingly. If Mbeki was just a good cadre of the struggle, which he is, then what I have said is just a hagiography of little worth. He offers more! There is merit to continuing the debate and work that he has sparked on the African continent because it raises truly substantive issues. This is not to glorify the individual, but to commit to the path of improving our world and especially our Africa.

Understandably, there is always interest in the human behind the public face. I am not in a position to comment a great deal on that since, for me, Mbeki's political philosophy is an integral part of the person I engaged with. He has been accused of many personal vices – aloof, secretive, manipulative and vindictive, among others. These are not the things that come to my mind when I think of my comrade. But any person who becomes a senior leader in a major organisation is going to appear to some as exhibiting one or more of these vices. Frankly, if they did not, then it is unlikely they had the strength, dispassion and determination to be a true leader.

The private person I interacted with enjoyed sport (we nearly got him to play golf), tutored me at various times on photography, how to tie my ties and always corrected my English spelling and grammar (a good lesson in humility for a white man!). I enjoyed our time together as it was both light and cerebral – a comradeship. I share with him a deep belief that no matter what other spiritual belief a person may have, there still remains the human responsibility to ensure that justice is done for all and all the time.

Africa, my Africa! I love these three words emotively – aroused some-where in the mists of youth – but it was Mbeki who allowed me to provide an intellectual base for this feeling. This is the second of the areas I refer to above. Africa is a complex concept, no matter how self-evident that may sound. What is the meaning of 'Africanist'? It can all too easily collapse into a facile nationalism, atavism, romanticism and even racism at its crudest. However, it is a historical fact; it has meaning on many fronts. So what is the essence of this meaning?

For me, Mbeki is a key representative of that cadre of African leaders who understood that the African condition would only change through the praxis of its leadership – the combination of the intellect and scholarship with political and social mobilisation. Historical fracture lines had to be grappled with. What is important about Mbeki in particular is his understanding that African political struggles – South Africa at the forefront – concentrated so many fundamental human tensions within themselves that they are crucibles for defining our approach to key issues of humanity. Mbeki was central in the equally important first democratic administration in South Africa, where these complex issues had to be dealt with as a concrete process of governance and reform. New political, social and even pyscho-sociological approaches had to be thought through. Of all our leaders, Mbeki not only understood these complex tensions best, but was also able to articulate these vexing propositions with a lyrical quality that could inspire a wider African renaissance.

Mbeki – along with Nkrumah, Nyerere, Mandela, Sisulu, Cabral, Fanon, among others – represents that calibre of African leadership who were able to avoid the three false paths to liberation that are all too often spawned by repression. These are a preoccupation with the status of being a victim or a desire to escape oppression by emulating the oppressor or a longing for a utopian African past. They understood that liberating Africa from its chains of colonialism and underdevelopment had to be done by Africans and that a liberated Africa would resemble neither its past nor the present of the former oppressors. Africa's liberation from the shackles of its recent history would once again make its own contribution to human civilisation as it had done powerfully in the past – it is in this sense that their political approach is profoundly Africanist.

So for me it is this positive, creative approach to Africa and its present position that Mbeki represents – maybe this will be his greatest contribution. He continues to point out the rank hypocrisy of the West's approach to Africa carried out under the cynical guise of promoting democracy. He continues to bemoan the weakness of African leaders who put short termism, and often personal gain above what is needed for a forward march in Africa's history. But there is another area – a subtle elusive area – that attracts me to his thought and again evokes the sense of comradeship. It is some form of ecological – in the sense of being across many disciplines – approach to politics and philosophy. Other South African leaders have grappled with it – Jan Smuts among them. It is a difficult path as it can collapse into its own immensity or retreat into the mystical. South Africa does lend itself to this, as it is such an amazing landmass, with antiquity and biodiversity in one place and time. Our land is a cornucopia of scientific possibility – inorganic, organic and human origins abound. We are an exploration into the meaning of existence – in both a fundamental sense and a socio-economic one. This is so exciting, and having some private hours on a plane to explore, dream and plan concrete use of this cornucopia are moments I will cherish forever.

However, pleasant moments for an old activist are not my point. This ability to integrate into our governance the exciting new understanding of human scientific endeavour is essential if humanity is to have a future. Mbeki is on this trajectory. If he were there alone, aloof and comfortable in an isolated ivory tower, then I for one would not hold him in high regard. He is not! He is capable of education, inspiration and discourse to learn more. Basically, he is a good communicator able to construct strategic political programmes. He is a universalist in order to be a better Africanist.

Comradeship and praxis make for good revolutionary leadership cadres. I am fortunate to have worked with Comrade Thabo Mbeki and his ilk. Africa, my Africa!

Interviewed July 2014, Cape Town

GERALDINE J. FRASER-MOLEKETI

❧❦❧

I left the country in 1980 and joined the African National Congress (ANC) in Zimbabwe, where I worked with Comrade Joe Gqabi, who was a member of the National Executive Committee (NEC) of the ANC. Comrade Joe served as the first chief representative to Zimbabwe and was involved in building relations with the Zimbabwe African National Union (ZANU) and the leadership of Zimbabwe. Historically, the ANC had strong links with the Zimbabwe African People's Union (ZAPU) and the Zimbabwe People's Revolutionary Army (ZIPRA), while the Pan Africanist Congress (PAC) was in alliance with ZANU. With Zimbabwean Independence in 1980, cadres of Umkhonto we Sizwe (MK) were infiltrated into Matabeleland with the ZIPRA comrades as they went into assembly points. Also, the newly formed MK cadres came through Southern Rhodesia, and in instances fought alongside ZAPU at Wankie and Sipolilo in 1967/68, en route to South Africa.

Thabo Mbeki worked closely with Joe Gqabi in building relations with the newly formed government of Zimbabwe and with the ruling party. They succeeded in building a strong relationship with the leadership of government, the two parties and the people of Zimbabwe. As stated earlier, historically, there was a sound relationship with ZAPU, who formed part of the original core of seven liberation movements.

My first encounter with Thabo Mbeki was in Harare in 1980. I reflect back now and ask whether I was most impressed by his humility or his tolerance and understanding of the youth who, in some ways, he almost humoured. On the particular day in question, I had been sent out on some errands and on my return to the office I found Govan Reddy there, who enquired whether Thabo Mbeki was coming to the office. I simply said that I did not know. Earlier that morning before I left the office I was introduced to a ZAPU comrade. So when I returned to the office and saw a person who was of a similar build reading newspapers I did not pay too much attention as I assumed it was the same person. I did not make a connection to the query by Govan Reddy and so I did not realise that this was in fact 'the' Thabo Mbeki reading the newspaper across the room from me.

Later that day when we left to go home, the three of us (the yet unnamed comrade, Comrade Joe and I) walked to the white Toyota Cressida that we would be driving. There were curtains on the back seat of the car as we were setting up the Ashdown Park house that the ANC had just acquired. I was quite clear that, since Comrade Joe was driving, I would sit in the passenger's seat and our guest would be on the back seat – with or on top of the curtains – because it should not be assumed that women should be in the uncomfortable space. As a militant 20-year-old at that time, I thought this was an important point as he might well be a chauvinist male and so I let him sit in the back seat while I got into the front seat.

Comrade Joe Gqabi looked at me askance and realised that I did not know our guest. He said as we were driving, 'Geraldine, I have not introduced you.' The guest replied, 'Ah no, Chief, she probably thinks it's just an old man with a pipe.' And he did have his signature pipe with him. Comrade Joe continued, 'Geraldine, this is Thabo Mbeki.' I nearly collapsed in the front seat. Here was a member of the leadership, Thabo Mbeki, sitting in the back seat on the curtains and I was sitting, until then quite comfortably, in front. The 'guest' behind me was the much talked about African intellectual, the voice heard on occasion on Radio Freedom, not to mention the son of one of our revered leaders, Govan Mbeki.

Our first stop was at an underground flat in Central Avenue in Harare. Comrade Joe wanted to either collect or drop something off. I turned around, thoroughly embarrassed, and asked, 'Do you want to sit in the front seat?' He responded, 'No, Chief, it is fine. I am quite comfortable at the back.'

So, in my first meeting with Thabo Mbeki, I made him sit on curtains instead of engaging with this ANC leader on the national, regional and global political situation. But Thabo Mbeki was clearly not concerned about where he was sitting. In an interesting way this reflects his reference to comrades as 'Chief'. Just as in the incident of the 'Chief' sitting on the curtains in the back seat of a car, he also was ready to build confidences and relationships where there was a lack of trust; this is an enduring trait. This also came through in what was referred to as 'quiet diplomacy' as President Oliver Tambo (O.R.) entrusted him to build the relationship of the movement with Zimbabwe and with the leaders of ZANU at the time. This was particularly sensitive and required great trust and confidence from all parties as the outcome involved the movement of cadres/personnel and arms through Zimbabwe, and the support of ANC cadres or operatives.

There are many views about Thabo and 'quiet diplomacy'. First of all, diplomacy by its very nature is silent and about building trust. Back then, he was the silent political diplomat whose mission was to build resilient relations between the ANC and ZANU and the government of Zimbabwe.

Thabo Mbeki is known not to suffer fools gladly but he had the patience and perseverance to build strategic relationships that were important for the movement.

Comrade Joe Gqabi was assassinated in Zimbabwe on 31 July 1981[1] as he was reversing the white Cressida out of the driveway of the Ashdown Park residence of the ANC in Harare. I was later detained and interrogated by the security police, who attempted to frame me for his murder under the pretext of obtaining information about the structures of the ANC in Zimbabwe and Botswana. The white Zimbabwean security police, McCullum and Gevisser, who carried out my arrest (at the ANC office in Angwa Street, Harare), told me during interrogation that the ANC claimed that it did not really know me. I replied: 'If you say that the ANC says that it does not know me, let the ANC say that. It is not for me to hear it from you.' They asked, 'But don't you think that it is strange that you were arrested in the ANC offices?' They tried to sow doubt, which was not an unusual tactic.

Unbeknown to me at the time, the ANC was involved in discussions

---

1 Joe Gqabi served ten years on Robben Island in the 1960s; was the 'chief defendant' in the Pretoria Twelve trial (1977); was assassinated on 31 July 1981 in Ashdown Park, Harare, by members of an apartheid 'death squad' (three assassins, including Gray Branfield – later a security contractor in Iraq where he was killed in April 2004). Julian Rademeyer, *Sunday Times* 18/04/2004.

with the government of Zimbabwe to secure my release from custody. This culminated in the movement sending a high-level delegation from Lusaka to Harare that consisted of the secretary general, Comrade Alfred Nzo, Comrade John Motsabi, a member of the Revolutionary Military Council (RMC), and Comrade Thabo Mbeki, who had been working closely with the Zimbabwean government. The delegation met with me prior to my release and before their departure back to Lusaka. While meeting me, they regaled us with various stories, much to the irritation of the Zimbabwean officers. When the officers asked whether they did not want to ask me any questions in their presence, they responded by saying, 'We will ask her all we want once she is released and back among us.' So that put paid to their threat that 'the ANC does not know you'. And 'the Thabo Mbeki I know', who sat on curtains on the back seat of the white Cressida, was part of the delegation to secure my release from police custody in Zimbabwe in September 1981.

Fast-forward to the 7th congress of the South African Communist Party (SACP) held in Cuba in 1989. That was the last illegal congress of the SACP. I was part of the delegation that came from Zimbabwe. The big debate was around the adoption of the 'Path to Power', the programme of the SACP. Of particular focus were the sections on the 'Seizure of Power' and the 'Prospects for a Negotiated Transfer of Power'. The mood of many of the cadres present and the particular militancy from those of us in the Frontline States, from the Camps and from within the country veered to quite a radical stance on insurrection as a key to the seizure of power. This was reflected, to an extent, in the debates in the lead-up to the 7th congress and during the congress. Of course it was captured in the songs and the mood at the time. It was at this congress that we collectively witnessed the brilliance of Thabo Mbeki as a negotiator and debater. His intellect and ideological depth were reflected in the way in which he chaired sessions of the Party Programme, 'Path to Power', and argued the issues at hand. He skilfully steered the debate and discussion, resulting in the inclusion under the section 'Prospects of a Negotiated Transfer of Power' of the assertion that *'Armed struggle cannot be counter posed with dialogue, negotiation and justifiable compromise, as if they were mutually exclusive categories. Liberation struggles have rarely ended with the unconditional surrender of the enemy's military forces ...'*

Then we entered government and we had to know our stuff as we were, after all, 'pioneers' of the budding democracy: the deputy president and later president had most likely read all the documentation and possibly reflected on the implications of decisions and beyond. We learned that we had a responsibility to familiarise ourselves with the subject matter and its implications. We had to be well prepared for cabinet meetings and not take anything for granted, because at the end of the day we knew that we were going to be with someone who had probably read more than us on the subject.

But there is another side to 'Chief': the very creative side that gave incredible meaning and depth to the country's coat of arms. He spoke very passionately about shaping the national coat of arms around our own history and 'our own Latin', the Khoi language. During this period, when he was quite immersed in the design and development of the coat of arms, I approached his office during the tea break in one of the cabinet meetings. I asked his personal assistant Mpho Ngozi for a few minutes to talk with the president on a public service matter. He was with Sydney Mufamadi at the time. On Mpho advising him that I wanted to meet with him briefly, his response was, 'I am trying to discuss creative matters such as a new coat of arms ...' and I retorted, 'And I must bring matters as mundane as the public service to your attention, Mr President.'

Well, without a doubt the final coat of arms did indeed capture creativity and brought to life our own extinct language and heritage.

With regard to the public service in South Africa, we had covered a lot of ground in our attempt to professionalise and modernise this area. But what it tends to be remembered for were the public service strikes even though the portfolio was much broader and, even with respect to public service labour relations, we had managed to achieve three-year multi-term wage agreements.

The 2007 round of wage negotiations was particularly difficult and it is quite clear that it was driven by a broader political agenda. The then secretary general of the ANC, Kgalema Motlanthe, was present with me in the informal meetings that were held with the general secretaries of the Congress of South African Trade Unions (COSATU) affiliated public service unions. The informal meetings were at first to try to avert the strike and later to end the strike. These marathon meetings went on through the night, and were out of the public eye, to try to reach agreement in principle while the more detailed discussions and technical agreement would be dealt with in the Public Sector Collective Bargaining Chamber (PSCBC).

We witnessed a protracted public service strike during this period that also affected essential service workers in spite of the collective bargaining agreement that excluded essential service workers from strike action. During one of the all-night discussions, I felt that we were not making any progress and that my union comrades were just dragging out discussions with no intention of resolving matters, even on those issues that we may have agreed upon. At one point, out of sheer exasperation, I made a call to the president and advised him that I thought that the discussions were quite frankly a waste of time as the union comrades were really negotiating in bad faith. I also stated that it would be prudent to end all discussions. The president asked me one question: 'Is the secretary general still in the meeting?' I responded in the affirmative. He then said, 'You should stay as well. I am confident that you will resolve the matters at hand. I am available if and when you need to confer on any of the matters at hand.' That put paid to my attempt to prematurely conclude the informal discussions. As an aside, I do believe that there is still a story to be told and written on the 2007 strike that will expose more details. In this particular instance, I would like to make two points: 'The Thabo Mbeki I know' had confidence that we would accomplish the task before us even when I thought we had exhausted all avenues. Secondly, he would be available if there was a need to draw on his advice or support at any time of the day or night. Well, looking back, one can say the 2007 strike did not bring government to its knees as may have been intended, but it did not come without a price.

I worked with different leaders: Joe Slovo, Chris Hani, Madiba and former President Thabo Mbeki. I will not draw a comparison of these leaders but will again make some anecdotal references. I know Mbeki can appear distant and even remote but that does not make him a dictator.

Mbeki may cast his gaze down or write down comments during discussions or debates in cabinet meetings to allow the discussion to go on up to a reasonable point, even if he may have a view at the time. And, mind you, it would have been a strong view that would have been informed by, in instances, his own in-depth research. We would know that he would question us on issues that we were presenting; he would require clarity and brevity in most cases and would not accommodate rambling. Again, this does not translate into dictatorship. He wanted rigour, preparation and readiness to defend your work. This does not mean that we did not have mediocrity among ourselves and, yes, he could be impatient and maybe a little intolerant, but that goes with leadership and I don't know an outstanding leader that did not have these characteristics. Some may just be able to hide them better than others.

This brings me to his leadership on the AIDS issue. This is clearly a complex and difficult subject and I will deal with it in passing. We clearly made mistakes in how we handled it and we came up against strong vested interests. There is a movie called *The Constant Gardener*, based on the novel by John Le Carré, about the dealings of the pharmaceutical industry and the power of vested interests. I think there are still lessons around how we communicated this matter and who communicated the messages. It should however be recognised that it was under Mbeki's watch that the largest antiretroviral programme in the world, at the time, was rolled out in South Africa.

It should also be acknowledged that, precisely because of the controversy around this issue, there was a debate within the ANC structures on AIDS and the roll-out of Nevirapine. So, in a controversial manner, it may have led to greater debate and awareness among the general population about the reality of HIV and AIDS. However, the last word has not been said.

To be quite honest, I think that those of us who were in government were too focused on government and we did not pay sufficient attention to the party structures. Interestingly, it was actually Thabo Mbeki who started the practice of spending one day a week at Luthuli House. The imbizos and 'Government Meets the People' initiatives were introduced under President Nelson Mandela and institutionalised by President Mbeki. So there should not have been a disconnect between government and the people in light of the targeted community outreach programmes in addition to policy changes, government programmes, the focus on the economy, to mention just some issues. On the other hand, there may be a view that we were, and are, confronting the challenges of a liberation movement that has yet to morph or transform into a governing party. Also, the prioritisation of government responsibilities were such that we did not spend enough time on building and strengthening the structures of the ANC to the extent required. We worked on the assumption that the party machinery and the secretary general, as the engine of the movement, would handle the responsibility of party building.

Now we are told, and they say it themselves, President Zuma and President Mbeki had come a long way together within the movement and worked together during some of the initial negotiations with the apartheid government. They were appointed as the ANC negotiators before the NEC of 1990 changed the decision, a story related by both of them. There is unfinished business that they should resolve and we probably failed as the NEC at the time to insist that they do so.

So, the 2007 ANC conference in Polokwane and what it represented was very difficult for me, after having been a member of the ANC for 27 years. It was an absolute shock to be at an ANC conference where the gesture of replacing a player used in a soccer match was shown as an indication to replace the leadership. Going to Polokwane, one still had a hope and a view that there would be an opportunity for policy debate. That was never done, because I do not think that there was either the appetite or the inclination to do so. There were discussions, but the big focus was on elections. I think that this is where the idea of a political slate of names was consolidated. By the second day, it was clear that there was a change in the political culture of the ANC as we knew it. We were astounded by the conduct, the way in which people engaged, the fact that at a point it was President Mbeki who stopped the debate on the secretary general's report because he thought that it would be too divisive. He also stopped the debate contesting the credentials because he viewed this as adding further to the polarisation of the conference. It was very, very difficult. I can almost say that it was quite traumatic, because we saw delegates to the conference of the ANC engaging in a way that could be described as quite alien to what we understood the traditions of the ANC to be. Now the seeds of ill-discipline planted in Polokwane have ravaged the ANC and have become the order of the day. On the other hand, we all know that democracy guarantees discontinuity and change. We probably need to change but we hope such change will bring and spawn greater depth within the movement. Having said that, it is recognised that the conference would be the arena for robust leadership contestation.

Thabo Mbeki is recognised for his work on the continent, as a leader and an intellectual. He has also contributed to us, as a country, recognising that our destiny is intertwined with that of the African continent.

A final but brief anecdote: while working as director of the Global Democratic Governance Practice of the United Nations Development Programme in 2013, I learned that President Thabo Mbeki was in New York. A young Cameroonian, Junior Professional Njoya Tikum, who worked with me at the time, was very keen to meet him. Through Mukoni Ratshitanga, who was with the 'Chief' at the time, we arranged to meet at the Waldorf Astoria. We spent several hours discussing African politics and so forth. At the end of the evening, Njoya requested a photograph and the 'Chief' obliged. Njoya posted his picture on his Facebook page. He relates that he was inundated with messages, requests and queries about how he was able to have an opportunity for this picture. He went on to say that he has even had invitations to events where the organisers may have wished to have Thabo Mbeki but, as a result of this photograph, he was invited. So, yet again, decades later Thabo Mbeki continues to avail himself to the youth, not only in Africa, but beyond.

It has been an honour for me to work with Thabo Mbeki – the same leader who sat on curtains on the back seat of the white Cressida in Harare back in 1980.

Interviewed May 2014, Johannesburg

FRANK CHIKANE

❧

I had the opportunity of working with Thabo Mbeki in government for a continuous stretch of more than 13 years between 1995 and 2008. I came in first as his special adviser when he was the deputy president of the country during President Nelson Mandela's presidency.

I must say that I was dragged in there 'kicking and screaming' as I did not want to be a civil servant, given the limitations that it puts on one's political engagement. As a civil servant, one can only talk about government and its policies, but cannot engage publicly on political issues that might venture into a critique of political parties or the government itself. Activist theologians in the Church would say that it will constrain your 'prophetic witness', that is, one's calling to speak on issues of justice irrespective of who is affected. But Mandela and Mbeki prevailed on me. Faced with this formidable duo, I really had no chance!

Within a year or so I was appointed director general in the office of the deputy president. And later during this term of government I was appointed deputy secretary of cabinet as part of the transitional management processes from Mandela's presidency to that of Mbeki. I must say that this was the best-managed transitional process from one presidency to another in our new democracy. It was consciously designed and developed in consultation with the key principals, Mbeki and Mandela, together with Professor Jakes Gerwel (the head of Mandela's office at the time) to ensure that the transition was seamless – and it was indeed seamless.

After the second democratic elections in June 1999, I was appointed as the director general for the presidency, which was now joined into one presidency, including the office of the deputy president. I was also made secretary of the cabinet. When the National Security Council (NSC) was established in the early 2000s, I took responsibility for the executive level of the council and chaired its security officials committee.

It was during this period in government when I really had an intense interaction with Mbeki – day and night, on both strategic and operational issues relating to the governance of the country, the renewal project of the African continent and the geopolitics of the world, and how this affected developing countries globally. I say 'day and night' as there was no 'day' or 'night' with Mbeki. One had to be on call 24 hours daily, as at times he worked around the clock. Some even said that he seemed to be more productive during the night than otherwise. The 'I am an African' speech, for instance, was the product of one such night!

Anyone who has had an opportunity of working with Mbeki, or interacting with him in whatever circumstances, will agree that he had a history that gave him vast experience and knowledge that many of his peers could not match, let alone those of us who came later in the game. His intellectual prowess was evident to all who worked with him. Even those who differed with him or even hated him cannot deny his extraordinary intellect and capacity to deal with complex issues that affected the country, the continent and the world.

Whenever the gap between me and Mbeki showed up during our work in terms of his wealth of knowledge and experience, I always reminded him that he had an advantage over me as he had been on planet earth about nine years or so before I was born. He also had the privilege of working with O.R. Tambo for many years, which privilege I did not have. And he had more experience on the international front than anyone I knew.

I tried to stretch myself to catch up with him or even overtake him by using the 'information highway' and all available modern technology, but I found him there already – surfing the Web and doing his own research, which was of such quality that even experts in whichever area of research he delved into felt highly challenged.

Because of this age difference, I had no possibility of meeting him when he transferred from the Eastern Cape to Johannesburg in the early

1960s to further his studies. When I was busy with my Standard 1 (Grade 3) and 2 (Grade 4), he was busy with his A levels, preparing himself for further study in the United Kingdom. While I was struggling to understand the strange military vehicles in the streets of Soweto following the declaration of the state of emergency in the early 1960s, he was organising youth and students around what was then called the PWV area (Pretoria-Witwatersrand-Vereeniging).

After he left the country in 1962 there was no possibility of our meeting for a period of more than 20 years, as one was barred from travelling from the latter part of the 1970s. The banning of the African National Congress (ANC) did not make it easier either.

As pressure piled up on the apartheid system, the apartheid government decided to withdraw banning orders and returned travel documents to those from whom they had been withdrawn to allow them to travel. That was towards the end of 1984.

With a passport in hand, we took the gap and accepted the invitation of the Swedish Labour Party to visit Sweden and attend the Labour Party conference as leaders of the United Democratic Front (UDF). It was at this point that one had an opportunity to meet Thabo Mbeki personally in London on our way to Sweden.

The arrangements for the meeting were unsurprisingly dramatic. It was 'cloak-and-daggers' stuff as we were not supposed to be known to have met Thabo Mbeki. I was moved from London Heathrow to the city centre where I was taken from one place to another – through basements of buildings where we changed cars – to ensure that we were not followed or tracked down to the venue. We then arrived at a house where we found Thabo Mbeki. He was typically relaxed and waiting for us. He was not different from the 'vintage Mbeki' some had described him to be or who was referred to as such in the media.

Though relaxed, the meeting became like a military-style 'debriefing, briefing and reporting' session. As we went through this process it became clear to me that they used any contact with people from home in South Africa to gather information about the developments in the country to inform their strategies and tactics. The scope was broad, given my involvement with the churches, the non-governmental organisations and communities over and above my role as the vice-president of the UDF. I also used the opportunity to understand the strategic operational approaches of the ANC then, given some of the challenges we were facing in the country as part of the liberation struggle.

Two months or so after our return, the whole leadership of the UDF was detained and charged with high treason. Some of us who were detained earlier ended up in the so-called Pietermaritzburg trial, and those who were missed in the first national security swoop ended up in the Delmas trial. Of the 16 leaders who were in the Pietermaritzburg Treason Trial, 12 of us were accused of being part of the 'ANC underground'. For the Pietermaritzburg trialists, the case took a year of their lives, but our extraordinary legal team made sure that the case collapsed. Six months after our release, a state of emergency was declared and many of us went underground.

Ironically it was during this period that I had an opportunity to spend more time with Mbeki as I left the country 'underground' and spent about six months outside the country, much of the time in Europe. The initial reason for leaving the country was to get an opportunity to write my final theology examinations with the University of South Africa (UNISA) outside the country to avoid being arrested if I did so in the country. But this was not to be, as UNISA insisted that I write the exam at the South African Embassy in the UK, which would have been a way of handing myself over to the apartheid regime.

I used the time outside the country to campaign against the apartheid regime in Europe and elsewhere in the world, using London as my base. As one would have expected, the *Weekly Mail* (a forerunner of the *Mail & Guardian*) picked up that I was in London and many thought I had gone into exile. It was during this time that I had more contact with Mbeki – that is, the last part of 1986 and the earlier part of 1987. At the beginning of 1987 I had a meeting with Mbeki to discuss the question of whether or not I should remain in exile or return home.

Earlier our church partners, who were concerned about the risks for me and my family if I returned home, made arrangements for my family to join me in Europe to discuss this matter. The expectations were that the family would be persuaded to remain with me in exile rather than return home.

My wife Kagiso knew how strongly I felt about returning home to continue with the struggle and my ministry to the people of South Africa, even if this had to be done from underground. In this regard, she felt that this decision should be left to me. Her standard approach on matters like these throughout our history was that she did not want to have a husband who felt he was not able to fulfil his mission (God's mission) because of her views and feelings, however difficult and challenging the circumstances were.

My discussions with Mbeki (as the most senior leader of the ANC I met) on this matter were high level, strategic and very intense. This included an analysis of the state of the country; the state of the struggle for liberation; what needed to be done; and the cadres necessary to advance this struggle. In strategic terms it became clear that my role back at home was more critical compared with remaining in exile. Based on these considerations, a decision was made that I return home rather than remain in exile.

It is important to state that the view at that stage was that the liberation movement needed more people to work inside the country rather than outside the country. In any case, I had left South Africa not because I was no longer useful there, but because we thought that I was going to write an exam in London. I had to return, notwithstanding the risks involved.

It will interest historians that the letter I wrote 'To All Those Who Care' in March 1987 and published in my autobiography, *No Life of My Own*, to explain this difficult decision does not refer to Mbeki or the ANC at all, as this was part of underground operations and could not be talked about then. A reference to that meeting would have been the best evidence to send one to jail for high treason.

I returned home underground in March 1987 and two months later I was appointed general secretary of the South African Council of Churches (SACC), which appointment made it possible for me to emerge from underground. This enabled me to interact with the ANC in a more formal and open way. Interestingly, there wasn't much interaction with Mbeki at a personal level during this time as we met more at formal events than operational. As the general secretary of the SACC I interacted more directly with the president of the ANC, O.R. Tambo, than his officials or colleagues.

On their return from exile, Mbeki arranged to pay me a courtesy call at home with other leaders of the ANC. From there on, I interacted with him as part of the leadership of the ANC, this time through and together with Nelson Mandela, who was now president.

Based on this historical account it is clear that the most intense interaction I had with Mbeki was when I was deployed in government. Accordingly, my reflection on 'The Thabo Mbeki I Know' will be based mainly on my work with him in government for a period of just more than 13 years.

The challenge I have about my contribution to this book about 'The Thabo Mbeki I Know' is that I have already written extensively about my experiences with him in my last two publications, namely, *Eight Days in September: The Removal of Thabo Mbeki* and *The Things that Could Not be Said: From A{ids} to Z{imbabwe}*, published in 2012 and 2013 respectively.

Although I tried to make the point that *Eight Days in September* was not a book about Mbeki but about my 'experiences in government' and that one of these experiences was the 'removal of Mbeki from office', many people view the book as being about Mbeki. The chapter that came closest to betraying the statement that this book was not about Mbeki was the last chapter, entitled 'Mbeki: The Person and His Legacy'. As I concluded writing, it became clear that the book would not be complete without such a chapter.

The chapter deals with my interactions with Mbeki as in this chapter, in particular I discuss how I came to know him and ended up working with him. The conclusion I made in that chapter, which sums up my understanding of him after working with him for more than 13 years, is that 'his perspectives on the world hinged on the issue of the right of Africans to determine their own destiny in a way they saw fit'. I further indicated that this perspective of Mbeki is demonstrated in the manner in which he handled conflict resolution processes in Lesotho, Democratic Republic of Congo (DRC), Burundi, Zimbabwe, Côte d'Ivoire, Sudan, and so forth, and his handling of the matter of drugs and HIV and AIDS.

The most controversial of these matters, where he was heavily criticised, were on Zimbabwe and HIV and AIDS. I do not intend to repeat the treatment of these matters here as they are extensively dealt with in the two books referred to above, and a summary of these matters will not do justice to the complexity of the issues involved. In this regard I would rather leave them as they are in those publications.

On his commitment to defend the right of Africans to determine their own destiny, Mbeki resisted external interference or dictates by former colonial powers and dominant countries in the areas where we had to deal with conflict resolution on the continent, all of which had colonial undertones. The vision of the African Renaissance was the best expression of his beliefs and commitment in this regard.

Furthermore, he was committed to defending the right of Africans to be treated equally, like all other human beings. This becomes clearer in his handling of the matter of the use of drugs such as Nevirapine and AZT (Azidothymidine). He challenged the approach of lowering the permissible 'risk and benefit ratio' in poorer countries as compared to rich countries. This put the lives of poorer people at higher levels of risk than rich people. In this logic, which even the World Health Organisation used, poverty becomes a determinant for the levels of risk that are permissible when dealing with treatment drugs. This was totally unacceptable to Mbeki.

Another aspect of this equality principle was in the way in which some of the Western powers selectively dealt with the matter of human rights to advance their narrow national interests. This is also seen in the manner in which they use the United Nations (UN) Security Council to advance their sectarian interests rather than the interests of the international community which the UN was created for. The same can be said about the International Criminal Court (ICC) where those who make decisions about referral of cases are not themselves signatories to the Rome Statutes, and thus remain outside the jurisdiction of the ICC. This is like having laws in the country for the poor and powerless that do not apply to the rich and powerful. This to Mbeki was like an apartheid system at a global level, and I deal with it extensively in *The Things That Could Not Be Said*.

Because of Mbeki's positions on the 'principles of equality', which he pursued with 'uncompromising zeal', he was identified as 'a hindrance to the interests of dominant countries in the global governance system', which is based on 'the relics of the colonial traditions and practices'. At one stage we even feared for his life, given the levels of irritation expressed by some of the Western powers. Some even felt that what befell Kwame Nkrumah could be the fate of Mbeki.

Interestingly, all the positions Mbeki held are within the policy framework, culture, and commitments of the ANC, which Mbeki simply pursued to their logical conclusions. One can say that there was nothing personal about it. He was just being a faithful cadre of the Movement or a well-schooled 'child' of the ANC.

As indicated in *Eight Days in September*, before I accepted the appointment to work with Mbeki I consulted comrades (who were mainly from exile) I felt would know him better. Besides the 'positive picture' they painted, especially his 'intellectual prowess', it is his 'knowledge and experience regarding the ANC' that one could not miss during the time I worked with him and beyond. One can boldly say that from beginning to the end, with all his strengths and weaknesses, he is a classic 'child of the ANC' – a classical cadre of the Movement!

He was born into a family of ANC diehards and staunch members of the Communist Party, and formally joined the ANC Youth League at the age of about 13. He moved to Johannesburg as an ANC cadre, and ended in exile where he spend 30 years as an ANC activist and leader, working with O.R. Tambo for many years. He often gives credit to O.R. Tambo for his speechwriting skills and capacity. If there is anyone who learned at the feet of O.R. Tambo it is Thabo Mbeki. One can in fact say that he is a product or disciple of O.R. Tambo.

Mbeki even imbibed some of O.R. Tambo's mannerisms, to the extent that when I suggested we change the length of the presidential political address at the national conference of the ANC, he said, 'No.' And the reason – 'that is how O.R. Tambo did it'. When I suggested that we have a workshop for his speechwriters and potential speechwriters to learn from him so that they could come up with the standards he expected, he said, 'No.' And why? 'No, O.R. did not do that with me.'

O.R. Tambo is one leader of the ANC who served at the apex of the organisation the longest during the most difficult time in the life of the ANC. He became secretary general in 1955 when Walter Sisulu was banned; deputy president in 1958; acting president in 1967; and then president in 1969. The character of the ANC we know today and the advanced policies we have were developed during his time. In fact one can say that the advanced revolutionary positions of the ANC were developed during O.R. Tambo's time and presidency. It is an ANC that is not about greed and material interests, but the interests of the masses of the people, particularly the poor. It is an ANC that was emptied of 'self' and filled with 'the people's interests'.

To appreciate this unique character of the ANC one just has to look at 'The Eye of the Needle' and the 'Ready to Govern' documents. 'The Eye of the Needle' deals with the quality of leaders and cadres the Movement needed in order to carry out the revolutionary task of the organisation, that is, the national democratic revolution (NDR). The other, that is, 'Ready to Govern', deals with the Movement's preparations for the takeover of government by democratic forces.

The vision of the African Renaissance and its programmes (NEPAD, APRM, etc.), which many think was just a fascination of Mbeki's, derived not only from the policy positions proposed for the new democratic government, but from the very DNA of the ANC – a party launched precisely to end tribal and ethnic divisions; a party whose name was changed from the South African Native National Congress (SANNC) to the African National Congress to emphasise the Africa dimension of it; a party that adopted an anthem, 'Nkosi Sikelel' iAfrika' rather than just 'Nkosi Sikelel' iSouth Afrika'. Even when he was invited to speak about South Africa, he would find a way to speak about Africa and its renewal.

For Mbeki, our national interest was the interest of the African continent as the ANC had conceptualised it. Our foreign policy perspective was based on the renewal of the African continent. With Mbeki, we mobilised the leadership of the African continent to make the renewal of the continent the major focus of the Organisation of African Unity (OAU), which became the African Union (AU). With Mbeki, we broke into the courts of the G8 club to make sure that they made no decisions about Africa without Africans, particularly about developmental matters. The Africa Partnership Forum (APF) was created to achieve this objective.

What is not talked about is the management of the transformation of the country from an apartheid system to a non-racial, non-sexist, just and equitable democratic country. From the outset, Mandela planned to delegate the day-to-day running of government to Mbeki. For the public, he took them into his confidence only towards the end of his term of office. But for me it was as clear as daylight from the first day of my service in the presidency. Mandela told me the day I reported at the Union Buildings that he wanted me not in his office but in Mbeki's office to create capacity there as he wanted to delegate his responsibilities to him. That was in 1995, about 18 months into his presidency.

While Mandela focused on matters of national reconciliation and healing, nation building and stabilisation of the country in terms of peace and security, Mbeki took responsibility for the nuts and bolts of the business of government and the transformation of the state. Mbeki also chaired most cabinet meetings on behalf of Mandela, especially towards the end of Mandela's term of office. These roles were not mutually exclusive as they worked as a team.

Here, one needed a strategic and pragmatic leadership that was able to steer the ship through stormy waters and sharks that were ready to cause us to be stillborn, consumed, destroyed, or to stop us advancing into the future. Mbeki was just such a pragmatic and strategic cadre of the Movement with the economic knowledge that was critical for his assignment.

He selected his advisers in a manner that would assist him in carrying out his responsibilities. Among these were Essop Pahad, who started as his parliamentary adviser and ended up being a deputy minister and later a minister. The second was Advocate Mojanku Gumbi who, interestingly, was not a member of the ruling party. Her presence helped us to keep an objective view about matters we were dealing with. His first speechwriter was Thami Ntenteni. His political advisers who also became speechwriters were Vusi Mavimbela followed by Titus Mafolo. His economic advisers, who dealt with the complex economic issues, were Moss Ngoasheng, followed by Professor Wiseman Nkuhlu. The team was later joined by Joel Netshitenzhe as head of the policy unit. I mention them because whatever I did with Mbeki, I was as part of a team of formidable advisers who ensured that we served Mbeki, the government, the country, Africa and the world with distinction.

The first task in government was to restructure and transform the apartheid state, including in particular the public service and the security services (the defence force, intelligence services and the police). This was more than the transformation of government. The second was the restructuring and transformation of the apartheid economy – a sophisticated economy designed to serve the white minority where the black majority were reduced to workers serving the interests of the white minority. The Reconstruction and Development Programme (RDP) served as the socio-economic policy framework for this reconstruction and development project.

Where one saw Mbeki at his best was in the area of managing the economy, which he did together with an ANC team, including Trevor Manuel, Alec Erwin, Tito Mboweni, and Maria Ramos, among many others. They were later joined by Moss Ngoasheng as the economic adviser to Mbeki. Interestingly, the first task that imposed itself on them was to defend the sovereignty of South Africa in terms of its economy against the advances of the International Monetary Fund (IMF) and the World Bank. They decided to use the skills and capacity of South Africans to rescue the distressed economy we inherited from the apartheid regime without the IMF and the World Bank.

As I have said elsewhere, the refusal to accept the offer of the IMF at the beginning of our democracy induced an arrogant response from a young Washington IMF official who said that, in five or so years, South Africa would come running to the IMF to ask for help. It is this arrogance, over and above the negative experiences of the roles of the IMF and the World Bank on the African continent, that made us decide to do whatever was possible to ensure that the IMF and the World Bank never comes to dictate how South Africa should run its economy, to defend our sovereignty and the gains of our struggle for liberation.

The 1996 financial crisis occasioned by the apprehension of investors in the early days of our democracy – including the resignation of Chris Liebenberg as the finance minister and his replacement by Trevor Manuel, and rumours about the health of Mandela – impacted on our currency in a manner that gave reason to the IMF to come back and offer their assistance again. Armed with the May 1992 policy conference resolution of the ANC, government declined the 'offer' to 'protect the integrity of domestic policy formulation' as well as 'reduce dependence on international financial institutions'.

This was how we ended up with our own restructuring of the economy called Growth, Employment and Redistribution (GEAR) to manage our macro-economic balances. This we had to do without lowering social expenditure, which is what normally happened when the IMF and the

World Bank got involved. Funds raised had to be used mainly for productive activities or projects that contributed in the growth of the economy, and not for social expenditure, which was a recipe for a debt trap. We also chose the sources of capital that made sense in terms of our business of government. We reduced the debt of the country again without compromising our social expenditure. This of course affected the steep of the graph followed but kept the growth sustainable.

Given the sensitivity of the project at that time and the urgency with which it had to be developed and implemented, the ANC government attracted attacks from its alliance partners, namely the Congress of South African Trade Unions (COSATU) and the South African Communist Party (SACP). COSATU described this as the '1996 Class Project'. But GEAR was ultimately adopted by the 50th conference of the ANC in Mafikeng in 1997. The conference resolved that 'The strategy for Growth, Employment and Redistribution (GEAR) is aimed at giving effect to the realisation of the RDP through the maintenance of macro balances and elaborates a set of mutually reinforcing policy instruments'. The conference further said that 'We are not pursuing macro balances for their own sake, but to create the conditions for sustainable growth, development and reconstruction'. This decision made GEAR part of the strategies of the ANC in dealing with the economy.

To deal with the arguments of commentators that GEAR was a change in policy from RDP policy framework, the conference resolved that 'The strategy for Growth, Employment and Redistribution (GEAR) aims at creating the environment of macro-economic balances required for the realisation of the RDP'. It said further that 'the GEAR does not seek to displace the RDP'. Clearly the conference considered GEAR as a strategy to achieve the objectives of the RDP, which was the policy of the organisation.

From 1996 onwards the economy grew up to more than 5 per cent, just shy of the target of 6 per cent to support the developmental policies and programmes of the ANC. The budget deficit targets were exceeded to an embarrassing level where we ended up with a budget surplus by the year 2003/2004. We also made great strides in the redistribution of resources via the national budget, social grants and other means. All these strategies put together made our fiscal policy positions the envy of many in the world.

What failed dismally was the creation of 'employment'. The mistake was the assumption that business would voluntarily come to the party based on the GEAR strategy and framework. That was not to be. In fact, the 'Ten Year Review' report published in 2004 showed that government succeeded where it had control. Where third parties were involved not much progress was made.

In this project of the management of the economy one saw Mbeki at his best. Cool, relaxed, but perceptive. He took into consideration all technical reports presented to him by his colleagues in cabinet and their technical advisers before he made his determination together with his colleagues. From where I stood this looked very collegial as opposed to what is presented of Mbeki as dictatorial and a lone ranger.

One instance that has stuck in my mind is the year when the Forum of Directors General (FOSAD), which I chaired, saw evidence that suggested we were going to have a budget surplus by 2003 in a country where the poverty levels were still very high. The irony of this is that the numbers were an indication of the success of the tight macro-economic policies government adopted. I brought this matter to Mbeki's attention, who immediately arranged for me to meet Trevor Manuel together with Alec Erwin, the minsters of finance and trade and industry respectively, to discuss the matter and manage it in a manner that benefited the country positively. We met within two weeks or so, and a month later there was a framework plan presented to the cabinet lekgotla to deploy the extra resources in a manner that would grow the economy faster and increase jobs.

If one uses the traditional models of leadership where the leader is singled out and made responsible for both successes and failures of government, one is bound to misunderstand Mbeki. That is why he was blamed for every controversial matter the ANC had to deal with. As a 'child' of the ANC, and having been brought up within the O.R. Tambo tradition, he acted in a manner that made sure that the party as a collective was always on board. In fact, the party led the way. Resolutions had to be adopted at the ANC conferences to enable government to act on those difficult policy issues. Even GEAR, which was within the macro-economic policy framework of the ANC, had to be endorsed by the policy conference of the ANC followed by the conference.

This is, in reality, where the gap between the public discourse and the actual historical facts come in regarding Mbeki's role in government.

The third challenge in transforming and restructuring the economy was the debt we inherited from the apartheid regime. The general policy position as we took over the levers of power was to refuse to pay the apartheid debt. What we found, though, was that because of the economic sanctions against the apartheid system the regime made loans from pension funds of South Africans. What stunned some of us was that only 6 per cent or so was foreign debt. The rest was domestic. Faced with this reality, we had to change our historical position in policy terms and commit to pay the debt.

This was one of the unpopular decisions that attracted attacks mainly from comrades and historical allies in the non-governmental sector. Some even suggested that these were mainly 'white' pension funds that were designed to maintain the inequalities between blacks and whites. But the ANC government stuck to its guns, recognising that a destabilisation of the pension funds would have a negative impact on the future of the country and the stability of the economy.

The one thing that one cannot take away from Mbeki – and many people have missed this point – is that he is a child of the ANC and that he comes from the Oliver Tambo tradition. Like Oliver Tambo, it was clear to all those who worked with him that Mbeki had no sense of money in terms of his personal interests. His focus was always on the government and the people rather than on him and his family. Having understood his family circumstances, his upbringing, and his life in exile, where he lived more for the organisation than for himself, one was not surprised about his perspectives about life in general.

In fact, after his marriage to Zanele Mbeki they lived apart most of the time because of their different deployments in terms of work. Besides, Mrs Mbeki was, for all intents and purposes, a breadwinner. From where I stood, it did not even seem as though Mbeki was worried about what was going to happen to them as a family at the end of his term of office. On the surface, it looked as if it was only MmaMbeki *o neng a kgaragatshega* (actively concerned) about getting a house where they would stay at the end of his term of office, unless this was a delegated or shared responsibility at home.

I am of the view that it was this lack of a sense of money for personal gain that saved him from those who would have wished to nail him for anything that might have looked like corruption in his life. If he was corrupt, they would have dealt with him a long time ago. Even the accusation about the arms deal could not hold water in terms of corruption affecting him personally. There were disagreements about the wisdom or not of acquiring the arms, but there was no evidence of corruption at a personal level.

The closest case, which does not make sense to me, was the allegation relating to the R30 million they say he organised, but gave R28 million to the ANC and the remaining R2 million to Jacob Zuma. For a corrupt person, this would not make sense. At least he should have left part of it for himself, if this allegation was correct.

One can submit therefore that Mbeki belonged to the Oliver Tambo generation that did not think of life in material terms. They thought of life in terms of what one could achieve for the people. They were all influenced by the ANC slogan of 'Power to the People'. In fact, one picture that comes to mind whenever I think of O.R. Tambo, is Tambo chanting the slogan. Power had to be people's power, not individual leaders' power!

Secondly, they had an aversion to personality cults, traditions where the individual is more important than the organisation. In speeches, they used the royal 'we' but in a literal sense of acting as a collective. That is why Mandela always made the point that what he was doing and saying was 'ANC policy' and not just his views and opinions. They never talked about 'my government' but 'our government' or the 'ANC government'.

As part of this culture and tradition, Mbeki resisted any talk about public relations strategies for himself. For the party, 'Yes.' For the election campaign, 'Yes.' But for himself, it was a categorical 'No!' Even when experts offered to help him with his communications strategy, he did not see any reason for this. He believed that people would judge him on his work. Mbeki did not see a reason for posing for cameras, nor did he plan how he was going to appear and communicate with the masses and the public. He believed that his work should speak for itself.

Some people would say that this was actually one of his weaknesses, because he assumed that the masses would understand him without using the media. Besides, he operated at such a high level intellectually that a medium for translating his thoughts and works would have been necessary.

I thought that Mbeki was one of those people who would have been doing outcome-based education without saying so. This is a case of a 'strength' that turns out to be a weakness in itself.

Another weakness with Mbeki was that he tended to expect that people would be like him. He made it with Oliver Tambo and produced the excellent speeches that were acceptable to the president without any assistance. For instance, he would appoint a cabinet, but having appointed a cabinet, he expected the members of cabinet to achieve the quality of work that met his expectations, that is, at his level. The reality is that some cabinet members could not meet the required high standards that were expected given that there was no formal training for one to be a minister.

If you are an adult and you submit policy documents or proposals to your chief [president] and he throws them away, you come again the second time and you still submit work that is qualitatively not at the level he expects. Even if he does this diplomatically, by the third time you give up and withdraw to yourself and then argue that Mbeki is difficult and not approachable as a president. The media adopted the same attitude because he would question their views as journalists.

The most sensitive for me was the way he dealt with his own intelligences services. When an intelligence officer said, 'Mr President, this is the story' and he replied, 'But there is something wrong about your story because I've got this alternative information about the same matter', and indeed he would prove you wrong. People then began to lose confidence in themselves, especially because he had too much information, and was way ahead of the 'officers' even before they briefed him. Mbeki would have interacted with everybody who was relevant, including heads of state, in gathering his information. He had his own early warning systems based on his vast network of leaders and individuals internationally.

To prove a point, read the text that he wrote on the problems afflicting Somalia in the *ANC Today*, which he published weekly when he was still the president of the ANC. I am of the view that no sitting president would write an absorbing and well-informed, intellectually stimulating article like that. Even if I was given time to conduct research linked to the same topic, I would not have been able to produce a text like that. But Mbeki could do it because he had so much general knowledge about politics on the African continent and the rest of the world. Mbeki had travelled the world over as part of Oliver Tambo's team and also the ANC's International Relations Department, which gave him an incredible amount of exposure.

When people felt that they could not approach Mbeki or say certain things to him, they came to me as the director general in the presidency or as secretary of the cabinet or just as a comrade, and I would go to him and say, 'Chief, you may know something that I do not know, but I have a responsibility to tell you the following ...' It did not matter to me whether the matter was thrown out of the window because it was seen to be of no substance or was wrong. But at least I would have raised it.

A matter that is now public knowledge, and can be talked about, was one relating to the attempted coup in Equatorial Guinea where we intervened as a country. I had to go to President Mbeki and say, 'Chief, I know that you see or read all this stuff but my information is that it is going to happen in six weeks.' Obviously, as president, Mbeki read a lot of things – including intelligence reports – but he could easily have missed something like this because of his busy schedule. In his response, he said to me, 'Yes, you are right, I have seen it, but I did not realise that it was possibly going to happen in six weeks.' We went back and checked and indeed I was right – 'in six weeks!' He then called the chief of intelligence and we worked on a plan to stop the planned coup.

Besides the fact that it was the position of the AU not to allow coups again on the African continent, there was a concern that there were rogue elements from the old order and some new-order South Africans who were involved. This was considered as a huge reputational risk for South Africa, especially because of our leadership in promoting the project of the renewal of the African continent. What was worse, though, was the fact that these South Africans were collaborating with some of the major Western powers to carry out this coup because of oil interests, which was contrary to our vision of the African Renaissance.

I am narrating this story to illustrate that people feared to approach him because they thought that he already had the information they were bring-ing. But in fact he may have missed some information because he is also a human being. His knowledge and capacity were strengths, but it could be disastrous if there was no back-up system from his own officials and colleagues in cabinet.

Another classical example of a strength that became a weakness was the fact that Mbeki did not believe that ANC cadres could do what they did in Polokwane. He carried this perspective along until Polokwane and ultimately to his removal as president. When he was advised otherwise he said no, an ANC cadre cannot do that, otherwise it cannot be the ANC. He missed the point that during the new dispensation the ANC cadres had changed in terms of self-interests. Besides, there were members who were disgruntled for one or other reason, who were determined to do their damnedest to remove him as he had become a hindrance to them for whatever reason – wrong or right. They did their damnedest, whatever the consequences.

Mbeki also missed the point that it was not the ANC cadre of Oliver Tambo who was occupying some of the strategic positions within the liberation movement. Besides the fact that some were already compromised, many of these cadres could disrupt a national conference, avoid discussing policy matters and just go to conference to vote. As the reports of chaos, violence and disruption of regional and provincial conferences reached him, they affirmed his belief that these were not genuine ANC cadres. He held this view up to the last minute in Polokwane, as if the cadre who would arrive at the conference was different from the one who was involved in regional and provincial conferences.

As the numbers came through from the provinces, it was clear that Mbeki would lose the election unless the delegates at the conference acted otherwise. He was advised again not to stand. But he took an even harder position to stand because he had been nominated by members of the ANC and had to respect the ANC. He said, 'Even if I lose, it is fine. If I withdraw and people who get elected by default destroy the country, people will blame me for withdrawing because they will say we were going to vote for you but you withdrew.' That was why he did not withdraw his candidature. Indeed he stood for the election and gave them an opportunity to vote for him or against him, and he lost.

Mbeki believed that those who voted in the manner they did could not blame him for whatever happened afterwards and what is happening in the ANC today. One should say, though, that there are those who still blame him for 'standing'. In their view, this exacerbated the situation. Others say that he caused them to do what they did because of what he did to them – whatever that is.

I must say that the two weeks leading to Polokwane were among the most difficult moments in my life in the presidency because although I was director general (DG) in the presidency I was also a member of the National Executive Committee (NEC) of the ANC. Before that moment I was able to separate my work as the DG from my position as a member of the NEC. This was made easier for me because Mbeki had a high level of understanding of his roles as head of government, head of state, and president of the party (ANC). In our interactions there was no confusion about the capacity in which we were acting.

Under normal circumstances I spent more time with him as DG than I did as a member of the NEC. Even when we were at an NEC meeting or conducting ANC business, we interacted as DG and president of the country as we continued running the country even when he was busy with ANC matters. That was why I would get office staff to be around on standby – not to do ANC work, but to do government work while he was attending to ANC business. I often had to go to him and say, 'By the way, Mr President, even if you are here paying attention to important matters of the ANC, we have to run the country!'

In a sense I spent more time with him than many members of the NEC. During this particular two weeks it was like being permanently in an ANC meeting, where I kept aloof unless there was a governance matter that required his attention. Although he operated more from Mahlamba Ndlopfu than from the Union Buildings to take care of many consultative meetings relating to the party, he still honoured all government engagements, including cabinet business.

My interactions with him were intermittent as I had to continue running the country. But those intermittent engagements were intense, focused, and brief. I had moments when I expressed my concerns about what was happening, especially the violence that went with it at the provincial conferences. I recalled my intervention within the meetings of the NEC of the ANC and through letters, warning about the new tendencies within the Movement of pursuing self-interests to the extent of becoming violent.

Given the fact that the waters were already bedevilled, no one listened.

I also tested whether or not he would want to continue as a nominee for the presidency, and he gave me the same response. 'Let us give the ANC members the opportunity to exercise their democratic right!'

We crossed over to Polokwane for the conference, and again we continued to have intermittent interactions. At the conference, the behaviour of some of the delegates was just disgusting. What was worse was that the conference was beamed live. In the words of one old and staunch member of the ANC who was not at the conference: 'I was so ashamed of the behaviour of my leaders that I shut down my TV and stopped listening to the radio. It was disgusting.' She wondered whether or not the delegates at the conference were really ANC members. 'I do not expect that from ANC members.'

The outcome was determined beforehand in the form of 'lists' and predetermined 'lists' of delegates – the electoral college. Every candidate was given the same medicine irrespective of who they were as long as they were not in the predetermined list or not in the prescribed list. The percentages of votes were roughly the same – like 40 per cent to 60 per cent depending on which list one was on. When Joel Netshitenzhe – a balanced cadre of the Movement who is not factional – was given the same medicine, I concluded that this election had nothing to do with electing the best that we had in the Movement to lead us into the future. It was about which list you belonged to.

And the rest is history!

Interviewed April 2014, Midrand

WISEMAN NKUHLU

I met President Mbeki for the first time when he returned to South Africa during the early 1990s. I knew a lot about him long before because, as a political activist in the 1960s, I was very much aware of the leadership of the African National Congress (ANC). What made me particularly interested in him was that he did his matric at Lovedale and he was expelled and, later on, I had a similar experience. That made me interested in his history and following up on him.

I worked for the National African Federated Chamber of Commerce (NAFCOC) in the late 1980s when one of our projects was the preparation of what we called an economic policy for a post-apartheid South Africa, which I was fortunate to coordinate. It was agreed among ourselves that before the unbanning of the liberation movement, we should meet leaders of the ANC. We had an opportunity under the leadership of Sam Motsuenyane to visit the ANC in Lusaka. We were met by Pallo Jordan, Max Sisulu and Tito Mboweni. Unfortunately, Thabo Mbeki was not there. We had been looking forward to seeing him there because we were sure that he was going to be part of the meeting but he had an emergency meeting elsewhere. So I was very much aware of him and I took a lot of interest in his initiative, especially since he worked mostly with Oliver Tambo.

On Thabo Mbeki's return to South Africa, we made contact in about 1992/93 when I became chairman of the Development Bank of Southern Africa (DBSA). At that time, Mbeki was deputy president of the ANC. As an economist, he was interested in making use of whatever research material, statistics and other relevant data were available even from the apartheid institutions like the DBSA. He was keen to gain access to material on the analysis of the economy to understand the nature of the apartheid economy. So I became a link then as chairman of the DBSA, making sure that he got whatever material was required to gain a better understanding of the role of the DBSA and the state of the economy.

Working with Mbeki also entailed meeting him at Shell House, the ANC headquarters in Johannesburg. It soon became clear that we were ideologically very much alike, strongly believing that our economic policies would have to be very pragmatic. The apartheid economy at that time was very dysfunctional. The debt was at its highest and growth had just collapsed. But really understanding those economic challenges and the structural problems was very important to Mbeki because if the ANC was going to be the future government in a few years' time, he needed to have a deep understanding of what we were inheriting. So it was a very good time for us to get to know each other.

From about 1992 we started meeting informally on a regular basis to talk about the economy and the DBSA. When he became deputy president, he had an informal group of people that he used to meet from time to time on Sundays to talk about the economy and other socio-economic challenges. There were people like Brigalia Bam, Eric Molobi, Aziz Pahad, Essop Pahad and Charles Nqakula in that group. I participated in those Sunday meetings on a regular basis. By the time he became president, we knew each other very well.

The debates during Nelson Mandela's presidency when Mbeki was one of the deputy presidents were, firstly, about the global economy – the fact that at the time liberal democracy was at its height. The socialist countries had just collapsed and there was a lot of excitement in the West about liberal democracy having triumphed. Given these dynamics, our debates were about how to position ourselves as a newly independent country aware of the fact that we had to avoid placing the country under the control of the World Bank and the International Monetary Fund (IMF) at all costs. The new government of the democratic South Africa inherited an economy that was very weak and bankrupt, with huge debt and a massive budget deficit. Because the economy was not growing, there was no possibility in the short term to actually grow out of that debt. If you are faced with that situation, one way out would have been to borrow from the World Bank and the IMF. But the government's fear was that the new South Africa would end up in the same situation as other African countries such as Zimbabwe that were, at that time, highly indebted to the World Bank, IMF and donor countries. As a consequence, their economic policies and socio-economic development programmes were being dictated by the World Bank and IMF, almost as if they had ceded their sovereignty.

So post-1994 South Africa was faced with the realities of how to respond to this grave situation. Deputy President Mbeki was aware that there was a need for urgent action to deal with socio-economic issues in terms of investing in education. The Reconstruction and Development Programme (RDP) had been developed, but the democratic government said that if we want our socio-economic development to be sustainable, we have to bite the bullet and delay implementing the RDP programme. The government had to avoid placing itself at the mercy of the international donor community by first correcting the deficit and placing South Africa on a strong footing so that the country could tackle poverty and the provision of social services on a sustainable basis.

This was how the elements in the Growth, Employment and Redistribution (GEAR) plan came about. It was never the intention to introduce economic restructuring that would cause more harm to our people. But we had fought so long for freedom; the Mandela presidency wanted our country to have the dignity and the ability to shape our own destiny, to determine our own socio-economic development path. The new government felt that the only way to do this was to first reduce the deficit.

At the time, it was a tough decision, but that is what leadership is about. When you are faced with having to get the country out of a very dangerous situation, the leaders – President Mandela, ably supported by Deputy President Mbeki – had to bite the bullet and turn things around, which they did successfully. Within a few years, the country was growing at 5 per cent and spending on electricity and housing increased phenomenally. The government made great improvements in access to education – universal primary education was achieved in a very short time. The economy was placed on a sound footing in less than five years.

It was impatience from the one side to blame Mbeki for implementing GEAR because it was a short-term recovery plan. As much as one tries to prepare detailed arguments to present to the ANC alliance, which I know that Deputy President Mbeki and President Mandela did in terms of trying to explain our grave economic situation, sometimes critics like those in the alliance can be blinded by ideology and economic dogma. When we told them that we should tighten our belts, they thought we were selling out to neo-liberalism. They did not have the courage nor the capacity to understand that the only way to get out of our economic crisis was first to tighten the belt before we actually got to our final destination.

As you will appreciate, we all came from an era of deep ideological commitments. All of us in the 1970s were strongly socialist, but as years went by we got a better understanding of the economic policies followed by successful countries, especially the Nordic countries, and also later on the Asian countries. One became aware of the need to keep a good balance in an economy to make sure that it raises enough tax and uses that tax base in the best possible way to advance the welfare of the people. But at the same time, you can only raise those taxes if you make it possible for the private sector to invest in the economy and to feel confident about the future. It was those kinds of balances that the ANC-led government had to make sure were understood.

The loan sharks at the World Bank and the IMF were ready to pounce. They wanted to be seen to be part of this South African 'miracle' because in those years we were being called successful and peaceful and we were associated with reconciliation. They wanted to be part of that and they wanted the government to borrow from them. They were short of countries to lend to because most African countries were now over-indebted. The South African government was under a lot of pressure with offers of assistance. But looking back, I still believe that it was the right thing for Mandela and Mbeki as leaders to get the country to live within its means. Once you have done that, the tax revenues can be used to improve the quality of life of the people. We saw it happening when Mbeki was the president of South Africa. From 2000 onwards expenditure on education, electrification, water and housing suddenly increased. We made the economic advances that we are all proud to talk about today. When Mbeki left government we had a surplus and we were in a strong economic position.

Then Deputy President Mbeki was singled out for harsh criticism by the alliance partners for implementing GEAR. He has always had this reputation of being an intellectual, a thinker, and he is also very articulate and is not a populist. He did his homework; he researched whatever subject matter he was dealing with. When he was asked to speak at a Congress of South African Trade Unions (COSATU) or a South African Communist Party (SACP) meeting, he would arrive well prepared, and when one is well prepared, it is very difficult for others to argue against you.

That was what I learned from working with Thabo Mbeki. When he sits down to have a discussion with you, in the first place he will give you enough time to state your case; he will never stop you because he is a good listener. Actually, you may sometimes think that he is not listening. He will allow you to speak at length. Then when he responds you realise that, regardless of the subject, whether it is a problem of poverty or conflict prevention, he has done much more research and has thought deeply about the matter and he has sympathy for your position. But, in the end, you will see for yourself that what he is saying makes more sense. I am certain that those were the kinds of interactions that happened in his engagements with COSATU and the SACP comrades. They had occasion to take the deputy president on, but their arguments were just not strong enough to be persuasive and in the end they had to allow these economic policies to be implemented and complain afterwards in the media.

I have never experienced Mbeki exhibiting any arrogance or intolerance. But, as his economic adviser, a number of times we spent days researching for a paper or a speech that he was going to present, be it the opening of parliament or some other occasion. We spent days researching and getting contributions from many people and thinking things through. In the end, we would agree that this was the best we could produce. And then we would give the paper to President Mbeki overnight, and he would say, comrades, you must be tired by now. Then we would leave him, believing that he would read the paper and go to bed. The next morning, he had a new paper. When you read it, it was much better than what we had produced. That happened a number of times because of the research and thought that goes into every statement that he prepares and every speech or presentation he makes. This was especially true when he had to speak to members of the ANC alliance or address parliament or the international community.

As his economic adviser, I never felt that my ideas were not being taken seriously. Input from other colleagues would be factored in, but of course he also brought his own side of the story on the basis of the work that he had done. On the strength of the arguments, in most cases we went along with his recommendations; he had just enhanced our arguments. He was an exceptional listener and very patient.

Moving on to a different matter. As I recall it, President Mbeki and President Obasanjo were heading different institutions of the developing world. Mbeki chaired the Non-Aligned Movement (NAM) and Obasanjo chaired the G77, and the Organisation of African Unity (OAU). Abdelaziz Bouteflika chaired. They were asked by the African leaders within the OAU to make a presentation to the G8 on behalf of the African countries about the cancellation of debt, because most of the African countries were heavily indebted at that time. But in thinking about the matter, the three of them felt that, in approaching the G8 countries, they needed to talk about a bigger vision. They decided that they needed to develop a renewal programme for the continent and place the issue of debt cancellation in that context.

In 2000 Mbeki, on behalf of the three presidents, started working on the paper, the Millennium Africa Plan (MAP). It was in that context that I was approached by the Reverend Frank Chikane to join the presidency as economic adviser; more specifically, they wanted me to work on MAP, on the African Renaissance plan. By the time I got to the presidency in October 2000, President Mbeki, working with other colleagues, especially Alec Erwin and Joel Netshitenzhe, had produced a draft MAP document. This was passed on to me to coordinate and to improve.

The document that President Mbeki had prepared was very powerful indeed in terms of presenting a strong argument about the fact that historically Africa had made a significant contribution to human progress, all the way back to ancient Egypt. He cited our contribution to human progress in terms of education and the contribution of our minerals, the wealth of the continent, to the welfare of the whole world, and that even then Africa was well positioned to continue to make that contribution. Another point was that African leaders were ready to take ownership and responsibility for the rebirth of the African continent.

For me, that was the most fulfilling time of working with Mbeki. I joined the presidency on 1 October and by the middle of October I had to call the first meeting of those representing Presidents Obasanjo and Bouteflika to discuss the draft MAP policy document. Mbeki and Obasanjo challenged us to unpack the concepts in the draft and develop them into more comprehensive plans. For example, when we were talking about improving Africa's leadership, what did that entail? We started unpacking how African leaders should conduct themselves in a democratic manner and be accountable to the people who elected them; this included other constitutional undertakings to their people and the international community.

Even at that early stage, Mbeki acknowledged upfront that Africa's problems were to a large extent the result of unfair trade relations with the international community, as well as unequal relations in general. The three presidents also acknowledged that we could not run away from the fact that the incompetence and corruption of African leaders during the post-independence era contributed to the malaise. If we were going to turn the African continent around they, as leaders, had to be role models in terms of taking ownership and responsibility for the problems in their countries. As leaders of the countries on the African continent, they had to become role models in terms of integrity; how they governed and also how they accounted to the people; and they had to respect the resources that were entrusted to them by the people. As African leaders, they should also be bold in tackling the unjust relationship between Africa and the international finance community. The World Bank, the IMF and the donors at that time were dictating economic policies, telling the continent what policies to adopt. That needed a lot of courage and we had to make sure that our research was thorough. Mbeki was adamant that that was the first thing we had to do.

Each time that we developed and unpacked the MAP concept document, we would report to Mbeki and we would say, 'Mr President, these are the concepts and this is our understanding of how we would move from the concept to an implementable programme.' We would have that conversation with him and he would have that conversation with Presidents Obasanjo and Bouteflika. The process involved all the directors general

(DGs) and ministers in South Africa because we were talking about what to do with mineral resources, energy, water, agriculture and so on. Mbeki was very open and we expanded his vision and in that way we felt that we were becoming partners in the roll-out of this vision that eventually became the New Partnership for Africa's Development (NEPAD). Every government department in South Africa was involved in contributing ideas to enrich the policy document. Around April/May 2001 we had produced the third version of the MAP document – it was now a much more comprehensive document of over 100 pages explaining what had to be done in each sector. Mbeki and Obasanjo felt that it was then time to have a much more comprehensive conversation about this MAP document.

We went to Abuja for a workshop, which Presidents Mbeki and Obasanjo encouraged DGs and other senior officials to attend to discuss the various aspects of the document. An important development at that time was that, for the first time, in addition to the three presidents who had initiated the project, we now had the president of Senegal, Abdoulaye Wade, and a representative from Egypt. President Obasanjo encouraged us to invite Mali and Mozambique. They were already thinking of extending the ownership of the process to more African countries.

During that early phase of conceptualisation, the focus of the MAP was merely to ensure that Africa takes ownership and responsibility for its own development and produces its own economic development plan for the first time, and to call on the international community to support an African-owned socio-economic development plan. We were pushing that line, and integral to that was the fact that the relationship with the developed world had to change. In the past, we had not been equal; they dictated the terms of the relationship. They would say that, because you are poor, underdeveloped and corrupt, your development priorities must be primary education and governance. And Presidents Mbeki and Obasanjo said that no country in the world had ever developed just on improving primary education and better governance. Countries develop because they concentrate on high-level skills; they invest heavily in research, they start with agriculture as a base, and they invest heavily in infrastructure. So they changed the manner in which things used to be done at the behest of Western powers. They challenged the dominance in terms of economic priorities being determined by the international community; these were now determined by Africans themselves. Amid all of that, around March 2001, Presidents Mbeki and Obasanjo introduced us to President Wade of Senegal who was working on his own African renewal initiative – Omega. They said that, in the interests of African unity, we should get in touch with President Wade's people and try to work together to merge the two initiatives into one. It was a very difficult process.

The difference between the two documents was that Omega only had to do with infrastructure, education and agriculture, and it was about getting more money from the development partners such as France – partners who would dictate to us. There was nothing about changing this donor-recipient relationship or about fundamentally changing this master-servant relationship. The president of Senegal wanted the French to come and build roads for us. In fact, during a meeting, President Wade actually said that he would not mind if there was a problem of corruption or incompetence because France could just send its engineers to build infrastructure for us. Our thinking was totally different. The issues of changing the leadership in Africa, how leadership was exercised, defining our own destiny as a continent, being role models with integrity, courage and doing away with corruption – none of these things were in Omega. The principles about corruption and good governance were in our original document. Those were the differences between the two sides represented by Mbeki, Obasanjo and Bouteflika on one side and Wade on the other.

But in any case, we started working on integrating the two documents. By the summit in July 2001, where the MAP document was to be presented, we as the steering committee had not completed the work. In an attempt to try to bridge the gap, we agreed to try to persuade President Wade, on his way to Lusaka where the last OAU summit was to be held, to travel via Johannesburg so that he could meet President Mbeki in Pretoria to discuss the matter of merging the two documents. It was not an easy meeting. But then again, President Mbeki being who he is, felt that firstly we should not compromise the key principles in MAP but that we should accommodate President Wade's sectoral preferences. In the end we tried to bring President Wade's priorities into the document without compromising the MAP principles. In the interests of Africa's unity and ensuring that the renewal of Africa was not delayed because of a misunderstanding between leaders, Presidents Mbeki and Obasanjo agreed that President Wade should present the MAP document in Lusaka, even though the three originating presidents had done much of the work.

President Wade spent two days in South Africa on his way to Lusaka and in those two days we had to finalise the merged document. Since there was no time to discuss the name, we agreed to call it the New African Initiative (NAI) and that was what was presented in Lusaka. After the Lusaka summit, at a meeting in Abuja in October 2001, it was agreed that the name of the initiative would be the New Partnership for Africa's Development (NEPAD).

I want to highlight that for me President Mbeki's contribution in promoting NEPAD became very decisive indeed. In approving NEPAD, there were two major challenges. First, the African scholars and civil society were very critical of NEPAD because they felt that it had been designed by African leaders without consulting the people. There was no participation by civil society in the development of NEPAD. Secondly, they were very sceptical about the commitments to good governance, the commitment to fight corruption, because there were leaders who were among the most corrupt on the continent.

Presidents Mbeki and Obasanjo, in particular, toured the continent consulting labour, civil society and others. They were very successful in this but it took some time. The year 2002 was very difficult, but by 2003 most of the African NGOs that participated at international level were supportive of NEPAD, which was really great. One thing that Mbeki applied his mind to was dealing with African scepticism and the concern that civil society had not been consulted. The two presidents tackled that issue head-on.

For the first time, African countries that supported NEPAD were telling the international world to stop deciding priorities for African countries unilaterally. Africa had a framework that spelled out our priorities and stated exactly what kind of support we wanted to guide international engagement with Africa. It was quite a big challenge to go to the G8 countries, to the World Bank and the IMF and persuade them to accept NEPAD. But Presidents Obasanjo and Mbeki were so determined, so brave and so committed to doing exactly this that the first thing they did was go to the

United Nations (UN) to get the UN to pass a resolution to that effect: from then onwards, the framework that would inform the involvement of UN agencies in Africa was NEPAD.

To me, that was a great success because Afro-pessimism was at its peak around 2000/1. This was soon after *The Economist* published an article that defined Africa as a 'failed continent'. The author argued that Africa was a 'hopeless continent'. Mbeki and Obasanjo were very much aware of that negative stereotype. That was why President Mbeki played a very important role in tackling Afro-pessimism and the negativity about Africa in forums all over the world. He prepared some of the most cogent arguments to deliver on these international platforms. His message to them was that you are wrong, Africa is turning the corner and that the twenty-first century was going to be Africa's century. The business community at the World Economic Forum was very negative. Mbeki addressed many World Economic Forums, civil society, the UN and so on. If you read those speeches now you will see that they played a very important role in changing perceptions about Africa.

It is important to note that Afro-pessimism was not only perpetuated by the international community; it was especially strong among African scholars who had accepted that we were a hopeless continent. If you read publications by African scholars during those days you will note that they were writing about acquiring additional aid, saying that our African leaders needed to be assisted by the World Bank and the IMF. Only a very small percentage of academics articulated the possibility of an African renewal and Africans taking responsibility for that renewal.

There is another issue that I would like to mention because it was a very important contribution by President Mbeki. He realised that the civil society's scepticism was justified, given what our African people had experienced over the decades. Civil society was saying that African leaders were corrupt, their word could not be trusted and now they were suddenly going to reform themselves and be advocates for good governance. It was against that background that the idea of the Africa Peer Review Mechanism (APRM) was proposed. The issue was, to really make NEPAD credible, why don't we as African leaders commit ourselves to regular reviews on the progress we are making in fighting corruption, improving governance, conducting free and fair elections and improving the management of our economies?

Mbeki and other African leaders agreed that members of the APRM panel would be eminent Africans who were really respected for their contribution to the economic development of the continent and who were not in any way linked to corruption on the continent. And that was how it came about. The panel was given complete independence to go to any country to conduct the review and deal with issues like ensuring democratic elections were free and fair and that human rights were respected.

As chief executive of the NEPAD secretariat, I was responsible for coordinating discussions at the level of the steering committee and coming up with the mechanisms for implementing the APRM. I had engaged the best expertise in Africa in developing these documents, trying to get the best practice of the highest quality on these processes. The person who was coordinating the preparation of the technical documents for NEPAD was Smunda Mokoena, a South African. Among the African experts who were at the centre of coordinating the discussion of the documents was Kingsley Amoako, chief executive of the Economic Commission for Africa (ECA). There was also Jani, who was with the United Nations Development Programme (UNDP) at that time. I had done the preparation and my steering committee had been approving the documents as they were being completed. The crunch came when the APRM framework and its implementation mechanism had to be approved by African heads of state at a meeting held in Abuja on 8 March 2003.

We, as the steering committee, had to meet a day before the heads of state meeting to recommend the documents to be formally adopted. The meeting was held, but members of the steering committee representing 15 countries backtracked. They were just not prepared to approve the document. Why hurry, they asked, because no other community in the world had a peer review that covered political governance. They asked why we wanted to be more advanced than Europe because in Europe, when they talked about peer review, they referred to addressing economic deficit and debt; no European country questions another on its governance. They asked why we wanted to be more advanced than Europe. For example, we were talking about the independence of the judiciary and non-interference in the election of judges and about the independence of the Reserve Bank.

When I got to Abuja everybody was saying they were not ready to approve the peer review framework.

I was really terribly depressed and confused about how I was going to approach the three presidents, because I had been assuring them all along that we were making progress and that they should go to Abuja because the documents were ready for signing. I had to call President Mbeki that evening to say, 'Mr President, I am sorry I have bad news. I had a steering committee meeting today and the members are not prepared to approve the documents.' President Mbeki said I should not worry, and then he arranged a meeting with Presidents Obasanjo and Bouteflika for that morning so that they could consult before the official meeting. At that point I was really panicking.

In the morning Presidents Obasanjo and Mbeki talked about everything other than the problem I had; I just sat there, listening and tense. Unfortunately, President Bouteflika did not arrive because his plane was delayed. After some time they called for Ethiopian Prime Minister Meles Zenawi to join them. When he arrived, they started discussing the problems linked to the peer review mechanism. The three presidents agreed that the undertaking had been made a long time ago; there was no turning back now. They said, 'Today, we are going to try to persuade our colleagues that the best thing to do is to approve this document and sign and commit themselves to the APRM process. If they do not, we will sign and then the process will start.' That was the most difficult moment in my whole career under NEPAD.

The meeting began and, as expected, president after president said that they were not ready to sign the document. 'What is the hurry?' they asked. And then Obasanjo intervened to say, 'Colleagues, we made this commitment a long time ago and the officials have done their work and I have looked at all the documents and the processes that they are suggesting and I am happy with them. Are there any clauses in this document that you are not happy with and that you want changed?' No president came up with a particular reservation about a particular clause, but they insisted they were not ready to sign. President Mbeki kept quiet. But after everybody had spoken he entered the debate and said, 'Colleagues, we understand your concerns, given where we come from, but it has taken us much time to reach this important stage.'

Mbeki reminded them that we had made this commitment at the launch of the AU in South Africa in 2002. That was when the commitment to design the APRM was made and it was announced as one of the outcomes of the summit. 'We said that we were going to complete this process and there is no way now that we can turn our backs. So if some of you are not ready we will understand, but I will sign on behalf of South Africa and President Obasanjo has said that he will sign on behalf of Nigeria. Prime Minister Meles Zenawi has said that he will sign on behalf of Ethiopia.' That was how the meeting ended; no other president supported the document.

I was still puzzled about what Plan B was after this had happened and, as we were taking the lunch break, Presidents Obasanjo and Mbeki, chatting casually as usual, said, 'Wiseman, bring the papers for us to sign,' and then the two of them signed the papers and then they went to lunch. As they were going out, more heads of state approached me and by the end of that day I had about 11 signatures. This is what I call strong leadership – keeping their commitment without being aggressive. The steering committee was made up of 15 heads of state at that time. Libya and Zimbabwe had decided not to participate in NEPAD.

For me, that was the climax in terms of demonstrating good and strong leadership and commitment to the renewal of the African continent. Mbeki persisted in tackling Afro-pessimism, determined to work with like-minded African leaders in taking the continent forward and working constantly in a relationship of trust with Obasanjo and Bouteflika. These were outstanding characteristics of the man. Mbeki made sure that whatever he had to do, he was well prepared and well read and ready. This commitment to integrity and fighting corruption and turning around the relationship with the developed countries from what it was before, a master-and-servant relationship, to a relationship of partners in the true sense of the word and to changing the priorities for the continent. Those are the outstanding contributions that I will always assign to African leaders such as Mbeki.

NEPAD was a hard sell to developed countries. After the initial introduction of the idea of a renewal plan for Africa, which the three presidents had mentioned in Japan, the next meeting of the G8 at which the African leaders presented NEPAD was in Genoa in Italy in July 2001. That was preceded by the adoption of the New Africa Initiative by the African leaders in the OAU in Lusaka in early July. One of the most important meetings in the development of the original MAP document was a meeting between Presidents Mbeki, Obasanjo and Bouteflika and the heads of the two Bretton Woods institutions; James Wolfensohn, the leader of the World Bank who was from the US, and Horst Köhler, the managing director of the IMF who was from Germany. We arranged to meet them in Mali around February/March 2001 and the purpose of that meeting was to appraise the heads of these two institutions of Africa's decision and they wanted them (the IMF and the World Bank) to commit to using it as a framework for engaging with Africa.

At that meeting, we presented the outline of MAP and talked about commitment to good governance, democracy, leadership, conflict resolution and then the economic sector priorities. Wolfensohn and Köhler listened and affirmed that they could not fault this approach and gave an undertaking to support Africa.

Then next major advocacy effort was in Genoa. Even in the address to the World Economic Forum attended by captains of industry and the UN, the advocacy was about changing the continent and putting the donor countries, the World Bank and the IMF on the back foot. Why the concerted advocacy? If you go to the United Nations, you are more likely to get support because the voice of developing countries is much stronger there. That was why the first resolution in support of NEPAD was from the UN. We had to get the UN behind us. But it took time. If you look up President Mbeki's and President Obasanjo's speaking engagements during 2001/2, you will understand what I am talking about; it was about selling a positive image of the African continent. It was really a very concerted effort on their part to be present wherever world leaders were gathered, whether it was big business or G8 leaders or the World Trade Forum.

In trying to work on the mindset of the developed countries, Mbeki, Obasanjo and others realised that the thinking in the developed countries was mainly controlled by the G8; they determined media opinion in the West. That was why there was this concerted effort to focus on the G8. President Mbeki would send either me or Mojanku Gumbi to every G8 meeting to make sure that African issues were on the agenda. We also tried to organise a one-on-one meeting between Mbeki and whichever president was chairing that G8. We would try to do that so that there would be a meeting of minds and that Africa would be part of the agenda. It was a concerted effort, commitment and engagement on behalf of the African continent, and I also think that they could not fault us on the progress that we were making on conflict resolution on the continent.

So the G8 sensed that this time around they were dealing with determined countries that were not dependent on aid and that Mbeki, Obasanjo and Bouteflika did not bring a begging bowl along when they attended G8 summits. It was easy for South Africa, Nigeria and Algeria to stand firm and take on the developed countries because, unlike most other African countries at the time, they were not indebted to them. If we had made the mistake in 1995 of borrowing from the IMF and the World Bank, South Africa would not have had the moral high ground to provide leadership to Africa, especially during the first 10 to 15 years of our freedom, and President Mbeki would never have had the chance to play a constructive role at the G8.

When it comes to good governance in Zimbabwe, all I can say is that I am a technocrat, not a politician. I tried to be a politician but it did not work. One of the things that the champions of NEPAD – that is, Mbeki, Obasanjo and Bouteflika – had said was that they would not tolerate any military coups or gross violations of human rights on the continent. With events taking place in both Sudan and Zimbabwe, it became very difficult for us and myself as a NEPAD technocrat to explain convincingly the position of the NEPAD leaders to the stakeholders in civil society. It was a challenge, because on my side I felt that there was a need to make a clear statement on Zimbabwe in those early days to the effect that this kind of conduct was not in line with NEPAD. But of course our political leaders saw things differently. They were not as forthright in dealing with the things that we were concerned with in terms of the international community.

That did create problems for us. In 2001 and 2002, I could stand on platforms and say with confidence that if there was any gross violation of human rights or an attempted coup, the NEPAD leaders would be there the following day; they would not allow it. But with the things that were happening in Zimbabwe and Sudan – and it became difficult to say such things – it presented me with a problem as the leader of the democrats on the NEPAD project. But the African leaders saw things differently. As a democrat I thought that they took longer than they should have to resolve the problems.

Mbeki and others continued to try their best, and around 2003/4 Africa's agenda was being articulated very forcefully and clearly. It was during that time that the Constitutive Act of the African Union was approved, which is a very progressive policy document compared to the Charter of the OAU. NEPAD and the APRM were also approved and implemented during those years. Africa was rising and there really was progress. The African leadership had regained respect and clearly there were leaders who were prepared to take leadership in resolving conflicts. We all know that enforcing peace in the Democratic Republic of the Congo (DRC) was a South African project. Again conflict prevention in Burundi was a South African project. Resolving conflict in Liberia was a Nigerian project. It was a concerted attempt by Africans to find African solutions to African problems during that time. But I am afraid that, with the departure of President Mbeki, and with Presidents Obasanjo and Bouteflika getting on in years, I do not see that kind of leadership emerging again. I do not see the Africans speaking with one voice on critical issues at an international level and taking strong leadership and committing their own resources to dealing with crisis situations on the continent.

As an example, if South Africa had waited for the AU to finance all the things that we were doing for peace to prevail in the DRC, it would never have happened. At some point Mbeki had to commit our own resources and make it happen, of course with the approval of the AU. That preparedness to go beyond the call of duty in resolving the conflicts on the continent, we do not see that happening any more. It was a big shock when the French president said Mbeki did not understand the soul of West Africa. I think that he was the one who had no understanding of the soul of 'Francophone' West Africa. President Mbeki had always worked closely with French-speaking Africa, not only with Algeria, but he had an excellent relationship with the presidents of Gabon and the DRC, and he also worked with Rwanda.

In the beginning, the idea was to have four presidents – including the Egyptian leader, partly for historical reasons – but President Bouteflika understood the French community very well and this was partly why he was part of the triumvirate. There was always consultation and there was a relationship of trust among the three presidents. The plan was that this core leadership would be made up of those four: Mbeki, Obasanjo, Bouteflika and Mubarak. Unfortunately, President Mubarak could not participate in the processes to the same extent as the others.

We were all shocked when Mbeki left office before his term expired. I just could not believe that it was the ANC that was doing that. Having had the privilege of working closely with two of its leaders, Presidents Mandela and Mbeki, and knowing not only the policies but also the values of the movement over many years, it was a really big shock. I was shocked by Polokwane and the behaviour of some of the people who were anti-Mbeki. But in the end, as a person who believes in democracy and the will of the people, I accepted the outcome. Perhaps we, as the people who had the privilege of working with Mbeki, were too busy in government and we did not spend enough time understanding the mood in the provinces. We thought that his record would speak for itself but that proved not to be the case.

I felt however that it was totally unjustified for Mbeki to be removed from office before completing his term on the basis of allegations that were erroneously made in court and he was never given an opportunity to defend himself by the NEC, of which he was a member and which is supposedly a democratic movement. The movement that he had served his entire life did not give him a chance to answer to those allegations in person. Mbeki was tried in absentia.

Mbeki is a human being who has weaknesses. It is a strange thing to say, but he is too rational, meaning that things to him are about facts. You have to convince him through argument for him to change his mind. Just telling him that people will not like something is not enough; there must be clear argument and facts to back up what you are saying. Rationality drives his world view. That is why he spends so much time studying, reading and making sure that he is properly informed before he takes a decision or makes a commitment. When you are a politician, you sometimes have to learn to be a little flexible; as a politician you cannot be completely rational. I would say that that was one of his weaknesses – he was too rational in his approach to politics.

One could say that he could have invested more in communicating and making himself better understood. As long as there are major opinion makers who still keep misrepresenting you, you must make an extra effort to actually reach out and communicate. So possibly on the issue of reaching out, he could have been much more persistent, even though he did communicate thoroughly in his weekly column in *ANC Today*.

I do not think that his reasons for standing for ANC president for a third term in 2008 were properly communicated. The ANC twisted it around, maintaining that he wanted to be president of South Africa for a third term. The fact that Mbeki had been advocating good governance and fighting against corruption within the ANC and suddenly he is doing this; that could have been communicated better, even though we know that the ANC's constitution allowed him to stand for a third term and Mbeki did not say he was running for the presidency of South Africa for the third time.

Interviewed September 2014, Midrand

IV

ADVISERS

ANTHONY MBEWU

⸺✦⸺

My grandfather was Professor Donald Mthimkhulu, who was a great educator and member of the African National Congress (ANC). He returned from exile in Zambia in 1963 to take me out of the country because he felt that there was no future for me with the apartheid regime intensifying its oppression. He took me to Zambia and then, in 1967, I went to the UK with my grandmother and my mother. I lived in the UK for 27 years. My family knew the Mbekis because my grandfather was the head of the Mindolo Ecumenical Centre in Kitwe, Zambia, and Edith – Zanele Mbeki's sister – was married to (Wilfred) Grenville-Grey who took charge of the Ecumenical Centre after my grandfather. So my mother and Edith were close friends and she knew Zanele because of that.

My mother knew President Mbeki in London because he was in and out between London and Moscow and elsewhere. At the time the South African community (in London) was quite closely knit. I was educated in England and I went to Oxford University to start my medical education. I was very fortunate to receive a full grant from the UK taxpayers; they provided me with an education as well as with a home in exile. I specialised in cardiology in Manchester. I did a research doctorate at the University of London and I got married in the UK.

I was in the ANC cell in Manchester and we were obviously involved with the British anti-apartheid movement – and then, much to our surprise, in 1990 F.W. de Klerk announced that Mandela was going to be released and political parties unbanned. So, having thought that I would spend the rest of my life in exile in the UK and that apartheid would gradually destroy my country, suddenly there was the possibility of going back home.

My family came to the country in 1992 and I visited the Groote Schuur Hospital in Cape Town and expressed an interest in coming back as a cardiologist. They were very supportive of the idea but for the next two years I heard nothing from them. When I wrote to them in 1994 they said that they thought that I was not interested. The assumption was that I would not come back, but I did. I came back two weeks before the elections in 1994.

In December 1994, Minister Nkosazana Dlamini-Zuma appointed me to the Board of the Medical Research Council (MRC). I served on that board for several years and I worked as a consultant cardiologist at the Groote Schuur Hospital from 1994 to 1996. It is a teaching hospital for the Western Cape but it was clear that there was not much transformation going on in the universities in South Africa. The then president of the MRC Walter Prozesky, who was a virologist, asked me if I was interested in applying to be head of research at the MRC. After agonising over the decision – because I had thought that I would come back to be an academic to train medical students – I decided to take up his offer. At that time, the controversies around HIV/AIDS were just beginning. The epidemic really took off around about 1990 but it was in about 1995/6 that various controversies arose in South Africa. These debates already permeated the medical scene abroad. I will provide the context.

In 1981 I was a medical student doing my clinical medical training at the University of London, having moved there from Oxford University. In the haematology wards at the Royal London Hospital, haematologists told us that patients with haemophilia required transfusions of clotting factors because they bled very easily. They told us that in the United States people were paid for blood donations whereas that did not happen in the UK. As a consequence, in the US diseases like hepatitis – at the time what was called non-A, non-B hepatitis – spread as a result of these blood donations because it was often people who were down and out or were drug users who donated blood.

As a young medical student, that shocked me because patients with haemophilia in the US were developing hepatitis because of the practice. The sort of people who donated blood in the UK were not likely to have these viral diseases. But many haemophiliacs in the UK would nevertheless develop hepatitis and other diseases. Within a year of those classes in the haematology wards at the Royal London Hospital, HIV suddenly appeared. I remember as a young medical student thinking that of course it was going to happen if one did crazy things like giving blood transfusions, which we knew were risky.

In England at the time, HIV first hit the haemophilic population but quickly moved into the gay population in London. Around about 1981/2, there was a distinguished London teaching hospital consultant who we later discovered was gay. He developed this mysterious illness in January 1982 and by Christmas that same year he was dead. I remember the panic in London at the time because this disease looked like a plague in that, particularly within the gay community and among the artistic community, people who became infected were dead within a year. It was a terrible, terrible time.

Within a year or two, we began to discover what needed to be done to halt the epidemic. It was obvious that the disease was sexually transmitted and, as with any sexually transmitted disease, the primary method of avoiding infection was to take precautionary measures such as using a condom, sticking to one partner, getting treatment very early on if you became infected with syphilis or gonorrhoea. As a medical student in London at the time, I lived in a small commune where I shared a room with a gay chef. Just before HIV hit the gay community, he told me that in London at that time they used to have parties where, from Friday night to Monday morning, you might have 50 different partners. When the gay community was affected, they realised that things needed to change. Multiple sexual partners, drug use and so on – all these things that were part of the scene in London at the time – were clearly fuelling the epidemic.

By the mid-1980s, the epidemic was beginning to come under control within the gay and artistic communities in London because they realised what they needed to do. They did not have a drug or a vaccine but they knew – as we later said in the 1990s in South Africa – about ABC (Abstain, Be faithful and Condomise). Change in sexual behaviour was the first method of control. I used to say to people that technically we have a cure for AIDS called the condom. If you and your partner are both negative and use a condom, the chances of your getting HIV are almost zero. So, in a sense, we had the solution back in the early 1990s when the gay community in England demonstrated that you could bring the epidemic under control through sexual behaviour change.

Around 1985 (HIV-positive) people often developed PCP (pneumocystis pneumonia), which was treated with high doses of cotrimoxazole, which we soon discovered was useful for people who were HIV-positive in terms of delaying the progression to full-blown AIDS. With hindsight, it was clear that cotrimoxazole reduced mortality in people living with HIV/AIDS by up to 50 per cent. It was actually the most potent in terms of dealing with HIV/AIDS. After 1985, AZT came in. It was a drug that had been used for cancer back in the 1960s but it was toxic in the doses used at the time. We started using it in people living with HIV using mono-therapy; people became resistant and dual-therapy came in the late 1980s and then, in 1987, triple-therapy – three antiretroviral drugs. It is often said that the major change in the HIV epidemic was when triple-therapy came in. It was called HAART (Highly Active Antiretroviral Therapy) – but it was not highly active, so this was quite a stupid name for it. We do not have any highly effective drugs against HIV yet and no cure, though people can live for many years on HAART.

I started to work at the MRC in 1996, which I think was about the same time that President Mbeki started the Partnership Against AIDS. As far as I know, that was the first multi-sectoral mobilisation strategy against the epidemic in South Africa. I think that Mbeki was one of the first who understood that this was not just a disease, but something that affected every sector of society and whose spread and impact was closely interwoven with all sorts of aspects of South African life, which was why he started the Partnership Against AIDS. At the MRC, we prioritised our research around the greatest health threats in the country at the time, which were HIV/AIDS, tuberculosis, malaria – in terms of continental malaria – and then increasingly non-communicable diseases such as heart disease, diabetes, strokes etc.

Walter Prozesky started the South African AIDS Vaccine Initiative in 1999. I went to Washington to the National Institute of Health and the World Bank and talked to them about South Africa developing an HIV vaccine. They were very amused by the idea. They told me that we clearly

did not know what was involved in developing a vaccine. But we nevertheless prioritised the whole agenda of government-funded health research
around the major health problems of South Africa. That was one of my
tasks, as well as building capacity for health research, particularly in terms of
training black and women scientists who, before 1990, had been completely
excluded from scientific endeavour.

Then the controversies began. For example, Minister Nkosazana
Dlamini-Zuma had to deal with the issue of whether we should be giving
AZT for prevention of mother-to-child transmission. The MRC was asked
to do research around this – literature reviews initially and then eventually original research. We did literature reviews around the issue of AZT
and provided those technical reports to the Department of Health, advising them of the pros and the cons. The next controversy that arose was
Virodene. The South African scientists who discovered this thing called
dimethylformamide, which actually seemed to be quite effective in people
living with HIV/AIDS, approached Minister Dlamini-Zuma. But then a
whole disinformation campaign began around Virodene; that it was highly
toxic, among other things. Also, the South African scientists who introduced
it had not followed the correct procedures in terms of testing on animals
first and then holding human clinical trials. So the thing was a big mess,
which was a pity because it looked like an agent that might have had a lot
of efficacy – but then again you were not allowed to say that.

When dealing with HIV/AIDS in South Africa and globally, there were
certain things that you were not allowed to talk about. The censorship and
the dialogue around HIV/AIDS was intense. I think that it is partly because
when the epidemic broke in the US, the first community that was hit was
the gay community. During the Reagan era, this disease was branded as the
'Gay Plague' – they called it GRID (Gay Related Immune Deficiency).
So from the start it was stigmatised as the disease that gays and drug users
got. The Reagan administration refused to marshal major resources around
research and it took the Ryan White Act to actually force them. So the gay
community, quite correctly, was very vocal in its activism about this disease
that was decimating them in the early 1980s and somehow it has maintained its heavy political overtones. That was how it began – the political
connotations around HIV/AIDS.

I mentioned earlier the panic that set in around HIV in London. The view of infectious disease specialists was that this disease would affect the heterosexual community and that there would be a major plague in Europe and the US among young sexually active people who often did not use condoms. By the late 1980s, it was clear that this was not going to happen. And to this day, HIV prevalence in the UK is of the order of less than one per cent; whereas HIV prevalence in the general population in South Africa is of the order of about 14 per cent. So everybody was surprised by the late 1980s in Europe and America that this thing that should have resembled the bubonic plague of 400 years ago was not happening.

By that time the pharmaceutical industry had begun to invest huge amounts in research. The first drug, AZT, was introduced, and big trials were done, which were a terrible mess. Industry was investing billions of dollars, as was the National Institutes of Health (NIH) in the US, in research around antiretrovirals and possibly other agents. But by the late 1980s it was clear that there was not going to be a major epidemic in Europe or the US and that suddenly became a problem. Medical research is driven primarily by commercial interests – not primarily by the major health problems that afflict a population. And that is true the world over.

In the late 1980s and early 1990s, suddenly this thing called Slim Disease hit East Africa. At first scientists in the US said it was not HIV/AIDS; it was just a severe immune deficiency caused by malnutrition, particularly by vitamin B12 deficiency. Because they lacked the equipment to test for HIV antibodies, the Bangui definition was developed based on AIDS defining conditions. We had the Bangui definition in Africa rather than actual tests. But by the early 1990s, the epidemic of immune deficiency in Africa was now labelled HIV/AIDS. So the American scientists decided that the epidemic in Africa was caused by HIV – that was the 'gospel truth' and it was blasphemous to question the causation of HIV/AIDS.

Many scientists at the time, including people like Luc Montagnier who discovered the HIV virus, agreed that AIDS was caused by HIV, but there were other aspects to consider. For instance, Montagnier asked why it hit Africa so hard but not the United States and Europe. What else was there that makes HIV prevalence escalate dramatically in African countries but not in European countries? Luc Montagnier talked about co-factors, possibly other viruses that together with HIV, caused AIDS.

Other scientists queried whether it was malnutrition in Africa, together with HIV, that destroyed the immune system. There were all sorts of ideas in the scientific community, but you were not allowed to talk about these in the scientific journals or other places because the so-called AIDS dissidents, like Peter Duesberg and others, were vilified and told that they were being irresponsible because they dared to ask such questions. The politics of AIDS was powerful because it first affected the gay community in the early 1980s and initially not much was done by the US government.

As I have said, the driver for this was largely a commercial one and not primarily a humanitarian one. It was an issue of antiretroviral drugs having to find a market. The disease had not materialised in Europe and the US and now suddenly Africa was the market. It was portrayed as a humanitarian issue but medicine and medical research are usually driven by commercial interests. South Africa happens to be one of the richest countries in Africa and surely those with commercial interests would exploit this fact.

Then along came President Mbeki who, having started the Partnership Against AIDS in 1996 and having mobilised and marshalled immense resources right across South African society around the epidemic, started asking questions about HIV/AIDS. Many of my US friends in the scientific community and medical profession applauded his enquiries because these were questions that they could not ask because if they did, they would not get grants, journals would ban their papers, their careers would be destroyed. President Mbeki, unlike other Western leaders, was actually willing to raise these pertinent questions.

In 1999, Mbeki assembled the Presidential International AIDS Panel and Minister of Health Manto Tshabalala-Msimang co-opted me on to that panel. We had two main meetings and after the second meeting, I was part of the writing group that had to write up the deliberations. Throughout the course of that International AIDS Panel, there was a furore: how could President Mbeki, who was not even a scientist, ask these questions and cast doubt in people's minds about the causation of HIV and AIDS? Incidentally, at no point did Mbeki ever say HIV does not cause AIDS. What he was trying to say was that a virus does not usually cause a syndrome in this manner. It was not just about a virus that you need to develop antiretrovirals against – it was about all the other aspects that determine the cause of an epidemic of HIV and AIDS.

I will explain with a parallel of another disease what I mean by that, or what Mbeki meant. Tuberculosis is a good example. TB is a disease that at the moment kills about 900 000 people globally. It used to kill about 70 000 people a year in South Africa, but that has come down to less than 50 000. You have to look at medical history and the cause of TB over the centuries. I talked to a very distinguished TB scientist about this, asking why the TB epidemic was so severe in South Africa. He did not say it is because of HIV, which is the answer that everybody would give, but that HIV is fuelling the TB epidemic. We have TB epidemics all across the country. In the Western Cape there are some of highest rates of TB incidence in the world, something like 1 000 per 100 000 of the population. But the HIV prevalence rate in the Western Cape is of the order of about 4 to 5 per cent. In KwaZulu-Natal (KZN) there is a very severe TB epidemic, although not as severe as the Western Cape, but the HIV prevalence in KZN is of the order of about 25 per cent.

So clearly TB in South Africa is not just about its relationship to HIV. In your Master's degree in Public Health, the first thing they do is show you the graph of the TB epidemic. My scientist friend said that because TB is a low and innocuous disease that kills you over a year or two, what happens when it enters a population is that its prevalence increases gradually over the course of about a hundred years and then it declines. It is a typical bell-shaped curve and the course for TB is about 200 years. The peak of the bell-shaped curve occurred in Europe in the middle of the nineteenth century. In southern Africa we reached the apex of the bell-shaped curve in the late twentieth century. If you look at the peak that occurred in Europe in the middle of the nineteenth century, there was a steady decline – a straight-line decline in the incidence and prevalence of TB. At one point you get the First World War and there is a slight peak and at another point you get the Second World War and there is a slight peak, but the decline continues. Round about the 1940s/1950s a drug treatment for TB called streptomycin comes in, but it does not make any difference to the curve. Then rifampicin comes in during the 1960s; it does not make any difference to the curve. What the public health people will say is that the key to managing TB is drugs. But the course of TB in a population is not primarily determined by the availability of drug treatment. It is determined by overcrowding, lack of sanitation, by malnutrition, by many social variables and challenges.

HIV is like that as well. So, yes, HIV causes AIDS but there are probably a lot of other things that contribute to the epidemic being more severe in southern Africa than in Europe and the United States. Yes, antiretrovirals are useful in the management of HIV and AIDS but they are not the primary solution. All the media hype around antiretrovirals is that they are life-saving drugs and that if we could only get our hands on antiretrovirals, the HIV epidemic would be contained, and of course that is not true. In the gay community in the US, HIV declined from 1980 mainly because of changes in sexual behaviour. The gay community was at the forefront of promoting the change in sexual behaviour, not the pharmaceutical companies.

The interesting thing about President Mbeki is that he understood a lot of this. He is not a medical doctor by profession; he is an economist. He is not a medical scientist, and yet he understood the multifaceted determinants of an epidemic like HIV and AIDS within a community and also the requirement to have an inter-sectoral response in terms of dealing with it, be it sports people, religious leaders, the media; be it better nutrition, social grants for women with young children, drug treatment, vaccines etc.

We wrote up the deliberations of the International Presidential AIDS Panel. Since then, our report has been suppressed. I am always amazed at the power of the global scientific community to suppress an issue that you are not supposed to talk about. It is a sort of self-censorship. What happens in our medical world is that, whether it is an experiment or something that somebody has written that is inconvenient, the best way to kill it is just to ignore it. Obviously it is more difficult to do now that we have social media and the Internet, but if you ask members of the public about the Presidential International AIDS Panel deliberations, they will ask you what that is. But the deliberations are available for those who care to read them.

The problem was that it was a dialogue of the deaf. On the one side, you had the so-called dissidents like Duesberg, whose views on HIV and AIDS I do not agree with, but he is one extreme. Then on the other side you had the more orthodox scientists who were growing increasingly hot under the collar because Duesberg and his company were threatening to question scientific dogma.

We had to write up our document presenting the views of the two sides and it raised a lot of questions, which required further research. The panel report was killed by simply being ignored. But of course the research was never done because it was not aligned to the commercial interests of the pharmaceutical industry. As an example, the question was asked, what is the role of traditional medicine in HIV and AIDS? There are more than 2 000 plants that are used in traditional medicines but they are of no commercial value to the bio-pharmaceutical industry so you just kill that one. Similarly, the issues around poverty and socio-economic deprivation, are they important in terms of the pathogenesis of HIV as they are important in the cause of TB? Again, influential people were not really interested. The only important thing was to roll out the antiretrovirals.

These issues continued after the Durban International AIDS conference as well as the whole question about whether to give antiretrovirals for the prevention of mother-to-child transmission. As I have mentioned, we had done our work at the MRC from about 1996 onwards in terms of literature reviews and then research around the issue. Eventually I seconded a colleague at the MRC to the Department of Health for six months to look into the issue, review the literature and write a technical report for government on the whole issue of prevention of mother-to-child transmission.

In 2000, President Mbeki asked us at the MRC to advise him. So we formed a group consisting of three senior scientists and research directors from the MRC, including one who had done a lot of work in behavioural change around sexually transmitted diseases like HIV, myself as the then executive director of research at the MRC, an expert on TB and HIV and AIDS, and an obstetrician and gynaecologist who was an expert on prevention of mother-to-child transmission of HIV. We four were called to Mahlamba Ndlopfu to advise the president. We discussed the issues around whether to give Nevirapine to HIV-positive pregnant women. I had already sent a research director to Uganda to look at the trials that were done there, which were disastrous. He spent six months writing up a technical report for the South African government. We were talking about the issues of possible toxicity, efficacy etc. Whenever I had spoken to or advised President Mbeki about HIV and AIDS, he had never told me what he thought. He always said, you're the expert, you tell me, which is very interesting. At one point in our group meeting he asked, so what should I do, should I give Nevirapine to HIV-positive pregnant women? After a bit of discussion he said: 'Tony, give me my marching orders.' So I said, 'Well, Mr President, you are the president of the Republic of South Africa, you decide these things. I am just here to give you technical advice.' He said, 'I know I am the president of the country, give me my marching orders.' So the four of us looked at each other and realised that he wanted to be told what he should do. So we advised him to start pilot sites around the country, introducing Nevirapine for HIV-positive pregnant women so that its efficacy, side effects etc. could be studied. Gradually, as you go along and if you discover that it can be given safely within the South African health system, then ramp up those pilot sites until eventually after a few years you have a safely administered programme right across the country.

Two months later, we had a panicked phone call from the cabinet office telling us that cabinet was going to decide on the matter that morning; where was the MRC's technical report? We said, but you have it; the Ministry of Health has it. They insisted that we send the technical report to the cabinet office and the cabinet decided to introduce pilot sites for Nevirapine prevention of mother-to-child transmission (PMTCT). At this point the Treatment Action Campaign (TAC) interest group panics and immediately takes out a court injunction, basically saying that government could not just roll out the pilot site approach. Anybody who works in the public health system knows that that is not possible; you cannot introduce an intervention amongst 1.1 million pregnant women at the drop of a hat. But it went to court anyway. The Constitutional Court ruled that it must be introduced right across the country immediately. But predictably it took three or four years before Nevirapine mono-therapy was available at every site where HIV-positive pregnant women gave birth.

In 2003 US President Bill Clinton and his aides came to visit President Mbeki. They asked about the whole issue of antiretroviral therapy for people living with HIV/AIDS. Health Minister Tshabalala-Msimang rang me up to say that there would be a ministerial task team and she wanted me to chair it. My colleagues in the medical profession told my wife, 'Well, Tony's career is finished because if he develops an antiretroviral programme that works, the president and the minister of health will be happy but the medical community and the AIDS activists would not.' So basically they said it was a poisoned chalice. Anyway, we worked from about August 2003; we had to do it in about eight weeks. The Clinton Foundation assembled the world's leading HIV/AIDS scientists from all over the world – about 50 of them – and we worked day and night to write the Operational Plan for Prevention, Treatment and Care for HIV/AIDS. We emphasised our comprehensive approach to HIV and AIDS treatment and that it was not just a matter of rolling out antiretrovirals. It was about the whole of the health system, all of South African society, and how to prevent HIV, treat people with HIV and AIDS and care for them. So it was a whole package. We included a chapter on traditional medicines, saying there should be research around this and it was impressive.

I went to a meeting in Geneva convened by the World Health Organisation (WHO) by what was called the '3 by 5 campaign'. They wanted to get three million people on to antiretrovirals by 2005. Jim Kim, current president of the World Bank (he is a medical doctor), and Zackie Achmat were in the audience. Jim Kim was saying that Professor Mbewu had written a Harvard AIDS treatment programme for Africa. Basically he was saying that I had written this complicated thing around antiretroviral toxicity because of the concerns of President Mbeki and the minister of health, and it was unworkable. This was total nonsense because what had happened was that, through the Clinton Foundation, we had ensured that we could introduce financially affordable antiretroviral treatment.

In 1997, it cost US$10 000 per patient per year – completely unaffordable. By 2000 the cost had come down to about US$3 000 per patient per year. Again, it was totally unaffordable, even for a middle-income country like South Africa. So in 2003 when we began writing the operational plan, the cost for treatment was about US$3 000 per patient per year. The Clinton Foundation negotiated with some pharmaceutical companies based in India and asked what the cost of goods would be. Now this is like a secret that has never been revealed in the history of therapeutic treatment over a period of 150 years: no pharmaceutical company has ever revealed its cost of goods, partly because they do not want to reveal the fact that they make super profits on some of their products.

So the Indian pharmaceutical companies replied that if we could guarantee one million patients on treatment for each of the Indian companies that participated, they would tell us their cost of goods. So they showed us their books, which had never been done before, which showed that while US$2–3 000 per patient per year was the cost for antiretroviral treatment on the market for people living with HIV/AIDS, their cost of goods was US$250. And so they said that if we could give them the US$250 plus a ten per cent margin, then we could do business. So through the Clinton Foundation we managed to get treatment for all of Africa at an affordable cost. Through the efforts of Thabo Mbeki, we achieved US$250 per patient per year by early 2004. The principal barrier to treatment was not Mbeki's political intransigence as most would like to believe; it was the financial cost. The South African government, led by Thabo Mbeki, made its decision in October 2003 that antiretroviral therapy had to be part of a comprehensive package of prevention, treatment and care, and it would be introduced in the South African public health system. In short, all the 2.2 million people we have on treatment in South Africa today are benefiting because of President Mbeki. It is important to note that antiretroviral therapy did not suddenly happen in 2009 when the new government took power; it began in 2004 and by 2009 we had 900 000 people on treatment. This was a result of President Mbeki's foresight and it is something for which he has not been given credit.

Early in 2004 I briefed the Science and Technology Portfolio Committee in parliament. I told them that South Africa had the largest antiretroviral programme in the history of the planet. The TAC activists in the audience were furious; they said that this was nonsense. But the figures were there for everyone to form an independent opinion – and not just the TAC as an activist group. Anybody in the health professions, but particularly those of us who are in research, know that when a new therapy is introduced to the market, the first thing you do if you are the medical director of a pharmaceutical company is look around the country for a champion for that product. It is usually a leading professor in that disease sphere. You then pay that professor through a grant to go to meetings around the country, to fly to international conferences. You fund his research as well and he becomes the champion of your product. You will not see that in the annual reports of the pharmaceutical companies but that is how they market their products. Drugs can only be administered when doctors sign a prescription. Medical doctors and professors are the gateway to a multibillion-dollar industry.

Similarly, if you, as the medical director of a pharmaceutical company, have a drug, particularly if it is an expensive drug that you want to introduce for disease control in a particular country, as well as finding a medical champion for that drug you will also identify a patient activist group and you will fund their programmes. For example, when Britain did not want to provide very expensive treatment for breast cancer, it was the cancer associations and the cancer activists who pressured the British government, saying that the treatment must be made available to the national health system; it was very expensive but it must be made available.

Sponsoring of the medical champion is usually a covert operation because pharmaceutical companies do not want to be seen to be pushing their products. That is the way it works. Why did the TAC and others not congratulate President Thabo Mbeki's government for lowering the cost of treatment to US$250 per patient per year by early 2004? The critics simply ignored this positive development.

If you want my opinion as to why there was such a furore in South Africa and globally when President Mbeki started asking questions about HIV and AIDS, my answer would be that I do not think that it was about HIV and AIDS. I think the threat that President Mbeki posed to the global order and the vested interests that work within that global order, be they governments or corporates, was not about HIV and AIDS; it was primarily about the whole issue of Africa. Here you have the second largest continent on the planet and with a mineral resource base larger than any other continent, with amazing agricultural potential, with more biodiversity than any other continent in the sea and on land – it should be the wealthiest continent. But for various reasons going right back hundreds of years to slavery and colonialism, it was a continent that was mired in disunity, in wars. Here was a man who came and said, 'Africa unite!' We had people before, like Patrice Lumumba and Kwame Nkrumah, who said that pan-Africanism was the key to our development. If we produce a quarter of the world's oil, then should we not have a say in the price of oil? If we produce half the world's diamonds, should they not be cut and polished in Africa? If we produce a quarter of the world's gold, shouldn't the gold price be set in Johannesburg rather than London or New York?

Here was somebody who was saying that the secret of the wealth of the US and why it became the world's biggest economy after 1870 was because in continental USA 70 per cent of trade is between the states of the USA and not with other countries, whereas in Africa in 1996, something like ten per cent of African trade was between African countries; and the rest was with the former colonial powers in Europe. Here was someone who was threatening to unite Africa so that we could use our mineral resources, our biodiversity, our human resources, our intellectual capital in order to build African countries in the African Union. That was the threat. HIV/AIDS was simply an instrument to tarnish his reputation. That is my belief. The historians will have to address the issue of whether the attacks and accusations thrown at Mbeki were bigger than the HIV/AIDS debates.

The momentum has not stopped. A good example now would be the issue of capital flight. It is non-governmental organisations (NGOs) in London and New York that have pointed out that Africa receives US$50 billion a year in aid from the Western world but US$100 billion to US$150 billion leaves Africa every year. The British NGOs have shown that something like 8 per cent of that capital flight is due to dictators stashing money in Switzerland. Something like 15 per cent is through international crime but 60 per cent is through mispricing etc.

I know that President Mbeki is very much involved in the Economic Community for Africa (ECA) in terms of looking at the whole issue of illicit financial flows. Here is someone who was saying, it is not aid that we need; it is not donations of antiretroviral drugs that we need – we just need a fair opportunity to trade with one another, to trade on the world markets without obstructive World Trade Organisation (WTO) regulations to choose who we partner with, be it China, India, Brazil, the US or the European Union. So I think the issue was not about Mbeki asking questions about HIV and AIDS; the threat was that here was a man who threatened to unite Africa. He argued that we would have to present a united front when we dealt with the pharmaceutical conglomerates. They should not divide us if we ask for a fair price for drugs and other medication. In terms of reducing the price of antiretroviral drugs, the partnership between the South African government and the Clinton Foundation benefited the African continent, not only South Africa. This is classic Mbeki.

They say hindsight is a precise science; actually it is not a very precise science. How did Mbeki's critics arrive at the number that 300 000 people lost their lives because of his position on HIV/AIDS? At one point they argued that he should be sent to The Hague. Why? Other heads of state knew not to ask these pertinent questions because the various vested interests are very powerful. In South Africa, we have taken on vested interests. For example, Nkosazana Dlamini-Zuma took on the tobacco industry, regardless that Margaret Thatcher was their consultant. We did not really win that war; that war is still ongoing. But we have had great success in halving the smoking prevalence in South Africa. In terms of the pharmaceutical industry and the global US$5 trillion health industry, it takes a very brave head of state to ask questions. All Mbeki did was to ask the correct questions and he wanted evidence and we provided him with evidence and then with technical advice, which he took. So why do people continue to accuse him of wrongdoing?

If you say that an AIDS denialist is somebody who asks questions about HIV and AIDS, then all HIV scientists are denialists because they all ask pertinent questions. There is no such thing as truth in science. A scientific hypothesis or a scientific theory is only true until an alternative explanation comes along and debunks it. Scientists all ask questions; scientists do not believe anything. They are not priests or bishops; science is not a religion, it is deeply sceptical and objective. It is about always asking questions and nothing is sacrosanct. There is no such thing as dogma in science. The dogma creeps in when the commercial interests want to use science in order to push a particular product and then you are not allowed to ask questions about its impact on human beings.

A disease being 'incurable' is used as a way of ensuring that people will pay a lot of money for products of the pharmaceutical companies. Cancer is 'incurable'; therefore oncology drugs must be very expensive. But of course, we already have a cure for 70 per cent of cancers. Thirty to 40 per cent of cancers are caused by diet and 30 per cent by pollutants. So if we clean up our diet and clean up the environment, we will eliminate 70 per cent of cancers. But nobody is going to make money out of that so we are supposed to keep quiet, eat junk food and take drugs.

To return to the question about cotrimoxazole, which I mentioned earlier, it is important to note that multivitamins are very useful for people living with HIV and AIDS and before antiretrovirals were available in South Africa, that was how we used to treat people with severe immune deficiency. It was by boosting them intravenously with multivitamins. One of the innovations in the operational plan for the prevention, treatment and care of HIV and AIDS and TB was that everybody who was HIV-positive should be on a multivitamin because it would probably delay progression. Secondly, once the CD4 cell count is below 500, they should be on cotrimoxazole because it can reduce AIDS mortality by up to 50 per cent. And then when the CD4 cell count drops below 200, you put patients on antiretrovirals. Now the set point has been changed to 350 and eventually the plan is that all HIV-positive patients will be put on ARVs regardless of CD4+ count.

The whole point was that it was comprehensive care. Other infections had to be treated and a proper diet had to be ensured. The strength of the South African programme was that it was a comprehensive approach. I suppose that all this input did destroy my career because of course the media tried to brand me as an AIDS denialist, which was not true. I applied for a lot of jobs, which I did not get because the media basically destroyed me, as they can do.

No one has given me and my team credit for developing the existing comprehensive plan with the support of President Mbeki. One of the wonderful things about this country is that not only did we liberate it after 1994, but because of the nature of the ANC, we were invited to be a close part of building this nation and we did it in the face of vested interests and scapegoating by the media. But the point is, what we have achieved in 20 years of democracy is remarkable.

It is utter nonsense to argue that President Mbeki is aloof, dictatorial and does not listen to other points of view. President Mbeki is a very warm and welcoming person – a good listener. I remember meeting him once when I was having problems with my boss at the MRC who had taken sides. I was under fire, and President Mbeki greeted me and took my hand in both his hands and he just looked at me and I thought, as a president you know what is happening, you know what I am going through. I was often privileged to be with him when he was on the election trail, addressing a meeting – I will always remember that when he stepped out of a house, the crowd would go wild. Mandela had an effect like that, but Mbeki had it too.

It is very interesting that President Mbeki is unpopular among white South Africans. Perhaps only 2 per cent of whites vote ANC. But among the majority of the people, he is immensely popular. It is almost as if they realise that this is the man who negotiated the political settlement from 1985 onwards in meetings in Zambia, Senegal, Switzerland and the UK. This is the man who was effectively the prime minister from 1994 to 1999 and basically stabilised an economy that was bankrupt, and he introduced all sorts of social programmes so that to this day our social spending is two thirds of the government budget. This is the man who introduced the Partnership Against AIDS and antiretrovirals for pregnant women and comprehensive care, including antiretrovirals, for people living with HIV/AIDS. This is the man who helped to found the African Union. This is the man who is going to do something about capital flight from the African continent. This is the man who was a talisman among other African heads of state; he was always the one they looked to for leadership.

The interesting thing is that the so-called common people understand better than any editor of a national newspaper or television station in this country what a hero he is, what an amazing man he is. He will be counted among them, the Mandelas, the Luthulis, the Mbekis – these are our national heroes.

Of course I was surprised when he was recalled! I could not believe it. I was at a medical conference in Mexico and I think that I saw something about it on CNN. So I phoned my son. I asked him what was happening in South Africa, so Thomas said not much. Then he said, 'Oh no, sorry, Dad, people are staging a coup against the president.' It was ridiculous, but not only that, it was disgraceful. It was a blot on our copybook because in these 20 years we have demonstrated that although we are a young democracy in terms of our governance structures, our political system, our electoral system, our Chapter 9 institutions, we are one of the most advanced, progressive democracies in the world. That (recall) was a step backwards. Hopefully it will never happen again.

What did strike me was the dignity with which Thabo Mbeki conducted himself because he knew that to try to fight this would have caused political mayhem. It must have been incredibly painful for a man who has dedicated his entire life to the people of this country and to the ANC, but he took the dignified route and said if my party recalls me, then so be it.

There has been a determined campaign, whether it is in the universities, in the media, in whatever avenue, to destroy the black intelligentsia. The only time a black intellectual will be quoted and is seen as credible is when their narrative fits in with the narrative of those who actually control the dialogue in this country. It is particularly striking for me, having been in exile for 27 years, where we had a global black intelligentsia who were writing about political struggle, who were producing music, who were putting on plays and doing all sorts of things from New York to Moscow to London to Johannesburg. Twenty years and there is silence. The black intelligentsia has been shut down because a certain group of people must control the discourse in this country. Freedom of the press or freedom of expression – that is nonsense when applied to the experiences of black people. Mbeki was not allowed to express his views about HIV and AIDS.

Interviewed July 2014, Johannesburg

GLORIA SEROBE

꙰

Because Thabo Mbeki led the process of undoing the very complex and sophisticated apartheid structure that caused untold horror and chaos in South Africa over many decades, I would like to talk about the Thabo Mbeki I know as a manager of this delicate process; a process that began changing the socio-political architecture of this very complex country. I would also, and more significantly, like to talk about Mr Mbeki as the champion of the difficult subject of gender transformation, of the emancipation of women.

I never had the opportunity of meeting Thabo Mbeki before 1990. This was mainly because I was never in political exile, nor was I ever involved in politics to the extent of having to meet the exiled or imprisoned political leadership. Until then, my understanding of him was of someone who was part of a team that African National Congress (ANC) President Oliver Tambo entrusted with many tasks, including that of head of International Affairs. It was also about him as a scholar and intellectual who had studied economics and political science at Sussex University. I was excited by politicians who appreciated the benefits of mixing politics and academic studies.

Also, growing up and studying as I did in the Eastern Cape, which was home to well-known intellectuals of the time, I understood him to have come from a home and family of scholars and political intellectuals, a man whose formally educated parents were involved in the political struggle of South Africa.

Untangling the messy web of apartheid politics in South Africa required all manner of skills from our politicians. We were a country in trouble and complex navigation was needed to remake South Africa, starting with the 1990-1994 political and constitutional negotiations. The depth of skills within the ANC proved critical to getting us through this difficult period. And so when 1994 came and we had a constitution to refer to, I could not but marvel at the political leadership behind it. This enhanced my respect for our political leadership, Thabo Mbeki among them.

I will forever be grateful to the ANC leadership for affording me the right to cast my first vote in 1994, at the ripe old age of 34.

My first encounter with Mr Mbeki was through his wife Sis Zanele Mbeki in 1990. A political activist in her own right, she had a passionate need to get us involved in contributing to the meaningful making of this new country, South Africa. Sis Zanele did an elegant job of making me think that I too had the responsibility and the necessary capability to make a difference, irrespective of my background. What she taught me then has remained entrenched in my head.

In April 1996, Minister Stella Sigcau appointed me as finance director of Transnet, under Saki Macozoma as the MD. This became my turning point in terms of my formal dealings with the political leadership. Transnet was and remains a 100 per cent State-Owned Enterprise, reporting at that time to Minister Sigcau. It was a company swimming in debt, 85 per cent geared, all underwritten and guaranteed by the South African government. It was choking under a huge pension fund deficit (only 22 per cent funded) of R17 billion, built up under the pre-1990 Transnet management and the apartheid government. They had created many different instruments, such that the servicing of this pension fund deficit was prioritised above all other debts. This meant that Transnet's investment backlog had accumulated to such high levels that the South African economy was almost at a standstill. Given the economy's dependence on Transnet's capabilities in rail, ports, aviation and pipelines, its inability to invest in these crucial sectors meant that the new South African government and the economy were held to ransom by Transnet's massive debt problem and operational inefficiencies. This was especially the case as all of the Transnet debt was guaranteed by the state.

Dealing with this chaos at Transnet meant working very closely with government. It made a big difference that President Mbeki's office was manned by highly respected professionals, people such as Moss Ngoasheng, an economist who was later succeeded by Professor Wiseman Nkuhlu; and on the legal side, Advocate Mojanku Gumbi.

President Mbeki's attention to detail and his ability to listen, as if we were the only problem he had to deal with in government, confirmed all that I had heard about him. Fixing the Transnet problem required sophistication and professionalism, rather than emotion and the sentiment of history; that is what we got from him and his office.

When, by the year 2000, we had successfully restructured the Transnet Pension Fund, fully equipped by the Transnet Pension Fund Amendment Act of 2000, and with the full backing of the government, the Transnet Board and all ten of the Transnet trade unions, it was not via a miracle but through an appropriate partnership with government.

Transnet's debt gearing ratio moved from 85 per cent to 50 per cent, a decent gearing for a company of that size and diversity; a diversity that included the aviation sector, known globally for high gearing. Only then, in the year 2000, could Transnet begin looking aggressively at its investment programme, something the South African economy desperately needed.

Under the new government, for the first time, the country was subjected to the rigour of credit rating processes – the kind of transparency the international and domestic investor communities need to make appropriate investment decisions. As Transnet itself was a subject of this credit rating process by Standard and Poors, Moody's and Fitch, its being a big part of the government debt guarantee book, we could now comfortably give the rating agencies a plan of how the Transnet debt problem was going to be solved, knowing full well that we were dealing with an office of the presidency that was consistent and predictable.

The Transnet experience is, I think, a good illustration of how the new government was able to move the country from the brink of bankruptcy in 1990 to the surplus levels of 1999. This achievement has got to be acknowledged as one of the finest works of President Mbeki and the teams he put in place.

President Mbeki seemed to believe strongly that in order for the country to move forward there had to be a genuine attempt to meaningfully include the

participation of women. The apartheid system was developed with precision and required enormous intellectual capacity to implement. In turn, the
reversal of this system required the same amount of precision and intellectual capacity, as well as an all-hands-on-deck approach; and that included
the capacity from women. The ANC policy on the emancipation of women
is very well articulated. But, like all policies, it could have sat on the shelves
and gathered dust if it had no champion. The privilege we had as women
was that this policy was championed from the highest office in the land; it
found itself in all manner of other policies. Even the private sector understood exactly what this meant.

Government led the charge. The appointment of women in key cabinet
portfolios such as foreign affairs, national intelligence, home affairs, agriculture and public works meant that the president believed in their capabilities
for the success of his delivery programme. There was a time when our
ambassadors to the major economies of the world were women – France,
the UK, USA, Germany, Switzerland etc. This was also at the time when the
job of ambassadors was being transformed from just political and ceremonial to being strong economic centres as well. The significance of this is that
the president was prepared to entrust his economic relationships with the
leading economies of the world to women. This was a profound affirmation
for us as women. The appointment of a deputy president in the form of
Phumzile Mlambo-Ngcuka was the highest point, and the biggest highlight
for us, the women of this country.

If there is any platform from which I can talk about engagement
at a deeper level with President Mbeki, it is with his formation of the
Presidential Working Group for Women. The president had formed a number of working groups to interact with non-governmental structures and
various strategic interest groups in areas where he needed to know what
the pressing issues were that government might have been missing out on.
Working groups were established for academics, trade unions, big business, black business, religious groups, youth and women.

The formation of the women's working group was the last and the most
complex, because the nature of women's organisations is such that they
cover all aspects of the life of a community. Minister Essop Pahad played
a key role because the working group was located within the gender office,

which formed part of his office. The group's formation took longer to put together as the presidency wanted to ensure that all women's interest groups were taken care of and that all their issues were covered. The final result was that the women's group became the largest group, made up of 58 organisations that included the Progressive Women's Movement, Jong Dames, Girl Guides, business and professional organisations, the Domestic Workers' Union, People Opposed to Women Abuse etc.

While women's organisations have many challenging issues to deal with, unlike business organisations, they don't have the necessary resources to run their programmes. The biggest challenge was therefore how to run and manage this working group effectively, such that our engagement with the president yielded meaningful results. This was the greatest opportunity for the women of this country to have so direct an engagement with the president – we could not afford to waste it.

I felt honoured and privileged when I was asked to be the chairperson of the working group. In all my travels, I am not aware of anywhere else in the world where one would find a president who was prepared to spend so much time tackling the issues of women. I therefore understood the privilege that came with the formation of the group and my appointment as chairperson. I was anxious not to waste this opportunity and to ensure the working group's capacity to deliver. We had to treat these meetings as if there was no tomorrow, especially because the working groups were not statutory, but rather related to the working style of a particular president.

The first thing we had to do was to make sure that this group did not meet only when we had the official meetings with the president. We had to meet many times, process our issues and be on top of things, before we met him officially. This meant that we needed to have a place to meet and prepare for our meetings. WIPHOLD (Women's Investment Portfolio Holdings) made their offices available. While most of the women's groups' offices were based around Gauteng, there were some in other provinces – the Girl Guides were based in the Eastern Cape, the Domestic Workers' Union in Cape Town, etc. These were mainly the NGOs, which did not have the resources for travel and accommodation. But those of us who had some resources made sure that our counterparts could attend these meetings – their mandates covered issues that could fundamentally change the lives of poor women.

These issues had to be covered and processed. By the time we were to meet the president, we were very well prepared and very clear about the priorities we wanted to place in front of him.

Our inaugural meeting with President Mbeki lasted from 8am to 1pm, followed by lunch, which he attended and did not seem to be in a hurry to leave. When by 3pm we dispersed, we had spent eight hours of quality time with the president – practically the whole day at the Union Buildings. He did one more thing, because I think our issues excited him; the other working groups were scheduled to meet three times a year. He decided that the women's working group should hold four meetings a year. You can imagine what that meant to our egos and psyche, and that set the tone for how the group was going to function.

Effectively this meant that the women met the president for five hours four times a year – 20 hours of dedicated engagement. Because we knew him to be an implementer, we knew that the issues we were discussing in those meetings were not just philosophical. They were the real, hard issues and solutions would be implemented. His leadership style and his strong work ethic that we experienced put us under immense pressure to generate workable solutions to taxing problems.

An illustration of this was his old-school use of notebooks. When he came to the meeting room, he had his notebook. It seemed that there was a notebook for each meeting. When he went back to his office, he filed the information about our working group, including the tasks we had agreed to. When the next meeting took place three months later, that old-school notebook would come out again with his copious recordings of what had to be done and who was responsible for implementation. An issue that we spoke about three months ago would be in front of him, and so when we started repeating things without having processed or addressed matters, he would remind us that the issue had been previously discussed and that there needed to be progress.

As a result, we decided that to match President Mbeki's focused working style we would also keep our own notebook. That then was his style of working: he was detailed, committed and thorough. He was always attentive, patient and had the ability to listen very carefully, ticking things off if they were done in a satisfactory manner. Because President Mbeki came from the old school, there was also the issue of the red pen. I too am a product of the old school and so I knew that if there was a red pen mark in his notebook, there was a problem. We also learned that we needed to apply our minds to what we were telling him because he was going to ask probing questions. As a group that did its work thoroughly, we enjoyed that because it made us feel that we were appreciated for getting things done. People who did not do their work saw President Mbeki as interfering and dictatorial. He had called us to hear from us what the pertinent issues impacting women were and it was therefore ridiculous to talk about him being intimidating or dictatorial. He had invited us to share with him our challenges and he wanted to find solutions to those pressing matters. There is nothing intimidating or dictatorial about such a focused approach to work.

Something that irritated President Mbeki was sweet talk. He did not want praise singing or whitewashing because it did not help to address the real challenges. He seemed to want to know about our challenges, raw and unedited. Because he is such a detailed person, after we had presented a set of problems to him, Mbeki would say things like, 'I also thought so before I researched further and therefore what you see on the surface is not what it is.' He would continue, 'This is what moved me from where you are now to where I am today. What do you think?' It was a constructive interaction – he would interrogate issues so that we could find answers together. The president would even direct us to existing laws or information that could help us to unlock our challenges. And so one of the things that we learned quickly was to study, conduct detailed research and understand the relevant pieces of legislation that had been passed dealing with gender issues. If you still had unresolved issues around the problem, he was there to assist. That was why he called us to form the Working Group for Women in the first place.

Mbeki never wanted to leave anything hanging. He was very comfortable with criticism, but you must know that he would respond if the criticism, was uninformed. Uninformed criticism would elicit a response based on informed knowledge. In many ways, it was more painful and embarrassing when that happened. An empty rant might have been easier to take. But what he was doing was bringing into the discussion constructive knowledge that you might not have had access to; sometimes that was more humiliating than if he had simply said, 'Don't talk nonsense.'

In order to be better organised, the Women's Working Group split into two groups dealing with social and economic issues respectively, although there were some cross-cutting issues.

We identified access to water and sanitation as a key area that impacted on a whole lot of others. For example, if you are living in a remote village and you have to fetch water at the river every day, it is likely that on your way you could meet up with some sort of crime such as rape. So, on the social side, we decided to prioritise issues that had to do with access to water and sanitation, especially in rural communities.

On the economic side, we recognised that the control of the economy was through banks, life insurance companies and retirement funds. The reason we raised issues about the banks, life insurance companies and retirement funds as part of our agenda was that the biggest pension fund in the country was the government pension fund, whose members include nurses and teachers, soldiers, police etc. It had 32 trustees. As a working group representing women, we wanted the composition of the government pension fund trustees to be reconfigured because all of them were men. Government appoints 16 trustees and the trade unions appoint the other half. You should have seen President Mbeki's face when we mentioned this fact to him − he was shocked beyond belief. To emphasise our point, we displayed a photo of the 32 male trustees on the projector to prove that we were not making up stories. Between government and the labour unions, they could not find one woman capable of being on this board of trustees − how did that happen?

So that was one of those issues that the presidency might not have seen if we had not brought it up. Trustees are custodians who preside over members' savings on behalf of those members, their spouses and children. They dictate through their investment strategies and asset allocation the direction in which an economy goes. The members are a mixture of men and women, sometimes on a 50/50 basis. How is it that on something that matters so much, there could be amnesia about the presence of women? The problem with not having women represented on the board of trustees was that the fund would not be directed to address women's issues even when it made economic sense. A lot of opportunities would be missed, not only for women but also for the government fund itself. It does not come naturally to men to raise those issues that could make a difference in the life of a woman.

This was a massive trillion-rand fund, and it just did not make sense that trade unions whose members include the Democratic Nursing Organisation of South Africa (DENOSA), which is made up of nurses, and SADTU, which is made up of teachers, both groups having a big component of women members, could not find a single woman to sit on the board of trustees. Men know how to carve out power for themselves and women do not and so when it comes to substance, we will never quite get there. President Mbeki was thoroughly embarrassed by this. He went to the ministry of finance, which was the one that had appointed the trustees on behalf of government, and because of his intervention, the National Treasury had to do the right thing to make sure that women were represented as members of the board of trustees of the government pension fund.

But the bigger issue under the economic theme was that of the experience of domestic workers, because it was mainly women who carried out this work. They often worked from their teenage years until they retired at around 60, after which they returned to their homes and that was the end of the story because they did not have a retirement fund. The reason that they did not have a retirement fund was because they would need an employer who was linked into the pension system. We set out to look for ways that we could set up a retirement fund for domestic workers and we shared our idea with President Mbeki. He welcomed our plan with open arms and asked us to consolidate it by conducting the relevant research ourselves as women, which we did.

Led by the Domestic Workers' Union, we came up with a plan whereby the employer would pay towards the domestic worker's retirement. If the domestic worker should leave to work for someone else, that new employer would then take over and make the contribution towards the retirement plan. It could not be made compulsory, but employers would be encouraged to support the plan. The domestic workers did not have any objections; they just did not have a structure to deal with this important matter. We formed what we called an umbrella fund and we ended up with Old Mutual handling the fund. We launched it officially and that was how the domestic workers' fund came into effect. It was a proud moment for us all and especially for the Domestic Workers' Union. We also had the intention of assisting women who were seasonal workers and creative artists – to include them in this fund. President Mbeki supported us doing homework on this.

But then Mbeki left office before we could finish this work, and there was no Women's Working Group to talk about these further plans. The work of the Women's Working Group came to an abrupt end when he left in 2008 because it was not a constitutional body and that was the end of it, much to our disappointment. Even though it was never meant to be a permanent structure, women felt the rejection, especially since some of the other working groups did continue functioning, and still do even today. The truth of the matter is that of those seven working groups that Mbeki established, the Women's Working Group delivered some tangible outcomes. For example, we had gone quite far with the water and sanitation project. We penetrated many municipalities because the delivery of water and sanitation turned out to be a local authority responsibility and we were trying to close the gap between the local authority, the water management services and the national department of local government.

Our interactions in the Women's Working Group were not light-hearted; we were implementing a lot of projects with the support of President Mbeki. The doors were opened to enable us to do our work and we did not waste the opportunities. The beautiful thing about the Women's Working Group was that none of us saw a business opportunity in the challenges that faced us. We were focused on fixing problems to try to lighten the burden on women, particularly poor women. We always felt good when we met with President Mbeki and had our ducks in a row to report back to him as the president of South Africa. We would even go so far as to spill the beans – telling him about who was not helpful within government departments. We had his ear and we were going to expose those public servants who were not helpful. Before we knew it, the ministers and DGs would be calling us to arrange meetings because the president had contacted them. President Mbeki could see that what we were trying to do was also helping to create movement in issues where government was not easily making an immediate impact. He understood that to accelerate service delivery in some of these key areas, he would need to use us and listen to what we had to say. We were like his equal partners and we made sure that we did not wait on government to deliver; we rolled up our sleeves, understanding that this was our country and we needed to work as partners alongside government. And fortunately we had a president who valued this kind of commitment and self-sacrifice.

When the working groups met, the ministers were invited to attend. In my other capacity in the Black Business Working Group, I would go to these meetings and find a whole delegation of relevant cabinet ministers there. But when it came to the Women's Working Group, some cabinet ministers were always too busy to attend. We took note of that because while we were in agreement that this was a woman-friendly government, some of the cabinet ministers did not think that a women's working group was that significant. We required these relevant cabinet ministers to attend but in the end we just ignored them and did what we had to do. I am mentioning this because we still have lots to do to get women's issues taken seriously, and that was why President Mbeki stood out. He thought that women's issue were part of his priorities.

The sad thing about the water and sanitation project is that when President Mbeki was recalled from office, we were about to get his approval for several items to be inserted into the budgeting process for February 2009. These were life-changing issues for the country because women in rural areas are affected even today. Those projects were going to make government look very good because they were not politically driven, they were not about electioneering. They were none of those things. They did not need legislation or to go to parliament for bills to be enacted. The policies already existed and we used these to good effect when we developed our projects. All that the president needed to do once he was satisfied was to take the matter through the ANC lekgotla process and then through the cabinet lekgotla process so that it fed into the budgeting process; that was all that was required. We had the credibility of 58 organisations and we had a comprehensive programme having done so much work on the ground, backed by those relevant municipalities that appreciated that kind of intervention.

A last word on this matter of the emancipation of women. The birth of women-led businesses such as WIPHOLD, Women's Development Banking, Nozala, Peotona etc. owes much to the enabling environment created by the ANC. But even more critical was the manner in which the head of state, President Mbeki, championed the need for these businesses – communicating as he did that this was critical to ensuring economic inclusion and the participation of women in the mainstream economy. Captains of industry had to take this seriously, recognising that this was not only a social but also an economic imperative.

The events of the ANC's Polokwane conference are best understood and articulated by the branch delegates of the party. It is fair to say, though, that because the ANC is the ruling party, we all followed the process with a keen interest, no differently from the Stellenbosch, Mafikeng or Mangaung conferences.

It is on the recalling of the president of South Africa in September 2008, six months before the end of his term that, as a citizen of the country, I can express my views.

It was really unfortunate that the ANC believed it to be a necessary act to take the country forward. Eight years later I still cannot understand what damage the ANC envisaged he would inflict on the country in his last six months, undoing all the work of the previous 14 years, work in which he had been intimately involved, work that he had driven and championed.

Once again, it was his statesmanship in this extremely complicated period that made me admire the man. As with his 'I am an African' speech, the speech that he made on his stepping down made me appreciate even more who Mbeki was and is – a child of the African National Congress.

In concluding, I would like to give my own personal views of President Mbeki, unrelated to work.

My ultimate hero in the world is my late grandfather, a Baptist Church pastor from Cape Town. Long after he passed on in 1985, the community of Gugulethu where he lived and practised has named our street NY 144 after him, something that excites me in the most unbelievable way.

I had the privilege of having time to learn everything I could from him – I was 26 when he passed on. I had the time to give him the joys and pride of what he would expect from his little princess. And so when his legacy is reflected in that street and the church both named after him, I cannot ask for more.

Back to President Mbeki: my biggest regret is that I never had the opportunity to work for him. My privilege is that at least in the Thabo Mbeki Foundation, of which I am a trustee, I am in a position to preserve his legacy. That is what South Africa deserves.

Interviewed April 2014, Johannesburg

JOEL NETSHITENZHE

❖

Political conscientisation for my generation happened in the early 1970s when we were still at high school. Then I went to medical school at the University of Natal in 1975 and there became actively involved with the South African Students' Organisation (SASO). Later, through contacts, we were able to start accessing Radio Freedom and became involved in all kinds of political debates. There was a lot of literature on people like Kwame Nkrumah, Frantz Fanon and others. It was like a building-up of political consciousness. While at high school the consciousness started merely with awareness of the apartheid system and youthful defiance; my understanding of the African National Congress (ANC) happened much later at university.

To cite a few instances. At the end of 1975, when we were really getting involved in SASO, we went to the SASO summer school. We also visited Steve Biko at his house in the evenings. There were all kinds of debates about the mission and constitutions of SASO and the Black People's Convention (BPC) and whether they recognised the liberation movement and whether they were for or against the ANC or the Pan Africanist Congress (PAC).

In early 1976 I became the secretary of the campus branch of SASO. Around the same period, Joseph Mdluli was killed while in detention in Durban and of course that generated a lot of discussion and anger. After the Soweto student uprisings in June 1976, we decided to demonstrate in solidarity and were arrested. Many of us felt that the country had reached a stage where we had to participate at a different level and by then we were in touch with people in the ANC underground.

A group of four of us left the country around September 1976 and were taken by underground operatives to Lesotho and later Swaziland. Towards the end of 1976, we went to the Umkhonto we Sizwe (MK) military camps in Angola and trained from December 1976 until March 1978, first in Luanda and then Benguela and Novo Katengue, where I became platoon commissar. Then I was selected to work at Radio Freedom. I always joke about this: it was not because of any qualities I possessed, but because I was one of the few people who could speak TshiVenda. They wanted someone who could broadcast in the language.

So in March 1978 I left the ANC camps and went to Lusaka where I started to work for Radio Freedom. That was when I met Thabo Mbeki for the first time – as the head of the Department of Information and Publicity (DIP), in President Oliver Tambo's office. Thabo Mbeki was responsible for Radio Freedom and other functions of DIP and therefore he would invite us from Makeni, where we were operating, to ANC headquarters in the town centre where we would discuss, among other things, the week's programmes and also debate the issues. He advised us generally with regard to the work of Radio Freedom. If my memory serves me well, Mbeki had a regular slot once a week in which he would also broadcast.

In terms of Thabo Mbeki's broadcasting impact, he had a deliberate way of presenting. As to whether Mbeki's voice itself would keep you enthralled as distinct from the substance is a different issue. I always joke about myself in the same regard because I think one of the reasons why I was shifted from Radio Freedom to *Mayibuye* towards the end of 1978 was because of my voice, which is not the best in the world. But Mbeki spoke slowly and deliberately and one of the most impressive things was that, as complex as his form of thinking was, he was able better than ourselves to present scripts for radio that were simple and easy to understand. He was very good at that and we learned a great deal from him. It was the simplicity, combined with substance and lots of crucial messages, that really impressed us.

Thabo Mbeki was also responsible for drafting almost all of the 8 January Statements from 1979 when the tradition, including a declaration of a year's theme, was introduced. Most South African languages were covered on Radio Freedom – in 1978 in Zambia, we broadcast in Venda, Tsonga, Sotho, Tswana, Xhosa, Afrikaans, English and Zulu. There were people like Reg

September, Solly Mokoetle, Thami Ntenteni and others, maybe about 12 people working in the team in Lusaka and elsewhere.

My impression of Mbeki is in part defined by an appreciation of his intelligence and sharpness of mind. In terms of communication, we would have all kinds of ideas about how to present the ANC's message over the radio to people in South Africa, but he would always question whether a particular approach was the correct one and advise on how some of the issues could be articulated. Listening to his presentations was a form of political education. I am not sure if this deserves any mention anywhere, but such was the impression he had on us, the young ones, as we were maturing within Radio Freedom and other structures, that many of us started smoking pipes – as a representation, in our minds, of deep reflection and intellectual posture. But the appropriate tobacco was not always available, so most of us abandoned the adventure.

Thabo Mbeki was a very accessible, very easy-going person and he did not have any airs. He interacted with us in a manner that encouraged critical thinking, always debating issues. I am not quite sure about his actual position then, whether he was already political secretary to Oliver Tambo or whether that came later, but what I remember is that he was operating in Tambo's office and he was put in charge of the DIP. And so he headed the work that we were doing at a supervisory and strategic level. When we had done our planning for the week, we would then debate the programming and the substantive issues with him.

People like Welile Nhlapo, who came later to Lusaka, will know this, given his seniority in the BCM leadership then. Among the dynamics in that period was the debate among the Black Consciousness people whether to establish themselves independently as an organisation or to join the ANC or the Pan Africanist Congress (PAC). Welile and his group came to meet with Thabo in Makeni in 1978, I think. The debate itself about the ANC and how it related to Black Consciousness ideas was an eye-opener, arising in part from the perspectives that Thabo was putting forward. For instance, he would argue with Welile and others that the ANC was more black conscious than the Black Consciousness Movement (BCM) itself, to the extent that while 'non-Africans' might have been members of the ANC since the 1969 Morogoro Conference, they could not become members of the

National Executive Committee (NEC).

At the end of 1978, I was shifted to work on the *Mayibuye* journal, which was launched then as a publication for distribution within South Africa. Joan Brickhill was its first editor. I still recall the first article that I contributed to *Mayibuye,* in the build-up to the centenary of the Battle of Isandlwana, which was in January 1979 and which the ANC declared the Year of the Spear.

I wrote the article about the Battle of Isandlwana and I thought it was quite good. At the time, Mbeki was kind of editor-in-chief of *Mayibuye:* we sent our copy to him for final approval. My piece was sent through, and he essentially rewrote it; improving it, not because there was anything wrong with it, but he enhanced the language, the prose and the overall presentation. Having done a bit of research and moving towards the conclusion of the article, I had a line that referred to a certain commander of the British forces who after they were defeated in Isandlwana either ran back to headquarters or sent back a message to report that 'the camp is in the hands of the enemy, sir!' So, in my conclusion, I said something like: 'It is just a matter of time before we will be able to report that the country is in the hands of the people, comrades!' I really thought that that was very beautiful. Mbeki enhanced the earlier parts of the article to link up with the conclusion. Afterwards, when the first issue of *Mayibuye* came out and when Oliver Tambo came to the DIP in Makeni, he came to greet me and commend me on a very beautiful article. I said Thabo Mbeki rewrote it and O.R. just laughed.

In the debates around the Year of the Spear, we tended to refer to King Cetshwayo's army, the Zulu army so to speak, as a people's army; and Mbeki said to us that we needed to have a debate about whether it really was a people's army; what a people's army really meant and what it represented; and in what sense even Umkhonto we Sizwe could be characterised as such.

These are just instances to illustrate how Mbeki always challenged us to reflect and to ensure that in whatever we presented we should be sure of what we meant and say it clearly. Later, in interactions with Oliver Tambo, one could see that Mbeki had learned from Tambo himself.

When later we interacted with people like Sizakele Sigxashe, who became the operational head of DIP, they told us about when they returned from universities all over the world where they had been trained in the 1960s and early 1970s. Oliver Tambo tested them on their ability to draft; and Thabo Mbeki emerged as the best among them. But, however well Thabo wrote, Oliver Tambo would still edit. In a sense one could say that there was a kind of transmission of education and a honing of skills, from Oliver Tambo to Thabo Mbeki, and then from Thabo to us. We were hardly conscious of the significance of all this, but it is in retrospect that we came to appreciate it fully as being like a little university.

It is difficult to comment on the relationship between Oliver Tambo and Thabo Mbeki as one was not often able to observe them in the same setting, except perhaps later when I became a member of the ANC's Politico Military Council (PMC) and attended some of the rare meetings at which both were present. It is of course a matter of public record that Mbeki contributed to most of the speeches that Oliver Tambo made as president. Furthermore, he was also responsible for strategising as political secretary in the president's office, which was responsible for a number of departments, including the DIP and political education. But the relationship between Thabo Mbeki and Oliver Tambo in my view, and I might be wrong in this, was one of reverence. I saw respect and reverence – and at times even nervousness on the part of 'the student'. I suppose Oliver Tambo's interventions in editing things that were drafted by Mbeki, or in challenging ideas that were being raised, made sure that there would be that appreciation that Tambo, as the president of the ANC, was in a different class altogether. I also think that age had something to do with it. People joke about referring to Mbeki as 'Chief'. In fact, members showed their reverence for Oliver Tambo in a similar way long before this; and if I'm not mistaken, this may have started with the previous president Albert Luthuli who was an actual traditional chief.

We did not often socialise with Mbeki in Lusaka. But there were instances when we visited his flat and sometimes we would find Abdullah Ibrahim there, who stayed at his place when he was in Lusaka, or you would find Caiphus Semenya and Letta Mbulu and they would be playing music. He attended some of the parties that we had and he would dance with us and have a drink. So Mbeki was able every so often to relax with the crowd.

The sense that one had of Mbeki was cool, strategic and measured, but around 1978/1979 – I do not know the actual details – I observed one time when he and Joe Nhlanhla sounded quite agitated as they were photocopying some important document in Makeni. We later learned that there were very intense debates taking place in the NEC about issues of strategy. There had not been a Strategy and Tactics document since the Morogoro conference of 1969 and there were all kinds of contestations around, for example, the relationship between mass and armed struggle and the role of the underground. Those who were members of the Revolutionary Council, especially those who came from MK, were emphasising the supremacy of the military struggle, and Thabo Mbeki and others from the political side were emphasising the importance of mass action. This, I think, illustrates how agitated Mbeki could become if he felt, especially at the level of the NEC, that people were not appreciating some of the ideas that he and like-minded people were putting forward.

Later, one was able to interact with Mbeki in the context of the South African Communist Party (SACP). Joe Nhlanhla, Joan Brickhill, one or two other comrades and I belonged to the same party unit as Thabo Mbeki and you can well imagine how we also learned from him in the context of that interaction. Among the things that remain etched in my mind, and in the context both of debates in that Communist Party unit and in other interactions, was the belief among some of us that the Freedom Charter essentially represented a socialist outcome to the struggle. But people like Mbeki and Jack Simons would draw our attention to other provisions in the Charter for us to appreciate that it was about a national democratic revolution. Others among us believed that the Freedom Charter promoted social democracy as manifest, for instance, in Scandinavian countries like Sweden. I remember arguing in one meeting that social democracy was a critical stage towards the attainment of socialism. Thabo Mbeki would argue that the concentration of private capital ownership in Sweden for instance – monopoly capital, that is – might be even more extensive and at a higher level than in many other Western countries: it was more about how they redistributed the income after it had been earned rather than an outcome of a particular form of ownership. In other words, things that appeared obvious and simple to us would be challenged by him, and this helped us to reflect and develop a keener understanding of the international and domestic environments.

I suppose it would possibly have been on Mbeki's recommendation that some of us were selected to go to the Institute of Social Sciences (popularly known as the Party School) in the Soviet Union for two years from 1982 to 1984. After that, we worked together in all kinds of forums, for instance, drafting, preparing and editing documents in the build-up to the Kabwe conference of 1985. In this period, I was asked to head what was called Internal Propaganda in the internal political committee and later the Politico-Military Council, incorporating *Mayibuye,* Radio Freedom, preparation of pamphlets and so on. Mbeki was, in all these functions, our locus of reference.

The other activity where we worked quite closely was in the preparation for the SACP congress that took place in Cuba in 1989. We were in the drafting team preparing the SACP programme, 'The Path to Power'. It was led by Joe Slovo, and Mbeki, Harold Wolpe, Jeremy Cronin and I contributed to the draft. He also chaired some of the sessions of the congress. He made a huge impact, especially when it came to debates on strategy and tactics. I need to emphasise that there was that keen awareness on Mbeki's part as we were debating 'The Path to Power' and the possibility of insurrection, that there was another possible route that was emerging as a consequence of the changing balance of forces both domestically and internationally. By then Mbeki and others had already started all kinds of interactions with representatives of the apartheid regime. At the party congress, the slant was more towards how to ensure that insurrection actually took place and then the debate about the transition and how long it would take for the national democratic revolution to transit to socialism. Those were the kinds of issues, but I think you could identify in the formulations introduced by Thabo Mbeki, among others, raising the possibility of substantive negotiations that he had background information that most of us did not have. Of course, no one wanted to raise this as a major issue at the congress; but it was a possibility that needed to be kept in mind.

Thabo Mbeki participated very actively in how issues needed to be formulated in the debates about the role of the working class and the emergence of the trade union movement, the relationship between the trade unions and the Communist Party, and the relationship between the ANC and the Communist Party. In chairing some of the congress sessions, he would discreetly guide the discussion in particular directions. Carefulness, elegance and precision in formulation – one could say that these were among the strongest contributions that Thabo Mbeki made in terms of our development within the DIP. We learned gradually, step by step, how to formulate things for presentation to society or to whoever else. One of the instances that we used to laugh about in Radio Freedom was the meeting in London between the ANC and Inkatha in 1979, an event that had agitated many of us young ones and the MK cadres in the camps. It was supposed to be a secret meeting but it would seem Mangosuthu Buthelezi decided to go public about it. So the ANC had to issue an official statement. Thabo Mbeki drafted the statement, and one of the lines that we used to joke about was the formulation that 'there was no secret meeting'. That did not mean that there was no meeting because the meeting did take place. So it was deliberately left open to interpretation.

By the mid- to late-1980s Thabo Mbeki became head of the Department of International Affairs (DIA), after Johnny Makhathini passed away. So in addition to being political adviser to Tambo, he was also head of International Affairs and he was travelling throughout the world. People like George Nene and Welile Nhlapo, who worked closely with him in this area, would confirm that around 1988 he was interacting with people from the underground inside the country, individuals connected to the apartheid regime, and also with various governments, including the UK and the US, which had all along sought to isolate the ANC as a 'terrorist' organisation. These governments were being pressurised and had started to accept that there would have to be change in South Africa. Tambo, who closely supervised what Mbeki was doing, introduced the debate about the possibility of negotiations, firstly, within the NEC, and later broadened it to include other cadres of the movement and the membership. There are many who felt that the time was not ripe for that to even be considered.

In the late 1980s, a special meeting was organised by Oliver Tambo. Thabo Mbeki was there, as well as a few other senior people, and some of us such as Jeremy Cronin from the Internal Political Committee, as well as Penuel Maduna and Ngoako Ramatlhodi, who had become the main speechwriter for Tambo. We were invited to start debating how to ensure that the ANC defined the road map that would need to be followed in negotiations in order for us to achieve our objectives. For instance, should we consider the Palestinian or Namibian approach, where there were outside powers to facilitate the negotiations process or should it just be among South Africans? It was out of that internal consultative process that the Harare Declaration emerged. By then secure communication was possible with the internal structures in South Africa and even those in prison. There were exchanges with some senior people in the United Democratic Front (UDF) but, more critically, with Mandela for political prisoners to make their own input. And when a certain stage had been reached, Oliver Tambo and Thabo Mbeki went around the Frontline States with a view to seeking their advice and influencing the Organisation of African Unity (OAU) to officially adopt the ANC position on this issue.

Tragically, a few days after that gruelling trip around southern Africa, Oliver Tambo had a stroke. The Harare Declaration was officially adopted by the OAU. It ended up being adopted by the United Nations (UN). The strategic plan that had been conceived under Oliver Tambo's leadership underlined, firstly, that substantive negotiations should be among South Africans and not mediated by anyone, as distinct from Zimbabwe and Namibia. Secondly, the Harare Declaration asserted that the outcome of the negotiations process should be an elective institution to draft a constitution and that there should be certain principles that defined what a new South Africa should look like. Thirdly, of course, before negotiations could start, the ANC and other liberation movements would have to be able to interact freely with the apartheid regime, which would mean the release of political prisoners and the unbanning of political organisations. One of the major contributions that Thabo Mbeki, under the tutelage of Oliver Tambo, made to the evolution of South Africa's body politic was in defining that road map.

In terms of geopolitics, it was important to understand the emphasis on negotiations being a South African process, because outside mediation could facilitate pursuit of the big powers' own self-interests as distinct from the interests of South Africans. One observation to make in this regard, which partly reflects the unique and varied South African patriotism within our society, is that this was one of the things on which the white Afrikaners were at one with the ANC. They did not want external forces such as the

US, Britain or the Soviet Union to be involved in the negotiations. In a sense this was an opportunity for the South African people to develop a profound understanding of their own self-interests, to look at commonalities and areas of divergence and how to bridge them as South Africans.

In the build-up to 2 February 1990, there was even more intense communication between the ANC team that was delegated by Oliver Tambo and the NEC to interact with the representatives of the apartheid regime. Those interactions took place in late 1988 and during the whole of 1989. In late 1989 to early 1990 the delegation was now directly from the regime, the National Intelligence Services (NIS) team, which was interacting with the ANC team that comprised people like Thabo Mbeki, Jacob Zuma, Aziz Pahad and Joe Nhlanhla. I think by then they were already signalling that the announcement of 2 February was going to take place. So for people like Mbeki, it was not a surprise; but it was a surprise for many of us who were at a distance.

We had developed a tradition by then of listening to or monitoring the major pronouncements of leaders of the apartheid regime. On 2 February 1990, I was at the offices of the Internal Political Committee (IPC), which was a branch of the PMC, when F.W. de Klerk announced the unbanning of political organisations and the release of political prisoners.

After listening to the speech, I decided to drive to the offices of the PMC where a meeting of the inner core of the PMC was taking place. There were people like Josiah Jele and Chris Hani and they were discussing military issues about problems of smuggling weapons into South Africa, developing new routes and so on.

So I barged in and informed them that F.W. de Klerk had just announced the unbanning of the ANC and the Communist Party. They asked a few questions, but their response was sort of, 'Oh, we see.' I left and they continued with their discussion. It was difficult for them to shift their mindset there and then; or maybe they realised that the change would not immediately render the armed struggle redundant.

Generally, it took time for people to absorb this information. If you had been planning and executing these military operations for some 30 years, you would not have been prepared for such a dramatic and sudden change. The PMC continued for a few weeks as if nothing had happened. Later we were invited to a special meeting of the PMC to discuss all these things that had taken place and their implications.

By this time the mood was a combination of hope and apprehension. In my view, what reinforced the sense of hope and, if you like, positive fore-boding was the following week when Mandela was released and the impact that he made on South African society. We observed it from Lusaka and celebrated it there. We spent the day of Mandela's release at Steve Tshwete's house having drinks, debating and musing about the implications. Thabo Mbeki, Jacob Zuma and others were already handling matters to do with Mandela and other political prisoners and their security as well as the ini-tiation of formal negotiations. They were also talking about which ANC team should be the first to reinforce the legal structures being re-established within the country. In the event, the team from the information and public-ity section was among the first to be asked to return to South Africa.

Prior to 1990, there was that team of Thabo Mbeki, Jacob Zuma, Aziz Pahad and others, who I would argue played a decisive role in clarifying the negotiations substance and process. But if that team had a weakness, it was about how to link up the negotiations process and all its technicalities to the mass of the people who supported the ANC and political change in South Africa. The initiation of the negotiations process pre-1990 had been a very secretive affair. One has a sense that the team continued with the same paradigm. What was missing in their style was actualising that linkage between the strategic and technical work on the one hand, and the totality of the leadership of the ANC, the mass democratic movement and the mass of South Africans on the other. The leadership from the mass democratic movement was more alert to this – and so it was a fusion of these styles that created a happy synthesis in the ANC's overall approach.

Cyril Ramaphosa, in particular, would have been a good negotiator on tactical issues, such as what you give and what you get. He was also, like Mandela, more alert to popular sensitivities and how to carry the mass of supporters along. However, in all the meetings, whether formal or otherwise, in all the bilateral discussions that we had with the leadership of the apart-heid regime and the National Party, the ultimate substance and guidance to the overall approach came from Thabo Mbeki. Everyone acknowledged that Mbeki was the most knowledgeable person in the ANC delegation.

Although Ramaphosa, as secretary general, led the delegation, and people like Joe Slovo made valuable inputs, Thabo Mbeki was the thought leader of the negotiations process.

We got into government in a situation in which the president's office had largely been denuded as De Klerk sought to get rid of the so-called securocrats after taking over from P.W. Botha. The president's office was then reconstructed into quite a small unit that serviced Mandela as president, as well as the cabinet. I think that the presidency was structured around the personality of the incumbent. But quite clearly that was not adequate to run the government and lead the process of effecting fundamental transformation. So the management of governmental issues, including the processing of policy at a senior level before it went to cabinet, resided in the deputy president's office. As a consequence, that office grew in terms of policy planning and strategising to become the engine of the presidency – and one is differentiating here between the president's office and the presidency. Thabo Mbeki was the first deputy president and his office became the engine of the presidency in determining what immediate policies needed to be introduced, how the democratic government was structured, how to submit important matters to cabinet, how to ensure that ANC cabinet members were able to plan for cabinet meetings in the Government of National Unity. For instance, many seminal pronouncements by Mandela in that period, including the speech that he delivered at the opening of the first democratic parliament, would have been drafted by Thabo Mbeki in interaction with the various ANC policy teams and the new ministers and advisers that had come in.

Initially there was no requisite capacity because we had never run a government before. There was a sense that many of the leaders were operating on the basis of what, in jest, I refer to as native intelligence: trying to get information, processing it and turning it into policy decisions; looking at the implications and the consequences; coming back, refining it and improving and looking at gaps in the structuring of government; getting information from ministers and advisers, because the old directors general were still there; and managing the process of easing some of the senior bureaucrats out as we brought in new ones who identified with the ruling 'party'.

With regard to the Growth, Employment and Redistribution (GEAR) plan, it was more about management of the macro-economic environment in a situation of political transition. It became clear that regardless of what the ANC and the government said and did, the confidence of the business community was not improving in line with the post-apartheid dividend. They accepted that there had been political change; they accepted that the constitution had clauses that would ensure that their property was protected and that if it were to be appropriated there would be legal processes. However, despite what the ANC said and did, they still did not want to invest in the new South Africa. Many were still even smuggling resources out of the country. Many wanted to relocate their businesses to Europe and other countries of the north. Many still thought that the ANC had something up its sleeve. And so there were moments in which, especially in 1995, confidence just plummeted. There were low rates of investment by domestic business, minimal inflows of capital from outside, and attacks on the rand. Further, when we went into government, the budget deficit was very high, and so macro-stabilisation measures had to be introduced, otherwise the social transformation process would have become unsustainable. There were a few things you could adjust by shifting resources, but if you were to ensure that more resources come into state coffers as a consequence of growth, then you had to stabilise the macro-economic environment. It was in that context that GEAR was introduced.

The content of GEAR was more about the actions that needed to be taken in order to slowly reduce the budget deficit, and to stabilise interest rates, inflation and all those macro-economic indicators. GEAR was necessary. If it had not been implemented but we still wanted to spend more resources on social transformation, we would have had to borrow from the dreaded International Monetary Fund (IMF) and World Bank. In this sense, GEAR was a temporary intervention to stabilise the macro-economic situation so that we would then be able to implement more far-reaching policies of economic restructuring, micro-economic interventions, comprehensive social programmes and so on. Its impact and the correctness of the approach were confirmed by history itself at the turn of the century around 2000/2001. By then it had achieved its purpose, and the trend in real growth in government expenditure changed dramatically.

As one has argued in many forums, including those of the SACP and the Congress of South African Trade Unions (COSATU), by 2001/2002, we were in a post-GEAR period. But you would still have critics who talked about the '1996 Class Project' and continued to refer to Mbeki as its figurehead. In my view, if there was any weakness in GEAR, it was more in its presentation and communication – in the sense that it was drafted as if it was the totality of economic policy, whereas it was a self-imposed macro-economic stabilisation programme. Perhaps that created the wrong impression. It might have been better to be frank and to say that we inherited a fiscus in serious distress and our macro-economy was in the doldrums and so we would introduce GEAR to stabilise these so that in the medium term we would have higher rates of growth – rather than promising some million jobs and so on in the same document. Otherwise, I have never doubted the logic behind it, and the outcome did prove its correctness. In my view, given his historical experience in the DIP, Thabo Mbeki could have played a more direct and active role in devising a better popular communication approach to GEAR.

I suppose that as Thabo Mbeki was easing into the presidency through the transition and the 'I am an African' speech in 1996, through to the Mafikeng national conference in 1997, when he was elected president of the ANC, there was perhaps consciously and subconsciously an effort on his part to assert his personality and his outlook on society. In that process, he tried to define a new trajectory for the country both in relation to economic issues, social issues, and also issues to do with psychology, identity and so on. By the time he became South Africa's president in 1999, he had already asserted the African continental outlook and he was interacting with some of the more progressive and advanced corps of leaders in the developing countries.

This was when platforms like the Smart Partnerships emerged. These were interactions with leaders such as Mahathir Mohamad of Malaysia, Ethiopia's Meles Zenawi and Olusegun Obasanjo of Nigeria. You could say these were the smart leaders of the developing world who were defining a new trajectory for developing countries in the context of globalisation. It is in that context that you would appreciate Thabo Mbeki's strategic outlook; that it transcended domestic and even continental issues and he was able to place his vision within the broader global environment: from G8

Thabo Mbeki at the MK camp in Uganda in 1990. (Courtesy Stanley Ndlovu)

General secretary of the ANC Alfred Nzo (left), Oliver Tambo, ANC president (centre), and Thabo Mbeki (right) in Lusaka. (Courtesy ANC Archives)

Thabo Mbeki with President Nelson Mandela at Mandela's last rally at the FNB Stadium in Johannesburg on 30 May 1999. (Getty Images)

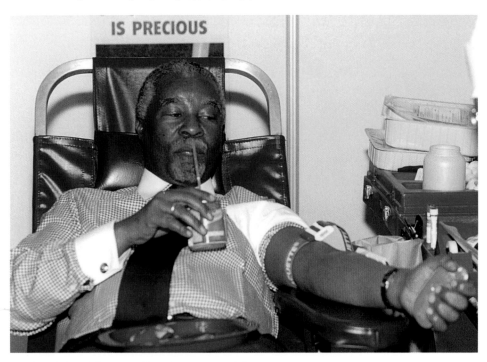

President Thabo Mbeki donates blood during a national shortage in 2001. (Getty Images)

President Thabo Mbeki with President George W. Bush in Pretoria on 9 July 2003. (Courtesy GCIS)

Thabo Mbeki with Ivorian President Laurent Gbagbo and South African Defence Minister Mosiuoa Lekota in Yamoussoukro on 11 January 2005. (Getty Images)

Thabo Mbeki with United Nations Secretary-General Kofi Annan. (Courtesy GCIS)

President Thabo Mbeki with Russian President Vladimir Putin. (Courtesy GCIS)

President Thabo Mbeki and Democratic Republic of Congo President Joseph Kabila on 14 June 2007.
(Courtesy GCIS)

Thabo Mbeki, president of the ANC, and his deputy, Jacob Zuma, at the ANC's 95th birthday bash at Witbank, Mpumalanga. (Courtesy Antony Kaminju/Times Media Group)

Thabo Mbeki joins Ladysmith Black Mambazo on stage during a performance. (Courtesy GCIS)

President Thabo Mbeki interacting with a community during an imbizo. (Courtesy GCIS)

President Thabo Mbeki and children having fun during an imbizo. (Courtesy GCIS)

Left to right, Dr Brigalia Bam, Zanele and Thabo Mbeki at the unveiling of the Tiyo Soga memorial in the Eastern Cape on 9 September 2011. (Courtesy Vusi Maqubela/Thabo Mbeki Foundation)

Former Presidents Olusegun Obasanjo and Thabo Mbeki during the 2012 annual Thabo Mbeki Africa Day Lecture. (Courtesy Shooheima Champion/University of South Africa)

Zanele, Thabo, Moeletsi and his son Karl Mbeki at the funeral of Epainette Mbeki.
(Courtesy Vusi Maqubela/Thabo Mbeki Foundation)

Thabo Mbeki and elders prepare for the funeral of his mother, Epainette Mbeki.
(Courtesy Vusi Maqubela/Thabo Mbeki Foundation)

Thabo Mbeki enjoys watching sport and has tried his hand at golf. (Courtesy GCIS)

Photography is one of Thabo Mbeki's favourite pastimes. He particularly enjoys nature photography.
(Courtesy Mukoni Ratshitanga/Thabo Mbeki Foundation)

to G20 and beyond, including the invitation to African countries to attend G8 meetings, and the conceptualisation of the New Partnership for Africa's Development (NEPAD).

In the meetings that we attended as part of the NEPAD drafting team we heard President Mbeki's elucidation of how Africa's underdevelopment could become a boon that Africa could exploit going forward because it meant that, for many years to come, infrastructure would need to be built on the African continent. Massive investment would be needed, leading to employment and the emergence of a 'middle class'. You would have, if you like, a virtuous cycle of Africa rising and benefiting from that process of advancement.

Having been in exile and having operated in places like Nigeria and elsewhere, Mbeki appreciated keenly the need to develop a network of leaders with the same strategic outlook with whom jointly to pursue the developmental state agenda. It is in the context of that strategic thinking and those interactions that NEPAD emerged; and so strong was its message that the developed countries, in spite of themselves, could not ignore it. That was why the G8 accepted that there would be African leaders at its meetings, and that a partnership would be formally declared between Africa and the G8. I think in part it was a product of Mbeki's strategic acumen. But, perhaps even more importantly, there had not been in many decades – some might say in history – as global and as universal a cause as the fight against apartheid, and that was as a consequence of the mobilisation of the international community; from east to west and in every capital on the globe. All of them came to the agreement that apartheid was a crime against humanity and needed to be got rid of. This provided the context for the ANC to develop not just networks across all these countries, but contacts at all levels of society, from the leadership to the student movement to the union movement. This was what made it possible for Mbeki to think globally and to link South Africa and the African continent to the global community – now in the context of post-colonial development.

In my view, at least in this context, there has never been a liberation movement with the kind of experience that the ANC had; and Thabo Mbeki was building on that. He had an appreciation of the global balance of forces, the global mood not only among the leaders but among the mass of the people, and how developing countries and an emerging South Africa could fit into that. The idea of Africa's Renaissance, and the development of NEPAD and the initiatives that Africa took became credible internationally, to the extent that even the Bushes of this world (and others) accepted that they could develop a partnership between the G8 and Africa for Africa's advancement. It was a major achievement that perhaps we have not fully appreciated.

The work that Thabo Mbeki was doing and his interactions with leaders like Meles and Obasanjo, and I think to some extent with Rwandan leader Paul Kagame, Uganda's Yoweri Museveni, Abdoulaye Wade of Senegal and Algerian Leader Abdelaziz Bouteflika, impacted on the refinement of the grand idea that was later called NEPAD. That we might be faltering in pursuing that grand idea today is, I think, a major tragedy for South Africa and for Africa as a whole.

In terms of addressing some of Mbeki's weaknesses and strengths, let us look at the issues of AIDS and Zimbabwe. With regard to HIV/AIDS, you will find some of these issues in the interviews that he conducted with Mark Gevisser. I think that one of his strengths, which can become a weakness, is the extent to which, before he develops ideas, he dips into minute detail. With issues of this kind, where medical science still had its gaps, one can become absorbed by minutiae and lose track of the bigger picture. That was the weakness in his approach to this issue. At least we were able to convince him to retreat from the public debate and accept what we thought and what we believed was the natural evolution of policy as we tried to attack the pandemic.

With regard to Zimbabwe, many factors come into play. The people who hate Mugabe also hate ZANU-PF and they had their own subjective reading of Mbeki's role and his capacity to change things quickly and neatly. And so many of them also developed a hatred for Mbeki for not producing instant results. They thus could not appreciate even the tectonic shift that was attained, particularly in the so-called harmonised elections of March 2008, with rules and regulations and practices that made it impossible to cheat. The outcome of that election, after many years of trying to normalise things, and partly as a consequence of Mbeki's (and of course SADC's) intervention, was a reflection of the will of the Zimbabwean people. That was a qualitative movement forward. Mbeki managed to steer things in such a way that Zimbabwe had the kind of democratic election that created a platform going forward for an improvement in how the country conducts its elections. Of course, there was the panic and violence that followed, particularly in relation to the presidential leg of the elections, but a qualitative shift had taken place. The negotiations that followed and the emergence of the multi-party government were not, in the strategic order of things, a step backwards, given the country's recent history.

The Western powers would criticise, but in private some of them would admit that they had no solutions except silly things like regime change or assassination. They would admit that patient and systematic approaches were needed in order to turn the Zimbabwean situation around. You get a sense, and sometimes it is one of the weaknesses of global politics, that some of the leaders tended to be guided by public opinion polls in their countries, and very superficial analysis of situations, rather than looking at the deep structural issues that required resolution.

Moving to domestic politics and in relation to Polokwane, I suppose that Mbeki might have made assumptions about the quality of the ANC's cadreship and membership, and their ability to differentiate between right and wrong. I think that he had not fully noticed how the liberation movement itself had changed. In brief, I would interpret what happened in Polokwane in that way. Some might say – particularly among those who supported him – that perhaps they were not frank enough about the actual balance of forces and they might have misled Mbeki. But then the matter had become one of principle. The bigger question was about a better appreciation of the changes that had taken place within the liberation movement in so far as the quality of cadreship and membership is concerned. It was this failure to appreciate changing internal organisational dynamics that was responsible for what happened in Polokwane. Post-Polokwane those internal dynamics are still manifesting, and the current ANC leadership has acknowledged as much. How you turn that around in the medium to long term is a discussion for another day.

I think that Mbeki assumed that the rationality of his approach would be what informed the thinking of the ANC as a liberation movement. This reflected a failure to appreciate the impulses that informed people's actions based on individual self-interest, among other things. And after the Polokwane defeat, I think that Mbeki believed that a liberation movement with the ANC's kind of history, a movement that had been rational in approaching challenges, would rationally handle the transition until he left government as dictated by the electoral cycles. He did not know that there would be other impulses at play. These started to manifest more intensely during the first half of 2008; and Mbeki came to appreciate that he was already trapped in the situation and could only operate on the basis of what his movement, the ANC, dictated.

It is difficult to articulate what happened when he was recalled from office because, although it is a few years since it happened, the sense of trauma from that period still lives with me today. The discussions unfolded at the NEC meeting of which I was a member. I did not quite understand why they wanted to recall him as the president of the republic. They were arguing about the distance between Luthuli House and the Union Buildings and so on. I was sitting through all this and participated in the discussion for what it was worth – to argue that we should not set a terrible precedent for the country; that if there was a feeling that change had to come, the election could be brought closer and we would then have a proper transition rather than being dramatic. It became clear in the course of the discussion that there might have been a lot of lobbying about what people would say and how they would ensure that the outcome happened as it did.

The recall of Thabo Mbeki was a tragedy for the ANC. It was a trag-edy, among other things, because it soiled the sense of stability, rationality, the measured approaches to issues, and the logic with which the ANC was historically associated. Once something like that happens, it embeds itself in the organisational culture. As I argued then, some might enjoy the glory of being perpetrators in a seemingly victorious moment, but they needed to be careful because having entrenched that destructive culture, they might, in time, become its victim. That experience, and the things that have happened since 2009, all speak to a liberation movement that needs fundamental re-engineering, restructuring, and reorientation. If that does not happen, the negative culture will become so systemic that the ANC – at least in so far as its outlook and standing in society are concerned – will die an ignominious death.

V

SOUTH AFRICAN AMBASSADORS

GEORGE NENE

❧❧

I was born and spent my early years in Soweto where I did my primary and high schooling. I matriculated at Morris Isaacson High in 1969 and then continued with my education by enrolling at the University of Zululand (Ongoye). I registered for a secondary teachers' diploma, which unfortunately I could not complete as I was one of those who were expelled. During my days as a student, I got involved in politics as part of black consciousness activity and was a member of the South African Students' Organisation (SASO).

Thrown back on to the streets of Soweto with nothing to do, I had to try to eke out a living and it was during this period that, together with friends, specifically Siphiwe Nyanda, Stanley Nkosi and Kgalema Motlanthe, I joined the African National Congress (ANC) and its military wing Umkhonto we Sizwe (MK). At some point Siphiwe and I were instructed by the ANC leadership in Swaziland to leave the country. My exile life started in January 1976.

I was among a group of new recruits, like others before us, who left Swaziland through Mozambique to Tanzania, which was the most used halfway station. From there you either went to school or to the army. I went to Russia where I received military training, after which I went to the first camp of the ANC in Benguela in Angola. In 1981 the ANC sent me to Mazimbu in Tanzania where I stayed until 1986, when I was deployed to Lusaka to join the Department of Information and Publicity (DIP) whose offices were in Makene. I became part of the machinery that produced the

ANC journal *Mayibuye*. The head of the DIP was Thabo Mbeki, with Pallo
Jordan and then Joel Netshitenzhe as his deputies. I was in the section that
produced, distributed and assisted in the smuggling of *Mayibuye*.

I did not see much of Mbeki in Makene and if you had been familiar
with our work schedule you would understand why this was the case. We
never had serious management committee meetings; Pallo was not a manager in the classic meaning of the word; Thabo was not a manager and Joel
was also not a manager and all three of them were our bosses. But whenever
we had time to meet, we knew that we would have quality discussions with
Mbeki.

As staff members, we devised a scheme to engage with him because only
a few of us knew where he stayed. So we just used to invade him during
the day when he was at work. One of the things we raised with him was
his non-attendance at funerals of ANC comrades in Zambia. We confronted
him and asked him how he could be a leader of the liberation movement
and not attend funerals. His argument was, 'What value will I add? Oliver
Tambo is always there as the president of the movement, symbolically representing everybody; I am doing better work here.' We said it does not work
like that. Slowly but surely we started seeing him coming to funerals and
other social gatherings relevant to our organisation.

I had met Mbeki earlier at the ANC conference in Kabwe; I was based
in Tanzania at that time. I was part of the delegation from Tanzania, deputis-
ing for Mendi Msimang, who was leader of the Tanzania delegation to the
Kabwe conference.

We participated with Thabo Mbeki in different commissions at the Kabwe
conference. Most of us attended the Strategy and Tactics Commission.
Obviously I attended the one on international affairs where we were dealing with the four pillars of struggle: international relations was one of the
four pillars. Since I was attending as deputy to Msimang, I had to go back
and report to the East Africa region. So I had to monitor all the commissions on behalf of our own delegation, and that was how I met and got to
know better most of the core leadership. There was what was described as
the 'second layer of leadership' and Mbeki was in the upper part of the second layer of leadership with Chris Hani and Pallo Jordan.

I was approached by Comrade Johnny Makhathini to join his department, the Department of International Affairs (DIA). Thabo Mbeki was not in favour of that but ultimately they found a solution that allowed me to move over to the DIA. At some point Johnny Makhathini said we should go to meet President Oliver Tambo. Johnny informed him that he had settled the matter with Thabo Mbeki and that was how I was redeployed to the DIA. As you know, Johnny did not live long because he did not take proper care of his diabetes; that was what killed him. Then Mbeki took over the DIA and that was when I really started to work closely with him.

Most of the ANC speeches were written by Thabo Mbeki, whether it was the ANC's January 8 speech or whatever. Mbeki would challenge us to offer input concerning the content. But the prerogative rested with Oliver Tambo to rubber-stamp, improve or discard those draft speeches. Mbeki would always remind us that we needed to prepare timeously for an upcoming event. I called him a 'little O.R.'. He took after President Oliver Tambo in terms of being a workaholic and very strict on quality and standards; he is very thorough. Obviously we also wanted to be in the second layer of leadership, so we were competitive in making sure that the quality of the work we gave to Mbeki was of a high standard.

We worked well during the day when he was not there, sharing ideas as we prepared the text. Most of the time Joel handed over these documents to Thabo personally and not to Pallo. The only reason for this was that Pallo, another workaholic and ANC intellectual, was always in his office, either reading, writing or conducting his research, and we hardly saw him, not even during lunch. Therefore we did not want to disturb him.

We did our best to reflect ANC policies and how to promote them in whatever the ANC needed to be conveyed in any given speech, which helped us to learn a lot about the ANC. Besides that, in the DIP we also learned a lot about international politics because we had to source information from different places in order to be able to produce *Mayibuye*. We also had to prepare reading material for the commissars in the military camps to share with the MK cadres because there was no information in the camps; there were no radios or television. That experience helped us to gain political background, including an understanding of how the media works.

But we learned more from Thabo Mbeki because he would engage us in discussions about the content to be published in *Mayibuye* or about drafting a speech. He had a particular way of doing things. For example, he would not call a meeting and say here is a draft speech. He would invite us to his house – it would be Tebogo Mafole, Joel, Bra Sydney and me. Then he would put a bottle of whisky in front of us and he would start a debate. We found out later that he would already have conceptualised the draft. We would argue until we were all tired, apart from Mbeki.

With reference to his not being tired after a hard day's work, I recall an occasion during the early 1990s when Mbeki travelled to Nigeria with Mandela, Joe Modise, Steve Tshwete and Stan Mabizela. I was ANC chief representative in Nigeria at the time. We made sure that Mandela went to sleep early and we continued with preparations for meetings with our Nigerian counterparts. I think that we held the discussions in Modise's hotel room and we must have been there until the early hours of the morning.

At 5am I heard somebody pushing a paper under my hotel room door: it was Mbeki. He had not gone to sleep after the debates in Modise's room and had finished writing the speech for Madiba. At breakfast Mbeki said, 'Mandela's speech is the product of my engagement with all of you because I collected all the ideas that we shared, took a shower and started typing.' So that debate in Modise's room enriched us because Mbeki's intellect and his experience was the way we, as a collective, learned in terms of recording our intellectual ideas as a liberation movement. Ours was also an intellectual struggle for ideas: Thabo, Pallo, Joel, Tebogo and others within the liberation movement personified and led this struggle through the production of knowledge. All you need to do is to read the content in *Sechaba* and *Mayibuye*.

We worked with Mbeki until we were repatriated back to South Africa. I was among the first group who returned in 1990 and was part of the first DIA staff at Shell House. The national leadership took a decision that at least 15 of us should go for training as diplomats in the UK, France, Germany and Norway. We also did a course on negotiations at the University of South Africa (UNISA). It was obvious that when we came back we would be part of the DIA. At that time we were working very closely with Thabo Mbeki. At that time, he was staying in a flat in Illovo, Johannesburg. We would work late in the office until it was time to go home to Soweto in a taxi organised for me.

Thabo Mbeki is easy to work with because he challenges you, but you will be uncomfortable if you have not prepared thoroughly enough to ask critical questions. I do not know whether it is a strength or a weakness, but he does not easily show his emotions. If he is angry with you, you will not see it because he will just withdraw, like most of those whose star sign is Gemini; I know because I am one too.

The people with whom I worked most closely were Makhathini and Mbeki. Makhathini was also a workaholic, but he lacked Thabo's finesse. Makhathini's strong point was that he was an excellent organiser and you needed this when your focus as a liberation movement prioritises international solidarity. But both Makhathini and Mbeki would tell you almost the same thing if they felt you were slacking; they would say, 'How can you be sleeping when Mandela is crushing stones in prison?' Even Oliver Tambo used to say that. I think that accounts for most of us being hard workers; I cannot sleep for more than four hours. I doubt that Thabo Mbeki sleeps for more than four hours a night, and I am told that Oliver Tambo never slept for more than four hours. I cannot sleep beyond four hours because I got used to it when I was in exile. If there was not much work, Oliver Tambo and Thabo Mbeki would look for work. I think that this is one thing that they shared: they worked too much. Even at present, my analysis is that Mbeki is working too much without taking a rest or a holiday, and in this respect he needs to be careful about his health.

My approach to the question about the leadership styles of our first two presidents, Mandela and Thabo Mbeki, is different and I say so when I am invited to ANC branch meetings where people argue that during Mandela's time the ANC government was very strong. They maintain that when Mandela left government human rights issues became weaker, whatever that loaded statement means. My analysis is that the challenges are different. You have to have both historical and political contexts. The context during Mandela's era was to allay white fears and those of the international community who thought that the country was going to explode. Therefore the focus of the Mandela era was more on social cohesion and nation building and he was guided by ANC policies in this regard.

One day in 1994 Mbeki received a call from the ANC leadership to say that he would be the deputy to Mandela. When he came back from answering the phone, he told us that 'These old people say that I must be the deputy president of the country; this means that I cannot sit and drink whisky in public with you in a hotel any more, but it does not mean that you must abandon me.' After the Madiba presidency the context had to change because we could not keep building a nation for ever just to cater for the needs of the white minority.

But whether it was Mbeki or somebody else who took power after Mandela that person would have had to come in with a vision of what the future of the country should be and there were a number of visions that originated from Thabo as the deputy president of the country. These were more visionary than issues of practicality, which suited Thabo Mbeki because he would think further than most of us. He would have been the best person intellectually to think through issues that led to the implementation of GEAR, the Growth, Employment and Redistribution plan. Mandela and Zuma were instrumental in promoting peace and winning Mangosuthu Buthelezi over. But transforming the country after inheriting a complex and bankrupt economy needed someone to grapple with the economic challenges, even though being in government was new to all of us. The question that Mandela then had to ask was who in his office could conduct the day-to-day business side of government effectively. I would put very little blame on heads of state for this delegation because they are supposed to oversee broad and inclusive issues. It is the directors general (DGs) and ministers in the presidency who will do the everyday work. So Mbeki, as the deputy president, had to be responsible for the day-to-day business of governing South Africa.

We had one big problem, which continues to haunt us even now. I think that the ANC did not properly manage the issue of the integration of the 'exiles' and 'inxiles' – the latter being those brave people who kept the liberation struggle going inside the country and challenged the might of the apartheid regime each and every day. For example, some of us from exile would arrogantly and naively ask, 'Who is this Chikane [the Reverend Frank]? He is just a reverend, how could he be made a DG in the office of President Mbeki?' But really all of us from exile knew very well that he was active during the days of the United Democratic Front (UDF). Of course, those 'exiles' thought that they knew everything about South Africa and had all the answers to the problems facing us. Even today the 'exiles' think that they know better than the 'inxiles' in terms of understanding our challenges, which is not necessarily the case. They remain prisoners of exile who live a life of exile in their own country. They need to wake up and be realistic, and time is not on their side.

As a liberation movement, we failed to prepare government officials or political activists for a consolidated transition so that we all approached the political management of problems facing our country from the same angle. In terms of internal dynamics, every minister, including the president or deputy president, had to have a mix to include, for example, people from Robben Island, political prisoners, the UDF, the June 16 generation or the Luthuli detachment in government structures. Each group approached challenges from a different angle because there was no school for public administration focusing on governance in a democratic South Africa. Public servants attended hastily arranged short courses on public administration. Many of us from exile believed that there was a need for counselling and debriefing. In hindsight, this was a major mistake because it did not happen – but there was no time, we had to get on with reconstructing and governing the country. As deputy president and also as president of the country, Thabo Mbeki had to address these complex issues.

A perfect example of this was my appointment as the ANC's representative in Nigeria during the early 1990s. I had to hit the road running at full speed. I stayed in Nigeria for almost ten years. The first representative in Nigeria was Thabo Mbeki when Olusegun Obasanjo was a military ruler. We worked very closely with Mbeki while I was in Nigeria. But then of course we went into democratic elections in 1994 and we closed the ANC office in Nigeria. Then Alfred Nzo and Thabo Mbeki called me to President Mandela's office where Mandela informed me of their decision to send me back to Nigeria as high commissioner for South Africa. By this time Thabo Mbeki was the deputy president. Obviously I had to consult with him regularly, but I had also made a lot of contacts by then.

And then Mandela became very angry with President Abacha of Nigeria. I was still in Lagos at that time, preparing to move to Abuja. There was no warning that there would be serious problems between Nigeria and South Africa over the Ogoni issue. It just blew up in our faces and it became a global issue and the then Nigerian foreign minister, Tom Ikimi, was a very stubborn man and, as you know, so was Mandela.

Thabo Mbeki told me to return home quietly so that we could discuss the issue while he sent representatives from the diplomatic services to talk to the Nigerians. He asked for my advice on what I thought should be done, but I really was clueless. I explained to him that the Nigerians told me that they had been told by their foreign minister, who was at the Commonwealth Heads of Government Meeting at the time (in Auckland New Zealand, in November 1995) not to welcome me into their offices until he got back. Mbeki's approach was that we had to find a way to handle the diplomatic fallout because we could not afford to have the two powerful African states moving apart.

We had to find a solution so that when the old man [Mandela] came back from the Commonwealth meeting we could discuss matters with him, and the South African diplomatic delegation that had been sent to Nigeria could simultaneously assist in closing the gap. At the same time, we could not be seen to be insensitive to what had happened in Ogoni. Mbeki had wanted to hear from me because I had met Ken Saro-Wiwa and I had spoken to the Nigerian foreign minister before he left for the Commonwealth meeting. I had even travelled to Ogoni just to understand who Ken Saro-Wiwa was. The chiefs in Ogoni were divided over Ken so there was no united position on this matter and the international press would have not picked up these internal divisions, which were based on the fact that some Ogoni chiefs did not want a young writer to be seen to be taking over their fiefdom. Some argued that Ken should be allowed to do his work and should be supported, while others said that he should first consult them. In the meantime, he was busy gaining international recognition and he was moving around embassies in Nigeria and that was how I met him. He came to brief me.

After three days of consultation at home, I returned to Nigeria and in the end I think that the fallout worked itself out after intense discussions between officials of the two countries. In fact the Nigerian foreign minister and I did not live far from each other. He actually invited me to his place and he conceded that the whole issue was not good but that there was nothing that he could do. He said he knew that Mandela was not happy with him. They never wrote to the South African government about the issue through our office, nor did the South African government write to the

Nigerians. In the end we just managed to smooth things out.

When I left Nigeria, I was told to go to Geneva. I did not return to South Africa as was normally the case – we would come home for debriefing before our next posting. I went straight from Lagos to Geneva. In Geneva, there are 43 UN-related organisations, so we often had cabinet ministers coming over. And then there was the annual Davos meeting. I think that Mandela attended two or three of them, but Mbeki had to continue to attend these important economic forums.

As the ambassador in Switzerland, I was the one who would have to brief him and take him through his programme for Davos. Once we had done this we would start our old Lusaka games of sitting and talking until the early hours of the morning. I learned so much because when you are in Geneva you need to be constantly in touch with the issues of the various international organisations. Mbeki is not shy about discussing issues openly so by the time that he left, you felt that you had learned a great deal. It was difficult to get all this crucial information from Mandela, not because Mandela would not share with us, but there was always a long queue of people when Mandela was in Davos – they all wanted to meet him, so there was no time to sit and engage with him.

I think that we need to differentiate between the two leaders. As Mandela said, 'Thabo is running the country; me, I am just the ceremonial head.'

We prepared documents and gave them to Mbeki, knowing that he would change them to suit his tune. He might not change the content as such, but he would change the style and so on. That was why when we were still in Lusaka we gave Joel the documents and we knew that he would rework them closer to Thabo's style, just as Thabo Mbeki would write a document closer to Oliver Tambo's style.

Heads of state do not read; essentially, they do not have the time. Mbeki, on the other hand, spent a lot of time reading and researching. His wife Zanele used say, 'Your friend is going to die in his library.' Once when I was with him in the UN General Assembly I noticed that he was carrying a thick book by Stephen King. So I asked, 'Chief, do you read Stephen King?' and he responded, 'You must read everything.'

President Mbeki, as head of government and the cabinet, continued to show the same leadership style as when he was the leader of the DIA in exile. He wanted to work with people who could be trusted to do their work so that he could do all the other things that were expected of him. He had a mixture of people working with him: ex-Robben Islanders, inxiles, exiles and UDF people, among others.

South Africans, including journalists, are very weak on understanding international issues. This is Thabo Mbeki's strength because of his long stay in exile and his experience in the international solidarity movement. I think that he was ahead of many of us in terms of international issues and that is why people, especially in the international community, still miss him today. I think that his understanding of how the world functions stemmed from his work in the ANC, and he earned the respect of the ANC cadres and the leadership as well as the international community. I worked at the UN for almost nine years and there was nobody there who did not know who Thabo Mbeki was, just as there were few people who could tell you that they did not know who Johnny Makhathini was. It is because of Thabo Mbeki's profound understanding of global issues that the international community has great respect for him.

Thabo Mbeki's recall happened when we were in the UN General Assembly where he was supposed to come to chair one of the committees. Nkosazana Dlamini-Zuma was already there and she informed us about the recall, and Ronnie Mamoepa and I had to reconfigure everything. We also had a discussion with Ambassador Dumisani Kumalo. Obviously I was not happy.

At Polokwane I think that the ANC was beginning to feel the stress of not having prepared for our return from exile. But then I have friends who tell me that I know nothing, so I took a cautious position because of my friendship with Mbeki. Maybe I should tell you what the Nigerians said to me when they gave me a farewell dinner in January 1999. They said that they were happy for South Africa and that Mandela had taken the country forward. Then they said, 'When the honeymoon is over in South Africa, the ANC will start tearing itself apart because there is power and there is money; then it will no longer be just about politics.' I dismissed this because I did not think that it was possible. But now I need to think about such possibilities.

Interviewed June 2014, Johannesburg

WELILE NHLAPO

❧

I enrolled at the University of Zululand in 1970 and on 21 March that year the students organised a commemoration of Sharpeville Day. Steve Biko came to our campus as president of the South African Students' Organisation (SASO), accompanied by Barney Pityana, who was the secretary general. After the singing and speeches, a few of us went to sit with Steve Biko to begin to strategise as university students around the central affiliation of our university to SASO. We had to look at how we needed to affiliate and what it actually meant. This was the first time that I met Biko and we really clicked and became very close. There was a lot of political activity during this time and of course Radio Freedom was feeding us a lot of information about the African National Congress (ANC).

Inside South Africa, the feeling was that a political movement was needed because the student organisation was not going to be able to handle issues outside student politics because both the ANC and Pan Africanist Congress (PAC) were banned. The idea was that we needed a political organisation that would also take into account, as SASO did, that it was a holding position because the political leadership was in exile or imprisoned on Robben Island. We were not looking for an alternative to the banned liberation movements. It was Biko's thinking that liberation movements had to unite and he was appealing to all of them to come together. He had met Robert Sobukwe, who was banned, and I subsequently met him in Kimberley to try to understand from him why there was disunity.

After the pro-FRELIMO (Mozambique Liberation Front) rallies of 1974

I decided to leave the country and went to Botswana as a refugee. Through Snuki Zikalala, I made good contacts with some ANC representatives in Botswana, but I stayed with the BCM group. We met activists from the PAC and the Unity Movement and engaged with them to decide which one we might join. Our impression at that time was that the ANC was not serious.

We met some PAC members who told us that they could provide us with training, so we decided to test them. They organised letters for us from Uganda under the pretext that we had full scholarships to study there and we organised passports. Under the PAC banner, we left Uganda and travelled to Khartoum, Sudan, and ended up in Tripoli, Libya. But in Libya they tried to convert us to Islam, which we resisted because we were students of Marxism. Later, we decided to return to Botswana via Dar es Salaam. By this time we had quarrelled with the PAC and they abandoned us at the airport.

While we were stranded at the Dar es Salaam airport, we noticed that a white man sitting in the lounge seemed to be interested in what we were discussing; it turned out that he was Joe Slovo. A gentleman by the name of William Tsotsi, a senior member of the Unity Movement, was also passing through the airport. He worked at the attorney general's office in Zambia. He could tell that we were South Africans and asked us who we were. We explained that we were on our way to Botswana. He told us that he could arrange transport and accommodation for us in Lusaka. Indeed, when we arrived in Lusaka, he had arranged transport and accommodation as he had promised. When we arrived at the airport in Lusaka we bumped into Thabo Mbeki who was returning from a meeting with ANC comrades in Tanzania. We went to greet him and he said that he would see us the next day. This was the first time I saw him. We were taken to the YWCA, but we did not know how we were going to get in touch with Mbeki.

Thabo Mbeki subsequently came to Botswana with Peter Maqabane. By that time Keith Mokoape was back in Botswana and he and Snuki Zikalala alerted us to his arrival. They arranged for us to meet Thabo Mbeki at a hotel. We sat with him and fired questions at him. There were many things that we wanted to know about the ANC and the liberation struggle because we were still trying to decide which liberation movement we were going to join. This was the first opportunity we had to meet and debate with

Thabo Mbeki and so our discussions were around the ANC, including the youth and student movement. We questioned him intensively about what had happened within the exiled youth and student movement because he was in the leadership. Mbeki was very impressive and he took the time to listen to us. He even clarified the issue of membership and this was when we realised that there was a clarity within the ANC compared to the other liberation movements.

When the 1976 student uprisings took place, activists inside South Africa alerted us to what was happening, but we were helpless while we were in exile in Botswana. With the little military training that we had received, we could not respond to the situation. We could analyse, but that was all. We would meet Keith and Snuki and share whatever information we received about the June 1976 events. Our engagements with them as ANC cadres helped us a lot, as did the discussions with Thabo Mbeki, in influencing our decision to join the ANC.

Ultimately we decided that being confined in Botswana was not taking us anywhere. I subsequently joined the ANC and went to Angola via Lusaka for military training. When I completed my military training in Angola in 1977, I was chosen to go to London to become the deputy editor of the *Sechaba* publication. Thabo Mbeki had come to Angola to attend the MPLA (Popular Movement for the Liberation of Angola) Congress. I had a short discussion with him relating to my new assignment because he was the head of the Department of Information and Publicity (DIP) which was responsible for publishing *Sechaba*. This meant that I was joining the DIP. I had already begun working with Radio Freedom.

We subsequently met Mbeki again in London and we had a lot of discussions because *Sechaba* was now becoming a monthly publication instead of a quarterly. I worked very closely with Aziz Pahad, who had been Thabo Mbeki's friend for a very long time. We started to interact with him socially and had robust debates with the Pahad brothers, Aziz and Essop. Thabo Mbeki had to engage us on matters relating to the content published in *Sechaba*, external publicity and other issues to do with the DIP.

The London office was responsible for the rest of Europe and for the creation of offices there. It was also responsible for engaging the anti-apartheid movements. The ANC leadership frequently passed through London, especially Oliver Tambo, and Thabo Mbeki came often as the head of DIP. We always had a moment to sit down and work out how to deal with issues and linkages with the work that was being done internally in South Africa.

In 1979, the Year of the Spear (Isandlwana), we started to design our pamphlets and radio broadcasts using all the new techniques that we were learning. I had to report regularly to headquarters in Lusaka. The Lancaster House talks began around this time and Mbeki came to London, where he spent most of his time attending the talks as an observer. One of our assignments was to link up with Edson Zvobgo and T.G. Silundika who were the spokespersons for ZANU-PF (Zimbabwe African National Union-Patriotic Front) and ZAPU (Zimbabwe African People's Union) so that we got to know what was happening in the discussions. We attended their press conferences and sat with representatives of the Zimbabwe liberation movements just to have a sense of what they were doing and so that we could also capture the process in the Lancaster House talks through *Sechaba*. ZANU had opened an office in London and we interacted with them. When the Patriotic Front was formed, we had to interact with it as well. Thabo Mbeki came to London for the Lancaster House talks more because of his connections with Solomon Mujuru and Dumiso Dabengwa, who were leading the military structures in the negotiations process. Mbeki met them almost every day and I was with him during these briefing sessions. They would brief him on the issues and the challenges that they faced during the talks with the British. At some stage we became aware of the political difficulties in the negotiations. We also realised that cracks were beginning to appear between Joshua Nkomo and Robert Mugabe and we became aware of the internal dynamics within the Patriotic Front.

The reason the Patriotic Front was created was so that the Zimbabweans could go to London to participate in the negotiations from a common position. The Zimbabweans were pushed into this but they agreed to form a united front because both were engaging the enemy. There were many difficulties and some heads of state like Julius Nyerere, Samora Machel and Kenneth Kaunda had to intervene to help smooth over the tensions between ZANU-PF and ZAPU. The African leaders did not want the Patriotic Front to break apart. Because of this rich historical background dating back to the Lancaster House talks, the Zimbabweans later preferred

President Mbeki to lead the peace talks as a representative of the African Union (AU) and the Southern African Development Community (SADC). Mbeki was familiar with the historical context and other important matters including the finer details related to the Lancaster House talks and the land issues in Zimbabwe.

In 1981, I was asked to return to Lusaka so that we could coordinate external and internal propaganda more efficiently. This meant that I had to work at the DIP. At this point, Thabo Mbeki was doubling up as Oliver Tambo's secretary until Anthony Mongalo came in to take over so that Mbeki could concentrate more on international relations. He ultimately headed the Department of International Affairs (DIA) after Johnny Makhathini passed away. Sizakele Sigxashe then took over the DIP.

At that time, we wanted to mobilise the internal and external wings of the ANC, while at the same time linking the two to make inputs into the content of our journal *Sechaba*. With Mbeki now responsible for the DIA, we focused on international mobilisation and solidarity. Being based in Lusaka made it easier to access information so that we could project our own operations to the international community through our publications. The main areas that we focused on were our international solidarity, internal mobilisation inside South Africa, underground work and the military offensive. The structure and content of *Sechaba* had to change to cover all those aspects. This also meant that I had to work very closely with Thabo Mbeki on international relations.

In 1982, while I was in Lusaka, we had to prepare for a youth conference. I was roped in to assist the organisers. When the conference took place, I was appointed head of the ANC Youth Section. But the person who was better placed in this arena, who had been involved in all the youth issues during the early days in exile, was Thabo Mbeki himself. So we relied quite a lot on him because he was familiar with relevant institutions that we were engaging as the youth and students section in the international arena. These included, among others, the International Union of Students, the Pan African Youth Movement, the All African Students' Union and the World Federation of Democratic Youth. As a student leader, Mbeki had built up relationships and networks with all these organisations.

I relied quite heavily on Mbeki on the role of the youth in the international arena and also on the relevant content focusing on diplomacy and international solidarity to be published in *Sechaba* and how to link these with internal mobilisation in South Africa. I had the advantage of having worked closely with the Anti-Apartheid Movement in London and I attended many conferences in Europe as part of my work for *Sechaba*. We had also taken out membership of the International Organisation of Journalists. We went to the youth conference in Prague and linked up with Essop Pahad, who was working for the *World Marxist Review*, and Moses Mabhida, who was working with the World Federation of Trade Unions.

I was roped into the organising committee for the ANC's 70th anniversary, representing the DIP. One of the tasks that we had to undertake in preparing for the anniversary was designing a new logo for the ANC – this was where the current logo originated. Thabo Mbeki also has a creative, artistic side that is not easily picked up. The DIP worked with lots of artists to share creative ideas about a new design for the ANC logo. The artists were drawn from places such as the camps in Angola and the Solomon Mahlangu Freedom College in Tanzania. We also had to design posters for external use because we were now going full out to promote the ANC in various media throughout the world. The new logo was ultimately adopted and we had to tighten our communication strategy because we were communicating our struggle to both the international community and to South Africa. Mbeki played an impeccable role in this regard.

In the mid-1980s, the engagements with the Afrikaners and the South African business community commenced and our major task was to mobilise and organise for a bigger meeting of all the different forces within South Africa. This meant that I had to work closely with Mbeki at the diplomatic level. He gave me a lot of his time and I really learned a lot from him in terms of international relations and diplomacy. In terms of internal diplomacy around alliance partners, there were a lot of discussions within the South African Communist Party (SACP) focusing on the relationship between the party and the ANC. There was tension from time to time because of the ANC's open-door policy, holding talks about talks with South African big business and prominent members of the Afrikaner community. I was in the same party unit as Thabo Mbeki, therefore there was a lot that we could share about the work that we were doing. But there was also this tendency to ostracise Mbeki because people were saying that there were secret meetings taking place between the liberation movement, the apartheid regime and the Western superpowers. The first official meeting between the ANC and the US authorities took place in 1986 and it was not a secret meeting.

At the same time, the ANC's Department of International Affairs (DIA), led by Mbeki with the necessary support from the office of Oliver Tambo, had to plan for and engage the different groups that were coming to Lusaka from South Africa. Because people wanted to know how we intended to take the country forward, these discussions and consultations with the ANC leadership were based around issues such as future constitutional principles as a basis for substantive negotiations in South Africa. The Constitutional Principles and Guidelines were developed and discussed quite extensively within the ANC during this period. As a result, in 1987, the ANC came up with its official statement on substantive negotiations following the Kabwe conference of 1985. There was no option: the liberation movement knew that at some point it would need to enter into substantive negotiations with the enemy. The constitutional principles were accepted and were later infused as part of the Harare Declaration. In addition, there was the UN Declaration on the formation of a democratic South Africa, which was informed by the Harare Declaration.

All these processes began from an internal ANC discussion about the strengths and weaknesses of the 1984 Nkomati Accord signed between apartheid South Africa and Mozambique. As an organisation, we had noticed that there was no blueprint for a political settlement that might lead to an independent, democratic South Africa, whereas there had been Resolution 435 for the independence of Namibia. African leaders, including Presidents Nyerere and Kaunda, advised the ANC to design a programme to inform the Frontline States about the formation of a non-racial, democratic state in South Africa. Luckily, as I indicated earlier, an internal process had already begun in terms of discussion of the Constitutional Guidelines and Principles during the mid-1980s, which influenced the Harare Declaration and, later, the UN Declaration. Thabo Mbeki and colleagues, on behalf of the liberation movement, suggested strategies on how to take all these international processes forward; how to engage the UN on the matter, identifying countries that were important to engage to support ANC positions at the UN; and also communicating with the worldwide anti-apartheid movements, which were key to mobilising international support for the ANC. Throughout these processes Mbeki had the support of Oliver Tambo who also led most of the ANC delegations.

At the time there were comrades who understood and appreciated Mbeki's work for the ANC and he earned a lot of respect from them. From my personal point of view, there were also some comrades who were envious of him. We spent endless hours debating and discussing geopolitical matters relevant to the struggle for national liberation. But there was always this unresolved issue of emphasis on a diplomatic approach versus the military approach. There was a very thin dividing line and this was where tensions arose in the approach to negotiations. There was also this undercurrent because people heard through the grapevine about negotiations taking place between the ANC and the apartheid regime. Some ANC activists were not happy about these secret negotiations. Their argument was that we needed to step up the armed struggle and defeat the apartheid regime on the battle front. That was why in Kabwe in 1985, before these talks began, we had to strike a balance between the two positions, that while we stepped up the armed struggle and insurrection, we also had to prepare for substantive negotiations. And that became a more acceptable position, which helped to kill the unnecessary tension and rumours about secret negotiations with the apartheid regime.

The actual substantive negotiations started in 1991. Tensions between various groups emerged. There were comrades who felt that they were being locked out of the substantive negotiations and were therefore very critical of the decisions adopted by the National Executive Committee (NEC) of the ANC. Of course, Thabo Mbeki, through the DIA, was to some extent the mouthpiece of the liberation movement for he was expected to communicate the movement's policy positions to the international community. That attracted a lot of anger towards, him which emanated from some comrades within the ANC.

To me, Thabo Mbeki appeared to be a very well-rounded human being. He socialised very easily. Many people do not know that he can dance; I have seen him dancing. He fitted in in social settings and he would engage with people. But when it was time to get down to business, he became very serious. He was very strict on deadlines that had to be met, because he was also working for President Oliver Tambo, who was also very strict on deadlines. He wanted things done on time and efficiently and he was a perfectionist. The only person who Oliver Tambo trusted with speechwriting was Thabo. The advantage that he had, unlike the so-called aloof Mbeki created by the media and others, was that he was very engaging and had an amazing capacity to listen to other viewpoints. From our own experience, that was what we saw in him. He always felt the need to engage, discuss openly and seek other people's opinions, and he very easily accepted other views if they were convincing and correct. He was the same even when he became head of state. This ability to listen also helped him formulate strategies that led to the ANC becoming a well-known liberation movement internationally and our contribution to international affairs was taken seriously.

Part of the problem that Oliver Tambo faced, which Thabo also faced (and which I think Jacob Zuma is going through now as president), is that there is a tendency for comrades within the core leadership of the ANC not to want to express their views – they want the president to lead all the time. When they were found wanting in their portfolios as ANC leaders or cabinet members, they would remark, 'If you had given us a clear direction earlier and said this or that as president, we would not have had such confusion. Your summary, what you are saying now, that is exactly what we had expected.'

Thabo Mbeki is so well read that you could not take chances with him. If he asked you to do something on behalf of the country or the liberation movement, you had better know your story. He was very impatient with half-baked ideas – a fact known by all of us comrades. He expected a high level of input on substantive issues that had to do with the well-being of the Republic of South Africa. There was a time when cabinet ministers relocated from Bryntirion Estate in Pretoria because there were no weekends there. He would call ministers and officials any time he came across anything that he wanted to share. For instance, if he came across a serious matter that compromised the people of South Africa, he would immediately contact the person responsible for that area and want to know whether they knew about the matter. If you were not aware, he would want to know why. If you did not address the matter, he would take responsibility and address it himself. I think that this was part of the problem: with him, the well-being of the people of South Africa came first.

But he had time to pay attention. He paid particular attention to the Forum of South African Directors General (FOSAD), which was the structure where all the DGs met as a collective to discuss the issues affecting South African citizens, and Mbeki relied on this structure for most of his information. That was why he had a lot of problems with some of his ministers because they were really not clued up on many of the issues he raised. The DGs were more informed because they had to deal with these practical issues on a daily basis. So he would lose patience with some of the ministers. You can interpret it in whichever way you want and call him aloof, arrogant or dismissive of others, but he demanded high performance and commitment on behalf of all South Africans. That was what mattered to him.

Some of us got used to his high expectations and his style of work, which he inherited from having worked with Oliver Tambo. You would give Oliver Tambo a draft statement or article and it would come back bleeding with remarks in red ballpoint: feedback from a typical teacher because he wanted to correct everything that was not relevant to the issue in question. Thabo Mbeki was that kind of perfectionist and this may have been too much for colleagues because he wanted things done in a particular way, and during that process he demanded that comrades sacrifice time.

For instance, we had to be available throughout the summer holidays when we were working on the draft 1999 Lusaka Agreement (to end hostilities in the Democratic Republic of Congo (DRC) through a ceasefire). We worked on that draft resolution over a matter of days and it was concluded on Christmas Day. All the South African ambassadors were on call, regardless of the fact that this was during the holidays, and they were called to receive the draft from the government residence. Some ambassadors were very angry because it meant that they could not enjoy their Christmas break. This was also the type of thing that Oliver Tambo would do as the president of the ANC. Oliver Tambo's draft 8 January statement was normally ready around Christmas Day and comrades such as Mbeki would be called to engage with it during the summer holidays.

In reflecting on Thabo Mbeki, I think that what is happening now that he is no longer president of the country is that the majority of South African citizens are beginning to appreciate him as both deputy president and president. In the past he was portrayed as this cold, aloof intellectual who wore suits and ties and spoke too much high English, recited poetry and smoked a pipe. They now appreciate that he was a man of ideas, he worked hard and he knew how to project issues. At the UN, when Mbeki was addressing the audience, the hall would be full because colleagues from all over the world knew that his speeches would be substantive in terms of content. At the meetings of the OAU, and later the AU, he commanded a lot of respect precisely because of the manner in which he handled issues affecting the African continent. Many leaders marvelled at his intellect and the way that he engaged with various subjects. There was much more appreciation for Mbeki from the external actors than from South Africa, probably because there were other internal dynamics at play at home.

You had to appreciate the ethical manner in which Thabo Mbeki handled the unconstitutional recall in 2008. I happened to be back from Washington DC, where I was South Africa's ambassador because, I had come to bury my deputy. On the day that we were returning home from the funeral, I heard the announcement about his recall on the radio. I had to go and see him that evening before leaving to go back to Washington because we were preparing for the FIFA Legacy Project and a final high-level meeting in the UN, which he was supposed to attend that week.

President Mbeki told me that a number of things were going to happen and asked me not to return to the US because we would need to deal with these issues. He also informed me that he was unlikely to travel to the UN. He thought that it was better if I waited so that I could brief Foreign Affairs Minister Nkosazana Dlamini-Zuma and the UN Secretary General and other relevant people. He was working on his response to both the international and South African public because he had earlier met the delegation sent by the ANC. It consisted of Gwede Mantashe and Kgalema Motlanthe.

Mbeki argued that stepping down as president of South Africa was not the issue, but there were legal and constitutional issues that had to be taken into account and the ANC leadership had not addressed these serious matters. In the South African constitution there is no provision for the resignation of the head of state. So the question was how to handle this. We could not go the route of an impeachment because it would have been a disaster. A vote of no confidence was not going to work because the opposition parties were going to be interested and take sides. Also, the ANC could not initiate a vote of no confidence because the likelihood was that internal divisions would have been even more apparent and the NEC's decision might be defeated during that vote in parliament. So Mbeki was more concerned about those issues that would gravely affect the ANC as a ruling party and he therefore worked independently towards finding a constructive solution that would not destabilise the country. He had to take me into his confidence because I had to return to the UN and explain to Minister Dlamini-Zuma and others.

Now moving to Zimbabwe: I do not think that President Mbeki could have or should have handled Zimbabwe differently. When I was the deputy director general for Africa, and later as the head of the Presidential Support Unit, I became very directly involved in the issues of Zimbabwe with him throughout the various stages: the discussions with the AU, the interactions with the Zimbabweans themselves and the often difficult engagements with international organisations. External forces were putting a lot of pressure on President Mbeki about the need to force Mugabe out of office, but Mbeki refused. For instance, the land restitution programme that was agreed upon with (Mark) Malloch-Brown, when he was head of the United Nations Development Programme (UNDP) and also endorsed by Kofi Annan at the UN, was compromised by the British. When Tony Blair, the British prime minister, started reneging, Mbeki had to engage Malloch-Brown who was kow-towing to pressure from Tony Blair's office.

If the British had addressed their part properly at the time, we would have not had that disaster of the taking over of farms by Zimbabweans. We were familiar with that willing-buyer willing-seller issue because we had been religiously following the Lancaster House negotiations while we were in exile and based in London and we knew what had become the points of tension, including the fallout between Nkomo and Mugabe. They differed fundamentally on what ought to be accepted and what had to be rejected. The other issue that caused friction within the Patriotic Front related to the interim phase, particularly with regard to the new constitution. So the historical background to the Zimbabwe issue was not new to us.

When the tensions emerged in Zimbabwe over the political negotiations, I think that Thabo Mbeki was correct and he put his foot down in engaging with Tony Blair. Mbeki insisted that they (Britain and the US) could not do as they pleased and prescribe self-serving solutions in Zimbabwe. I know that in his engagements with President Bush and his administration, when I was ambassador in the US, President Mbeki adopted a tough stance for he was not willing to be bullied by the Western superpowers.

I was privy to the long letter that Mbeki had written to President George Bush. President Mbeki phoned me and asked me to sit next to my computer because he was sending me a copy of the letter that he was sending to the US ambassador in South Africa to be transmitted to Washington. He wanted me to know the contents of the letter so that I would be familiar with them if I was summoned by the Americans and asked about the issue. I must say that the letter was very rough politically speaking, as Mbeki did not mince his words. I must admit I was scared after reading it. Some of the things that he articulated in the letter led me to say to myself that 'the president is asking for trouble' by standing up and being counted. But that was his approach.

Most people would agree that President Mbeki really showed patience, because as discussions continued he had come to an agreement with Blair and Bush to leave the issue for him to handle. But because Bush and Blair were both close to the end of their terms in office there was an eagerness to engineer a regime change and hit out at Mugabe. Mbeki had to respond to stop this unacceptable behaviour. During this period he also had to delicately try to coerce the parties in Zimbabwe to enter into negotiations. The first constructive attempt to try to find a resolution to the Zimbabwean crisis took place on the day of the 9/11 attacks in the US. We were in Zimbabwe on that day when the news came through that the World Trade Center had been hit by two planes. It was a Southern African Development Community (SADC) initiative after it was agreed that the regional body should intervene in the matter. These were the discussions between commercial farmers, the opposition and the Zimbabwean government.

I believe that Mbeki's handling of the issue was the most prudent because any slip at that time would have led to a major disaster. It was during this period that I first heard of something called 'regime change' and I started to understand the dilemma that Nigerian President Olusegun Obasanjo was facing as the chair of the Commonwealth. It was not surprising that the Commonwealth failed to address the matter.

When I was stationed at the UN I worked very closely on the Zimbabwe issue with Ibrahim Gambari who was appointed by Kofi Annan, and the UNDP representative Agostinho Zacarias in Harare. There were a lot of problems after the human settlements issue erupted. We had to interface with President Mbeki who was dealing with the same issues. Even when the Zimbabwe issue blew up in Kofi Annan's face, Mugabe told Kofi Annan to rather back away from the problem. But we were in the thick of it at the UN. Gambari and I had to engage the Zimbabweans and also hold discussions with Mbeki to get a better understanding of how the issue could be addressed. We needed to compare notes and find out whether the Western powers were repeating the same message to Mbeki that they were relaying to Kofi Annan.

Mbeki wrote a hard-hitting letter to ZANU-PF about the way it had lost its revolutionary zeal and why it was facing these political problems. At this stage, Mbeki was having serious problems with them as a ruling party. But he maintained a different level of engagement with the Zimbabweans because of the relationships between the liberation movements during the years in exile. He knew them at a different level and he could see the challenges that they were confronted with. He had known some of the people who were in the Zimbabwe military for decades. He also knew the intricacies of the Lancaster House negotiations, which I think informed his thinking on the Zimbabwean question. I think that the manner in which he handled Zimbabwe under those circumstances was the best way, otherwise he would never have been able to muster a political agreement in Zimbabwe. He was even able to handle Morgan Tsvangirai's group and some of their external sponsors because he understood the internal dynamics.

It was public knowledge that Britain was one of Morgan Tsvangirai's main sponsors through Freedom House. The Movement for Democratic Change (MDC) was being sponsored through the so-called Freedom/Democracy programmes. The role of influential external players was a long-standing problem and Mbeki knew about it.

I worked with Mbeki on all these important matters dating back to the defusion of tension after the fallout in Kisangani between Rwanda and Uganda over the DRC spoils when they deployed forces across each other's borders, which almost led to a serious war. Mbeki sent then retired ministers Alfred Nzo and Joe Modise, supported by Billy Masetlha and myself, to hold discussions with both the Rwandese and the Ugandans to convince them not to go the military route. The peace structure that emanated from this was Mbeki's brainchild. It was a security arrangement coordinated by Tanzania's Ben Mkapa between the three countries – Rwanda, Uganda and the DRC.

There were a lot of things that Thabo Mbeki did towards conflict prevention in the African continent. These peace initiatives were informed by his thinking and strategies, which he discussed with a number of people. He had a very consultative approach. In terms of diplomacy, I learned a lot from him and at least some of us who worked with him appreciated the fact that he gave us the space to think and say whatever we thought without any fear of retribution. We would differ and engage and debate, and in the end decisions would be taken and implementation would go ahead. My experience of him is quite different from what I have heard and read in various media and other platforms and I have come a very long way with him.

I would say the same about the Pahad brothers, Aziz and Essop, whom I believe are misunderstood. People think that they are just friends and lackeys of Mbeki – something that is belied by the way in which they argue with Mbeki, the manner in which they differ and engage robustly. This was something I witnessed while we were still in exile in London. I had also seen it in government and I still observe the same now that Mbeki is out of office. Nothing changed; they still debate robustly among themselves the way they used to way back then. To me, you have got to engage and understand an individual before constructing your own perceptions about them. Whatever you hear about that individual, you must be personally informed. Mbeki is consultative and believes in a collective, but if he does not get results he becomes impatient and will move on his own ideas. He consulted his colleagues in the ANC and those in the cabinet, but people would later claim that they were not consulted, which was not being very honest.

When it came to international and conflict prevention matters, President

Mbeki consulted widely and he never dealt with any conflict situation without discussion with the affected neighbouring countries or even external elements that might have had an interest, such as the former colonial powers. He did not shy away from engaging them as equals and many of them were not used to this style. They were used to dictating terms to Africans. He wanted to make sure that when we moved on an issue we would know that there was buy-in. He often emerged as one of the few honest brokers who took everybody's concerns on board. He sat for long hours listening to people, unpacking issues and engaging them so that there would be a clear understanding of where the problem was. That has always been his style.

Mbeki, in my view, was willing to risk his own popularity, which was never an issue for him. He was always about principle and acting on the right side of principle in the interests of the people he served. But if you did not want to be pushed to do your work on behalf of the South African citizens and you did not want to work towards deadlines, then you would naturally have a problem with him. People chose to define him as an aloof and cold character and ruthless at the best of times. To be honest, I do not know where these things came from.

People asked what was the problem between Jacob Zuma (JZ) and Mbeki when Zuma was relieved of his duties as deputy president in 2005. I worked with the two of them on the Burundi crisis and we managed the issue even during that demanding period. JZ continued to work on the Burundi problem until the end. Some Barundi felt that because JZ was no longer deputy president, he had to be withdrawn from the facilitation team. Mbeki did not entertain this idea. I have witnessed mutual respect between JZ and Mbeki but, indeed, there was a time when the relationship became quite icy.

But I still needed to consult both of them on the Burundi question, first individually and then together. I had to brief them and seek their advice on how to proceed on the Burundi situation. I had been given the task of checking with both of them because some of the affected parties in Burundi were saying that they did not want JZ and they were now playing their own political games. Anyway, there was not much left to do, but when the need arose we would travel to Burundi. The programme and the support that had always been there would continue and JZ was required to complete the assignment. That was the agreement that was spearheaded by President Mbeki. Even at that time of the fallout, the fall-back in terms of protecting the conflict prevention work continued. When the presidential inauguration took place in Burundi, both JZ and Mbeki were there. They were both given due respect at the inauguration because they had both worked very hard to deliver the peace process.

When Polokwane happened, I was in Washington. But in the build-up to it, I was still at the UN. People who used to come in and out of New York would indicate that there were political tensions in the ANC branches and they would talk of a political fallout. Of course the *Mail & Guardian* was having a field day, so we would get some of what was going on through it. In the UN itself there was a lot of concern, particularly among African colleagues. They would ask what was happening to the ANC – a trusted liberation movement as far as colleagues from other parts of the continent were concerned.

I had to try to understand what was happening because colleagues were hearing all sorts of conspiracy stories and they would come and ask me about them. As the official South African representative at the UN, I was trying to distil and understand these issues and the tensions. People who came from South Africa said there was a problem in our liberation movement and others asked me which side I was on. 'Which side are you on?' – this was new language to me.

I went to Polokwane in order to gain an understanding of what was happening. What I saw there really shook me. I even said to Dr Nkosazana Dlamini-Zuma, 'My sister, this thing that I am witnessing, we will never be able to recover from it.' This was after I had seen a group of young people singing at the time of voting; it was pouring with rain and they were directing rude gestures at Nkosazana, accusing her of refusing to support Jacob. This open defiance and the derogatory language and the shouting down of Terror Lekota as the chairperson really shocked me. I was sitting with the international guests at the opening ceremony and they kept asking me, 'What is going on?' I was really worried that what was started in Polokwane would be difficult to repair: the insults, the shouting down of the ANC leadership and the derogatory songs. But then came the recall the following year and I had to watch this political drama unfolding.

There are certain internal dynamics that one has to take into consideration. I am of the view that the main mistake that a lot of opportunistic people made was that they decided on their own that there was a problem between JZ and Mbeki and they therefore felt the need to take sides. They instilled the idea that one would succeed over the other or that there was a lot of sympathy for one over the other, and this really smacked of political opportunism. This was the beginning of factionalism as we know it and we thought we had got rid of such problems while we were in exile. As far as I am concerned, this issue of the voting slates was actually institutionalising factionalism within the liberation movement. If there was one person who was very sensitive about the issue of factionalism it was Oliver Tambo and we were always taught to be vigilant and warned against it.

One special moment that I will always remember about Thabo Mbeki was the time we almost got into big trouble in Lusaka. It had to do with a statement that was issued after the official meeting between the ANC and Inkatha, which took place in London in 1979. They had a bilateral meeting; after that Inkatha had a meeting with the Foreign Service Office to brief them, and Inkatha presented a different document, giving the impression that there was an agreement that they would be the internal wing of the ANC and that they had managed to convince the ANC against the armed struggle.

Suzanne Vos was stringing for the *Sunday Times* and we were alerted to the fact that she was publishing a story about a secret meeting that had taken place in London between the ANC and Inkatha. Maggie Smith, who was working for the *Rand Daily Mail*, was asked about this meeting and when she came to alert us we had to decide what to do. We had to meet quickly and Oliver Tambo decided that a statement needed to be issued, but the question was how to handle this matter because the proceedings of the meeting had not even been reported to the NEC. The story was indeed written and published by newspapers about the secret meeting between the ANC and Inkatha and the supposed outcomes of it. As we were brainstorming how to deal with the issue, which was now part of the public domain, Mbeki turned around said, 'But there was no secret meeting.' We were taken aback and said, 'But, Chief, there *was* a meeting between the ANC and Inkatha.' He responded, 'Who came with the idea that there was a *secret* meeting? What took place was planned a long time ago, so why do they give the impression that it was a secret meeting? In any case, it is no secret that we got instructions from the NEC that we must engage the Inkatha.' Of course, we understood what he was saying immediately.

So we decided to issue a press statement that read as follows: 'It has come to the attention of the ANC that there is a report in the *Sunday Times* which carries a headline that there was a secret meeting between the ANC and the IFP.' The statement went on to say, 'There was no secret meeting.' And we left it at that. But then we inserted several paragraphs on the strategy and tactics of the ANC, including the Four Pillars, based on the armed struggle, international solidarity, the underground and the role of the masses and reaffirmed our positions. This way we thought we could counter the newspaper reports about all the so-called agreements that were supposedly rubber-stamped by the ANC and Inkatha. Those ANC members who had received the reports of a secret meeting became quite confused when they read our statement that said that there was no such meeting. The question became, was there or wasn't there a meeting between the two organisations, particularly because the final decisions taken during the official meeting had not yet been tabled before the NEC?

We in the ANC propaganda wing were not prepared to fall into the trap set by the British Broadcasting Organisation (BBC) and others. When they asked us about it, we simply gave them the same short answer, 'No, there was no secret meeting.' This was the only way to defuse the issue, which had become quite tense when people heard that the ANC had been convinced by Inkatha to move away from armed struggle and that Inkatha would now be the custodians of ANC policy and raise the flag of the ANC inside the country. When Oliver Tambo saw our statement, he was amused by our approach and thought that it was quite a naughty way of handling it, but it worked in terms of public relations. This was because those who attended the official meeting were still compiling their report that would be officially presented to the NEC, which had sanctioned the meeting.

Interviewed April 2014, Centurion

THANDI LUJABE-RANKOE

※

Thabo Mvuyelwa Mbeki showed leadership qualities from an early age. He had foresight and influencing and negotiating skills.

In 1968 a group of us was sent to Bulgaria to attend a youth festival. In the bus, on the way to our destination, we were loudly singing our freedom songs when Thabo suddenly stopped us and told us to calm down. He wanted us to arrive as dignified and disciplined youth. Because of our excitement, our response at the time was 'he thinks he is better than us'.

Thabo Mbeki was appointed to head the African National Congress's (ANC's) Department of International Affairs (DIA), after the death of the previous office bearer, Johnny Makhathini. This appointment brought him into contact with statesmen all over the world in his relentless efforts to isolate apartheid, a move that the ANC regarded as crucial. In his role as head of the ANC's DIA, Thabo Mbeki was best known for his charm, statesmanship and ability to keep his composure even in the face of provocation and seemingly insurmountable obstacles and pessimism about our cause – a trait that would serve him well as president in later years.

The first ANC Chief Representatives conference took place in Gran in Norway, from 15 to 21 March 1989. Thabo led the delegation. I was the ANC Chief Representative in Norway at the time. He demonstrated his leadership capability by strengthening the ties with the Norwegians, building on their support of the liberation struggle. In his calm, collected and thoughtful manner he managed to organise funding from the Norwegians and build the credibility of the ANC so that our office in Norway was able to run more or less like any other institution's foreign office.

In those days, Thabo was still fond of his pipe.

In 1991, the ANC leaders who had been incarcerated on Robben Island were released. Thabo accompanied them and their wives on a trip to Tanzania and then to Norway. I discovered at that time what a soft heart he had. After the second day he told me that the leaders and their wives did not have any warm clothes and requested that I assist, which I did. I felt that he showed the signs of a disciplined, caring and selfless cadre.

During my term in Tanzania, he came a few times to consult with Mwalimu Julius Nyerere regarding peace in Burundi. There was mutual respect between the two leaders. When Mwalimu Nyerere passed on I had just been posted to Botswana. Thabo invited me to travel with his entourage to Tanzania for the funeral. I appreciated how thoughtful and strategic his actions were in the way that he selected the members of his entourage. I shall never forget that. Thank you.

Thabo Mbeki has always been good at developing relationships. He had an excellent relationship with former President Mkapa, who took over from Mwalimu Nyerere. This is what former President Mkapa had to say about him and his governance: 'I commend the ANC Government for its many successes against formidable odds. In particular, the successful pursuit of the Reconstruction and Development Programme (RDP), which has brought water, electricity, telephone lines, houses and better health and education to many South Africans. Above all, the dignity, respect, justice and other basic human rights denied for so long to the vast majority of South Africans have finally been won.'

Thabo Mbeki was the president during my term of office in Mozambique and, again, he built excellent relations with former President Chissano. A lot of constructive and exciting things happened during this time, numerous agreements were signed between the two countries, and I was proud to be South Africa's High Commissioner to Mozambique. Thanks once again for entrusting me with the conduct of diplomatic relations with a neighbouring country with whom we continue to share ties of solidarity.

A sad moment for me was Polokwane. Thank you for selflessly thinking of the country first. A true leader puts others before himself. Keep on leading your dream of the African Renaissance.

I am very proud of the way in which you continue to serve our continent with diligence and integrity. The qualities you have possessed since I have known you in your youth have matured along with you, hence you are the logical port of call as a trusted broker in seeking the resolution of some seemingly intractable conflicts on our continent. This faith in your abilities is not misplaced; your name is among the pantheon of leaders who have built Africa.

DUMISANI KUMALO

❧

One of Thabo Mbeki's qualities – in fact, it is the first thing you notice about him – is that he listens. He is the kind of person who listens with his body. Had he been a Catholic, he would have been a priest and everybody would have gone to him for confession. Truly, he listens with his whole body.

You never forget meeting Mbeki for the first time. I met him in 1977 in New York when we were in exile in the US and he came there on behalf of the African National Congress (ANC). He was always active in the United Nations (UN). Remember that in the UN they listen to member states only and officially it was the apartheid government that was recognised, but because the ANC had extensive international networks and the ability to get the other African countries to represent our cause, the UN was an important place to pursue the liberation struggle. As a result, the liberation movement fought hard to have South Africa's issue (the struggle) recognised in the UN. Thabo Mbeki would accompany Oliver Tambo to the US twice a year and they were hosted by Johnny Makhathini, who was the ANC representative in New York.

One of Thabo Mbeki's legacies is that he gave us our identity while we were still in exile in the US. Mbeki was the first person to remind us that we are all Africans. Ellen Johnson Sirleaf, the current president of Liberia, used to lecture at the University of Denver and she organised a conference there where Mbeki gave a talk to African students from all over the US. Mbeki's presentation focused specifically on the meaning of being an African and this was because of an existing problem among foreign African students in the US. For instance, the Nigerians in the US would proudly proclaim, 'I am a Fulani, a Hausa, Yoruba or I am an Ibo man', very much in tribalistic terms, in the same way as they would say at home that I am 100 per cent Xhosa or Zulu or Venda etc. During the lecture, Mbeki pointed out the dangers posed by ethnicity among Africans.

One of the commendable things achieved by Mbeki and Johnny Makhathini was to forge links so that all the African diplomats in the UN, as official members of the African Group, were officially representing the cause of the ANC and other liberation movements fighting against racist, white minority governments in Africa. Embassies were deemed a restricted, exclusive space reserved for a particular country. But for us as South Africans in exile we had full access to, for example, the Nigerian mission and to many other African missions in New York. This African Renaissance was not an approach solely championed by the ANC. For implementing the goals of such a renaissance you needed the support of member states. The strongest link in the UN, the Nigerian mission, was like the ANC mission in the UN. In 1973, when the UN officially declared apartheid a crime against humanity, Nigeria chaired the committee against apartheid.

Because of African solidarity, important resolutions were easily passed and the representatives of the apartheid regime at the UN were concerned about how the ANC got these crucial resolutions passed by the General Assembly and the Security Council because it was not an official member of the UN and the liberation movement did not represent a sovereign member state. The genius was to consolidate African solidarity and say, 'We are Africans,' and the anchor was that the liberation struggle was an international struggle. For as long as there was an official African representative at the UN, all the liberation movements were represented.

This was Oliver Tambo's genius, and he was ably supported by Johnny Makhathini and Thabo Mbeki in getting all our African friends to represent us in various multilateral organisations such as the UN, the Non-Aligned Movement (NAM) and the Organisation of African Unity (OAU). The ANC in exile was linking not only with the ambassadors based in the UN but also with their capitals in the African continent. It was therefore no coincidence that Mbeki was based in Lusaka. I am of the view that Thabo

Mbeki's speech, 'I am an African', should be understood within this historical context. It is predicated on African solidarity, which flourished during
the dark days of apartheid.

After the democratic elections of 1994, Alfred Nzo, as the minister of for-
eign affairs, told me that President Mandela had appointed me to represent
South Africa in the UN. On the eve of my departure, I had to meet with
Deputy President Mbeki and I will never forget what he said to me. It was so
true and it stayed with me for all the ten years that I was in the UN. He said,
'When you go there [to the UN], there are Africans and you are all represented there and you have to make sure that you join forces with the Africans.'
It also helped that South Africa was chairing the NAM and therefore we were
able to draw in the Cubans, the Indians, the Pakistanis and other developing
countries, so we had a voice at the UN that was bigger than we were.

An example of how we used our power at the UN when we were in government occurred during the Iraq invasion. There were only three African
countries in the UN Security Council – Angola, Guinea and Cameroon
– but their presidents were getting briefings from President Thabo Mbeki.
Although South Africa was not a member of the Security Council, the
African countries were in constant contact with Mbeki because he was
like the African envoy. I was chair of the NAM. I would harass the Security
Council using African representatives from Guinea, Cameroon and Angola
– they were the ones who would speak out on our behalf.

Regarding the developments in Iraq, President Mbeki spoke with authority because he had sent a South African team of experts in nuclear weapons
to the country. Since South Africa was chair of the NAM, we were able to
impose ourselves on the debate. The toughest story behind the scenes was
that the US and the UK needed nine votes to implement their destructive
agenda in Iraq, but they could not get the nine votes from the UN Security
Council. The countries that were blocking them were Angola, Cameroon
and Guinea Conakry. The presidents of these African countries had had
direct discussions with Mbeki and they really could not give way on this.
The ambassadors of Chile and Mexico were declared personae non gratae
by the US because they refused to vote with them. It was the toughest
fight and ambassadors who were there – and I know that one of them has
written a book – will all tell you the same. It was brutal, but the powerful

countries just could not get the nine votes. And Africa was supposed to be the easiest region to convince. But Africa stood very firm on this one. This was one time when Mandela was really upset and he kept pressure on President Bush Jnr and British Prime Minister Blair.

There was also the story about Colin Powell trying to exert more political pressure in order for the US to achieve its main goals and objectives. But as the NAM, we would not allow the UN Security Council to hold the meeting without inviting South Africa as the chair of NAM. Colin Powell approached Kofi Annan, who later informed me that Powell said he did not want to make 'this Kumalo guy happy' by calling for a closed meeting; he said that they were going to do their bidding in an open meeting. And of course Powell embarrassed the US and showed all the world that weapons of mass destruction did not exist. I was in touch with Mbeki throughout these happenings at the UN.

We knew from our South African experts who had gone to Iraq as part of the inspection team that there were no weapons of mass destruction. As the chair of NAM, I met Hans Blix (head of UN Monitoring, Verification and Inspection Commission) regularly and he indicated that Powell was concocting false stories. When powerful countries want something in the UN, they will manipulate the Security Council.

President Mbeki did not focus his attention only at the UN; he was also paying attention to conflict prevention on the African continent. There was the Ouagadougou Agreement in Côte d'Ivoire. A cabinet minister in the government of the president of Burkina Faso, Blaise Compaoré, informed me that this agreement was the result of Mbeki's genius because he flew to Côte d'Ivoire, took President Gbagbo into his plane and they stopped in the north and picked up Force Nouvelle leader Guillaume Soro and then proceeded to Burkina Faso where they all sat down and drafted the peace agreement.

We had problems with the Ouagadougou Agreement when the French challenged its legality because they (the French) could not believe that an agreement between political adversaries in a Francophone country had been reached without France's involvement. So the French fought very hard to try to belittle the agreement, but they did not succeed because the African leaders rallied around it and embraced it and it became an African agreement. And this was made possible because of President Mbeki's ability to listen to what both Gbagbo and Soro had to say about their political differences. I know this for a fact because I led a UN Security Council delegation to Côte d'Ivoire twice. We knew that the French were trying their best to bring in Alassane Ouattara as their proxy and he is now the President of Côte d'Ivoire because they wanted to keep their stronghold on the cocoa (and coffee) industry.

I once asked a French ambassador at the UN, who was a friend of mine, why they were hassling us so much on the Ivoirian issue. He said, 'Listen here, my friend, if you are in a café in Paris, just remember that one of every five cups of coffee is made from coffee from Côte d'Ivoire and that is how much Côte d'Ivoire means to the French.'

Kofi Annan's people were really uncomfortable because President Mbeki would go personally to Côte d'Ivoire, for instance, on a conflict prevention mission, and Annan's people at the UN would submit incorrect reports. I was always in touch with President Mbeki and I would go to the Security Council the next day and say that my president was there and this is what he reported to me. So they hated us for always submitting a report that contradicted theirs.

One day when historians write the history of South Africa at the UN, they will say that the decade from 1999 to 2008 was one shining and exciting moment for South Africa but, like every shining moment, it went dull afterwards. It was one shining moment when South Africa truly put Africa on the global map and this was because of President Mbeki. When I went to the UN, the first thing I did, without even being familiar with the issues, was to chair the meetings as a representative of the chair of NAM on the dissolution of Yugoslavia and the creation of countries like Croatia, Slovenia etc. That was why I took a Security Council delegation to Kosovo, and when we got to Belgrade we were told by the president there that he knew President Mbeki. He was really very well known and it was because of the work that he did on international solidarity during the liberation struggle.

Mbeki was a great friend of French President Jacques Chirac and people do not realise that President George Bush Jnr was also a good friend. The two of them always met whenever Mbeki went to the UN. They were close buddies.

All these links that Mbeki forged with such a wide network of people also helped us when I was in a battle over Zimbabwe, when the issue came to the Security Council and Mbeki was defending the right of the

Zimbabweans to decide their own political destiny. The British were doing everything in their power to get their way in Zimbabwe. They had meetings where they would negotiate in Pretoria and the next morning the French and British ambassadors at the UN would inform me that Morgan Tsvangirai had agreed to a particular position, but they would say that they knew that he did not mean it. They would even proclaim that their version would appear in the newspapers and it always did. Then a few days later Tsvangirai would make a statement denying what he had promised in private discussions. I was always protected by President Mbeki and our minister of foreign affairs. Many times the powerful Western nations went to Nkosazana Dlamini-Zuma, who was my minister then, and pleaded with her to get me out of the UN. And Nkosazana would say, 'I did not send him there, it was President Mbeki.' I had two books that I used to carry with me all the time and I would recommend them to young people. The two documents that guided me during my tenure at the UN were the South African Constitution and the UN Charter. The preamble to the South African Constitution says something about restoring South Africa to its rightful place among nations – and its rightful place was to be as stubborn as hell at the UN.

One thing that South Africa did, as president of the Security Council, which had never happened before, was to invite 16 African heads of state to a meeting. It was the first time that the African leaders had met in the Security Council to address serious matters about conflict prevention and peace in Africa. This demonstrated how much Mbeki valued the views of people he worked with. The idea that he did not consult and that his views were sacrosanct and could not be challenged really is a myth. He is a good listener.

To me, this goes back to a story I was told once about Mbeki. When he was a schoolboy, he used to go to his mother's shop back in his hometown and write letters for the elders in his community. The women who went to the shop would ask him to write letters for them to their husbands who were migrant labourers residing in far-flung areas within South Africa. The young Mbeki had the ability to listen to those women's narratives and to understand the messages that they wanted to convey to their husbands. That is really something special. Regardless of what political detractors say about Mbeki, he has the ability to listen and also to explain something in a way that everybody understands.

I think that the fact that Mbeki was able to stand up to the mighty US and Britain goes back to his ability to listen and to understand where his opponents are coming from. He is then able to articulate his case in a manner that opponents will hear because he really paid attention, and that is what makes him so great in negotiations for peace. When you have warring factions that you are trying to bring together in a peace deal you have to be able to listen to each side's case before you can suggest solutions. So Mbeki was able to listen to Mugabe and Tsvangirai. The others, as representatives of the UK and the US, were simply dictating terms to these two leaders as if they were children.

On conflict prevention in Zimbabwe, Mbeki believed that it was a matter of fundamental principle that the people of Zimbabwe had the right to choose their own destiny; it was not for the UN Security Council to decide for them. Kenya provides an example of double standards at the UN. After the 2007 elections, when people were being killed as Kibaki and Odinga jostled for political power, there was never a meeting in the UN Security Council to try to enforce regime change in Kenya. Why? The British and the Americans were not going to allow it. The American ambassadors told me very clearly that I had to understand that in Kenya the Americans supported Mwai Kibaki and the British supported Raila Odinga. What was really unfair was that Kofi Annan was the special envoy on Kenya brought in by the British and the Americans to try to resolve the political disputes, but he never once submitted a report on the Kenyan issue to the Security Council. When it came to Zimbabwe, they were reporting to the UN every day. These were the double standards that were questioned and challenged by President Mbeki.

So our issue was that we would never allow an African country to be subjected to the kinds of selective political pressure that the powerful countries were imposing. When the liberation movement was still in exile, its interests were always taken care of because African countries represented our struggle when we were not members of the UN; it was therefore important for South Africa to continue representing Zimbabwe at the UN, with the support of President Mbeki of course. Now that we had won our struggle for liberation against white minority rule we could not forget other African countries that needed us. The other thing that the British hated Mbeki for was that he always reminded them about the Lancaster House agreement. He was familiar with the terms of this agreement because he supported the Patriotic Front.

Another interesting matter related to the Zimbabwe issue concerns the then ambassador of Burkina Faso, Michel Kafando. He used to sit next to me at the UN and on the day that he was supposed to vote on Zimbabwe, and he was going to vote with me, he was called by President Compaoré, who instructed him not to vote with South Africa. He came and told me about this. But he defied Compaoré and did vote against the UN resolution.

There was a lot of political pressure from France. Because of the positive role South Africa played in NAM, Indonesia and other NAM member states were there with us. When the resolution was vetoed by China and Russia, the Russian ambassador at the UN called me at six in the morning and suggested that we should meet. He informed me that President Mbeki had spoken to his president (Putin) and carefully explained to him why South Africa was not going to allow this resolution to go through. Condoleezza Rice was very shocked because the confident Americans thought they had it in the bag when suddenly Russia, China and South Africa voted against it. I will maintain even today that the decisions we took at the UN about Zimbabwe were correct. If regime change had happened in Zimbabwe, then it could have happened to any other African country – including democratic South Africa.

We were also right on Myanmar. We followed the decisions of the Association of Southeast Asian Nations (ASEAN), particularly what Indonesia and India were saying, and in principle we stood with them. South Africa was part of the international world when Thabo Mbeki was the president of the country. In the spirit of international solidarity, we consulted our international colleagues. President Mbeki's viewpoint and advice about particular geopolitical matters were highly sought after by international leaders. But, I am sad to say, it did not happen with Libya in 2011. With Libya, the Americans were able to turn South Africa's vote. They got Nigeria and South Africa to vote the wrong way and now look at the mess in Libya.

How the Zimbabwe matter ended up in the Security Council is really fascinating because one has to ask oneself whether this tiny country in southern Africa posed a threat to global peace. What happened behind the scenes was that there was a G8 meeting in Asia, which was attended by President Mbeki. He met with the presidents of Russia and China while he was there. The way the UN system works is that instructions are then forwarded to the ambassadors in the UN and they are told how to deal with the matter.

Somalia was falling apart, but the Security Council was not addressing the matter. Mbeki and others wanted it put on the UN agenda. Somalia was a threat to international peace and security yet this important issue was not on the UN Security Council's agenda. Yet the Western countries and their supporters were focused on Zimbabwe where citizens had voted in an official election. The fact that Zimbabweans elected a different person was, according to the dictates of Western powers, perceived as a threat to international peace and security by these same powers. At the end of the day you could not take away the right of the Zimbabweans to choose whomever they wanted.

The other pressing matter was that the African Union (AU) was always being marginalised at the UN because of the dismissive attitude of these Western countries. With the support of President Mbeki, we always argued that the decisions of the AU must be taken seriously by the UN Security Council. We could not have a situation where African countries took decisions and then the Security Council ignored them.

When he came to the UN, President Mbeki would never deliver a speech that I had not seen. In fact I would sit with him all night while he wrote the speech. He would tell me that I was the one who was in the UN and so I always told him what the situation was. He gave me the freedom to manoeuvre and I would always report back to him. I would often talk to Advocate Mojanku Gumbi because she was always there with him. South Africa would never vote in the Security Council without informing Nkosazana Dlamini-Zuma, our minister of foreign affairs. There was nothing about the UN that President Mbeki did not already know. He knew the system because he had worked it over so many years during the struggle and he knew many of the people there.

We used to get about 30 to 40 bilateral requests whenever Mbeki came to New York for the UN General Assembly. One time, Ariel Sharon, prime minister of Israel, personally complained about me to President Mbeki and Nkosazana Dlamini-Zuma. He told Mbeki that 'your ambassador here' refused to have the Day of the Holocaust on the UN agenda; my point was that this could not happen when you did not have a Day of Slavery on the UN agenda. The Israelis wanted a bilateral with Mbeki, knowing that I would be there to take notes and Sharon complained in my presence.

When President Mbeki came to New York, I would host a lunch and invite African heads of state. That was how President Robert Mugabe sat down with Jack Straw (the British foreign secretary) and the papers in the UK were full of pictures of Jack Straw eating at the same table as Mugabe. Mbeki and Straw's friendship dated back to their student days in England.

There are other stories to tell about Mbeki outside the hardcore geo-politics and work environment, so let me tell you a funny story. We were in Algeria for the OAU summit in 1981 that decided that African countries that engineered coups could not be members of the OAU. The summit was held at a brand-new hotel that had just opened in Algiers and they had never before hosted a summit of this size. Nothing worked at that brand-new hotel. All the presidents' clothes were taken to be ironed/pressed, and because it was a new hotel and the staff were inexperienced they somehow mixed up all the pants and the jackets. Not only was there a mix-up with Mbeki's suit, but the meeting was about to commence and there was no food. We discovered that the hotel staff were the only ones who had food and they were eating in a little canteen. Mbeki said to his team, let us go and eat, and he led us to that little canteen. We sat down and we ate with the workers. The ministers who accompanied him were upset about this matter, asking how we could take the president to eat with the workers. Meanwhile Mbeki was sitting and enjoying his lunch with the Algerian workers.

In Monterrey, the favourite dish was something called *cabrito,* which is lamb. It is braaied and it is really a wonderful meal. We told Mbeki that the only thing to eat was *cabrito* and he said we should bring it. President Chirac was eating McDonald's and was most surprised to see President Mbeki eating *cabrito* with Trevor Manuel and others.

Mbeki's recall from office was very sad. Nkosazana Dlamini-Zuma was in the ANC meeting that took the decision to recall Mbeki and so they called us to tell us that Mbeki was no longer coming to the UN. But Nkosazana came to New York and Trevor went to Washington and this messed us up because we had made arrangements ahead of time for these official gatherings. But what could we do, we had to manage the situation. The powerful countries knew that South Africa was no longer going to give them a hard time after Mbeki was recalled and they were right.

In terms of personality, Thabo Mbeki is the simplest, most humble of people. He is none of those things that are said about him. The description that he is aloof does not fit. One of the things that I was well known for by ministers like Pravin Gordhan and Trevor Manuel was that, because I like jazz, I used to have a table at the Blue Note Jazz Club in New York. When these ministers came to New York they knew that if they wanted to see me on a Saturday night, they would find me at the Blue Note Jazz Club. When Mbeki was in New York, he was a permanent member of that table. We were always at the Blue Note until 3am. I am mentioning this because it reveals that Mbeki was not always serious; he could let his hair down, so to speak.

In terms of Mbeki's legacy, I have always said that if you looked at the national symbols of South Africa – the flag, the crest, the coat of arms, the Constitution – you would find that they carry Mbeki's contributions on his creative side.

I have had the pleasure of travelling all over the world. I chaired a committee on behalf of East Timor, a little island in the middle of the Pacific. Xanana Gusmao told us that everything he knew he had learned from President Mbeki when they were students in exile in London.

I think that we do not appreciate Mbeki now and that is why it is important for us to write about the man we know, because South Africa does not appreciate its own. We may not appreciate Mbeki now, but one day the country will sit back and really come to appreciate him and his contribution to this country, the African continent and the world.

Interviewed July 2015, Johannesburg

NOZIPHO JANUARY-BARDILL

❖

I first met Thabo Mbeki in the mid-1980s when I was living in exile with my family in London. My long-time friend Sheila Sisulu was visiting and, uncertain of the London underground system, she asked me to accompany her to the home of our late president Oliver Tambo in North London where he and Thabo Mbeki were working for the liberation of our country. I couldn't believe my luck. I had grown to admire and respect both of them as my leaders in exile who chose to devote their entire lives to the fight for racial justice, equality and freedom in South Africa. Witnessing the much-written-about mentor/mentee relationship between the two men, albeit briefly in a relatively short meeting, was an experience that has remained etched in my memory for many years.

President Mbeki's brother Jama, whose death remains unsolved, had sometimes spoken of him during earlier years in Lesotho. Jama Mbeki, like many South Africans, had chosen to study at the University of Botswana, Lesotho and Swaziland to escape the wrath of the apartheid state for daring to get involved in the African National Congress (ANC) led liberation struggle and to avoid bantustan tertiary education. The popular Jama, a formidable leader, was elected president of the Student Representative Council during my first year of study. I remember him leading the student body to hold a successful 'sit-in' when the late Prime Minister Leabua Jonathan declared a coup after the 1970 parliamentary elections in Lesotho.

Decades later, after many years in Lesotho and London, and totally involved in the transformation of our now free South Africa, I had a different encounter with President Mbeki. I had been back in the country for seven years when in December 2000 I was approached by the then director general of the department of foreign affairs, Sipho Pityana, to serve as Ambassador Plenipotentiary in Bern, Switzerland, the Principality of Lichtenstein and the Holy See (Vatican).

I was one of many women whom the president had identified to change the white and male character of South Africa's political representation abroad. We had been preceded by a cohort of South Africa's most iconic women such as our then minister of foreign affairs, Dr Nkosazana Dlamini-Zuma, High Commissioner Lindiwe Mabuza, Ambassadors Barbara Masekela, Ruth Mompati, Thandi Rankoe, Maite Nkoana-Mashabane (our current foreign minister) and Nozipho Mxakato-Diseko to name a few. The president had also appointed women speakers in parliament: my former boss, Dr Frene Ginwala and Baleka Mbete (now chairperson of the ANC). President Mbeki did not just talk about gender equality and women's empowerment; he actually put his money where his heart is.

I was flattered by the affirmation and honoured to have been asked to represent President Mbeki in this small and beautiful alpine country whose international stature belies its small size, largely due to its importance as one of the world's major financial centres, as well as its hosting of a large number of international diplomatic, economic and sporting bodies, including a number of key United Nations (UN) multilateral agencies. With a long history of political neutrality, Switzerland had also gained notoriety in some quarters for refusing to apply economic sanctions against South Africa when the ANC called for them. The presidency had given me a clear directive to engage more with our former adversaries than our friends, and I was to find out that there were indeed some who seemed to mourn the demise of the old South Africa and hadn't quite got around to believing that a black government could be trusted. More encouragingly, there were also many individuals and institutions that positively supported the changes that were taking place in South Africa.

Serving abroad was an honour and a privilege. It required Thabo Mbeki's brand of South African activism and the president's commitment to hard work, professionalism, appreciation of knowledge, learning and confidence. We knew we were serving a president who had a love of and passion for international relations. We knew that he would not settle for mediocrity and underperformance by any of us. We were also working for a woman minister with a razor-sharp mind and equally impressive directors general in Pityana and Dr Ayanda Ntsaluba who set high standards of performance and knew exactly what they wanted and expected of us. During Heads of Mission conferences, when representatives came home to be briefed, we looked forward to the president's guidance and leadership and his ministers' analyses of their portfolios and what was expected of us to successfully implement the government's foreign policy.

In this regard, the weekly 'Letter from the President' in the newsletter *ANC Today* became an important tool for all diplomats. It was a compulsory read to keep abreast of topical issues at home, abroad and at the UN. It helped us understand what the president's positions were. We looked forward to reading *ANC Today* because it gave us confidence and ammunition to manage sometimes intricate political questions from the governments and people of our accredited countries. Even the controversial AIDS debate, which was hard for many to articulate in the face of incessant criticism was explained in the president's letter. The president's ability to write these letters week after week and do the million other things that his job demanded was both admirable and inspiring. I was told that he often wrote his own speeches, sitting up till the early hours of the morning to finish them. I witnessed this myself when I invited him to Bern for an official visit, piggybacking on his invitation to give a keynote address at the Geneva-based International Labour Organisation (ILO) annual conference. I had scheduled a briefing meeting with him for half an hour and, as we finished, he took out his own laptop and swiftly left us to go and finalise his ILO speech, which had been drafted by one of his deputy directors general.

When, in 2004, after ten years of freedom, ambassadors were asked to remain in their posts and plan formal celebrations of South Africa's decade of freedom with the people of the world who had walked the long road to freedom with us in the anti-apartheid movement, we deepened our under-standing of the real values of the president, the ANC and the government. We were told that it was important that we acknowledge and applaud the role of the international community in the demise of apartheid and can-didly inform them what the new government had done to fulfil the dream of a free and democratic South Africa that they still shared with the people of this country. The missions rose to the occasion with the support of the department and its principals, and successfully implemented the president's mandate. I documented our work in Switzerland and was able to present him with a book, *People to People – Celebrating Ten Years of Freedom in South Africa*. I had been inspired by his incessant desire to write.

In that same year, Presidents Mbeki and Mandela, Archbishop Tutu, Minister Nkosazana Dlamini-Zuma and South African Football Association president Danny Jordaan and his team led a delegation to the headquarters of FIFA to present the country's bid for hosting the 2010 World Cup tournament. The president had asked the embassy to host a dinner after the presentation and on the eve of the announcement to mobilise the South African vuvuzela-carrying crowds who had flown in and colonised the famous Dolder Hotel in Zürich. Like a true commander in chief, he and his delegation left the party at midnight to ensure that he was back home with the people of South African at 2pm the next day when the announcement of the winner was made by Sepp Blatter. The rest is history.

I cannot conclude this piece without commenting on the president's vision of an African Renaissance and the leading role he played in the establishment of the New Partnership for Africa's Development (NEPAD) and the African Union (AU). Nearly 20 years into our democracy, it would be dishonest to believe that NEPAD did not offer a degree of hope for African governments and their people, men and women. NEPAD was central to our foreign policy at the time and we had to convince our local stakeholders of its importance in the growth and sustainability of the African continent. The focus on developing Africa's economic capacity through good governance as a prerequisite for stability, investor confidence and support from developed nations was met with both excitement and scepticism; but Mbeki was determined to encourage all to extricate themselves and the continent from underdevelopment and marginalisation in an increasingly globalised world. The promotion of women in all NEPAD objectives and activities encouraged African leaders to recognise and value the abilities of women to play a central role in the development of our continent.

President Thabo Mbeki had internalised the principles of gender equality, women's empowerment and non-discrimination. He may very well have been ahead of his time in a society that is still not ready for this ideal.

His legacy will continue to inspire many who believe in his vision. His current work on the continent is testament to his selfless commitment to peace and stability that the people of Africa so deserve.

VI

CADRES AND COMRADES

MONGANE WALLY SEROTE

❧❧

The first time I sat in a meeting with Comrade Thabo Mbeki was in the 1980s in Botswana. I was then the chairperson of our underground political committee in the area. The Movement had escalated the struggle for the liberation of our country at all levels by coordinating the underground, armed, mass and international struggles against the apartheid regime. The apartheid regime was reacting like a wounded bull against all the front areas where the fighting forces of the African National Congress (ANC) were based, taking the fight against the apartheid regime the length and breadth of the country.

The issue on the agenda of the meeting was to discuss the comrades who were saying that, in self-defence, they would begin shooting from Botswana into South Africa because of the manner in which some of the security forces in that country were acting against comrades. We were divided on the issue; some did not agree with that position. There was therefore enthusiastic debate among the different units. We were seeking a common understanding so that we could act from a common point of reference. Headquarters had sent different leaders to participate in the discussion.

The meeting was held at night in one of our underground houses. Comrade Thabo, who was in the area for other matters related to the struggle, attended the meeting. We gave a briefing about the situation and the circumstances we were working under. Basically, there was an agreement among all of us who were deployed in Botswana that, because of the escalating political and armed struggle in South Africa, forward areas like

Botswana had to defend and protect their sovereignty and national interests against the regime's so-called 'hot pursuits'. The protective measures that Frontline States like Botswana took against cadres in their countries included arresting us, sending us back to the rear, shooting cadres, and rumour had it that some cadres had been sent back to South Africa. We were all edgy about this. It was therefore not surprising that some comrades expressed ultra-radical positions with regard to our situation. It was an extremely dangerous position to take; it would diminish the element of surprise against the apartheid forces but, equally dangerous, it would completely alienate the Batswana who already had become victims of the apartheid regime's hot pursuit tactics.

As comrades were reporting, I was watching Comrade Thabo. He was listening carefully. As he listened he was busy with his tobacco pouch, pipe and pipe cleaner. We used to smoke heavily in meetings in those days. Nkosazana Dlamini-Zuma had not come into the picture yet to put a ban on smoking in buildings. Comrade Thabo lit his pipe, the rum-and-maple aroma filled the room, and smoke from the puffed pipe curled up to the ceiling and around the space in the room.

In hindsight, I can say that he responded in typical fashion. He gave examples of the advice he was about to give us by relating several incidents that happened elsewhere, illustrating the differences between strategy and tactics. What stuck in my mind for ever was how he eventually advised us specifically in terms of the situation we were facing. He described how Batswana were a very nationalistic people, and how they would be most committed to fight against the apartheid regime. I cannot remember whether he explicitly stated that the position about 'shooting from Botswana into South Africa' was wrong, but the examples he gave about happenings elsewhere, and the observations he shared with us regarding the Batswana, were stated in simple terms, yet they were profound answers to a very tense and dangerous situation. He told us stories about Batswana that clearly illustrated that they were our strong and committed allies.

There was this thing about him, which cut him as being a bit distant; distant from what I struggled to understand. Some called him an aloof intellectual, others called him a snob. I took a decision that I was going to listen carefully to him, to his voice. Nowadays this is called 'watching the space'.

The meeting ended quite deep in the night. He left, but I remained, thinking about his pipe, the smoke, the aroma and his stories. How did he know that Botswana was our strong and committed ally; did that arise only from their being nationalistic?

We lived and worked in Botswana. We were called *matlola trata* – 'those who jumped the fence'. We were referred to in derogatory terms as 'refugees'. 'Bo ekse', the phrase is used in township lingo, derived from Afrikaans, more or less meaning the 'hey yous'. ('Ek – I , sê – say', literal translation.) The foreign minister of Botswana, Mme Machiepe, was quoted in papers as having said that if South Africa knew where the ANC cadres were, it should point out the areas or houses and the Botswana police would arrest them. It was true that some comrades had been shot and wounded, some had been arrested and sentenced, some had been sent back to the rear and the radio continuously stated that anyone seeing people in tackies (canvas shoes), denim jeans, and talking Afrikaans must report them. It was also a time rife with rumours.

Pik Botha, then South African minister of foreign affairs, had sent many threats to the Batswana that South Africa would have no choice but to embark on hot pursuit missions. It was around that time, 1985, that the South African Defence Force (SADF) mounted a major attack on the capital of Botswana, Gaborone, killing 12 comrades and destroying property. Several other attacks were mounted against Botswana and other southern African countries.

Comrade Thabo had said that, given everything that was going on in the region, he thought that Botswana would prove to be the only front area we could use to escalate the struggle. By the late 1980s, his view was proved correct. Leaders within any organisation are profiled and are known throughout its ranks. Comrade Thabo's profile in the Movement was that he was the youngest in the National Executive Committee (NEC); he was not only close to but he was also being mentored by President Oliver Tambo; it was known that he had been at a university in England and that he had been deployed in the front in Swaziland, from where he was transferred to headquarters in Lusaka, Zambia. His having been in London and being referred to as an intellectual was really said tongue in cheek. As he sat there, in that underground house, busy with his pipe, pipe cleaner and tobacco pouch, suit, tie and all, I thought about the manner in which he had been referred to as being intellectual and aloof. The way he had discussed the situation in Botswana with us, and the fact that later when he was vindicated by events, made me change my views about him. Not only that, but I began to understand what an intellectual must be.

That was why I put my ear to the ground for that, his voice. We infiltrated men and women, weapons and messages into South Africa but it became apparent in our engagements with those comrades who were operating and living inside the country that the ability of the Movement to operate from most of the front areas was diminishing, and the load of those operations was now placed on Botswana. Many home-based operatives were transferred to Botswana. I decided that there were certain issues that Comrade Thabo Mbeki understood, being a member of the NEC and the Politico Military Council (PMC) at headquarters, and being Oliver Tambo's speechwriter. I knew I must listen to that voice and take it as a guide regarding the front areas. Of course it was not the only voice; there were other leadership voices. What was most inspiring was that Comrade Johnny Makhathini would say something in New York; the same drift on other matters would be said by Comrade Mac Maharaj in London and by Comrade Thabo or Comrade Pallo in Lusaka. When the members of the PMC came to front areas – as did Comrade Thabo or Comrade Reg September, or Comrades Nkadimeng or Ntate Motsabi or Mme maMophosho, or Comrades Cassius Make, or Ronnie Kasrils, or Joe Jele, or Joe Modise, or Chris Hani, or Lehlohonolo Moloi (then known as Comrade A) – you felt and knew that leadership was in control of the struggle. There was strong coordination in the front areas and in the underground, mass and international fronts. These sectors of struggle were sustained by those voices, and by O.R.'s voice, which reached us every 8 January. I have no doubt that all front areas took the 8 January statement by Oliver Tambo as the ultimate order for action in a certain direction. 1979 was declared the Year of Isandlwana and the armed operations in South Africa escalated.

When I was deployed in London after having been active in Botswana for ten years, there was overwhelming support for the ANC in Britain and Europe. The discussions, debriefings and briefings that one had with the different levels of the Anti-Apartheid Movement (AAM) were nuanced so that at times there was a need for thorough explanation for whatever agenda was on the table. One therefore had to commit to reading and studying policy positions of the Movement on different subjects.

Thabo was a master at this and it was this observation that made me commit to a flexible intellectual approach to the struggle. It was necessary and essential that cadres of the Movement were trained to become intellectuals, which is fundamentally different from being an academic, but different also from being an intellectual for the sake of being intellectual. The intellectual within the Movement had, on the one hand, to be theoretical in approach to the issues on the table, which must be related to the advancement of the Movement; on the other hand, that theory had to transform to practice, the objective being to investigate the truth in any of the opposing views and finding what would be appropriate to serve the interests of the advancement of the Movement. To engage the issues of sanctions, the cultural and sports boycott, disinvestment and strong opposition to the apartheid regime from an AAM position, one had to, in the same breath, also ensure that one spoke to the restricted nature of the armed struggle being waged through Umkhonto we Sizwe (MK), as also one must emphasise the non-racial approach of whatever activity the Movement engaged in and emphasise the fact that it was Movement policy to ensure the unity of the black and white citizens of South Africa. Radical positions that were not contextualised in reality were clearly counter-productive.

At one point some ANC leaders, who resided in Britain or were visiting London on different missions, expressed views opposed to lesbianism and homosexuality and spoke publicly about the subject in a most negative manner. There was a serious backlash from members of the AAM that could have threatened the strength and unity of one of the most important supporters of the ANC. I cannot recall whether Comrade Thabo Mbeki was already in London when this backlash happened, or whether he came specially from Lusaka to engage the issue.

The Regional Politico Military Council (RPMC) of the Movement, which was based in London and headed by Comrade Aziz Pahad, was convened to discuss this matter with some leaders of the AAM. Comrade Thabo led the discussions in that meeting. I gleaned from how he summarised that this was a subject about which most South Africans were ignorant and, I suspect, held very backward positions about. His summary focused on the fact that our approach to the subject must be on the basis of human rights. All of us have the right of choice and association. I came to realise after the discussions that prejudice is most damning and cruel. It does not only emanate from utter ignorance but is also most potent in breeding evil and cruelty.

In the three years while I was based in London, there were many encounters with Comrade Thabo on issues of sanctions, the cultural and sports boycott, disinvestment, the underground and the armed struggle. The Liberation Movement and the AAM had become the hammer and anvil for the apartheid regime; the regime's neck was now on the anvil. The content of the Movement based in South Africa complemented that of the Movement based externally, and as the isolation of the apartheid regime intensified, the theories that informed the strategy and tactics of the Movement, when practised, yielded evidence of the quality outcomes of tits objectives. The AAM was very strong then, with a large following in Europe, the US, Latin America and Cuba – which stood out, with its most progressive internationalist policy – the Caribbean Islands, Asia and in Africa. Apart from a few countries, the African continent was fully behind the struggle for the liberation of South Africa and Namibia. In the many examples that Comrade Thabo gave about the continent, he conscientised one to pay particular attention to the happenings on the continent and to regard the continent not only as an African space and place that was extremely important for the liberation of South Africa, but also important for Africans within the global village.

1987-88 was the volcano-like moment of eruption in southern Africa. The SADF was defeated in Angola by the joint forces of the Cuban and Angolan armed forces, and finally the region was freed from the clutches of imperialism and apartheid. For South Africa and Namibia it was no longer an issue of whether the countries would be free, but when it would be that the peoples of those countries seized power and determined the destinies of their countries. It was not too long before Comrade Thabo put the issue of the African Renaissance not only on the agenda of South Africa, but also of the continent and the world.

It was in 1988 when some members of the RPMC led by Comrade Thabo met with the emissaries of the apartheid system sent by Die Groot Krokodil (P.W. Botha). We convened at a hotel in Kent, organised by the Gold Field mining company. I had recently come back from further military training in Moscow and it did not take long for me to realise that this was a very serious meeting. As I have said, in 1985, the SADF had mounted a major attack on Gaborone, killing 12 of our comrades. That meant that those of us who were on the ground after the attack had to turn our defensive mode into an offensive one. We did everything possible to regain that ground. By that time, Comrade A, the chief of operations of MK, had become head of the Botswana RPMC and had taken complete charge of the ground forces in Botswana. He was a focused, no-nonsense leader who led from the front and sifted operatives and deployed them. I worked closely with him and aspired to be a good soldier. We met at night, in the early hours of the morning, in houses, in the bush and in cars; at times we walked briefly together, said what we had to say and parted. Botswana was fundamentally changed as an operational area; our operations were strictly underground. That was the context from which I came when I was deployed in London. Apart from the SADF attack in Botswana, the 1980s manifested what we had anticipated from the apartheid regime: it swung into total violence in the townships and villages. This occurred not only in South Africa but also in the front areas as Comrade Thabo had warned, and in fact we quickly became the only functional front, for all intents and purposes.

I had to learn how to work in London. I went for training where one day one of our instructors said out of the blue: how relevant would the armed struggle be if the political prisoners in your country were released? As the commander of the group, I really felt that he was talking nonsense. He asked us to discuss this among ourselves and that he would listen to our presentation a week or so later. As we discussed this he came back with another surprise: he wanted us to discuss the relationship between nationalism and socialism. Before we could tackle that subject, which we felt most enthusiastic about, he told us that the citizens of East Germany were demanding to be reintegrated into West Germany, and that the numbers of those who were participating in the demonstrations and protests in favour of the integration were growing rapidly. We were not shocked; we were numbed. The implications for our struggle were serious. He later told us about glasnost and perestroika, saying the implications were that the Soviet Union could disintegrate.

These matters were very fresh in my mind as I sat in the meeting led by Comrade Thabo in Kent. I had to use the background of all the other meetings that I had attended as my compass to navigate the discussions at hand. I listened to him carefully. I sensed that the few of us sitting there represented the mighty voice of the Movement. I was keenly aware that these talks were very high level. The global situation as I have described it hovered at the back of my mind as I followed the discussions in the room, the talks about talks.

Then I heard Comrade Thabo put the conditions for the negotiations: '... the release of all political prisoners; the unbanning of all political organisations ...' It was most interesting to watch the leader of the other side, Professor Willie Esterhuyse. He was sharp and at times nervous. The stakes were indeed very high on both sides. A team spirit emerged between Comrade Thabo and Comrade Aziz; they complemented each other and their emphasis on issues indicated that the Movement was now on the move. The strategy had been outlined and the tactics were on the table.

Where does one learn these skills? As I watched Thabo in that room, the tone of his voice, the incisive logic, the carefully constructed sentences which, although plain and simple were describing complex and extremely serious matters that carried the lives and being of a nation in them, I truly did not see an alternative to what was happening. I even understood that we had reached the turning point in our country. The many things that Comrade Thabo said in the meeting implied that all of us must quickly move away from the past and that our minds must now focus on the present and the future, for that was what we had been catapulted into. It felt as though the frames of a film were unrolling before our eyes.

Perhaps universities will have the basis, in retrospect, to learn from these events, and use these experiences to create courses for study by young Africans. Otherwise, there was no university in the world that could have taught any of the discussions that were unfolding in that room. Those discussions carried the weight of the lives of the people of South Africa, southern Africa and the African continent.

From then on, it felt as if we were in a runaway train, rattling on its track at non-stop pace and when it stopped, in what seemed a short space of time, we were in South Africa. The negotiations for non-racialism, non-sexism and democracy were unfolding; Madiba was now on the national stage. O.R., Tata Sisulu, Oom Gov and other Rivonia trialists were there some-where, now in the background and then at rallies, and although Comrade Thabo was not very visible, one knew that he was there somewhere, pipe, tobacco pouch and pipe cleaner all to hand. I pictured him listening, think-ing, probing, consulting, he and Comrade Zuma a formidable team.

And then one day Comrade Thabo was the deputy president of the democratic South Africa, under President Mandela. I kept asking myself in those days: what is wrong with saying HIV/AIDS has three characteristics: the virus, the weak immune system and the opportunistic diseases? I asked myself, what is wrong with saying the world must support the Zimbabwean people in deciding their own destiny? I explored these thoughts in *History is the Home Address*, an epic poem. It felt as if we had very quickly arrived at a very dangerous moment in South Africa. It felt familiar, it felt like that African moment when leaders are assassinated, when the hand that squeezes the trigger is African, but the mind that plots is far away from where the act happens. It had already happened in South Africa – Comrade Chris had been murdered.

I understood what President Mbeki was saying about these two extremely important issues relating to South Africa and southern Africa respectively. The manner in which the world vilified him about these two issues cast my mind back to the not-so-long-ago history of the continent: Kwame Nkrumah, Amílcar Cabral, Mondlane, Sékou Touré, Machel … but there were also other voices that were most worrying because they were from among our ranks; they too were vilifying him on the same two issues. They even went further; they were asking that President Mbeki be charged for genocide because 350 000 children had died while he refused to roll out the antiretrovirals.

There is a corruption charge against Deputy President Zuma; President Mbeki 'relieves the deputy president of the State of his duties'. All of us cadres of the ANC are thrust into a deep hurt and pain … What is going on?

How time flies! Seven months before completing his tenure as presi-dent of our Movement, the ANC recalls President Thabo Mbeki. President

Mbeki resigns. We are further thrust into a deep quandary and pain. We are most fearful for our Movement. I do not think that it is an illusion to think that the Movement is scuttling. It is not because President Mbeki is not there that the Movement is scuttling. It is not because the Movement is divided. It is not even that it is just a perception that the Movement has scuttled into factions. It is that all of us, members of the ANC, must remind ourselves that we inherited the Movement, the ANC. It was a united fighting force when we took over from those who had, as our leaders, prepared it to lead and fight for freedom. We are under an obligation to hand it over to the coming generations, as it was given to us: united and fighting for peace, security and freedom, not only for South Africa, but for the continent and for the world. President Zuma knows and understands this. President Mbeki knows and understands this. I thank President Mbeki for his far-sightedness that, when he was recalled, he set a new precedent on the African continent. He resigned and handed power back to the ANC.

Now the ANC must give power back to the people!

SNUKI ZIKALALA

※

I know Thabo Mbeki as a committed African National Congress (ANC) cadre and liberation leader. I know him as one of the few ANC leaders who was tasked by the ANC to rebuild the underground structures of the movement and instil confidence among the masses of South Africa who were deprived of leadership after the banning, arrests and persecution of political leaders of South Africa in the late 1960s and early 1970s. I know Mbeki as an African patriot, selfless, passionate in his quest for a peaceful African continent. I know him as a man who yearns for and works towards an Africa that is democratic, stable, non-racial, non-sexist; an African continent that strives to develop sustainably. I know him as a committed citizen of the world, consistently and patiently propounding ideas of unity, a fighter against the deification of arms, a strong believer in a world at peace with itself.

I first met Thabo Mbeki in 1974 when I was exiled in Botswana. I had the pleasure of interacting and working closely with him from then until 1977 when, together with Keith Mokoape, another committed cadre, we were declared prohibited immigrants by the Botswana government. The South African government provided the security police of Botswana with information relating to the underground activities of Umkhonto we Sizwe (The Spear of the Nation), or MK as it was known, after an agent had infiltrated the movement and then fled to South Africa where he provided the racist authorities with detailed information about MK activities in Botswana.

Between 1974 and 1978, Mbeki was assigned by the ANC leadership to establish a strong underground presence in Botswana and Swaziland. Because of his intellect and revolutionary zeal, he was able to persuade the Botswana government to allow a small contingent of ANC activists to be accommodated and to do political work within the country. This was around the time when a radical change in the geopolitical landscape of southern Africa occurred, occasioned by the fall of the Caetano regime in Portugal, the colonial masters of Angola and Mozambique. The independence of Mozambique in 1974 inspired the oppressed people of South Africa. The Black Consciousness Movement (BCM) organisations, the Black People's Convention (BCP) and the South African Students' Organisation (SASO) went so far as to organise a Viva FRELIMO rally, thereby identifying themselves with FRELIMO, the Mozambique Liberation Front.

Thabo Mbeki's deployment in Botswana proved to be very strategic as he was able to interact with BCM activists who had sought refuge in Botswana, having fled the country after being hounded by the apartheid regime. The BCM leaders included Bokwe Mafuna, Harry Nengwekhulu, Papi Moloto, Tebogo Mafole, Welile Nhlapo and others. With Mbeki, we paid unannounced visits to BCM activists' houses and held intense intellectual discussions about the future of South Africa and the role that the youth ought to play in bringing down the apartheid regime. Discussions would go on for hours, with Mbeki explaining in detail the importance of a well-organised united front to fight against apartheid. We would marvel at the way he propounded the theories of Karl Marx and Friedrich Engels, or the theories of the Black Panther Movement and how these could be applied in the South African context.

The BCM activists were extremely critical of the ANC at first. They had planned to form their own liberation movement that would intensify the armed struggle inside South Africa. They accused the ANC and the Pan Africanist Congress (PAC) of having run out of ideas and believed that the BCM had the potential to lead the struggle for liberation. However, with a great deal of patience and irrefutable facts, we eventually managed to convince the majority of them that the ANC was indeed a home for all South Africans who had the desire and will to fight for a non-racial and democratic South Africa.

Together with the top leadership of the ANC – Ruth Mompati, Dan

Tloome, Duma Nokwe and John Motshabi – Thabo Mbeki would meet community leaders, trade unions and student organisation leaders who had been requested to visit Botswana under the guise of touring the country. Discussions ranged from building strong organisational structures for the ANC, trade union movement, student and church organisations, to setting up clandestine MK bases within the country. These community leaders were not met in large groups but as a few selected individuals who had no idea of the presence of the others.

Thabo Mbeki would come out of these meetings in the early hours of the morning and ready himself to attend official meetings with Botswana government officials. His visits to Botswana and the intellectual discussions he had with university professors and students from the University of Botswana changed the mindset of many.

The Botswana government and its officials respected Mbeki's acumen and intellectual prowess. Sir Seretse Khama, the first president of independent Botswana, was always impressed by Thabo Mbeki's deep understanding of African politics and the role of the then Organisation of African Unity (OAU) in supporting the liberation movements in their struggle against colonialism. This was also the case when President Masire took power in Botswana.

The seminal events of the Soweto student uprising of 1976 posed enormous challenges for the ANC. Thousands of students and other young patriots fleeing the country sought refuge mainly in Botswana and Swaziland before proceeding to other African countries like Zambia and Tanzania. With foresight, the ANC had set up a nucleus office in Botswana led by Isaac Makopo, Keith Mokoape and myself. We had to establish a well-oiled machinery that would receive, accommodate and dispatch these young people further north. While in Botswana, Thabo Mbeki led from the front. He would accompany Keith and myself during our regular visits to police stations and prisons where some of those who had fled South Africa were detained by the Botswana authorities. He led discussions with the angry detained youth, convincing them that the ANC was their home and that they had the choice either to go for military training or to further their education.

In 1977, having been declared prohibited immigrants, Keith and I left for

Zambia where we were part of the ANC Revolutionary Council. Thabo Mbeki was appointed head of communications when he was in charge of the Department of Information and Publicity. It was here that he changed the profile of the ANC, which became more visible owing to the communications strategy that he, together with the leadership of the ANC, had crafted and implemented.

When I was studying in Bulgaria, Mbeki and his wife Zanele visited the country. There, at a human level, Mbeki showed his humility. Despite being an ANC leader, Mbeki and his wife took a bus from the city of Sofia to the student town Dervenitsa to experience how students lived. They met some of our South African students, including my wife Pinkie and son Vusi.

Much later, in 1997, as group executive of the South African Broadcasting Corporation (SABC) News, we launched SABC News International, a 24-hour pan-African news channel with 13 correspondents throughout Africa, Europe, Latin America and the Caribbean. Thabo Mbeki, as president of the country, wholly supported the initiative. He gave a keynote address, warmly welcoming the launch, which he believed could serve as a critical building block in helping us realise the vision of the African Renaissance. As a journalist and senior reporter in the 1990s, I covered his political activities as best I could, including when he became president of South Africa and the ANC.

That is the Thabo Mbeki I know. The Thabo Mbeki Foundation and the Thabo Mbeki African Leadership Institute are the current pillars of the pan-African agenda.

ANDILE NGCABA

⚏

As a young underground activist in the late 1970s, I realised that going into exile was becoming unavoidable. After a series of trips to Maseru and other Frontline States in late 1979, it was clear that I would soon have to move out of the country.

Prior to going to exile I was a simple young electronics technician at Philips, based in Martindale down the road from Coronation Hospital in Johannesburg, South Africa. While working at Philips I got the opportunity to spend time in different divisions of the company, such as medical electronics, scientific instrumentation, Private Automatic Branch Exchange (PABX), data systems, consumer goods and lighting. I quit my job abruptly in 1981 and decided it was time to go into exile.

It will be important for me first to discuss the important role of Information and Communications Technology (ICT) in the liberation struggle prior to 1994. These are important matters that came to the fore in 1990 in order to engage the apartheid regime. It is also important to provide this context because Thabo Mbeki played a crucial role in spearheading the development of ICT during the post-1994 era. This issue will be discussed in the latter part of this paper.

I left South Africa to join Umkhonto we Sizwe (MK). I was part of the generations who took an oath to fight to liberate South Africa. After I left South Africa I went to Maseru, where I survived the 9th December 1982 massacre in which 42 people were killed by the South African Defence Force (SADF). After that I was sent to Angola to undergo general military training, thereafter specialising in military communications systems. Communications has always been close to my heart even prior to my work at Philips. This was the perfect opportunity. MK Military Communications used Soviet technology and we were oriented towards the Warsaw Pact military doctrine. Little did I know that military electronics and communications were far more interesting than what I had been doing at Philips. I was fortunate to be amongst the few who were selected to be trained in special military communications by Russian radio engineering instructors. Some refer to it as Signal Intelligence (SIGINT), Electronics Intelligence (ELINT) and Communication Intelligence (COMINT).

Special communications is high-speed, low-power consumption radio technology with complex frequency modulation. It transmits high volumes of data in nanoseconds using the ionosphere as a reflective layer and this makes it nearly impossible to intercept. Many have tried without success.

As part of MK's communication platform, we also made use of high-power transmitters whose antenna field would be equivalent to the size of two rugby fields. This was the earliest phase of the 4th Generation Military electronics and communications warfare. These transmitters used valve technology. To give a sense of the size of the valves, each one was larger than a two-litre Coke bottle. Today's military radio is very advanced and modern electronic systems are weaponised. They are microwave, sonic and electromagnetic weapons.

While in Angola I became the Chief Commanding Officer of Communications. I stayed in the camps in Angola throughout the 1980s, except for a few special missions. One example was the visit to the Polisario Front with President Oliver Tambo. Sahrawi Arab Democratic Republic in Western Sahara is a desert with temperatures averaging 42 degrees Celsius and a different terrain in which to conduct guerrilla warfare. We were used to operating in an equatorial rainforest region where you were guaranteed malaria at least once or twice a year.

My electronics background enabled me to train and work with younger MK recruits coming into exile to join the liberation movement. We established a fully fledged Military Communications Academy named after Ruth First. It was situated in Malanje and in Viana outside Luanda. We also worked with the People's Armed Forces for the Liberation of Angola

(FAPLA) and Cubans in developing a broader communications strategy. During this period there were Cubans and Russians as well as the ANC and the South West Africa People's Organisation (SWAPO) in Angola. Hence, when it came to military communication there was a lot of coordination of activities required. We possessed a great deal of advanced technology and were able to share communications and logistics with other friendly forces and, similarly, they would share with us. In that way we enhanced each other's expertise in the areas of SIGINT and COMINT.

The military communications system of MK was amongst the most sophisticated at that time. The MK communications network systems were there to connect headquarters in Lusaka and Luanda to Maputo with regions such as Gaborone, Dar es Salaam, Mbarara, Maseru, Manzini, and from the camps such as Caculama, Pango, Cacuso and Caxito, Quibaxe and Quela to Luanda. The systems were also designed to communicate with underground communications units inside South Africa. We ran all the long- and short-distance communications, strategic and tactical communications and conventional and unconventional military communications. During this period, we made use of one of the best encryption systems of that time. It was a mathematical algorithm that you can only use once.

We had to outsmart the apartheid regime because they also possessed high-level communication and interception systems. The apartheid forces had just invented radio frequency hopping technology and they had also deployed a SIGINT and Electronic Warfare (EW) platform to try to monitor and destabilise our and the Frontline States' border communications. This was a critical battle front for MK because of the constant movement of guerrilla forces who had infiltrated South Africa through the Frontline States. The apartheid regime also had a system called Military Area Radio Network (Marnet), which was widely used by farmers together with security forces operating along border areas of the Frontline States. They also deployed a tropospheric scatter communication system to cover both air and ground along the border with all Frontline States. The South African regime attempted to launch a reconnaissance satellite that was supposed to provide reconnaissance and surveillance systems to the SA Air Force when they planned cross-border air attacks. The satellite was built at Howteq in Grabouw near Cape Town and was supposed to be launched at the Overberg

Test Range (OTB) near Cape Agulhas as a polar Low Earth Orbit (LEO) satellite launch. These plans never materialised. When the ANC took over in South Africa in 1994, the Howteq facility was one of my responsibilities. We subsequently used it to train young South African graduates in satellite and space communications and remote sensing.

During this phase of the liberation movement Thabo Mbeki was working with Oliver Tambo in Lusaka. He was responsible for the Department of Information and Publicity (DIP), which included Radio Freedom amongst other media. Radio Freedom broadcast from Madagascar, Angola, Ethiopia, Zambia and Tanzania. The audience, of course, was the oppressed masses inside South Africa.

The ANC leadership was also conscious of the fact that the enemy possessed highly sophisticated communication and interception systems. One of the critical issues at the time was the communication of military intelligence from different sources back to headquarters in Lusaka, particularly from the military units operating in the Frontline States, units on the ground and from certain key individuals operating within South Africa. We had to build an appropriate communications system that would enable this to be done swiftly without any interception from outside forces. In guerrilla warfare or conventional military operations, communication becomes your heart and your nervous system, without which you are not going to succeed. People often talk about the fact that the ANC was in different parts of Angola, Tanzania, Zambia and other places, but they never ask how we communicated information as a liberation movement and how this helped us to keep going.

I knew of Mbeki from his writings and his role in the office of President Oliver Tambo. Within the MK training camps he had accumulated huge amounts of respect for his intellect. The National Liberation Movement cadres and leadership had a culture of regularly writing and publishing political, socio-economic and geopolitical articles and papers. This was common practice through magazines such as *Sechaba*, *Dawn*, *Umsebenzi* and *African Communist*. It was an exciting period of analysing articles by comrades such as Jack and Rae Simons, Mzala, Mark Shope, Thabo Mbeki, and others. This culture of dialogue permeated several levels within the ranks of MK and broader movement.

I was in the regional command at that time and we knew that Mbeki was one of the strategists and writers supporting President Oliver Tambo. The Angolan region was represented at the ANC Kabwe conference in 1985. Key issues, among others that we wanted discussed and adopted, were the strategy and tactics cadre policy about developing comrades in the areas in which they were most skilled. Following the Kabwe conference, the leadership and others came to Angola to communicate major political decisions adopted there.

In March 1985 Mikhail Gorbachev was elected as secretary general of the Communist Party of the Soviet Union. He started implementing policies such as perestroika ('restructuring') and glasnost ('openness'), which generated waves in the geopolitical sphere all over the world. In our region and in the UN Security Council, Resolution 435, calling for the independence of Namibia, was talked about in every corridor. The campaign behind Resolution 435 was gaining traction. What speeded up things was the battle of Cuito Cuanavale in southern Angola, which began in August 1987 and lasted for about seven to eight months. This battle changed the balance of power in the Southern African Development Community (SADC) region. A date for Namibia elections was set and Namibia gained its independence in 1990.

Around 1987 the leadership from Lusaka began to arrive at the camps to brief us as the regional command on what was occurring at the time in our region, on geopolitical issues globally, and what was to follow in the years to come. Developments in the OAU National Liberation Committee, SADC and Frontline States were also discussed in the briefing. These briefings were very important, in particular for us in the trenches who were not aware of everything that was happening due to the remoteness of our camps.

Later we were informed that the ANC leadership was involved in discussions with different African heads of state and that there was going to be an opportunity to engage the apartheid regime in preparatory talks about the new political dispensation in South Africa. They told us that they were meeting all the heads of state in the region in preparation for the Harare Declaration in August 1989 and that there was positive support from the OAU and the leaders of the Frontline States. Thabo Mbeki played a critical role in this initiative with the support of President Oliver Tambo.

Imagine being in the trenches in Angola for a lengthy period of time waging the military struggle. We listened to their political briefing but we thought to ourselves that we were still going to be in the trenches for a very long time. The concept of negotiations seemed to us a remote possibility or nearly impossible. In my view, ultimately nobody would refuse to go home if political conditions were conducive, but the political message from Mbeki and the others took a lot of us by surprise because we thought it was too good to be true or too early to succeed. We had seen Angola gain independence in mid-1975, Zimbabwe in 1980 and Namibia was scheduled for 21 March 1990. Many of us thought it might take us another ten years or so to achieve victory in South Africa. There was almost a feeling that we should not place too much on what Thabo Mbeki and his colleagues had said about the possibility of substantive negotiations with the apartheid regime. If the political negotiations did not happen and we had to go back to the trenches, MK soldiers would be devastated and lose the determination to fight the enemy. We had to almost condition ourselves that it might not happen and believe we were being set up by the apartheid regime. We trusted our leadership and this process did unfold as they planned.

Also during this period, Jonas Savimbi's UNITA (National Union for the Total Independence of Angola) were conducting ambushes against MK convoys. UNITA had placed landmines on every road that connected towns in the east and north of Angola and they had members of the SADF embedded in their combat units. They felt that the best way to deal with the ANC was to destabilise MK in our rear in order for us to be weaker on the frontlines; this is a classic military strategy that has been used countless times in history. They never succeeded.

Whilst Mbeki and others (for example, Pallo Jordan and Zola Skweyiya) were perfecting their negotiation strategy through the development of constitutional guidelines, in late 1988 the leadership of MK in both the Angola region and from headquarters gave me the task of closing down Eastern Front Malanje military camps. I remember that the last convoys of more than 200 trucks, tanks, armed personnel carriers, rocket launchers and all the arsenals of MK were being withdrawn through mountainous territory. One particularly dangerous zone was a pass we called 'Ten Per Cent', because it was as steep as the line in a percentage sign. It was infested with anti-tank landmines and it was a good spot to conduct ambushes. Regular rainfall was also a great disadvantage in this equatorial terrain.

It was in that last military convoy when one of our Russian Kraz trucks with a full load of more than 300 Katyusha rockets fell down the mountainside. In order to get the truck back we had to disassemble it and bring it back in parts from the bottom of the steep valley – a distance of more than two kilometres – and reassemble it again on the road. We were lucky that during the rescue operations none of the rockets exploded and no one was hurt or killed. The whole task took more than a week. We experienced many combat encounters in Ten Per Cent.

The next time I met Mbeki was when we were preparing to go back to South Africa in 1989. The ANC and the South African government were engaged in secret talks in which Mbeki led the ANC delegation. I was fortunate enough to be asked by President Oliver Tambo and Mbeki to be among the first cadres to establish the ANC headquarters at home. My role was to set up covert communications in order to ensure that the pre-negotiations reports that would be coming out of the talks about talks with the apartheid regime were transmitted from South Africa back to Lusaka without being intercepted by foreign intelligence agents. There was huge world interest in what was happening at the time in South Africa. Global intelligence communities were interested in finding out if there was a connection between the fall of the Berlin Wall in November 1989 and the end of the Cold War with what was happening in southern Africa. During the pre-negotiations phase, everybody wanted to know how and when substantive and real negotiations would begin and what the preconditions were.

Mbeki was part of the ANC advance delegation when we came back from exile in 1990 for the preparatory talks about substantive negotiations. My role was to send and receive communications between Johannesburg and Lusaka. This was a regular communications route because President Tambo was based in Lusaka. We were required to forward messages back to ANC headquarters in Lusaka every time we met with the apartheid regime. The reports could not be sent in an open line of communication. We used very advanced military technology that could not be intercepted by the apartheid regime or any world superpower intelligence group that wanted to find out what the ANC was thinking regarding the future of a non-racial, democratic South Africa.

Between 1990 and 1994 I took on a civilian role within the ANC HQ in Johannesburg as head of the Information Systems Department. I had to design and secure ANC HQ computer systems and communications, starting with the president's office. It was during this time that we also set up communications systems for all the offices of the ANC to function efficiently. The computer systems were to be set up in such a way that the ANC's information was secure when the Johannesburg office communicated with the Lusaka office and with other offices in the country.

Before returning home I was briefed in Lusaka by President Tambo on ensuring that the contents of communications must never be intercepted by enemy forces. In fact, we had to conduct counter-SIGINT in order to ascertain that the process of negotiations started by the then South African government was genuine. The ANC leadership gave me this mandate and explained my role. I was told that representatives of South African security and intelligence would meet us in Johannesburg. We were the first group of five people to walk into the belly of the beast.

Envisage departing Lusaka Airport to land at what was then Jan Smuts Airport and being transported in Ford XR6 cars to the Pretoria Holiday Inn on Beatrix Street by the apartheid regime's intelligence officers! These were the same cars they used to abduct underground activists in the early hours of the morning during the worst days of apartheid. Even though we were assured of the authenticity of the negotiations occurring at the time, being driven around by the same people who had gone out of their way to kill us all over Africa was rather disconcerting, but also liberating. However, this time we were going to meet and discuss the future of our country, and the tables had turned.

We started our engagement with them at the Holiday Inn on Beatrix Street. We needed to be assured that when our leadership arrived in the country they would not be harassed at Jan Smuts Airport. The most important thing was to confirm that we would bring our own communication systems into the country, and that they had no right to know the type of equipment or technology we were using. We also had to get them to agree not to search our bags when we next landed at the airport. In the following trips I knew I would bring most of our own equipment technology to set up our own communications systems. Some of the kit didn't come through Johannesburg, but was brought through our covert routes from Botswana. I told the South African intelligence agents that we did not need anything from them in as far as communications systems were concerned. What was critical was to agree on how we would communicate between the two sides in order to ensure that no other services would manage to break our respective communications. We confirmed with them that we had our own technology and our own systems and facilities to look after our leadership and delegation.

It was also important that communications between us and the regime communications people be kept secret from foreign interests. When the first group of ANC leaders returned to South Africa in 1990 for preparatory talks with the South African government, we were already prepared. We operated from Anderson Street and the Munich Re building (now Luthuli House) in Sauer Street and we later moved to Shell House. In Johannesburg we always met our South African communications intelligence counterparts at the snake park in Midrand. We had to make sure that when the ANC leadership arrived there was a whole host of things in place. For example, we could not have a situation where people who had left in the 1960s were harassed about whether or not they had IDs, and we also had to ensure that people were not harassed for staying in 'white' areas. By the time leaders like Mbeki arrived, we had established a very efficient system so that they could get straight to work. That was what we had to do throughout the negotiations: we had to make sure that the communications systems were up and running and very secure.

When we ultimately left Lusaka to return to South Africa I shared my thoughts with comrades, asking what would happen if the apartheid regime had deceived us and locked us all up upon arrival in South Africa. Or perhaps even killed some of us? After all, we were all considered terrorists by the South African state. We were however assured that Mbeki and others had been engaging with the regime about modalities, terms of reference and other conditions relevant to our homecoming. So we were going into this trusting that Mbeki and other leaders, who had started this political process long before it was visible to many, had a clear view as to where

things were going and knew how to manage counterparts in the South
African government. We also had to assume that the apartheid regime's
security and intelligence officers would talk to us and respect us as genuine
representatives of the people.

As I established the Department of Information Systems in the ANC
HQ in Johannesburg in the early 1990s, I simultaneously founded a
research institute called the Centre for Development of Information and
Telecommunications Policy (CDITP), which was located at Wits University
Corner in Braamfontein, Johannesburg. This was the ICT policy research
centre of the ANC. We worked with a number of international organisations
in the ICT sector. It was again at this time that I represented the ANC at
the International Telecommunications Union (ITU), which recognised the
ANC as a national liberation movement. The Department of Information
Systems of the ANC provided computer and telecommunication training
through the African Institute of Technology (AIT) – an organisation that
was established within the ANC headquarters. The Information Systems
Department convened a number of stakeholder events and conferences. It
was at this time that I accepted a request to join Info Dev, which is part of
the World Bank, as one of its advisers. The period between 1990 and 1994
was a very busy era. As a representative of the ANC at the ITU one had to
regularly brief Thabo Mbeki who was then the head of International Affairs
of the ANC.

After the high level committee of the ITU finished its work, an additional plenipotentiary conference was convened in Geneva in 1992. This
conference restructured the ITU into three bureaus: namely Standards,
Development and Radio Communications. The secretary general of the
ITU, Pekka Tarjanne, asked me to serve on his committee that had the
responsibility of developing a global telecommunications regulations framework. We subsequently published a report entitled 'Why, What and How to
Regulate Telecommunications'. This became a preferred model on how to
separate policy and regulations in the ICT sector globally.

After the 1994 democratic elections, I took on the role of director general (DG) of communications. This responsibility was defined under the
Post Office Act of 1958 and was called Post Master General. Amongst
other functions, I was responsible for securing the communications and

information systems at the Union Buildings. I would be the one to ensure that both President Mandela and Deputy President Mbeki's computer systems and communications were working all the time. I had to be very selective about the people that I put in place to make sure that computers, telephones and servers were managed in a secure environment because of the sensitive information being exchanged. At this point, there were old staff who had worked with the previous government. The possibility of information being leaked was high and had to be contained at all times. Many of them had been working in the Union Buildings for more than 20 years and this made the situation even more difficult. To share just one example, while we were running IT systems at Shell House, at one point the computers and the printers gave problems while we were trying to print out the list of the people going into cabinet after the first democratic elections in 1994. However, our communications system was very secure and the list was never leaked. Such roles and functions in any government system require people who are both militarily and intelligence trained in handling sensitive information without which you run a big risk.

In modern information warfare such as social engineering, remote viewing and psychological warfare, it is the manipulation of information that changes the landscape between adversaries. At the request of Mbeki, we all went into government and assisted with upgrading the communications systems. Some of us were trained in both military and civilian environments and a lot of people who went into government in 1994 realised that the ANC communications systems were more technologically sophisticated and more secure than those of the former apartheid government. The use of the Internet in government at the time was non-existent. The sphere of communications systems was very unstructured and outdated. We were among the first people to use the Internet to communicate within the movement. As DG of the department of communications, I assisted the cabinet and director general in the presidency Jakes Gerwel and others with anything they needed in terms of information and communications systems. The ANC had a lot of knowledgeable people who had to leave Shell House to go into government in Pretoria, which resulted in the ANC headquarters being left with a skeletal staff. The government's schedule was very heavy, and so we did not go back to our respective units in Shell House because most of our time was spent in Pretoria and Cape Town. This was one of the new challenges we now had to face.

In 1994, at the ITU plenipotentiary conference in Kyoto, the South African government officially took its seat amongst other nation states. By this time both the ANC, as a national liberation movement and young democratic government, was recognised in the UN system in Geneva.

In 1995 G7 ministers responsible for ICT met in Brussels to discuss global information society issues. This was where the concept of the Digital Opportunity Task Force (DOTforce) was informally discussed. The president of the European Commission, Jacques Santer, invited South African Deputy President Thabo Mbeki to address the delegates at that event. In his address Mbeki said that there were more telephones in Manhattan than in sub-Saharan Africa. He was trying to illustrate dramatically the need to bridge the digital divide. Following that event, everyone in the global ICT sector was talking about what Mbeki had said in Brussels. That same year President Mandela opened the largest ITU Telecom conference in the world in Geneva.

As a result of Mbeki's Brussels speech, the 21st G7 summit took place in Halifax in 1995. It took a resolution to support the South African government's initiative to host the Information Society and Development (ISAD) conference, which was held in Midrand at Gallagher Estate in 1996. Al Gore addressed the audience via video link. The conference was opened by Deputy President Mbeki.

The 1996 ISAD conference was a success and led to further global debate on issues concerning the information society. The following year Malaysia hosted INET 97. The Internet and the knowledge economy were central issues at that conference. Malaysia hosted an African Symposium within INET 97 where Mbeki's speech was again prominent. It was after that meeting when the Internet Corporation for Assigned Names and Numbers (ICANN) was established in September 1997 in Los Angeles. The Government Advisory Committee (GAC) had no more than five members at the time. Mbeki made sure that South Africa was part of the first GAC. Today GAC has more than 150 countries participating. The debate about Dot Africa started at that time. Deputy President Thabo Mbeki followed these developments very closely and had an excellent grasp of the techno-economic issues involved.

During ISAD, Mbeki and Gore had a conversation about the future of the Information Society and the activities that were taking place within what was now the G8, as Russia had joined in 1997. In 1998 the World Trade Organisation (WTO) was leading a telecommunications liberalisation process that aimed to facilitate an environment where countries licensed more than two mobile operators within their borders. This liberalisation debate, coupled with independent regulations, formed the foundation blocks of what we see today in the ICT sector. Mbeki was well informed about these developments.

In 1999 the ITU announced that the South African government would host the November 2001 25th ITU Telecom event in Africa. That conference was officially opened by Mbeki and brought together 20 000 participants. In late 1999 the Japanese government was planning to host the 26th G8 meeting, of year 2000, in Okinawa. This was an interesting year with regard to technology. Japan invited Deputy President Mbeki to attend that G8 meeting. They also convened the DOTforce meeting in Okinawa. Italy did the same in 2001 when they hosted the 27th G8 meeting in Genoa. Canada followed with the 28th G8 2002 in Kananaskis. DOTforce issues were discussed during all these meetings.

Parallel to this, Mbeki was leading the New Partnership for Africa's Development (NEPAD) initiative that was formed during the 37th AU heads of state meeting in Lusaka in 2001. The NEPAD Information and Communications Technologies secretariat has been very active in global debates about the future of ICT. All these events culminated in The World Summit on Information Society (WSIS), which was held in Switzerland in 2003 and in Tunisia in 2005. The important role South Africa played under Mbeki's leadership in shaping this geopolitical landscape was immense and we are still benefiting from it, in particular in the ICT and Internet sector.

One can argue that our involvement as an African country on driving geopolitical directions in the global information society has had a profound benefit for our domestic policies. This can be seen in the institutional framework and legislation.

Under Thabo Mbeki's leadership we established the following:

ISSA   Institute of Satellite and Space Applications

NEMISA	The National Electronic Media Institute of South Africa
ICASA	Independent Communications Authority of South Africa
USAASA	The Universal Service and Access Agency of South Africa
COMSEC	Electronic Communications Security (Pty) Ltd
ZADNA	The ZA Domain Name Authority
ZACR	The ZA Central Registry
CSIR	The Meraka Institute operating under CSIR

Also, Mbeki and Joe Nhlanhla, as the minister of intelligence, asked me to assist in establishing the National Communications Centre (NCC). Its sole mandate was foreign SIGINT collection. The NCC had no domestic SIGINT responsibility. Moreover, the African Network Information Centre (Afrinic) was established using the budget of the department of communications. The benefit of this can be seen in the growth of the Internet in Africa. It was Mbeki who launched the first legal and official digital signature recognised by South African law. We were among the first countries in the world to do this.

One area that we could not get right was the State Information Technology Agency (SITA). The former Infoplan management moved first and reorganised themselves to become the sole provider of information technology to government. We came into the process late. They included the SANDF as one of their primary clients. In my opinion you cannot develop and execute a military or defence cyber strategy within that civilian environment. Cyber warfare is a very specialised field. Also the permanent exclusive model in IT was opposite to what everyone else in the world was doing. IT and Internet only work when there is competition. Even with Telkom, we gave them a five-year exclusive period while they had to reorganise themselves before introducing competition and liberalisation. This approach was acceptable to the WTO.

The former Infoplan management was trying to secure their long-term incentives and retirement. I still hope that this was the only reason. We were very busy addressing other pressing challenges at that time, so I suggested to my colleagues that we let it go. I probably provided the same advice to Mbeki who was keenly interested in such matters. My views still stand that IT services work best in a competitive environment. The role of SITA should be confined to IT standards. When we were planning to go into government in the early 1990s the global debate was about the separation of regulations and standard-making from services. Similarly, there should be a separation of policy and legislation from regulations.

As we are navigating the second decade of the 21st century, global information society issues have become even more complex than before. Internet and mobile communications are driving this rapid change. The global and domestic information society institutions that were established in the 1990 require fundamental change. The Internet of today is very different. It has no borders or jurisdiction and therefore it cannot be regulated like telecommunications or mobile. As South Africa, we need to take our rightful place in the domestic, regional and global discourse on Internet governance issues. The Internet is one big influencer when it comes to geo-politics, trade, commerce and development. A classic example is that cyber warfare is becoming a critical domain in the theatre of war and conflict. Some countries already have ministries responsible for cyber space and all business will soon have a Chief Digital Officer (CDO) as the second most important person to the Chief Executive Officer (CEO).

Thabo Mbeki recognised that to address both macro and micro issues of government and the national economy you needed an efficient state. He recognised the role played by ICT in the socio-economic development of any nation. He was the sponsor and supporter of all issues related to the development of information technology and national communications infrastructure and systems. We were fortunate to have a sound relationship with him, as well as with Pallo Jordan and the late Dr Ivy Matsepe-Casaburri when she was appointed minister of communications. When the G8 started to invite African leaders to its meetings, we were included because of Mbeki in what was called the DOTforce. We worked closely with the president's office to keep Mbeki up to date on what was happening and to discuss how we could get support from the G8 to drive the communications and information agenda in Africa, and how these could be used for socio-economic development on the continent.

It is very important to emphasise that Mbeki's work with other African leaders was immeasurable. Today there are over 900 million mobile phones in Africa and there will soon be a billion. President Mbeki drove the development of the Internet and good information technology policies because he was conscious that we are living in an information age. He enabled us to build a sophisticated government communications system. He would meet with us as directors general and elaborate how the state should be run efficiently by using information technology.

President Mbeki also created an advisory structure called the Presidential International Advisory Council on Information Society and Development, which included global CEOs and senior executives from technology companies around the world such as Oracle, Microsoft, Cisco, IBM, HP, SAP. He chaired the weekend meetings of the Advisory Council, which dealt with developing trends in the ICT sector and possible opportunities the country could take advantage of in pursuit of economic development and poverty eradication. In his time in office as both deputy president and president, the country made major advances in information technology. In this regard, South Africa became part of the international world, punching above its weight even at the G8 summits.

On Mbeki's exit from office. This set a wrong precedent in the movement's culture, a culture whose foundation is based on unity, rooted in intellectual discourse and diversity of views. In my years of experience working with leadership communications I have been exposed to both simple and very complex situations, which were always resolved in a conciliatory way that built unity. The recalling of Mbeki created a loss of institutional memory because many people left the state institutions as a result. This knowledge is what we need as we continue to navigate the transition between apartheid and democracy. We need every hand on the deck as we build a competitive, modern, knowledge-based economy and modern cyberspace that will drive an efficient state or e-government and information society. Building our country's knowledge-based economy and an efficient state is what this first post-apartheid generation needs to focus on; to do this we will need all the competent men and women we have as a country irrespective of political belief, race, gender or religion. Also, this expertise is crucial for us to survive the globalised digital economy and its increasingly complex geopolitics. A nation's best assets are its people. It is only a growing modern Internet-driven knowledge economy that can create jobs and eradicate poverty. We need an economy that works hand in glove with an efficient public sector. Any analysis that separates domestic political economy from geopolitical economy is bound to be faulty. Foreign Direct Investment (FDI) and domestic private sector investments are the main drivers for growth. Today, both national and even party politics are strongly influenced by the geopolitical economic landscape.

There is a metaphor that I think is applicable in this case. Someone asked the French about the impact of the Napoleonic wars on Europe some 200 years ago. The French gave a detailed explanation about having to create borders. Then another person asked the Chinese the same question about the Napoleonic wars, and their reply was that it was too early to draw conclusions. I think that over time history is going to correct itself. Reconciliation and unity will always prevail. History has many such examples. Russia took 70 years following the Bolshevik revolution to celebrate the Tsar Nicholas II, the Orthodox Church and some of the great writers of that time. It took decades for China to recover from the devastation of the Cultural Revolution, and for the country to reach its current levels of economic growth. In Ghana it took 50 years for Jerry Rawlings to restore the memory and dignity of Kwame Nkrumah. The recall of Mbeki was a historic event and there will come a time when the national liberation movement will see the need to rebuild unity, social cohesion and reconciliation and recognise what is in the best interests of all South Africans and our beautiful continent of Africa.

Interviewed July 2014, Johannesburg

JONAS GWANGWA

❖

Thabo Mbeki: 'Gwangwa is right … Gwangwa you are on … Direct the show.'

This was Mbeki's view on using culture and the creative arts as a weapon in the struggle for national liberation in South Africa. In 1976 I embarked on a concert tour of Botswana with Caiphus Semenya and Letta Mbulu, where I decided to stay and did not return to the United States. I formed a band – Shakowe – with some young musicians from the region who I also tutored, and which featured Dennis Mpale on the trumpet and Steve Dyer on the tenor sax.

Shortly thereafter the band, with fellow musician Wally Serote, formed a cultural organisation, which African National Congress (ANC) cadres, together with a few other South Africans and Batswana, formally named the 'MEDU Arts Ensemble'. The organisation produced a massive, politically commanding festival that showcased various artistic disciplines by South African artists – music, dance, painting, sculpture, poetry, photography, film and video – all with political undertones.

This festival later went to Amsterdam in the Netherlands, where it was called 'Culture in Another South Africa' (CASA), and became hugely popular. The South African apartheid government was not happy about the growing support for the festival, and in 1985 military commandos crossed the Botswana border illegally and raided Gaborone, killing 12 people, Batswana included, in the process.

In 1977 the ANC was invited to a festival of arts and culture – the World

Black Festival of Arts and Culture (FESTAC) – in Lagos, Nigeria. Artists affiliated to the ANC from many different countries and from various artistic disciplines attended. They did not know one another, and passionate argument soon ensued as to how to go about their participation in the festival. I suggested that a single production incorporating many artistic disciplines could be the ace up the sleeve of the liberation movement, but comrades disagreed very strongly with this methodology, calling for a diversified deployment of groupings in the various disciplines. In the end, Thabo Mbeki, the chief representative of the ANC at the time, had the last word. He concurred with me and hence his prophetic words expressed in the opening paragraph.

Afterwards Mbeki instructed me to draft a cultural memorandum for the ANC in exile that would herald the formation of *Amandla*, the enthralling worldwide ANC cultural ensemble tour to which I devoted ten years of my life. With the support of Mbeki, who valued the role of culture in the liberation struggle, I served as the composer, arranger, musical director and director of the ANC's *Amandla Cultural Ensemble*. This subsequently led to the enthusiastic development of a highly talented, but untrained and underdeveloped group of ANC cadres under the banner of *Amandla*. Many of the prospective recruits had never seen a professional stage show, let alone performed in one. Together with knowledgeable colleagues, we created a professional company from Umkhonto we Sizwe (MK) youth in the Angolan training camps.

Coupled with an intensifying interest in culture, this period saw rising numbers of workshops, festivals and seminars devoted to the subject, as well as interviews and public pronouncements by leading ANC officials, and the high-profile CASA conference held in Amsterdam in December 1987.

The Amandla Cultural Ensemble undoubtedly grew stronger and was a major part of this burgeoning interest in culture. It came to be considered within the ANC as one of its greatest achievements in this sphere and Thabo Mbeki was always supportive of such creative endeavours. At its inception, *Amandla*, the stage production of the Ensemble, denoted a call to action, a no-holds-barred demand for the world to open its eyes to the reality of the war tearing South Africa apart, and an insistence that the world rise up to stand with South Africans against this most heinous oppression.

The message still rings strong and true, and now calls on all South Africans not to forget that we come from dire struggle, from the fiercest determination, and to use our shared history and our shared determination to forge ahead on the road to reconciliation, and to continue to shape a prosperous future for all who call this land home.

The Amandla Cultural Ensemble travelled and performed in every corner of the globe, on every continent, in many countries and regions, cities and towns for a decade – from 1980 to 1990.

Of ex-President Thabo Mbeki, who gave me the go-ahead, and the first real support for the formation of Amandla, I attest: 'Our friendship continued for many years from then on. I often stayed at his place in Lusaka, where my wife even sent him his tobacco – it was not available there. We have over the years enjoyed numerous New Year's Eve parties at his home, a solid camaraderie and great conversations.'

SMUTS NGONYAMA

After the unbanning of all the political parties involved in the liberation struggle in the early 1990s, African National Congress (ANC) leaders could enter South Africa and openly engage in overt political meetings. It was during this time that I established contact with many leaders. Amongst them there was a leader whom I deeply admired through his written articles and the communication that was coming through the underground channels. This person was Thabo Mbeki, a renowned political strategist, together with some of the other credible leaders of the ANC.

Later on, I became the regional chairperson of the ANC for the Border region, a wide area that covered East London, King William's Town, as far as Fort Beaufort in the east. In the north, it included areas such as Aliwal North. Indeed this was one of the biggest and strongest political regions in the ANC. This position required constant consultation with leaders such as former President Thabo Mbeki, Chris Hani, Steve Tshwete, Charles Nqakula and other veterans of the ANC who originated from the area. This region was one of the areas identified as the seedbed of the struggle against oppression. This position also allowed me, constitutionally, to become a member of the National Executive Committee (NEC) and to participate in all its deliberations. Later on, during the negotiation process for a new democratic South Africa, as facilitated through the Congress for a Democratic South Africa (CODESA), I also had the opportunity to be closely exposed to many of the tried-and-tested doyens of our revolution, amongst whom was Thabo Mbeki.

When I met Thabo Mbeki, I liked him as a leader and as a deep revolutionary, and I came to identify him as a very strong and deep thinker, particularly as an intellectual. I saw him as a balanced person who, at all times, sought to listen to the views of everyone in the NEC before he made his interventions, which always seemed to be appreciative of the various points of view that had been raised by others before him. He would, however, present a proposal that, on many occasions, would be accepted as a sound position.

Thabo Mbeki was deeply respected by all the members of the NEC; at least, that was how I observed it to be. The committee was non-racial in character and it was constituted of some of the distinguished leaders of the party such as Joe Slovo, Ronnie Kasrils, Albie Sachs, Dullah Omar, Ahmed Kathrada, Mac Maharaj and Gill Marcus. I am mentioning these as an example in order to illustrate the non-racial character of the NEC, which also included many representatives from minority communities, although the list is much longer. However, everybody accorded President Mbeki great respect and this respect was not only confined to him. Various leaders were also accorded the respect they deserved, characteristic of the internal discipline and cohesion within the NEC. This kind of respect was also demonstrated towards Mbeki by the elders of the ANC such as Madiba, Walter Sisulu and others. When Thabo Mbeki stood up to speak you could sense, from the full attention given to him by the NEC members and by the leadership in general, that indeed he was a voice of reason within the Movement. It was clear that he was serious about South Africa and her people, irrespective of skin colour, gender and class. Above all, he had a deep passion for the revolutionary alliance. Surprisingly, 'the Chief', as he was affectionately called, was unassuming and humble despite the huge respect he was accorded, and displayed no traits of a personality cult or arrogance and aloofness as some, who were not acquainted with him, would want to make us believe.

The Thabo Mbeki I came to know is a man who always had the progress, unity and cohesion of South Africa as a nation at the core of his concerns. He was not concerned about his own popularity. However, he gained popularity with many groups, whether it was representatives of the working class, the communists, socialists, or the bourgeois, young and old, among the members of the ANC. He would address issues head-on, and deal with what he believed was pertinent for the country at that time. *Thabo Mbeki would tread where even angels fear to tread.* His thinking was informed by the desire to develop South Africa to the best of the country's potential. He did not like proposals that ventured on to unnecessarily dangerous ground for the sake of cheap popularity. In short, he is not a populist. Many have come to know that 'the Chief', as one of his hallmarks, is a workaholic; for him, what needs to be done for the people has to be completed within reasonable time and should be of good quality. For him, time cannot be presented as an excuse for not finishing a target that has been set. He always sets high standards, going without sleep if need be. With Mbeki, every task has to be finished and be done properly.

I soon discovered, as I worked closely with him at the NEC level and later on as head of his office in the ANC, that Thabo Mbeki is also an astute negotiator. This was evident at CODESA when the question of an Afrikaner Volkstad was raised during the negotiations for a democratic process in South Africa. Mbeki led a committee that was engaging with right-wing Afrikaner groups that were calling for the establishment of a separate self-governing state and, because they saw that their concerns were being taken seriously and were being listened to, they remained at the negotiating table and finally became part of the democratic South Africa. Mbeki acted in this way because he believed all the participants needed to be listened to, despite the general opinion that this was an unreasonable proposition by right-wing Afrikaner groups. However, he respected them as fellow South Africans who had the right to raise their issues, although some of these demands may have been regarded as outrageous. He motivated us during NEC caucus meetings to continue to engage until we could find a solution and, indeed, by doing this, an otherwise stormy political crisis was averted.

The so-called conflict between the ANC and the Inkatha Freedom Party (IFP), a feature of the unpalatable encounter amongst our peoples in the provinces of KwaZulu-Natal and Gauteng, emerged at the same time as the unbanning of the ANC. In order to bring an end to this bloodshed, under the leadership of Nelson Mandela, Thabo Mbeki and Jacob Zuma motivated in favour of negotiations with the IFP to try to find a peaceful solution to this unnecessary conflict. Through the leadership of Jacob

Zuma, together with Mbeki as well as Nelson Mandela, it was possible to broker peace between the ANC and the IFP, saving many lives.

As I worked in Mbeki's office at Luthuli House, I discovered that he was a quintessential diplomat who was driven by the motto of 'Africa first'. From the time of Nelson Mandela's presidency, critics indicated that South Africa was punching above its weight, because soon after South Africa became a member of the multilateral institutions it came to be regarded as a progressive voice, especially on behalf of the underdeveloped and emerging nations. South Africa did not take up positions of expediency, but rather defended positions of rationality and consistency. Thabo Mbeki had a particular passion for and interest in the evolution of South Africa's foreign policy on which he had a strong influence. His focus was to place South Africa strategically and significantly on the continent of Africa. It was precisely because South Africa during apartheid had regarded itself as an appendage of the Western world in Africa and had never in any way aligned itself with the former Organisation of African Unity (OAU), that Mbeki instituted the 'Africa first' political philosophy, and developed his idea of the African Renaissance for a liberated South Africa.

With regard to Zimbabwe, Mbeki refused to lead an attack against the president of Zimbabwe, Robert Mugabe, in order to appease the West, nor did he unconditionally support the Zimbabwean government in order to be popular with Mugabe at the expense of rationality. Instead Mbeki's approach placed the people of Zimbabwe first. His policy was about the achievement of a truly democratic government and society in Zimbabwe. Thus, the focus of discussions was on free and fair elections, a functional opposition, and with this in mind meetings were held with both President Robert Mugabe and the leader of the opposition, Morgan Tsvangirai. The essence of this approach was to respect the sovereignty of Zimbabwe and therefore facilitate a solution within international democratic principles. It was not driven by a regime-change solution as was requested by Western powers. Mbeki's approach was then labelled by his critics as being so-called 'quiet diplomacy'. Out of this came the custom of trying to denigrate any approach by South Africa that attempted to find solutions through peaceful means, respecting democracy and sovereignty, labelling it 'ZANUfication'. However, looking back, we can now draw lessons from the unfortunate negative consequences of regime change in Iraq, Libya and, perhaps, Syria that will be evident for many generations to come.

With regard to the above, it may be interesting to point out that in 2001 Mbeki took an unpopular and brave stand regarding the proposed invasion of Iraq on the basis of the presence of weapons of mass destruction. He approached President George Bush Jnr, the president of the United States of America, and Prime Minister Tony Blair of the United Kingdom, calling on them both to pursue all relevant avenues of negotiation as against the option of invading Iraq, which could lead to bloodshed. When the USA and the UK finally invaded Iraq, South Africa, led by President Mbeki, did not support this action. Fundamentally, South Africa did not believe that such heavy-handedness would advance universal peace and believed that such action had no respect for the 'sovereignty of state' principle. Approaching matters in this context is typical of President Thabo Mbeki, who was not afraid to defend a principled position, which he considered to be of fundamental importance even when going against the position held by the world's most powerful nations. Hence, the statement that South Africa was 'punching above its weight'.

With regard to foreign policy, Mbeki pursued the welfare of South Africa, and that of Africa in general, as a priority. China is a good example of this. Although Mbeki encouraged diplomatic and economic relations with China, I remember vividly how, in one of his arguments presented during an NEC meeting, he made it clear that the rules of engagement included having China as a strategic partner and ally but not to allow for any possibility of economic imperialism that could emerge from this relationship. He made the point that Africans and South Africans must set the agenda and not allow themselves to be relegated to being inferior partners. Mbeki was the first African leader to be part of the G8. He was invited to participate in these international meetings because the Group of Eight world leaders recognised the political respect he enjoyed and the influence he had within the African continent. In all the positions that he held in advanced international and multilateral forums, he was invited, as the president of South Africa, to represent Africa.

I am also of the view that working with Mbeki was empowering because his ability to question and apply reasoning to all issues meant that he constantly challenged the ideas and decisions of ANC members to ensure that the best possible policies were implemented. Mbeki is a good listener and people who worked with him knew that when he said, 'Is that so, is that so, Chief?' it meant that he was listening deeply and appreciating the views advanced. He is known to ask the following question: 'Do you think, comrades, that people understand this line of reasoning?' because he always wanted to ensure that the people of South Africa and the continent of Africa were placed first in all policies and strategies and, therefore, wanted to ensure that their aspirations be encapsulated in the positions that were adopted. South Africa, for Mbeki, was to be a democratic, non-racist, non-sexist prosperous society, and he would always question whether policies were taking the country backwards or forwards towards the realisation of this strategic objective. He would probe before he started to engage. When he ventured on a course of action at the conclusion of discussions, participants would feel fully empowered by his perspective. It is this brave and listening character that to some extent made Thabo Mbeki unpopular to people who felt that their lines of argument should be regarded as the gospel truth, either by virtue of who they were or by the ideological positions that they held.

As a good example of this character, at the first ANC conference to be held in South Africa in Durban in 1993, Thabo Mbeki persuaded the ANC that the retention of economic sanctions would hurt the South African economy at a time when the political mood in the country was changing for the better. Because the negotiations were underway, Mbeki posited that it was no longer useful to call for disinvestment, but there was the need rather to put building blocks in place to ensure robust economic growth. He understood that the desire from 1994 onwards to redress the injustices of apartheid through the provision of housing, services and employment en masse was laudable, but not immediately possible through state expenditure because of the inheritance of a huge budget deficit from the apartheid government. He committed himself, through his actions as the deputy president of South Africa, to articulate the Freedom Charter and the Reconstruction and Development Programme (RDP), ensuring that there was no deviation from these fundamental policy positions. If there were deviations from the plans due to challenges relating to available resources, these should be of a tactical nature and not of a fundamental nature.

It was in this context that the NEC of the ANC adopted the Growth, Employment and Redistribution (GEAR) programme in 1996. This strategy would mean less spending of scarce resources by the state, but also included strict fiscal policies to meet the basic needs of the people of South Africa. The cabinet at the time implemented this policy as official ANC policy. However, this policy position did not endear Mbeki to some of the members of the alliance partners, after he and a few others were identified as the main proponents of this policy position. During this time, the budget was driven by three objectives that were fundamental to the strategic goals of our movement and these were: (1) the eradication of poverty, (2) the growth and development of our economy, and (3) the construction of a people-centred society. These were based on the principle and practice of human solidarity as expressed by two documents: *Ready to Govern* and the *Reconstruction and Development Programme*. The ANC called on the government to address the issue of macro-economic balances. In other words, it was requested that development should be financed using the available South African resources rather than depend on borrowed money, which would increase the level of debt. Unfortunately, this approach was denounced as 'neo-liberal' and a betrayal of the revolution to the so-called Washington Consensus, as those who were subscribing to this alternative school of thought warned that debt would be increased on the basis of a 'live now, pay later' view.

Another interesting observation was that President Thabo Mbeki would take personal notes during the NEC meetings. He would not interfere while people spoke but paid close attention to the contributions of his colleagues. For some time, he suggested that he present the political overview statement by the president only at the end of meetings to avoid influencing discussions. However, as meetings progressed, a consensus emerged that this system should change and it was requested that the presidential political overview statement be presented at the beginning of the meeting. This decision was taken after it was realised that the president's statement could bring up important issues that the NEC had not taken into consideration during the course of discussions. I remember vividly how an NEC member from KwaZulu-Natal by the name of Dumisani Makhaye, who has now passed on, protested strongly about the fact that the NEC had changed the tried-and-tested procedure and requested that an opportunity be given to the president to present his political statement first and to then continue with the discussions by analysing the statement from different angles. Hence the procedure was changed back to the original.

With regard to the debate about the political character of the ANC as an organisation and its socialist leanings, Thabo Mbeki would explicitly state, without any fear of risking his popularity, that although the ANC was in alliance with the Congress of South African Trade Unions (COSATU) and the South African Communist Party (SACP), it was not itself a 'socialist' organisation. I clearly recollect the debate on this topic within the context of the discussions about the 'Green Book' during one of the 2007 NEC meetings. This was an interesting debate that enriched many within the ANC – an interesting debate indeed! It was typical of the NEC, which had robust debates, at times tense, but nevertheless they never seemed to be acrimonious.

The ANC under Mbeki saw itself as an omnibus for all the people of South Africa. It needed to address their diverse interests from the worker to the capitalist, regardless of race, gender or creed. Mbeki considered it very important to keep the ANC focused as a national democratic revolutionary organisation. This meant that the ANC would be open to the evolutionary process of positive change without compromising the development of the nation and democracy. This was the historical character of the ANC, which Mbeki revived and unpacked for the government of his day.

Ilima/Letsima is an old, pre-colonial African practice where people living in the same village would come together and plough one another's fields and assist in the growing of crops. Each field owner's harvest would be their own, but anyone who might experience a poor harvest would not go hungry because of the communal involvement in food growing. Thus it is underpinned by the philosophy of communal well-being and reciprocity. This concept of *Ilima/Letsima* led to Mbeki's idea of the new patriotism, which he thought necessary to be imbibed by all in South Africa to ensure the building of the nation and common national identity as well as the growth of the economy. Mbeki's positions while president of South Africa always stemmed from careful study of the issues at hand and the results of the balance of evidence.

When the ANC launched the volunteer campaign announced during the 90th anniversary of the ANC, it was the resolve of President Mbeki to ensure that the ANC went back to the original discipline and selflessness that was characteristic of the 1952 campaign for the defiance of unjust laws. He said, 'We must draw inspiration from, and emulate, the great heroes and heroines of our country who, at that time, volunteered to defy the apartheid system as part of the intensification of the struggle for our liberation.'[1] He went on to say, 'What characterised the volunteers of that defiance campaign was a spirit of dedication, courage and sacrifice ... they did not act for material rewards of any kind, including personal popularity. They sought only to serve the people of South Africa.'[2] President Mbeki was calling for this high level of discipline and dedication to serve the people and he believed that this volunteer campaign was meant to strengthen the links and the cooperation between the government and the people. He believed strongly that, 'historically, our movement has always depended on the concept that the people are their own liberators'.[3] 'The struggle was never conducted on the basis that the people would be reduced to a state of paralysis, transformed into mere observers, the object instead of being the subject of change, even as we have been building our non-racial and non-sexist democracy, we have insisted that ours must be a peoples-driven process of change.'[4] He stated that 'one of the objectives of the volunteer campaign Letsima/Ilima was to rebuild the sense of community among all our people and not atomisation that could lead to the breakdown of family life and individual isolation and alienation'.[5]

President Mbeki linked this to what Nelson Mandela called 'the RDP of the soul'. The Letsima campaign directly addresses this question and he said further, 'we are convinced that, as this campaign takes firm root among the people, it will help to also rebuild further and strengthen the value system we all seek'.[6] For him, this was critical to ensure social mobilisation against crimes against people, including murder, rape, domestic violence and the

---

1 *ANC Today,* Vol. 2, No. 5, 1–7 February 2002, 'Letsema Volunteer Campaign – giving effect to the concept and goal of a new patriotism'.
2 Ibid.
3 Ibid.
4 Ibid.
5 Ibid.
6 Ibid.

abuse of children. President Mbeki felt very strongly about this moral decay that needed to be vehemently rooted out of our societies.

President Mbeki coincided with George Soros' perception by which 'one of the greatest defects of the global capitalist system is that it has allowed the market mechanism and profit motive to penetrate into fields of activity where they do not properly belong', a process that was 'corrupting politics through the promotion of self-interest'. Mbeki concurred with Soros when he said that this had led to 'the failure of politics' and had become 'the strongest argument in favour of giving the markets even freer rein' over politics, transforming 'all social activities and human interactions' including political processes, into 'transactional, contract-based relationships and valued in terms of a single common denominator: money'.[7]

Thabo Mbeki considered education and the regeneration of the African continent to be of the utmost importance. He further emphasised the concept of new patriotism and called on the people to become their own liberators, putting on the mantle of selflessness as they build the new Rainbow Nation at peace with itself. The *ANC Today* publication appeared on the ANC website on a weekly basis. When it was mooted, he embraced the idea and committed himself towards the initiative, believing that this would be a good platform to express the ideas and opinions of the ANC and its leader and to encourage discussion and debate, not only within the ANC but also in broader society even outside South Africa. The weekly publication included a 'Letter from the President', which he would write personally every week without fail. This letter became a point of attraction for many who read and subscribed to this publication. 'Welcome to ANC Today' was the first letter Mbeki wrote. Others included:

- African People Central to Success of Recovery Plan
- A New Patriotism for a New South Africa
- Health for the Poor is a Fundamental Human Right
- One Step Closer to the African Union
- We Must Move to a Caring and People Centred Society
- Humanism

---

7 Soros, George (1998). *The Crisis of Global Capitalism: Open Society Endangered.* New York: PublicAffairs.

- The Challenges of Freedom
- Important Steps to Different Democratic Practice in Southern Africa
- Sport is a Valuable Part of a Democratic Society
- Our Commitment to Africa … Land Reform
- World Economic Forum
- UK … wants SA to succeed
- Let us Speak of Freedom
- The Task Facing the ANC Two Years into our Second Term
- Launch of the Government's Integrated and Sustainable Programme
- Africa's High Road to Unity and Rebirth
- Strong Support Expected from G8 Leaders for Africa Recovery Plan
- Despite Difficulties South Africa is on Course
- … Transformation … Peoples of the World Unite for Equality, Justice and Dignity
- Southern Africa must Press Ahead with Integration
- Tell No Lies, Claim No Easy Victories
- Region Unites to Support Zimbabwe's Efforts and Progress
- Acts of Terror must be Condemned Unreservedly
- Japanese Support for African Development
- Breaching the Digital and Development Divide
- Religious Leaders Who Immersed themselves in the Struggle
- South Africans have Reason to be Positive
- Our Obligations to Peace and Development in Africa
- The Truth Stands in the Way of the Arms Accusers
- Ending Poverty in the Global Village and at Home

The themes of the above letters indicate President Mbeki's concern for the people of South Africa. The issues of integration, eradication of poverty, and human rights for all from the cradle to the grave were his central focus and, in addition, he emphasised the place of Africa, and southern Africa in particular, in world relations. Mbeki was driven by these passions during his time as president of South Africa, and still is today.

It was also apparent that Thabo Mbeki's approach was to move the ANC, as the governing party in South Africa, from a revolutionary movement that had achieved its goals of overcoming the apartheid regime to a political movement capable of good governance and ensuring the ongoing development of a free and democratic society. He believed that the elected representatives should be accountable to 'the people; their political organisations and the legislatures to which they belong'[8] and he emphasised that all elected representatives have a standing obligation to maintain regular contacts with the people. He maintained that, after being allocated specific constituencies or wards, their work must focus on changing the quality of lives of their people. Mbeki warned against an approach that would lead to false promises and rhetoric, and a corrupt and bloated government bureaucracy, class conflict, and racial and economic antagonism and disintegration. For him it was important that the people governing South Africa must be 'new cadres' who put good governance first and were not involved in populist politicking and corruption. A government of informed leadership and integrity was, for Mbeki, the foundation of democracy and freedom. He based his thinking on the fundamental values, principles and discipline of the ANC.

On 21 September 2008 Thabo Mbeki gave his resignation address to the nation. His patriotic responsibility and dedication to the peace and stability of South Africa would not allow him to cling to power at the expense of the stability of his beloved South Africa and his glorious movement, the ANC. Even though many felt that the decision by the ANC NEC that cut short his presidential term was unjust, unconstitutional and legally challengeable, Mbeki would not follow that path. In his address to the nation he stated: 'The current government that I have been privileged to lead has been obliged, by decision of the ruling party, the ANC, acting within its rights, to end its tenure a few months ahead of its popularly mandated term. In the interest of the masses of our people and country, personally I have accepted this eventuality without resistance or rancour, and acted upon it accordingly. I trust that all of us, members of the National Executive, will respond in similar fashion.'

In conclusion, Thabo Mbeki's dedication to democracy extended to all of Africa, and his stance at the African Union (AU) was that democracy

---

8 Ibid.

must be defended and, to that end, governments resulting from coups in African countries could not and should not be tolerated. The people of Africa must have a legitimate democratic voice. After Thabo Mbeki's tenure as the president of South Africa ended, he continued to work for liberty and democracy of the country. He also continued his involvement in matters of international diplomacy, especially within the continent. Mbeki's dedication to the development of true democracy is rooted in education and, to this end, he started the Thabo Mbeki Foundation. The Foundation seeks to support efforts that promote the achievement of an African Renaissance by enabling progressive change throughout the continent. It creates platforms for dialogue to promote positive change by a new cadre of thought leaders dedicated to Africa's political, social and economic renewal.

Thabo Mbeki has also been invited to mediate for peace in countries like the Ivory Coast, South Sudan and many others. In the Ivory Coast, he was able to negotiate for the establishment of a peacekeeping force in the country. His involvement with South Sudan was part of a United Nations mandate. These examples demonstrate the esteem and respect that Mbeki commands internationally for his insights, diplomatic ability and his commitment to peace. These are some of my humble reflections about a true leader of the people, a true son of the soil. I have come to know a true human soul who dedicates his time, energies, emotions, mental capabilities and his entire life to serve the people of South Africa. I am honoured to have been asked to contribute these reflections about Thabo Mbeki.

MAVUSO MSIMANG

The Thabo Mbeki I know is a quintessential African National Congress (ANC) person who draws his inspiration and purpose for life from his inalienable association with that organisation. It is the ANC that has shaped his mission in life and moulded his understanding of the political world and, in particular, his vision for Africa.

The Thabo I know understands that from its founding day the ANC proclaimed itself the 'African', rather than the 'South African' National Congress. The founders well understood the limitations attendant on a geographical circumscription that reduced the big prize that was the object of the struggle for emancipation – and eschewed the narrowness. At the founding of this century-old organisation the sine qua non for success was the unity of the black nationalities: 'Zulu, Xhosa, Sotho hlanganani', the 1912 delegates chanted in unison. Tribalism was repudiated. Even as they waged a struggle for national liberation, their vision of a united Africa was prominent in their thinking.

Quite early in his life – it has been said in jest that he was born in an ANC office! – Thabo Mbeki will have been conscious of the fact that Swaziland, Lesotho and Botswana – whatever names the British had chosen to call them at the time – were represented by senior emissaries at the founding ANC conference; also that Zimbabwe and Zambia, at the time also christened in colonial nomenclature, had gone on to form their own anti-colonial ANCs modelled on the African National Congress of South Africa.

Thabo Mbeki's approach to politics epitomises the values of his organisation's founding fathers. Yes, it was only 'fathers' who did the founding. The change in this gender exclusion was to come about as a result of the struggles waged by women themselves, fighting for their own emancipation. It is a project in which they were joined by their male counterparts.

The Thabo Mbeki I know is a formidable intellectual powerhouse. I realised this in the late 1960s and 1970s in Lusaka, Zambia, when a group of us regularly engaged in weighty and often animated discussions, analysing the essence of imperialism, colonialism and racism. We paid a lot of attention to Mbeki's thinking when discussing these and other political issues, namely, the liberation wars raging in Asia, Africa and Latin America; power blocs of the time – The North Atlantic Treaty Organisation, the South East Asia Organisation; etc. We debated the Sino-Soviet dispute and the US invasion of Vietnam, which we were all convinced would end in ignominious defeat for the Americans.

The Thabo Mbeki I know has unquestionable integrity. It is a Mbeki whose public actions are informed by a lofty sense of values; a Mbeki who is trustworthy and trusting. A Mbeki, I must admit, whose 'trusting business' I often thought was product of naiveté. It is actually born of a belief, intrinsic in his psyche, that an ANC comrade is incapable of duplicity or engagement in activities that could have the effect of subverting the objectives of the organisation.

I will never forget the 'hoax email' saga. Incredibly, people who should have known better seemed to believe spurious allegations about the authorship of this twaddle. Thabo Mbeki probably understands better today that trust can be misplaced.

In many ways Thabo Mbeki reminds me of O.R. Tambo, his mentor. He, too, found it difficult to comprehend how an ANC leader could be anything but an individual fully committed to the objectives of the revolution. It is a misjudgement that would occasionally prove costly to the organisation: witness, for instance, the impact of the highly disruptive activities of the Gang of Eight. They were eventually expelled from the organisation.

In Mbeki we have an Africanist, an individual with a lot of empathy and a great vision for black people and their continent. I vividly recall the evening of 31 December 1999 when Mbeki asked a small group of friends who had assembled at his official residence what they thought the agenda for his administration should be. We all proffered suggestions: the development of an HIV vaccine; improvements in the education system, somebody said; putting in place a world-class public transport system, someone offered; and so on it went. Mbeki's response was simple but categorical: *It has to be the start of the African Century.*

It was a mission he was to pursue with singular vigour. Witness the role South Africa played in peacekeeping efforts and in the development and building of infrastructure projects in Africa. We saw the birth of NEPAD – the New Partnership for Africa's Development.

To this day Thabo Mbeki continues to raise alarm bells over the trillions of dollars that are transferred out of the continent in dubious commercial remittances but also simply fraudulently. Africa and the world owe Mbeki a huge debt of gratitude for his initiative to keep the Timbuktu Manuscripts in safe storage. As is known, Timbuktu was an ancient centre of learning and home to a university and boasted a vast collection of manuscripts containing priceless written records. It's gratifying to know that most of them survived the jihadist invasion of the city a few years ago.

Mbeki's vision of an Africa united in development extends to the diaspora. During his administration strong links were forged between South Africa and the Caribbean states, progressive African-American organisations and peoples of African origin elsewhere. His belief in solidarity with African patriots impelled him to bring home to South Africa embattled President Jean-Bertrand Aristide of Haiti following his illegal removal from office in a coup d'état.

Asking me to talk about the Thabo Mbeki I know invites a comment on workaholism. His nocturnal scribbling has over the years produced a phenomenal wealth of writings, some of them literary masterpieces. His 'I am an African' speech, delivered in parliament during the inauguration of the Constitution of South Africa in 1996, ranks among the best speeches made by a political leader anywhere. Written in flowing poetic prose, it nudges citizens towards an inclusive patriotism, and in that act shatters silos that were constructed by the myopia of the *ancien régime,* including its colonial predecessors.

The Thabo Mbeki I know was prolific as ANC president, writing the weekly ANC Newsletter, January 8 ANC anniversary statements, conference strategy documents and discussion papers, political reports, etc. It makes profound sense that the Thabo Mbeki Foundation should want to archive these masterpieces, documents of value to historians, academics and many others who will come after our epoch. These are records of the tumultuous events that defined South Africa's emergence from the long night of repression to the joyful birth of democracy, and its early childhood.

The Thabo Mbeki I know is a voracious reader of everything: publications, literature and poetry. Ahead of most in his generation, he quickly appreciated the tremendous value of the Internet. He loves jazz and classical music and enjoys occasional mbaqanga – quite eclectic, as a matter of fact. He is a student of history and takes a keen interest in heritage matters.

If you will let me, I will also tell you that the Thabo Mbeki I know is a fun person. He is witty and can unleash a wicked jibe if provoked to it – it is not easy to be on the receiving end of his humour. He shares no common space with foolishness. He can be unconventional, to a point of irreverence at times. I suppose high office has tampered some of these traits. Protocol can be unforgiving in its restrictions. How unfair that this should happen to Thabo. The sight of Thabo in stiff formal dress – starched shirts, dark suits, black ties and cufflinks! Heaven forbid!

Back in the Lusaka days, when we lived in Makeni, we used to frequent a watering hole called The Pelican. We imbibed cold Mosi beer to pulsating Congolese music from a live band that entertained patrons until the wee hours of the morning. With no budget to meet the finer products of Scottish distilleries, Mbeki adjusted easily to the plentiful Zambian breweries' offerings. Not being quite a great dancer, he consoled himself by imagining that he was much better than me at it me. I prefer not to challenge this highly contentious claim.

I hope one day I will understand how the Thabo Mbeki I thought I knew ended up with his calamitous take on the devastating HIV/AIDS pandemic. Equally worrying is why his ANC colleagues on the National Executive Committee, the Working Committee and in cabinet did not challenge and correct his disastrously misguided views. Were these people intimidated by his intellectual prowess? Did they not, as leaders in their own right, appreciate the gravity of the strategy? Could it be that they knew but feared that differing with the leader might cost them their jobs? This reluctance by ANC leaders to take a stand against indefensible positions that betray the principles of the ANC saw 199 men and women who represent the ANC in the National Assembly vote in support of a blatantly unconstitutional and shameful Nkandla report by Police Minister Nathi Nhleko that overturned the Public Protector's findings that President Zuma had wrongfully benefited from the security upgrades in his homestead, and must remedy the situation by paying back monies that were due.

The Thabo Mbeki I know is a good listener. I can cite several instances when he changed course following advice from comrades. I respect the Thabo Mbeki I know for all the things I have said. And for others too many to cite here.

VII

SUPPORT STAFF AND MEDIA

THAMI NTENTENI

✦

'It is also the fate of leadership to be misunderstood; for historians, academics, writers and journalists to reflect great lives according to their own subjective canon. This is all the more evident in a country where the interpreters have a much greater pool of resources to publish views regarding the quest for dignity and nationhood' (Nelson Mandela at the commemoration of the twentieth anniversary of the death in police detention of Steve Biko, East London, South Africa, 1 September 1997).

John Kenneth Galbraith, the eminent and celebrated economist, makes this interesting observation about the philosophical approach of certain individuals to truth and reality: 'In any great organisation it is far, far safer to be wrong with the majority than to be right alone.'

This is the route often taken by political opportunists who are prepared to sacrifice ethics and principles on the altar of political correctness and expediency. They are the political chameleons whose views and opinions are not informed by their knowledge and their understanding of reality but rather take positions on the basis of what seems to be the prevailing conventional wisdom of the day, or to please the powerful authorities of the day who have the power to dispense patronage. These individuals have as their sole aim not the service of truth or to expose maleficent conduct but the hope that they will be rewarded either financially, with positions or social status. Not so with Thabo Mbeki, who speaks and writes about truth and reality informed by his own reading and information at his disposal. As shall be obvious later, such a stance requires courage and conviction as it attracts the vilification of those whose comfort zones are threatened by this truth.

A further quotation: 'In all life one should comfort the afflicted, but verily, also, one should afflict the comfortable, and especially when they are comfortably, contentedly, even happily wrong. There is something wonderful in seeing a wrong-headed majority assailed by truth.' (Dell, Jim (2011-05-12). *Memorable Quotations from John Kenneth Galbraith* (Kindle Locations 59-62). Kindle Edition.)

But what needs to be interrogated is the process by which one arrives at the truth and the development of human knowledge and progress. Neil deGrasse Tyson, the astrophysicist, proposes what he calls 'simple rules' that should guide one:

- Question authority. No idea is true, just because someone says so. Think for yourself.
- Question yourself. Don't believe anything, just because you want to. Believing something does not make it so.
- Test ideas, by the evidence gained from observation and experiment.
- If you have no evidence, reserve judgement.
- And perhaps the most important rule of all, remember you could be wrong.

He goes on to make this profound statement: 'Have scientists known sin? Of course, we have misused science just as we have every other tool at our disposal. That's why we can't afford to leave it in the hands of a powerful few. The more science belongs to all of us, the less likely it is to be misused.'

The above quotes serve to lay the foundation and provide context to write about the Thabo Mbeki I know. This is for the obvious reason that I cannot think of Thabo Mbeki outside of his intellectual and erudite capabilities. I have referred to the views expressed by economist John Kenneth Galbraith and astrophysicist Neil deGrasse Tyson to give context to my understanding of Mbeki and his philosophical outlook on life, his approach to truth and reality. According to my understanding of Thabo Mbeki, these quotes define the values that he subscribes to in his unending quest for knowledge and the improvement of the human condition.

Thabo Mbeki is an African intellectual whose passion for the continent and its people has found expression in his actions, writings and utterances. Some years ago, there was an article in a newspaper that defined Mbeki as an enigma. At the time and even now, I believe this is the easy route taken by a lazy journalist who is trying to avoid doing his/her homework. It is easier to describe Mbeki as an enigma rather than engage in the challenging intellectual discourse that his ideas and thinking never fail to provoke. For one to engage in intellectual conversation with Mbeki, one must have read a great deal. In an insightful and informative piece on Mbeki entitled 'Just say Yes, Mr President', Anthony Brink observes that '… Mbeki reads up on things for himself before forming opinions, and he doesn't just rely on what he's told by ignorant slobs in high positions posing as experts who are too lazy to do the reading he has, is apparent from his complaint in the *Sunday Times* on 6 February 2000: "What do you do if … university people, professors and scientists … haven't read … won't read? What do you do?"' Yet one must concede that it takes extraordinary courage, bravery and belief in oneself to even express one's thoughts and go against that which is conventional wisdom and the prevailing and dominant ideas of the day, that is, 'to be right alone', if you like.

History bears testimony to the fact that human knowledge and progress would not be possible, and science would not have advanced to the level at which humanity is today, if everybody conformed to any idea simply because some authority or expert said it is so. Through studying the history of science we know that science has only been able to advance human knowledge because there were those who had the courage to raise questions and challenge the notion that 'the world is flat', those who had the courage to question authority because they believed that 'no idea is true, just because someone says so'. But this does not suggest that one questions ideas from a basis of ignorance but rather from an informed position that is the product of investigation and searching in order to arrive at the deeper meaning of phenomena.

In the days of old, those who were regarded as non-conformist and questioned the official version of reality as seen through the eyes of the powerful and those in authority, the self-appointed custodians of knowledge, were called heretics. Today they are called 'dissidents' or 'denialists' and are 'burned' at the stake of public opinion by 'writers and journalists, [who] reflect great lives according to their own subjective canon. This is all the more evident in a country where the interpreters have a much greater pool of resources to publish views regarding the quest for dignity and nationhood.'

On 16 February 2000, Frank Gaglioti wrote a tribute to Giordano Bruno in which he said: 'Four centuries ago today, on February 16, 1600, the Roman Catholic Church executed Giordano Bruno, Italian philosopher and scientist, for the crime of heresy. He was taken from his cell in the early hours of the morning to the Piazza dei Fiori in Rome and burnt alive at the stake. To the last, the Church authorities were fearful of the ideas of a man who was known throughout Europe as a bold and brilliant thinker. In a peculiar twist to the gruesome affair, the executioners were ordered to tie his tongue so that he would be unable to address those gathered … His life stands as a testimony to the drive for knowledge and truth that marked the astonishing period of history known as the Renaissance – from which so much in modern art, thought and science derives.'

To this day, according to Frank Gaglioti, it is important to note that Giordano Bruno's writings remain 'on the Vatican's list of forbidden texts.' (https://www.wsws.org/en/articles/2000/02/brun-f16.html)

Writing in *Business Day* on 22 August 2007, Steven Friedman thought that Mbeki wasn't just South Africa's smartest leader ever, but that he 'may well be the world's most intelligent head of government'. Allister Sparks expresses the view that 'Mbeki is an exceptionally intelligent man, one of the sharpest and brightest analysts I have ever met' (*London Guardian*, 9 April 2004). Peter Bruce had this to say: 'Mbeki is arguably the most intelligent national leader this country has ever had' (*Financial Mail*, 17 November 2000). In an editorial in *Business Day* on 14 August 2007, Bruce adds: '… arguing with him is hard, because his opinions are informed: what's difficult about tackling Mbeki is that he is so obviously an enlightened man. He reads, he is erudite, he's good company.'

The opinions expressed above serve to define the essence and character of Thabo Mbeki.

But it is not so much the question that Mbeki is 'obviously an enlightened man', who reads and is erudite that one must engage. It is more to understand why he inspires such anger and even hatred among his detractors. The answer to this question may well be provided by a professor of politics at the University of Cape Town, a certain Robert Schrire. In his Wolpe Trust Lecture in Cape Town on 23 September 2008, Schrire says: 'Mbeki is not an intellectual. This is a good thing. I am scared of intellectuals as leaders. We need simple-minded people in government … One emotion he exhibits is a visceral hatred of the West. He likes being an Englishman but hates the West.' There, the cat is out of the bag. It would be interesting to know when Schrire became afflicted by this irrational fear of 'intellectuals as leaders'. Is it a realisation that he arrived at prior to the democratic elections of 1994, which ushered in a predominantly black democratic government in South Africa? Further, does this fear extend to the leaders of the West such as Abraham Lincoln, Franklin D. Roosevelt, Andrew Jackson, Otto von Bismarck, Napoleon, Churchill or any of the latter-day leaders of the Western world who are highly regarded and respected in their societies for their intellectual capabilities? We will return to this matter in the course of this essay.

I have known Thabo Mbeki since the early 1980s, around 1983 to be exact, when he became the director of the Department of Information and Publicity of the African National Congress (ANC) and I was the director of Radio Freedom. This means that I have known him for the best part of 31 years, both in exile during the days of the liberation struggle and here at home when he was deputy president of the republic and I was the director of communications in his office. It is not often that one keeps a vivid recollection of an encounter with another individual over such a long period of time, unless there is something compelling and significant about it. During the time I was exposed to Mbeki I can say without fear of contradiction that it was a learning experience for me. It was a relationship that was characterised by mutual respect, dignity and a common belief in the justness of the struggle of the people of South Africa for their liberation.

I soon came to the realisation that Mbeki was an independent thinker, but at the same time he respected my views and opinions without being judgemental. There were numerous occasions when I learned from Mbeki that in the process of problem solving things are not necessarily what they seem to be at first glance, but there is always a deeper meaning and one must strive to discover that meaning. I learned that Thabo Mbeki was concerned and preoccupied with detail and had the ability to focus and anticipate events as well as continuity and respect for institutional memory. I noticed that Mbeki paid attention and was quick to pick up words of wisdom expressed by others.

I recall such an occasion when we were in the company of an African-American pastor in the United States whom I considered to be well read and he was concerned about the conditions of African-Americans in the United States. In the course of a discussion with Mbeki he used a Chinese proverb to the effect that '... many people are attracted to the noise that one tree makes as it breaks but remain unaware of the millions of other trees growing silently nearby ...' The pastor continued '... you know, Mr Deputy President, when you watch television in the United States and it features black people, either they are singing, involved in athletics and sport or dancing – not that there is anything wrong with that – but we never feature in scientific and other programmes which debate aspects of human progress and development ...' The pastor also observed that in life '... there are those people who are pace-setters, they are not destined to win the race but they set the pace and just towards the finishing line, they allow others to claim the victory'.

Mbeki was immensely impressed with the views expressed by this pastor and he later asked me: 'Thami, did you hear what that pastor said and what do you think?' We then proceeded to engage and dissect the views in order to get to their essence and deeper meaning. I really relished such moments because those were the periods that I can now identify as contributing to my own intellectual growth.

There are numerous other anecdotes that one could relate but time and space do not allow. But I will touch on two that relate to me per-sonally. At some point during our time in exile, the then director of the ANC's Department of International Affairs, the late Johnny Makhathini, proposed to Mbeki that I should join his department and be posted to the United States. The other occasion was when the Youth Section proposed that I should be the ANC youth representative at the World Federation of Democratic Youth (WFDY) in Budapest. On both occasions, Mbeki and I discussed these proposals. His considered opinion was that the work that I was doing as director of Radio Freedom would suffer if I left and somebody else took over. Not that there was no one who could do it, but because it would break continuity and whoever took over would have to start almost from scratch. But his main concern was that all our energy and focus should be directed internally – meaning South Africa – rather than externally. He expressed the view that to a very great extent the ANC had won the support of the international community. But he added, 'I am aware that this might seem as if I am denying you the opportunity to grow in another direction, but I ask you to think about what I have said and give me an answer. Should you decide that you want to go, I will not stop you.' I thought about this long and hard, but I could not come up with arguments of my own to contest his views. His arguments made sense to me and after careful thought I informed him that my decision was to stay. This is important because Mbeki did not impose his views on me, he used the strength of argument to convince me that his views were correct. That has been the nature of my relationship with Thabo Mbeki.

That is why the view of an autocratic and authoritarian Mbeki presents itself as strange to me. It is strange because I have on numerous occasions had debates with Mbeki pertaining to the approach to his speeches, certain issues pertaining to media and communication and sometimes he sought my opinion on policy matters. Obviously the final decision was his but never once was I made to feel that my opinions were not appreciated or undermined.

But I had come to understand that when I engage with him I should offer informed opinions based on what I have read. I realised that Mbeki 'does not suffer fools gladly', which may partly explain the reason for his vilification and supposed aloofness by his detractors both in politics and in the media.

This is inclusive of the political discussions and decisions that were taken when we discussed his speeches which, it must be said, he writes himself and usually in the early hours of the morning after we have spent the best part of the night discussing and debating what angle he would take. During these times I also acted as his editor; this does not define Mbeki as autocratic or authoritarian.

To return to Schrire. The learned professor holds the view that 'Mbeki is not an intellectual [and] … one emotion he exhibits is a visceral hatred of the West. He likes being an Englishman but hates the West.' It is Schrire's right to hold this opinion, but it begs the question, what informs it? When Thabo Mbeki expresses himself through his speeches and writings, he puts his views and ideas in the public domain. When ideas are in the public domain, they cease to be private and become public property. When ideas capture the imagination of people, they serve as a motive force, an engine to galvanise people towards action. They stimulate their creative capacities and catapult them towards progress and changing their circumstances to improve the quality of their lives. On the other hand, they expose the writer to the harsh and sometimes vitriolic criticism of his peers. But the criticism must be informed and be pitched at the same level as the ideas being criticised.

On 8 May 1996, on the occasion of the adoption of the Constitution Bill by the Constitutional Assembly of the Republic of South Africa, Mbeki made one of his highly acclaimed speeches, 'I am an African'. This speech is important because Mbeki defines who he is and what his attitude is to those who came from Europe to colonise our country. He says: 'I am formed of the migrants who left Europe to find a new home on our native land. Whatever their own actions, they remain still part of me ... I am the grandchild who lays fresh flowers on the Boer graves at St Helena and the Bahamas, who sees in the mind's eye and suffers the suffering of a simple peasant folk: death, concentration camps, destroyed homesteads, a dream in ruins.'

His concern is '... at times, and in fear, I have wondered whether I should concede equal citizenship of our country to the leopard and the lion, the elephant and the springbok, the hyena, the black mamba and the pestilential mosquito ... a human presence among all these, a feature on the face of our native land thus defined, I know that none dare challenge me when I say: I am an African.' (Mbeki: 1998: 31-32)

He did not say: 'I know that none dare challenge me when I say: I am an Englishman or I aspire to be one.'

If only the learned professor had taken time to read 'I am an African' he would never even have suggested that Mbeki hates the West and all he wants in life is to be an Englishman. The problem is that professor does not read work written by Africans. Schrire expressed his view in 2008 and Mbeki articulated his views in 1996. Surely the professor would have known by then that Mbeki does not aspire to be an Englishman. One can only conclude that there are those who would prefer to obscure the reality of South Africa, which is that it is a country consisting of two nations, as Thabo Mbeki pointed out. 'One of these nations is white, relatively prosperous, regardless of gender or geographic dispersal. It has ready access to a developed economic, physical, educational, communication and other infrastructure ... all members of this nation have the possibility to exercise their right to equal opportunity ...' Furthermore, '... the second and larger nation of South Africa is black and poor ... this nation lives under conditions of a grossly underdeveloped economic, physical, educational, communication and other infrastructure. It has virtually no possibility to exercise what in reality amounts to a theoretical right to equal opportunity, with that right being equal within this black nation only to the extent that it is equally incapable of realisation ...' Mbeki then gives the nation an ominous warning: 'What is happening in our country which pushes us away from achieving this goal [national reconciliation] is producing rage among millions of people. I am convinced that we are faced with the danger of a mounting rage to which we must respond seriously. In a speech, again in this House, we quoted the African-American poet Langston Hughes, when he wrote, "What happens to a dream deferred?" His conclusion was that it explodes.' (Mbeki: 1998: 75–76)

These words were almost prophetic. The events of the opening of the year 2016 with the racist bile spewed by Penny Sparrow calling black people monkeys have vindicated Mbeki. The *Sunday Times* of 10 January 2016 had a screaming headline on the leading page 'JAIL THE RACISTS' – clearly the chickens have come home to roost. But, interestingly, those who accused Mbeki of being preoccupied with race, seem to have suffered from collective amnesia; none seem to remember that Mbeki warned South Africa that 'a dream deferred explodes'.

It is because Mbeki raises these uncomfortable truths and disturbs the comfort zones of some white professors, who would rather close their eyes to the South African reality, that he has been so maligned. Mbeki offers this ominous warning to South Africa that 'a dream deferred' is bound to explode. However, those who are content to bask in the glory of wealth born out of a history of inequality and deprivation are quick to accuse

Mbeki of being preoccupied with race.

Kenneth Galbraith makes this observation: '... it is my conclusion that reality is more obscured by social or habitual preference and personal or group pecuniary advantage in economics and politics than in any other subject ... out of the pecuniary and political fashions of the time, economics and larger economic and political systems cultivate their own version of truth. This has no necessary relation to reality ... what it is convenient to believe is greatly preferred. It is what serves, or is not adverse to, influential economic, political and social interest ...' (John Kenneth Galbraith, *The Economics of Innocent Fraud: Truth for Our Time*)

Hopefully, when historians write about the modern history of South Africa, they will note that during the darkest days of struggle, when the defeat of the apartheid system seemed like an impossible dream, when the dark night of oppression seemed so long and that dawn would not break, at a time when it was easier to give up hope and abandon the struggle, when the rewards of being in the struggle were death, imprisonment and exile, history will be kind to Mbeki and others by noting that throughout these trials and tribulations they never wavered, they steadfastly believed and they were always there for the people. You might not say the same about the likes of Schrire.

History must, in the same vein, also pose the question to those who have been so eager to 'cast the first stone ... those who are without sin', those whose criticism of Mbeki has been so vociferous, those who now bask in the sunshine of a liberated South Africa enjoying ill-gotten wealth; history must ask whether they were in the same trenches with Mbeki during those difficult days.

Mbeki's unswerving belief in the capacity of Africa to rise and claim its rightful place within the community of nations is best expressed in his own words:

'... as Africans, our struggle is to engage in both the total emancipation of our continent from the social, political and economic legacy of colonialism and apartheid ... to reclaim our history, identity and traditions and on the foundation that our ancestors built for all of humanity, rebuild our societies to ensure that they are developed and prosperous' (Thabo Mbeki, *Exploding the Myth about Africa*).

BHEKI KHUMALO

My journey extraordinaire to meeting and working for Thabo Mbeki had its origins in 1976 when my father, a Tembisa resident originally from Nkandla and staunch supporter of both the Inkatha Freedom Party (IFP) and Nelson Mandela, berated and beat me up in authentic Zulu fashion. The reason was that I, a skinny stripling, had instinctively joined fellow children from my neighbourhood in a black power salute. That was among my fellow born-unfrees in support of the uprisings that started in Soweto and spread throughout the country, affecting both primary and high schools alike. Those forests of fists of hope helped to change the face of South Africa. Countless hundreds shed their blood so that our nation was able, one day, to speak for the first time of born-frees. We had no notion of this, but we nevertheless joined the protests.

At the time I had no inkling that this black power movement had its origins and influence in events that were fast unfolding in the United States following years of stagnation instead of 'reconstruction' after the Civil War. That was the country where W.E.B. Du Bois in 1903 predicted that the problem of the twentieth century would be the problem of the colour line. It was as if Du Bois had our country specifically in mind, namely the social engineering and brutal institutionalised racism applied by the minority for nearly a century – until our freedom arrived in 1994.

The racial supremacy and colonialism of the Dutch and British settlers had been replaced in history by a thoroughgoing, home-grown South African-based racial segregation that Kader Asmal (an African National Congress

(ANC) international law expert for whom I also worked) called arbitrary, capricious and discriminatory. It is this unique phenomenon that prompted the liberation movement led by the ANC to categorise our country's racial configuration as 'colonialism of a special type'. Most of this, of course, went over the head of young 'Mthofi' Khumalo when he raised his fist with the rest of them in Tembisa in 1976. Yet it was a cause that moulded his whole life, and led him to people like Mbeki.

My father did not forgive me till on his deathbed in 1984, a year after the formation of the United Democratic Front (UDF), where I played my part in responding to the ANC's call to render the country ungovernable and the apartheid system unworkable. My father punished me for showing nascent signs of political consciousness to the extent that he banished me, ignominiously, to the Siberia of Nkandla between 1980 and 1983 where I was expected to study, perhaps far away from the hustle and bustle of the politics of the township. This much-resented attempt at putting the brakes on my political activism was finally defeated when, upon my return, I immediately joined the Congress of South African Students (COSAS), the South African National Students Congress (SANSCO), the UDF and later ANC structures. I held numerous local, regional, provincial and national leadership positions. In this I was driven by the 1961 declaration by Umkhonto we Sizwe (MK), under the command of Mandela, that the time had come to fight and not surrender. Such times do present themselves in life, hopefully not often.

It was a combination of my aborted attempt at being a journalist on the then *Weekly Mail* – courtesy of the state of emergency and the threat of police arrest – and my numerous roles as spokesperson for various UDF and ANC structures, including education ministers Sibusiso Bengu and Kader Asmal, that landed me the position of spokesperson to Thabo Mbeki. In 2001, shortly after the opening of the new school term and after consequently being on television and radio quite a bit as spokesperson for Professor Asmal, I applied for a job as chief director and spokesperson to the deputy president, Jacob Zuma. He was a fellow 'homeboy', from Nkandla, and had not had his run-ins with Mbeki. No luck. I drew a blank. However, the panel recommended me – no doubt supported by Tony Heard, then special adviser to Essop Pahad and the presidency – for consideration as spokesperson to Mbeki but at the same rank of director that I had occupied in education. With the sad passing of Parks Mankahlana, a superb pioneer presidential spokesperson, the post needed direction and someone with iron filings on their teeth to handle the storms ahead on AIDS, defence acquisition (derogatorily called the arms deal), Zimbabwe and other matters. It was to be a baptism of fire, but worth every minute!

I remember walking jauntily into Asmal's office, chuffed, to tell him about, for me, a most auspicious development. A man short in stature but strong on convictions, he rose to his bare five feet at his desk. He threw his head back and pealed with loud laughter in disbelief. In his half-Irish way, he uttered words to the effect of, 'Who do you think you are, to think you can work for Mbeki, a man with scant regard for other people, a cold person who will never take you seriously and who will sideline you?' This was deflating. Asmal seemed to forget that he saw me for the first time at the Gauteng provincial conference of the ANC where I was able to engage in complex theoretical debates of the organisation to the extent that he asked my name and gave me his business card, having asked if I could work for him as his spokesperson. He seemed then conveniently to have forgotten that I was remotely visible on a panel at Fort Hare University interviewing him as a candidate for the job of vice-chancellor after he came back to South Africa from Ireland in the early 1990s – a job even he, such a brilliant person, failed to clinch.

The vagaries of fate, however, had decreed that, in time, he would find me sitting there in education, my having worked for Bengu before Asmal took over in 1999. My next stop was to be at Mbeki's side. Despite Asmal's tugging at my coat sleeves, I told him that I was nevertheless determined to take up the job offer with Mbeki. I remembered with some foreboding that when Mbeki, then ANC director of international relations, came to Fort Hare, where as political education officer of the campus branch of SANSCO and Students' Representative Council (SRC) vice-president, I had with supreme confidence told him that the leadership of my organisation, the ANC, was in cloud-cuckoo-land if it thought the National Party, representing the last vestiges of supremacist Afrikanerdom, would voluntarily give up power. Of course, in one of the firsts in history of a rigid volk having the prescience of enlightened self-interest, it did, sharing in the

Government of National Unity, until F. W. de Klerk's precipitate withdrawal.

When two weeks passed without my even having met Mbeki, I started regretting having joined the presidency. I was totally unsighted. Asmal's words came back to haunt me. On the face of it, the Asmal judgement seemed correct. At least, until Zamikhaya Maseti, then director in Mbeki's office, introduced me to the president. What Mbeki said, in the studied cordiality that was his hallmark – and wearing a somewhat strange yellowish suit – disarmed me totally and ended my incipient feelings of reserve and even prejudice. He said with a typical lack of emotion, 'This is the man I usually see on television and hear on the radio ... I have appointed you spokesperson so you can go back to your job.' That was the end of the brief encounter with Mbeki. This is the same theme Mbeki turned to after the euphoria of the landslide victory of the ANC in the 2004 elections when, at the victory party at Gallagher Estate, he called on us, assembled party faithfuls, to 'go back to work' as the people had spoken. It was as if he was impatient that we were partying instead of being immediately at the coalface tackling his favourite subject of the triple evils of poverty, inequality and underdevelopment.

The same spirit was evident when we gained our first-ever two-year stint as a non-permanent member state of the United Nations Security Council. At the presidential end-of-year function in a tent on the west lawn of the Union Buildings, Mbeki cut through the euphoria and said there was more work to do now that we had achieved this important milestone for South Africa and Africa. It was his way. Undramatic and industrious.

My first real encounter in battle with Mbeki was in dealing with the April 2001 announcement by Steve Tshwete, then minister of police, that three senior leaders of the ANC – Cyril Ramaphosa, Tokyo Sexwale and Mathews Phosa – were involved in a plot to undermine Mbeki by spreading rumours that he had been behind the assassination of Chris Hani in 1993. Ray Hartley, in *Ragged Glory: The Rainbow Nation in Black and White*, page 152, noting that 'Hani was a rival for power within the party', added that 'the plot allegations undermined Mbeki's reputation, confirming the stereotype that he was a Machiavellian operator who would do anything to hold on to power'. The *Mail & Guardian*, the paper for which Mbeki played a crucial role in fund-raising in 1987 and described by the conservative

R.W. Johnson in 1990 as 'the main mouthpiece of the white pro-ANC liberalism', went further than that and asked in April 2001, as it did in 1996, if Mbeki was fit to rule.

It was dauntingly adverse circumstances like this that often meant flying by the seat of my pants. As the newly appointed spokesperson I had to field press queries, while simultaneously building a rapport not only with Mbeki but also with the security establishment that is prone to being suspicious of newcomers, even those from the Congress movement. This often meant having to ensure that one had the green light on the messaging from the often disparate, and sometimes conflicting, interests in various arms of the state. In this I found the formidable Frank Chikane, Joel Netshitenzhe, Mojanku Gumbi and Lucille Meyer – my immediate supervisor – to be reliable pillars and the guiding lights for the entire duration of my stint as spokesperson. The person who asked Mbeki perhaps the most telling personal question during the period was Tim Sebastian, the inimitable host of the BBC's most feared programme, *Hard Talk*. Sebastian asked Mbeki if he was a shy person. This question, planted by Smuts Ngonyama and myself, caught Mbeki totally unawares, his proverbial pants down, to which he replied that he was not a showman. This answer to this seasoned BBC journalist aptly describes the person I came to serve in the presidency.

This reality is reflected by the over-reported encounter between Thabo and his father Govan Mbeki when they saw each other after almost three decades. Thabo did not show any public emotion, which people were ordinarily expected to show in such circumstances. The other, and in my view less dramatic but enlightening, encounter is described by Thabo himself, writing a preface to a book, *Oliver Tambo Remembered*. He tells how he went into exile in 1962, only after 'Walter Sisulu directed me [Mbeki] to meet two of our leaders, Duma Nokwe and Govan Mbeki [note: rather than mention him as his father he chose to refer to him as a leader of the ANC], who conveyed the instruction rather than a proposal of the movement, that I should leave the country.'

It can be suggested that Thabo Mbeki saw himself and his father primarily as fighters in a sacred, historic cause, with not much room for the ordinary father-and-son sentiments. The feeling seemed to be mutual between them. Govan was a lifelong communist, with all the seriousness and detachment from sentimentality that usually goes with that. Crown prince of the ANC for some years, Thabo was a realist and even matter of fact about the heavy political responsibilities thrust upon him, and seldom showed emotion in public. Occasionally his speeches would reflect his dislike in others of unnecessary shows of emotion and showmanship in public. He particularly disliked public grandstanding, which of course made things difficult for those, like me, desperately dedicated at all costs to building his image after Mandela. His humour seemed gentle and subtle on the surface, but it had a bite – with some teasing – in delivery. He could laugh readily in a slow, deep, mildly infectious way. He did this in private, in the company of his close associates and advisers, rather than in public.

It was his deportment, his polite way of dealing with his staff, his routinely referring to us as 'chief', that endeared him to all of us. We in turn all called him 'The Chief'. He was the able person in charge, the chairman of the board of SA Inc. As someone who has worked at senior levels of both the public and the private sector, I have come to experience first hand values–driven leadership. I have seen this strongly evident in the presidency of Mbeki. Mandela was, of course, in a class of his own, in all history. To be fair, I spotted, in varying degrees such attributes in both Deputy President and later President Zuma, and in the quiet, undramatic Motlanthe. Mbeki's mentor, Oliver Tambo, an icon of the ANC, clearly had the same undramatic, businesslike leadership style as Mbeki – and also immense influence politically.

The strength of the ANC is in the manner in which its leaders conduct themselves in the course of their political and official work. It is this attribute that built the ANC into the formidable force it has become. Mbeki was driven to the point of being obsessed with what his biographer Mark Gevisser correctly called in *The Dream Deferred* '… the crisis of expectation of black South Africans awaiting liberation and who now found themselves often with less even than they had before, and thus on the brink of dangerous explosion. This more than anything else symbolised Mbeki's concern about the plight of our people, just like black Americans, whose dream of emancipation had sagged, rotted and festered into inner-city ghettoes like Harlem.'

It is therefore not a surprise that Mbeki brought to bear the might of his intellectual faculties in matters that have to do with the economy. Most of us made the mistake of defining the future of our country merely on the basis of the political landscape. In this we were not alone, we were influenced, narrowly and in my view inappropriately, by Kwame Nkrumah's dictum: 'Seek ye first the political kingdom and all else will follow.' It is Mandela, Tambo, Mbeki and Zuma and other leaders of the ANC who recognised that the time had come to find a political solution to our country's problems. In this they worked with the one-time apartheid regime to produce the political outcome of the 1994 breakthrough. This is crucial given the events that are happening to countries that were ruled by a strong political centre such as, among others, Egypt, Iraq and Libya.

It is the strength of the ANC, confident in its mass appeal, that allowed Mbeki, during the early years of Mandela's presidency, to work with Tito Mboweni, Trevor Manuel, Maria Ramos, Alec Erwin and others to tackle the economy that was in endemic crisis, with public sector debt ballooning out of control; GDP growth lagging; inflation, critical for bringing down interest rates, was in the 10s and even 20s; more importantly, the country's national foreign reserves were negative. We had a net open forex position that exceeded US$25 billion. In those horror days of forex volatility, we were adding up to US$1.0 billion per day to our national liability. We were going broke, fast. We had arguably inherited a slag heap in the early 1990s, and it took time to turn this around. By 2001, the government public debt was among the lowest when compared with its peers. As these obstacles were being systematically removed, government's credibility grew over time. South Africa's credit ratings improved, economic growth picked up and by 2004 our GDP had grown by 5.5 per cent.

Mbeki and his team engineered the historic turnaround, steadily and impressively executed. I recall that during 2003 the rand had gone to the dogs at above R10 to the dollar. We were on a state visit to China and we were visiting the industrial city of Shanghai where we were bombarded with a litany of questions about the structure of our economy. I asked Alec Erwin, who at face value seemed unperturbed, whether we had it in ourselves as a country to survive these shocks. He gave me a crash course in economics, on those meandering streets of Shanghai, a lesson that to this day I have not forgotten and which I found useful when I did my executive development programme at Wits Business School and which has stood me in good stead in my current job. The key is to continue to pursue prudent fiscal management even in the face of two disparate ideological extremes.

The other issue that was the subject of contestation during the Mbeki years was the issue of peace and stability on the African continent. Mbeki, himself a revolutionary pan-Africanist, understood that he needed to win over and work with these sections of the liberation movement whom we hated in our townships. These often opposed school, rent and consumer boycotts that we organised in the 1980s. It is this issue, of what I thought constituted co-option with reactionaries, that I never quite understood and appreciated at the time I worked for Mbeki. I was a proud product of the structures of the UDF whose grassroots structures were festooned over every street of our country in the 1980s. We indeed wrongly saw these organisations as reactionaries rather than progressive allies of the national democratic struggle – euphemism for the ANC's national democratic revolution. Mbeki was ahead of the times. He was able to charm these organisations in the same way he did the Afrikaners who met the ANC in Dakar in 1987. Mbeki realised, soon after 1994, that these organisations, though not part of the Congress movement, were critical to the real reconstruction of our country.

It is no secret that black intellectuals in academia, the media, and in business were dominated by the members of these organisations. The close working relationship Mbeki developed with, inter alia, Mojanku Gumbi, Dikgang Moseneke and Mathatha Tsedu of the Black Consciousness Movement has surprised those of us who traditionally come from the Congress movement. This orientation accounts for all the good work that Mbeki – including decimating these organisations to the point of extinction – did to an extent that the African agenda is the cornerstone of our foreign policy.

This also drove his Millennium Africa Plan (MAP), which towered above Senegal's Omega plan and which, renamed the New Partnership for Africa's Development (NEPAD), Mbeki pursued with Nigeria's Olusegun Obasanjo, Algeria's Abdelaziz Bouteflika, and Senegal's Abdoulaye Wade. The African Union (AU) has been a de facto permanent presence in all the G8 summits since then. In 2004 we took a trip of 18 hours to the US to attend a bilateral meeting with the government of the US led by President George Bush Jnr and also in support of AGOA (Africa Growth and Opportunity Act), and returned to South Africa for four hours before travelling for more than 18 hours to Japan to attend a meeting of the Tokyo Conference on African Development (TICAD) and then returning to spend three days, without sleeping, in Kinshasa so that Mbeki could continue his efforts to broker a cessation of hostilities in the aftermath of the assassination of the abrasive Laurent Kabila, Joseph Kabila's father. That was how it went in those hectic days. In one of those bizarre moments, having not slept for days, Mbeki summoned his physician, Dr Sithebe, to give him an injection so that he could continue for a few days without sleeping, which Sithebe, also in a moment of madness, refused and instead offered him Berocca, which didn't work, good as it was in ordinary circumstances.

Let it be noted, as I conclude, that Mbeki, remarkably, gave me a free hand in my role as his spokesperson. That was liberation. Others had been more restrictive. It bred a sense of responsibility. It accorded the necessary seniority and scope in a not-easy job. If there is one area about which I wish to be really critical in relation to Mbeki – apart from the myths, mysteries, harm and realities of what became the HIV/AIDS debacle, with so much already written and said about it that I shall leave it at that for now – it is the underlying manner in which he dealt with the politics of the tripartite alliance and his glaring failure to deal with the succession.

Joe Slovo was fond of saying that 'hindsight is the most perfect and irritating of all sciences'. We can't go back to fix that which was unaddressed during his presidency. With 'hindsight' he should have spent his time and used his charm to win over the tripartite alliance and consolidate his base in the ANC rather than use Lenin's famous statement 'better fewer but better'.

This for me is disappointing in the leader who, boldly and more than anyone else, was central to the secret negotiations that produced a democratic outcome in 1994 and a man who led the country extremely well as South Africa's de facto prime minister since the dawn of majority rule. He inadvertently behaved like a modern-day version of his Shakespearean tragic hero Coriolanus, the Roman general who went to war against his own people. Mbeki's growing, disparate ranks of opponents in the ANC were emboldened to strike back with unity of purpose, scenting and seizing success by a margin that was not at all overwhelming.

Mbeki could also, in limited respects, even be seen as a Brutus figure, in Shakespeare's *Julius Caesar*, who made errors of judgement that made him ultimately, in defeat, fall on his sword. He was no political assassin; on the contrary. That was others' speciality. Yet, in my view, some of his judgements, and also appointments made ahead of the Polokwane conference, were tragic and led to the groundswell whose results still haunt my beloved organisation, the ANC, to this day.

Some columnists (e.g. John Scott) when referring to Mbeki have intoned 'all is forgiven'. He was an outstanding, strong-minded and independent president, an earnest man with a mission and a vision.

MPHO NGOZI

⊰⊱

I started working with Thabo Mbeki when he was the deputy president of South Africa. The then director general in the presidency, the Reverend Frank Chikane, had called me and informed me that I was the appointed candidate for the position of private secretary to Deputy President Thabo Mbeki. He then informed me of my appointment to meet with the deputy president. After receiving that call I was filled with mixed feelings and confusion, but I told myself that the deputy president was a human being after all and therefore there was no need for me to be intimidated by working with him. I knew at that time that I was ready to work in that office, but I did not know the amount of work or the man I would be working with.

My first meeting with Deputy President Mbeki was on a Saturday morning at his official residence, Oliver Tambo House. As I arrived at the residence I was received by an official who introduced me to the man himself. Deputy President Mbeki offered me some refreshments, I promptly responded, 'Please, Mr Deputy President, tea will do.' I had always privately complained about his unkempt beard, and thought this was my best opportunity to ask him to shave or trim it. Yes, I did, but the surprised Mbeki looked at me and laughed with his pipe in his mouth. After a brief discussion, he shook my hand and warmly welcomed me and congratulated me on my new position.

This was the day that profoundly changed my life; at a professional level, I gained a strong work ethic, principles and values and for this I give credit to Advocate Mojanku Gumbi, the legal adviser, and the Reverend Chikane for their guidance through the years. It would be wrong for me not to mention Ms Lyndall Shope-Mafole, who mentored me. I recall her telling me that the work that I was doing at the IBA (Independent Broadcasting Authority) as head of secretariat had prepared me for the future. Indeed, when I was invited for an interview at the Union Buildings, I informed her that I had got the job and she responded with a smile: 'This is the future I was talking about.' I worked with Deputy President Thabo Mbeki from March 1998 until April 1999, and from 1999 to 2004 when he was elected president.

On my first day in the Cape Town office, Deputy President Mbeki asked me to bring him a pie. In my wisdom, I judged that no deputy president should be eating a pie and with great confidence I instead ordered a healthy sandwich for him. I proudly walked into his office with a tray with coffee and the healthy sandwich. He took one look at the sandwich and asked me whether I knew what a pie was. I was taken by surprise and I swiftly left the coffee on his desk and took back the sandwich and requested the security personnel to hastily purchase a pie as per the request of the deputy president. On the second day, then Deputy Minister Essop Pahad walked into my office and asked me if the deputy president was in his office and I responded in the affirmative. Pahad knocked on the door and let himself in. Barely a few minutes later, Mbeki walked out to ask me who had given the deputy minister permission to enter his office without checking his availability. I explained that Dr Pahad did not ask me whether or not he could enter and that he just let himself in. In a very polite manner, Mbeki asked the deputy minister to go back and ask me because I was his secretary and not a flower pot. He turned to Dr Pahad and said, 'Chief, go back and talk to her. I do not talk to people unless she says so. She manages people.' That was the kind of boss he was.

This little encounter gave me an incredible sense of being valued by my boss. He had effectively affirmed me and my role in his office and he demanded that my office be respected. Over the years Mbeki taught me one valuable lesson that I have carried with me to this day and that is that when you are in a position of responsibility, you must think, read and use your intelligence.

President Thabo Mbeki was a historian and a teacher. For the period that

I worked with him I very quickly learned about South African and African history. He taught me that Africa was an important continent and that we had to take ourselves as Africans seriously and deal with African challenges as Africans. When I started working for him, I was clueless about the names of the various presidents on our continent. I was ignorant about the role of the United Nations (UN) and his role in the transformation of the OAU (Organisation of African Unity) to the African Union (AU). But the more we engaged with all these issues, the more I took interest and the more I learned. He taught me how to relate to senior government officials in a polite but firm manner. Because he placed his trust in me, my confidence grew.

The president taught me the difference between a head of state and a head of government. I learnt that the representatives in English-speaking countries were referred to as high commissioners while the French referred to them as ambassadors. I also learned that in our country the African National Congress (ANC) was the only organisation that had a secretary general and that all other organisations had general secretaries. I had to get this seemingly irrelevant information correct in my communications with different parties and stakeholders.

Often the president would call me into his office and ask me to call another president that he needed to talk to, only mentioning his name. If he did not mention the country, I would return to my desk to start a frantic search for the person I was to call and the country they came from. But, with time, I learned who each president was. In the beginning I was overwhelmed by all these big names, but Mbeki helped me to find the confidence to handle all kinds of situations.

Because he was a teacher, he also wanted to know your views. President Mbeki is a fantastic researcher and this intimidated all of us. When you talk to President Mbeki, you must know your facts and never go to him with the aim of dabbling in small talk. Advocate Mojanku would always say that I was a bully but that was because I was taught by the president to stand my ground and he gave me the power to exercise my responsibilities in the best way I could.

President Mbeki never left us with insufficient knowledge or at least an understanding of why we were doing what we were doing. We had to read and watch news. We had to know what was going on in the rest of the world. He would wake you up at 2am and, for example, he would say, 'Chief, do you think we can go to Lesotho tomorrow morning?' and the first person we would call was Deputy Foreign Affairs Minister Aziz Pahad, and then we would call the Reverend Chikane and Advocate Mojanku to say we are leaving at 8am. My husband would throw me out of the room complaining that the presidency did not know the difference between day and night; he would say, 'Don't do your work in my room.'

As a person, I learned from him. Once we went to Japan and on inform- ing him that I was going out to explore the city, he told me about the geishas. I was so fascinated and I doubt I would have known what they were had he not told me about them. This again was his ability to use his knowledge on cultural issues to teach us about the different places we travelled to. President Mbeki loves archaeology and palaeontology. We vis- ited the Sterkfontein caves with Professor Tobias of the University of the Witwatersrand. If you told him that there was no space in the diary, he would say, 'Chief, you know how to manage these things, find the space,' and then we would go to these meaningful places like the Cradle of Humankind. I have cherished those teachings. He was strict, but a wonderful and pleasant person to work with. Working in President Mbeki's office also taught me that you never worked *for* but rather *with* him: he never referred to himself but to a collective.

President Mbeki had a way of empowering us by giving us a sense of responsibility and making sure that we were well informed, and that we read and understood documents so that we could make intelligent and sen- sible inputs. Because of the perfectionist that he is, we got to learn to edit documents thoroughly before they reached him. Every day was a learning process. We learned to interrogate and ask questions before presenting a document to him. This way, we could almost pre-empt what he would ask and how we would respond. In the process, we were forced to fully understand how government worked. Mbeki moved from the fundamental premise that each of us has the capacity to think and use our intellect and he would engage us on pressing issues, even though we thought that they were way above our heads as junior staff members; he wanted to know what we thought. The president had a way of making sure that before taking any decision he would get people at all levels to make a contribution. He was highly consultative. Even as secretaries, he never left us out. He consulted all of us every step of the way. He never had the attitude that Mpho is just a secretary and therefore has nothing meaningful to contribute. You had to prepare thoroughly. There could be no fumbling, because he would listen carefully and then interrogate you on your decision so that we were all sure that what we wanted to achieve was well thought out.

If you want to understand the depth of President Mbeki's love for education and history, you need only look at the manner in which he gave his heart and soul to preserving the Timbuktu Manuscripts. We were in Mali and he said, 'Chiefs, we must get those documents and we must make sure that they are preserved.' For him, historical documents are important – any history that is documented and archived is important. He committed himself to the Timbuktu project because he possesses a historical conscious-ness. I believe that Mbeki could not imagine that the wealth of knowledge contained in the Timbuktu Manuscripts could simply disappear. We got to understand that, in part, the manuscripts proved the fundamental point that was being ignored in history books: that Africa made a major contribution to the world in terms of knowledge and was not the 'dark' continent that history books told us about. This helped us to appreciate our continent even more.

When the president and his team began working on South Africa's coat of arms, he got me involved. One day he asked, 'Do you know how to draw a Secretary Bird?' Baffled, I told him that I was not a good artist. He then sent me to the Botanical Gardens in Cape Town to do research on South African indigenous plants. But as we were working on the design of the coat of arms, researching birds and plants, he asked me, 'Why should we use animals in the highest symbol of the country when in fact there are human beings that we need to recognise: the Khoi and the San people?' This was how we came to have the Khoisan figures and their language on the South African coat of arms.

One morning as I walked into the Union Buildings I heard a report that some white boys had stolen the coat of arms symbols from the West Wing entrance. I reported this matter to him and he asked me why I thought they wanted the symbols. I said that I thought it was racist tendencies of silly white boys who did not recognise our symbols; it was vandalism. He looked at me and said, 'Ma (as he would sometimes refer to me if he was not calling me Chief), don't you think that they took those symbols because they want to have them in their own homes and cherish them? We should not always be cynical and negative about the things that white people do. Sometimes they just want to own some of the processes during this time of change.' I got to learn that the president never worked on assumptions. He worked from the very basic premise that all human beings are inherently good.

I doubt that anyone who worked with Mbeki will deny that he is among the most humble of people. This side of him could be seen even during mealtimes. I got to know that when a buffet was served, he never wanted anyone to dish up for him; he wanted to make his own choices. I learned never to interfere with that. But some people would take me to task for not serving the president and I had to ask them to allow him to be a human being, to do what everyone else did.

It did not matter whether he was in the company of the world's most powerful leaders or whether he was sitting with a community of elders in the villages, Mbeki had a very deep respect for the elders. It amazed me how he moved so comfortably between the two worlds with such ease. From quoting Shakespeare and talking high politics in powerful Western countries to talking community politics in the rural villages in South Africa, he always seemed at ease. In the villages, it came to him naturally to give up his seat to an older person or to a woman; it was almost automatic for him to take his place on the floor.

As a president he was very sympathetic, very sensitive, very humane but also very strict on issues related to protocol. He once told me: 'I am not a doctor, I only have an honorary doctorate.' I did not know that when you have an honorary doctorate, you cannot be called 'doctor'. The president made it very clear to me that to become a doctor you must earn a PhD; you must work for it. He would say, 'I am not going to be addressed as Doctor, I am Mister Thabo Mbeki.' He was very strict about adhering to the rules and regulations, the Constitution and the law. He never wanted to do things that were not in line with protocol. He would say, 'Ma, I am not a member of parliament and so we must request the Speaker to invite us to address Parliament. I cannot just show up uninvited.'

I became conscious of the fact that President Mbeki's biggest passion was to see that people genuinely had a better life, so this thing of 'a better life for all' was not merely a slogan for him. It was a genuine concern and one that challenged him deeply. That was why he had the imbizos. He thought that they were opportunities to talk directly to communities to hear for himself what their concerns were and how they could be addressed, especially communities in far flung areas of the country. The president was very passionate about gender issues and about children and that was why there was an official women's and children's portfolio in the presidency.

When the president was thinking about establishing the National Orders and how they should be handled – the bestowal, the venue and the ceremony itself – he called me and said, 'Chief, do we have time?' I responded, 'Time to do what?' He said, 'To find a venue.' I wondered what we needed a venue for. He then explained that we needed to find a venue for the National Orders ceremony and that it needed to take place at the seat of government, which was either the Union Buildings or Tuynhuis. I wondered why the president would want to look for a venue when all he needed to do was instruct us to do so. But then I realised how close this project was to his heart and that was why he wanted to pay attention to the detail and format that this ceremony should take. He solicited our opinions and made sure that every detail was carefully implemented as befitted a ceremony of this nature. The National Orders, to him, were part of the transformation of South Africa and he paid careful attention to what they signified, what they should achieve and how they should be handled.

In reply, I informed him that I had an hour to spare and so we took a walk through the entire Union Buildings, into the gardens and around the Police Memorial. As we were walking, I could see the pleasure on his face; mostly he moved from his office to his car and seldom got the opportunity to get out into the fresh air to explore his surroundings in this way. As we were walking back up the mountain around the Union Buildings, I was huffing and puffing, and it must have been obvious to him because he laughed and with this naughty look on his face, he turned to the security team and said, 'Chief, bring a car around to pick up Madam. She is too tired to walk up the hill.' President Mbeki then turned to me and said, 'Chief, you must start exercising.' My response was, 'When? We work so hard and we literally leave the office very late in the evening – short of sleeping in the office.' He could not help but burst into laughter.

Mbeki's respect for people is beyond doubt. I often marvelled at the way he treated every human being with whom he came into contact with utmost respect. For example, it is well known that Mbeki smokes a pipe, but one thing he never did was ask me to get him a match when he needed to light his pipe. He would rather ask one of his male colleagues for a match. In his mind, he could not ask a lady to do that. One day on our travels in Brazil, we arrived in his hotel suite and he said, 'I want to smoke my pipe now.' The problem was that one of the ambassadors had come to visit with their baby. The then minister of health Dr Dlamini-Zuma, who had been promoting the no-smoking campaign, was also there. I asked both the minister and the ambassador with the baby to give us some time without giving them my reasons. As they were leaving, the president laughed and asked, 'How did you know that those were the two people I did not want to be in the room while I smoked?' I responded, 'The champion of no-smoking and a baby could not be in the same room when you smoke.' This was how sensitive he was and he never used his powerful position to disrespect or undermine his fellow human beings, no matter who they were.

The president had a deep obsession to get the economy to grow. He believed that solid economic growth in South Africa and the rest of the African continent would naturally lead to a better Africa. In working on this matter, he had assembled different consultative groups. He consulted broadly to try to understand what other people thought about how to grow the economy. In all his international, continental and domestic travels, we had to involve people who would add value to everything he did. He always consulted people whom he thought would enhance or help his own understanding of what he needed to do on any issue.

Around President Mbeki, we had to be thorough and logical in all we did because when he quizzed you about a decision, you needed to have solid answers for him. At times, he would ask questions that we were totally unprepared for or to which we had not sufficiently applied our minds. For example, on one trip from London, he asked, 'What route are we taking?' At that time, he was using a small plane that needed to be refuelled. I told him that we were going via Libya. On receiving this information, he said,

'No, I am not going there. Find another route.' I told him that this meant that I would need about two hours to resolve the issue and get clearance to reroute our flight. All he said was, 'Chief, this is your job, but I am not going to Libya.' I knew that the reason that he did not want to go via Libya was that if Libyan leader Muammar Gaddafi got wind of the fact that President Mbeki had landed in his country, he would have wanted to host him in an elaborate ceremony that would not only have been a disruption to our schedule but an inconvenience to the Libyans.

Because of his hectic travels, we had to learn our geography very fast. He always wanted to know how we came to the conclusion that going via a particular country was the shortest route and so we would go back to our maps and check and recheck and come back with a more coherent and logical suggestion. For President Mbeki, there was no need to waste time and money when we could use the shortest routes to get where we needed to be. I became so good at this that when the pilots briefed me about a route, I knew immediately whether we were taking the best route. Mbeki's intellect does not allow him to take things at face value and we had to learn to think on our feet.

I was only 34 when I began working for Deputy President Mbeki and I had a son who was one and a half years old. I used to leave the office around 2 to 3am and was expected to be back in the office the next day at 8 o'clock. If I was not in the office on time and the president was late, the Reverend Chikane would say that there was no room for mistakes. We never knew what sleep was because we were working with a person who was passionate about the work he was doing for our country and so we all got used to sleeping for only an hour or two. The little secret we had, which we did not want to share with Mrs Mbeki, was that there were times when he would say, 'Chief, do you think that I can have a burger and some chips?' and this was around 2am. I would try to say to him, 'But, Chief, burgers and chips at 2am?' His response would be, 'Mpho, your stomach does not know what time it is; let us just eat please.'

But that was Thabo Mbeki. If you have not come close to him, you would not know this side of him – the human part of him. The man I am talking about is a man of integrity and respect, who has a very sharp and superior intellect. He does not know the difference between day and night.

If he had things to do, he would work for days on end with very little rest. It got to a point where I had to find a strategy to get him to rest without saying to him, 'It's time to sleep.' I would have to trick him into going to sleep by offering him a morning or day off. I would say, 'Chief, I think tomorrow you can sleep until the afternoon and we in the office can have breakfast at 14:00' – that was the only way that he would agree.

It will surprise many people to know that President Mbeki does not know the meaning of possessing money even though he is an economist by profession. If, for example, you told him the price of bread, he would be shocked at how expensive it was. At times, someone would bring him money that they owed him for something that they had perhaps wanted to buy while on a trip but did not have cash on them at the time. When I counted it, it might turn out to be about R500. For him that was a lot of money. Happy to have received his money, he would then call me and say, 'Chief, who do we owe?' If, for example, he had borrowed R100 from one of the presidential security personnel to buy something that he saw while on a trip, I would point out that he needed to pay that person. At times he would tell me that he wanted to go to a shopping mall to buy music (classical or jazz) CDs or books etc. But when we got there, he might not have the money on him, which meant I had to use my credit card. Sometimes I would tell him, 'Chief, you cannot take so many books, I do not have that kind of money on my card. This money is for my children.' I knew that I would always get my money back from him. He was not doing this to make life difficult for me but he just never carried money on him – he did not own a credit card or a mobile phone, which might have been helpful in such circumstances. Even if he wanted to buy sweets or vetkoek from the mamas or gogos selling in the stalls in the communities, we always had to lend him the money. It was almost as if he had no use for money and I put this down to the fact that he only knew how to live on the allowance or stipend, a pittance, given to him by the ANC while in exile. As far as Mbeki was concerned, his job as president of South Africa paid for everything for him and at times he never understood why he needed a travel allowance because food, accommodation and transport were provided for him by the state.

Besides his love for music and books, President Mbeki also loved cricket.

When I started working with him, I knew nothing about cricket. He would come out of cabinet meetings and the first thing he would ask me was, 'What's the score?' Thankfully, Ricky Naidoo, who used to work in the office, became his reliable source of information on cricket matters.

My fights with President Mbeki began when it was time for his health check-ups because he was scared of doctors. You could see it on his face when the doctor came into the office carrying his medical kit. On the days of the check-ups, I had to make sure that I took the afternoon off because it often needed a lot of persuasion and fancy footwork to get through what Mbeki saw as an ordeal.

But there was one thing where President Mbeki put me to shame. When during the morning you needed to enter his suite in a hotel where we were staying, the first thing that struck you was how he kept everything in place. He would have pulled his bed covers neatly into place, placed his beautifully folded pyjamas on top and his morning slippers would be lined up neatly on the floor; nothing was out of place. The hotel staff responsible for cleaning often found the room tidy.

On these trips, it was our job to make sure that his clothes were pressed and ready. On one occasion we had to go to Lesotho. We thought that we would be returning home the same day, but as it turned out the talks continued into the following day. The problem was what was the president going to wear the next day? One of our colleagues in the presidential protection unit, Ben Ditlhakanyane, gave us one of his shirts. I pressed it and gave it to the president to wear to the meeting. That morning, I took the soap that is normally found in hotel bathrooms and washed the president's shirt so that he could have a clean shirt the next day after wearing Ben's shirt. I tell this story because I do not think he even asked where we got the shirt from and he did not make a fuss because the only thing that was on his mind was the job at hand.

There were some instances where the president would ask us to save him and cancel a meeting, but he would also want to know what excuse we were going to offer. The reason for this was so that he could corroborate the story if he ever needed to. Nothing that the president did was about him, including his birthday. He needed to be reminded that it was his birthday because he never thought that it was important. We often had to remind him to eat, cut his hair; shave and, most important of all, go to sleep. This was not because he did not care, it was because he was so obsessed with work and delivering on the mandate given to him by the people of South Africa that he often lost all sense of time. The Thabo Mbeki I know worked tirelessly to reconstruct South Africa and Africa, and his contribution towards the African agenda is highly respected.

I worked for this man with pride and respect. I still respect him and his wife Mama Zanele for their professionalism and the wealth of knowledge that one has sponged from them. During his downtime, which was very rare, he enjoyed photography and loved butterflies. At some point, we agreed that we would produce and label dresses for women decorated with brightly coloured butterflies. I am not sure that we agreed on the label and I am still waiting for the butterfly designer label dresses.

Anybody who has worked with President Mbeki will tell you that there was one thing he refused to do and that was to conflate his government and ANC work. He made it clear to those of us in the presidency that we were public servants and that he did not need us or our help during political rallies and other official ANC events. I knew that when he went to do his ANC work, I needed to allow his PA in Luthuli House, Sibongile Mahlangu, to take over. If, for some reason, we had to be at an ANC event, it would be only because there was some government work that the DG, the Reverend Chikane, needed us to complete and it would require that we interacted with the president to get it done. None of us would be seen to be doing ANC work.

During the World Conference Against Racism in Durban in 2001, Oom Gov, his father, passed away. The conference was due to adopt resolutions on the Friday night. We were supposed to leave for Port Elizabeth to attend the night vigil and, because he was the eldest son of Oom Gov, he had to be at home. I approached him and told him that we needed to leave. He asked me if I could give him an hour; he was hoping that by then the resolutions would have been passed. I agreed, but the meeting was not getting any closer to finalising the resolution. An hour later, I went back and looked at him with my usual bullying eyes and, once again, he asked for an hour to which I agreed. The third time I walked into the room, he looked at me with intimidating eyes, but I said, 'We are leaving now, resolution or no resolution, because Mrs Mbeki has called wanting to know when we are leaving Durban.' He said, 'No, no, Chief, just leave Zanele alone. I called my mum and she said that it is okay if we come when we are done.' I exploded. I said, 'Chief, I am not asking you now. I am telling you that we are packing up and we are going.' I told him that the resolution would be taken regardless of whether we were in PE or in Durban and that the minister of foreign affairs would call him, but that there was no question: we were leaving because he was the eldest son and we had to respect our traditions as Africans. He looked at me and could see that I was dead serious. 'We are going; it's not negotiable any more,' I told him. He asked me to call Advocate Gumbi so that she could intervene and she also tried to get an extra hour, but I refused and we all left immediately. I had to put my foot down. As an African, and in support of Mrs Zanele Mbeki, I understood the importance of his being home during the vigil. Hence I decided to do what I had been employed to do: to run his life.

TAU THEKISO

I never had an opportunity to meet Thabo Mbeki when I was in exile, but I had the perception that he had no clue about what was happening in the military camps. In 1993 I was appointed to the security team of the then chairperson of the African National Congress (ANC) and that was when I came to know the man we call Chief. During this time, ANC leaders were engaged in CODESA (Convention for a Democratic South Africa) talks and we would spend long days at Luthuli House. The seventh-floor boardroom was turned into our mini bedroom due to late nights and early mornings.

Working with President Thabo Mbeki was priceless; one has good memories that cannot be erased. I remember that during one of the election campaigns, we had quite a hectic day and were driving to Hillbrow for an election rally. I was sitting in the main car and referred to as number one bodyguard at that moment. As we were driving, the president asked me to give him ideas on what he should tell the potential voters as he wanted fresh ideas. I took the opportunity to tell him about the views of the people on the ground and what they expected from their government. When the president took to the stage, he said exactly what we had discussed in the car and I was thrilled to hear positive responses from the crowd. This to me proved that indeed he was serious about ensuring that the ANC must always be people centred and it was never about him as an individual.

At one of the rallies in Msinga, KwaZulu-Natal, a community member complained about the cellphone network coverage in the area. I went

outside and called Mr Mandla Mthembu from Vodacom and he promised
to send technicians. While we were still inside the tent, a Vodacom van went
past the venue to install a signal booster. During a local radio interview that
same evening, one of the callers thanked the president for the signal and
I was surprised when I received a thank-you call from the president the
following day around 23h00. He even mentioned the initiative made by
the security in parliament. That was just TM for you; he always gave credit
where it was due.

During the election campaign of 2004, a certain lady asked the president
for money, and the president turned around and asked, 'Chief, do you have
any money to give to the lady because I only have dollars in my pocket.'
We laughed because we knew the president never carried any money, thus
he could not have had any dollars.

After the elections the president slaughtered a cow for us as a thank-you
gesture. During the celebrations my team finished the 'hot stuff' within the
first hour. I announced that the whisky was finished and that they should
drink beer. The president heard me and offered money for more whisky
and I was very surprised when he gave me R10 000 instead of R1 300. It
was a feast.

One evening in early 2000 President Mbeki was invited to attend a
National African Chamber of Commerce (NAFCOC) dinner and he was
not keen to go. He called me and told me he was not in the mood to attend.
I asked him why, and he said that when he attended this function every year
he sat at the same table with the same people having the same discussions.
He pleaded with me to come up with any excuse for him not to attend.
I contacted the organisers and gave a story why the president could not
attend. The organisers were not happy at all. I went back to the president
and suggested that he should attend. We were about to leave the house
when we received a call that the power at the venue had gone off and it
was such a blessing. Although we had nothing to do with the power failure,
we took the credit because it worked for the president as the function had
to be cancelled. The president then asked us: 'Chief, tell me, did you have
anything to do with this power cut?' We all laughed.

Not once did I ever hear the president raise his voice at his staff. He
always felt immensely guilty when we finished work late because of his

official commitments. He is the real Chief. He is a father to many of us and to us he will always be the president. President Mbeki trusted us to do our work and showed us respect, which made it really easy to work with him. I recall one day driving from Pretoria to Johannesburg and just as we got to the Woodmead area, we discovered that the car he was in (the main car), had a flat tyre. Normally, in such a situation, we would make contingency plans and transfer him to another car so that he could proceed. But typical of President Mbeki's humble nature, he refused to do that and instead he rolled up his sleeves and chose to stay and assist us in fixing the tyre.

The other lesson we learned working with him was that there was no hurry, even though everybody will tell you that he is militant with time and dislikes keeping people waiting. But on the road, he insisted that we never drove above the speed limit to the extent of disrupting other drivers on the roads, which is why we always set off early; he would rather arrive earlier than late. There were times when we might have been forced to use some speed, but generally the instruction was to weave through the traffic with as little 'siren noise' as possible.

When we went to imbizos (community meetings), we knew that the president was genuine when he said that those meetings were for the communities and therefore he did not want to make a grand entrance. He wanted to be part of the community so that everyone could talk openly and interact with him. So in our planning for the imbizos, we had to make sure that as far as possible the president's security detail blended in with the community.

President Mbeki respected security functions and never interfered with any decisions taken by security. This is a man who never chose which vehicle or aircraft he was transported in. During the Sudan talks, we had to travel to Kenya for a signing ceremony. We activated an advance team from Pretoria at short notice and the team did its work as expected. The team of ministers and protocol briefed the president on arrangements and we briefed the chief of protocol on security matters. We then learned that the ministers of foreign affairs and defence wanted the president to fly with the president of Sudan in his aircraft.

We quickly briefed the chief of protocol and legal adviser Advocate Mojanku Gumbi on the risks and implications. When the ministers suggested to the president that he should fly in the Sudanese aircraft he asked, what is security saying? Advocate Gumbi told the president that security objected to the suggestion and the president told the ministers to respect security as they were the experts in the field.

I learned how President Mbeki loved the ANC. During the National General Council (NGC) meeting at Pretoria University in 2005, the president went home to rest after some heated debate and intense hostility towards him. When we reached home I asked the president to write about the supposed role of the president in the appointment of ministers, mayors and councillors. My request was prompted by the level of an acrimonious debate where the president of the ANC was blamed for everything that went wrong – even though the organisation had a full-time secretary general who was supposed to address some of the issues affecting the effective functioning of the ruling party. The president responded by saying that there was no need for him to write about that because every member of the ANC knew about the process and the role of the president. This was a man who maintained principles as opposed to being a populist.

In honour of his legacy, I named my son after him and I hope that Mvuyelwa will follow his namesake's teachings, principles and values and advance the agenda of the poor in the African continent.

MIRANDA STRYDOM

❧

While working as a journalist I can state upfront, without hesitation, that any journalist who was looking for glitz and glamour in covering President Mbeki was sorely mistaken. In fact, he was a journalist's worst nightmare. He was not fond of giving sound bites for the sake of it, nor was he concerned with public relations appearances in the media. You could never second-guess him because you were bound to get it wrong especially if you did not research issues well and were too lazy to read widely. To convey his message correctly required a great deal of reading, critical analysis and questioning. Having said that, though, if he detected that you were genuinely out of your depth, Mbeki had a way of explaining issues in such a way that you got the background story. Perhaps this had to do with the fact that he headed the African National Congress's (ANC's) Department of Information and Publicity (DIP) in exile and therefore knew how the minds of journalists worked and how the media functioned.

More challenging was working through President Mbeki's speeches, sometimes littered with poetry but within that would be the essence of the message he was trying to convey. Journalists' failure to think deeply in order to understand and grasp the underlying message would undoubtedly lead to conveying a half-baked story to the public and result in flawed interpretations by commentators and analysts of what the president had said. The poem 'The Fool' that he cited in what journalists may call an infamous speech in the year 2000 is one I cannot forget because I have often wondered whether we would have understood him better had he not used

400

that poem to ask the important question that became controversial almost throughout his entire term as president of the Republic of South Africa. I am also of the view that some intellectually inclined citizens might have understood his message and therefore understood why he chose to use this particular poem to emphasise his point. But I will elaborate on the 'The Fool' later in the section on the HIV and AIDS controversy.

The process of interpreting, simplifying and condensing President Mbeki's speeches to digestible sound bites for the public often caused many headaches for journalists and the media fraternity; it was not an easy task, especially if you had a minute and a half to try to explain this very complex mind. Many journalists will attest to this and some would complain that he was too 'abstract'. I am reminded of the day we had gone to the launch of Southern Africa's Largest Telescope (SALT). Because we had been on the road for days and did not get sufficient time to read up on SALT, we really battled. The president spoke about the gamma rays and quasars and the scientific world of astronomy. At the end of his speech, my colleague Dumisani and I looked at each other, quite defeated. Dumisani asked, 'Sisi, what has the president just said?' We were not sure how we were going to simplify this into a minute and a half news story for the SABC. We ran around asking the academic experts who were readily available to help us to put it into simple, everyday English language. My heart went out to the editors who had to translate this story into the various languages.

Long before I was assigned by my bosses at the South African Broadcasting Corporation (SABC) to cover the presidency, I was among the journalists who sided with those who blasted Deputy President Mbeki for the Growth, Employment and Redistribution Strategy (GEAR). I had been working as an economics reporter at the time and was also working closely with the labour movement. Convinced as we were at the time that GEAR was wrong, no amount of explaining from the side of the government swayed us about the correctness of this strategy and so to me, like some of the journalists then, Mbeki was going to be problematic for the country. Of course, I am now embarrassed about the arguments that I advanced in my articles at the time; they were full of nonsensical ramblings because I did not understand then that we had inherited a bankrupt country from the apartheid regime.

During the 1999 election campaign period, I was assigned to cover him as he crisscrossed the country and this was essentially the beginning of my journey in Mbeki's 'shadow'. For weeks, he delivered a consistent message. He lamented the slow pace of delivery, tore into lazy councillors and public servants and decried his very own ANC comrades whom he accused of abusing their ANC membership for their own personal gains. His most popular phrase at the time was, 'there are careerists in our movement. Some among us use our ANC membership for our personal gains.' For us as journalists, these were 'juicy' sound bites and, looking back, I am not sure whether many of us understood the depth of Mbeki's concern in terms of corruption and the abuse of political power for economic gain by well-connected members of the ruling party. Little did we know at the time that President Mbeki was already detecting very deep levels of corruption starting to affect his beloved ANC, and that possibly his utterances and public stance would later lead to his early exit from office.

Those of us who covered the presidency during Mbeki's time soon became conscious that it was never going to be easy. In many ways President Mbeki carried a very heavy burden. He began his term of office with the popular question in both local and international media of whether he could fit President Mandela's 'very big shoes'. This question was posed regardless of the fact that the then Deputy President Mbeki controlled the day-to-day business of the government during Mandela's presidency – a point publicly corroborated by Mandela himself – and Mbeki ended his term in government under circumstances that were not expected.

President Mbeki came into office with his own leadership style after journalists and the media had become used to Mandela's leadership. At some point Parks Mankahlana, who was Mbeki's spokesperson at the time, informed me that after one of the first few press conferences after Mbeki became president of South Africa, he wanted to know from him 'where are the black journalists?' As we understood it, it was not that Mbeki did not want the white journalists to cover the presidency; he was concerned and probably refused to believe that black journalists were not capable of covering the work of the presidency. Therefore it was not a coincidence that an increasing number of black journalists, myself included, were assigned to cover his presidency together with our white counterparts.

It was not going to take us long to learn that what keeps Mbeki awake at night is what would happen if 'the dream is deferred'. Even as he took the oath of office, it was clear that his African Renaissance agenda would remain the mainstay of his presidency. And these remained the overarching objectives of his term: accelerated service delivery with a focused approach on economic growth and the African agenda. He explained to the crowds gathered at the Union Buildings for his inauguration, 'We trust that what we will do will not only better our own condition as a people, but will also make a contribution, however small, to the success of Africa's Renaissance, towards the identification of the century ahead of us as the African Century.' Even before he could say 'so help me God' Mbeki was involved in conflict prevention and peace efforts in the Democratic Republic of Congo (DRC). Barely a few days after being installed as the president of the Republic of South Africa, we set off to Zambia where the warring factions in the DRC conflict were locked in tough negotiations to cease the fire that had drawn in the armies of several African countries. On arrival in Zambia, the parties gathered at the Mulungushi Conference Centre were close to signing the Lusaka Ceasefire Agreement, but the situation in the DRC was still tense and the warring factions were holding stubbornly to their positions in last-minute horse-trading and Mbeki was working tirelessly behind the scenes.

For us as journalists camped out at the hotel in Lusaka, any hopes of getting a sound bite from the newly installed president of South Africa were but a pipe dream. I was soon to learn that our new president was not in the habit of speaking out of turn to journalists, especially where he thought that the peace process would be jeopardised. This was to be the lesson that I would learn about his approach to mediation going forward: no matter how hard you tried, President Mbeki held firm to his principle that his mediation would never be conducted via the media and as journalists we had to live with it. He profoundly respected and protected the parties he was negotiating with and operated on a need-to-know basis. So we were not able to send 'cooked' sound bites to our media houses regardless of tight deadlines and schedules. Despite the Lusaka Ceasefire Agreement, the political problems in the DRC festered, a point I will return to later.

President Mbeki was clear in his mind that without peace in Africa, there was very little hope of achieving the renaissance of the continent. Even as we received news of the passing of Tanzanian President Julius Nyerere only four months into Mbeki's presidency, it became clear that the new generation of African leaders that was emerging understood the responsibility that the founding fathers of the Organisation of African Unity (OAU) had placed on them. Speaking during Mwalimu Nyerere's memorial in October 1999, President Mbeki made a solemn promise that, 'Because of what you [Nyerere] have done: Africa shall be at peace! Africa will prosper! No longer will her children be the despised of the earth!' Several journalists and a fairly large South African government delegation, led by President Mbeki, set off during the early hours of the morning of Mwalimu Nyerere's funeral. As the plane came in to land in Tanzania, dark clouds hung over the stadium where Mwalimu's body lay. It was a very poignant moment in Africa's history and it struck me that the baton had now been handed to President Mbeki and his generation of leaders. And as I watched President Mbeki going to pay his last respects to Mwalimu, his body language told a story of a son who had lost his father. He walked with his shoulders drooped almost as if he was carrying something heavy on them and perhaps he was; the African Renaissance vision that Nyerere had earlier endorsed and placed on his shoulders.

It was Mbeki's generation that would proclaim the twenty-first century as the 'African Century', and so began another chapter in Africa's history. As we ushered in the new millennium, there was a buzz in the air about Africa's Renaissance. President Mbeki and some of his colleagues unveiled the New Partnership for Africa's Development (NEPAD), the continent's economic recovery blueprint. As journalists we were confused about this plan that had gone through several name changes: first it was the Millennium Africa Plan (MAP), we then heard that Senegalese President Abdoulaye Wade had his own plan called the Omega Plan, then after that we were told that it was called the New Africa Initiative (NAI), until they finally settled for NEPAD. I think that many of us saw this as some grand, ambitious plan, and because as Africans we were conditioned to think that Africa was beyond repair, it was not a story that grabbed many journalists and media houses at first.

By the year 2000, President Mbeki was already mobilising the continent and we travelled to various countries where he delivered one address after another to universities, diplomats, business and many other communities. The theme remained the same: the African agenda. By the time NEPAD was adopted in Abuja in 2001, the roadshow moved into full gear. We travelled the length and breadth of the globe, at times living out of our suit-cases for long periods of time. Because our SABC crew flew commercially, travel was very difficult at the time, especially on the African continent; direct flights to most countries were almost non-existent. Sometimes, we literally had to fly into Europe first to connect to other African countries. I recall travelling to Kananaskis, Canada, during a G8 summit where the Africa Action Plan was adopted. This was seen as a major boost for NEPAD because it detailed plans to support the African continent. But as is usually the case during G8 summits, there were large groups of protesters protest-ing around different issues: debt relief, climate change, free trade. Among these many groups was one that was supposedly an 'anti-NEPAD' group.

At the end of the G8 summit, Bheki Khumalo, the presidential spokes-person at the time, organised a press conference at the hotel. Besides the international media, there could have been around three or four other South African journalists. I think that the last question from one of the journalists was what was Mbeki's reaction to the people who felt that NEPAD was a 'neo-liberal' document. Well, this press conference turned into a university lecture. Mbeki took us step by step to make sure that the journalists left the 'lecture room' with a full understanding. Our team was under severe dead-line pressures but Mbeki took his time delivering the lecture and was not concerned about our plight. He explained to us the impact of debt relief; he went through the need for infrastructure development in the African con-tinent and the need for better education, health, sanitation, water etc. He explained the kind of resources that the continent possessed and asked why they could not be used to develop the African continent and whether we thought that it was unreasonable for African leaders to demand fair global trade terms. He explained how many countries got into debt through the Structural Adjustment Programmes developed by both the International Monetary Fund (IMF) and the World Bank and how African countries needed to be freed from these debt traps. For people like me, it was not new because we had been listening to President Mbeki for months on end and all we wanted was to run out to file. But you could see that Mbeki had the other journalists in the 'lecture room' thinking hard.

So we gave up worrying about our deadline and sat through the lecture. It seemed that Mbeki was not going to let us go until we fully understood.

It was as if he was pleading with the media to understand that Africa is not the 'hopeless' continent that some described it as. He spoke like his life depended on our understanding of this issue. It was among the few times that I had seen Mbeki in that mood. I got a sense that perhaps he temporarily lost his patience with the same recycled negative narrative and stereotypes about the African continent. After what seemed like eternity, equally surprised by this, Bheki Khumalo then turned to him and said, 'Phew, Mr President, I have never heard you speak like this,' and with that he closed the press conference. This was when I understood that his African Renaissance vision was not just a slogan or dream. If I was going to report on this president, I should have known that I was going to eat, sleep and drink the African Renaissance.

As we travelled from one G8 summit to another – Kananaskis (Canada), Evian (France), Heiligendamm (Germany), St Petersburg (Russia), Gleneagles (UK), Sapporo (Japan) – we came to understand clearly Africa's position in the global economy. We could easily summarise it even in our sleep. But some commentators and analysts were quick to dismiss NEPAD. The popular narrative was that, after all, Africans were used to going cap in hand to beg for money from Western countries. Others pointed out that developed countries were suffering from what they called 'donor fatigue'. These comments did not deter President Mbeki and his colleagues. As far as they were concerned, the time had come for Africans to determine their own future. They were not begging for donor funding or money from Western countries. Africa was determined to show the rest of the world that it was taking steps to transform itself and that was how the African Peer Review Mechanism (APRM) was developed. But the African leaders went beyond that to pay particular attention to the conflicts on the continent. At the time, several conflicts were raging and these were linked to geopolitics and hence the involvement of some powerful Western countries that benefited. President Mbeki and his colleagues adopted the approach that it was important to engage the powerful nations as Africa sought to transform itself.

I recall, for example, when George W. Bush was announced winner of the 2000 US presidential elections. We had to stop over at the Embraer aircraft manufacturers in Brasília with a South African business delegation. We were en route to Florianópolis to attend a Mercosur Summit. During the luncheon that was co-hosted by Embraer and Mercedes-Benz, Mbeki stepped out to make a phone call to Bush to congratulate him. But the central message of the phone call was to ask Bush, as the leader of the most powerful nation in the world, not to forget that he had a responsibility towards the African continent.

By this time, African leaders were preparing to transform the OAU into the African Union (AU). For all intents and purposes, the AU launch ceremony, which was held in Durban in 2002, signified a major turning point in Africa's history. President Mbeki was the first chairperson of the newly established African Union and many saw this as Mbeki's moment to truly embed the vision of the African Renaissance in the minds of the African masses and to send a clear message to the rest of the world that indeed Africa's time had come. Also, we had just returned from the G8 summit in Kananaskis a few days earlier where the Africa Action Plan was adopted and so the mood was one of hope.

It was during these interactions with the developed north and powerful Western countries that one really got to understand that President Mbeki detested the notion that Africans were incapable of thinking or doing things for themselves. Often, during our interviews with him, we picked up a deep level of agitation where he felt African intelligence was being held in contempt. Whether he was sitting in Buckingham Palace with Her Majesty in London, in the Oval Office with President George Bush in Washington DC or in the midst of policy makers in the European Union in Brussels, Mbeki maintained a consistent message about an Africa on the rise. He loathed any attempts by Western powers to talk down to Africans. He preached the gospel that Africa was no longer interested in a 'donor/recipient' or 'paternalistic' relationship with the north, and constantly hammered home the demand for fair trade, debt cancellation and market access and really this was what NEPAD was about and one may ask the critics, what is neo-liberal about this essential demand? To elaborate my point, President Mbeki's speech to the European Parliament in November 2004 stands out in my mind. I recall the silence in the house as he delivered this speech in his usual calm way, but the message was powerful as he reminded the lawmakers about their own EU Regional Policy in an effort to get them to understand NEPAD. One European MP commented afterwards,

'That was one hell of a speech but it embarrasses us as Europeans.'

At the same time that there was this great push to re-engineer the relationship with the developed north into a partnership of equals, President Mbeki and his colleagues simultaneously sought to restructure relations with countries of the south, which could be seen as re-energising the South-South Cooperation. Mbeki and his colleagues used platforms in countries like Cuba, Chile, Brazil, China, India and many others to mobilise the global south towards this common vision. This was also seen in the formation of the IBSA (India, Brazil, South Africa) Dialogue Forum in 2003. At some point the G8 was even talking about the possibility of expanding itself to become the G13 to include China, South Africa, Brazil, Mexico and India. There was a point where Presidents Hu Jintao, Lula da Silva, Prime Minister Manmohan Singh, President Felipe Calderón and President Mbeki (the G5) would be formally invited to attend the G8 summits and would take this opportunity to have their own side meetings.

After several attempts by the African leaders to get the Congolese into a dialogue, South Africa was officially tasked by the AU with hosting the Inter Congolese Dialogue in 2002 in what became known as the Sun City talks, where parties had gathered to hammer out a new path for peace in their war-torn country. The dynamics of what went on at Sun City still need to be fully chronicled in a book; suffice to say that this was one story that made me understand Mbeki's methodology in mediation and conflict prevention. At times, when all hope was lost, President Mbeki would be the person to bring back some level of sanity to the situation. On its own, this took an incredible amount of endurance, the patience of a saint and tolerance, which many of us could not fathom. So many times we journalists would hear such comments as, 'These people do not want peace; Mbeki should leave them to kill one another.' At this point, it would only be the mediator and his team that would know the 'real' story behind the scenes and none would speak to us, the media, unless it was absolutely necessary. Most of the time, it was on a need-to-know basis.

When the Congolese finally reached an agreement on 16 December 2002, after months of laborious negotiations, it was a moment that will for ever remain etched in my mind. Mahlamba Ndlopfu burst into ululation as the women of Congo danced and cried from sheer joy in the early hours of the morning. By some strange coincidence, this also happened to be on the day that South Africa was celebrating Reconciliation Day. This moment cannot be fully described in words. And once the transitional government had been installed and the country finally held elections, President Mbeki attended President Joseph Kabila's inauguration in 2006. We had been in Kinshasa throughout the rerun of the presidential elections and the fighting that broke out during that period. By the time President Mbeki arrived, we could say that we had got swept into the euphoria because the DRC had not held an election in almost four decades and the Congolese were feeling hopeful. We had also interviewed people like Nzanga Mobutu and Joseph Kabila and both of them sent out messages of hope. Mobutu's point was that they were painfully aware of the history of their fathers (Mobutu Sese Seko and Laurent Kabila) and that as the younger generation they were pre-pared to fight to create a new Congo. People like François Lumumba, the son of Patrice Lumumba, had also been part of the dialogues and processes towards this new Congo. So no one at the time could help but feel a sense of excitement about the developments in that country.

President Mbeki was on his way to Washington to meet President George Bush. We excitedly settled down to conduct an interview with him. I wanted to know how he felt after having worked for almost a decade on the DRC conflict. Of course my mind had gone back to those early years when President Mandela tried to get Laurent Kabila and Mobutu Sese Seko to talk on the *Outeniqua* in 1997, the 1999 Lusaka ceasefire talks, the Sun City talks and the back and forth between South Africa and Kinshasa. I am not sure whether I expected him to share in the excitement, but as only President Mbeki can do, his answer sobered us up. He basically said that the real work was yet to begin and that there was a need to work harder to make sure that the peace did not unravel. He also told us as journalists that among the issues that he was going to discuss with Bush was the need for further support for the DRC. But all this was said in that 'business as usual tone', no hint of celebration.

Another conflict had erupted two years prior in Côte d'Ivoire, that is, in 2004. The media reports we were receiving suggested that the French army had opened fire in retaliation for the gunning down of nine French soldiers by the Ivorian military. But when we arrived in Abidjan the story was com-pletely different from what we had read in the media. Our interactions with university students and civil society groups awakened us to a far deeper problem in that country. We managed to lay our hands on footage that showed unarmed youths being gunned down by French troops in front of Hotel Ivoire. For South Africans, the pictures were reminiscent of the 1976 student uprisings and we said as much in our reports. Also, thousands of Ivorians had taken to the streets to form a human shield around President Laurent Gbagbo's residence to protect him from what they believed was an attempted coup, led by the French. It was President Mbeki who was asked by the AU to go in to mediate.

The French military had sealed off the airport in Abidjan but as the South Africans troops arrived, and much to the fury of Paris, they were compelled to clear the way. This was one time one fully appreciated the South African National Defence Force because when those military vehicles drove through Abidjan, the French troops retreated within minutes to their bases. The Ivorian people jubilantly welcomed the South Africans. As journalists, we travelled in and out of Côte d'Ivoire for weeks thereafter. At some point we flew into the rebel-held territory of Bouaké. Some of the South African officials expressed nervousness about this particular trip to Bouaké because this area was known to possess huge supplies of arms and they feared that this was putting President Mbeki's life in danger. But none, including the French, would dare stop Mbeki, who was determined to go on a fact-finding mission. When we landed in Bouaké, many of us did not expect what we found there. At times, being a television reporter helps because when you cannot find the words to describe a situation, you allow the pictures to speak for themselves. I had only ever seen such a massive outpouring of people onto the streets when Madiba was released from prison in 1990. Once we had transmitted these visuals, we received numerous calls from South Africa from people who could not believe what they had seen on television. Bouaké came to a standstill as people poured onto the streets; they hung from trees and rooftops all the way from the airport to the hotel. Banners with 'President Mbeki our saviour' were visible all along the way. I recall that I was pushed into Deputy Foreign Affairs Minister Aziz Pahad's car to get us through the crowds; we would have completely missed the story had we tried to make our own way to the hotel. The short trip to the hotel was a nightmare as we tried to navigate through the massive crowds of people hoping to catch a glimpse of President Mbeki.

At the hotel, Mbeki sat through hours of discussion as he listened patiently to the views of the people. Fully armed with this new information, we set off back to Abidjan, and this was another mission. The entire SA delegation had to be airlifted from the hotel because the crowds of people had swelled in numbers and to get through them was near impossible. At the end of all the back and forth, the Ivorians eventually signed the Pretoria and later the Ouagadougou Agreements. To this day, I believe that the French never saw it coming.

In 2003, try as we may, our SABC crew could not get a flight into Liberia. Former Liberian President Charles Taylor had stepped down and handed over to his vice-president, Moses Blah. President Mbeki, Mozambican President Joaquim Chissano, Togolese Prime Minister Koffi Sama and Ghana's President John Kufuor were going to attend the handover ceremony. As we understood it, African leaders, particularly President Obasanjo, had been negotiating with Taylor to step down. Since we could not get there, our only option was to source material from media houses that had made it into Monrovia. It was pouring with rain in Liberia as President Mbeki led Charles Taylor onto the plane that was to take him into exile. President Obasanjo had made his plane available for Taylor's exit. The long and the short is that this action finally paved the way for the installation of Africa's very first woman president, Ellen Johnson Sirleaf, a few years later. Even as we attended her inauguration in 2006, the images of the day that Taylor was escorted out of the country remained vivid in our minds.

Mbeki, together with leaders such as the then Nigerian President Olusegun Obasanjo, Ghana's President John Kufuor and others, were often deployed to the hotspots. For example, in 2001, the Southern African Development Community (SADC) Task Force on Developments in Zimbabwe met in Harare. The late war veterans' leader Chenjerai 'Hitler' Hunzvi, who had become the bugbear of the West, Britain in particular, also attended the meeting. Morgan Tsvangirai and others were also present. This was about the time when the tensions over the land issue had erupted and for weeks while I was deployed in Zimbabwe we were chasing stories of war veterans pushing into white-owned farms and reporting on the 'land grabs', as they had become known in the media.

But as it turned out, this was also the day of the 9/11 attacks in the US and so the world's attention shifted. The meeting in Harare continued, but Zimbabwe slid off the media radar for a few weeks. By the time we got to the Commonwealth Heads of State and Government Summit that took place in Coolum in Queensland, Australia, in 2002, no other issue was as hot as the Zimbabwean story. At every turn, the main topic was about Zimbabwe and all other issues that came out of that particular meeting barely made it into the news. It was after that meeting that Zimbabwe was suspended from the Commonwealth. A troika made up of Presidents Olusegun Obasanjo, Thabo Mbeki and Prime Minister John Howard was tasked with handling the Zimbabwe issue. But the divisions over Zimbabwe were seen even in the media, with one British journalist reporting after the troika was announced, 'two blacks, one white', and continuing with something like 'it is a reflection of the racial divisions within the Commonwealth'. The South African media had an opportunity to interview President Mbeki in Brisbane where he had gone to address business people. We asked him about his views on this 'two blacks, one white' issue. He said: 'It is unfortunate. I think that the suggestion that there is a racial divide is wrong.' He went on to say that the journalist's statement suggested that 'the blacks on the one side approve of violence and land grabs in Zimbabwe etc. It is unfortunate and wrong.' He explained that the way that the troika was constituted was to have President Mbeki as the outgoing chair, John Howard as the chair at the time when the meeting was convened and Obasanjo as the incoming chair. I narrate this story to demonstrate the intensity of the feelings towards Zimbabwe at the time extending to journalists who were taking sides.

Meanwhile, President Mbeki, as the leader of the 'African powerhouse' was being forced from all sides to remove President Robert Mugabe. Suggestions of military intervention and regime change were seen as Mbeki's only solution. The more he refused to succumb to these options, the more pressure mounted. Never had an African leader been under such enormous pressure to remove another – to effect regime change on behalf of the British. And this campaign was unrelenting over many years. This was the beginning of the most strenuous years of reporting on a president who was loathed by those who felt he was not taking the bait. Added to that was his so-called AIDS denialism. Nothing could have prepared us for the difficulties that came with covering such a head of state.

His colleagues and people close to him say that President Mbeki is a workaholic. I can confirm this. Holidays and long weekends often just passed us by because they did not exist for journalists assigned to cover the presidency. I can say without fear of contradiction that those who accused him of being a 'jet-set president' were misinformed and had very little knowledge about the magnitude of the work on his plate.

One story I recall was when we had to go to Sudan in 2004. Because our crew often travelled in advance, we had to leave on the day after Christmas. And so while we were spending Christmas day with our families, we were also packing to leave for Sudan the next day. A series of meetings was to be held in Khartoum and at some point we were to travel to Darfur because Mbeki needed a deeper understanding of that conflict. We all came back humbled by what we had seen. We did not dare complain about having missed the Christmas holidays with our families. Big men were driven to tears after witnessing the painful existence of the people in Darfur.

We returned to the hotel in Khartoum and, if my memory serves me well, I think that Mbeki went to Naivasha in Kenya to participate in the signing of part of the Comprehensive Peace Agreement, which was on 31 December 2004, New Year's Eve. Obviously our team could not go to Kenya because Mbeki was travelling in the presidential plane and it was impossible for us to try to get a commercial flight at that time of year and be back for the next engagement in Khartoum. So we remained behind. Among the people there was Minister Mosiuoa Lekota, who was the minister of defence. The hotel did not have a bar where we could sit and relax over a drink, other than soft drinks, while we waited for the president and his delegation to return. So we spent the evening imagining, with envy, what people in South Africa might be doing. I could hear Minister Lekota complaining, 'No, man, this is New Year's Eve; we could be at home marinating the meat for a braai and cooling the beers, and we are sitting here – no braai, no cold beers,' and everyone was rolling with laughter.

When Mbeki finally arrived after midnight we were waiting in the lobby to see if we could get a short interview about the signing ceremony so that we could file for the morning news bulletins. As he got out of the car we could see that he was exhausted and all he said was, 'Happy New Year, Chiefs,' and when we asked for an interview, all he could say was, 'Please, go and sleep, let's talk in the morning,' and off he went to his room. We hardly slept because we had to be up very early to prepare for the day's events. Such was Mbeki's work ethic; it did not matter whether it was holiday time or not, Christmas, New Year or whatever, work had to be done on behalf of the people of the African continent.

We also had to learn to think on our feet because of the fast pace at which he moved. For example, we once had to go to Côte d'Ivoire straight from another assignment. When we arrived in Abidjan, we were informed that President Mbeki was going to Yamoussoukro, which was a quite a distance from Abidjan. We decided that since our hotel was already paid for and it was too late to phone the SABC office in South Africa to ask them to book us a hotel in Yamoussoukro, we would sleep in Abidjan, wake up early and ask the driver we had hired to take us to Yamoussoukro, which was what happened. Because of the situation in Côte d'Ivoire at the time, the presidential protection unit had brought in cars from South Africa on an Ilyushin cargo aircraft.

When we had filed our story and were preparing to return to Abidjan, we were told that President Mbeki was urgently needed in Kinshasa; there were complications between Jean-Pierre Bemba and Joseph Kabila. We were told that if we needed a lift and were prepared to get onto the Ilyushin aircraft with the vehicles, we could proceed to the next assignment in the DRC. The problem was that our luggage was at the hotel in Abidjan and the Ilyushin aircraft was leaving Yamoussoukro the following afternoon. We called our driver, gave him money to settle our bills and asked him to collect our bags from Abidjan. We loaded ourselves into the Ilyushin aircraft, which meant spending the night sitting on the floor of the aircraft because it was used only to transport equipment and did not have seats or any form of comfort.

We arrived in Kinshasa in the early hours of the next morning, freshened up and got to work immediately. Mbeki spent the entire day in different meetings and finished late that evening. As soon as his plane had taken off, we packed up and got back into the Ilyushin aircraft and arrived home in South Africa as part of the cargo. President Mbeki's mediation work was very unpredictable; anything could happen at any time. As journalists we had to learn to sleep with one eye open.

As Mbeki was trying to transform the different sectors of South African society, he also tried to do the same with the media. Pre-1994, very few black journalists were found in newsrooms, let alone black female journalists. At some point, a number of us would meet regularly at our favourite watering holes either in Yeoville or Newtown to discuss the formation of the Black Journalists Group – we called it the BJG, but then the Forum for Black Journalists (FBJ) was formally established. The objective of this forum was to find ways to address the challenges that black journalists were facing in newsrooms: many were being thrown in the deep end with very little training or support. They felt marginalised and there was a sense that they were just filling the 'quotas'. It was Deputy President Thabo Mbeki who addressed us when we launched the FBJ in 1997. This was only three years into our democracy when race relations in the new nation were still in a very delicate and sensitive state. Among the things the deputy president said to us was, 'We have the responsibility to tell the people the truth. Part of that truth is that we are set on the path towards the transformation of our country. Deviation from that path would constitute a betrayal of the interests and aspirations of all our people, both black and white.' In truth, transforming the newsrooms was never going to be an easy task for those in leadership positions in the media at the time.

As time went by, a decision was taken between the South African National Editors' Forum (SANEF) and government during a meeting at Sun City in 2001 that a presidential press corps be established. Essentially this would be no different to the White House, Downing Street or even what is known as the Royal Correspondents who report on the British royal family. The problem came when it was time to conduct security clearance. The media was not happy about the extent of the vetting that would be required. To put this into context, in other countries a certain level of security checks is done – I guess to avoid risky situations like the one shown in the movie *Air Force One* where guys posing as journalists hijack the American president's plane. All the same, we launched the presidential press corps in 2003 after the various media houses had nominated the people that would be on this team. Mbeki had wanted it to work and said, 'There is no reason why it [the Presidential Press Corps] shouldn't [work]. It will depend entirely on all of us.' And because Mbeki had worked in the international media space for decades while he was head of the ANC's DIP, he would have had a deep understanding of the power of some of the international media houses. By going along with the idea of forming a South African presidential press corps, he saw it not only as an opportunity for journalists to be empowered in this space, but also that the information that the public was consuming was coming from our own South African journalists.

Unfortunately, I was not privy to what might have happened to cause the presidential press corps to collapse.

The collapse of the presidential press corps posed an interesting dynamic when we were out of the country as journalists. For example, if we were at a G8, we would watch as the planes of the various leaders landed. Almost all of them had their press corps accompanying the delegation. In fact, on Air Force One there was always a vehicle specifically assigned to the White House correspondents. The invited leaders such as Presidents Obasanjo, Hu Jintao and Prime Minister Manmohan Singh would also arrive with their press corps. Then would come Mbeki with just his officials and security and that was it. I often wished that the press corps had worked because I felt that the industry would have been far more enriched with the incredible information and experiences of learning about the dynamics between the various countries at an international level. On the few occasions when there would be more South African journalists on an assignment, we would actually get excited because then we knew that at least the public would get fed first-hand information from more of us rather than just from the SABC, and thus South African editors would not have to rely only on the international media angles.

The result was that there was the danger of media houses falling back into the old tradition of relying heavily on the international mainstream media for their sources of information. The disadvantage we had as the SABC press corps was that reliance on the mainstream international media often made it difficult for us to report on what we saw on the ground if it did not conform to those angles. For example, after one of the SADC summits, leaders came out to say, 'Land is important in the region since the majority of the people of SADC live in rural areas, and depend on agriculture for their livelihood.'[1] Within minutes, some media houses were running with the angle that 'Africa's leaders endorse Mugabe's land grab'. Try as we may to tell the editors that this was not what the leaders said, it was just not easy.

---

1 SADC Heads of State and Government Summit communiqué, Blantyre, Malawi, August 2001.

On this same day, it so happened that the rand had taken quite a knock. As we were waiting to do a live crossing with a radio station, I was listening in to the interview that was being done. The presenter pressed this economist to say that the rand had fallen because the markets were concerned about the position that African leaders had taken on Zimbabwe's land question. Unfortunately for the presenter, the economist said, 'Not at all. You may have been following what is happening; the rand's fall has to do with the emerging market uncertainty, which we have been following for a few days now.' This kind of situation happened regularly and it took a while before there was a mindset change. In hindsight, one wonders whether the collapse of the presidential press corps did not add to the perceptions of President Mbeki's being aloof, detached and unapproachable, but that is a debate for the media itself.

To come back to the poem I mentioned at the beginning. Of all the so-called 'controversial' issues that arose under Mbeki's watch, none could have been as difficult as the HIV and AIDS issue because it followed us as journalists, particularly in the UK and the US. At almost every press conference in those countries, Mbeki was asked about this issue. Naturally, we also tried to find out for ourselves why President Mbeki was taking an unpopular stance. Nothing made sense to us because there seemed to be no logic in the argument bandied about that Mbeki and his government were out to kill ordinary people. It made no sense that he would simply deny people the drugs for the sake of it when he could see that people were dying in numbers.

But the confusion deepened even further during the first meeting of the Presidential Advisory Panel on AIDS. Earlier I mentioned that I often wondered whether his use of poetry to advance his argument was not perhaps one of the reasons people lost his central message. We often wondered whether it was possible that the poem 'The Fool' could be interpreted to mean that Mbeki did not believe that HIV caused AIDS. Essentially, by citing the poem, Mbeki was telling the scientists that because he was not an expert on such matters, he needed their assistance to understand what the country was up against on the AIDS issue. He wanted to know what had caused the explosion of AIDS in sub-Saharan Africa and questioned whether there were other contributing factors to the exponential growth in cases of AIDS. If issues such as poverty, nutrition, sanitation etc. were exacerbating the situation, then it was clear that, as government, it had to respond differently rather than merely feed people with the drugs; it needed a more holistic approach.

What struck me as odd was that within ten minutes of his delivering his speech at the meeting of the Presidential Advisory Panel, 'analysts', 'AIDS activists' and others were already lined up to give their reactions to Mbeki's speech in back-to-back interviews. He came in for heavy criticism for saying 'HIV does not cause AIDS'. The problem was that we had listened attentively to his arguments, we had read and reread his speech because we were flabbergasted by the claims that the president could come out with such a statement. We went back to our archival material, which included previous comments and interviews with the president, and nowhere could we find this statement that journalists and so-called experts attributed to Mbeki. I say this in jest, but truly, I think as a journalist I became more the FOOL after the conference because I had never seen anything like it before with no one, including myself, questioning the factual inaccuracies of some of the statements attributed to President Mbeki. The only other time that I and many others in the media found ourselves FOOLS was when some international media houses went all out to convince us that Saddam Hussein was harbouring weapons of mass destruction, which have yet to be found, but that is another story to tell. The question that remains unanswered is whether the truth was and still is the casualty in this matter.

One day on a visit to the UK, Mbeki and Tony Blair held a press conference on the lawns of 10 Downing Street. And as was expected, a journalist asked, 'Mr Mbeki, how could you say that HIV does not cause AIDS, when it is evident that so many people are dying?' Mbeki very calmly replied, 'When did I say that?' The journalist stammered and stuttered until she was only able to say, 'Well, it is written everywhere'. But he probed her even further, asking, 'But be precise, if it is written everywhere, when did I say that?' And when she had no way of continuing with her line of questioning, Mbeki simply responded, 'I did not say that' and they moved on to the next question which, if I am not mistaken, was on Zimbabwe.

At some point, the press conferences had become predictable; we knew that AIDS and Zimbabwe were always the opening or closing questions.

And we were adept because if we wanted to ask any other questions, we waited until all the questions on AIDS and Zimbabwe were done so that we could ask whatever it was that we needed to ask. But everywhere he went, Mbeki found himself trying in every way to explain why he was asking critical questions. This issue of Mbeki and AIDS became so intense that one prominent international media house was even questioning his mental state.

But there were instances where Mbeki was admired for what some in the medical field saw as 'bravery'. In Dublin one year we met two medical students at our hotel and we got chatting. They asked, 'Why are you South Africans not hearing President Mbeki's arguments on the HIV and AIDS issue?' At first I thought it was just another of those discussions where we would be told how our president was killing people. But as I listened on, these two medical students told me that Mbeki was asking all the correct questions. I must admit that in the beginning I was a little lost because they went into some heavy medical analysis that included scientific terms that flew right over my head. But they went into detail to explain to me why they thought that Mbeki was correct in asking his questions. As journalists, we were in the privileged position that we were exposed to very different views on our travels, which gave us a little more insight into some of the dynamics. In the end, like everyone else, we chose to remain silent, probably out of fear of discussing this issue. But if we analyse the archives closely I think that I have a sense of which way history will judge Mbeki on his position on the HIV and AIDS issue.

There were times when we were out of the country when our office would ask us to try to get an interview with President Mbeki on issues that may have been topical back home. Back in 2005, we had to travel to Argentina and Chile and then we were going to Qatar where the G77 was being held. The media was running a story back home that the then national director of public prosecutions, Advocate Vusi Pikoli, would be on Mbeki's plane with him to Chile to brief him on the decision to charge Deputy President Jacob Zuma. Our SABC newsroom called us and gave us the heads up and said we should leave our hotel and see if we could get a shot of Pikoli getting off the president's plane and record the story. But when we got to the airport, there was Pikoli standing in the receiving line like the rest of us waiting for the presidential plane to land. Later that day, at the press conference following the bilateral meetings, Pikoli and his Chilean counterpart were called up to sign a bilateral agreement that the two governments had been working on over some time. Pikoli, as we understood it, was among the many people who were part of the South African delegation, which included a business contingent. Whether Mbeki and Pikoli spoke somewhere in some corner during that trip, I would not know, but what was not true was that Pikoli was on that plane that day.

From Chile, President Mbeki returned to South Africa, but he was due to travel to Qatar to attend the G77 so we proceeded to Doha. Minister Dlamini-Zuma was already in Qatar by the time we arrived. We then got a message that the president would no longer be coming to Qatar and we also heard the reason: he was going to address parliament to announce his decision to relieve his deputy, Jacob Zuma, of his duties. We could not believe this because there was no hint that it was coming. On the day, the South African delegation was probably the least focused of all the people attending the G77. Most people's minds would have been on what was happening back home. In the end Minister Dlamini-Zuma had to deliver President Mbeki's address on his behalf. I cannot remember whether we even got an opportunity to get Minister Dlamini-Zuma's reaction to what had happened back home.

As time went by, we also started to hear murmurs of political tensions that had arisen in the ANC's 2005 National General Council but again we were far from it. But as we were approaching the 2007 national conference of the ANC, we heard that two camps had emerged in the ANC: the so-called Zuma camp and the Mbeki camp. But not once did President Mbeki ever give us a hint whether he was standing for another term as president of the ruling party. Our newsroom at the SABC had asked us a couple of times to put the question to him but he never came out clearly on this.

It was not until we went on an official visit to Namibia a few weeks away from the Polokwane conference that we thought we needed an answer from him and we pressed him to say whether or not he would stand. This time, he surprised us and came out clearly to say that he was going to stand for president of the ANC because there were people who wanted him to stand and the ANC constitution did not prescribe a term limit on this position. At the time, Minister Nosiviwe Mapisa-Nqakula was also in

Namibia and our newsroom asked us to get a sound bite from her about the ANC Women's League's position on the ANC's presidential election. All she could tell us then was that 'we need a leader with integrity' and she left it at that despite our best efforts to get her to tell us who they were backing.

As the Polokwane conference was approaching, we had to travel to the Commonwealth Heads of State and Government meeting in Uganda. By this time, the ANC's nomination process had started but it seemed nobody was sure which way it was going. It was not until we landed back home and were getting off the plane and we overhead one ambassador saying, 'Things will change in Polokwane,' that we realised that Polokwane was going to be a major story. And indeed it was; many observers, ANC veterans and even foreign dignitaries said that they had never expected what they saw in Polokwane. The rest, as they say, is history. After that conference all sorts of speculation was flying around and it was for that reason that we needed to try to separate fact from fiction because some of it seemed far-fetched, or at least that was what we thought. All the same, we were under enormous pressure because President Mbeki had moved into top gear and we were moving at an even faster pace because he was determined to make sure that he wrapped up many of the things that he promised to deliver before he left office.

There were farewell imbizos (community meetings) taking place throughout the country, various leaders such as Venezuela's Hugo Chavez, were coming to the country, the Zimbabwean negotiations were ongoing and many other major assignments were happening. By this time, the press corps had already been running several stories in which we reminded the nation that it was his last year in office. For example, during the imbizos that year, many local communities in the various provinces were bidding President Mbeki farewell because they would no longer be interacting with him as head of state in those settings. He was also going to be attending the last G8, AU and other summits as the president of South Africa.

But, as it turned out, the NEC of the ANC was meeting as we were preparing to leave for New York for what would have been Mbeki's last address to the UN General Assembly as head of state. Among other things, he would use the opportunity to lobby the support of other leaders for the 2010 Soccer World Cup and he would be briefing the UN about the Zimbabwean Global Political Agreement that had been signed a few days earlier. We also expected that President Mbeki was going to travel to Iran after the US. For any journalist, this was a big story because at the time Iranian President Mahmoud Ahmadinejad was under severe pressure over his nuclear enrichment programme and this issue was in the news every day. I mention this because we were surprised to learn later that there were some people in the country who genuinely believed that President Mbeki's mistake was that he wanted a third term as head of state. This was misleading because Mbeki was focusing on a third term as president of the ANC of which he was a member, and had a constitutional right to do so.

On the evening of the NEC meeting, we packed and unpacked our bags several times because we were supposed to get on to the flight the very next day. We were getting different stories with each phone call from the SABC: 'No, the president is not being fired, you guys must proceed.' The next call that came through we were told, 'It looks like he will be fired, so we think you should stay.' At the time, I think that we naively believed that these were just rumours because, as we understood the policies of the ANC, Mbeki ought to have been at that meeting as a member of the NEC and afforded an opportunity to argue his side of the story, as would happen in any democratic movement. All the same, the uncertainty about our trip went on for a few hours until eventually the news broke that he was definitely being recalled from office. The editors called me and asked me to be at the Union Buildings to do a live crossing. By this time, I had a fairly good idea that President Mbeki was not about to put up a fight, especially because it would have gone totally against everything he had been advocating about the renaissance of Africa. Asked to foretell what he would say in his resignation speech to the nation, I knew in my mind, even as I did the live broadcast on the eve of his departure, that he would thank the nation for the confidence it had shown in him and encourage South Africans to continue to work hard towards rebuilding the country.

On the evening of 21 September 2008, Mbeki walked into the SABC building in Tshwane and was ushered into the make-up room. I walked in while they were busy preparing him and in his usual calm way he asked, 'Chief, how are we?' I detected no anger or pain; he just looked like the usual Mbeki who had come to the studio to do an interview on any day. I answered, 'Fine, Mr President,' not knowing what else to say to him at this time. I could not imagine what he must have been feeling because his face gave nothing away. As I predicted, he said more or less the things that I had expected him to say in his resignation speech. While Mbeki was sitting in the studio and reading his resignation speech, the ANC leadership was on the other channels explaining the reasons for the recall. The journalists had all gathered around the television sets in the newsroom. When the president got to the end of his speech, I went into the studio where he was. I am not sure what I was expecting him to say or do. When I got there, the SABC staff had been taking pictures with him. Under his breath, one staff member asked, 'What just happened in our country?' But we all pretended not to hear the question. With that, Mbeki's term ended seven months before he was due to step down. From this point, he was now a former president and as he was leaving with Smuts Ngonyama and Snuki Zikalala behind him, we shook hands and nothing was said. I guess nothing could be said.

The following day, the president's spokesperson Mukoni Ratshitanga informed me that there was a meeting of all the security chiefs. I rushed to the Union Buildings but I was the only journalist there. As I arrived, the meeting was about to finish and as they came out, I ambushed them to ask what the president, by now, the former president had called them for. They explained that he had informed them about his recall and that he called on them to make sure that they continued to carry out their constitutional responsibilities.

And when I was done with those interviews, I thought that I could ask to take shots of the president cleaning out his office since it was his last day in the Union Buildings. I had also asked Advocate Mojanku Gumbi if I could do an interview with her about the meeting; I did not think that the president would want to speak to me at that point. Fortunately for me, Advocate Gumbi said, 'The president will speak to you,' and I followed her to his office. As I entered his office, I saw that it was already cleared out and all that remained on his desk was a newspaper, which had a lead article about his recall. I could not believe the speed with which the cleaning out was done. Even as I did that last interview with him, Mbeki showed no signs of anger. He remained calm and spoke in the same measured tone that we had become used to over all those years. He explained the same thing that the security officers had told me. And with that came the end of a long and often difficult journey that we had travelled in reporting on the president we had come to know as 'Chief'.

It is perhaps a reflection of President Mbeki himself as one who questions and debates all the time, because his recall became a major talking point on the rest of the African continent. Since we then covered President Kgalema Motlanthe's seven-month term, we continued to travel on different assignments on the African continent. We were totally amazed at the debates that were taking place about President Mbeki's recall by the ruling party. There were many African analysts, journalists and academics who were in awe of the manner in which he left. At the same time, we were bombarded with questions about the constitutionality of his recall because the South African population had voted him into power and therefore he represented all citizens of South Africa, not just the ANC. The South African constitution does not have a clause on how to deal with a 'recall' of this nature. In addition, many on the African continent wondered why South Africans were silent on the Supreme Court of Appeal's outright dismissal of Judge Nicholson's ruling that led to Mbeki's 'recall'. Some argued that the actions taken by the ruling party were in conflict with the Constitutive Act of the African Union. So, not only did we find ourselves constantly being quizzed about our president's 'controversial' positions on HIV and AIDS and Zimbabwe, we were now having to face questions around the constitutionality of his recall from office and its implications in terms of the AU Constitutive Act.

After all that I have said above, to claim to know Thabo Mbeki would be to grossly deceive the reader. This is because even though I reported on him and the office that he occupied over so many years, I will be honest and say that I did not get close enough to know whether he likes tea or coffee, for example; as a presidential correspondent representing the SABC, together with my colleagues, I was always operating more in his shadow, so to speak. But one of the many lessons I learned from this journey was what he always preached: 'Remain loyal to principle.' Whatever the popular view, stick religiously to the truth and to fact, which was what he had asked of the Forum for Black Journalists back in 1997. Whether we managed to do that, we leave it to the media industry to make the call.

VIII

ACQUAINTANCES

ALBIE SACHS

⊰⊱

The bit I remember vividly is my confusion about surreptitiously shaking hands with Thabo, just below the level of the tablecloth in the jam-packed Sandton Convention Centre banqueting hall. The part I am more hazy about is exactly whose 80th birthday we were celebrating that evening. I think it was the renowned Advocate George Bizos and maybe one other distinguished South African. But certainly the atmosphere was jolly, and to everyone's surprise, Thabo had walked in with the birthday boy[s], a big smile on his face. My heart had leapt. It had been a dreadful time for him, voted out of his position as African National Congress (ANC) leader at Polokwane, deposed or about to be deposed as president of the country. Should I go over to his table to greet him? He had been my friend and comrade for decades, now he was down, down, down. On the one hand, as a sitting Justice of the Constitutional Court, protocol and the separation of powers required me to stay at arm's length from the highest representative of the executive. On the other hand this was a birthday party, and we had been through so much together! And there was a bigger problem, too, my ambivalence about him, admiration, anger, disappointment and love all mixed up.

I thought immediately of an exquisite moment of Thabo at his sensitive, thoughtful, soulful and gracious best. It was at the opening of an art exhibition in one of the buildings of the presidential residential compound in Pretoria. As he walked to the dais he noticed a portrait of the artist Dumile Feni in the collection, and told us a story. His voice was distinctively that of Thabo, modulated, rich and a bit hesitant as he searched for the right word.

427

It was the early 1970s, he said, at the height of the Vietnam War. People all over the world were sending goods to help Vietnam. There was a trainload of medications from the UK, and a trainload of food and clothing from France. What could we in the ANC in London send on behalf of the people of South Africa? We had nothing, he told us. So in desperation we thought of a picture. Dumile used to spend a lot of time at the ANC office, so we asked him if he could do a drawing for us. Yes, Dumile replied, as long as we didn't tell him what he should draw. We of course agreed to his condition. And he produced a most beautiful drawing. We had it wrapped, and sent it off, feeling embarrassed at how meagre our little parcel was. Thabo stopped to clear his throat. Some months later, he resumed, we received a letter from Vietnamese President Ho Chi Minh. It was addressed to the ANC office in London. In the letter, Ho Chi Minh said that his country had received wonderful gifts from people all over the world, which he highly appreciated. But the gift that he valued above all was the drawing from South Africa. That drawing, President Ho Chi Minh told us, was now hanging in his office directly above his desk.

And then I remembered the speech Thabo made on the lifting of sanctions against the apartheid government. He was facing 2 040 extremely sceptical, if not hostile, delegates at the ANC's first national conference on South African soil in Durban in 1991. His presentation was masterly. There was huge international pressure, he informed us, from friends as well as from enemies, for the ANC to agree to lifting sanctions as a response to the steps De Klerk had taken to end the ban on the ANC and other organisations and set negotiations in motion. The conference delegates were resistant, almost to a man and woman. Without sanctions, and with the armed struggle suspended, we wondered, what pressure would be left on the regime? Thabo stood impassively at the microphone and spoke for about 20 minutes, quietly and logically. No vivas, no revolutionary songs. Just precisely phrased and thoughtfully presented struggle logic. He explained that Scandinavian countries that had given us enormous support over the years had now said they were going to lift economic sanctions to encourage De Klerk to continue with negotiations. If we insisted on sanctions remaining in place, he observed, and they were nevertheless lifted, we would appear to have lost the battle. Rather, he argued, we should go along with sanctions being progressively lifted on a step-by-step basis as tangible advances were made towards the democratisation of our country. In this way we could remain in control of the process rather than appear to be defeated by it. It was magisterial, Thabo at his most thoughtful and persuasive best, singlehandedly turning the boat of our opinion around.

I recalled too the exquisite cadences of his famous 'I am an African' speech in the new democratic parliament ... But other memories, far less flattering, jostled for acknowledgement. I couldn't blot out an exchange of letters between Thabo and my late brother, Dr Johnny Sachs. Johnny had been a member of the ANC Health Committee in London for many years, working with people like Nkosazana Zuma, Ayanda Ntsaluba, William Makgoba and Max Price. One of their achievements had been to help formulate an advanced and progressive ANC position on how to give humane and practical support to comrades living with HIV. This was in the 1980s. Ten years later Johnny had been one of a group of medical scientists who had written to Thabo in his capacity as president of South Africa, setting out in firm but polite terms the scientific case for accepting that the virus indeed existed and in fact caused extreme debilitation of the immune system leading to death. Johnny showed me Thabo's response. After a gracious opening recalling their earlier comradeship, the letter descended into a series of prolix and barely readable sentences contending that there were more plausible explanations for the pandemic of death than the existence of the virus ... I could hardly bear to think of the tragic consequences of his imperious refusal to acknowledge what science and bitter daily experience on the ground was proving every day, every hour.

And I also couldn't help thinking about the day when he had spoken at the inauguration of South Africa's wonderful new Constitutional Court building on the site of the Old Fort prison in Braamfontein. His office had asked for some notes, and we had sent him a few paragraphs on the history of the site, where Gandhi, Luthuli, Tambo and Mandela had all been locked up. We suggested possible formulations on the extraordinary quality of the architecture and on the meaning of the building as a sign of the country's commitment to constitutional democracy and fundamental rights. Top judges from all over the world were there, as well as a full complement of diplomats.

But when he came to speak I could hardly believe my ears. No joy, no celebration. Apart from half a sentence granting some passing praise to the architects, his speech was a toneless exposition in support of his views on how important it was for the judiciary to be responsive to public opinion. To make it worse, his researchers had inserted a quotation in support of his approach from a notably conservative and allegedly anti-immigrant Australian judge. This was followed by citing American Professor Robert Bork, whose nomination to the US Supreme Court had been rejected after he had said that he agreed with the outcome of the famous *Brown v Board of Education* case, but not with the Supreme Court being the body to declare segregation unconstitutional.

Could it have been, I wondered, that Thabo had been angry with us because we had recently declared a decision of the cabinet, presided over by him, to deny all but a few prisoners the right to vote, to be unconstitutional? To his credit, Thabo never once defied a decision of the Court, however much he spoke out against it. And when inside the building after the formal opening, he, together with Zanele, was warm, gracious and deeply appreciative. But what pique had brought him to addle a proud and meaningful occasion with a sour and obscure homily? Some people try to hide their weaker qualities and put their good ones on display. With Thabo I often felt the reverse was happening ... Morose and obstinate in public, sensitive and gracious in private.

Anyhow, at the banquet I had to make a decision. I found myself standing up, as my body impulsively moved forward, my heart leading and my brain and conflicted memories staying behind. Thabo was my friend, my comrade. Each individual in the struggle had had moments of exaltation and desolation. Now he was there in front of me at a party. We had been through so much together, in so many countries, over so many years. His contribution had been enormous. So I walked to his table, sat down next to him, and put out my hand in greeting. He clasped my outstretched fingers and pulled them down below the rim of the tablecloth, and warmly shook them. I was surprised by the clandestinity of his gesture, wondering whether he wished to protect me from possible criticism for being too close to him, or whether the habits of secrecy were simply ingrained in him. Or was it just shyness? Well, I decided, with Thabo you often just couldn't tell. But the subterranean human contact seemed to be very meaningful to both of us.

DANNY SCHECHTER

❦

On The Mountain Top with Thabo Mbeki: An American Activist/Journalist
Remembers an Explosive Meeting

It was a cold, snowy day on a Swiss Alp in a scenic town called Davos
where a form of German is spoken, and the World Economic Forum
sparks world attention once a year. I was there as an invited journalist. It
was a chance to observe the global power elite in action as it pays a pretty
penny to be seen at this opulent venue, the world's most prestigious networking party.

At one session, I noticed a familiar face at the back of the room, a woman
I had met in the 1970s in Cambridge, Massachusetts. Her name: Zanele
Mbeki, now the first lady of South Africa. Somehow we gravitated towards
each other into a warm embrace, or in South African parlance, a 'howzit?'
session. She knew my history as an American anti-apartheid activist and as
a media critic. I told her about a study I had just seen showing a dramatic
drop in media visibility for South Africa, then under her husband's leadership. I was concerned about it, and thought her husband should be as well.

She agreed. 'You must come see him and tell him yourself, and,' she said, 'he
will listen to you.' 'When?' I asked. 'Tomorrow,' was her definitive response.
'Give me your number and I will call you.' I did, and then she was gone, but
not before I told her that, given the high snows and my lack of transportation,
I'd need someone to pick me up. She nodded as she was whisked away, leaving me to continue my anthropological 'infiltration' alone.

431

I had known Thabo Mbeki since the 1960s when I was a graduate student at the London School of Economics. We are the same age. He was going to school in Sussex then, but was well known as an African National Congress (ANC) partisan and theorist, a son of ANC veteran and Robben Island inmate Govan Mbeki, whom I later learned was a key member of the secretive 'high organ' that led the movement behind bars. His family had pushed him into exile to protect him from predictable barbarity had he stayed in those dark days. We met again on many occasions and I knew that he became a key strategist who initiated meetings with the country's white business elite in the late 1980s that were credited with breaking the ice of negotiations that in a few short years led to the fall of apartheid.

In one interview, years before it happened, he told me apartheid was unravelling. He knew of what he spoke because he was driving a secret negotiating process. Many had called for the system's fall but, truth be told, Mbeki helped push it over the edge. We who watched from afar noted the daily violence and the lack of progress, but he provided optimism when it was in short supply.

Nelson Mandela may have been the world's best-known political prisoner, and Oliver Tambo the most visible liberation movement leader, but it was the enigmatic Thabo Mbeki, known by his beard, pipe, Scotch, and persuasive diplomacy, who played the key behind-the-scenes role breaking the logjam.

'TM', as he was known in the Movement, had the temperament and focus to cultivate the ANC's enemies, wow the liberals and even, at times, co-opt the angriest in the Afrikaner far right, reaching out to military and business leaders and anyone with the guts to attend off-the-record conferences in England, Senegal and South Africa. He was known as a good listener, not always an easy skill, even if later his critics said that he only listened to himself.

Many on the ANC left may have distrusted him but he, too, had been branded a terrorist. His outgoing style and the substance of his problem-solving approach won the confidence of those who feared the firebrands. His pragmatism was seen by the business world as a safer alternative to all the purveyors of anti-system ideology and sloganising. Later, he helped steer the Mandela presidency with skills he learned in decades of exile. Some accused him of selling out, but realism was his real religion. He manoeuvred in environments he did not create. Just as he made peace with people who wanted to kill him, he embraced, perhaps over-embraced, neo-liberalism as the only option on the table. Capitalists thought they could deal with him in an era when Soviet communism collapsed. They found him supportive.

The revolutionary moment seemed to have passed, quickly displaced by the need for reconciliation and the lure of reform. Nationalisation, however much it had been used by Afrikaners to consolidate their control through a strategy of parastatals, and called for in the Freedom Charter, was pushed off the table with the ANC under heavy lobbying by the corporates, the multinationals, the mining empires and foreign governments, the International Monetary Fund (IMF) and World Bank and internal personalities eager to move up into well-paying positions.

Most of the press focused on public political talks, not behind-the-scenes economic wrangling. Mbeki, meanwhile, was on a mission to assure a stable political transition and prevent a race war. In the public eye, Madiba was the front man, the media icon on the outside; Mbeki, his deputy president, was the go-to person on the inside.

Then he became South Africa's president. Elected by a bigger margin than Mandela, with his backing, he was known for strategic brilliance and personal stubbornness; he was trying to move the country from the joy and shock of its great change into a period of institutional transformation. Soon he was subjected to far more scrutiny than Mandela, who enjoyed a god-like aura and, paradoxically, elicited higher hopes and lower expectations.

He invited me to his inaugurations, not as a journalist but as a self-important guest. At one point, I even sat behind Libyan President Gaddafi, shades and all. He had orchestrated Mandela's elevation – now it was his turn. At a concert outside on the lawn of the Union Buildings, I was pushed away by security goons as the president dropped in for a visit.

Despite the crowds, I shouted out, 'Hi, Thabo!' and to my surprise he stopped in his tracks, brought the entourage to a halt, and reached out to shake hands and ask how I was. The crowd around me seemed to be caught off guard by this spontaneous moment of interracial solidarity. No one knew me, except him. So, yes, we knew each other, but like many ANC boosters, I was disturbed by what I took as his downplaying of the HIV/

AIDS crisis, and distressed by a speech I heard him give at the Durban AIDS Conference in 2000 where he was practically booed by disappointed activists while many in the media denounced him as out of touch and a denialist. There was more to it than that. There always is.

The story making the rounds was that he had investigated the discourse on AIDS late at night while surfing the Internet. Suspicious of claims that seemed to reflect the interests of big pharmaceutical companies that overcharged for their medications, and Western governments that ignored the many diseases of poverty that killed so many more Africans, he tried to discuss the many deeper questions that were not being raised. Mistake – even if he was right, or partially right. He was branded a conspiracy nut, even when he wasn't. (It was not as if the AIDS epidemic was brought under rapid control by establishment-approved remedies.) Nevertheless, he was depicted as uncaring, overly intellectual, detached and dogmatic.

To raise questions in that period was akin to some of us denying the Holocaust. That clearly pissed him off but his reputation took a dive in an environment of political correctness and some hysteria. The issue had by then become highly emotional and many were convinced that there was only one way to fight AIDS: hand over the national budget to buy overpriced AIDS medicines. He rejected that. Without revisiting the details of the debate, it clearly hurt Mbeki's reputation, and ever since mainstream media narratives of the world have looked at him negatively. Once they brand you, they keep you branded in a simplistic world of good guys and bad guys.

That was not good for South Africa and its need to attract investment and preserve its image as the 'rainbow nation', a model for Africa and the world. So now, people like myself who study news narratives were reporting that South Africa's portrayal had turned very negative, and Mbeki's leadership was being blamed. I had one of the studies and wanted to discuss it with him along with some thoughts on how he might turn the situation around.

At around midnight I had a call from an operative at the 'South African control room' that coordinated the president's visit to inform me that Mbeki would see me at eight in the morning and that, yes, hooray, a car would be sent to fetch me. Meanwhile, outside snows swirled and streets quickly became clogged; it was COLD. I wondered if this was the time or place for a discussion of sunny South Africa.

The car was there on time, and we headed slowly for the hotel through the blizzard. The Swiss are experts in moving snow around so we made it there quickly. Soon, another visitor turned up: the powerful financier, George Soros. We knew each other too, and I made some small talk while thinking that now I would have to wait for this VIP to see him first. To my surprise, Soros was left to cool his heels, and they took me first. I don't think he was too pleased to be upended by a lesser mortal. That incident may be why George, who backed some of our media projects at one time, never did so again. Big money is often linked to big egos.

In going in to see him, I thought to myself that I had to get his attention or this encounter would become just one more useless hand-shaking reunion. I went radical. To insure a 'tell', I thought I first needed a 'show', as in show and tell, but with a little drama thrown in.

The first words out of my mouth, after I thanked him for seeing me, were to ask if I could be 'candid, *really* candid'. Mbeki said, sure, noting we had known each other a long time. Knowing that I was not seeking a job, I wanted to incite, not impress. I then told him point blank that I felt he was 'fucking up' big time on the media front. The room went silent. He started smiling.

His aide/colleague went ballistic, outraged by my invective, not realising it was calculated. 'You can't talk to the president that way,' he shouted at me. He was disgusted at my lack of propriety and etiquette. I could sense him wondering, 'Who is this insolent American?' There was a jolt of electricity in the room. He feigned insult. If Mbeki wasn't there, he might have clobbered me. When I spoke to the president as 'Thabo', deliberately using his first name, which showed familiarity, that pissed him off even more.

I later learned that an amused Zanele was listening in the back room.

To my delight, Mbeki intervened, told his staffer that it was okay, and to back off, that we were old friends. The underling did so, but smarting with looks to kill.

I then explained that I had only a few minutes and I was worried about surveys that showed how poorly South Africa was being perceived in the world, and that he should fire whoever was doing his press relations, and

I told him about my media monitoring site, Mediachannel.org. He knew about all the documentaries I had made about South Africa and the *South Africa Now* series I produced out of New York for three years.

This gave the aide – first name Justice – an opening to come back at me in asking what I wanted and how much I was charging. I asked him if he had heard anything about money, and that I was a journalist, not a PR man pitching a client. I wondered if Soros heard all the yelling. A now amused Mbeki jumped back into the conversation. He looked at the data in a study I showed him, and said quietly and reflectively, as he is wont to do, 'You are right. We are not doing well in our communications. My guys are screwing it up.'

He then told me about his frustrations with the advice he was getting, and agreed that more needed to be done, and more creativity shown. He asked me if I could meet with his team the next time I was in South Africa and I said I would, but I was not looking for a job. I suggested he might arrange a university lecture for me, which might give me a chance to share what insights and advice I might have on a voluntary basis.

After a good 20 minutes of solid back and forth, he agreed that my idea was doable, that the problems were real, and that he would follow up. Later Zanele congratulated me on how I got through to him, with a bemused twinkle in her eye. I was encouraged but, sorry to report, whatever good intentions there may have been at the time I heard nothing more from him or his control rooms. There was no follow-up at their end. I am sure he got busy.

Unfortunately, the media animus was not turned around, with or without my input, and years later he lost support in the public and the party. What happened happened! He took a big but possibly preventable fall. It just goes to show that people in power don't necessarily have power over all the people around them, many of whom are yes-men or use their access to advance their careers. Politicians can't be expected to manage everything, especially their own media images, even though Mbeki had a reputation as a micro manager, even a control freak.

When you are a nation's leader you are always reacting to a parade of unplanned events, more than acting proactively. In his case, he was clearly more obsessed with programmatic detail than media perception. He really didn't have time to listen to me or others offering all kinds of advice that his insiders often wanted to blunt or sideline. That impresses me about him to this day.

He was playing a political game that you don't always win. South Africa has not been the same since. Thabo's many detractors soon realised that things could get a lot worse, and many soon recognised how much they missed him, flaws and all. The same thing happened in America to Bill Clinton after his sex scandal. His media image had sunk, dropping him from hero to zero. But by the time he left office few Americans wanted him to leave. In that case, a lot of media savvy and professional energy was invested in rehabbing his shattered image.

Clinton was known as the 'Comeback Kid' and he did come back. Thabo did not, although he has continued to do excellent work with his institute, initiatives in Africa and thoughtful lectures. I met a South African TV producer, a fellow in his institute, who said it was the best experience of her life. But Mbeki seems to have recognised too late that in public life perception trumps reality. It wasn't just the press that put him down but many comrades and colleagues who got caught up in paroxysm of populism and in some cases tribalism. He became a symbol of a crisis-ridden status quo. He had turned many off by his stiffness and distance, even his erudition, perhaps an indication of his own contempt for insincerity, but not always necessarily a winning formula for a politician. He became, alas, perhaps more of a manager than a movement militant. His refusal to pander led to his being denounced as 'arrogant'.

At the same time, he wanted to be a 'thought leader' offering ideas that were often pioneering if provocative. In the same way that he fashioned a strategy for fracturing the official white wall of unity behind apartheid, he pioneered a historic thrust into Africa with his 'I am an African' speech and the initiatives that followed. That was gutsy and ambitious, if not always successful. I met and was impressed by some of the South African peacekeepers in the Democratic Republic of Congo when I was making a film in Goma.

I learned from Thabo Mbeki even as I had the luxury of being critical from a world away. Many took his thoughtfulness as a sense of superiority, but that didn't make him a bad leader. He marched to his own drummer as in a speech I heard him give on the anniversary of the Freedom

Charter where he chose to remember the socialist and feminist writer Olive Schreiner. I wasn't sure why he chose that occasion to deliver it, but he believed it was relevant to add women's rights to the discourse.

When he went deeper and refused to recycle old slogans, there was often pushback and putdowns as if he was out of touch. By dumping him the way they did, his detractors claimed to be saving democracy.

Look what they ended up with.

Mbeki may have overestimated the prospect of rationality guiding politics and at the same time underestimated his own support. He was treated shabbily, not even allowed to finish his term. Since then, the country has marched steadily downhill. They called it a 'recall'; I saw it as a decapitation. Even his critical biographer, the journalist Mark Gevisser, is striking a more balanced note these days about a man he often skewered: 'Too often Mbeki's critics forget, when decrying the way Black Economic Empowerment created a few black millionaires but left everyone else in the dirt, about the tens of thousands of black people who entered the middle class as a consequence of his policies: not Ramaphosas or Sexwales, but bank clerks and copywriters, medics and accountants. Certainly, these include a fair number of unqualified civil servants who grow fat on corrupted tenders and teachers who care more about their salaries than the social good, but they also encompass an entire generation of people ...'

Fast forward to 2012. I was back in South Africa, documenting the making and meaning of the movie *Long Walk To Freedom* based on Nelson Mandela's autobiography and being filmed by producer Anant Singh.

I interviewed many of Madiba's comrades who suffered with him and struggled with him. I knew I couldn't tell the story without Thabo's participation. He wasn't giving interviews but agreed to meet. At his home office in Johannesburg, he sat behind a big desk taking frequent calls about a planned trip to Ethiopia. He seemed bummed out, especially with his successor. On the wall, I noticed a historic picture of Mandela in the early 1960s meeting with Algerian revolutionaries in North Africa. I pitched hard for his participation, and he agreed to give me a half-hour.

We ranged over many issues but the one that fascinated me the most was his assessment of the challenges the country faces. Usually it is his brother Moeletsi who raises an economic critique but Thabo has one too. Here was the man who seduced and befriended the white business elite, who dined with them in Davos and elsewhere, now reflecting on how he feels they betrayed the country.

I think that the fundamental problems of South Africa have remained unchanged since that transition in 1994. When people talk about national reconciliation, national cohesion and all that, the fundamental problems of poverty and inequality have to be addressed. What is it that needs to be done in order to eradicate poverty? What is it that needs to be done to bridge these enormous gaps in terms of wealth, of income, of opportunity? Between black and white, men and women, and all that. That's what the country must address.

One of the problems, one of the challenges that South Africa has never been able to solve in all of these years since its liberation, is the attitude of white capital. Even today there are large volumes of investable money that South African companies are holding in cash, and not investing in the economy. And this has been the situation ever since 1994; it's driven by a fear that it's inevitable that there will be a crisis. And because there will be a crisis inevitably I must hold as many of my assets in liquid form as possible, so that if I have to run, I can upend the factory because I can't move it, but at least the money I can run away with. It's a persistent problem.

Danny: Well, I'd love to discuss this with you because we have the same problem in the US. The 1 per cent versus the 99 per cent, with the corporate people basically moving money offshore and not creating jobs, with big banks playing their own game and not serving the people.

Thabo: I think that fundamentally the legacy is about political liberation. I think that the liberation for which Mandela and others sacrificed so much created a space for us as South Africans indeed to change our lives for the better. The challenge we face is, how do we do it? And I think it would be quite correct if people said that we are moving too slowly with regard to all of these things we are talking about. Poverty eradication, reduction in levels of inequality, quality of education, women's emancipation, all of these things. But I think that's a question that as South Africans all of us must answer. What is it that we must do to make sure that indeed we build, we take advantage of that liberation, to build a better South Africa.

I learned a lot from Thabo Mbeki even as I remain critical. He was willing to admit errors and revise policies. He was reflective and hard work-ing. He took unpopular stands like supporting Haiti and its beleaguered and then deposed President Aristide. He believed in Nkrumah's dream of pan-Africanism. He had a vision of a renaissance.

He wasn't perfect. He said so himself. He lived in an often hostile world of big powers, imperial interests and self-serving narrow-minded politicians who used the ANC and the state to benefit themselves because 'their time' had come. He deplored corruption, but how to control it? He tried to ride (and rule) the many contradictions in his own party and country. His political end, when it came, was tragic for South Africa; alas, no longer the beloved country.

I never got to know him as well as I wanted. But, then, that was a com-plaint many others might make as well.

ANNE PAGE

❧

The Thabo Mbeki I Know ... is mysterious

He always has been – since he first appeared in UK press headlines at the time of the Rivonia Trial. Here was the 20-year-old son of a man accused of treason, a death sentence at risk. Yet no hint of personal emotion clouded the mature delivery of speech after speech he made at the time, whether to students at Sussex University – the first time I met him – or on television, or from the plinth at Trafalgar Square to a *vast* crowd (said to be the biggest since the Suez Crisis).

To most observers, Thabo seemed much like the other students at the trendy new university on the south coast – a symbol of the swinging sixties where the clever and fashionable daughters of prominent politicians were much photographed in mini-dresses and academic robes.

His rural childhood, intensive early political education, the adventurous journey abroad were all masked as Thabo Mbeki studied and partied, worked and played, while always raising consciousness of South Africa. We learned more than dancing from the songs of Dorothy Masuka and Miriam Makeba. Some time later Thabo disappeared. I learned only decades later from Mark Gevisser's biography some of what might have been happening to him. Then he popped back into my by now married life, arriving unannounced at our house near the African National Congress (ANC) office in Islington, north London, often with Abdul Bham, always hungry for both food and new ideas, picking up the discussions of the day with my journalist husband Bruce Page.

In and out of London for years and years, Thabo would be the main speaker at solidarity meetings in Friends House, or the Conway Hall, or Caxton Hall. We would embrace, exchange news, and off he would go again, gipsying around the world, homeless, without apparent means, exiled.

And yet … in 1974, he married Zanele in a historic British castle, owned by her then brother-in-law. It was in great style, with a ceremony in Xhosa in the chapel, the bride charming and modest as ever, and Adelaide Tambo, *in loco parentis*, in a wonderful floating peachy chiffon outfit.

But the peripatetic life resumed. We became aware that Thabo's skills – at negotiation, communication, presentation – were increasingly critical in helping to bring the South African struggle to the forefront of international attention again. In 1985, he arranged for Oliver Tambo to attend the Labour Party conference in Bournemouth as the special international guest. At an already dramatic meeting, where Neil Kinnock finally got the Labour Party back on track, the ANC delegation was of more than usual interest. Their first meeting with white businessmen from Johannesburg had just taken place in Zambia. Thabo and I walked for hours on the seaside promenade as the dusk turned to dark. His conviction that major change was on the way was infectious, and I too was sure of it from then, though many others, much closer to the action than I was, remained doubtful for years.

Via the UK press and television, we could see that Thabo Mbeki, now chief spokesman for the ANC, was in New York a lot, raising the anti-apartheid temperature in the United Nations, the Western and international media, and in diplomatic circles. His fluency, earthy manner and not least his trademark pipe combined to attract supporters and sceptics alike into expecting, and therefore helping to bring about, change in South Africa. I was not surprised when I met him in South Africa in the early 1990s to find his compatriots at ease with him as he relearned the country and the people he had not been among for 30 years. I had no home nor cellphone in those days of my own return, but friends were uniformly thrilled if they received a phone message for me from Thabo.

The mystery returned much later when Thabo was president. This man had been so open to ideas and discussion, so understanding of other points of view, so careful in leading argument, so persuasive, so able to articulate emotions and to inspire love. Yet when in office, publicly, and not only on the AIDS issue, he seemed to become closed, lacking empathy. His great initiatives – in the African Renaissance, in launching the Constitution, in economic and social policy – became clouded by unexpected misjudgement, even intransigence, elsewhere.

Always responsive when I called on visits to South Africa, Thabo would talk to me about some of the myriad issues confronting him. But when a friend gains such high office it is hard to be fully at ease, and we avoided contentious matters. Now as we enter our old age, we are, happily, recovering more ordinary relations. His delight in the successes of the young Africans emerging from his Leadership Institute is palpable. His role in resolving conflict elsewhere on the African continent is meaningful. His popularity seems to rise as time passes. He is able to play the piano. Perhaps the mysteries will unfurl along with the years.

IX

FRIENDS FROM OTHER COUNTRIES

AMI MPUNGWE

꧁꧂

Thabo Mbeki and I became comrades long before we had personally met. The intensity of the nationalist and pan-Africanist struggles
of the 1950s and early 1960s not only evolved a common political culture across the continent, but also had a significant equalising effect on
our generation – our development as individuals was underpinned by the
demand for Africa's total liberation and it's rebirth in a post-colonial, post-
apartheid environment. When Thabo and I started working together closely
in the late 1970s, we would regularly reminisce about the political events of
the 1950s and 1960s, as they continued to inform and inspire the political
struggles on the continent and beyond. And the clarion calls for 'Amandla'
in South Africa, 'Harambee' in Kenya, 'Uhuru' in Tanganyika, 'Kwacha' in
Malawi and Zambia etc., are still fresh in our ears, as Thabo and I keep on
imagining and working for Africa's prosperous future.

The Thabo Mbeki that I know is therefore, first and foremost, a great
student of history, particularly as it relates to African nationalism, pan-
Africanism and Africans in the diaspora. He is both a student of this history
and a product of it – I have known and interacted with Thabo for close to
40 years now and I know him as a strong and committed pan-Africanist. He
still shares Julius Nyerere's assertion that 'African nationalism is meaningless,
anachronistic and dangerous, if it is not, at the same time, pan-Africanism.'
Although the African National Congress (ANC) was prohibited by the
Pretoria regime from attending the 1958 All African Peoples Conference
that was held in Accra, Ghana, it sent a memorandum in support of the

pan-African movement. Ever since, members of the ANC, and Thabo in particular, have drawn inspiration from the resolutions of that conference. The conference's slogan, 'Hands-Off Africa', still resonates with Thabo and drives his political thought to date. His involvement in the South African struggle has always been informed by the ideas of pan-Africanism, including the struggles of the Africans in diaspora, and he remains profoundly committed to the indivisibility and universality of human rights, freedom, justice and dignity in South Africa and elsewhere in the world.

Thabo's pan-Africanist tendencies first became apparent when he became actively engaged in student politics while studying in the UK, far beyond the limitations of the South African or African struggles alone. It is quite clear to me, apart from Titans of the South African struggle, the likes of Julius Nyerere, Harry Nkumbula, Kenneth Kaunda, Sam Nujoma, Joshua Nkomo, Ndabaningi Sithole, Haile Selassie, Gamal Abdel-Nasser, Kwame Nkrumah, Abubakar Tafawa Balewa, Nnamdi Azikiwe, Jomo Kenyatta, Modibo Keita, Sékou Touré, Patrice Lumumba, Ahmed Ben Bella, Houari Boumédiène, Habib Bourguiba and Dr Sylvanus Olympio, became a major source of hope and inspiration to young Thabo as he was maturing fast during the South African and pan-Africanist struggles of the 1950s and as an adult in 1960s and 1970s.

Through his active involvement in pan-Africanist activities, at different levels, Thabo is also an active and committed internationalist. The Bandung Conference, held in Indonesia in 1955, which gave rise to the Non-Aligned Movement at the height of the Cold War, has always inspired Thabo. The growing solidarity within the pan-African Movement, the Afro-Asia Group, the Afro-Arab Solidarity Group and the Afro-Caribbean Solidarity Group, to mention just a few, also helped to shape Thabo's worldview, in the context of his pan-Africanist political thought and activism.

At an organisational level, Thabo was involved in the establishment of the pan-African Freedom Movement for East and Central Africa (PAFMECA) in Mwanza, Tanzania, in 1958, which transformed into pan-African Freedom Movement for East, Central and Southern Africa (PAFMECSA) in 1962, and brought together the nationalist movements in East, Central and southern Africa, with the view to coordinating their respective nationalist struggles at the sub-regional level. He was also involved in the establishment of similar pan-Africanist movements elsewhere in Africa – the Casablanca Group, the Brazzaville Group and the Monrovia Group (the latter having been formed in 1961, with the view to reconciling the ideological differences between the Casablanca and Brazzaville groups). Thabo was, therefore, part of the significant ideological debates that took place in the freedom/nationalist movements as well as in the regional and continental organisations at the height of the Cold War, as he worked out his own pragmatic way forward. Indeed, Thabo is a genuine product of the Non-Aligned Movement as he does not subscribe to any extremist ideology.

Thabo and I, in our separate ways, were deeply influenced by all the major political developments of our time, including the activities of the East and Central African Good Neighbourliness Conference, which became famous for the adoption of the Lusaka Manifesto of April 1969. Although the manifesto stressed dialogue with the oppressors and colonisers as a preferred option for resolving the southern African conflicts, it also provided a framework for resorting to armed struggle when dialogue failed.

The birth of the Organisation of African Unity (OAU) in Addis Ababa in 1963 entailed the disbandment of all regional blocs, including PAFMECSA and the Casablanca, Monrovia and Brazzaville groups. Consequently, the Lusaka Manifesto was carried forward through the OAU-sponsored Mogadishu Declaration of 1970 and the Dar es Salaam Declaration of 1975. Thabo was involved in both declarations. In between, and due to the intensity of the southern African liberation struggle, the Frontline States Group also evolved in the early 1970s, initially out of the regular, bilateral consultations between Kenneth Kaunda and Julius Nyerere (known as the Mbeya/Mbala summits).

The immediate consequence of the growing intensity in the liberation struggles was the arrival thousands of freedom fighters in Tanganyika – which was the first country to gain independence in the sub-region – following the banning of the various political parties and liberation movements in East, Central and southern Africa states.

One of the first arrivals was the former president of Namibia, President Hifikepunye Pohamba, who arrived in Dar es Salaam on 9 December 1961, Tanganyika's Independence Day. The president of the ANC, Oliver Tambo, arrived a month later, in January 1962, and Nelson Mandela arrived a month after that. He was followed by a host of other leaders – Sam Nujoma, Agostinho Neto, Joshua Nkomo, Ndabaningi Sithole and Potlako Leballo. The late Dr Eduardo Mondlane founded FRELIMO in Tanganyika in 1962 and a lot of other liberation movements were either based or headquartered in Tanganyika.

Thabo also escaped South Africa through Tanganyika, where he obtained his first passport, en route to the UK for further studies in November 1962. Boarding the same flight to London from Dar es Salaam as Kenneth Kaunda, Julius Nyerere entrusted the 'young' Thabo to Kaunda. In those days, boarding a plane at 20 would make anyone an 'unaccompanied minor'! Unfortunately, Kenneth Kaunda had to abandon Thabo on arrival at Heathrow because Thabo had issues with his Tanganyikan passport. The former British colonial official who issued the passport had indicated Thabo's citizenship as 'undetermined'. He was rescued by his hosts, some hours later.

Interestingly, it would be Kaunda, 32 years later, in 1994, who would advise President Mandela to appoint Thabo as his deputy president, identifying him as someone 'the whole region knows and trusts'. Thabo had come to know the senior leadership in the region and on the continent well before he assumed powerful positions in his own country.

Though Thabo and I grew up separately, the nationalist and pan-Africanist political culture that characterised and informed our upbringing would form a solid basis for our relationship. Our initial contact came during my student days, at the University of Dar es Salaam in the early 1970s. In those days, the University of Dar es Salaam was a hotbed of Third World intellectual activism, spearheaded by the TANU Youth League activists and the University Students' African Revolutionary Front (USARF), whose early student leaders included the likes of Yoweri Museveni and John Garang. The teaching faculty included reputed pan-Africanist scholars, like Walter Rodney, Wadada Nabudere, Yash Tandon, Abdul-Aziz Jalloh, Issa Shivji and Nathan Shamuyarira. My own Political Science and International Relations major, was on 'Imperialism and Liberation in Southern Africa', completed under the supervision of Professor Nathan Shamuyarira, which in today's world would be considered nothing short of 'terrorist training'!

Many of the leaders and cadres of the liberation movements, including

Thabo, appeared as guest speakers and lecturers and publications like Sechaba and ANC Today became part of our core reading materials. The External Service of Radio Tanzania was another major source of information about the struggle being pursued by the different liberation movements. We also had access to the senior leadership of the Dar es Salaam-based OAU Liberation Committee and liberation movements. It was in this context that Thabo distinguished himself as a pan-Africanist intellectual and a political thinker and strategist, in addition to being a committed freedom fighter.

My contact with Thabo became more regular when I joined the Tanzanian Foreign Service in 1975. I started my career as a Desk Officer for Australasia and South Pacific Islands. My immediate task was to oversee Papua New Guinea's independence from the Australian administration, which was achieved in September 1975. It also involved monitoring East Timor's liberation process from the Portuguese (under FRETELINI – which had close links with its African counterparts, particularly FRELIMO and the MPLA). Equally important, my brief also involved maintaining close links with the anti-apartheid movements in Australia and New Zealand, particularly the campaign against sporting tours to South Africa. It was in this role that I again connected with Thabo, as did political campaigners like Trevor Richards of New Zealand's Halt All Racist Tours (HART), who became very close to both Thabo and I. We also worked closely with the likes of Abraham Odia and Jean-Claude Ganga, the president and secretary general of the Supreme Council of Sports in Africa, particularly during Africa's boycott of the Montreal Olympics in 1975 and the adoption of the Gleneagles Agreement in 1977, which sought to isolate apartheid South Africa from the world of civilised sports.

During this period, Thabo's political acumen became evident to me and I found myself encountering his strategic footprints in the ANC's major publications and in my numerous conversations with many other ANC cadres, old and young, including the likes of Thomas Nkobi, Alfred Nzo, Mendi Msimang, Essop Pahad, Jacob Zuma, Chris Hani, Aziz Pahad; Kader Asmal, Johnny Makhathini, Tony Mongalo, Thami Sindelo, Mojo Motau, Ruth Mompati and Eddie Funde. Even other campaigners used his positions and strategies to bolster their own – Sam Ramsamy, on the sports boycott, and Abdul Minty, on the comprehensive arms embargo against South Africa, to name but two.

Following the liberation of the Portuguese colonies of Mozambique and Angola in 1975, and with Zimbabwe's independence pending, the liberation base and frontier in southern Africa moved from Tanzania to Zambia. Consequently, I was posted to our high commission in Lusaka in December 1979. In the absence of a Tanzanian diplomatic mission in Salisbury, Lusaka became our 'listening post' and my initial assignment was to cover the Zimbabwean independence process from Lusaka. Thereafter, I covered all matters related to the Frontline States' liberation support in southern Africa, in particular the intensifying struggles in South Africa and Namibia, through the ANC and SWAPO offices in Zambia as well the ongoing conflicts between FRELIMO and RENAMO in Mozambique and MPLA and UNITA in Angola.

One of my early moves was to re-establish contact with Thabo, who, at that time, was heading up the ANC's Department of Information and Publicity (DIP). He was basically the ANC's frontman in the diplomatic world of Lusaka (and anywhere else they needed him) and had become a key assistant to Oliver Tambo, the then president of the ANC.

I reconnected with Thabo in December 1979, at a cocktail party hosted by Hage Geingob, the current president of Namibia. I have always found Thabo very approachable and extremely accommodating, particularly in light of our differences in age and position, and things were no different on that evening. Thabo is urbane, well read and well travelled – a very polished and sophisticated diplomat. His profound love for the arts, culture and literature is amazing. He always enjoys thinking out of the box, in search of new and innovative ideas about any subject of discussion, particularly on matters related to the liberation struggle in southern Africa and the Third World's role in the global political economy. Thabo would always approach the liberation issues in the pan-Africanist and Third World context, bearing in mind the collective strength of those bodies in support of the liberation process in southern Africa. But he was also humble, modest and prepared to listen, his focus always 'the battle of ideas' on the liberation of Africa and its prosperous future.

As a political officer at the mission covering Zambia, Botswana and the rest of the southern African region, I benefited immensely from Thabo's analysis of the unfolding situation. Thabo always enjoys analytical conversations about our region and our continent and the solid state of relations between Tanzania and the ANC, as well as the deep level of collaboration between and among the Frontline States and liberation movements, further leveraged the depth of our personal relationship. In the process, he became and remains a trusted brother, comrade and mentor.

Having been the ANC representative in Zambia, Botswana, Swaziland and Nigeria, as well as representing the ANC at many international conferences, Thabo quickly became very actively involved in the intricacies of diplomatic operations in Lusaka. In addition to this, in terms of the established Frontlines States' operational culture, Thabo was of ministerial rank and was often sought out as a 'struggle diplomat'. His workload ensured that I sustained substantial 'collateral damage' on an almost daily basis, as Thabo would usually make my residence his final stop on his diplomatic rounds, often quite late at night, and would not be in a rush to go home. Our exchanges would usually last into the early hours of the morning!

While at my residence, Thabo would make phone calls to contacts inside South Africa, something that could have cost me my job – the destination of the calls was more than a little suspicious – had I not kept my ambassador aware of what was transpiring. That was the time that the South African police and intelligence had infiltrated the Mandela Football Club and Thabo was constantly pleading with Winnie Mandela and others to keep their distance from the club.

I have never seen Thabo so depressed as when Presidents Samora Machel of Mozambique and P. W. Botha of South Africa signed the Nkomati Accord, on 16 March 1984. Thabo was aware that the regime had tried to sign similar 'peace accords' with Lesotho, Botswana and Swaziland, but without success. We held numerous discussions to find the way forward after this major setback and to rekindle the spirit of solidarity in the region. At one stage, Thabo sought to mobilise the youth within the Frontline States and liberation movements to march to the summit of Mount Kilimanjaro. There they would place a Liberation Torch which, as Mwalimu had put it in 1958, 'would shine across the borders and bring hope where there is despair, love where there is hatred and dignity where there is humiliation!'

However, soon after this the Pretoria regime came under increasing domestic and international pressure and delegations from South Africa began to arrive in Lusaka, initially to sound out ANC's appetite and readiness for a negotiated settlement. The church leaders were the first to reach out to the ANC in exile, followed by journalists, academics and business leaders. Thabo was the key contact person and this flurry of activity further intensified as South Africa became increasingly ungovernable and the Cold War tensions continued to thaw, putting significant pressure on the Pretoria regime to abandon its anti-communist cover for sustaining apartheid. It was a difficult time for Thabo, particularly because he was still involved in an intensive campaign to isolate South Africa. Only a person of his profound commitment, unquestionable integrity and intense thoughtfulness would have been able to pursue both initiatives without a sense of betrayal or compromise.

Dr Frederik van Zyl Slabbert, the leader of the then Progressive Federal Party (PFP), was among those Thabo met with during this period (he visited Thabo in Lusaka in 1984). Van Zyl Slabbert would go on to play a key role in organising the Dakar Conference of 1987, a meeting between white South Africans (mostly Afrikaner politicians, academics, clergy and businessmen) and the ANC, with Thabo playing a central role on behalf of the ANC. It was the sum total of all those contacts and consultations that gave impetus to the formulation of a framework for a negotiated settlement in South Africa.

However, the hazards of a diplomatic career meant that I would miss the most exciting phase of our struggle against apartheid. In October 1985, at very short notice, I was transferred back to Dar, to become personal assistant to President Ali Hassan Mwinyi, who had just been elected to office, replacing Mwalimu.

My six-year stint in Lusaka, where I had my most intensive and regular interactions with Thabo, was the highlight of my entire diplomatic career, not only because I was dealing with the most strategically sensitive issues facing the whole of southern Africa but also because it was out of my posting in Lusaka that I attained optimum career growth. Thabo may not be aware of this but he certainly contributed significantly to my development.

In Dar es Salaam, having taken up my new role at the president's office, I maintained regular contact with the local ANC representation in Dar es

Salaam, through the likes of the late Stan Mabizela, Manala Manzini, who later became the chief of South African security and intelligence, and the last man out, Thanduyise Henry Chiliza, who finally closed the long history of ANC presence in Tanzania and returned to a united, non-racial, non-sexist, democratic South Africa in 1994.

The thawing of Cold War tensions, accelerated by the fall of the Berlin Wall in November 1989, limited the Pretoria regime's ability to continue to prevaricate over Namibia's independence and the dismantling of apartheid in South Africa. Mikhail Gorbachev's perestroika (restructuring) and glasnost (openness) revealed the decline of Soviet power and, therefore, weakened the Western world's justification for supporting the apartheid regime. At the same time, the ANC's ongoing offensive in the US, where Thabo was now playing an active role, had made significant inroads both on Capitol Hill and with corporate America in New York.

Those who believed in the Frontline States' 'Domino Theory' strategy – a theory that, it is worth noting, was heavily contested by the ANC – argued that the fall of Mozambique, Angola and Zimbabwe had to be followed by the fall of Namibia and finally South Africa. When Jimmy Carter came to power as the 39th president of the United States of America, in January 1977, he immediately dispatched Andrew Young, the first black US ambassador to the UN, to southern Africa, to enquire from Mwalimu Julius Nyerere, the chairman of the Frontline States, as to what the new US administration could do to accelerate the ongoing liberation process in southern Africa. According to Andrew Young, Nyerere wanted the US to simply support in the acceleration of the Zimbabwean independence process by putting pressure on the British and 'leave Namibia and South Africa to us. We shall resolve them in our own way!' It is apparent that, on the basis of the 'Domino Theory', Mwalimu could clearly see the fall of Southern Rhodesian white minority rule, paving the way for a sharper and dedicated focus on Namibia's liberation and later 'Le Grande Finale', the dismantling of apartheid in South Africa. And so it was that after nine years of prevarication, the Pretoria regime had no choice but to commence the implementation of the UN Security Council Resolution 435, of September 1978, for Namibia. At the same time, the consultations between the various representatives of Afrikaans organisations and the ANC, now under Thabo's leadership, had gained substantial momentum, with an increasingly clear sense of direction.

As a committed pan-Africanist, Thabo was keen to see that the Namibian transitional process started and proceeded well. After extensive consultation, we agreed that I should get the Tanzanian government to mobilise the rest of the Frontline States' governments to establish a Frontline States Team (FROLISOT) inside Namibia, to assist SWAPO in ensuring that the process was carried out in strict compliance with UN Security Council Resolution 435 (1978).

Indeed, I became a member of the Tanzanian team which went around all the Frontline States and consulted extensively with governments and liberation movements on mechanisms for setting up such an observer mission, its mandate and function. The Frontline States Team was deployed in April 1989 and I was appointed Deputy Chief of Mission for the Tanzanian team.

After operating inside Namibia for three months, I flew back to Tanzania in mid-June, to brief the government on the status of the transitional process. As Thabo and I had maintained close and regular contact, my trip to Dar es Salaam was scheduled to coincide with an ANC delegation's visit to Tanzania (led by Oliver Tambo, the delegation was to include Thabo, Penuell Maduna, Steve Tshwete and Ngoako Ramatlhodi). The objective was to brief the Tanzanian government on the progress made from the series of the private talks between the ANC and the South African government, including the different Afrikaner formations. At the same time, Thabo had requested me to brief O. R. Tambo and the ANC team on the ongoing transition taking place in Namibia. At that stage, it was quite clear that the Namibian process was on course and South Africa would follow suit, sooner rather than later.

In the evening, I invited Thabo, Penuell Maduna, Steve Tshwete and Ngoako Ramatlhodi to my house for dinner and further discussions on ANC's proposals for South Africa's transitional framework. Prior to this, the ANC team had met Mwalimu and the OAU secretary general, Salim Ahmed Salim, to 'test the waters' and it all looked positive. In the course of our discussions, it was clear that the 'liberation train' was now heading towards its final destination, South Africa. It was, therefore, imperative that the ANC began to consult with its internal membership and external supporters, particularly the Frontline States, to get the buy-in it would need for the next step in the process.

In the course of our discussions, it was revealed that the intensive consultations between the ANC and the Pretoria regime over the years had enabled the ANC to develop a three-phase framework that would direct and govern the South African transitional process:

PHASE 1: *Creation of atmosphere for free political activities.* This entailed the unbanning of all political parties, the release of Nelson Mandela and other political prisoners, the suspension of death sentences, the return of exiles and refugees, the removal of troops from the townships, etc.

PHASE 2: *Creation of atmosphere for free negotiations.* Requiring the regime to repeal all discriminatory and repressive laws, etc.

PHASE 3: *Convening of an all-parties' conference.* Here broad political consultations could take place and front-end constitutional principles could be agreed. These would inform and guide political parties and ordinary South Africans as they elected a constituent assembly that would have the mandate to write the constitution for a new South Africa. This was necessary as none of the political parties would have, during the transitional stage, a democratic mandate to write a new South African constitution.

Our discussions continued until about 5am in the morning as we tested every angle of the transitional framework, the process and the intended outcomes. This was the first time that we'd had a comprehensive framework that looked realistic and gave hope for the early eradication of apartheid, through a negotiated settlement. It was a fine outcome after almost five years of intensive, behind-the-scenes consultations and negotiations.

As I drove the delegation back to their hotel, I asked Thabo whether the ultra-conservative and extreme right-wing faction of the apartheid regime would accept and/or support the proposals. Thabo assured me that, in their extensive consultations, even the Broederbond was on board, including personal assurances from its leader, Professor Pieter de Lange.

It was an exciting night! However, back at the hotel, close to 6am, we found President Tambo pacing up and down in the lobby, seemingly worried that he may have lost his entire team over the night – there were no cellphones in those days! Later that morning, the ANC delegation left Dar es Salaam for Maputo and the other Frontline States, to undertake similar consultations and spell out the way forward as agreed in Dar es Salaam.

Finally, a summit of the OAU Ad Hoc Committee on Southern Africa was convened and issued the Harare Declaration on 21 August 1989, which basically endorsed the proposed three-phase framework. The Harare Summit also resolved to submit the adopted declaration for further endorsement by the Non-Aligned Movement, the UN General Assembly, the UN Security Council and the Commonwealth. The responses from these bodies were extremely positive and the UN General Assembly, for instance, adopted a Declaration against Apartheid and its Destructive Consequences in Southern Africa on 14 December 1989, which was crafted along the same lines as the Harare Declaration. Thabo's active involvement and leadership were quite evident in all these initiatives as he crisscrossed the world to mobilise support for the transitional framework.

Very much consistent with the agreements reached between the ANC and the apartheid formations, as presented through the Harare Declaration, President F. W. de Klerk made goodwill releases of political prisoners such as Walter Sisulu and Ahmed Kathrada at the end of 1989 and announced the release of Nelson Mandela, the unbanning of the political parties and the end of the state of emergency on 2 February 1990. The great success of the Namibian transitional process, leading to her independence on 21 March 1990, meant that the focus shifted entirely to South Africa as the two sides worked so closely to implement the provisions of the Harare Declaration, largely through the Groote Schuur Minute of 4 May 1990 and the Pretoria Minute of 6 August 1990, both of which Thabo was actively involved in drafting.

In summary, everything that Thabo had briefed me about in Dar es Salaam in June 1989, relative to South Africa's transitional framework, unfolded and was implemented as per the plan. It clearly demonstrated Thabo's deep involvement and massive influence over the entire transitional process.

Following the independence of Namibia, which also marked the end of the Frontline States' Mission to Namibia, I returned to Dar es Salaam. Thabo was by this time spending more time at home, inside South Africa, dealing with the various aspects of implementing the fundamental provisions of the Harare Declaration. However, Thabo and I sustained regular communications and continued to meet at various international forums for briefing sessions which focused on the Frontline States, OAU and Commonwealth meetings, in particular.

While significant progress was being made inside South Africa towards the dismantling of the apartheid system and the ushering in of a non-racial, democratic era, spearheaded by the mainstream democratic formations headed by the ANC, the 'forces of the status quo', largely composed of right-wing Afrikaners, took various measures to disrupt the process, including fuelling so-called 'black-on-black' violence. Thabo and his colleagues in the ANC had to contend with various violent acts during the negotiation process, particularly following the commencement of the Convention for a Democratic South Africa (CODESA) at the World Trade Centre in Johannesburg, in December 1991, being the implementation of phase three of the Harare Declaration.

At the same time, the other political formations in South Africa that had 'missed the bus', like the pan-Africanist Congress of Azania (PAC), tried to justify their relevance by making unrealistic demands (demands outside what had been envisaged in the Harare Declaration). For instance, quite late in the day, the PAC demanded that the negotiation process for the dismantling of apartheid be conducted by a 'neutral chair and at a neutral venue'. The then PAC Secretary for External Affairs, Gora Ebrahim, was the strongest proponent of this approach and travelled across Africa to mobilise support. He tactfully exploited the collapse of the Nkomati Accord to drum up Africa's distrust in the genuine intentions of the Pretoria regime.

Gora Ebrahim managed to gain traction in some African capitals, including some of the Frontline States, by tapping into the apprehension felt by some of those looking in on the process. Even within the ANC there were concerns and these intensified when a small section of the ANC leadership, led by Thabo, begun mobilising for a 'phased lifting of sanctions', soon after committing the movement to accepting the 'suspension of the armed struggle'. Fortunately, Thabo had kept me abreast of the rationale behind this strategy. It was basically intended to leverage the ANC's strategic leadership over the entire negotiation process and its outcome. The phased lifting of sanctions was to be used as a 'lever for change', by 'incentifying the regime' each time it achieved a prescribed milestone.

At the same time, the strategic initiative was meant to get countries like the United States, which had instituted the Comprehensive Anti-Apartheid Act of 1986 but subsequently became too slow to deal with the fast-changing situation, to be able to, according to Thabo, 'break their own laws, by lifting certain classes of sanctions' in support of the positive progress that was being achieved on the ground. And indeed, the US responded positively and in accordance with the ANC's plan.

Prior to this, I vividly recall Thabo making the most compelling case on these highly controversial issues, in the wee hours of the morning during ANC's first national conference to be held inside South Africa since its banning 30 years earlier. The conference was held in Durban in February 1991. I was aide to the Tanzanian delegation to the conference, led by Comrade Kingunge Ngombale-Mwiru of the Chama Cha Mapinduzi (CCM), and, therefore, touched the South African soil for the first time ever.

Although Thabo had successfully put the case for the phased lifting of sanctions there were still serious misgivings over the Pretoria regime's real intentions within the ANC and in many African capitals, including my own. There was a feeling in some quarters that the ANC was giving up 'too much, too soon'. I personally had to put in extra effort to convince my political seniors to support the ANC's position on 'suspending the armed struggle' and 'phased lifting of sanctions' within the Frontline States, the OAU and Non-Aligned Movement's circles. On the eve of the Frontline States' ministerial meeting, held in Gaborone, Botswana, in August 1991, I even arranged for the then deputy foreign minister of Tanzania, now the secretary general of the CCM, Colonel Abdulrahman Kinana, to meet with Thabo, to appropriately appreciate the ANC's position on the two issues. Abdul Kinana, a teetotaller, paid a heavy price for that meeting – it took all night! However, once convinced, Colonel Kinana successfully assisted in mobilising his colleagues in the Frontline States. The Zimbabwean foreign minister, the late Professor Nathan Shamuyarira, my former professor at the University of Dar es Salaam, had initially remained quite hawkish, but we finally managed to soften his position in support of the motion. Thereafter, my former professor remarked to me, 'With these kinds of complications, it is time for some of us to pass over responsibility to your generation!'

Our next significant stop in our long journey of close collaboration was the Harare Commonwealth Heads of Government Meeting (CHOGM) of October 1991. As an ANC cadre, Thabo was staying at an obscure hotel in downtown Harare. As Senior Foreign Services Officer seconded to the Tanzanian president's Office, I was staying at the Harare Sheraton, which was also the conference venue. Consequently, Thabo would hold most of his meetings in my room and on some days I even had to pay for his taxi fare back to his hotel! To date, I am not even certain whether Thabo has ever carried a wallet. All the years that I have known him, money has never been an issue and, indeed, the one topic that Thabo and I have never discussed.

Since the transitional process inside South Africa had almost reached a point of no return and everything was pointing in the right direction, Thabo used the larger portion of his time at the Harare CHOGM to update the various foreign ministers and heads of state on progress in the implementation of the Harare Declaration. Through Thabo, the ANC also lobbied and successfully managed to secure the lifting of the Commonwealth cricket boycott against South Africa, a feat that made Steve Tshwete 'abandon' Thabo in Harare and rush back to Johannesburg to pop open some Champagne.

I spent the post-CHOGM time in Harare catching up with Thabo on the ANC's preparations for governing in South Africa – De Klerk's term was ending in April 1994 and it was quite evident that the next set of elections would be under a democratic and non-racial dispensation of some sort. Thabo was quite clear that although the ANC was certainly assured of the majority of the vote, post-apartheid governance in South Africa would require participation by as many different parties as possible – to avoid alienating any section of the population. He considered a winner-takes-all system as both undemocratic and unrealistic in the context of South Africa's distorted and lopsided racial and power structures. Thabo, therefore, elaborated on the ANC's commitment to have a post-apartheid governance structure that would involve the participation of any political formation that garnered 5 per cent of the vote or more. The sum total of these parts would then become a Government of National Unity (GNU). In the end, in spite of the ANC's majority position, it also invited and included Buthelezi's Inkatha Freedom Party and De Klerk's National Party to be part of GNU.

In January 1992, I was appointed to head up the Directorate of Africa and Middle East in the Tanzanian ministry of foreign affairs, and given a promotion to a full ambassadorial rank. Among my many responsibilities on the continent, the eradication of apartheid and resolving the Rwandese conflict, which had been unfolding since October 1989, were paramount. The following twenty months, until August 1993, I was fully occupied with mediation efforts for Rwanda, through the Arusha Peace Process, which I coordinated and chaired. However, I still sustained close and regular contact with Thabo and other ANC leaders. On Thabo's 'instructions', sometime in April 1992, I'd hosted Nelson Mandela at the Lake Manyara National Park for five days, when he was going through his marital separation from his estranged wife, Winnie Madikizela-Mandela. That availed me with a unique opportunity to get closer to Madiba and further deepen my political contacts and relations with the ANC leadership. This became quite handy when I was posted to be Tanzania's first high commissioner to the post-apartheid, united, non-racial and non-sexist South Africa, under President Nelson Mandela in 1994.

As I indicated earlier on, the growing success of the South African democratisation process also continued to attract disruptive interventions, largely sponsored or carried out by the right wing. These included the Boipatong Massacre of June 1992 and the Bisho Massacre of September 1992, both of which posed serious threats to the peace process, as the ANC, which was the main victim of the attacks, severally threatened to withdraw from the transitional process.

Thabo and I were in Dakar, Senegal, for the OAU summit in June 1992. The major issue on the agenda was the establishment of the Mechanism for Conflict Prevention, Management and Resolution in Africa. This was the next step after the 1990 declaration by the OAU Heads of State and Government on the Fundamental Global Changes and Africa's Response and the 1991 Abuja Plan of Action on Regional Economic Integration. It was concluded that none of the lofty ideas and grant initiatives would succeed if there was no peace and stability in Africa. Unfortunately, both the OAU ministerial council and summit failed to adopt the mechanism, largely due to petty politics, and the matter had to be postponed to the next summit in Cairo, the following June.

Thabo also spent time updating various delegations on the latest developments in the implementation of the Harare Declaration. He elaborated on the violent acts that were threatening smooth implementation and, in particular, Julius Nyerere's latest efforts, in London, to convince Nelson Mandela not to fall into the regime's diversionary ploy by withdrawing from the transitional process, as many ANC cadres had opted to do. Thabo found himself in a precarious situation, as he fully agreed with Nyerere's analysis and conclusion but Nelson Mandela insisted on the ANC's withdrawal from the talks. Ultimately, and fortunately, the ANC remained in the process, after receiving some specific guarantees from the regime.

I also took the opportunity to brief Thabo on the Rwandese peace talks that Tanzania had scheduled to launch in Arusha, soon after the Dakar OAU summit, on 10 July 1992. Even in the middle of South Africa's complicated transitional process, Thabo's commitment to various pan-African issues remained solid and he maintained an immense interest in the Rwandese process until its conclusion on 4 August 1993.

Thabo and I also worked very closely at the Cairo OAU summit in June 1993, where we finally concluded the work that we had carried forward from the Dakar summit and managed to adopt the OAU Mechanism for Conflict Prevention, Management and Resolution. The mechanism specifically underscored Africa's commitment to resolve its own internal conflicts, a commitment that was dear to Thabo, evidenced by the fact that to date he continues to participate in attempts to resolve a number of internal African conflicts. The adoption and implementation of the Harare Declaration was clear testimony to that commitment and the capacity that existed within Africa.

Soon after we had successfully concluded the Rwandese peace talks, with the signing of the Arusha Peace Agreement for Rwanda on 4 August 1993, after 13 months of non-stop, round-the-clock work, I was posted to Pretoria, in October 1993, as a representative at the Tanzania Liaison Office for South Africa. Through Thabo, as ANC head of international affairs (at that stage, almost operating jointly with Foreign Minister Pik Botha), arrangements were made for the Frontline States to establish liaison offices in South Africa to oversee the transitional process, as was done in Namibia, offer advisory assistance to the ANC when and where required, and prepare the ground for the establishment of diplomatic relations with South Africa, soon after the establishment of a non-racial, democratic dispensation.

As the Tanzanian representative, I became part of the OAU observer team, which was deployed around the country to observe the electoral process. Joe Lwegaila, the veteran Botswanan diplomat with whom I had served during the Namibian transition, was the OAU chief of the observer mission in South Africa.

In spite of all the threats of violence and boycotts, largely by Buthelezi's IFP, the elections went well and were declared free and fair by the South African Independent Electoral Commission and all other local and inter-national observers. Nelson Mandela was sworn in as the first democratically elected president on 10 May 1994.

With a skeleton staff of only two officers, I had to host both the sitting Tanzanian president, Ali Hassan Mwinyi, and the Father of the Tanzanian Nation, Mwalimu Julius Nyerere. As was to be expected, President Mandela was extremely busy, both before and after his inauguration. However, through Thabo's intervention, at 6.30am on 11 May 1994, a day after the big event, I accompanied Mwalimu for a meeting with Madiba before the latter left town, presumably to form his new government. Thabo arrived at Madiba's Houghton residence at the same time as we did, but with his shirt hanging out, his hair not properly combed, not wearing socks, etc. It was quite clear that Thabo had worked through the night. The Thabo Mbeki I know is a workaholic and a night owl who would not stop working simply because the night was getting younger. As a matter of fact, Thabo gets sharper and more efficient as the night gets younger, and many of us have paid a heavy price for hanging around with him during those odd hours. When Mwalimu saw Thabo, he whispered to me in Swahili: 'Hawakulala hawa. Utalalaje … utapataje usingizi wakati unabeba jukumu zito kama hili …?' (These people never slept … but how do you sleep when you have inherited such a huge responsibility?)

After brief pleasantries, Mwalimu informed President Mandela, in the presence of Thabo, that he had two pieces of advice to share as they assumed power in South Africa. 'You may choose to ignore the first piece of advice, but, please, Mr President, don't ignore the second one!' he stated. 'The one that you may ignore is about your relationship with your neighbours and Africa in general ... I know the Americans will very soon be coming and whispering to you that "... you are not like Burkina Faso, you are like us." Please, Mr President, don't listen to that! Don't behave like a big brother to your fellow Africans, because if you do, they will resent you. However, don't pretend to be a small brother either, because if you do, your fellow Africans will be suspicious of you. If Lesotho is providing leadership on an issue, please, Mr President, follow Lesotho, but if there is an African crisis and nobody is taking any action, then, please, Mr President, South Africa should not fold her arms. You must intervene! You should not behave like a small brother.' Mwalimu paused. 'But, as I said, you may ignore this advice! The advice that you should not ignore, Mr President, is about the Reconstruction and Development Programme, the RDP. Please, Mr President, stick to the RDP, don't abandon it, because it defines the true meaning of liberation as it focuses on the provision of education, health, water, housing, etc. Please, Mr President, don't ignore this advice, stick to the RDP!'

Driving back to the hotel, I turned to Mwalimu and said, 'But, Mwalimu, the RDP is the ANC's own governance blueprint. Why did you become so emotional about it, to the point of insisting that they shouldn't abandon it?'

Mwalimu, emphatically, replied, 'Ambassador, I am very worried about South Africa, because they have an affluence that the rest of us in Africa do not have, but they also have a poverty that the rest of us in Africa don't have ... I am very worried that the post-liberation leadership in South Africa will be sucked into affluence and begin to forget the poverty that the RDP seeks to address!'

It was clear that both Madiba and Thabo got Mwalimu's message and before we left Thabo made arrangements for Mwalimu to visit Soweto and see 'poverty' and later fly to Sun City to see 'affluence'. When informed that the Presidential Suite at The Palace of the Lost City at Sun City costs about US$4 000 per night, Mwalimu turned to me and whispered, 'Ambassador, I am glad that we are not spending a night here. If we were I would have requested you to pitch a tent for me somewhere!'

In the diplomatic life, the presentation of credentials is always the most solemn of occasions. However, on the day that I presented my credentials to Madiba, with a deep sense of genuine happiness and excitement, he broke through all the usual diplomatic formality, emotionally remarking, 'I am glad that President Mwinyi sent you, a person who knows our struggles as well as our aspirations …!'

During our tete-a-tete, rather than discussing bilateral issues between South Africa and Tanzania, President Mandela wanted to know why the former Zambian president, Kenneth Kaunda, was still in active politics! Thus clearly demonstrating the closeness of relations between the Frontline States.

My special relationship with Thabo and, through Thabo, with Madiba, was extended to almost the entire senior leadership of the ANC and the new South African government. It was as if the limitations of my diplomatic accreditation were simply just not part of the equation.

On 5 January 1995, while I was on holiday with my family in Cape Town, I got a call from my office that I had to take the first available flight and meet Deputy President Mbeki, in Pretoria, immediately. I was in Pretoria by midday, my head spinning, only to find out that I was scheduled to meet with the deputy president at 8pm. It turned out that I was to travel to Dar es Salaam the following day to deliver an urgent message to President Mwinyi and, I was, therefore, invited to spend the night, as Thabo and I finished our discussions too late for me to secure any hotel accommodation.

At about 2am, Zanele woke me up to inform me that Thabo had just received a message that Joe Slovo had passed away and that he wanted me to accompany him to Joe Slovo's residence. Minister Sydney Mufamadi joined us. To say that this was an unusual situation – the high commissioner of one country accompanying the deputy president of another to the home of a recently deceased struggle hero – is laughable as an understatement.

Thabo's ascendency to deputy president and my own posting as Tanzania's first high commissioner to South Africa did not change or modify the nature of our relationship. For Thabo, in particular, it was as if nothing had changed; always close, warm and very personal to me, even when I attempted (usually in public) to invoke some diplomatic courtesies.

Thabo would ban me from meeting him at the office – our meetings were always conducted at his residence where a lot of his cabinet ministers

and senior officials got to know our special relationship! Like our days in
Lusaka, I would still remain the last entry of the day in Thabo's diary and
our conversations would last till late at night. Thabo would remember all
the details many months, even years later, as he is always thorough in narrating incidents and experiences.

On a few occasions, Thabo would, to my profound discomfort, make
public references to our private conversations on a range of issues. It is a
sign of someone who is genuine and sincere, with a great deal of intellectual
honesty, but it had unintended consequences. The late South African foreign minister, Alfred Nzo, for instance, would jokingly refer to me as more
of 'an adviser than ambassador to South Africa.' His deputy, Aziz Pahad,
would be more 'threatening' and on several occasions he warned me that
I risked being declared 'persona non grata' in South Africa because 'each
time you have a conversation with our deputy president on some African
or global issue, we get into trouble the following day!'

However, in reality, Aziz's 'threats' only ever earned me an invitation to
Off The Record, a fine pub that used to be run by the Department of
Foreign Affairs at the Union Building, to further elaborate on issues at hand.

This kind of special relationship, reflecting the closeness of the relations that existed between Tanzania and South Africa, extended to many
ministers and other senior officials in the new South African government
– Trade and Industry Minister Alec Erwin always addressed me as his 'special adviser' on Africa – the ultimate dream of any diplomat! It also helped
me to effectively represent my various constituencies to the South African
government, when I concurrently became the dean of the entire diplomatic
corps, the dean of the Commonwealth, the dean of the African Group and
the dean of the SADC Group!

In spite of his hectic schedule and heavy responsibilities, Thabo always
had time for me and was accommodating, even to unusual requests. Close
to the commencement of the Commonwealth Heads of Government
Meeting (CHOGM) in Auckland, New Zealand, on 10 November 1995,
there was a lot of tension across the Commonwealth and especially within
Africa over the ruling by the military tribunal of General Sani Abacha's
regime in Nigeria to execute Ken Saro-Wiwa, a writer and leader of the
Movement for the Survival of the Ogoni People (MOSOP).

Based on his extensive contacts and profound knowledge on Nigeria, where he had served as ANC representative in the 1980s, Thabo had undertaken more trips to Nigeria than any other African leader in an attempt to dissuade the Abacha regime from executing Ken Saro-Wiwa and his colleagues. As my president (H. E. Ali Hassan Mwinyi) had two hours in transit at O. R. Tambo International on his way to Auckland, I hired a suite at the Holiday Inn, then in the vicinity of the airport, and asked Thabo to come and brief him on what had transpired during his numerous visits to Nigeria, with the view to formulating a common African position on the matter. Thabo gladly honoured my request, much to the sincere appreciation of President Mwinyi. Unfortunately, Ken Saro-Wiwa and his ten colleagues were executed on the eve of CHOGM 1995, on 10 November 1995, and Nigeria was suspended from the Commonwealth.

In April and May 1997, President Mandela and Thabo were deeply involved in reconciling the various conflicting groups in the DRC, through peace talks held at Ponte Noire, DRC, aboard the SAS Outeniqua. Thereafter, Mobutu escaped into exile to Morocco through Togo and Laurent Kabila took over power on 16 May 1997. President Mandela then left it to Thabo to sort out the mess left behind by Mobutu's sudden escape.

On Friday, 30 May 1997, Thabo called to inform me that President Mandela had instructed him to immediately take a break and that he wanted me to organise a trip to Zanzibar the following day. He insisted that the trip had to be strictly private and, therefore, he didn't want any welcoming ceremonies or formal receptions. He even refused to be accompanied by a medical doctor or any other aide, apart from a very minimal security detail. I communicated all of this to President Salmin Amour of Zanzibar, but on arrival we were welcomed by a large, cheering crowd, much to Thabo's fury! Noticing my profound embarrassment, he lightened the situation by remarking that, 'Chief, if you are a fool, you would think this crowd is for you but it is actually for your host!' Thabo is basically a very modest person and hates pomposity, particularly when exhibited by people in leadership positions. Later that evening he spent a long time lamenting the many African leaders who are so obsessed with ceremonies and status at the expense of the real issues hampering Africa's transformation and growth.

When the short break took us to Lake Manyara National Park,

Ngorongoro Crater and Serengeti National Park, Thabo's deep love of nature as well as cultural heritage became evident. We visited the Olduvai Gorge, one of the key paleoanthropological sites in the world, which provides strong evidence that Africa is indeed the cradle of humankind. A few years later, as South Africa's president, Thabo procured financial and technical assistance to help preserve the Timbuktu Manuscripts in Mali.

Thabo is a deep thinker, a philosopher, a visionary and a political strategist of repute. On 16 October 1997, I accompanied Mwalimu Nyerere to Cape Town where he addressed the South African parliament and later met Thabo at his Cape Town office. Here Thabo shared his views on the African Renaissance with Mwalimu and what needed to be done for the continent to take its rightful place in the global community of nations, after the end of apartheid, at the dawn of the 21st century. Mwalimu listened attentively to Thabo and, when he finished, his response was, 'You have a recruit here ... you have a faithful messenger here ... send me around to spread the word!'

As we were driving back to the hotel, Mwalimu excitedly remarked to me, 'That young man is the hope for Africa. He is the future of Africa. This is the leadership that will take Africa to the next level.'

Indeed, there was a special relationship between Thabo and Mwalimu that grew partly from Mwalimu's close ties with Oliver Tambo. Mwalimu was both a political and father figure to Thabo and he considered him a mentor and role model for selfless, ethical, principle-based leadership. Mwalimu's total commitment to Africa's liberation, respect, dignity, pan-Africanism and Third World solidarity sits very well with Thabo's own political convictions.

When Mwalimu Nyerere lay critically ill at St Thomas's hospital in London in September/October 1999, Thabo followed his condition on a daily basis. In fact, it was through Thabo that I first learnt of Mwalimu's death, even before I received a communication from the foreign office in Dar es Salaam. It was about 11am and he was on his way to parliament in Cape Town. He wanted to make an official announcement in parliament and wanted to get my view on this idea. I strongly felt that, to avoid any embarrassment to President Mkapa, the official 'breaking news' on Mwalimu's death should come from Dar es Salaam rather than Cape Town, advice that was well received by Thabo. As a gesture of profound respect for Mwalimu, Thabo, who was now the president of South Africa, declared five days of national mourning, with the national flag to fly at half-mast. He was the first dignitary to visit the high commission to sign the condolence book.

Thabo's feelings of personal loss became even more evident when he defied the five-person limit, per delegation, for the heads of state who were to attend Mwalimu's funeral in Dar es Salaam. President Mbeki's response was simply, 'No, Ami, just tell Dar es Salaam that the restriction would not apply to the South African delegation … If your problem is accommodation and transport, then we will just arrive early in the morning, travel to the funeral by bus and then fly back to South Africa!'

Indeed, Thabo led a 40-person delegation to Mwalimu's funeral that arrived in Dar es Salaam early in the morning and returned to Pretoria late in the evening. It included Foreign Minister Nkosazana Dlamini-Zuma and Home Affairs Minister Nkosi Mangosuthu Buthelezi.

It was quite some coincidence that 14 October 1999, the day that Mwalimu died, was also supposed to be my last day in the office, pending my early retirement from the diplomatic service, a decision that was strongly contested by both Mwalimu and Thabo! I was, however, of a strong view that, having spent the greater part of my career on liberation issues, the eradication of apartheid, the establishment of a non-racial, democratic order and seen the rise to the presidency in South Africa of both Nelson Mandela and Thabo Mbeki, I had reached the pinnacle of my career. No other diplomatic posting in the world would have led to the same sense of achievement.

I could feel that the political Thabo took my leaving the diplomatic service for the private sector as an act of betrayal. However, I know he also appreciated the private sector's strategic role in driving the African Renaissance. He therefore, rather unwillingly, accepted my decision, drawing comfort from the fact that I would divide my time between Dar es Salaam and Pretoria, where my kids were still attending school. And, in spite of my being out of public service, I found that I still had unhindered access to President Mbeki each time I was in Pretoria and our agenda would remain the same: 'Solving Africa's problems!' He remained a friend, a comrade, a brother and a sparring partner in the 'battles of ideas' regarding various African challenges and opportunities.

It is quite clear that commitment to Africa and Third World solidarity are key ingredients to developing a close relationship with Thabo – during his presidency this deep commitment, particularly on matters of peace, stability and dignity, sometimes even ended up overshadowing the most pressing domestic issues. He is a deep thinker, with an enormous capacity to unpack complex issues and render them easily comprehensible. As a visionary, he anticipates and plans for the future with a high degree of success. He provides strong and reliable leadership on most African and Third World issues. His intellectual prowess is unmatched by anyone of his generation of African leaders, which at times either intimidates or disarms people. As a result, Thabo does not tolerate mediocrity, a factor that often earns him false accusations of being arrogant, uncaring and extremely cold. At times, partly because of his cutting-edge ideas, Thabo turns out to be the most misunderstood of politicians, perhaps even more so in South Africa than elsewhere in the world.

My long relationship with Thabo has not been without differences of opinion but these have been surprisingly few in number. For instance, when he was deputy president, he refused my repeated appeals for him to balance his time in Pretoria, Cape Town and on foreign visits, with regular visits to the provinces and rural areas, arguing that, as the leader of government business in parliament, he needed to spend more time in Cape Town and Pretoria. We certainly differed significantly on our respective interpretation regarding the political events that ultimately led to his ousting as ANC president at the Polokwane national conference in December 2007 and later his recall as president of South Africa in September 2008.

In my view, Thabo grossly underestimates the work that was done to mobilise people against him. This work was done by his bitter rivals within the Congress of South African Trade Unions (COSATU) and the South African Communist Party (SACP) through the ANC structures as a 'punishment' for 'abandoning the Freedom Charter and, therefore, betraying the revolution' by embracing what they considered to be 'neo-liberal' economic policies as represented by the Growth, Employment and Redistribution (GEAR) programme. This is in spite of the fact that both COSATU and the SACP could not offer any alternative policy to GEAR when challenged to do so by Thabo and his colleagues. But Thabo has a different view, and ended up giving me a long lecture on the ANC's ability to self-correct, stretching way back to 1912, when it was formed.

When Thabo was recalled from the presidency, I was in Hong Kong. I flew back to Johannesburg immediately. As expected, being the statesman that he is, Thabo had handled his recall gracefully and with dignity, without any sense of anger. I pleaded with his ANC colleagues, who were planning to quit the ANC and form a breakaway party, not to break ranks but rather sustain the competitive tension within the ANC, because the group that carried the 'coup' in Polokwane were united by what they didn't want and that was Thabo Mbeki. I argued that when they had to define what they wanted, they would discover that they all had different ideas and different ambitions. Soon, after the dust had settled, some may even want to rejoin the so-called Thabo Mbeki camp. And, indeed, what is happening in South Africa today proves my point. It is gratifying to know that, because of Thabo, the majority of the South African people today have come to appreciate the significant role that committed, ethical, creative and honest leadership plays in national development. Thabo Mbeki has proven that he is not just a great South African leader, but an African hero, and as such he enjoys respect and admiration wherever he goes on the continent.

ANDERS MÖLLANDER

❧

My first reaction when asked to write a chapter for a book about Thabo Mbeki was that it was a great idea to produce and publish such a book, with or without my contribution. I felt that a lot of negative publicity had clouded the public perception of Mbeki in later years. To revisit his contributions to developments in South Africa during what were perhaps its most crucial years seemed like an excellent idea. My own first meetings with Mbeki were in the early or mid-1970s when Sweden was beginning to extend humanitarian support to South African refugees under the care of the African National Congress (ANC) in neighbouring African countries. I was first involved as a young bureaucrat in the Swedish International Development Cooperation Agency (SIDA) and later foreign ministry headquarters in Stockholm, and then on my first posting abroad to Dar es Salaam. When I was posted to the Swedish Embassy in Lusaka in 1977, my predecessor told me that Thabo Mbeki used to visit him at home on an irregular but not infrequent basis. The visits provided opportunities for us to be informed of important developments about the ANC and its struggle against the apartheid regime. We were also given the opportunity to ask questions and test ideas in a relaxed environment.

These visits continued after my arrival in Lusaka and, as others have testified later, Mbeki had the ability to make us feel like friends although what brought us together was important business. It would seem when he arrived on these visits that he and his companions just happened to be passing by, but more often than not they brought an important issue to be discussed

473

and/or forwarded to our headquarters. I shall give you just a few examples that stand out in my memory.

In 1979, Mbeki informed us about aborted talks in London with the Inkatha movement. The remarkable piece of information for us was that the ANC had been informed by a Swedish intermediary that the talks were to be held at Inkatha's instigation. So when they arrived in London, the ANC delegation had opened by asking what Inkatha wanted to discuss since they had asked for the meeting. It then transpired that Inkatha had been informed that it was the ANC that had asked for the meeting! I also learned from this information about initiatives on the part of some quarters in Stockholm to complement Swedish support to the ANC with support to Inkatha. Decisions about this support were taken outside the established channels. Mbeki's information made it possible for some of us to react and to give our views on the advisability or otherwise of these decisions.

Similarly, it was Mbeki who in 1979 alerted us when the ANC suspected that the International University Exchange Fund (IUEF) had been infiltrated by South African intelligence. I wrote to Stockholm about this and was at first rather sternly rebuffed. After what later transpired, it is clear that we should instead have thanked the ANC for warning us because Swedish funds were being diverted from the IUEF. It was later alleged that some of these funds were used by the apartheid regime to fund its death-squad activities.

When Zimbabwe won its independence in 1980, Mbeki was paving the way for ANC relations with the incoming Zimbabwe African National Union (ZANU) government. It appears that he was one of few international observers who saw the ZANU victory coming. As Sweden had good relations with both ZANU and the Zimbabwe African People's Union (ZAPU), and a measure of diplomatic protection, we could perhaps more easily travel back and forth to the country during this sensitive period. As I and other Swedish officials did so, we were able to share some of our impressions with our main interlocutor in the ANC in political and foreign affairs issues.

After a spell in Bonn, then West Germany, I was back in the ministry for foreign affairs in Stockholm in the mid-1980s, again on the southern Africa desk. It was during this time that I was approached by Mbeki on a very sensitive issue. He wanted to know whether Sweden could assist in helping the ANC in exile to communicate secretly with the leadership inside South Africa, including and especially with Nelson Mandela and others on Robben Island. He was not explicit, as I remember it, but said the need was increasing. He said that they could ask others, but would prefer to get this help from Sweden. He specifically mentioned a technique that he had learned about that made it possible to minimise text to hide it in inconspicuous communications. I forwarded the request to my superiors, but was later told that we were not in a position to assist.

I should perhaps have connected this request with another piece of information from Mbeki at about the same time. In his inimitable way, he approached me to ask what I thought one should make of the fact that a certain university professor with known connections to the apartheid regime had asked to see him. As we have learned later, this was one of the early attempts by the regime to establish channels to the ANC in exile. The idea was probably to give me and therefore Sweden a hint of what was happening. It was at the time very hard to believe that the regime would want to talk to the ANC in order to prepare for negotiations.

In 1986, Mbeki and I both took part in the People's Parliament against apartheid in Stockholm, which was Prime Minister Olof Palme's last public appearance on an international platform. I remember being struck by the immediacy of the rapport between Palme and Oliver Tambo in their talks on the margins of the meeting. I am making this point to illustrate that the rapport created in the field by Mbeki and others was indeed mirrored at the highest level.

In 1987, Mbeki was again the one to pass a warning to us in Sweden, when we most needed it. He had observed that Allan Boesak was a frequent visitor to Sweden, where he obviously enjoyed support. Now the ANC were beginning to have some misgivings about his affairs. Mbeki had run into Boesak in New York where Oliver Tambo was to give a speech in the legendary Riverside Church in Harlem. It later transpired that Boesak had used funds from donors in the Nordic countries for his own private projects.

When the ANC was unbanned in 1990, I had already spent almost three years at our legation in Pretoria. It was of course great to welcome ANC leaders like Mbeki back home, but also a nervous time as violence was rife, and especially directed against the ANC. I thought of this when I visited Mbeki at a flat he rented on top of a building in downtown Johannesburg. I was reminded of visiting his home in Lusaka. When I remarked that his was the only one in the row of houses without a guard at the gate, Thabo told me that it was to him, as an African, that the guards of his neighbours would come when they ran out of cigarettes or needed a small loan. So they will obviously also protect us, he said with that great smile of his.

In 1991, the ANC was able to hold its first congress in South Africa in over 30 years. I was there in Durban and saw a side of Mbeki that I had not seen before, that of the astute popular politician. He moved among the delegates, shook hands, stopped to talk and had his picture taken by young delegates, most of whom had of course never seen him before. He received a very high number of votes for his seat on the Executive Committee.

In the run-up to elections in 1994, it was clear that the foreign policy priorities of the ANC had to change from those of a liberation movement to those of a country and a government. Sweden moved from having been one of the movement's main priorities, as we were a major supporter and donor in the West, to one of many partners in foreign policy and trade. Some of my fellow Swedes found this difficult to understand. They must have noticed, though, as I did, that there were often signals that our common past had not been forgotten.

In the 1990s the Swedish government gave the highest priority to the sales effort of our fighter aircraft JAS Gripen and I was asked to accommodate the wish of Saab to have a private meeting with Thabo Mbeki when he visited Stockholm as deputy president. He agreed, but reluctantly, saying, 'I'll do it for you, Anders,' pointing out that he had consciously stayed away from the preparations for the purchase until it was time to take political decisions. The meeting with the Saab directors took place in Mbeki's suite at the Grand Hotel. I had arrived in advance and we had talked in a corner of one of the rooms. Mbeki then took my hand, as African men do, as we walked into the meeting with the Swedish company directors. I wonder to this day what they thought. Mbeki listened to the directors outlining the advantages of their product and then said thank you and prepared to stand up. Did he not have any questions? 'If I do, I can call Peter Wallenberg representing the principal owner of the company,' was the answer.

Arriving in 2005 at the president's house in Pretoria to present my let-
ters of credentials as Swedish ambassador to President Thabo Mbeki was
of course a great professional finale for me, having been involved with the
ANC and Mbeki since the very beginnings of Swedish official aid to the
ANC in the 1970s. It was not lessened by being addressed in Swedish by his
Chief of Protocol Billy Modise, who had studied in Sweden and been the
ANC representative there for many years.

Developments in Zimbabwe became a difficult issue during my years
as ambassador in South Africa. Mbeki's role as the Southern African
Development Community (SADC) mediator was criticised and little
understood. In a meeting with one of his closest advisers in the matter I was
told the following. Many, including Mandela and Mbeki, had tried to intervene with Mugabe when political opposition was being curtailed, often
violently. All such efforts had seemingly failed. When opposition leaders
were beaten up, SADC obviously felt the need to try again to intervene.
The issue was discussed and it was decided that the incoming chair of
SADC's organ on politics, defence and security, the Tanzanian president,
should be sent to talk to Mugabe. He did so, but came back to report that
Mugabe would only be willing to talk to Thabo Mbeki. Mbeki's team then
decided to set a minimalist agenda, one that would at least guarantee a reasonably fair and transparent election process. One of the results of the South
African negotiations was a ruling that votes should first be counted locally
and the results immediately posted outside the election hall. When voters
and observers were able to take pictures of the results it became impossible
to later change the results. The opposition gained a majority in parliament
and the ZANU government eventually had to accept the result and enter
into a power-sharing arrangement with the opposition.

The HIV/AIDS issue is another one where I suspect that Mbeki may
have been at least partially misunderstood. I had to explain to my headquarters and to almost all visiting politicians and journalists that to the best
of my knowledge Mbeki had looked at the issue with the same critical eye
that he used in other matters. He thus came to question why AIDS was
more prevalent in southern Africa than anywhere else and was worried
about the high costs of treatment. He was eventually told, as I understood it,

by the ANC's governing bodies to refrain from publicly questioning common wisdom in the matter of how the disease was contracted and what the preferred treatments were, but did so only after securing the right for South Africa to use so-called endemic and cheaper products.

During my years as ambassador to South Africa, we had a visit from Bosse Ringholm, former minister of finance, who had come for a meeting between the Social Democratic Party of Sweden and the ANC. We met Mbeki alone and had the opportunity to ask him what he thought of the ANC's prospects in the upcoming elections. Common wisdom at the time had it that the ANC would take a serious beating, mainly because the movement had seemingly been unable to deliver services and jobs in relation to the very high expectations of the population. 'We have asked ourselves the same question and have done extensive groundwork as a party,' was Mbeki's answer. 'The feedback we get is that people may complain of the speed of delivery, but they have not forgotten who freed them from apartheid, they have seen that up to two million houses have been delivered to the poor, along with services, increased pensions and child grants. They are aware of where the bottlenecks are, and are directing their anger principally at non- or poorly performing local politicians. We have thus struck a number of our local politicians from the electoral rolls.' He gave us a figure of the ANC's expected result in the elections, which we could later see was correct almost to the decimal point.

One of many reasons I hope that Mbeki himself will write a book about his career is that I would like to know what led to the very rare but obvious miscalculation on his and his advisers' part when going for re-election as ANC president at the ANC congress in Polokwane in 2007. When arriving there, it was soon obvious to all that a majority crowd had been assembled to cheer Mbeki's rival, the ousted former Deputy President Zuma. To meet these delegates with arguments and references to achievements as listed above was futile and was met by booing and general behaviour of a kind not seen at earlier ANC congresses, certainly not at the one I had attended in Durban in 1991.

Meeting Mbeki later at his home in Johannesburg during a private visit in 2009, I had the opportunity to inform myself about his view on a few things of the past, including his role before and during the negotiations leading to a new constitution and eventual elections and transfer of power. One of the things he told me concerned the background to the so-called 'sunset clauses', which were offered by the ANC at a late stage, assuring the white administration of job security. Mbeki explained that it flowed from a comment solicited from President Nyerere as one of the leaders of the Frontline States. Nyerere told the ANC that they must realise that when going into negotiations on a new constitution leading to general elections (i.e. one man-one vote), they were going to be the stronger party. Thus, they must be prepared to offer the other side some perhaps painful concessions. Mandela's message from jail was along the same lines.

When we left Lusaka in 1980, Thabo and his wife Zanele organised a party for me and my wife Birgitta. Thabo gave me a tape with South African jazz that he had himself recorded. It was lost when we later moved to South Africa in 1987. We had a mysterious burglary in our container of furniture and personal belongings. If, as I suspect, the tape ended up with the security services of the apartheid regime, together with personal letters and records, maybe it would be possible for me to have it back. Perhaps someone who reads this would know how.

With the few examples given above – all selected to accord with the title of this book, i.e. *The Thabo Mbeki I Know* – I hope that I have been able to convey a part of a bigger picture, namely of the important role that Thabo Mbeki played in relations between Sweden and South Africa. With his great communication skills, his charm and professionalism, he has helped us as a partner to be informed of important developments and considerations on the part of the ANC and later the government of South Africa. And in the process he has gained many friends in Sweden. I am only one of many who could write similar accounts of those times.

RANDALL ROBINSON

❈

I first met Thabo Mbeki when he was a young man in exile, attempting to win international support for the battle against apartheid. I, too, was a young man then, based in Washington, DC and attempting to do my part to end US support for the apartheid state. By that time, I had already read a great deal about Thabo's legendary father, Govan Mbeki, whom the apartheid authorities had tried so hard to break, and who was then one of South Africa's most famous – *and revered* – political prisoners. In time I would come to know and respect Thabo's younger brother Moeletsi as well. Thabo quickly became one of the most important links between black South Africa and the international community. His dignity, intellect and powers of analysis were such that we all fully expected that his would one day be a place of great weight and influence in a future South Africa.

Much has been written about the extraordinary impact of Thabo Mbeki in his role as deputy president during the Mandela presidency. And much, rightly, has been written about the transformative contributions he made to his country during the two terms that he served as president of South Africa. In addition to his admirable service as president of the most powerful black nation on earth, however, Thabo Mbeki has proven himself to be even more – as his writings, speeches, and work regarding the ideal of an African Renaissance make clear. His vision and impact not having been given life by any particular office, Thabo is neither obsessed with nor dependent upon any particular title. As gargantuan a challenge as the struggle against apartheid was, and as fulfilling as its replacement by democracy must have been, his concerns did not end there. Neither did he limit the investment of his energies to the interests of South Africa only. His African Renaissance work shows that his is the heart of a philosopher, visionary, and poet, and his mind that of an experienced pragmatist who understands what people of African descent have to do – and be – if we are ever to escape the elastic reach of colonialism and slavery.

Thabo believes, and I agree, that Africans' embrace of an African Renaissance is as crucial to us as water is to life. Indeed, in 1998, while still deputy president, Thabo said this at Gallagher Estate in South Africa: 'The beginning of our rebirth as a continent must be our own rediscovery of our soul, captured and made permanently available in the great works of creativity represented by the pyramids and sphinxes of Egypt, the stone buildings of Axum and the ruins of Carthage and Zimbabwe, the rock paintings of the San, the Benin bronzes and the African masks, the carvings of the Makonde and the stone sculptures of the Shona.' He continued: 'A people capable of such creativity … must be its own liberator from the condition which seeks to describe our continent and its people as the poverty-stricken and disease ridden … In that journey of self-discovery and the restoration of our own self-esteem, without which we would never become combatants for the African Renaissance, we must retune our ears to the music of Zao and Franco of the Congos and the poetry of Mazisi Kunene of South Africa and refocus our eyes to behold the paintings of Malangatana of Mozambique and the sculptures of Dumile Feni of South Africa …'

These words provide an important glimpse into Thabo Mbeki's mind and soul. And we have all, at different times, and in different places, witnessed compelling variations on this theme. In 2004, for example, with no international media to record him and no global applause to encourage him, Thabo Mbeki's choices on a matter discussed below yielded important insights into the character and convictions of the man that South Africans had chosen to lead their nation: Two hundred years earlier, Africans enslaved on St Domingue (now Haiti) had risen up and, in an extraordinary display of spiritual fortitude, military prowess and blinding determination, defeated the armies of Spain, England, and France in a gruelling war that lasted some 13 years. St Domingue was at that time by far the most valuable colony of any European power anywhere in the Americas – including the 13 North

American colonies combined. Western, slave-owning powers, therefore, had no intention of letting this slave-led revolution succeed. But St Domingue's fighters had no intention of returning to the pathological depravity of slavery either. The slave revolutionaries won. On 1 January 1804, the Republic of Haiti was born. And Western powers spent the next 200 years humiliating and destabilising Haiti for its temerity.

With this as a backdrop, the year 2003 unfolds and Thabo Mbeki has been president of the most powerful black nation on earth for four years. The demands on his time are enormous. He has a powerful, complex nation to lead. Most significantly, an election is looming in 2004. Halfway around the world, Haiti is planning its January 2004 bicentennial celebrations to commemorate its glorious 1804 Revolution, and they have invited the world's leading democracies to Haiti to help celebrate this extraordinary event. Western powers, in response, launch a relentless campaign to 'deep six' Haiti's bicentennial celebrations, telling international invitees that 'it is not safe' to travel to Haiti. Soon, one after the other, heads of state, heads of government and other dignitaries from around the world begin sending their regrets to the government of Haiti.

President Mbeki could have followed them all and sent an exquisitely worded congratulatory message printed on special parchment to the government and people of Haiti. He could have commissioned an extraordinary Haiti/South Africa sculpture to be placed in some public space in Haiti. Indeed, he could have sent a member of his cabinet to Haiti's bicentennial celebrations – or done like so many other nations and sent no one at all. Instead Thabo did what he knew would mean most to the ten million people of Haiti: he and Mrs Mbeki travelled halfway around the world and placed at the disposal of the government and people of Haiti, the power, the prestige, the respect and honour of the Republic of South Africa – the most powerful black nation on earth – as they, the Haitians, remembered and honoured their glorious revolution.

Once there, Thabo could have sat politely through the ceremonies, offered the perfunctory smile when appropriate, and then simply returned to his own country. Instead, he and Mrs Mbeki participated in the full array of magnificent reverential, ceremonial, educational and other activities that the Haitian government and people had so carefully and thoughtfully put together.

And then he spoke.

He spoke to the hundreds of thousands of Haitians who had flocked to the National Palace on their bicentennial morning, swaying and singing beautiful folksongs in celebration of who and what they were. He spoke to the foreign ambassadors living in Haiti who, like him, were seated on the outdoor dais, facing the crowds. And he spoke to the government, led by President Jean-Bertrand Aristide, that the people of Haiti had elected to lead them. He said, among other things, 'Today we celebrate because from 1791 to 1803, our heroes, led by the revolutionary Toussaint L'Ouverture and others, dared to challenge those who had trampled on these sacred things that define our being as Africans and as human beings.

'Today we are engaged in a historic struggle for the victory of the African Renaissance because we are inspired by, among others, the Haitian Revolution.

'We are engaged in a struggle for the regeneration of all Africans, in the Americas, the Caribbean, Africa and everywhere, because we want to ensure that the struggle of our people here in Haiti, in the Caribbean, in the Americas, Europe and Africa must never be in vain.

'Accordingly, together with the leadership and people of Haiti, we are determined to work together to address the problems facing this inspirational home of African freedom, and achieve stability and prosperity in this important site of African heroism – and wherever Africans are to be found.

'We trust and are confident that in both the leadership and people of Haiti we will find equally determined partners so that together we can here help to recreate a model country, informed by the wise words of the 1805 Constitution of Haiti that we have "an opportunity of breaking our fetters, and of constituting ourselves as a people free, civilised and independent".

'In this way, we will contribute to the renaissance of Africans everywhere in the world and ensure that we are no longer an object of ridicule and pity, nor a toll of exploitation to be discarded at the fancy of the powerful, but that we become what we really and truly are: proud and confident human beings who occupy their pride of place as equals among all peoples of the world.

'We wish the people of Haiti, all Africans and people of goodwill throughout the world, joyful Bicentenary Celebrations of the great Haitian

Revolution whose victory was proudly proclaimed this day, January 1, two hundred years ago.'

Travelling so great a distance to honour Haiti, its revolution, and its people – no enthralled international media recording his every move, no global fanfare urging him on, and probably despite having been urged by Western powers not to attend – spoke volumes about Thabo Mbeki's decency as a human being, and his character as a leader.

Most of all, it highlighted the sincerity and clarity, the meaning and power of the African Renaissance ideal that lives in his heart.

May the descendants of Africa everywhere understand the importance of the ideal of the African Renaissance that Thabo holds out to us.

And may we hasten to work with him in order to bring into being this gift that only we can create – by knowing and striving together.

X

ACADEMICS

BEN TUROK

⇥⇤

G iven the regrettable and ignominious removal of Mbeki from the presidency, it is difficult to view his political contribution in a proper perspective. I hope that this book will help us all to get a balanced view of his enormous contribution to our history.

I can offer only a few anecdotes about that contribution. First is his work on the New Partnership for Africa's Development (NEPAD) and the African Renaissance. He pioneered both and persuaded the whole of Africa that its destiny lay in its own initiatives. Of great importance to South Africans is that he reminded us that we are part of Africa and not Europe, and that out destiny lies here. He reminded us that during the struggle years, we were inspired by the work of Nkrumah, Nyerere and Kaunda and that we ought to follow in that tradition.

Of course NEPAD was primarily a developmental programme with a strong economic basis. At first it made a huge impact, but slowly the enthusiasm faded and Mbeki himself seemed to lose interest. A major reason for this failure was the division of responsibility between two ministers, foreign affairs and trade and industry, leading to passing the buck between them.

This legacy is now being taken up by the United Nations Economic Commission for Africa and there is much optimism about the new plans. But the seeds were sown by Mbeki.

I also want to comment on my own reactions to three major speeches. The first, 'I am an African', stunned the National Assembly both for its poetry and for its content. It has been interpreted in many ways, but the

487

essence was that it was a reminder, which is needed from time to time, that even though our country has a very diverse population, the African people are the vast majority, and as we build a country united in diversity, respecting all racial groups, we have to ensure that the cultural heritage of our African people is given the necessary status and recognition.

Another speech that stands out in my memory is the one about 'two nations'. This too stunned the National Assembly since it reminded us that no matter how we promoted unity and the rainbow nation ideal, the foundations of inequality remain intact. This is a tough lesson for the country to swallow. Our legislation is meant to serve all our people without discrimination, yet if we do not legislate for advancing the condition of the majority, we shall fail. The weakness of the speech, however, was that the socio-economic policies pursued by the government under Mbeki did not begin to remedy the legacy of underdevelopment even though he understood this condition perfectly.

The next anecdote refers to his speech at the Nelson Mandela Memorial Lecture at Wits University when he castigated conspicuous consumption, corruption and greed. It was a very strong statement, and the audience, which included many senior personalities in government and the private sector, was also stunned at his boldness. That speech remains a point of reference even now. Again, insufficient measures were taken to put his criticisms into effect.

Two other speeches stand out in my recollections, the speeches at the African National Congress (ANC) Policy Conference in Midrand when he drew a clear distinction between the democratic road and the socialist road, declaring unambiguously that the ANC was not a socialist movement. Here again he stunned the audience of over a thousand cadres and there was a great deal of agonising about that statement afterwards. Finally, I recall a remarkable speech he made at a conference of the World Bank at the International Conference Centre in Cape Town. I was invited to present on a panel at one of the sessions, but we all, about a thousand participants, gathered in the main hall to hear a keynote speech by Mbeki. I had been uneasy about the speech since Mbeki's government had been supportive of the World Bank's structural adjustment programmes, which I had opposed over many years.

To my delight, Mbeki recounted how at Sussex University he had been taught the theories of underdevelopment and that the policies of the International Monetary Fund and World Bank on fiscal discipline should be resisted since they would only stall the economy in developing countries. It was a brilliant performance that again stunned the orthodox economists present, including Nick Stern, the acclaimed guru of international economic theory who was due to report on his global scenarios. What also made a huge impact was Mbeki's warning that 'the poor are at the gate, and if those who have the key do not relent, the poor will break it down'.

So what do I make of this enigmatic man who was on the world stage for so many years? What puzzles me is that he came from such a radical tradition, including leadership of the Communist Party in exile; he fully understood the dilemmas of the Third World and in his mind and heart identified with their leaders and peoples, yet he was unable to take South Africa into a posture that would be consistent with its history, at home and in exile. As we struggle to develop an economic programme that will lift us out of the stagnation now gripping the economy, as we toss around several alternative economic policies, one is reminded that here was a man who had both the brains and capability to solve these challenges, but is not around to do anything about it.

WILLIE ESTERHUYSE

❧

The African National Congress (ANC) was for many years my enemy, given my political, cultural, educational and religious background. The social network and capital I shared with my fellow Afrikaners made what has become known as the 'construct of the enemy' the only justifiable manner in which the ANC could be described. And Thabo Mbeki was a rising political star in the ANC. He was my enemy. Mankind's history tells the story of how powerful the impact of the construct of the enemy could be on human relationships, interaction between groups and the machinations of states in the games of power humans sometimes play. In fact, many famous myths reflect this particular human condition. The biblical myth of Cain and Abel provides an excellent example in this regard: brother against brother; herdsman and tiller of the soil at odds with each other on the issue of land (in my opinion).

The course of events in South Africa during the eighties of the previous century made a meeting between me and Thabo Mbeki – or 'talking to the enemy' – inevitable. A possible meeting (1985), organised by Professor H.W. van der Merwe from the University of Cape Town, which would have included Professor Sampie Terreblanche, was cancelled. President P.W. Botha summoned me and Terreblanche to his office and in a friendly but very firm manner told us: 'We don't talk to murderers.' Two telephone calls in 1987, one from London (Fleur de Villiers on behalf of Consolidated Goldfields) and the other one a few weeks later from Pretoria (an official from the National Intelligence Service) put me on a course that made meeting Thabo Mbeki and talking to him just a matter of time.

I met Thabo Mbeki for the first time during the weekend of 21 February 1988, the second dialogue session between a few Afrikaners (academics and businessmen) and members of the ANC in exile. These dialogue sessions were called 'talks about talks': informal, unmandated and confidential but nevertheless important for they were aimed at understanding 'the other'. The first session took place during the weekend starting 1 November 1987. Aziz Pahad, Tony Trew, Wally Serote and Harold Wolpe were the ANC participants. Willie Breytenbach and Sampie Terreblanche accompanied me, the three of us hailing from Stellenbosch.

The second meeting took place in impressive surroundings: the Eastwell Manor Hotel in Kent. I had heard a lot about Thabo Mbeki. I had also made a special effort to collect and read everything written by him or about him. It made me nervous! I wondered whether we as Afrikaner participants would be a match for him. Known for his charm and composure, he was – as I was informed by someone – resolute and unwavering in his purpose of destroying the apartheid system.

I remember the moment of standing in front of him, being introduced by Michael Young, the dialogue group's independent (British) convener. I took his hand, trying to make a mental note of my first impressions: body language, the tone of voice, eye contact, expressiveness and signs of 'reaching out'. At the back of my mind a question that made me smile: 'What would P.W. Botha say if he could have witnessed the handshake?' I was advised by my contacts from the National Intelligence Service not to say too much, but rather to listen carefully and make detailed notes. 'He is an important ANC leader. We need a comprehensive profile of him,' my contact emphasised.

Not knowing much about 'profiling', I carefully prepared an opening remark that I had learned by heart: 'It is a pleasure to meet with you. I have heard that you studied at Sussex University and that you are an economist with an appetite for political philosophy and literature.'

It was a waste of time. I did not get the opportunity to say what I learned by heart. Mbeki, cordial and confident, took the initiative. Taking my hand in a firm grip, he said, as I recall it: 'Oh, the professor of philosophy from Stellenbosch.' Later: 'I've read your book *Apartheid Must Die* (1979). It was a risky book for you to have written. Apartheid was supposedly intended to protect Afrikaners, but your book actually says that apartheid would lead to their self-destruction.'

By 1988 the book was outdated. He nevertheless floored me. I wrote in my notebook that night before going to bed: 'We have a common goal: the end of apartheid. Would the two of us also learn to find common ground about the route to this goal, given the ANC's violence option?' The next day (a Saturday) he provided me with a (partial) answer to my question: 'Violence generates violence. Apartheid is a violent system – structurally and in practice. Why blame only the ANC?' Thabo Mbeki, at our first eye-ball-to-eyeball meeting, unintentionally inspired me to make one of the most important and resolute decisions I have ever made: to trust him with information that at that stage was very sensitive, namely my contact with the National Intelligence Service. I asked myself: Should I not just walk up to him and without much ado tell him: 'Yes, I am a professor of philosophy from Stellenbosch. But take note: I am well connected with the Spooks of Pretoria.'

My first impressions of him? In my notebook: 'Friendly. Charming. Serious. Controlled. Attentive to what was being said. Glints of humour in his eyes. Steel in his teeth.' Underneath a tree in the icy grounds of Eastwell Manor, I told him – in a serious tone – that our dialogue group actually also amounted to 'talks within talks', one form of dialogue involved the whole group; the second was private and personal between him and me and related to my National Intelligence connection.

I stressed the fact that I had no mandate and that I had no knowledge of the National Intelligence Service's game plan. He looked at me with his piercing dark eyes, all emotions completely under control. 'You are aware that you're taking a risk by informing me? Why are you doing it?' I replied: 'Not informing you is a greater risk. What do I do if the talks leak out, and also if it should take longer than was anticipated and we make progress?' He said: 'Good. I hear you.' Just that.

Trust and confidence building is also about the sharing of risks. It does not mean that you are in full agreement with the person you trust and have confidence in. I was asked by the National Intelligence Service at the beginning of 1989, after P.W. Botha's stroke, to get a reliable and confidential telephone number from Thabo Mbeki. The National Intelligence Service wanted to explore direct talks with the leadership in exile. Mbeki was their point man. I made the arrangements with sardonic irony: We must meet in London on the Day of the Republic – which was 31 May. We met in a pub, the Albert, where he gave me the telephone number on a piece of paper which I still have. Included were a few Afrikaans words.

Mbeki, more than anyone else from the ANC, helped me to 'deconstruct' my concept of 'the enemy'. He liberated me in this respect. His role in the complex and even dangerous preparatory process for a negotiated settlement was pivotal, if not more important than anyone else's in the ANC. If he 'seduced' me – and even Van Zyl Slabbert – as some nowadays claim, it was for a good cause: an inclusive, negotiated settlement of the deadly conflict that was raging like a bushfire throughout our country. The Mbeki I got to know many years ago is the Mbeki I still trust. And have confidence in: an African leader with an inspiring and well-founded vision – Africa's development and renaissance, led by committed African leaders.

JOHN STREMLAU

❧

My interest in Thabo Mbeki as an African National Congress (ANC) stalwart, advocate for liberation, national leader and world statesman began in the 1970s when I was an international relations programme officer with the Rockefeller Foundation in New York.

The Foundation in 1978 launched a multi-year independent national commission to critically assess US policy towards South Africa. And one of its first decisions was to reach out to the ANC to understand how it envisioned eventual majority rule in South Africa. That was how I first became acquainted with Thabo Mbeki who was handling foreign affairs for Oliver Tambo.

We met numerous times during the years following and I became a great admirer of his intellect, his vision. He was always willing to listen and debate, demonstrating a deft ability to adapt to changing circumstances and compromise, but without ever betraying the enduring principles of the ANC and its democratic Freedom Charter.

But I must say there were some odd moments in our conversations and one anecdote, which I will share, was indicative of challenges he and the ANC faced. Around 1985 I arranged to meet Mr Mbeki at a Capitol Hill coffee shop in Washington, DC. We had a long and probing conversation because by that stage he was interested in the kind of black leadership development grants that the Rockefeller Foundation was making in South Africa. I was able to go back and forth a couple of times a year to work with United Democratic Front/Black Consciousness Movement affiliated, community-based organisations to give them a little help. There was enough in the US-South African relationship of the day to allow me to operate, but I was always under a lot of threat and constraints; nevertheless, we were working with oppressed South Africans.

He wanted to know what was happening and I wanted to share our findings with him. Afterwards, as we stood outside to say goodbye, sirens screamed as a motorcade worthy of a major head of state zoomed past with flags flying. But it was not a head of state at all, merely the Reagan administration giving undue prominence to Jonas Savimbi, the rebel leader in Angola. And I thought: Here I am standing next to a man with the potential to one day be the democratically elected leader of Africa's most important country, South Africa. First, however, Mbeki and the ANC had to overcome such political absurdities as the US ties to the likes of Jonas Savimbi or, worse, the racist minority in South Africa.

Well, Thabo Mbeki did have a way with words and with ideas and had empathy and a sophisticated understanding of the complexities of American politics, while building support among liberal/progressives concerned about South Africa and committed to changing US policy.

Mbeki also understood that from my perspective I feared escalating race war in South Africa would exacerbate racism in the United States. One could only imagine the effects of nightly television news reports of full-scale civil war in South Africa barely ten years after America's own civil rights struggle, and amid the still simmering sediments of slavery and related racist tendencies. A situation where progressives demanded the US support South Africa's freedom forces, where opposing conservatives demanded respect for America's traditional Cold War ally, the white minority racist regime that still enjoyed widespread sovereign recognition, could prove politically poisonous and polarise communities across America.

Talking to Thabo Mbeki, however, convinced me that violence was not inevitable and could be prevented, if only we could bridge these differences. And what I admired most was his ability to see all sides of a problem and to talk them through. That was what drew me to him as a source of hope despite prevailing current events.

South Africa is a complicated place and in ways sometimes familiar to Americans, which led me to believe the two nations have a special relationship, interdependent politically, socially and culturally, as well as because of their extensive economic ties. How this is perceived and by whom in US politics continues to evolve, often in surprising ways.

In 1989, although a registered Democrat, I had an opportunity to join the incoming Republican administration of George Herbert Walker Bush, serving as Deputy Director for Policy Planning in the State Department and into President Clinton's Democratic administration. My first week on the job I found a request pending from F.W. de Klerk for a meeting with President Bush, with Policy Planning tasked with drafting a recommendation for Secretary James Baker to give the White House. Policy Planning recommended the request be declined as De Klerk had not yet shown sufficient willingness to compromise with the democratic forces. The recommendation was accepted, which did not please De Klerk and it was a straw in the wind of change.

Why was that happening? James Baker was a shrewd politician and realised that the Reagan administration had been bedevilled by the antiapartheid legislation. Baker was smart enough, and I think that the elder Bush was also smart enough, to see which way history was moving and by that stage Mbeki was pushing on an open door, even though these were Republicans. Mbeki's work, together with many ANC comrades and allies in many nations, was finally bearing fruit.

Diplomacy is a little bit like water polo; a lot of the kicking goes on underneath the surface. You do not understand until you actually see the score of who is ahead and who is behind. I was surprised and thrilled by the release of Mandela and the changes that followed, culminating with the 1994 election. So when I had the opportunity in 1997 to accept a teaching position at the University of the Witwatersrand (Wits) as head of International Relations I took it, confident that the ANC, a nationalist-based organisation and, true to the Freedom Charter, an inclusive, non-racial, democratic organisation, was capable of leading the country and Africa to a better place.

Upon reaching Wits in 1998, however, I found the Department of International Relations paid very little attention to Africa and post-94 foreign policy. All the curricula materials were from Europe and America. My department was nearly all white male, and Africa was as marginal as it would be in a US university course on foreign policy and international relations. So my dual objectives were to try to do what I could while I was holding this position: first, to transform the faculty and, secondly, to transform the curriculum so that it would be more appropriate to a democratic South Africa – an influential force for good on the African continent.

Fortunately I had a great deal of help in doing this job from Deputy President and later President Thabo Mbeki. Of course he didn't know this at the time, but many efforts to engage other African leaders and regional organisations, as well as the rest of the world, generated an endless stream of teachable moments and issues for students to reference and debate. It was a heady time for IR students and faculty alike and we tried to make the most of it, including launching a Centre for Africa's International Relations reflective of South Africa's new foreign policy priorities. It was especially exciting and inspiring to our legions of young African students, and certainly made my job a good deal easier!

Moreover, there are important aspects in the back story of the ANC's ascension internationally that continue to inform IR teaching and research. Although we still live in a world of sovereign states, with norms of non-intervention and sovereign equality important restraints preventing the strong forcing their will on the weak, the United Nations (UN) Security Council's historic decision to declare apartheid a threat to international peace and security was the first time that an internal affair of a member state was internationalised to this degree. As US President Jimmy Carter subsequently declared when addressing the UN General Assembly: 'The abuse of power within states was too important to be left to those states alone to solve. Today's human rights abuses generate tomorrow's refugees along with new threats to the peace and security of the offending regime's neighbours.'

As President Mbeki assumed the reins of South Africa's post-apartheid foreign policy, his actions showed a new recognition that peace with justice in Africa will require a rebalancing of the sovereign rights and obligations to protect and advance human rights. Though, to be legitimate and sustainable, he maintained such issues are best resolved through negotiation rather than the use of force. In the absence of magic formulas, real-life crises also become 'teachable moments' for practitioners and scholars alike.

An attribute of President Mbeki that I have watched play out is that he does not put himself above other leaders or interlocutors internationally. But he expects the respect of an equal and he will give that reciprocal recognition himself as a way to move forward. When he started talking about the African Renaissance and I was teaching new classes of increasingly majority black students, I was able to explain why the field of international relations is so relevant to their lives. It was also exciting because Africa was opening up to cooperation with South Africa, which was no longer a pariah state. The country had a new president with another resounding democratic mandate and bold foreign policy priorities beginning with being a good neighbour to Southern African Development Community (SADC) partners and extending to the rest of the African Union (AU). Globally, South Africa would also seek close ties with those countries further abroad, especially if demonstrably committed to taking collective progressive action in sync with Mbeki's vision of an 'African Renaissance' and his New Partnership for Africa's Development (NEPAD) and Peer Review Mechanism. No wonder this fired the imagination of Wits students, tomorrow's South African leaders.

At the same time, South Africa's new and activist foreign policy conveyed to the major powers: Don't you tell us how to do these things. We are ready to decide among ourselves the norms, the institutional reforms and the political resolve to advance and consolidate this new pan-African way of thinking. There were of course setbacks and contradictions, but Mbeki deserves credit for forging strategies and actions that have sought to insulate Africa from foreign meddling and greater African regional activism to reduce if not remove opportunities for such meddling. And students easily grasped a foreign policy rooted in Mbeki's vision of African collective action which, in effect, said: Look, it is time for us to grow up and take care of our neighbourhood and ourselves and to insulate ourselves from the horrors and abuses of foreign intervention and foreign dependency that have ravaged and stunted the growth and possibilities of a prosperous, democratic African future.

Undergraduate enrolment in International Relations suddenly doubled, with similar increases at the postgraduate level, although initially the new majority came from universities in East, West and Central Africa. By the time I stepped down in 2006, the majority of the teaching staff had become much younger, far more expert on Africa's international relations, and were by slim majorities predominantly non-white and female. As with our postgraduate cohort, several new staff came from other African countries, important assets for teaching and research about Africa's international relations and disseminating Mbeki's ideas for critical debate and consensus building.

My successor, Professor Gilbert Khadiagala, is doing a great job and continues to develop the curriculum faithful in tone and substance Afrocentric. Mbeki's pioneering efforts to advance an African Renaissance, collective African initiatives to solve African problems and the expanding roles of the AU and Regional Economic Organisations are priority interests for teaching and research.

During my years with the Carter Center in Atlanta, from 2006 to 2014, I had almost no contact with President Mbeki but had ample opportunities to see and benefit from the widespread positive effects of his Africa policies. Most notable was when the Carter Center observed the 2006 transitional election in the Democratic Republic of the Congo (DRC). This election was possible only because of Thabo Mbeki's initiative and commitment to finally bringing all of the key Congo antagonists together at Sun City which, after much wrangling and constant pressure from South Africa, produced a historic peace agreement with provision for the DRC's first fully open national presidential election.

William Swing, formerly a US ambassador to South Africa, was the head of the United Nations (UN) operation in the Congo during this critical period and recounts how throughout the complex peace operations in the DRC, the biggest UN peace operation ever mounted, for the first time in any UN mission, the lead state was not a Western major power; the lead state in this case was South Africa.

Swing told me that any time the UN needed helicopters, weapons, communications equipment or virtually anything else, including sound advice, he knew he could always turn to Thabo Mbeki for help. Mbeki committed his nation to a huge investment because of his strategic sense that the future of Central Africa would never be secure if there was not a peaceful Congo, a work still in progress.

And there have been other peace efforts to Mbeki's credit in the troubled

Great Lakes Region. During his presidency, Deputy President Jacob Zuma was the AU's special envoy to Burundi. He invited several academics to join an informal Burundi advisory group, which may not have contributed much to peace, but revealed how difficult and complex this task was that South Africa had voluntarily undertaken to try to prevent another deadly conflict and to advance regional security. After recounting in great detail the many factional leaders, and their strengths and weaknesses militarily and politically, an exasperated Jacob Zuma quipped that if he had 20 or 30 ANC cadres he could solve the matter very quickly, but the factions were so unwilling to compromise. It was a reminder of South Africa's special genius for debate, compromise and consensus building, skills never gained easily and in need of constant sharpening domestically and internationally, as Thabo Mbeki advocates.

One foreign policy problem that has not been amenable to persuasion and compromise has been in the protracted political crisis and repression in Zimbabwe. Political developments in Zimbabwe also raise complex and contentious domestic political issues within South Africa. Mbeki's initial reaction to seizure of white-owned farms during the early phases of the crisis following the 2000 election reminded me of my fears in the 1980s that racial tensions among South Africans might have serious negative repercussions within America. Land is such a sensitive issue in South Africa that President Mbeki's first responsibility, I believe, was to protect the safety and integrity of the South African people and to find a way to insulate the country from a fight over land in imitation of or as an extension of what President Mugabe was doing in Zimbabwe. So I regarded Mbeki's initial diplomatic moves to be quite deft in reducing a threat to South Africa's domestic peace and tranquillity, even though his subsequent efforts in support of power-sharing and peaceful political reforms were unsuccessful and the crisis has passed to his successor, including the many problems arising from the many Zimbabweans – estimates range from one to three million – who have sought refuge in South Africa since the crisis began.

Of course not just Zimbabweans, but many people from other African countries emigrate to South Africa because they want to flourish and prosper here. And while the influx is not an unmixed blessing, it is a credit to the country's successful transition and to the leadership of Mandela and Mbeki that South Africa became so appealing a destination for others. No one is rushing into Nigeria in droves, nor are they rushing into China; they are rushing into South Africa because it promises economic opportunities, the rule of law, and democratic governance. These values matter internationally, as I am reminded when I reflect upon the life and times of Thabo Mbeki's political activism and public service.

Mbeki is a great representative for Africa globally. From my perspective, he was the first foreign policy president able to advance South Africa's national and regional interests and values eyeball to eyeball with any leader, however powerful, anywhere on the planet. Historically, Africans have been the world's shock takers, ever and often horribly the object of exploitation and even now to the havoc of climate change caused by others. Africa's economies are small and its politics balkanised and rooted in a history Mbeki knows better than anyone.

Mbeki's grasp of the hard realities and driving passions at the heart of world affairs covers so many areas, but none more important for Africa than the legacy and persistence of racial hegemony and prejudice. This was evident when he chose to be the only head of state to go to the 200th anniversary of the Haitian revolution. Now that I have lived in the American south, I realise what the Haitian revolution meant for the dignity of black people. With the repression of African-Americans in the American plantation-culture oligarchy, whites in the South's cotton belt states were scared to death of another uprising like that which occurred in Haiti. And yet I think that President Mbeki did not want that history to be forgotten. That is why I commend him for attending the 200th anniversary; other leaders should have attended too but they did not. Mbeki has that special sensitivity to what the struggle for dignity and equality is about.

Thabo Mbeki was a founding father of a new kind of pan-Africanism: more pragmatic and more engaged, including promoting greater collective involvement in the internal affairs of African states for failing to meet their sovereign obligations under relevant international instruments. Africa obviously remains a gaggle of sovereign states, but Mbeki often reminds all that these were mostly demarcated by colonial powers with little concern for the peoples residing there.

Integration is difficult and takes time, yet Mbeki's leadership in the establishment of the AU, and the development, if not the recent testing, of the African Charter on Democracy, Elections, and Governance (ACDEG) helped establish the authority and legitimacy for unprecedented experiments of African collective engagement. Experience since then has shown, however, that when provisions of the ACDEG have been invoked in efforts to stabilise and advance democratic governance in fragile states such as Madagascar, Burundi, Burkina Faso or Central African Republic, the process can be fitful, ragged and at best of only limited success. To Mbeki's great credit, however, new pan-African structures and procedures are in place and are being tested albeit with many difficulties.

Lest we forget, 1994 marked a successful internationalised transition to democracy in South Africa, but also the failure by regional and international organisations to take preventive action when warned of impending genocide in Rwanda. One small by-product has been the adoption of new norms that sanction collective intervention to prevent genocide and other crimes against humanity, now commonly referred to as the 'Responsibility to Protect' or R2P. While this idea has generated support among scholars, Mbeki's approach is rightly cautious. And the moral hazards of applying R2P continue to be hotly debated in the case of Libya.

The public needs to debate such matters and it helps when there are statesmen of Thabo Mbeki's calibre at the focal point of such debates. South Africa has been reluctant to use force but, at least under Mbeki, was willing to invest substantially to advance peace in Africa, most notably in the DRC. This, of course, is very different from the 2003 intervention George W. Bush undertook in Iraq, which Mbeki reportedly lobbied Bush not to do, based on superior South African intelligence regarding alleged weapons of mass destruction. Mbeki deserves credit for trying.

Mbeki's outreach to candidate George W. Bush is also instructive. Given his close working relations and friendship with Bush's presidential opponent, the then US Vice-President Al Gore, Mbeki might have been expected to give Bush a cold shoulder. Yet who was the only foreign leader to venture down to Crawford, Texas, to meet presidential candidate George W. Bush in 2000? It was Thabo Mbeki. Why did he do that? Because if George W. Bush were elected he would be in charge of the most powerful nation and Mbeki would not be intimidated but only seek what he believed to be in South Africa's best interests.

When President Mbeki resigned and returned to private life in September 2008 I was far away in Atlanta, Georgia, at the Carter Center. While I found it difficult to comprehend the internal ANC politics that precipitated the resignation so close to the end of his second term of elected office, much less the judicial ruling that precipitated the ANC Executive Committee's recall and the unanimous overruling of that judgment by the Supreme Court of Appeal three months later, the bottom line for me seemed startlingly clear and carefully drawn by Thabo Mbeki. He chose not to fight the decision but rather to place the interests of the ANC and the country ahead of his own, thus preventing what appeared to be an obvious risk of conflict that could have ruptured the party and even destroyed the still fragile democracy to which he had dedicated his life. As his resignation resulted neither from a parliamentary nor a popular vote, and may raise constitutional issues in the course of South Africa's democratic development, his committed service to party and country is for me very clear, and a positive example to others in or aspiring to high office in Africa or abroad.

Informed Americans compared Mbeki's response to the decision taken by the ANC Executive Committee to the reaction of US Vice-President Al Gore when the US Supreme Court ruled that George W. Bush had defeated him in the 2000 US presidential election, even though Gore believed, and it was later confirmed, that he had received more votes than Bush. Gore did not question the legitimacy of the Court's ruling, just as Mbeki accepted the legitimacy of ruling of the ANC Executive. In both cases we have leaders willing to put the national interest ahead of their own. It is across Africa, however, where I believe Mbeki's example should resonate most positively and powerfully.

I recall the indefensible and costly price the people of Ivory Coast paid when incumbent president Laurent Gbagbo defied what independent impartial international election observers, including the UN and the Economic Community of West African States (ECOWAS), determined was his decisive defeat in the 2011 election there. Ghana's former President John Kufuor was in Abidjan to observe the election and at a private dinner the night of the vote appealed to Gbagbo to put the interests of the nation first, whatever the results. Gbagbo dismissed the suggestion, saying

he would lose all his friends and not know what to do if out of office. The
country and he would have been better off had he followed the example of
Thabo Mbeki, an example that today is being advanced by a growing number of former democratic leaders seeking democratic solutions in troubled
countries from Madagascar, the Great Lakes Region, across the Sahel and
elsewhere. Progress has been clearly evident in Ivory Coast and in each of
its Mano River Region neighbours. All remain 'works in progress' as democratic development is difficult for all nations and never done, even in the
world's oldest and richest countries. And in Africa we know there are still
too many ageing autocrats who refuse to play by the rules, even those they
once wrote for themselves, which make the good examples set by Mbeki
and other diehard democrats all the more vital for Africa's achieving its full
political potential.

Finally, the attributes I came to know and admire in Thabo Mbeki remain
clearly evident in his continuing public service, even while out of office
these past eight years. He remains active on issues of regional peace and
security and economic cooperation, which are vital for Africa's self-determination and sustainable development. They illustrate his continuing belief
that Africans are capable of pursuing for themselves a progressive agenda
provided there is, in his words, 'sufficiently strong, cohesive and determined
international collective leadership'.

Two examples especially impress me. One was his 2011 appointment to
chair the African Union High Level Implementation Panel (AUHIP) for
Sudan and South Sudan with a sweeping mandate but few resources to
assist the democratic transformation of Sudan. South Africa under Thabo
Mbeki's leadership had worked very hard on behalf of South Sudan's bid
for independence and was a key international stakeholder in the 2005
Comprehensive Peace Agreement that everyone hoped would be the foundation for sustainable peace and development for both countries. When
conflict persisted, within and between them, the AU turned to Mbeki who,
along with AUHIP members, former presidents Abdulsalami Abubakar of
Nigeria and Pierre Buyoya of Burundi, have tirelessly tried to bridge differences in multi-track negotiations still continuing in 2016 but without any
definitive successes.

What we cannot know is whether, without the patient and persistent peace work of the AUHIP, the Sudanese situation would have been far worse. But this serves as another important illustration of Thabo Mbeki's tenacious commitment to finding common ground, as earlier demonstrated in his efforts to bring democracy to South Africa and peace in the DRC.

A second example of the former president's continuing ambition to advance Africa's development is in his efforts to curtail illicit financial flows that are costing Africa as much as $50 billion annually, twice the amount received in official development assistance. Since February 2012 Mbeki has chaired the High Level Panel on Illicit Financial Flows under the joint auspices of the African Union Commission and the United Nations Economic Commission for Africa. Although the problem is daunting, the work of his panel is already having a positive impact on governments, as evident during the July 2015 Financing for Development Conference in Addis Ababa and in guiding the Addis Tax Initiative adopted following the conference.

Difficult as it will be to develop sufficiently strong institutional mechanisms, hard data, and the political resolve for effective collective action, Mbeki as usual seeks a 'win-win' outcome of benefit to citizens, governments and socially responsible business leaders. Extensive research and analysis, though still quite path breaking, already reveal that among the most likely culprits – the corrupt, criminal and commercial – the commercial actors are the ones most responsible for illicit financial flows. And the hope is that businesses involved in fraudulent transfer pricing and other bad practices will be responsive to media exposure and pressure from governments, civil society and socially responsible business leaders.

The stakes for Africa are huge. Illicit financial flows drain poverty-stricken countries of much-needed foreign exchange reserves, result in lost tax revenues, cancel out investment inflows, exacerbate poverty and undermine the rule of law. Ever the tireless lobbyist for African self-reliance and collective action, Mbeki hit the ground running, calling on heads of state, finance ministers, customs officers, central bankers, civil society and corporate leaders in Mozambique, Tanzania, Kenya, Ethiopia, Mauritius, Tunisia, Liberia, Ghana, Nigeria, Nigeria, Congo and, of course, South Africa, which has a big illicit financial flow problem of its own. Mbeki is also reaching out to major rich countries that in dollar terms suffer far bigger losses, most notably to key people in Washington, New York, Paris and Brussels. As one of the technical experts involved told me: 'We have to recognise that every single thing we are doing is political and we need to play our cards right in multiple markets around the African continent. Mbeki has been a stimulus to this thinking, and I have admired how he operates, always moving the ball forward and doing so with intellect and diplomacy.'

Mbeki, ever patient and disciplined, is usually able to see further and more clearly than the rest of us. But what I have found over the years so appealing about him is the sense he conveys of always trying in his own life to live up to the founding ideals of the Freedom Charter and the ANC, backed by a deeply personal conviction that recalls a verse from 'Invictus', which many associate with his ANC comrade Nelson Mandela:

> It matters not how strait the gate,
> How charged with punishments the scroll,
> I am the master of my fate.
> I am the captain of my soul.

Interviewed July 2014, Johannesburg

CHRIS LANDSBERG

❖

Thabo Mbeki is arguably the foremost international stalwart and states-man of his generation in Africa. He is in all probability the most influential pan-Africanist of his time – Africa's uber diplomat, the man who brought us the African Renaissance with his fierce belief in African self-determination. He embarked on a quest for strategic partnerships between Africa and the outside world, a new South-South solidarism, a North-South dialogue based not on neo-patrimonialism but on mutual accountability and responsibility, and a transformed global governance order in which Africa and the South would have a greater voice and their interests pro-tected, and bilateral relations anchored not on hegemony but on mutual respect and common interests. Although the memory of many observers is ephemeral, the legacy of Thabo Mbeki's presidency and his political life outside the formal trappings of government is destined to permeate the political scene for decades to come.

While detractors have regarded him as aloof and unapproachable and have focused on his controversial positions on HIV/AIDS, referred to by critics as his 'denialism', in reality they know very little about the man and his times. Mbeki was the real force of the politics of policy, power and state-craft during the golden era of African diplomacy after the Cold War. Nor has the foreign policy front been spared the critical gaze of sceptics and cynics, ever eager to discredit a figure known more for his quiet-spoken approach than loud proclamations.

Here is a man who was utterly misunderstood by many, especially those who liked to box him in ideologically. Yet labels like 'liberal', 'conservative' and 'radical' do not do justice to understanding Mbeki. The Mbeki I know harboured a world view that was born from complex policy projects, and his ideological orientation was made up of divergent strands, including liberalism, constructivism, realism and radical Marxism. Indeed, his political formation is more usefully read in terms of arguments for modernisation. One can claim that Mbeki subscribed to a 'progressive' outlook, with which he was able to articulate a strong transformational and developmental foreign policy agenda. In the realm of ideology, Mbeki will be remembered for a unique yet misunderstood contribution. He was a man who paid a heavy price for originality and political innovation in an alliance that was often committed to old-style, rigid ideological strands. Indeed, he was 'recalled' as president in 2008 for the unique ideological views he believed in. He left office with dignity; he left quietly and simply continued his work in promoting the African Renaissance. He demonstrated the difference between positional and strategic leadership, and the fact that one could continue to influence agendas without the formal trappings of power.

This perspective of Mbeki as a progressive leader is corroborated by his participation in the Progressive Governance Forum, a platform for centre-left governments that was started by US President Bill Clinton and British Prime Minister Tony Blair in 1999, and joined by the likes of Göran Persson of Sweden, Ricardo Lagos of Chile, Stanislav Gross of the Czech Republic and Helen Clark of New Zealand. Mbeki was, in fact, the only African leader in this grouping at the time. During the July 2003 Progressive Politics conference held in London, Mbeki singled out the core issue of multilateralism – including the question of strengthening the United Nations (UN) and its effectiveness – as central to the developing world's understanding of progressivism.

The Mbeki I know is a man who did not run away from deep and contentious waters. From an almost obsessive belief in economic growth and redistribution at home emerged the notion of a developmental foreign policy with strong emphases on welfare and growth goals. For Mbeki, growth versus redistribution was not an either/or choice: the two stratagems went hand in hand. Those who accused him of 'talking left whilst walking right' had better take heed of the fact that he had no qualms about trying to reconcile the roles of the public sector and the market. He was no Reaganite or Thatcherite; those who claim that he was were plainly mischievous. There is no evidence whatsoever that Mbeki ever came out in favour of a limited role of the state. The issue for Mbeki has always been what role the market and private sector had to play for the state to realise its developmental goals. It was precisely because he regarded the state as the lead agent in any such development that he focused on the South African state and its machinery. Indeed, modernisation of the state will come to be recognised as one of his most strategic and significant legacies as he left as part of his legacy an intricate web of government clusters and structures that sought to bring about coordinated and integrated governance.

The Mbeki I know is Africa's true renaissance man. As a staunch believer in the African Renaissance, Mbeki promoted an economic framework that included the continent putting its own house in order. With his policies he put flesh on the skeletal bones of the African Renaissance vision. Whether to partners in the African Union or colleagues at home, he called for a massive infusion of capital through investment, aid through trade, and debt alleviation for the developing world. Such viewpoints owed more to Anthony Giddens' 'Third Way' than to laissez-faire capitalism or Karl Marx's command economy, but it was this consistent striving for the ideals of a developmental, fast-growing meritocratic state, allied to notions of social capitalism and a continental vision, that was to ensure he left a well-considered and clear, if somewhat controversial, legacy.

A key to Mbeki's political legacy is the nature of his political and diplomatic leadership styles. Here was a president with a tremendous intellect and a tireless capacity for work – he was one who burned the midnight oil throughout his life. Aristocratic in his demeanour, he does the nightshift now that he is out of office as much as he did while in office. As head of state he was an original thinker with a fierce determination to succeed, coupled with a single-minded dedication to his modernisation, development and transformationist Renaissance project. He was often stoic in his approach as he focused on his mission and vision of an African Renaissance. Formidable powers of intellectual persuasion, which often overawed his ministers and confidants alike, helped to establish his unrivalled dominance in the cabinet. The Mbeki I know never shied away from an intellectual, policy or political debate. He was, and remains, a stickler for detail, and he prepared meticulously.

The Mbeki I know is a policy and institutions man, one who took a hard-headed view and didn't shy away from tough decisions with their often uncomfortable trade-offs. Here indeed is Aristotle's political animal personified, a devoted politician who brought a strategic dimension to South Africa's domestic and foreign policy, and to Africa's place in the world. He was disciplined in thought and in deed. He never said more than was necessary; yet every word had its place in his orations.

Institutions and rules were the warp and weft of his administration and his Thabo Mbeki Foundation after leaving office. This belief in institutions, not populism, combined with his intense individualism, led many to conclude that he was obsessed with centralisation of power. Certainly, he appeared disconnected from the crowds and masses and did not pursue fame or popularity. Instead, he found comfort in statecraft, seeking out the interstices of power and resources, and weaving into them the threads of carefully strategised policy. As president, Thabo Mbeki was most at home engaging with the nexus of power, tackling elites head-on or revelling in the company of advisers, experts, philosophers and fellow statesmen. He did not lack confidence in the company of his peers, whether from the West or the developing world.

As a student of statecraft, I can say without any equivocation that I know no other statesman who was as devastating with the pen as Mbeki. Every word meant something in his communications. He could literally write mini-dissertations when he engaged fellow heads of state or world leaders. One thinks here of the Mbeki-Mugabe papers, published in *New Agenda* magazine; Mbeki's correspondence with former Canadian Prime Minister Jean Chrétien; Mbeki's engagements with former British Prime Minister Tony Blair on Zimbabwe; and his back and forth with former US President George Bush Jnr regarding the 2003 invasion of Iraq.

To those responsible for carrying out his orders, he was a tough disciplinarian, a man who did not take kindly to what he perceived as ill-discipline and political laziness. Loyalty and obedience were his watchwords, and he dealt with all cabinet members in a hard-nosed fashion, always expecting them to engage in rigorous policy debates on behalf of South African citizens.

Rather than populist flamboyance, Mbeki's gravitas came essentially from his command of political strategy. A tight group of trusted policy advisers ensured that he kept a persistent focus on his goals, in both domestic and foreign policy. The coterie included individuals such as Foreign Affairs Deputy Minister Aziz Pahad and his minister in the presidency, Essop Pahad, brothers who played vital roles in crafting strategy alongside legal adviser Mojanku Gumbi and Sydney Mufamadi, then minister of provincial and local affairs, and former Minister of Defence Mosiuoa Lekota. On the implementation side were Frank Chikane, director general in the president's office, and ambassadors Billy Modise, Dumisani Kumalo and Kingsley Mamabolo, and of course Foreign Minister Nkosazana Dlamini-Zuma. As president, Mbeki enjoyed a following in elite policy-intellectual circles outside government, both at home and on the rest of the continent. His supporters regarded him as a visionary leader, a Renaissance man, and clever Machiavellian in the true sense of political statecraft – the one who understood power. His detractors, on the other hand, saw him as a manipulator, a plotter, a centraliser and a dictator, one who would stop at nothing to crush his enemies, Machiavellian in the bad sense. The existence of such a sharp disparity in viewpoints was crystallised at the time of his downfall. Whatever his merits or faults, Mbeki clearly was a fiercely single-minded head of state, determined to realise the goals of his political modernisation project. Remaining to the end an enigmatic figure, he had established himself as *primus inter pares* (first among equals) in a range of fields, including economic, social and education policy. But it was in the realm of foreign policy that he came to be viewed as a statesman in his own right, a man with a forceful diplomatic stature.

When Mbeki took over from Mandela in 1999, he faced the world with fresh confidence and belief, convinced that Africa could be approached from a position of strength. Having shaken off South Africa's image of pariah of the continent, armed with a credible political settlement at home and a respected new constitution, the country could hold its head high in Africa and the rest of the world. Bold geo-political and geo-economic considerations loomed large in Mbeki's scheme as he developed a clear foreign policy narrative driven by ambitious domestic and external strategic, developmental and transformational goals. He could be quite ambitious in his goals, and always showed the self-belief and determination to realise them.

Over the years a clear political narrative developed in Mbeki's world view. The narrative was developed along the themes of redress and development, through a dialectical approach that explicitly linked state and economy on the one hand and peace and development on the other. It made use of statecraft and diplomacy to promote first peace, then democratisation and development and, lastly, state-building. Mbeki applied this ambitious strategy in the Comoros, Zimbabwe, Iran, Iraq, Sudan, Côte d'Ivoire and many other countries, straddling the region, the continent, the South, the North and the global terrain. He promoted collective self-reliance in a democratic and accountable Africa, and almost single-handedly canvassed the industrialised powers for a strategic partnership with Africa. He staunchly believed in African autonomy and self-determination. For him Africa had to show the mental and intellectual confidence to develop its own agendas, and drive its own emancipation projects. 'African solutions for African problems' was not just a throw-away line. It was a principled line, and a point of conviction.

The Mbeki known to me was someone who stayed faithful to his developmental agenda. In line with this, he had, since 1999, emphasised domestic economic growth in order to play a meaningful role on the continent, realising that the one could not proceed without the other. This was the very area in which Mbeki sought to make a unique contribution, addressing the dichotomy of the country's domestic and internationalist roles by aligning its foreign relations with domestic goals. In real intellectual fashion, he was the one who brought us the idea of South Africa having been turned by apartheid into a country of 'two economies' and 'two nations'. According to this characterisation, South Africa was divided between the more developed, largely white, globally competitive economy and peoples, and the other more underdeveloped, largely black nation and economy, in which the majority of people struggled for survival.

The Mbeki I know was a man who presided over a government that used to think. In fact, the Mbeki government acted like a serious, well-oiled think tank, and often did the work that academics and intellectuals used to do. Two examples come to mind that vindicate this. One was the idea of transforming the state into a developmental state. This idea was put on the agenda by the government, not by academics and intelligentsia outside of government. The other example was that even before he became head of state, Mbeki elevated African considerations to the top of his foreign policy matrix. By the time he left office, South Africa had been pursuing an 'Africa first' foreign policy for several years. The fact that South Africa in 2009 had diplomatic relations with 47 of the continent's states is but one testimony to the sincerity of this policy.

Throughout his presidency, Thabo Mbeki championed a new African continentalism, as he sought to influence the inter-African system, not in the direction of supra-nationalism or federalism, but towards functionalism and a rules-based continental order. The Mbeki administration constantly made links between the national interest and the continental interest, and during his 14 years in government as deputy president and as president, Mbeki was the chief promoter of a new African rulebook.

As deputy president, Mbeki championed the African Renaissance as a doctrine for the continent's renewal and its reintegration into the global economy on its own terms. While critics caricatured the African Renaissance concept as 'wishy-washy' or 'airy-fairy', for Mbeki this was no mere rhetorical device. It was a statement of intent, signalling a quest for 'the self-determination of Africans by the Africans themselves'. To be sure, Mbeki was not so naive as to believe that any rebirth was already underway. The African Renaissance was to become an inspiring vision, and he was in position to prescribe policies that could create the conditions for it. By 1999, the vision was being translated into a concrete programme of action, first through the Millennium Africa Programme (MAP) of 2000, and then as part of the New Partnership for Africa's Development (NEPAD) in 2001. Mbeki was the chief architect of both these programmes, as well as a central player in the making of the African Union (AU) in 2002. If nothing else, as modernisation projects, MAP and NEPAD achieved the goal of putting Africa on the international agenda. Mbeki and his continental allies Olusegun Obasanjo, Joaquim Chissano, Abdoulaye Wade, Meles Zenawi – and, later on, John Kufuor and Jakaya Kikwete – all crisscrossed the globe, engaging in their own brand of African developmental diplomacy and searching out commitments from the industrialised powers in the areas of aid, trade, debt relief, market access and the massive resources needed for

Africa's conflict resolution and peace diplomacy challenges. At this time, Mbeki rather ambitiously campaigned for an injection of $64 billion a year in economic stimulus packages to Africa, and it is worth pointing out here that many local civil society formations were sceptical of these approaches.

No supporter of Muammar Gaddafi's grand federalist vision of a United States of Africa, Mbeki preferred a more confederalist and functionalist idea that regarded the continent's sub-regions as the building blocks of continental union. Similarly, his African Renaissance extended across a wide spectrum of competences and identities of Africans in the diaspora, including the Caribbean, the Americas and Europe. Together with his partners Obasanjo, Chissano, Konaré and others, he advocated that the diaspora be recognised as the 'sixth region' of Africa, alongside North Africa, West Africa, East Africa and the Horn, Central Africa and Southern Africa.

The Mbeki I know was a true visionary, also in terms of his contribution to South-South solidarism. His was not just another variant of nostalgic South-South diplomacy. With his South-South cooperation strategies, Mbeki set out to reinvigorate political and economic links between Asia, South America and Africa, emphasising developmental and poverty reduction goals through trade expansion and economic growth and modernisation through infrastructure development and technical cooperation. He is associated with the idea of a 'G8 of the South', the notion that the developing world needed to form countervailing blocs to rival the hegemony of the West.

Mbeki's strategies urged states to go beyond mere sentimental and solidarity politics and to become more focused on substantive economic dimensions. One could argue that Mbeki was to Africa and the South in the late twentieth and early twenty-first century, what post-independence Indian Prime Minister Jawaharlal Nehru was during the age of decolonisation. During his reign as president, Mbeki became the voice of Africa and countries of the South in a way that India's first prime minister had been for Asia and members of the British Empire half a century earlier. Whereas Nehru championed political solidarity among countries of the Third World, Mbeki championed a developmental and economic pact between countries from the South. An almost fierce anti-colonial and pro self-determination slant punctuated Mbeki's policy statements, as did the views of Nehru during the 1950s. In his University of Havana address, Mbeki reminded his audience that 'Africa, together with the other developing regions of the world, is a victim of the skewed distribution of the benefits of the global economy, a situation that is characterised among others by the absence of a fair and just global order with regard to such important matters as trade, finance and technology' (Mbeki, 2001b).

The Mbeki I know was instrumental in the establishment or revival of a number of South-South formations, notably the Non-Aligned Movement (NAM), the G77+China, the New Asian-Africa Strategic Partnership (NAASP), and the India-Brazil-South Africa (IBSA) Dialogue Forum established in 2003. In the case of IBSA, for example, Mbeki was not interested in just another trilateral ad hoc project. He wanted IBSA to be a substantive project between serious strategic partners. Mbeki was clear that the trilateral forum had to be based on common interests on the global and trilateral levels, as well as common values such as democracy, peace and human rights. Mbeki insisted that IBSA should seek to enhance cooperation in the areas of trade, energy, transport, health and social development. At the global level, Mbeki insisted that the three powers from the South needed to seek a soft-balancing towards countries of the North, and to defend common interests in multilateral institutions such as the World Bank, International Monetary Fund (IMF), World Trade Organisation (WTO) and the United Nations (UN).

The Mbeki familiar to me regarded forums from the South as platforms for the developing countries to adopt 'common positions' on strategic matters such as the transformation of the global political, security and economic architectures.

The Mbeki I am accustomed to was one who also left a strong legacy in a more complex and dispersed dimension in North-South dialogue. In essence, he sought to reformulate development as a universal and strategic challenge facing international society, to change the international economic balance of power, and to extract significant financial resource commitments from the North. During his time as president he was almost single-handedly responsible for putting on the agenda the idea of a 'strategic partnership' between Africa and the outside world. But it was an Mbeki who was more than prepared to back up ideas with action. Mbeki convinced fellow

African leaders from Nigeria, Ghana, Mozambique, Senegal, Algeria, Egypt, Ethiopia and others to join him in the quest for partnership with the outside world.

Mbeki and his government approached the industrialised powers with much self-assurance and boldness. Indeed, if the chief goal of South-South strategies was to turn the South into a more cohesive bloc, and so to engage the North more effectively, then the goals of North-South strategies were just as ambitious. He pushed for a new, non-paternalistic partnership with the North, guided by the principle of mutual accountability and mutual responsibility, meaning that both African and northern industrialised states had certain political obligations to bring about this new comradeship. This was a central tenet of Mbeki's North-South strategies, namely to extract commitments from the developed countries in favour of the development and modernisation of Africa and the South.

The Mbeki I know was a man who spared little effort in giving stature and prominence to South Africa's global standing, and often referred to his country as 'an agent of progressive change in the world'. We now turn to Mbeki's international political transformation project. We recognise the need to democratise decision-making in the international arena. This global democratisation project included the restructuring of key multi-lateral institutions such as the UN, the international financial institutions, and international trade organisations.

Politically, Mbeki never wavered in challenging the unilateral conduct of the US during the eight years of George W. Bush's presidency. Also, in the contentious nuclear weapons debate, South Africa consistently supported the terms of the UN's 1970 Nuclear Non-Proliferation Treaty, insisting that the states with nuclear weapons (USA, France, Britain, Russia and China) commit to arms control and disarmament and that those without show dedication to non-proliferation. At the same time, Mbeki's government steadfastly defended the right and privilege of all states, including those the US had dubbed 'rogue states', to develop their nuclear capacities for civilian use and energy purposes. Mbeki paid particular policy attention to international socio-economic and development issues, identifying the fundamental need to restructure the world economic and political orders.

Under Mbeki's execution of foreign policy, South Africa established solid credentials as a pivotal state in Africa. He stepped down as president with his reputation as Africa's uber diplomat firmly entrenched. He left behind a legacy of consistent support for multilateral solutions to regional conflicts. It is this vision – at the time unpalatable to many, but to be vindicated in the future – that explains his policy of 'quiet diplomacy' towards Zimbabwe.

Mbeki was more prepared than Mandela to send peacekeepers abroad, and this has increased South Africa's credibility as a major geo-strategic player in Africa. He used his consensus-building skills to serve as chief mediator in Côte d'Ivoire and the Democratic Republic of the Congo. He was the first chair of the AU and chair of the NAM. He was the intellectual architect of NEPAD, the African Renaissance and the chief designer of the AU and its regulations. Under his leadership, South Africa hosted two high-profile UN conferences on racism and sustainable development. South Africa was elected president of the influential Group of 77 developing countries at the UN, and won a two-year seat on the UN Security Council from January 2007.

Mbeki's distinctive impact on South Africa's foreign policy is likely to be felt for a very long time in the future. His modernisation and development project has had a profound impact on the country's global standing and trajectory, and it is plausible that the Mbeki years will come to be viewed as a watershed era by historians interested in seeing beyond the facade of self-interested party politics and superficial journalism.

PATRICIA MCFADDEN

❧

L et me admit from the very outset that this has been one of the most challenging pieces of writing I have done in a very long time. In fact, I cannot remember a task and/or pleasure more demanding than this, for several reasons. Reminiscing about someone who lives and breathes life, particularly in the ways that Thabo Mbeki exists as a phenomenal African leader, man, comrade, intellectual and friend, dare I say the last, presents its own landmines and delights. However, after some gentle nudging from the organisers of the collection of 'remembrances', I decided, why not just take the plunge and say some of the things that I feel and know about this very special African.

I would like to begin with the first remembered meeting with Thabo Mbeki in Lusaka sometime in the late 1970s. I was attending a CODESRIA (Council for the Development of Economic and Social Research in Africa) conference on development, and we were housed at the student hostel of the University of Zambia. Someone mentioned that Thabo Mbeki would like to talk with me, and I was both elated and anxious. Why would this powerful person in the Movement want to speak to me, an activist and budding scholar?

Let me contextualise my relationship with the African National Congress (ANC) at that point in time. By the mid-1970s I was already active in the ANC both in Swaziland and in Tanzania, the former being the place I was born and where I had encountered the Movement through South African teachers in high school in the south of Swaziland. My history teacher in particular, Mr Mbatha, a South African exile, insisted that we learn about South

Africa and whatever he knew about the African continent, besides preparing us for the Cambridge history papers that were standard in Swazi higher education. For me, already highly sensitive to colonial arrogance and the racial exclusions that characterised British colonial presence in Swaziland in the 1960s, radical ideas on South Africa and the continent were like a match to a wick. My radical instincts blossomed, nurtured by parents who worked hard to protect us from the humiliation of white supremacy by teaching us to be open and dignified.

By the time I met Thabo Mbeki in the student hostel that afternoon in Lusaka, I had already worked as an ANC activist on the campus of the University of Swaziland for several years, having been employed as an assistant lecturer by the university when I completed my BA degree at UBLS (University of Botswana, Lesotho and Swaziland). I was recruited into the Movement by a courageous and dedicated comrade called Mpule Mogudi, who was a student at the university and who had befriended me and supplied me with copies of *Sechaba,* the ANC magazine, and other revolutionary literature.

So I accepted the challenge and took the step forward into the fray, met the people I would work closely with in the South African Congress of Trade Unions (SACTU), led by Comrade John Nkadimeng, who became a father figure and gentle adviser to us all, as well as by Stanley Mabizela, who was the chief representative of the ANC in Swaziland at that time. He was an amazing man, on the frontline of attacks by the boers who had a close working relationship with the Swazi regime and who came in and out of Swaziland without much difficulty, slaughtering comrades and Swazis who supported the struggle with an impunity that still enrages me many years later.

During my years as a university student and assistant lecturer in Swaziland, and later in Dar es Salaam, I heard about Thabo Mbeki and knew that he was a rising force in the Movement, often pictured in Movement literature and public media at the side of Oliver Tambo (whom we all affectionately referred to as O.R.), who was loved and deeply respected by all. I had read Govan Mbeki's *The Peasants' Revolt* in my teens, and had been in awe of the women and men who were standing up to the repressive South African settler colonial state. As the son of Govan, Thabo would inevitably be unique in particular ways, and while the unofficial biographer (Gevisser) implies that the political activism of his father left Thabo 'homeless', I think that that is an unfortunate misrepresentation of the real meaning of what many South African combatants gave up for national freedom. In the *Economist,* an unidentified author claims that 'Mr Mbeki followed in the steps of his distant father by sublimating his emotions into the anti-apartheid struggle, which became his life' (*Economist,* 2007). Only someone who had never participated in the life-and-death struggles for freedom that black people have had to endure and survive across this continent, could glibly describe one's participation in a liberation movement as 'sublimation of emotions'. Fighting for freedom and justice demands passion and dedication; it requires a love so intense for the belief that one can win that it sears itself into your very soul. Like Thabo Mbeki, I know the intensity and exhilaration that drives the instinct and determination to survive centuries of evil, so that a new day can dawn for oneself and for all those who have pinned their hopes and dreams on your courage and fortitude. And we did survive and are here to tell the truth of it, including stories of bravery and courage, especially of comrades whose lives were brutally snatched away by the vicious forces of apartheid, among whom was my youngest brother Keith McFadden and his comrade Zweli Nyanda on 22 November 1983.

While I was undertaking the MA in Sociology at the University of Dar es Salaam during the mid-1970s, I often visited Mazimbu and the Solomon Mahlangu College, attended ANC meetings, caught glimpses of Thabo sometimes, but I do not recall actually engaging in a conversation with him. I often had discussions with his brother Moeletsi, who also worked in the trade unions and often came to the university campus for seminars and meetings of the Organisation of African Unity (OAU) Liberation Committee. That is why that encounter in the student hostel at the University of Zambia was so memorable; and the irony of it is that after all the intrigue and mystery that had surrounded Thabo Mbeki in the Movement, when he came into the hostel and greeted me, he turned out to be this quietly spoken, warm and very kindly man, whose laugh is the clearest evidence of his humaneness, and who made me feel as though I was the most interesting person in the world; that he was happily giving me all his attention for as long as I wanted it. I think that anyone who has come close enough to Thabo Mbeki to recognise who he is will concur with my assertion. Now I laugh at myself and my ageing memory, because for all its significance in terms of my future relationship with him over the many years since, I cannot for the life of me remember what we talked about. I had picked up a bottle of whisky at the airport (not the most expensive, of course, I was an assistant lecturer who earned a small salary, but it was whisky after all) which we drank from the lid of the bottle – there were no glasses in the hostel room – not knowing how Mbeki's simple preference for single malts would become the bugbear of aggrieved white liberals across the world after he became the president of South Africa. It was an unanticipated yet prescient little gesture that often stops me in my tracks when I read the vitriol of people who hide their prejudices and bitterness over the demise of colonial white privilege behind a supposed critique of Thabo Mbeki as a 'cold and remote bourgeois type', claiming that he is 'an enigma' who has been 'disconnected ... from his roots and his country, and how this has influenced his opinions and behaviour' ('Mystery Man', *The Economist*, 29 November 2007).

While refreshing my memory during the preparation for this article, I came across some very illuminating biographical data about Thabo Mbeki's childhood, which led to an 'aha' moment that I decided to include in this reminiscence. When Thabo was a boy, he was exposed to music while living with his maternal uncle Michael Moerane, who was a music teacher and composer of classical music. I think this was the origin of his love of reading and music. Reading this, I remembered hearing an interview with Sibongile Khumalo speaking about the music of Princess Magogo, the mother of Mangosuthu Buthelezi, and I realised once again just how rich and sophisticated the history of the South African black middle class is. The autobiography of Phyllis Ntantala (Jordan), *A Life's Mosaic* (University of California, 1993), reiterates the difficult but necessary choices that already established African middle-class families made in choosing to fight for the freedom of their country from settler colonialism. In the preface to her narrative, Phyllis states unequivocally that 'Like Trotsky, I did not leave home with the proverbial one-and-six in my pocket. I come from a family of landed gentry ... [and] I could have chosen the path of comfort and safety, for even in apartheid South Africa, there is still that path for those who will collaborate. But I chose the path of struggle and uncertainty.'

Among the most significant features of Thabo Mbeki's political career, prior to, during and since his occupation of the highest position in South African society, was his unwavering stance, policy initiatives and continuing activism for gender equality and the particular entitlements of South African women. The record speaks for itself. Suffice to say that while I have argued consistently that gender mainstreaming would never be adequate in terms of redressing the exclusions that African women in South Africa and across the African continent face, and more radical action is required to initiate and sustain the deep-level changes that would transform women's lives and realities, I am nonetheless among the first to acknowledge that Thabo Mbeki stands head and shoulders above most of his contemporaries in terms of pushing for and defending the programmes and policies that have enabled some black women in South Africa to get beyond lives of survival and to become part of the middle classes. He was and continues to be unwavering on women's rights, often recognising by name the amazing women who participated in and contributed to the liberation struggle. He called consistently for the emancipation of women and for government to 'put the critical matter of the emancipation and empowerment of women at the centre of the democratic order' in South African and African society. He has been and continues to be emphatically against gendered violence, and had the courage to state in a speech on 9 August 2008 that 'More often than not, rape and child abuse are committed by people who are known to the victim. Very often, some of the criminal perpetrators are husbands, fathers, relatives, family friends or acquaintances.'

During his tenure in office, he doubled his cabinet to eight women, which included Nkosazana Dlamini-Zuma as one of the first female foreign ministers on the continent. Nonetheless, the issues of gender and equality remain deeply contentious, and for those who still think that black people should not enjoy the benefits of class upward mobility, a depressing moralism defines their critique of the increasing presence of black women in the upper classes of African society generally. From my perspective, one of the key achievements of the Mbeki government was the relocation of women's issues and entitlements to a more central position within the policy and advocacy platforms of the newly independent South Africa – most dramatically articulated in the South African constitution. It also created new openings and possibilities for black women to become members of the middle classes in various ways, as businesswomen, intellectuals, professionals and educators. These are tremendous milestones that must be acknowledged.

Moreover, as someone who has been vilified and attacked for my radical views, particularly on race and sexuality, I feel particularly proud of Thabo Mbeki's stand on the inclusion of LGBTIQ rights and entitlements in the constitutional dispensation of the new South Africa. This was a first not only on the African continent, but among liberation movements as well, and the interview that Thabo gave on the eve of South African independence on the ANC's commitment to an inclusive and free society in his country stands out as one of the most significant moments in my memory of that time. A few of us in the Movement had spoken, often under our breaths, about the homophobia and the feudalistic attitudes of most comrades towards gay and lesbian people and women. Although I have consistently critiqued heterosexuality as a radical feminist who understands that my complete freedom is essentially dependent on the freedom of all humans to love whom they will, Thabo Mbeki's reiteration of this fundamental principle of a liberated society served to strengthen my stance on the matter. An article by Peter Tatchell on 'The road to LGBTIQ rights in independent South Africa' mentions that he had been advised by David and Norma Kitson to write to Thabo Mbeki, who was 'the most liberal (open) minded of the ANC leaders and senior enough to be able to push for a radical rethink of official policy' on LGBTIQ rights, further confirms his distinctive strengths as a very special (heterosexual) man.

This might not seem significant to those who take heteronormativity as a given in our deeply feudal and patriarchal societies, but having the courage to speak up for the inclusion of everyone beyond the grand populist declarations that have characterised the moment of independence across this continent, is a distinction that must be applauded and reiterated. In his response to Tatchell, Mbeki said: 'The ANC is indeed firmly committed to removing all forms of discrimination and oppression in a liberated South Africa ... That commitment must surely extend to the protection of gay rights ... As a movement, we are of the view that the sexual preferences of an individual are a private matter. We would not wish to compromise anybody's right to privacy.' With the further involvement of Albie Sachs and other brave and freedom-loving South Africans, the rights of LGBTIQ persons were enshrined in the South African constitution under Chapter 2 – the Bill of Rights – as part of the Equality Clause. On a continent that remains virulently homophobic, this particular inclusive clause stands as a shining landmark of the special contribution of people like Thabo Mbeki to a different Africa in the future.

While I have spoken of the moments of personal and political encounter with Thabo Mbeki during and after the liberation struggle, I do have several issues on which I do not agree with him. I have always critiqued the NEPAD programme, largely because it caters for the African middle and upper classes in terms of aspiring to promote even further the entrenchment of capitalist enterprise and the extraction of African wealth at the expense of the working people; and, ideologically, I disagree with the liberal stance adopted by his 'I am an African' speech, which I think was totally unnecessary and which in effect transposed the South African compromise with white settler privilege onto the rest of the continent, a gesture that speaks dramatically to the persistence of a sense of South African exceptionalism and exaggerated benevolence towards whites generally.

Therefore, while I agree fully with Vusi Gumede's critique that 'Thabo Mbeki, in a 1996 speech, "I am an African", described being South African fundamentally in historical terms ... the speech was not helpful in directly dealing with the National Question ...' ('An Elusive South African Nation: The National Question Revisited', UNISA, October 2014), I think the difficult but inevitable challenges posed by white class privilege must be contextualised within a more contemporary understanding of the National and Continental Question, given the persistence of white economic and social privilege that has pervaded the continent since 1994.

These and other issues, including the burning question of land and its redistribution, especially to young South Africans who will have to 'return to the land and learn afresh how to feed themselves with wholesome and nutritious food' in order for South Africa to have a viable future, these are matters over which we will argue and from which we will learn, as we move forward towards different and more wholesome societies in our region and continent. I have no doubt that Thabo Mbeki will continue to be at the cutting edge of our immediate and long-term future; and each time he asks me 'are we all right' and I say 'yes' – I know that I am among the privileged people who understand what a gift Mbeki has been and continues to be to all Africans in this very significant time of Africa's history.

NOTES ON CONTRIBUTORS

❧

Barney AFAKO is an advocate of the Courts of Uganda. In 2009, he worked closely with President Thabo Mbeki on the African Union Panel for Darfur, and since then as a legal adviser to the AU High-Level Implementation Panel on Sudan and South Sudan. He is also a Senior UN Mediation Adviser and a Tribunal Judge in the United Kingdom.

Brigalia Ntombemhlophe BAM was born in the village of Qogwana, in the Eastern Cape. Her education spans teaching, social work, communications and management. She left South Africa to work in Switzerland and campaign against apartheid. During her time there she worked at the WCC, the World Young Women's Christian Association and the International Union Federation. After 21 years she returned to South Africa and was appointed deputy general secretary of the SACC, later becoming its general secretary. In 1999 she was appointed chairperson of the IEC of South Africa. She serves on numerous boards of companies as well as non-governmental organisations in South Africa and abroad. She is the current chairperson of the Thabo Mbeki Foundation.

Mangosuthu BUTHELEZI was born into the Zulu royal family as the son of Princess Magogo kaDinuzulu, King Solomon's sister, and Inkosi Mathole Buthelezi, the king's prime minister. He joined the ANC Youth League at the University of Fort Hare and completed his studies at the University of Natal. On the advice of Inkosi Albert Luthuli, he responded to the call of the Buthelezi Clan and returned to Mahlabathini in 1953 to take up his hereditary position as Inkosi, but he remained deeply involved in liberation politics. In 1970, he was elected chief executive officer of the Zulu Territorial Authority. In 1972, he became chief executive councillor to the KwaZulu Legislative Assembly and from 1976 to 1994 served as chief minister of KwaZulu. In 1975 Prince Buthelezi founded Inkatha yeNkulukelo yeSizwe, which quickly grew into a formidable liberation organisation. After the first democratic elections in April 1994, Prince Buthelezi was appointed national minister of home affairs and served in this capacity under Presidents Mandela and Mbeki. During the first ten years of democracy, he was appointed acting president of the country on numerous occasions. Prince Buthelezi continues to serve as a member of parliament, as the traditional prime minister to the Zulu monarch and nation, and as the president of the IFP.

Frank CHIKANE's former appointments include deputy president of the UDF, member of the NEC of the ANC, commissioner of the IEC, director general in the presidency and general secretary of the SACC. He was also involved in the development and promotion of the African Renaissance vision, which gave birth to NEPAD and the African Peer Review Mechanism. Chikane is currently a pastor of the Apostolic Faith Mission of South Africa (AFM) in Naledi, Soweto, the president of AFM International, and he consults with companies that do business on the African continent. He is the visiting adjunct professor at the Graduate School of Public and Development Management at the University of the Witwatersrand and serves on a number of non-governmental organisations and company boards, including Kagiso Trust, Sci-Bono Discovery Centre, Amarick Mining Resources (Pty) Ltd and Suntrace Africa (Pty) Ltd.

Dumiso DABENGWA was born in Bubi, Zimbabwe, in 1939. He holds a diploma from the Institute of Administrative Management, UK. An early member of ZAPU, he was sent for military training in the USSR in the mid-1960s, specialising in intelligence. He was later head of military intelligence for ZIPRA and saw active service against the Rhodesian and South African regimes in 1967/68. He was a member of parliament from 1990 to 2000, serving as deputy minister of home affairs during that period, and has held directorships of a number of Zimbabwean companies. He is current president of ZAPU, elected unopposed in 2010.

Alexander (Alec) ERWIN was born in Cape Town in 1948. He matriculated from Durban Boys' High in 1965. He graduated with an Honours degree in economics from the University of Natal and then lectured at the university. He was involved in the rebuilding of the non-racial trade unions in Natal, becoming general secretary of FOSATU in 1979, education secretary of COSATU in 1985 and of NUMSA in 1987. He was involved with the National Peace Accord from 1992 and was one of the 20 COSATU leaders seconded to the ANC in 1993. He was appointed deputy minister of finance in 1994 and subsequently served as minister of trade and industry and public enterprises until his resignation in September 2008. He is currently involved in business and academic work.

Willie ESTERHUYSE is a leading South African writer, philosopher and intellectual who played a significant role in opening dialogue between the ANC and the apartheid government, which contributed to negotiations that finally led to the interim constitution that laid the basis for democracy in South Africa. Professor Esterhuyse holds a DPhil from the University of Stellenbosch. His academic career spans more than 50 years and he has served in many leadership positions and held several corporate directorships. The recipient of a number of distinguished awards, he has published extensively over a wide area on philosophical and political issues.

Geraldine Joslyn FRASER-MOLEKETI is an African leader committed to development that is more inclusive and economic growth that is more sustainable. She is special envoy on gender at the African Development Bank, which is recognised as the premium institution on gender equality and economic empowerment in Africa. She was previously director of the UNDP's Democratic Governance Group. She served as minister of public service and administration for two consecutive terms and as minister of welfare and population development in South Africa's first democratic government. She has been a member of the ANC for the past 35 years and was the national deputy elections coordinator of the ANC for the first democratic elections in 1994. She was elected to parliament in April 1994 and served in three consecutive parliaments until her resignation in September 2008. She serves on various boards and is a fellow of the Institute of Politics, Kennedy School of Government, Harvard University. A strong supporter of intergenerational dialogue, Geraldine mentors young women and men across the continent.

Jonas Mosa GWANGWA was born into a musical family in Orlando East in Johannesburg in 1937. His cultivation as a musical enthusiast was fostered during his years at St Peter's High School in Rosettenville, Johannesburg, where he first met Father Trevor Huddleston, rector of the school and the priory there. In 1954, Father Huddleston gave Gwangwa his first trombone. Gwangwa was a passionate political activist who dedicated his life to fight for the freedom of black people in

South Africa. In 1961 he joined the *King Kong Musical Orchestra*, which saw a very successful run in London's West End. At this time Gwangwa acquired a scholarship from the African Music and Drama Association, and in the same year he enrolled for a Bachelor of Music at the Manhattan School of Music in New York. There he was reunited with Hugh Masekela and Miriam Makeba. Gwangwa now heads Barungwa Productions and is looking to inspire the next generation of South African musicians.

Nozipho JANUARY-BARDILL has extensive experience in both the private and public sectors where she has served with distinction. Her past appointments include: corporate affairs executive at the MTN Group; South Africa's ambassador to Switzerland, Lichtenstein and the Holy See; deputy director general, Human Capital Management at the Department of International Relations and Cooperation; and chief director/adviser to the Speaker of the South African parliament. Currently she serves as an independent non-executive director on the boards of Anglo Gold Ashanti, Credit Suisse Securities Johannesburg, and Mercedes-Benz SA. She is also a senior special adviser to the executive director of UN Women and the head of UN Women Southern Africa. She is on the advisory board of 4GAfrica (Switzerland) and serves on the fund-raising committee of the Nelson Mandela Children's Hospital Trust and on the board of Phenduka, a literacy project for children in Alexandra township.

Bheki KHUMALO was President Thabo Mbeki's spokesperson between 2001 and 2005. He has worked for Siemens, Sasol and Anglo American and for cabinet ministers of education, minerals and energy.

Dumisani Shadrack KUMALO is a journalist and diplomat and the founding father of the Thabo Mbeki Foundation. Before going into exile in 1977 he worked as a political reporter for the *Golden City Post*, *DRUM*, and the Johannesburg *Sunday Times*. He sought asylum in the United States, where he continued to work for South African liberation and democracy. As project director on the American Committee on Africa (ACOA) and its sister organisation The Africa Fund from 1979 to 1997, he played a key role in the mobilisation of US sanctions against apartheid, helping to build the divestment movement that led to numerous divestments from US banks and companies that did business with apartheid South Africa. After apartheid ended he returned to South Africa and was appointed director of the United States Desk in the department of foreign affairs in 1997. In 1999

Kumalo was appointed as South Africa's Permanent Representative to the United Nations. Upon his retirement, Ambassador Kumalo was appointed CEO of the Thabo Mbeki Foundation.

Chris LANDSBERG holds an MPhil degree from Rhodes University and a DPhil (International Relations) from the University of Oxford. He is a professor and current SARChi Chair of African Diplomacy and Foreign Policy at the University of Johannesburg.

Thandi LUJABE-RANKOE was born in 1936 in Tsolo in the Eastern Cape and educated at Lovedale College in Alice, Eastern Cape. She was in exile for 33 years, much of which was spent in Norway liaising with the Norwegian government in supporting the anti-apartheid movement. She returned to South Africa in 1994. A seasoned diplomat, she was appointed South Africa's first high commissioner to Tanzania in 1995 and subsequently served as high commissioner to Botswana and Mozambique. From 2010 to 2013 she was engaged in teaching new ambassadors at the Academy in the Department of International Relations. She has published two books: *A Dream Fulfilled: Memoirs of an African Diplomat* and *Two Nations One Vision*.

Tiksie MABIZELA was born in the village of Tsomo in the Eastern Cape to teacher parents and grandparents on both sides of the family. She completed her high-school education at the Lovedale Institution and cut her political teeth at a young age in the Society of Youth Africa, the youth section of the then All-African Convention. She studied nursing in East London and Port Elizabeth and at Natal University. She married Stanley Mabizela in 1966 and joined him in exile in Swaziland in 1968. They later moved to Mozambique, Tanzania and Zimbabwe, before she and her husband returned to South Africa in 1990.

Mahmood MAMDANI is Executive Director of the Makerere Institute of Social Research, Makerere University, Kampala, Uganda, and the Herbert Lehman Professor of Government at Columbia University, New York City.

Ketumile MASIRE was Botswana's second president, serving 18 years from 1980–1998. Prior to this, he was a leading figure in the independence movement and then the new government, and played a crucial role in facilitating and protecting Botswana's steady financial growth and development. A former teacher, farmer and journalist, he became a member of parliament in 1966 and later vice-president and minister of finance and development planning. In 1980 he succeeded the late Sir Seretse Khama as president of Botswana, and in 1984 won the presidential elections under the ruling Botswana Democratic Party. During his tenure as president, Sir Ketumile Masire was chairman of SADC and co-chairperson of the Global Coalition for Africa. He became the first vice-chairman of the OAU in 1991. He remains active as an elder statesman and has intervened in diplomatic initiatives in a number of African countries, including Rwanda, the DRC, Ethiopia and Lesotho. In 2007, he established the Sir Ketumile Masire Foundation, which exists to promote peace and good governance, innovation and alternatives in agriculture and children's welfare.

Anthony MBEWU is a specialist cardiologist, research scientist, and chief executive officer of the Government Printing Works. He was executive director of research at the MRC from 1996 to 2005 and president of the MRC from 2005 to 2010. From 1994 to 1996 he was a consultant cardiologist at the University of Cape Town, and honorary professor in cardiology and internal medicine from 2004 to 2014. Professor Mbewu lived in the UK for 28 years, where he trained in medicine at Oxford and London universities. He holds a research doctorate (MD) in preventive cardiology from the University of London and completed the Programme in Management Development at the Graduate School of Business of Harvard University. In recognition of his outstanding contributions in the health field, he was elected a foreign associate of the Institute of Medicine of the National Academy of Sciences of the USA in 2009 and is a founding member of the Academy of Science of South Africa, and a Fellow of the Royal College of Physicians of the UK. In the national arena Professor Mbewu has served on the boards of numerous medical and health bodies and chaired the ministerial national task team that prepared the Antiretroviral Plan for HIV/AIDS in South Africa. He has published 50 peer-reviewed papers, mainly in international journals, and presented over 40 papers and posters at national and international research meetings.

Patricia McFADDEN is a Radical African Feminist who has worked for Justice, Freedom and Lives of Dignity for all people, especially for African women, most of her life. Born in Swaziland, she lives actively as a Vegan, growing her own organic vegetables and herbs and treating all living creatures with respect. She currently works as a scholar/writer/activist/teacher at the Thabo Mbeki African Leadership Institute (TMALI) at the University of South Africa.

Anders MÖLLANDER is a retired Swedish diplomat. He last served as Sweden's ambassador to South Africa from 2005 to 2008. His career involved several earlier postings in southern Africa (Dar es Salaam 1975–77, Lusaka 1977–80, Pretoria 1987–92, Luanda 1992–95), as well as positions in the ministry for foreign affairs related to southern African matters. He has thus occupied himself with Swedish southern Africa policy both at the practical level in the field and in policy formulation at headquarters almost uninterrupted for almost 40 years. Interactions with Thabo Mbeki have taken place since 1977.

Ami R. MPUNGWE graduated with a BA (Hons) from the University of Dar es Salaam in 1975 and immediately joined the Tanzanian foreign service as a career diplomat. In 1994, he became Tanzania's first high commissioner to South Africa. He had also served as personal assistant to the president of Tanzania and as director, Africa and Middle East, in the foreign ministry. His career was largely dedicated to the liberation and peace processes in southern Africa and the Great Lakes States. In December 1999, at age 48, Mpungwe took early retirement from the diplomatic service to join the private sector, where he also sits on a number of boards. In 1999, he was decorated with the Order of Good Hope, South Africa's highest award to foreign citizens, for his contribution to the liberation and for promoting closer ties between South Africa and Tanzania.

Mavuso MSIMANG was born in Edendale, Pietermaritzburg on October 19, 1941 to teacher parents. His father, Walter, taught agriculture for over 20 years at Indaleni High School in Richmond, KZN. Mavuso joined the African National Congress in 1958. During his brief stint at Fort Hare he was appointed to the ANC underground High Command. After student disturbances he was advised to leave the country to study abroad. When the ANC leadership was arrested on Rivonia Farm in 1963 Mavuso changed his mind and opted to undergo military training, which he subsequently did in Moscow. He was in the first group to arrive at the Kongwa Camp, in central Tanzania in 1964. In 1965 Mavuso was assigned to Zambia to set up a radio communication station and to participate in reconnaissance activities along the Zambezi River. He was appointed head of Umkhonto weSizwe (MK) military high command in charge of communication. After the 1969 Morogoro Conference Mavuso was appointed Secretary to the Presidency. Resuming his academic studies Mavuso obtained a BSc, majoring in Biochemistry and Entomology at the University of Zambia. He later obtained an MBA from the US International University. On returning to South Africa in 1993 Mavuso undertook several public-assignments that included the leadership of SA Tourism, SANparks, the State IT Agency (SITA) and the Department of Home Affairs.

George NENE was born and grew up in Soweto. He was a member of the South African Students' Organisation during his university days and joined the ANC and MK in the early 1970s. Forced into exile in January 1976, he underwent political and military training in the ANC and served in various capacities within the movement. He joined the department of foreign affairs in the democratic government in 1994 and was appointed the first South African high commissioner to Nigeria. In 1999 he was appointed South African Ambassador Extraordinary and Plenipotentiary Permanent Representative to the United Nations in Geneva. In 2003 he was appointed deputy director general in the department of foreign affairs responsible for multilateral affairs. Ambassador Nene has served on international boards and represented South Africa in a senior capacity at both the G5 and G20.

Joel Khathutshelo NETSHITENZHE is the executive director of the Mapungubwe Institute for Strategic Reflection (MISTRA), an independent research institute. He has an MSc in financial economics from the University of London (SOAS) and a diploma in political science from the Institute of Social Sciences in Moscow. Between 1994 and 2009 he served variously as head of communication in President Nelson Mandela's office, CEO of Government Communications (GCIS) and head of the Policy Unit in the presidency. From 2010 to 2015 he served on South Africa's first national planning commission. He is a member of the NEC of the ANC and serves on the boards of the Nedbank Group, the Council for Scientific and Industrial Research and Life Healthcare Group.

Andile NGCABA is the founder and chairman of Convergence Partners Investments and executive chairman of Dimension Data Middle East and Africa. He holds a Master of Commerce, majoring in information systems, from the University of Witwatersrand. The University of Fort Hare honoured him with an honorary doctorate in commerce and Nelson Mandela Metropolitan University appointed him adjunct professor affiliated to the faculty of science. He has been actively involved in public policy development at national, continental and global levels through his activities on various bodies, including the ITU, ICANN and the AU. His latest venture is the establishment of The Cortex Hub in East London, South Africa, which will be competing globally in producing IT entrepreneurs who are able to develop local and global solutions. He serves on the boards of a number of companies, including Seacom, New Dawn Satellite Company and FibreCo, and serves a number of national, regional and international policy-making bodies in an advisory capacity in the technology and science sectors.

Lulama Smuts NGONYAMA matriculated at Healdtown High School and subsequently obtained a BCom from the University of Fort Hare and an MPhil in political economy from the Nelson Mandela Metropolitan University. As a student activist, he was involved in MK's underground activities. After an early career in banking, he began his political career in provincial government before becoming national spokesperson for the ANC in 1998 and an MP in 2009. In March 2015 he was accredited as the ambassador of the Republic of South Africa to the Kingdom of Spain.

Mpho NGOZI joined the office of Deputy President Thabo Mbeki after working as head of secretariat at the Independent Broadcasting Authority from 1994 to 1998. She worked as personal assistant to former Deputy President Mbeki from 1998 to 1999, before being promoted to director, personal support service in 1999. In 1999 she transferred to the KwaZulu-Natal premier's office as chief of staff for then Premier Sbu Ndebele. Two years later she returned to the presidency as the chief director, protocol and ceremonial. She is currently employed in the presidency as chief director, events management.

Welile NHLAPO served as South Africa's ambassador to Washington, DC, until his appointment as national security special adviser to President Jacob Zuma in November 2009. In June 2011, he became South Africa's special representative to the Great Lakes countries. He began his political activities in the BCM but went into exile in Botswana in 1974, where he later became the ANC chief representative. He joined the department of foreign affairs in 1994 and has held ambassadorial posts in a number of African countries as well as serving as permanent representative to the OAU and UNECA. In 1998 he was appointed deputy director general responsible for Africa in the department of foreign affairs and in 2001 he was appointed head of the presidential support unit.

Lumkile Wiseman NKUHLU is chancellor of the University of Pretoria and chairman of Rothschild (South Africa). He has served on the boards of many financial and educational institutions, fulfilling the role of chairman on a number of occasions. He was economic adviser to President Thabo Mbeki from 2000 to 2005 and in this capacity he led the technical development of NEPAD's policy document and also served as chief executive of the NEPAD secretariat. He qualified as a chartered accountant in 1976 and has made a unique contribution to the accounting profession, including two terms as president of the South African Institute of Chartered Accountants. In recognition of his contributions to socio-economic development, education and business, he has been awarded honorary doctorates by eight South African universities.

Thami NTENTENI matriculated at Morris Isaacson High School in 1971. In 1973 he registered for a BComm (Law) degree at the University of Zululand (Ngoye). He soon became involved in student politics and joined the South African Students' Organisation. His student activism attracted the attention of the university authorities and consequently he could not complete his studies. He returned to Morris Isaacson High School as a teacher in 1975. Morris Isaacson was one of the schools at the centre of the June 16 uprising in 1976. During this period Ntenteni was recruited into the underground structures of the ANC by his lifelong friend and comrade George Nene. In February 1976 he left the country to join the ANC in exile where he underwent military and journalistic training in the then Soviet Union. The journalism training prepared him to join Radio Freedom of which he became director in 1983 and it was at this time that he came into contact with Thabo Mbeki who was then director of the ANC's Department of Information and Publicity.

Olusegun OBASANJO became president of the Federal Republic of Nigeria in 1999 following the demise of the military dictatorship of General Sani Abacha. Leadership was first thrust upon him in February 1976 when he narrowly escaped an assassination attempt that killed Nigeria's military ruler Murtala Mohammed. Outside Nigeria, Obasanjo has been central in the regeneration and repositioning of the AU. With former South African President Thabo Mbeki he led the creation of the African Peer Review Mechanism and NEPAD. After serving his country for eight years and regaining the respect of its continental peers and the international community, he stepped down in 2007. His role as Africa's ambassador-at-large continues.

Anne PAGE is honorary consul for South Africa in the East of England. She was information officer for the Anti-apartheid Movement from 1963 to 1966, and founding editor of *Anti-apartheid News* from 1965 to 1970. A graduate of the University of Cape Town, she is the special representative in the UK of the University of Fort Hare.

Aziz PAHAD is a former deputy minister of foreign affairs, a position he held from 1994 until he resigned from government in 2008. He has served in various structures of the ANC from the time of his exile in the 1960s to the present. In September 2014, President Jacob Zuma appointed him as special envoy to Gaza. Pahad is also chairperson of the Concerned Africans Forum and a trustee of the Thabo Mbeki Foundation.

Essop PAHAD has been involved in the struggle against racism and apartheid for more than 50 years. Currently, Dr Pahad is the director of Vusizwe Media and the editor of *The Thinker*, a quality pan-African quarterly journal covering broad socio-economic and socio-political issues in South Africa and the African continent. He has held numerous political offices as a member of the National Assembly from 1994 to 2008, including parliamentary counsellor to the deputy president (1994 to 1996), and deputy minister in the office of former Deputy President Thabo Mbeki (1996 to 1999). In 1999 Dr Pahad was appointed minister in the presidency with specific responsibility for the Office on the Rights of the Child, Office on the Status of Women and Office on the Status of Disabled People, as well as the National Youth Commission and the Government Communication and Information System. Dr Pahad was minister in the presidency until 2008. He has published numerous journal articles and is co-editor of *Africa, The Time Has Come* and *Africa, Define Yourself*, a collection of speeches of former President Thabo Mbeki. He holds a BA degree in political science from Wits University and an MA in African politics and a PhD in history from Sussex University.

Pedro PIRES was elected as the third president of the Republic of Cape Verde from March 2001 to September 2011 having served as prime minister between 1975 and 1991. In 1956, he left home to study in Portugal but five years later, together with a group of African youth, he left Portugal clandestinely to join the African Party for the Independence of Guinea and Cape Verde (PAIGC), which was led by Amílcar Cabral. With the proclamation of independence of Guinea-Bissau in 1973, he was nominated as assistant minister for defence. In October 1974 Pires returned home to lead the Cape Verdean branch of PAIGC in talks for the independence of Cape Verde. Cape Verde became an independent state on 5 July 1975, with Pires serving as the country's first prime minister. President Pires won the Mo Ibrahim prize for good governance in 2011.

Randall ROBINSON is a writer, foreign policy advocate, and professor of law at Penn State University. Founder and former president of TransAfrica, the Washington-based black foreign policy institute established to promote more enlightened US policies towards Africa and the Caribbean, Robinson was the founder and leader of the Free South Africa Movement. Among his works are the bestsellers *The Debt – What America Owes to Blacks*; *The Reckoning – What Blacks Owe to Each Other*; *Unbroken Agony – From Revolution to the Kidnapping of a President*; and his most recent work of fiction *MAKEDA*. He is the recipient of 19 honorary degrees and has been honoured by the Congressional Black Caucus of the United States Congress, the Martin Luther King Center for Non-Violent Change, the United Nations, and the government of South Africa, among others.

Albie SACHS's career in human rights activism started at the age of 17 when, as a second-year law student at the University of Cape Town, he took part in the Defiance of Unjust Laws Campaign. He started a practice as an advocate at the Cape Bar aged 21. Most of his work involved defending people charged under racist statutes and repressive security laws, and he himself was raided by the security police, subjected to banning orders and eventually placed in solitary confinement without trial for two prolonged spells of detention. In 1966 he went into exile. After 11 years of studying and teaching law in England, he worked in the legal field for a further 11 years in Mozambique. In 1988 he was blown up by a bomb placed in his car in Maputo by South African security agents, losing an arm and the sight of one eye. After recovering from his injuries, he devoted himself full-time to preparations for a new democratic constitution for South Africa. In 1990 he returned home and played an active part in the negotiations that led to South Africa's becoming a constitutional democracy. After the first democratic election in 1994, President Nelson Mandela appointed him to serve on the newly established Constitutional Court. A prolific author, Albie Sachs has received many awards in recognition of his work in the field of human rights.

Salim Ahmed SALIM is a Tanzanian diplomat and politician who is the serving chairman of the board of trustees of the Mwalimu Nyerere Foundation and chairperson of the board of the Mwalimu Nyerere Memorial Academy. He is also a member of the Panel of the Wise of the African Union and chairs a number of the boards of African NGOs dealing with humanitarian and security issues. In his long public career he has served as ambassador to Egypt (1964), India (1965–68), and China (1969), as well as Permanent Representative to the United Nations

(1970–80), where he also served as president of the 34th session of the United Nations General Assembly. Other positions held include minister for foreign affairs (1980-84), prime minister (1984-85), deputy prime minister and minister of defence and national service (1985-89). He also served for three successive terms (1989 to 2001) as secretary general of the OAU (now the African Union).

Danny SCHECHTER was an activist who became a journalist recruited in London for an underground anti-apartheid mission inside apartheid South Africa. He worked as a producer for CNN and ABC News before creating and producing the *South Africa Now* TV series from 1988 to 2001 and then made many films about the fight for freedom in South Africa. Danny Schechter died in March 2015.

Gloria Tomatoe SEROBE was born in Gugulethu, Cape Town, in 1959. She obtained a BCom degree from the University of Transkei and holds an MBA degree from Rutgers University, New Jersey, USA. She is a founding member and executive director of WIPHOLD and chief executive officer of Wipcapital. Her professional experience includes positions at Exxon Corporation in the USA, Munich Reinsurance Company of SA, the Premier Group and Standard Corporate and Merchant Bank. She was the executive director finance of Transnet Limited and was a member of the Transnet Board and its major subsidiaries. She serves on several boards, including Sasol Mining, Hans Merensky and Old Mutual Emerging Markets. She is a trustee of several trusts, including the WIPHOLD NGO Trust and WIPHOLD Investment Trust. She is an honorary member of the Actuarial Society of South Africa and is a member of the SAICA Advisory Council. In the past she held many non-executive directorships and has won a number of personal leadership awards.

Mongane Wally SEROTE participated, during 18 years in exile, at various levels in ANC structures in the mobilisation, planning and negotiations in the struggle for the liberation of South Africa. He spearheaded the organisation and mobilisation of cultural workers throughout the 1980s and early 1990s, which resulted in the formation of national organisations of writers, photographers and film-makers, among others. From 1990, he was head of arts and culture in the ANC. He has written a number of novels and published poetry collections, essays and plays, and has been awarded national and international awards in this regard. As a member of parliament and chair of the parliamentary select committee for arts and culture, he initiated and facilitated the research and debate for Indigenous Knowledge Systems

(IKS) to be accepted as a tool for the social and economic upliftment, nationally. He was awarded a Master of Fine Arts at Columbia University in New York as a Fulbright scholar.

John STREMLAU is the former vice-president for peace programmes at The Carter Center (2006-2015). During this time, he oversaw the Center's programmes to advance human rights, democracy and conflict resolution globally; regional cooperation in the Americas; and promotion of grassroots democracy, rule of law, and social justice in China. From 1998 to 2006 he resided in South Africa where he was Jan Smuts professor and head of international relations and the founding director of the Centre for Africa's International Relations at the University of the Witwatersrand, Johannesburg. Previously, he served as senior adviser to the Carnegie Commission on Preventing Deadly Conflict in Washington, DC (1994-1998), deputy director for policy planning in the office of the US Secretary of State (1989–1994), strategic planning officer for the World Bank (1988-1989), and an officer of the Rockefeller Foundation (1974–1987), directing its international relations division from 1984 to 1987. At the Rockefeller Foundation his responsibilities included administering a special trustee-supported programme to fund black leadership development in South Africa. Dr Stremlau publishes extensively on foreign affairs and is a frequent media commentator on international network news programmes. He authored *The International Politics of the Nigerian Civil War* and has edited several books.

Tau THEKISO is a member of the ANC, former MK combatant and former head of the presidential protection unit. He started working with Thabo Mbeki as a close protection officer in 1993 when he was still the chairperson of the ANC. He continued working as part of the close protection detail of Thabo Mbeki when he was deputy president. He was appointed the head of the presidential protection unit in 2004, a post he held until his retirement in 2010.

Ben TUROK has been a member of the liberation movement for many decades. He was an accused in the 1956 Treason Trial, served three years in prison and was in exile for 25 years, returning in 1990. In the 1994 democratic government he was first head of the Commission on the RDP in the Gauteng provincial cabinet and then moved to parliament in 1995. He was the co-chair of the committee on ethics and members' interests of both houses in parliament. Professor Turok has three degrees – in engineering, philosophy and political science. He is the author of 20 books on Africa's development economics and politics, has lectured at many universities across Africa, and presented papers at numerous conferences and seminars, including at the United Nations and the European Parliamentary Assembly. He taught at the Open University in the UK for many years and at the University of Zambia, and is visiting professor at the University of KwaZulu-Natal. He is the editor of *New Agenda, SA Journal of Social and Economic Policy*, published by the Institute for African Alternatives, The UN Economic Commission for Africa commissioned him to initiate a major study in 10 countries on value addition in Africa's natural resources, which was the basis for the Economic Report on Africa 2013, and is the lead consultant for a UNECA study on mineral value chains in South Africa. His book *With My Head Above The Parapet* has received a great deal of media attention. His latest book is *Changing the Colour of Capital*.

Meles ZENAWI joined the Tigrayan People's Liberation Front (TPLF) in 1974. He was chairman of the TPLF and the Ethiopian People's Revolutionary Democratic Front (EPRDF) between 1989 and 1991 and led the overthrow of the previous Derg regime in 1991. He served as chairman of the EPRDF and president of the transitional government of Ethiopia from 1991 to 1995. Meles was elected prime minister of the Ethiopian Federal Democratic Republic on 22 August 1995 following the general elections that year. He served as prime minister until his death on 20 August 2012.

Snuki ZIKALALA holds a BA Hons degree in industrial sociology from the University of the Witwatersrand, and a Master's degree and PhD in journalism from Sofia University in Bulgaria. While in exile, Dr Zikalala joined Radio Sofia and *Troud* Newspaper in Sofia. When he returned to South Africa in 1991, after 17 years in exile, he worked in diverse broadcasting media before joining the SABC initially as a labour correspondent in 1993. After holding a number of key positions in broadcasting and communications, he was appointed group executive of the SABC News and Current Affairs Division, tasked with taking charge of Africa's largest news organisation. After leaving the SABC in August 2009, Dr Zikalala established a media company – Szassociates – which does media consulting, and later established the Independent Pan African News Online.

ABOUT THE EDITORS

Sifiso Mxolisi NDLOVU is an executive director at the South African Democracy Education Trust. He has a PhD in history from the University of the Witwatersrand and an MA in history from the University of Natal. He is the editor-in-chief of the multi-volume *Road to Democracy in South Africa* series. He is also the author of *The Soweto Uprisings: Counter-memories of June 1976* and has published articles in international journals that include *History and Theory*, *Area Studies Review*, *South African Historical Journal* and *Soccer and Society*. He is a professor of history at the University of South Africa and also a member of UNESCO's Scientific Committee responsible for revising and updating the *General History of Africa* series.

Miranda STRYDOM was born and raised in Swaziland. She arrived in South Africa in 1995 where she started working as an economics reporter for SABC Radio. She later joined *Business Report* until she was recruited to the news team of the newly launched e.tv News in 1998. Miranda was appointed business editor for the *Sowetan* newspaper and, after a short stint as communications adviser to then Minister of Public Enterprises Jeff Radebe, she returned to the SABC as a member of the presidential press corps. She left the media industry in 2011 to join the Thabo Mbeki Foundation.